A SUPPLEMENT

FROM UNPUBLISHED MSS.

TO

BURNET'S HISTORY OF MY OWN TIME

H. C. FOXCROFT

HENRY FROWDE, M.A.
PUBLISHER TO THE UNIVERSITY OF OXFORD
LONDON, EDINBURGH
NEW YORK

A SUPPLEMENT TO

BURNET'S

HISTORY OF MY OWN TIME

DERIVED FROM

HIS ORIGINAL MEMOIRS
HIS AUTOBIOGRAPHY
HIS LETTERS TO ADMIRAL HERBERT
AND HIS PRIVATE MEDITATIONS

ALL HITHERTO UNPUBLISHED

EDITED BY

H. C. FOXCROFT

AUTHOR OF 'THE LIFE, ETC. OF SIR GEORGE SAVILE, BART.
FIRST MARQUIS OF HALIFAX'

OXFORD

AT THE CLARENDON PRESS

M.DCCCC.II

OXFORD

PRINTED AT THE CLARENDON PRESS
BY HORACE HART, M.A.
PRINTER TO THE UNIVERSITY

INTRODUCTION

ON THE TEXT OF BURNET'S HISTORY

By far the larger portion of the ensuing work is drawn from a source of which the existence at least is well known to all students of seventeenth-century history. The remarks of Dr. Routh[1] and Miss Strickland[2], of Lord Macaulay[3], Professor Von Ranke[4], and Dr. Osmund Airy[5], have emphasized the fact that there exist in the British Museum fragments of Dr. Burnet's *History*, derived from an original version which differs in many respects from the text as eventually published. The observations of Von Ranke, notwithstanding their value, were in one respect unfortunate; his report has been erroneously accepted as exhaustive; and, despite his own ardently expressed aspiration for a complete edition of the manuscript, it has been assumed that he had noticed the chief differences between the early version and the received text. As a matter of fact the quotations of the distinguished German refer exclusively to two important passages[6]; he states specifically that he became acquainted with the document very late in the progress of his monumental work; and his language leaves us in doubt whether he had ever seen either the original papers or a complete transcript.

---

[1] Preface to Burnet's *History*, ed. 1823, p. xviii.

[2] *Queens of England*, vol. viii. (1845) p. 444; vol. x. (1847) pp. 290, 356 (and note), 414; vol. xi. (1847) pp. 17, 68, 70, 199, 307, 319. The description of the MS. is on p. 356, vol. x, note.

[3] As Macaulay did not employ the Harleian MS. in the preparation of that first instalment of his *History* which ends with the Revolution settlement, and which appeared in 1848, there seems some reason to believe that his attention was originally directed to it by the comments and quotations of Miss Strickland. The MS. is described near the beginning of the second instalment, issued in 1855; in the course of which it is frequently mentioned (see ed. 1858, vol. iv. pp. 19, 20, 56, 66, 81, 278; v. 32, 133; vi. 166, 172, 176, 206-7, 211, 276, 372).

[4] *Eng. Gesch.* ed. Leipzig, vol. vii. 1868, App. ii. pp. 184-99.

[5] See his quotation of Von Ranke, *Dict. Nat. Biog.* vol. vii. p. 405.

[6] The 'Characters' of the English Court in 1663, and the Post-Revolution Settlement.

The manuscript is described as No. 6584 in the catalogue of the Harleian Library; which collection, formed by the first and second Earls of Oxford between the years 1705 and 1741, was acquired for the nation in 1753. The papers in question constitute a substantial folio volume containing 350 leaves, the great majority of which bear writing on both sides. The cover, till within the last few years, was a British Museum binding of the eighteenth century; and though the authorities lay no stress on the circumstance, the present editor inclines to deduce that the papers reached the Museum in loose quires, and were there arranged for the binder. It is at least certain that about June 6, 1781 [1], Dr. Gifford (assistant librarian to the British Museum from 1757 to 1784) perused the manuscript; that he divided the work, after a somewhat arbitrary fashion, into eight 'Numbers' (of which the second is obviously misplaced); and that he prefaced each 'Number' by a small inserted sheet of his own memoranda, in which attention is drawn to a few of the more salient discrepancies between the succeeding 'Number' and the published text. Not content with this, he has inscribed, in ink, and upon the margin of the actual manuscript, occasional references to the printed version [2]; while in two instances he has taken upon himself to add, in a similar manner, substantial annotations.

Upon a close investigation, the original manuscript falls into three main divisions.

1. Folio 2 is a separate sheet, headed 'Materials,' and including some citations from the ensuing manuscript, with comments derogatory to the Whig party. The query appended by Dr. Gifford, 'Whether this is not yᵉ Bishop's own handwriting?' may be unhesitatingly answered in the negative; but it approximates in a marked degree to the somewhat peculiar script of Robert Harley, founder of the Harleian collection; and Mr. Cartwright, whose familiarity with Harley's hand is probably unique, 'feels no doubt whatever' that the writing is in Harley's autograph.

2. (A) Nos. 1, 3, 4, 2 (the first three named of which are in one and the same clerical hand, all four being corrected by

---

[1] Date appended to Dr. Gifford's notes on f. 1.

[2] He quotes the pagination of an early octavo edition.

the pen of Burnet himself[1]) are clearly distinct fragments of a single clerical copy, which we shall designate throughout this work as Transcript A. Of these fragments the earliest includes events from 1660 to 1664; the next in date relates to the year 1683; the third is concerned with events from the end of 1684 to the autumn of 1686; the last named narrates incidents from the middle of the year 1689 to the close of 1695.

(B) Nos. 5–8, on the other hand, compose a single continuous fragment (ranging in subject-matter from 1684 to 1696) of a later transcript, which we shall designate as Transcript B; and which was evidently copied from the preceding version [2] by a number of clerks working, it would appear, simultaneously [3]. There are no author's corrections, though this copy, like the former, betrays in many places (and in some portions with peculiar frequency) the characteristic mistakes of hasty and illiterate scribes; but a few of the pages present slight emendations or notes, apparently in the hand of Harley [4].

So much for the Harleian manuscript; but investigations in the Bodleian Library have unearthed additional material, of great interest in this connexion. Among the mass of Burnet papers acquired by the University in the year 1835 for a total sum of £210 [5] (which include the now well-known 'autograph'

---

[1] There can be no reasonable doubt on the subject; though the separation of the individual letters for purposes of clearness differentiates the writing somewhat from Burnet's current hand. The revision has been rather carelessly made; two corrections, on ff. 129 (*b*) and 55 (*a*) respectively, are obviously erroneous.

[2] Cf. ff. 119 (*a*) and 120 (*b*) with ff. 164 (*a*) and 167 (*a*) respectively. In each case it will be found that Transcript B carelessly adopts *both* the original reading and Burnet's correction of the same.

[3] The narrative is continuous, but is in a great variety of hands. The fresh writing always *begins* at the top of a folio, and the opening words generally, if not always, coincide with the commencement of a folio in Transcript A; on the other hand, the portion assigned to any one hand frequently terminates halfway down the folio.

[4] The minute slips of paper gummed on ff. 93 and 146 respectively were probably used as markers. On one is written, 'Russel's trial. E. of Essex'; on the other 'To Ld Oxford. Russell's execution.' The first is now (1902) missing.

[5] Catalogue of acquisitions. The papers (Mus. Add. D. 15–24) in all probability originally descended to David Mitchell, brother-in-law of Sir Thomas Burnet; cf. Brit. Mus. Add. MSS. 11404, f. 101 with *Hist.* i. 32–3, note (we give the folio pagination). Those of the Burnet MSS. which (as we must suppose) were rejected by the Bodleian authorities seem to have been sold at Evans', July 21–6, 1838 (see Auction Catalogue, Nos. 1015–22, 1025, 1027–8); and the British Museum then acquired Add. MSS. 11402–4, 11569, 11570. The source of Mr. Morrison's three autographs is not known. As late as April, 1887, the British Museum purchased

copy of the published *History*[1]) there was found a long autograph fragment of Burnet's original draught, extending from the battle of Oudenarde to the conclusion of the work; and also the original draught of the Bishop's own Autobiography, on which the Life by his son is principally founded. The historical fragment seems to have hitherto escaped the notice of students; the Autobiography is, we find, twice cursorily mentioned in the notes appended by Dr. Routh to the edition of *Burnet's History* (so far as it relates to the reign of James II) which he published in 1853 from the Bodleian autograph of the *History*.

The questions suggested by the preceding details may be thus briefly summarized. In what manner can we account for the existence of the two Harleian transcripts, and under what circumstances can they have fallen into the hands of the Harley family? What is the historical relation between this early draught and the work as eventually published? To what extent do the two versions correspond? in what respects do they differ? and how far can the variations be said to throw light upon the origin of the so-called ' editorial castrations' which have occasioned so much comment?

Three preliminary facts, of great interest, can be at once established. This first draught, or original Memoir, which constituted the basis of Burnet's published *History* and was commenced in the year 1683[2], when Burnet was forty years old, may be confidently identified with the 'Apology,' 'Memoir,' or 'History' of which Burnet, anno 1687, in his published correspondence with Lord Middleton, threatened the publication. We find, moreover, that in October, 1688, Burnet, anticipating possible disaster to the impending expedition of the Prince of Orange, left private directions[3] for the posthumous publication of the work, which he had brought up to date; and, in the last place, that the narrative was continued at irregular intervals from that period, first to the Peace of Ryswick, and finally to that of Utrecht.

---

an early manuscript version of the *Lives of the Hamiltons* from a Dr. Lippmann (Brit. Mus. Add. MSS. 33259).

[1] Used as the basis for Dr. Routh's *Burnet's James II*, and the Clarendon Press edition of the *History* now in progress.

[2] *Hist.*, Airy's ed., ii. 474; *infra*, p. 1.

[3] See *infra*, Appendix III.

The portion of this original draught which we assume to have ended with the Peace of Ryswick, and within which fall the entire series of the Harleian fragments, first demands our attention ; since it appears probable, that this initial portion was on its first completion regarded as an integral whole ; and that its fortunes were at once more complicated and more curious than those of the subsequent part.

There can be no doubt that the ' Secret History ' (as Burnet himself terms it) was throughout originally committed to paper by Burnet's own hand. The Harleian fragments show that he revised at least one clerical copy of the portion anterior to the Peace of Ryswick [1] ; and the motives for such a duplication are not far to seek. Burnet, with characteristic garrulity, seems to have freely advertised the existence of his ' secret ' Memoirs [2] ; and as—partly perhaps in deference to importunate curiosity [3], partly on design to obtain critical suggestions [4]—he appears to have shown it, in confidence, to several of his acquaintance [5], common prudence must have suggested the preparation of a duplicate.

The question now arises, whether among those to whom Burnet, during the closing years of the seventeenth century, submitted the first portion of the original draught we must include Robert Harley. The circumstance could throw no light upon Harley's *possession* of the fragments, which must in any case have been secured subsequently, and from a surreptitious source ; but it is not in itself altogether improbable. The Bishop, in earlier years, had been intimate with Harley's family [6] ; and though, by 1699, the trial of Fenwick had proved for both a parting of the ways (so that Burnet ranked as a staunch if independent supporter of the Court, while Harley led the antiministerial opposition), still the final identification of Harley with the Tory party [7] remained a

---

[1] The writer of the *Occasional Letter*, who says there was only one clerical transcript (see *infra*, p. xv, note 1), may allude either to the original draught, or a first recension.

[2] Preface to the Elliot *Specimens*, p. 6.   [3] *Ibid.*

[4] *Hist.* i. 3-4 (folio pagination) and Dartmouth's note.

[5] *Ibid.*

[6] See the interesting correspondence published by the Hist. MSS. Comm., *Longleat MSS.*, vol. i.

[7] To which we owe the unfavourable comments of Burnet's published *History*, see vol. ii. 109, 255, 270, 291, 381, 486-97, 553-62 (folio pagination), and the virulent juvenile

remote contingency ; and his extensive knowledge of Parliamentary forms would have lent to his criticism of a work, so frequently concerned with parliamentary proceedings, a special value. That Harley, during the summer of 1699, did, whether in legitimate or clandestine fashion, peruse Burnet's Memoirs, is at any rate certain. Mrs. S. C. Lomas, who has kindly devoted some study to the sheet of rough and almost illegible notes[1] prefixed to the Harl. MSS. 6584, argues very conclusively that the initial dates represent the period of their composition ; and show us Harley, during the recess of 1699, collecting from Burnet's original Memoirs materials for the renewed attack on the administration, which he carried into effect during the ensuing session.

But, as we have already hinted, it is not altogether necessary to conclude that Mr. Harley derived his knowledge of the Burnet Memoirs from an act of confidence on the part of their author. A remarkable anecdote is extant, which may throw light upon a possible source of Harley's knowledge, and the probable genesis of the second Harleian transcript.

It was towards the close of the seventeenth century—probably between 1697 and 1700[2]—that Burnet temporarily confided his Memoirs—presumably the Harleian clerical transcript

---

satires of Burnet's son. See also the bitter observations of Oxford himself, *Hist. MSS. Com. Rep.*, XI. pt. v. p. 322.

[1] Printed *infra*, as Appendix VII. The references to the Burnet Memoirs have been appended as notes. We may here add—1. That Sʳ Wʳ Yᵉ is probably Sir Walter Yonge, who long represented Honiton in the Whig interest. 2. That the list of charters given is presumably the list of charters granted by William III. Such a list was demanded by a committee of the House of Commons (which included Harley) during the ensuing session ; was laid before the House, Feb. 7, 1698/9 ; and should appear in the Journals, from which however it is absent (*Com. Journ.* vol. xiii. pp. 8, 164, 176, 183, 203, 220, 224. See also *Registers of the Privy Council*, Feb. 2, 1698/9, May 18, June 15, Aug.

29, 1699 ; *Beauties of England and Wales*, vi. 494, xv. (1) 604–5). 3. That the affair of the Royal Oak Lottery took place in the spring of 1698/9 (see *Commons Journals*, xii. 497, 588, 623–4, 644, 646, 665 ; *Statutes at Large* (1769), iv. 15 ; and a curious little tract called *The Arraignment, Trial and Condemnation of Squire Lottery*, alias *Royal Oak Lottery*. Printed and sold by A. Baldwin . . . 1699). 4. That 'marshal' law is *military*, not 'martial' law ; and that the Mutiny Act was in abeyance for nearly four years from April 10, 1698.

[2] Dr. Cockburn, *Specimen*, pp. 64–5, says he had seen the extracts 'about nine or ten years before 1705' (Mr. Airy, note to *Hist.* i. xxi. of his edition, misreads the passage). But few memories are accurate at a distance of twenty years ; the *Specimen* is dated 1724.

which we describe as A—to the custody of a certain Lord
W. P.; who is very plausibly identified by Dr. Bliss with
Lord William Paulet, second son of the Duke of Bolton [1]. In
him the work appears to have excited an interest which prevailed over the punctilios of honour. Desirous of retaining
a copy, he hired, before the return of the manuscript, a number
of clerks; and dividing among them, with every possible precaution of secresy, the papers in question, he managed to
secure, within a very short time, a complete transcript; which,
from the circumstances of its origin, must necessarily have
presented many of the peculiarities observable in our Transcript
B. We know nothing of the relations existing between
Paulet and Harley; but it does not appear incredible that
the clandestine copy may have been lent by the one to the
other.

Meanwhile, the indiscretion of Paulet was destined to bear
fruit elsewhere. Among his hirelings was an impoverished
Scotch nonjuror, in episcopal orders, of the name of Elliot [2],
who had been compelled by want to assume lay attire and
labours; and who, exasperated by the tendencies of the work,
political and religious, found means to record, upon 'some
clean paper,' which he had concealed under his cuff, a few
illicit extracts from the sheets before him. These evidently
related to the years 1679–81, and are, as it happens, missing
from the Harleian fragments [3].

These extracts Elliot seems to have almost immediately [4]
communicated to a former acquaintance of Dr. Burnet, Dr.
Cockburn the nonjuring pamphleteer, a nephew of Bishop
Scougall of Aberdeen. The act was represented as a mark
of peculiar confidence on the part of Elliot, who was under
obligations to Cockburn; and we presume it was intended

---

[1] Preface to the *History*, ed. 1823.
Lord William was a pall-bearer at the
Duke of Gloucester's funeral, Aug. 9,
1700; sat in Parliament 1688–1729;
became a Teller of the Exchequer
1715; and died Sept. 25, 1729, aged
63 (*Collins' Peerage*, 1812, ii. 382).
[2] See Hew Scott's *Fasti Ecclesiae
Scoticanae*, vol. i. pt. 2, p. 552; Robert
Elliot, minister of *Lessuden*, deprived

27 Aug. 1690 for refusing the oaths.
[3] All this from the anonymous preface
to the Elliot *Specimens*.
[4] Probably during the year 1697, when
Cockburn, who spent almost the whole
of the period between 1696 and 1709
in exile, happened to be in England.
Cf. p. xiv, note 2, with the Rev.
Alexander Gordon's article on Cockburn, *Dict. Nat. Biog.* xi. 189-91.

that the latter should make some controversial use of this material. Cockburn, however, finding that the papers owed their existence to a double. breach of trust, very properly refused his countenance ; and recommended their destruction, or at least suppression. Elliot[1], 'disappointed and disgusted,' declined the hint; and himself drew up, between August, 1699, and August, 1700[2], some exceedingly virulent annotations, which he appended to the extracts. He then placed the whole in the hands of an anonymous friend ; a 'brother' (whether brother in blood, in law, or in orders does not appear) of the celebrated Jacobite controversialist Charles Leslie. This nameless recipient[3], before returning the manuscript, took a complete copy.

Within the next few years, Elliot seems to have died ; and his papers, in some unexplained fashion, fell into the hands of his friend Leslie. Among them, Leslie found Elliot's autograph copy of the Burnet extracts[4]. How far Leslie himself was aware of the circumstances under which they had been obtained is not perfectly clear; but he certainly knew that the transaction was clandestine[5].

It was in the winter session of 1702–3 that the Bishop of Salisbury (who, in the eyes of nonjuring Anglicans in general and of Leslie in especial[6], had long been the most obnoxious of living divines) filled the cup of his ecclesiastical iniquities by a strenuous opposition to the first Bill against Occasional Conformity. At a moment of such acute crisis, when Burnet stood exposed to clerical odium as a supposed renegade to the interests of his order, the temptation of publishing certain sweeping strictures on the clergy, included in the Elliot extracts, proved too strong for Charles Leslie. To a tract

---

[1] All this from Cockburn, *Specimen of Remarks*, p. 64. His statement that the extracts contained great part of the Preface to the *History* is clearly a lapse of memory.

[2] There are allusions to the trial of the Bishop of St. David's, Aug. 3, 1699; and to Burnet's charge of the Duke of Gloucester, which lapsed with the boy's death, Aug. 1700.

[3] Who places the incident about 'fifteen years' before 1715. See the preface to the Elliot *Specimens*.

[4] This, and a fair copy, are probably in the Bodleian ; see *infra*, p. lxiii.

[5] See *New Association, Part II*, p. 22 ; *Cassandra*, No. ii. p. 23.

[6] See *infra*, p. xxii. note 2. (R. F. Leslie's *Life of Leslie*, which is strongly biassed, and seldom gives authorities, should be read with caution.) Lathbury's *Nonjurors*, pp. 210-1, is valuable on the main question.

entitled *The New Association, Part II*, which probably appeared in the first days of April, 1703 [1], he appended the sub-title ' With . . . the Discovery of a certain Secret History not yet published '; and in the body of the work, without actually mentioning names, he animadverted, in sufficiently intelligible fashion, upon the author of this ' most virulent and voluminous Secret History.' Part of it, Leslie explains, he has already seen ; the author ' dares not publish [it] whilst it may be disproved. But intends to leave it as a legacy and libel against the Church and the Crown . . . so much of it as I have seen . . . is the lewdest libel that ever my eyes saw drop from the pen of any atheist, or the most spiteful dissenter, against the Church and the Crown, and all clergymen whatever, of whatever degree or profession.' He proceeded to quote a selection from the passages most likely to prove offensive in the eyes of his readers ; compared his author to Archbishop Williams as described in Clarendon's newly published *History* ; contrived to insert a trenchant reference to Burnet's early papers on polygamy and divorce ; and described the circumstances which had brought the extracts into his own possession as providential [2].

It is clear that a publication of this kind could not long escape the notice of Burnet himself. We are informed, in fact, that ' as soon as he read it he knew himself to be the person meant, which put him, as any one may believe, into a passion ; nor was he long aguessing how his Secret History came to be known ; which made a rupture of old friendship, and was like to have produced other ill-effects [3].' Whether, on discovering Lord W[illiam]'s indiscretion, Burnet may have insisted on the return of the illegitimate copy ; whether he then may have made arrangements for the destruction of this, and his own clerical transcript ; whether his arrangements can have been in part frustrated by the treachery of an agent ; and whether imperfect fragments rescued from the intended holocaust can have been offered to Harley, when he became known as a collector of historical MSS., we have no means of knowing ;

---

[1] The ' Supplement ' (written after the body of the work had gone to press) is dated March 25, 1703.

[2] *New Association, Part II*, pp. 5, 22.

[3] Cockburn, p. 65.

but such a supposition would at least afford a plausible explanation of the Harleian fragments [1].

The question next arises, can any connexion be traced between Leslie's pamphlet and Burnet's first revision of his manuscript *History*? It seems unlikely that Leslie's revelation *occasioned* the recension; since we have Burnet's own evidence to the fact that the task was undertaken before the appearance of the Leslie tract, though possibly but a few days previously [2]. For such a revision indeed there must have already existed quite sufficient motives. A resolution of imitating the method of de Thou [3], by placing the events of the author's *life* as a supplement to those of his *time* (which is specifically adduced both by himself and his biographer), must have involved the complete remodelling of a narrative, in which the two strands were originally interwoven; while the criticism of his friends [4]—the emulation inspired by the stately eloquence of Clarendon's *History*, which had appeared during the preceding year [5]—a desire of repelling the charge of literary negligence, so delicately (we might almost say so flatteringly) insinuated by one of the two distinguished men who, during Burnet's life, had shed a lustre on the title of Halifax [6], may have induced a critical review of his own pedestrian narrative.

But if Mr. Leslie's tract did not supply the impulse for the revision, it probably affected its character. The recension of the reign of Charles II, within which fall the passages censured by Leslie, was completed by the month of August, 1703; and in this recension [7] the passages stigmatized by Leslie, with others of a similar tenor, are sensibly modified; while

---

[1] The Harleian fragments are not mentioned in the copious manuscript memoranda of Humphrey Wanley, Harley's librarian; which extend, with some breaks (July 18, 1716-Jan. 11, $17\frac{19}{20}$ July 15-Oct. 28, 1721), from March 2, $17\frac{14}{15}$, to June 23, 1726, and contain notices of all acquisitions as made (Brit. Mus. Lans. MSS. 771-2).

[2] It was probably begun in the spring of 1702-3; i. e. before March 25, 1703. Cf. heading of Bodl. Add. MSS. D. 18 (1702) with *Hist.* i. 1, ii. 474 in Airy's edition; 1683 + 20 = 1703. The second part of the *New Associa-*

tion appeared in April, 1703; see *supra*, p. xiii, note 1.

[3] See *infra*, p. 451; Life in *Hist.* ii. 671; the anonymous *Occasional Letter* of 1704, p. 13.

[4] *Hist.* i. 4.

[5] See Burnet's speech of Dec. 3, 1703; *Hist.*, Airy's ed., vol. i. p. 53, note b.

[6] See Life in *Hist.* ii. 725-6. The character may possibly be by Montagu.

[7] Contained in the original readings of the Bodleian autograph and quoted in the textual notes to Airy's ed.

thè Preface, written (or at least rewritten) on the occasion, excuses such censures on the clergy as remain.

Nor does it appear that Leslie's influence in the matter ended here. A pamphlet, by an anonymous author, which, without naming the Bishop, undertook his defence[1], was answered by Leslie, anonymously, in the second number of *Cassandra* (1704). In this work, to which he appended the sarcastic portrait of Burnet entitled the 'Character of an Enthusiast,' he contrived to insert, not very consequently, all the remaining 'Elliot' extracts. One of these, which described the murder of Archbishop Sharp, probably evoked the resentful intervention of the Archbishop's son Sir William, who wrung from Burnet a promise that the strictures it contained should be modified[2]; and the passage in question has, it appears, actually undergone a second and final recension[3].

Meanwhile, during the course of these alterations the first revision was rapidly proceeding. On Sept. 15, 1704, Burnet completed the recast narrative, as far as the end of the fourth book in the reign of William and Mary. On the first of May, 1705, he resumed his pen[4]; and the period of the Peace of Ryswick was reached by June 15 in that year[5].

Moreover, concurrently with this elaborate revision of the earlier portion, the rough draught of the later *History* went steadily on. In June, 1708, as his son tells us (*Hist.* ii. 669)[6], Burnet wrote his so-called 'Conclusion'; in 1710 he executed the proposed autobiographical appendix; and with 1713 the work reached its termination. The revision of the latter portion

---

[1] The *Occasional Letter*, No. 1 of 1704. Leslie's biographer treats the author 'as Burnet's apologist or amanuensis,' if not 'Burnet himself'; the latter a quite inadmissible hypothesis. The occasional writer describes Leslie's extracts as either false, or at best grossly exaggerated, though the work, so he maintains, remains unaltered. He says the author never had more than one copy taken, and that by a person yet alive, whose attestation to the effect that he had never revealed its contents the writer had seen. This account is clearly either misinformed or disingenuous, and probably merely emanates from some party hack, writing upon second-or third-hand information.

[2] See Cockburn, who however supposed, no doubt erroneously, that Sharp had seen the extract in MS.

[3] See on this the curious letter from Canon William Stratford to Edward Lord Harley, Nov. 15, 1723 (Portland MSS., vol. vii. *Hist. MSS. Com. Rep.* 367-8). Leslie's tracts are also probably the source whence the quotations in Hickes' Preface to *Three Short Treatises* (1709) are derived; also the *Examiner*, Nos. 41, 50, 51; *Spec. Saris.*, p. 10.

[4] Bodl. Add. MSS. D. 19, f. 126.

[5] *Ibid.* f. 235.

[6] On Burnet's own authority; see last page of the Bodleian transcript.

probably occupied the last two years of the Bishop's life; but it was never extended to the autobiographical supplement itself[1].

We now come to the interesting and important question, upon which circumstances have already compelled us to trench, How far and in what respects does the earlier draught differ from the first recension? And are these differences of such a nature as to render the earlier version of other than literary interest?

We must preface our remarks by the explanation, which can excite no surprise, that the variations decrease in importance as the interval between composition and correction lessens. The divergences are extensive in the earliest of the Harleian fragments (1661–4) and very considerable in the remainder (1683–96); the Bodleian draught, concluded only two years before the Bishop's death, is of much inferior interest; while the original of the famous 'Conclusion' differs very little from the version eventually published. This premised, we may pronounce—

I. That, in the first place (as we have already observed), the recension is marked by an entire change of plan. The Life of the author, which in the original sketch had formed the thread by which the various episodes were connected, was now postponed to an appendix; and it will be observed that, throughout the published *History*, Burnet's own experience appears to be cited only where it becomes desirable to throw light upon the sources of his information, or to exonerate his public character from charges publicly made[2]. The fact that he had omitted much matter relating to himself is mentioned by Canon Stratford in the letter quoted below[3]; who states (on what authority he does not say) that these alterations

---

[1] The revised 'Conclusion' is missing from the autograph *History* (Bodl. Add. MSS. D. 20).

[2] See *Hist.* i. 595. Of the necessity for such self-defence a few instances may be given: (*a*) For the episode of the crown matrimonial (*Hist.* i. 692-3) see Hickes, *Some discourses*, pp. 12-3, and Burnet's *Reflections* on the same, p. 55. (*b*) For Burnet and the copy of Magna Charta (*Hist.* i. 32-3, 812) see Hickes, *Some discourses*, p. 21;

Burnet, *Reflections*, p. 68; Dartmouth's and Airy's notes to *Hist.* i. 33. (*c*) For Burnet and the flight of James II (*Hist.* i. 799) see Hickes, *Some discourses*, p. 25; Burnet's *Reflections*, p. 128; Burnet to Herbert, Eg. MSS. 2621, f. 83 (*infra*, App. IV, p. 536). (*d*) For Burnet's attitude towards Scotch Episcopalians (*Hist.* ii. 25-6) see pp. 66, 80; Burnet, *Reflections*, p. 114.

[3] *Infra*, pp. xxiv-v.

were made on the advice of Secretary Johnstone[1]. We thus discover in the first draught, more especially in the earlier portions, much valuable autobiographical information missing from the final version, and sensibly modified even in the original Autobiography. Moreover, the abandonment of the original design has destroyed to a great extent the unity of the work. In the pages of the published *History* the various episodes, severed from their original context (that is, from the order in which they came to Burnet's own knowledge), are arranged without either art or insight in a series professedly chronological ; they lose the ingenuous simplicity of the Memoirs, without attaining to the organic coherence of a literary or scientific masterpiece. We notice, too, that the transposition has been in some cases very carelessly executed; and confusing repetitions or discrepancies are not uncommon [2].

II. We have next to consider another class of alterations— the deliberate substantial modification of statements originally made. Such changes are very much more numerous than Burnet's own assertion, on p. 3 of his Preface, can in any way suggest ; and we must charitably suppose that the passage in question, written at the moment when he began to recast the work, eventually escaped his notice.

The variations to which we refer may be roughly grouped as follows :—

(*a*) Amplifications and corrections inserted in the final version on the strength of subsequent information or recollection. These are very frequent ; and often correct obvious errors, fill up considerable gaps, or supply needful subsidiary details lacking in the original narrative.

(*b*) The necessary omission of prophecies, reflections, or censure, falsified by the event.

(*c*) Omission of subsidiary detail, often vivid and charac-

---

[1] Portland MSS., vol. vii. *Hist. MSS. Com. Rep.* 367–8.

[2] Instances :—the list of politico-religious crises given in *Hist.* i. 310–21 does not tally with p. 656; the reference to Monmouth's sale of his jewels is twice given (*ibid.* 631, 640) ; the connexion between his landing and the close of the session is mentioned three times (*ibid.* 639, 640, 641) ; Admiral Russell's mission is described twice in slightly different language (*ibid.* 746, 763) ; the reasons for filling the sees of the deprived bishops are reiterated (*ibid.* ii. 71, 76).

teristic, in some cases through a respect for the delicacy of the persons concerned [1], in other cases as obviously from an excessive respect for the dignity of history. In certain cases the eventual excision has been so rigorously or so carelessly done that the curtailed narrative of the printed *History* does not make sense [2].

(*d*) Changes due to the desire of deprecating censure, whether deserved or undeserved. Among these we may mention—

(1) The softening of those diatribes against the characteristic errors of the Anglican clergy, to which we have already referred, and which had raised such a storm of resentment.

(2) The lessened space devoted to members of Burnet's own family—to George Hutcheson, Lord Warriston, and 'Secretary' Johnstone.

(3) The omission of various references bearing on Burnet's early intimacy with Lauderdale [3]. These alterations, though natural enough, are not in all instances perfectly ingenuous.

(4) In general, the more lenient treatment accorded, throughout the *History*, to individual character. We shall see reason to suppose that in a second revision the process was carried further.

(*e*) Alterations due to a change of standpoint on the part of the writer. These, though of great interest and importance, are by no means so extensive as Von Ranke's imperfect researches led him to suppose. The principal classes are—

(1) Changes occasioned by the modification of Burnet's views on the subject of passive obedience. For this see Appendix I, *infra*.

(2) Changes occasioned by the gradual transformation and definition of parties, which had occupied the whole reign

---

[1] As in the case of the graceful character of Lady Russell, who survived the Bishop; the portraits of Lady Balcarres and Lady Essex are also to the point.

[2] Instances :—Leighton's motives for preaching in Latin (*Hist.* i. 136) ; the fate of Fairfoul and the comments it evoked (*ibid.* 134) ; the escape of Lord Grey (*ibid.* 549).

[3] See for instance Harl. MSS. 6584, ff. 10 (*b*), 11 (*b*), 14 (*b*) (three times), 16 (*a-b*), 23 (*b*), 45 (*b*) ; *infra*, pp. 17, 18, 23–4, 25, 41, 98.

of William, and which had practically reached its final stage early in the reign of Anne. This process, which found Burnet, though a warm adherent of the Revolution, yet detached from party ties, left him identified with the reconstituted Whig section, of which Lords Marlborough and Godolphin were allies and Lord Nottingham an opponent[1]. The alterations (which mainly occur in the account of the Revolution, and the subsequent settlement, and are most noticeable in the references to Churchill, Nottingham, Sancroft, and possibly to Portland [2]) are, as Von Ranke says [3], very significant ; they impair the historical value and the self-consistency of the final narrative ; they reflect upon Burnet's political judgement ; in some instances they are hardly to be reconciled with those professions of a 'full and free impartiality [4]' in which Von Ranke traces something of 'clerical unction' (*geistlicher Pathos*). But regarded as a whole, the severe strictures of the distinguished German seem somewhat overstrained. Twelve agitated years of fluctuating political relations, of unsparing political conflict, and bitter party recrimination, are apt to modify our estimate of men, measures, and events ; and though the omission of Nottingham's domestic virtues and the condonation of Churchill's public vices cannot be defended, it must be admitted that these instances of partiality are practically unique. Nor should it be forgotten that Burnet's intimacy with the Marlboroughs (which followed on his admission, as tutor to the Duke of Gloucester, to the household of the Princess Anne) had placed him under considerable obligations to Churchill's friendship [5] ; and had exposed him, in full measure, to the fascinating influence of the most seductive intellect in Europe. A curious instance of his gradual subjection is to be found in his account of Marlborough's disgrace. Originally this was ascribed to detected

[1] Even Swift admits that it was only during the last ten years of his life that Burnet can be described as party mad (*Works*, ed. 1824, xii. 189).

[2] See Appendix VI, *infra*. Portland was of course associated with the Whig junto in the severe proceedings relative to the Partition Treaty, 1701.

[3] *Eng. Gesch.* ed. 1868, vii. App. ii. pp. 184-9.

[4] *History* (Preface), i. pp. 2-4.

[5] See *infra*, p. 494, and note.

treachery, of which Burnet had been informed by William himself; next, Burnet concedes that a discontented man may be unjustly aspersed by the interpretations of political go-betweens ; finally, the charge is dismissed as quite unfounded, and the Churchill version of the affair is accepted without demur [1].

III. In the third place, we are concerned with the changes of phraseology, which are almost innumerable. It is clear that the style was throughout revised with an anxious and painful deliberation [2]; and we can only regret that the result, by general consent, should prove so singularly unsuccessful. The truth appears to be that Burnet, by temper and training an orator, never expressed himself with the force, the lucidity, and the eloquence which constitute a fine literary style, save when under the immediate influence of strong, though restrained, emotion. His Essay upon Mary II, his diary of Lord Russell's imprisonment, the noble exhortation with which his *History* concludes, are admirable in their respective kinds. On a lower level, he was capable of rendering with considerable vivacity any keen immediate impression ; and the ' Characters,' as originally sketched (upon which Von Ranke has passed so high an eulogy), often evince the happy strokes of a quick and practised observer. But what Burnet was capable of doing upon the spur of the moment, or under the stimulus of mental and emotional excitement, he was quite incapable of doing in cold blood ; he had some literary instinct; but of literary tact or literary judgement none. This explains the astonishing inferiority of the laborious published Characters—an inferiority which Von Ranke regards as inexplicable (*räthselhaft*). Burnet's untiring exertions have rectified structural errors, corrected grammatical blunders, removed provincial peculiarities, averted verbal repetition; but they have blurred and distorted the sharpness of the original outline, and rendered the general literary effect at once feeble and incoherent. The unsatisfactory result is intensified by a curious distaste, which seems to have grown upon Burnet in later years, for the use of conjunctive particles. This gives to the

---

[1] See *infra*, p. 373 and note.   [2] Cf. Autobiography, *infra*, p. 487.

History in its final form an oddly disjointed character; and often renders it difficult to trace the connexion of events [1].

We have thus discussed at length the relation between the original Memoirs of Burnet and the first recension of the *History*. Two points remain for consideration; the nature of the second revision (commenced in the year 1711), to which Burnet himself is witness [2], with its bearing upon the authenticity of the so-called ' editorial castrations '; and the circumstances which led to the substitution of the well-known ' Life ' by his son for Burnet's own autobiographical appendix. To elucidate these questions, we must refer to events connected with the first publication of the *History*.

The Bodleian autograph of the *History*, which represents the first recension, contains numerous alterations (mostly of a literary tenor, but in some cases calculated to minimize personal censure) in the hand of Burnet himself. These are embodied in the text of the edition now in progress, the original readings being relegated to the textual notes; and the Preface [3] regards the text so amended as authoritative. This conclusion is, however, misleading. The text of the present edition, though of first-rate value for historical purposes, is unquestionably not the text which Burnet finally sanctioned. In a codicil to his will, dated Oct. 24, 1711, and published (apparently by his family [4]) within a year of his death, the Bishop bequeathed to his second son, Gilbert, all his private papers, with directions that none should be published save ' a Book entitled *Essays and Meditations on Morality and Religion* [5] ' and ' the *History of my own Time*, together with the Conclusion and the *History of my own Life*.' Of this *History*, so the Bishop explains, he leaves two copies, ' one in my own hands (*sic*) and another ·in the hand of a servant. In the reading these over ' (he proceeds) ' I have made several amendments, deletions and additions, having read over sometimes the one copy and sometimes the other ; so I order the two

---

[1] This was carried still further in the second revision. Can Burnet have been influenced by the strictures of Swift ? See *Works*, ed. 1824, iv. 184.

[2] *History*, Airy's edition, ii. 474.

[3] Airy's ed., i. p. ix, note.

[4] The biographical sketch which accompanies it is usually ascribed to his son Thomas ; the original of the will is at Somerset House (Fagg, 58).

[5] See Autobiography, *infra*, p. 489, and Appendix III, *infra*, p. 526.

copies to be compared together, that so all the alterations that I have made may be taken into the printed edition . . . [This is to appear] six years after my death, and . . . not . . . sooner. But as to the printing it after six years or the delaying it longer, I refer that to such directions as I may give him by word of mouth, only I require him to print it faithfully, as I leave it without adding suppressing or altering it in any particular, for this is my positive charge and command.' The publication of the will had been no doubt necessitated by the curiosity as to the contents of the Bishop's posthumous *History*, which the Leslie revelations had occasioned [1]. This excitement was now further stimulated by the republication of the ' Elliot ' extracts (from the secondary copy described *supra*, p. xii) with a dedication to Leslie, and the explanatory preface of the nameless ' brother ' above mentioned ; and by a series of ribald skits on the deceased historian, of which the wittiest is ascribed to Dr. Arbuthnot [2].

The six years mentioned in the Bishop's will expired with the year 1720, O. S. ; and we may presume that Mr. Gilbert Burnet, then Rector of East Barnet, commenced thereupon to prepare for the publication. It seems certain that he obtained some editorial assistance [3] ; and a Jacobite rumour, current at Paris, named as his colleagues the Bishop's cousin, Mr. ' Secretary ' Johnstone, then living in extreme old age in retirement at Twickenham, and a Mr. Cunningham (query the historian ?) [4]. We give the story for what it is worth ; as

---

[1] The pamphlet containing the will ran through at least four editions, the last of which appeared in 1717.

[2] This is the *Notes . . . of the Six Days* (preceding Burnet's death), which represents him as revising his *History* to the last. For the relations between Burnet and Leslie see Burnet's printed speech against the Occasional Conformity Bill of 1703, p. 4 ; *infra*, Autobiography, pp. 499, 506 ; Leslie's *Leslie*, pp. 96–101, 241, 408, 451 ; Burnet, *Hist.* ii. 538–9 ; Leslie's *Good Old Cause* and *Letter to the Lord Bishop of Sarum.*

[3] The prefatory notice mentions ' editors ' ; while it is clear from Brit. Mus. Add. MSS. 11404, f. 96, and J. Sinclair's answer to Beach, that Thomas Burnet was not concerned in vol. i.

[4] *Journal des Sçavans*, Paris, Nov. 26, 1726, p. 699. Johnstone was certainly consulted concerning the business aspect of the second volume (Bodl. Add. MSS. D. 23, f. 155), and betrayed some acquaintance with Burnet's revisionary zeal (Dartmouth's note to *Hist.* i. 4). Cunningham (no doubt the diplomatist and historian, though the early confusion which identified him with the editor of Horace appears in the *Journal des Sçavans*) was the ally and agent of Carstares (though no friend of Portland), and was thus presumably an enemy of Johnstone ; while his rooted antipathy to Burnet, whom he never mentions without a sneer (see his subsequent *History*, i. pp. lxiv, lxv, 29–

regards Cunningham, at least, it would seem very improbable.

We have seen that, according to the terms of Burnet's will, the task of eliciting the Bishop's final version from the two manuscripts in which it was imbedded devolved on his editor. This tedious process might have been effected in one of four methods :—

1. The autograph copy might have been selected as the basis, and revised by the clerical copy.

2. Or the reverse method might have been pursued.

3. Or a fresh transcript might have been derived from the one version and collated with the other.

4. Or, after the collation had been made, a fair copy might have been produced for the use of the printers.

The editorial notices prefixed to each volume, which promise to deposit the clerical transcript corrected by Burnet in a public library, describe that MS. as the copy from which the work had been printed ; but this may only mean that the transcript in question had been selected as the basis of the text. The actual 'printer's copy' is among the Burnet papers in the Bodleian [1] ; and Dr. Routh, who maintains that a cross reference given in the Autograph does not correspond with the pagination of this second copy [2], infers that the printer's version was a transcript subsequently made. His view derives some force from the fact that the printer's copy is not—as Burnet's instructions suggest his own copy to have been—all in one hand ; but as, when carefully studied, it reveals corrections in Burnet's autograph, the identification seems complete. Its first volume, with which the original editors alone concerned themselves, is full of deletions and alterations (all so made, that the original readings, like those of the Autograph, are clearly legible). Some of these are obviously transcribed from the final readings of the autograph copy ; others are not so authenticated. Were all these last made by Burnet himself in this transcript ? or did the editors, from motives of caution or timidity, defy the Bishop's instruc-

---

30, 46, 50, 60, 79, 83, 88, 103, 114, 118, 124, 145–6, 254, 258), belies the tale.
[1] Bodl. Add. MSS. D. 15, 16.

[2] Routh's *Burnet's James II,* 475 ; he does not give the references.

tions already published by the family, and retrench some passages which they feared might be offensive? That they did so seems very probable; though the charge originally emanated from political malignity.

The editors of this first instalment were not unnaturally anxious to secure the services of Bowyer the elder, the most famous printer of the day. Mr. Bowyer, himself a Jacobite, who had but a few years before enthusiastically undertaken the republication of Leslie's works, employed as press-reader the Rev. John Blackbourne, an impoverished nonjuror, eventually advanced to the rank of bishop in the sect. Blackbourne, to whom the 'copy' of the first volume was entrusted, soon convinced himself that the text had been tampered with; and on his advice, Bowyer declined the task, which was entrusted to another firm. Blackbourne, however, retained a transcript of all those passages which he assumed to have been posthumously deleted, but some of which are really marked for omission even in the Bodleian autograph; he made at least one subsequent copy, which passed into the possession of his employer, and is now in the Bodleian Library [1]; and he seems to have freely trumpeted abroad the supposed falsification.

It is not therefore surprising that the appearance of the volume in the end of the year 1723 [2] should have been the signal for vociferous accusation. In this connexion we note an extremely curious letter written Nov. 23, 1723 [3], by Dr. William Stratford, Canon of Christ Church, to Edward Lord Harley, eldest son of Lord Oxford (then still alive). Stratford, who abuses the book with considerable asperity, and refers to a severe criticism passed upon Burnet's conduct by Lord Oxford, observes, in so many words, 'There are great omissions from the original draught . . . such as chiefly related to himself.' He refers to the Leslie publications; and hopes 'the omissions will be supplied out of true copies of the original which are still extant.' To what does Stratford allude? To the originals

---

[1] For all this see Nichols, *Lit. Anec.*, i. 282, 251-3, note; Macray, *Ann. of the Bodl.*, 329-30. Blackbourne's own copy is in Rawl. MSS. D. 404, ff. 1-10. The 'Bowyer transcript' is a copy of the printed *History*, vol. i, with the MS.

insertions, given by Bowyer to Gough. For three other copies see *infra*, p. xxviii.

[2] With title-page dated 1724.

[3] Portland MSS., vol. vii. *Hist. MSS. Com. Rep.*, 367-8; cf. *Hist.* i. 382 (Lord Dartmouth's note).

of the Elliot extracts? or does he refer to Blackbourne's MSS.? Hardly, since few of the 'castrations' relate to Burnet. Then had he seen the Harleian fragments either in Paulet's or Harley's custody? If so, was Harley's own son (as the form of the sentence suggests) ignorant of their existence?

Nor were these charges of fraud made only in private circles. As early as Nov. 1726 the Parisian journal already mentioned, while reviewing in a strong Jacobite strain the French translation of 1725, maintained that the editors 'en ont re-tranché un grand nombre d'endroits injurieux à des personnes respectables'; adding sarcastically: 'ce qu'ils ont laissé fait assez voir l'indulgence de ces reviseurs.' Again, in the year 1733, the anonymous editor of the *Memoirs* and *Characters* of John Macky the spy (in a preface of which the political animus may be guessed from the terms of the dedication to Frederick Prince of Wales) taunted the Bishop's youngest son Thomas, on whom, by the death of his elder brothers, the editorship had devolved, with the non-appearance of the second and of a (mythical) third volume; and made a direct assertion that the *History* had been largely falsified [1].

It does certainly appear that the violent storm of party resentment excited by the contents of the first volume [2] had intimidated the Bishop's family; who seem moreover to have had some reason to suppose that the publication was not very favourably regarded in high government quarters. The pecuniary straits of the family were however pressing; and necessitated in 1734 the issue of the second and final volume [3].

---

[1] For Macky see the above work; also McCormick, *Carstares Papers*; and cf. his *Memorial*, pp. 138-40, with *Hist.* ii. 93. Macky has been wrongly identified by Miss Strickland with John Mackney, the Bishop's steward (*Queens of England*, viii. 374, note). His editor's remarks apply to the supposed omission of certain 'characters' from the *History* (he says Macky's own 'characters,' but this is absurd) and the suppression of the Bishop's early opinions on polygamy and divorce, which he reprints from a previous publication of the original MS. The existing account, *Hist.* i. 261, may have been altered after the composition of the original draught, the corresponding portion of which is not now extant; but as the autograph and published versions of the *History* exactly correspond, the editors are here at least blameless. The introduction of Burnet's affairs into Macky's volume is gratuitous and suggests personal malignity.

[2] See the various pamphlets evoked by it; also *Hist. MSS. Com. Rep.* XIII. iv. 496.

[3] See Bodl. Add. MSS. D. 23, f. 156 et seq.; Brit. Mus. Add. MSS. 11404, ff. 62-3.

In the ' printer's copy[1]' of this, as of the former volume, are many deletions, which however have been prudently obliterated, or in some cases altogether erased. These ' castrations' have never been published ; the original readings are for the most part still legible in the Autograph, and will no doubt be reproduced in the edition now in progress. The proposed autobiographical appendix meanwhile had, as we have seen, never been revised by its author ; and the circumstance afforded a specious, perhaps a legitimate pretext, for the substitution of a ' Life' by the editor, founded on this and other sources. Motives more remote may however be suspected. The Autobiography, which is both garrulous and imperfect, evinces in a high degree that mixture of childlike self-complacency and childlike self-reproach which had so often brought upon the author the charge of excessive egotism ; while the fragment unluckily concluded with the Bishop's devout reflections upon the exemplary success which, up to the year 1710, had attended his efforts for the due education of his family. As it chanced, the subsequent stages of Mr. Thomas Burnet's youth had not been such as to rejoice the heart of an anxious parent ; from 1712 to 1715 he had been notorious among the ' men about town' of his generation[2] ; and though, by the year 1734, he had long since carried into effect that ' reformation' of his own manners which he had once wittily contemplated as ' a greater work than his father's[3],' and was to die some twenty years later in the odour of judicial sanctity, it was natural he should wish to avert the laughter of the town by the suppression of so premature a paean.

To this second volume of the _History_, which, with its accompanying ' Life,' appeared in 1734, Mr. Burnet prefixed a renewal of his brother's promise to deposit the MS. in some public collection ; and more particularly specified the Cotton Library. Two years later, the non-fulfilment of this promise evoked an anonymous ' Letter to Thomas Burnet, Esq.,' usually

---

[1] It is hard to explain a curious transcript of _Hist._ ii. 1–293 in Thomas Burnet's hand (Bodl. Add. MSS. D. 17). It differs both from his father's autograph and the printer's copy, and is probably a tentative editorial version.

[2] Swift, _Works_, ed. 1824, iii. 5 ; the _Notes . . . of the Six Days_; and various other contemporary skits.

[3] Nichols, _Literary Anecdotes_, iii. 353.

ascribed to Mr. Philip Beach, son of a nonjuring Dr. Beach, between whom and Bishop Burnet a somewhat notorious controversy had existed[1]. This pamphleteer, whose information was presumably derived from Mr. Blackbourne[2], asserted that he had before him 'an authentic collection of very many passages castrated in the manuscript from which this book was printed . . . after the Bishop's decease. . . . The manuscript meant is that which was wrote by the Bishop's amanuensis and corrected throughout by the Bishop himself.' Of these so-called 'castrations' the pamphleteer gave a preliminary selection, with references to the MS., which coincide with the pagination of the printer's copy ; and he threatened that unless the MS. should be laid open to the public, the whole of them should be published by himself. The answer to this challenge, which issued during the same year under the name of 'J. Sinclair,' is not very convincing ; it insinuates, without actually asseverating, that all the deletions were really made by the Bishop, upon charitable motives ; affirms in so many words that the passage on the misfortunes of the Dalrymples, printed in Beach's pamphlet, had been so expunged ; and makes a 'palpable hit' by the insinuation that the deposition of the MS. would at this conjuncture become the signal for a publication of the most authentic deletions. Mr. Beach's retort, however, ruthlessly analyses the arguments of Sinclair, and quotes a further instalment of the reputed 'castrations.' There, for the time being, the controversy closed. Rumour continued to assert that the second volume, of which no 'castrations' had become public, had been manipulated at the instance of the Duchess of Marlborough[3] ; but Mr. Burnet held his peace, and kept the manuscript[4] ; and it was not till forty years after his death, in the year 1795, that the *European Magazine* published some further specimens of passages 'suppressed' in the first volume[5]. The original

---

[1] See Life in *Hist.* ii. pp. 311–3 ; Hickes, *Some discourses*, pp. 15, 16, and Appendix ; *Hist. MSS. Com. Rep.* XIII. vi. 29 ; Bodl. Add. MSS. D. 23, f. 55.

[2] Who survived till 1741.

[3] See Dartmouth's note on *Hist.* ii. 90 ; Hardwicke's on *Hist.* ii. 91.

[4] The edition of 1753 (misprinted as 1755 in the preface to the edition of 1823) seems to be merely a pirated venture.

[5] Beach's first selection of passages included the 'castrations' of *Hist.* i. 28, 35, 39, 97, 189, 203, 207,

source of this publication seems to have been a transcript in the possession of Lord Hardwicke, of which, previously to 1775, Lord Onslow had obtained a copy; into this copy, at some date before 1788, by Lord Lansdowne's permission, the Swift notes had been transcribed; and the indiscretion of his copyist may have occasioned the eventual appearance of the excerpts in the pages of the *Magazine*. Finally, in the Clarendon Press edition of 1823 the 'castrations' of the first volume were for the first time included in the text, from a collation of the 'Onslow' and 'Bowyer' transcripts[1].

On a review of the whole evidence it seems impossible to avoid the conclusion that some, though by no means the whole[2], of the 'suppressed passages' were in fact unwarrantably deleted. It may indeed be fairly urged that all the variations can be paralleled by changes avowedly licensed—that they could all be sufficiently explained by the Bishop's own desire of averting censure or resentment, by the growing timidity, the more lenient charity, the stricter decorum of old age. Nor can it be denied that the action of Mr. Beach was calculated to place an honest no less than a dishonest editor on the horns of a dilemma. The suppression of the Autobiography may perhaps be adduced as an argument on either side; since if it evinces on any hypothesis a defiance of the Bishop's instructions, it is none the less possible to argue that, where such defiance seemed imperative, it was at least frankly avowed. On the whole, however, it seems difficult to believe that the editors did not, as a matter of fact, introduce some unwarranted changes, substantial as well as grammatical, into the text prepared for the printers. The reduced circumstances of Burnet's family and the pecuniary dangers of

---

257, 297, 320, 328, 357, 369, 380, 382, 508, 511, 524. His second instalment referred to *Hist.* i. 89, 177, 267, 414, 416. The *European Magazine* for 1795 (pp. 39-41, 158-9, 374) quotes three of the above (*Hist.* i. 28, 35, 39); and adds *Hist.* i. 26, 27, 30, 34, 39 (Montrose), 40, 52, 59, 102, 126. Quotations from the Swift and Onslow notes appear in the *Magazine*, 1795-7.

[1] See Preface, edition 1823, pp. vii, x, xvii. It does not seem to be generally known that Dr. Birch had also a complete copy of the castrations (Brit. Mus. Sloane MSS. 4238.

[2] The following only among the so-called 'editorial castrations' of the first volume are deleted in the Bodleian autograph—*Hist.* i. 28 (*sexies*), 30 (*bis*), 39, 77, 143, 267, 396, 433, 669, 764 (*bis*) (see Mr. Airy's edition, *in locis*). But it reveals many other genuine deletions (*ibid.*).

prosecution for *scandalum magnatum* suggest a possible motive; while the continued failure to deposit the MS. as promised, and the non-existence of any explicit statement on the part of Burnet's friends to the effect that the provisions of his will had been scrupulously observed, seem evidence, circumstantial indeed, but sufficiently damning.

The documentary appendices to the present volume call for little comment. The three valuable 'Meditations' (revealing to us the sentiments with which Burnet approached the several crises of his second marriage, the expedition of the Prince of Orange, and his own elevation to the episcopate) are here reproduced, from Mrs. Salmon's transcripts of the autograph originals, by kind permission of Mrs. Morrison. Two of them, we shall find, are specially mentioned in the Memoirs and Autobiography respectively; and their existence is noted by the *Hist. MSS. Comm. Rep.* ix. p. 160, and by Dr. Airy (*Dict. Nat. Biog.*). The Herbert Correspondence, from the autograph originals in the British Museum, gives Burnet's contemporary reflections during the great expedition. These also are mentioned by Dr. Airy. The Harley Notes are printed as Appendix VII; and editorial notes too long for the body of the work appear on pp. 515-9 and 540-4.

The plan of the present work is indicated in the scheme of Contents; but it demands some further explanation. Considerable embarrassment arose as regards references to the *History*. Convenience would have prompted the citation of the edition now in progress, to which this volume is an appendix; but as only two instalments have yet appeared, it seemed best, for the sake of uniformity, to quote the folio pagination, which is given marginally in all the Clarendon Press editions. For the same reason, the text quoted is always that of 1833; and references to the existing two volumes of the edition now in progress or to Routh's reprint of *Burnet's James II* are always specifically given to 'Airy's' and 'Routh's' edition respectively.

It was the wish of the Delegates that the original draught or Memoirs should be reproduced in as condensed a form as possible; and that the present publication, while final for historical purposes, should ignore merely literary variations.

Where possible, therefore, the text of the *History* is taken as a basis; and only substantial variations are recorded, in type comparatively small[1]. In all such cases the reader will of course accommodate the punctuation of the *History* to the exigencies of the new matter. Passages which differ largely from the received version or are not represented within its scope are printed *in extenso*, and in larger type; with parallel references to the *History* in a separate set of footnotes. The forward references remain valid till cancelled by a backward reference, or by a fresh indicating letter[2]. Throughout the original Memoirs the spelling and punctuation have been modernized; and (on the suggestion of Dr. Firth) the marginalia have been employed as subject headings: where these are defective they have been supplied, within brackets, by the Editor, where possible, from the *History*.

The Autobiography, on the other hand, is printed as Burnet left it; save that the marginalia have been transferred to the text. It is singularly characteristic; and while the interest of the Memoirs is dependent on that of the *History*, to which they are an indispensable complement, this quaint and curious piece of self-revelation—unique perhaps in the case of a man, high in ecclesiastical office, and verging upon his threescore years and ten—should attract on its own merits the attention of the literary world.

The synopses of parallel passages, and of passages peculiar to the Memoirs or Autobiography, have been carefully compiled; and it is hoped they may prove a convenient means of reference. As they serve, to a great extent, the purposes of a subject index, the final index is mainly personal; but readers are referred, in the latter case, to the exceptional items ranged under the general headings 'Affairs English, Irish, Scotch, Colonial, and Foreign,' with their subdivisions.

Finally, the sincere thanks of the Editor are due for the valuable advice of Dr. Firth and Mr. Doble; while a work of so complicated a nature is specially obliged to the vigilance of the proof-reader.

---

[1] By this means an amount of matter which would naturally occupy more than a thousand pages is reduced to half that number.

[2] The text and foliation of Transcript A are always preferred.

CONTENTS

PART I

REMAINING FRAGMENTS OF BISHOP BURNET'S ORIGINAL MEMOIRS

Contents

PART II

BISHOP BURNET'S AUTOBIOGRAPHY

APPENDICES

I. SYNOPSIS OF SUBJECTS COMMON TO THE REMAINING PORTIONS OF THE EARLY DRAUGHTS, AND THE HISTORY (AND LIFE) AS PUBLISHED.

[NOTE.—Passages in which the differences between the two versions appear very important are italicized.]

(EVENTS PREVIOUS TO THE RESTORATION.)

[1] The account of them given in the *History* does not appear.

(Reign of Anne.)

II. SYNOPSIS OF SUBJECTS PECULIAR TO THE EARLY DRAUGHTS.

I. The Memoirs.

(Events previous to Restoration.)

(Reign of Charles II.)

(1660–4.)

(1678–81.)

II. The Autobiography.

ADDENDA

THE ELLIOT-LESLIE EXTRACTS

WHILE this work was in the Press, the editor's attention was called (by the courtesy of Mr. W. H. Allnutt) to certain Burnet entries in the newly published Catalogue of Rawlinson MSS. D. Among the papers there described is a MS. copy of the Elliot extracts and comments, which may be confidently identified as Elliot's own draught; and attention is drawn to a duplicate (Rawl. B. 453, f. 45) which is probably his fair copy. These identifications derive stress from the fact that the text, in certain trivial instances, is that of Leslie, who used Elliot's papers, and not that of the anonymous editor (1715), who employed his own transcript. How Rawlinson became possessed of the papers does not appear; himself a non-juror, he had facilities for acquiring such MSS. The title differs entirely from that adopted in 1715; it runs as follows: ' A Sample or Proof sheet Being a Collection and faithful relation of a few passages taken out of a Voluminous History written by Dr. Gilbert Burnet, representing the Affairs of Church and State within Britain and Ireland in his time, and design'd to be published for a postumus (*sic*) work, with some Remarkes upon them [by a hater of lies and falshood [1]]. Dedicated to all true Churchmen of England.' (The mottos are, Hor. Car. III. vi. 45–7; Ps. lii. 3 et seq.)

The following variations from the edition of 1715 (quoted on pp. 98–109) affect the actual quotations :—

P. 100, l. 3 from bottom, *read* 'these and the present time'; last line, *for* 'ran' *read* 'run.'

P. 101, l. 8, *for* 'either' *read* 'neither'; *and adopt all Leslie's readings.*

P. 102, l. 8, *for* 'with' *read* 'in'; l. 18 *transpose* 'only' *to after* 'lords.'

----

[1] Added, as an afterthought, in the fair copy only.

P. 103, l. 18, *for* 'were' *read* 'was.'

P. 104, l. 10, *for* 'a' *read* 'the'; *before* 'fate' *insert* 'dismal.'

(N.B. 'on' *for* 'in' (l. 9) *and the omission of* 'passing into' *before* 'an unchangeable' (l. 12) *are slips of the present editor*.)

P. 106, l. 8, *omit* 'house.'

P. 107, l. 4, *after* 'fulsome' *insert* 'stuff'; l. 9, *before* 'health' *insert* 'good'; l. 18, *for* 'as he should' *read* 'which he would ever.'

P. 9, n. 1, *add* 'A generous recantation of his censures on Leighton will be found in Hickes' unpublished retort to Burnet's *Vindication* (Bodl. MSS. Rawlinson D. 841, p. 48).'

Pp. 40–1, 'Burnet's projects of reform,' add reference to *Hist.* ii. 669.

P. 108, l. 4 from bottom, *add* '(see however *supra*, p. vii, n. 4).'

ADDENDA ET CORRIGENDA

Introduction, p. viii, l. 8. The Editor learns that since Dr. Routh's time, the 'Autobiography' has been used by Mr. H. W. C. Davis, M.A., Fellow of Balliol College, Oxford, in a Lecture on Bishop Burnet, delivered at St. Margaret's, Westminster, during the early part of the year 1901, and printed (pp. 147-91) in *Typical English Churchmen*, published in 1902 by the Church Historical Society through the Society for Promoting Christian Knowledge.

Text, p. 91, ll. 12-13, *for* 'Ahoab and Musaphia [? Mustapha]' *read* 'Aboab and Musaphia,' *and add this note :—*

'ISAAC ABOAB DE FONSECA (Isaac Avu haf), a Portuguese Jew, *b.* 1606, was carried to Amsterdam in his seventh year. He migrated, about the year 1642, in the capacity of Rabbi, with a band of Jewish colonists to the Dutch possessions in Brazil; where he remained till the discreditable abandonment of those colonies in 1652,—for which see Burnet, *Supplement, infra*, p. 199. He became one of the heads of the Jewish community at Amsterdam (in which capacity he helped to excommunicate Spinoza), and was a leading light of the great Jewish college in that city ; where he died in 1693. He left behind him a few translations from the Spanish into Hebrew, and vice versa ; with some 886 sermons. Graetz describes him as a distinguished and popular preacher, but as very deficient in originality of conception and force of character ; and stigmatizes his influence over the Jewish community in Amsterdam as little less than disastrous.

'DYONIS (BENJAMIN) MUSAPHIA, *b.* 1616, *d.* 1675, a physician, scientist, and lexicographer, spent some years in the service of the Danish king, Christian IV. He had philosophic leanings; allowed himself some heterodox doubts ; and was regarded as "half a Spinozist." None the less he engaged in active controversy with Christians ; figured at Amsterdam, in later life, in the character of Rabbi; and about the time of Burnet's visit fell, together with the above-mentioned Aboab, under the spell of the pseudo-messias Sabbataï.

For the sources of this correction and note (Jöcher : *Allgemeines Gelehrtenlexicon*, i, p. 670, and Continuation, v. 243 ; Graetz : *Geschichte der Juden*, x. 9, 11, 24, 27-8, 129, 175-7, 202, 226-7, 243-4), the editor is obliged to the courtesy of a learned correspondent.

Supplement to Burnet.

PART I

REMAINING FRAGMENTS OF BURNET'S

ORIGINAL MEMOIRS

(From Harl. MSS. 6584; the *Specimens* of Robert Elliot; and
Bodl. Add. MSS. D. 21)

INTRODUCTORY NOTE

[SINCE the opening 47 folios—amounting, on a rough calculation,
to about 47,000 words—are missing from the initial ˈNumberˈ of the
Harl. MSS. 6584, the first portion of Burnet's original Memoirs, extending from his birth in 1643 to about the year 1661, is not available.
We may however conclude, with little fear of error, that ff. 195-9 of
the Autobiographical Appendix, printed in Part II, give a fairly representative, though very much condensed rendering of the more personal
details contained in the lost fragment. This fragment must almost
certainly have further included some form of Preface: a Summary
recapitulation of the affairs in Scotland ... to the Restoration of King
Charles II ˈ (see printed *History*, i. 5-21, 26-45, 49-65, 83-9; nearly
all the passages omitted in this list emerge at a later stage in the
original Memoirs); with the characters of the leading Scottish statesmen
at the time of the Restoration (see *ibid.* 101-5) and the career of the
ˈDrunken Administrationˈ (*ibid.* 105-7, 108-28).

The earliest portion of the original Memoirs which is yet extant, and
which is printed below, is contained in the initial folios of the existing
Harleian MSS. 6584. It forms part of Transcript A (see Preface), and
represents ˈNo. 1ˈ of Dr. Gifford's eight sections; beginning abruptly with
p. 94, and concluding abruptly with p. 179 of the original pagination
(ff. 3-45 of the present enumeration). The leaves are written on both
sides, in a neat clerical hand, corrected throughout by Dr. Burnet himself
(see Preface). Incidental allusions to the recent marriage of the Princess
Anne, with the impending sixth anniversary of her sister's wedding,
restrict the period of composition within the terminal dates July 28 and
Nov. 4, 1683 (O.S.); but an explicit statement on f. 38 (*a*) that a certain
brief passage at that point was *added after the doctor's return from
France*, which took place about Oct. 20 (*Hist. MSS. Com. Rep.* vii.
291 *b*) in that year, suggests that the bulk of the narrative was actually
written during the early part of August, 1683, at the end of which month
he had started for France (*ibid.* 289 *b*, 366 *a*, 290 *b*). The most probable
inference would seem to be that Burnet commenced his Memoirs after the

execution of Lord Russell, July 21, 1683, perhaps in consequence of the satisfaction expressed by the dead man's family with the terms of the little 'Journal' of Russell's last days, which Burnet had drawn up for them. It is, however, possible that the initial and now missing portions of the Memoir, though certainly composed in 1683 (see *Hist.*, ed. Airy, ii. 474), may have been written earlier in the year. Roughly speaking, the contents of the present fragment fall within the years 1661–4, and correspond, though with innumerable variations as well in substance as in arrangement, to *Hist.* i. 93–101, 128–208. The first imperfect sentence alludes to the benefits Burnet had derived from his introduction to Nairne and Charteris.]

HARL. MSS. 6584, f. 3.

[Obligations to Nairn and Charteris; the Edinburgh ministers.]

[That I fell into such hands after I had so long cast off] ᵃ all restraint [1], and was now beginning to take my ply, was so great a blessing to me ᵃ and had such effects on me, that to this day I count myself bound in my daily thanksgiving to God to thank him for the happy providence of my falling into their acquaintance and friendship; and though I had but two or three days' conversation with Mr. Charteris at this time, yet the impressions that it made were very deep. For the other ministers of Edinburgh, I neither admired their persons nor their sermons, and much less their conversation which was all made up of news. Their sermons were subtle divisions of very ordinary matter hung full of quotations of Scripture, but there was nothing in them that struck either on my fancy or reason, or that went to my heart; they were plain dull things sometimes set off with an appearance of quickness and wit, which made them rather worse than better.

[Characters of Douglas and Hutcheson.]

The two eminentest of them were Mr. Douglas [2] and Mr. Hutcheson ; ᵇ the former was a bastard of a bastard, but

---

ᵃ Cf. *Hist.*, fo. ed., i. 216 (Airy's ed. i. 386).   ᵇ *Ibid.* 34.

---

[1] In the *History*, Burnet introduces his obligations to these two divines sub anno 1665, in connexion with the later intimacy which resulted from his settlement at Salton, in their common neighbourhood.

[2] For Robert Douglas see *infra*, f.

17 (*b*) ; Article on Robert Douglas (by A. C. Bickley), *Dict. Nat. Biog.*, where the Harl. MS. is quoted ; Mr. Airy's notes on *Hist.* i. 34, 109 (fol. pagination); *Lauderdale Papers*, i. 4, and introduction ; also *Lauderdale Papers*, i. 34, 36, 54–90 (*passim*), 292, 295, lxxxii.

it is believed his father was Mary queen of Scotland's son,
for he was born soon after she was conveyed out of the castle
of Lochleven, and was educated with great care by the gentleman that helped her away, so that it was believed there
were more than ordinary endearments between them, and
that this son was the fruit of these. It is certain Mr. Douglas
was not ill-pleased to have this story pass ; he had something
very great in his countenance, his looks showed both much
wisdom and great thoughtfulness, but withal a vast pride ;
he was generally very silent, I confess I never admired anything he said. I wondered to see him express such mean
compliances with some silly women of their party, as I have
seen him do to my own mother and sister. He went over
when he was a young man chaplain to a regiment in
Germany, where, for want of other books, he got the
Scripture so by heart that he could not only repeat any
part of it but could have readily quoted chapter and verse
for every passage in it[a] ; and this was his great faculty in
preaching, that he laid all the Scriptures relating to any
point together, but it was a skeleton of bones, for he neither
connected them well nor made he lively reflections on them ;
his chief excellence in preaching was that he would have
made his matter look towards the present times with such
dexterity that though it was visible what he meant, yet he
could not be questioned upon it. He was a man of great
personal courage [*f.* 3 (*b*)] which he shewed often in Germany
more signally than became his profession, yet he was a very
mild good-natured man (though that did not appear much
in his countenance) and he was of an unblamable conversation as to all private matters. The other[1] has written
many books ; as, on Job and St. John's Gospel two folios, and

[a] *Hist.* i. 34.

---

[1] For George Hutcheson, by marriage Burnet's cousin-germane, of
whom, in the printed *History*, no
character is given, see *Hist.* i. 276,
281, 290–1, 295–7; Mr. Airy's notes
to *ibid.* 51, 109, 276, 281 ; *Lauderdale Papers*, i. 4, 34, 77, 83, 295;
Pearson, *Life of Leighton* (*Works
of Leighton*, 1835, i. 36 and note).

3 books in octavo on the 12 lesser prophets; he had a great subtlety in his preaching and drew out one thing very ingeniously from another, which I thought was like wire drawing and ever despised it; he affected great mirth and was much given to raillery, but it was neither grave nor witty and he seemed to be a very proud man. ^a He married my cousin-germane^a so that I was well acquainted with him, but could never have any great value of him; yet the duchess of Hamilton[1], and some others whom I esteem very much, have told me that he was a much better man than he appeared to be upon a general acquaintance, and that the more any one knew him, they would value him the more.

[*Burnet's family recommend the law.*]

This is all that is particular to myself that fell out this year, only in the beginning of the next year ^b(my brother Robert dying of a fever) all our family set on me to return to the study of the law; they flattered themselves and me so as to think that I might grow eminent in that profession; and they, being zealous presbyterians, were afraid of my conforming and so desired to see me in another employment, but I thank God their importunities had no effect on me, so I went on. But now I will give an account of public affairs.

[*Middleton goes to Court.*]

Cf. *Hist.*, fo. ed., i. 128–30 (Airy's ed. i. 230–2) (*from* 'Middleton went up' *to* 'unusual and so unreasonable').

After 'pride' *add* 'he reckoned that Lauderdale and Crawford could not stand long before him, and[2].'

[*f.* 4 (*a*)] *For* 'The earl of Crawford still pressed' *read* 'Crawford, who told me all this story, pressed.'

Om. 'The earl of Crawford was glad . . . excuse him.'

For 'prison' *read* 'the castle of Edinburgh.'

Om. 'that was not a time . . . insist on it.'

For 'as fully satisfied the king' *read* 'that nothing could be made of them.'

---

^a Cf *Hist.* i. 276.   ^b Cf. Life (appended to *Hist.* ii), p. 674.

---

[1] See *Hist.* i. 295.   [2] Cf. *Lauderdale Papers*, i. 105.

For 'he was set at liberty' *read* 'he was confined to his house¹ which lasted till the next sessions of parliament'; *and om. next sentence.*

After 'because' *read* 'a few days before he left Scotland.'

After 'from Tweeddale' *add* 'at his house of Pinkey, 4 miles from Edinburgh'; and *om.* 'upon the complaint . . . ready at hand.'

For 'Middleton was now raising the guards . . . granted by the parliament' *read* 'Middleton was made general of the forces that were now a raising (for the English garrisons were removed, and the citadels which they had built in Scotland were slighted)' (cf. *Hist.* i. 107).

After 'himself as general' *add* 'and delivered by them to the paymasters of the army.'

[*f.* 4 (*b*)] *After* 'opposed this' *add* '(and was seconded in it by Lauderdale).' *Om.* 'with great advantage . . . treasury.'

For 'and as to what . . . . king was master' *read* 'that the £40,000 was the best and surest branch of the revenue, that though a great part of it was to go to the establishing of the forces, yet it was not able to be so employed.'

After 'to the treasury' *add* 'for the payment of the guards and preferring them to other payments'; *and om.* 'But the earl of Middleton knew . . . year's end.'

For 'unless . . . masters of the army' *read* 'except in time of war. These things were unanswerable.'

After 'unreasonable' *add* 'for it had been a much easier thing for him to have got himself made treasurer than to have gained such a point.'

[*Lord Lorn's estate.*]

ᵃ The next particular brought in debate was concerning the estate of Argyll. The king had great inclinations to restore the lord Lorn, so that much pains was taken to persuade him that all the zeal that he had expressed for his service was only an artifice between his father and him to secure the estate, which way soever the world might turn; but in managing this they committed great errors, for it was said that Lorn had searched the king's pockets and locked him up as a prisoner while he was in Scotland; this the king knew to be so false, that it made the other things laid to his charge to be the less believed. So they, finding that this was not like to take effect, betook themselves to another method that was likely to be more effectual. The late marquis of Argyll had designed to raise his family to an absolute

ᵃ *Hist.* i. 130.

---

¹ For the reason of this see *Lauderdale Papers,* i. 102. This was the 'house at Bothans,' not the 'house of Pinkey' specifically mentioned below.

power over the Highlands; and the marquis of Huntly being the next in power to him, he intended to take his estate into his own hands, which he effected in this manner. The marquis of Huntly had married his sister, so during their friendship he was bound with him for some of his debts. Afterwards Huntly both neglecting his affairs and engaging in the king's service, (by which he was likely to be ruined considering the violence of that time) Argyll pretended that for securing himself he was forced to buy in prior debts and mortgages, for which he said he had paid great sums of money, but it was said by others that he had them almost for nothing; it is like he never paid so much himself as he said, nor so little as his enemies gave out, but in conclusion he transacted for about £20,000 of his debts, and made his son bind with him for the payment of these debts. So now it was moved that the king ought in honour and justice to restore the marquis of Huntly, and then they reckoned those debts [*f.* 5 (*a*)] of his for which the lord Lorn was bound would sink him. Lorn upon this offered to clear the accounts between his father and Huntly, and that he would not pretend to a farthing, but that which he should prove his father had in effect payed for Huntly's debts, but that was not much considered. So Huntly had a grant given him of all that part of Argyll's forfeiture that concerned his estate, by which he was neither liable to his own grandfather's debts, nor to those for which Lorn was engaged ; and this was the true occasion of all the hardship that Lorn was afterwards put on which raised such a clamour against him[1]. After this Montrose put in his claim upon this account; when the late marquis of Montrose was in armes his men had wasted and burnt Argyll's estate, upon which Argyll got Montrose's estate to be charged with that damage, and possessed it till his son compounded with him for it, so he now pretended that he ought to have all that restored to him and got a grant of a part of Argyll's estate to reimburse him worth between

---

[1] See *infra*, f. 120 (*a*).

5 or £6,000. After that a great many others put in their claims, pretending their estates had been ruined by Argyll's means for their adhering to the king's service, and it being easy to swell up an account of losses, they put in such pretensions that all Argyll's estate could not have satisfied them. To all this Lorn answered that if the king intended any grace for him, a stop must be put to all further grants out of his father's estate, otherwise it would be quickly out of the king's power to give him anything, especially considering the great debts that lay on it; so a stop was put, and Middleton saw it was in vain to press the matter further.

Consultations concerning episcopacy.

Cf. *Hist.* i. 130 (*from* 'The point of the greatest importance' *to* p. 132, *end of paragraph*).

Om. 'and honester.'

Insert 'that' *before* 'one synod' *and* 'many others.'

Om. 'Sharp assured . . . indemnity passed.'

For 'and that the supporting it . . . engaged in' *substitute the following passage* (cf. with *Hist.* i. 107–8): 'and that after that the keeping of Scotland quiet would be all that the government there could do; whereas if the king would let them alone with their beloved presbytery, he might have the hearts and affections of the nation entirely united to his service in all other things; and that Scotland being a poor kingdom, all that the king could expect from it was the hearts and hands of so many people; [*f.* 5 (*b*)] this Lauderdale made his constant topic to the king, that whatsoever he intended to do at any time in England, he might govern Scotland so as to have them all sure to assist him in it; and showed him how certainly his father might have made himself master of England if it had not been for the trouble he brought on himself from Scotland.'

Om. 'The king went . . . design [1].'

For 'and having called . . . the way of that nation' *read* 'and was only apprehensive of some disorder that might follow on the change.'

After 'inclinations of the nation' *insert the episode of the letter in white ink* (*Hist.* i. 108); *reading instead of* 'a daughter of the earl . . . among her papers' *only* 'her whom I afterwards married which I have in my hands [2]'; *and for* 'he saw the king was indifferent' *to the end of the passage, reading* 'pressing her to take care to have many of the presbyterians to signify to the king their aversion to episcopacy and their firmness to him in all other things if he would not

---

[1] The passage is also omitted in Airy's edition.

[2] Lady Margaret was living when Burnet wrote this, though in a state of imbecility; for she died early in 1685; see *infra*, f. 117, and Autobiography, ff. 208–9. Burnet's assertion therefore, in the published *History*, that he found the letter *after her death* must be a slip of the pen, unless we suppose the anecdote to be a subsequent insertion.

touch them in that point; but he pressed her to engage them to make full declarations of their affection in all other things; so that in this letter it both appears that he had at that time a great zeal for presbytery, and that he was beginning to possess the king with that which he esteemed afterwards his masterpiece, that the chief use the king ought to make of Scotland was to engage them to assist him in any design that he might come to have in England.'

Then resume p. 132 *from* ' The result of the debate.'

For ' that might have such effects . . . affairs ' *read* ' in so important a thing.'

For ' the main body of' *read* ' the whole.'

[*Men sought out to be bishops.*]

Cf. *Hist.* i. 132-4 (*to* ' dealt falsely in the covenant ').

Begin ' And thus was the matter concluded. [*f.* 6 (*a*)] So nothing remained but the calling up such a number of men as might be first consecrated in England and then sent down to consecrate the rest'; *then* (*omitting from* ' Sheldon and the English bishops' *to* ' that matter wholly to him,' p. 133) *proceed* ' Sharp now took off the mask and owned,' &c.

After ' love and moderation' *return to* p. 132, ' There was but one of the old bishops,' &c., *and after* ' Galloway' *insert* (cf. *Hist.* i. 26) ' that was a very learned and good man and one on whom old age had a very extraordinary effect, for he who was hot and fierce beyond expression in his youth, was now become very mild and gentle in his old age, but he was always more a scholar than a wise man, and he was now under some of the ill effects of age, for he was beginning to sink much.'

Om. ' he had come up . . . primacy of Scotland.'

After ' episcopally ordained' *insert* ' and the bishops required some uneasy conditions of those whom they ordained.'

Om. ' with others . . . about him.'

After ' of ordaining' *read* ' in his chamber.'

For from ' and that without demanding' *to end of following paragraph read* ' without requiring any conditions of them; for all that he took was fees. This was so foul a thing, so like simony, and so contrary to all ecclesiastical orders, that nothing but regard to his old age, and the merit of his former life and his sufferings, kept them from proceeding against him; so it was resolved [*see* p. 133] that he should only be made bishop of Orkney which has a good revenue, and it was intended he should never go thither.'

For ' The former of these . . . own function' *read* ' The former was a prudent and good-natured man, very facetious, and of a most obliging behaviour; he was also a very good physician, which gave him a great interest in the country where he lived, but it was never thought he had a deep sense of religion, nor was his life exact.'

Om. ' very good.'

[*f.* 6 (*b*)] *For* ' he, who had passed his whole life . . . almost a changeling' *read* ' he very soon lost both his understanding and his memory. Whether it was that he was falling under the infirmities of old age, or that he indulged himself too freely in eating, drinking, and sleeping, I know not; certain it is, that he became very soon the object of all people's scorn or pity.'

After ' himself from suspicion' *insert* ' and to keep his benefice.'

After 'sacrament' *insert* 'he used to renew it, with this ceremony.'

After 'falsely in the covenant' *add* 'He was designed to be bishop of Galloway, and it was thought the respect to his birth would make him the better received there; he was also a good plain preacher and a man of estate.'

Bishop Leighton's character.

[a] But there was another Scotch clergyman[1] then in England who for his health had gone to The Bath, on whom, because I have known him so particularly and esteem him beyond all the churchmen I ever yet knew, I will dwell a little longer. He was son to Dr. Leighton, a Scotchman that lived in England, and was censured in the Star-chamber for a seditious book that he had writ against the bishops of England: he was sent by him to be educated in the college of Edinburgh, because he looked on the English universities as much corrupted; so [b] he was bred under all the prejudices to episcopacy and the church of England that a father of hot principles and inflamed by ill-usage could infuse into him. [c] He was a man of a most quick and piercing apprehension, he had a life in his thoughts and expressions that were inimitable, [d] only his language was too fine, too much laboured, and too full of figures and sentences: this was the effect of study in his youth, and became a habit, or rather nature, in his old age. [e] He spoke Latin with a readiness and purity that I never knew in any except sir James Langham[2], and he was a great master of the Greek, [*f.* 7 (*a*)] and had almost all their poets by heart; he had the Hebrew very well, so that I have met with many curious criticisms from him which I have found never in any

[a] Cf. *Hist.* i. 134.   [b] *Ibid.* 135.   [c] *Ibid.* 134.   [d] *Ibid.* 135.
[e] *Ibid.* 134.

---

[1] It will be remembered that when this was written Leighton, who died June 28, 1684, was still alive. To Mr. Airy's note, *Hist. in loco,* we may add, that traces of correspondence between Burnet and Leighton survive in *Hist. MSS. Com. Rep.* xi. pt. 6, p. 148, Brit. Mus. Add. MSS. 23135, f. 96, and Bodl. Add. MSS. D. 23, ff. 34–54, of which the two latter are shortly to be published by the Scottish Historical Society; and that Burnet's enthusiastic admiration of Leighton, intimated to

the world during Burnet's lifetime in the Preface to the *Life of Bedel* and the *Pastoral Care,* drew upon him the bitterest censures of the Jacobite High-churchmen, who regarded Leighton as a fanatic (see *Some discourses on Dr. Burnet and Dr. Tillotson* [1695], by [George Hickes, D.D.], pp. 23–4). We see trace of a desire to deprecate such a view, in the variations between the original and later versions.

[2] See *Hist.* i. 267, and Mr. Airy's note on that passage.

author; [a]he spoke French like one born in France[a], though it is now 45 years since he came out of it. He had read the fathers so exactly that [b]I never happened to talk with him of any particular relating to ecclesiastical learning, but he was as ready at it as if he had just come from studying it[b]; and he was most conversant in the lives of all the devout men that have been of all religions, and out of them all he formed the highest idea of devotion that I ever yet met with; for he had laid together with great judgement all the extraordinary passages of bishops and churchmen, and had read most of the lives written in the latter ages, and had picked out of them what was most remarkable and imitable among them, and used to say that when he met with a good passage, he did not much care whether it was true or not, so that it raised in him some good thoughts. He was sent again by his father into Scotland in the year [16]38 [?], and was at the assembly of Glasgow; he told me he was even then disgusted with their heats and the manner of their proceedings, but these prejudices were not yet strong enough in him to overcome education. Some time after that [c]he took presbyterian ordination[c] and signed the covenant, [d]and was minister at Newbottle within four miles of Edinburgh, [e]where the earl of Lothian dwelt. [f]He led so exemplary a life, that it was rather like a pattern framed out of fancy, than what a man could really attain to. He entered upon a course of [g]almost perpetual fasting[g], for though he had a quick and craving appetite, he never eat above what seemed necessary to keep him alive; he never allowed himself any sort of diversion, except riding abroad; [h]he was never merry, nor familiar with any, but lived in a perpetual reserve and silence, and every word he spoke had an impression of religion on it. Those that knew him before me and [i]I that have now lived one and twenty years in greater intimacy with him than he has been ever observed to live in with any person, must say this of him, [k]that I

---

[a] Cf. *Hist.* i. 135.   [b] *Ibid.* 134.   [c] *Ibid.* 135.   [d] *Ibid.*
[e] *Ibid.* 136.   [f] *Ibid. supra.*   [g] *Ibid.* 134.   [h] *Ibid.* 135.
[i] *Ibid.* 135, 138.   [k] *Ibid.* 135.

never saw him angry at anything, [a] nor ever perceived in him any concern for anything in this world, or the least appearance of pride or vanity; [b] and I scarce ever heard him speak an idle word [b], and never once found him in any other temper, but such as I would wish to be in when I were to die. He has a heart the fullest [*f.* 7 (*b*)] of all the melting affections and devotions in religion, and yet has nothing of enthusiasm, or of a schismatical temper under it; [c] he had the most universal charity for persons and things that I ever knew in man. [d] He had such a way in preaching that I [n]ever knew any come near it; his thoughts were the most ravishing, his style the most beautiful (if not too fine), but his way of uttering them so grave, and so tender together, that I never heard him preach without trembling for one great part of the sermon, and weeping for another; and I confess his way of preaching was so much above all others that I had ever heard, or anything that I could ever hope to attain to, that for some time after every sermon that I heard of his I both preached myself and heard all others with a sort of indignation; and yet he really seemed so to undervalue himself that he always chose to preach to mean auditories, and when he was tied to a charge he used to employ every man he could get to preach for him [d]. And though he never made any so much his own friend as he did me, yet he was a friend to a great many, and was very full of tenderness and Christian concern for them, and I see it still lives with him. [e] He soon came to see the follies of the presbyterians; he hated their covenant and their rebellion against the king, their imposing of oaths, and their fury against all that differed from them, and their rough sourness and narrowness of soul, and he openly preached up an universal charity; he would never meddle in their matters, but withdrew from them, and only minded his pastoral care in his own parish [v]. They saw he grew to hate their ways, but the reputation he was in was such that they durst not let it be thought that he was against their courses; [f] yet he openly

[a] Cf. *Hist.* i. 134.   [b] *Ibid.* 135.   [c] *Ibid. infra.*   [d] *Ibid. infra.*
[e] *Ibid.* 135-6.   [f] *Ibid.* 136.

declared himself for the engagement in the year [16]48 that
was made for delivering the king; and when after the defeat
of that army some that were in it came to profess their repentance for it, in his church, according to the order of the
general assembly, he, being to exhort them to a true repentance, told them they had been in an expedition in which he
was afraid they had been guilty of much swearing, drunkenness, oppression and other sins, besides the neglect of God
and religion, and charged them to repent seriously for those
things, but did not say one word of the unlawfulness of the
expedition.   He likewise openly owned his esteem of all the
episcopal party[a], and when my father was absconding [*f.* 8 (*a*)]
for refusing to swear the covenant[1] he visited him often; he
wished that the presbyterians would have questioned him for
these things or put him again to renew the covenant that
so he might have found a fair colour for breaking with them,
but they thought it more advisable to let him alone.   [b]At last
he grew so weary of mixing with them that he left his
charge, and retired into England; he would never engage in
janglings, so he would not declare against them, but thought it
was better to leave them[b].   He likewise found that his English
accent, and that politeness to which he had accustomed
himself, made him less capable of doing good among the
commons; and so he thought he could not hold a living
with a good conscience, where he was as a stranger and
almost a barbarian to the greater part.   [c]Soon after that the
mastership of the college of Edinburgh fell vacant, and that
being in the town's gift the offer of it was made him.   It was
an employment separated from all ecclesiastical matters, so
he accepted of it[c]; but though the heads of the college were
generally considered as members of the presbytery, yet he
never went to their meetings, and continued to live in great
reservedness with all people.   The English judges and
officers then in Scotland courted him much, and endeavoured

---

[a] Cf. *Hist.* i. 136.   [b] *Ibid. infra.*   [c] *Ibid. infra.*

---

[1] His reasons for doing this will be found in Bodl. Add. MSS. D. 23, ff. 124-5.

often to hear him preach; upon that he gave over all preaching in the pulpits of Edinburgh (for which ᵃthe lowness of
his voice furnished him with a very good excuse), but ᵇhe
preached often within the college, and did it for the most
part once a week; but finding crowds break in upon them
from the ţown ᵇ, he ordered that the gates should be shut when
he preached; yet the judges were too great to be shut out,
so once when he came into the pulpit, and saw them there,
ᶜinstead of preaching in English he did it in Latin ᶜ, and so was
delivered from their company. ᵈHe went often into England
in vacation time, and once or twice over into Flanders;
he grew a little acquainted with all the great preachers about
London and the high-flown men about Cromwell's court;
but he often told me, he could never be taken with anything
he observed among them, and that all he heard from them
was dry unsavoury bombast stuff. He was much taken with
some religious men he saw in Flandêrs; some of them were
Jansenius's followers, and he thought they were men of
extraordinary tempers; he did not stick to declare himself
freely against the humour of magnifying and widening con-
troversiesᵈ of all hands, not excepting those with the papists,
and did often preach up a greater largeness of charity¹. [*f.* 8 (*b*)]
ᵉThus he had lived above twenty years in Scotland, and was
the most admired man that was in that kingdom. He had
a brother, sir Elisha Leighton, very like him in face and wit,
but the most unlike him in better things that could be, for
though he will talk of the highest notions of religion, and
heat himself with them as if he were in a rapture, yet he is
a very bad man in all respectsᵉ. He has a vast deal of wit,
but by his rambling way of discourse he will sometimes run
out into great impertinences, pursuing wit when he cannot

ᵃ Cf. *Hist.* i. 135. ᵇ *Ibid.* 136. ᶜ *Ibid.* ᵈ *Ibid.* 137. ᵉ *Ibid.* 136.

---

¹ Burnet, in his published *History*
(see i. 137), has somewhat extenuated
Leighton's complacency towards the
Church of Rome as suggested above
and on f. 8. It must however be
remembered, that when Burnet and
Leighton met for the last time, a few
months after this passage was written,
Burnet had found his old friend much
more strongly impressed with the
errors of Popery. See *Hist.* i. 138-9,
589.

hit on it; he is an eternal talker, and will often say as lively things as ever I heard; I will set down at present, for a taste, one of the best of his sayings that occurs to me. [a] He is a papist—that is to say he goes to mass—(having declared himself one when he thought it was his interest to do so), [b] but he believes nothing of popery. [c] So one asked him once if he believed transubstantiation; he answered, he did not know whether he himself believed it or not, but he was sure the king believed it; and when the king asked him how he came to think that, he said, 'Sir, you believe Christ is present in an unconceivable manner'; to which the king assenting, he said, 'Then you must believe transubstantiation, for that is the most unconceivable manner that ever was yet hit on.' He was a man of a facetious conversation, [d] and was much with the earl of Bristol and the lord Aubigny, and knew the secret of the duke's being a papist, for he was his secretary; [e] but his great design was to raise himself [e]; for he had no spite nor ill-nature in him, and thought of nothing but plenty and pleasure, and would have stuck at nothing that could have procured him these. [f] He, seeing that his brother was not only episcopal, but had tender and favourable thoughts of many things in the church of Rome, resolved that he would get him to be made a bishop, and fancied he would soon be the eminentest man in Scotland, and this would help to support him at court. So he pressed my lord Aubigny and all the popish party to put the king on making him a bishop. His brother was truly the most averse from it that could be [f], for he hated both pomp and business, and was often running away from London, having come thither from The Bath in his way to Scotland.

Sir Elisha at first thought this was only a shyness of his brother's, but when he saw how positive he was in it, he was almost mad at it, and got it to be so much pressed on him by all hands that he at last yielded to it. [g] The English clergy found him more learned and [*f*. 9 (*a*)] more thoroughly

[a] Cf. *Hist.* i. 136.   [b] *Ibid.* 137.   [c] *Ibid.* 138.   [d] *Ibid.* 136.
[e] *Ibid.* 137.   [f] *Ibid.*   [g] *Ibid.* 138.

theirs in the business of the common prayer than any other
of the Scotch clergy, and though they did not much like his
strictness, yet they thought that such a man as he was might
give a credit to episcopacy at its first entry into Scotland.
Lauderdale was not much concerned, only he saw he did not
love Sharp whom he hated, and so he hoped he would balance
him. [a] Leighton, seeing what the state of the bishoprics of
Scotland were, found that Dumblane was a very small diocese
consisting of about 24 parishes, that the revenue of it was
very low (not £200 a year), and the deanery of the king's
chapel was united to it; so he made choice of that, and
resolved to have set up common prayer in the chapel[a].
This made Middleton very desirous of engaging him to it,
for he could not find any of the rest that were willing to
undertake so hard a province.   Thus he was pressed to it on
all hands.   [b] The secret of this matter was never known, and
is not too honourable for his memory, yet I set it down
frankly as I had it both from himself and his brother, but it
will soon appear how much they were mistaken in him that
pressed his advancement in hopes of his favouring popery.
[c] The truth on it is he was much charmed with his brother[c],
and it was long before he thought he was so ill a man as he
afterwards to his great grief knew him to be.

[The Scottish bishops consecrated.]

Cf. *Hist.* i. 139–40 (*to* ' new modelling of a church ').
For ' Sharp was very uneasy at this' *read* 'Sharp seemed to resent this very
much and spoke big, as if he would never submit to it.'
Om. 'who thought it went too far , . . fierceness.'
For 'The English bishops did also say' *read* ' To this it was answered.'
[*f.* 9 (*b*)] *Om.* 'thrown off that order . . . greater matters.'
Om. 'He did not think orders . . . being of a church.   But.'

[Leighton's schemes.]

[d] After that he had some private discourses with Sharp,
about the method in which they intended to proceed; but
he was surprised to find that he had laid down no scheme at
all, but only this, that they should be established by next

---

[a] Cf. *Hist.* i. 138.   [b] *Ibid. infra.*   [c] *Ibid.* 137.   [d] *Ibid.* 140.

sessions of parliament, and so be lodged in their bishoprics, and then every man must do the best he could. ᵃ As for Fairfoul he could never endure to talk with him, for he had always some merry tale ready, and this was all he could ever get of him. So he found the two things that he designed were never like to take effect; ᵇ the one was to set a higher spirit of religion and devotion on foot ᵇ both among the clergy and laity, and to look well to the universities, particularly to the professions of divinity, that so those who were trained up for holy orders might be well formed and prepared, whereby the nation might see they were like to be the better for that order; ᶜ the other was that some reasonable terms might be offered to such of the presbyterians, who could not be induced to submit to that order, ᵈ that so they might not be turned out but suffered to die out, and so in little more than twenty years most of them would be gone off the stage, and they dropping thus one after another, if care was taken to have worthy men ready to put in their rooms, he thought the change would be more insensible to the nation, whereas if they went more violently to work it would raise a great fermentation, which perhaps would never be quite laid to sleep. But all that he proposed signified nothing.

[*Leighton loses heart.*]

Cf. *Hist.* i. 141 ('By these means' *to end of paragraph*).

After 'that affair' *add* 'and in all that has been done since.'

For 'and that they were not . . . church' *read* 'in the way in which [*f.* 10 (*a*)] they set it up.'

For 'He who . . . hand in it' *read* 'The churchman that managed the design (Sharp)'; *om.* 'and the rest. . . selfish.'

[*The meetings of the presbyteries forbidden.*]

Cf. *Hist.* i. 141–2.

For 'were of a piece with this melancholy beginning' *read* 'helped to fix this melancholy prospect in his mind.'

For 'openly' *read* 'more openly' *and om.* 'and to prepare. . . against them'; *and for* 'Some were talking' *read* 'and [Sharp] fear[ed] lest in presbyteries they might have entered.'

For 'since the king . . . episcopacy' *read* 'a letter might be sent from the king to the council ordering.'

ᵃ Cf. *Hist.* i. 141.   ᵇ *Ibid.* 140.   ᶜ *Ibid. supra.*   ᵈ Cf. with this, *ibid.* 273–6.

For ' the ministers' *read* ' some of them (i.e. the presbyterians).'

For ' once' *read* ' secretly.'

For ' without any advice' *read* ' without so much as communicating it with the other bishops.'

Before ' when king James' *insert* ' if, as '; *and for* ' some of them protested . . . no remedy' *read* ' they would have sat still, pretending that their sitting there with a bishop was but like a submission granted in civil things to an usurper.'

Om. ' by a sort of connivance . . . legal authority.'

Om. from ' which was too great a turn' *to end of paragraph.*

1662. *Episcopacy settled in Scotland.*

Cf. *Hist.* i. 142 (' The bishops came down' *to* p. 143, *end of paragraph*).

For ' soon after their consecration' *read* ' in March.'

For ' a few days before them' *read* ' privately, only with his man.'

[*f.* 10 (*b*)] *For* ' and was not easy . . . forced it on him' *read* ' nor would he ever go before men of quality.'

After ' function' *add* ' and I was full of many sad thoughts upon it.'

After ' arrival' *add* ' Middleton came down and.'

Before ' Sharp hoped' *insert* ' Lauderdale told me that.'

Om. ' but he would enter . . . one Wishart,' *and read* ' Afterwards one Wishart, a weak and insignificant but candid and good-natured old man, was preferred to it.'

For ' that it seemed but justice' *read* ' so Middleton thought it was but justice' (cf. *Mr. Airy's edition*).

[*They were brought into parliament.*]

Cf. *Hist.* i. 143 (' The session of parliament' *to* p. 144, *end of paragraph*).

Om. ' by the earl of Middleton' *and* ' the king . . . so much.'

For ' something before them . . '. or to the church' *read* ' some extraordinary occasions.'

Om. the simile of the harpies.

Om. ' This was plainly . . . negative voice upon them' (*the sentence inserted is merely repetition*).

For ' Nor did it escape censure' *read* ' Others made a more pleasant but malicious observation.'

Om. from end of sentence to ' imposing upon conscience.'

[*f.* 11 (*a*)] *For* ' had never carried . . . by this act' *read* ' thought the clergy ought to have their share in the exercise of all ecclesiastical authority, and that therefore it ought not to have been vested singly in the bishop.'

For ' and submitting' *read* ' the government as it was established by law, since that was an approving of the bishops having the sole power of jurisdiction.'

For ' All the bishops . . . fit to assume' *read* ' even when the bishops themselves intended not to pretend to anything more than a negative vote.'

[*Scruples concerning the oath of allegiance.*]

Cf. *Hist.* i. 144 (*from* ' Soon after' *to* ' and supremacy').

Om. ' for their words . . . senses.'

[Conduct of the earl of Cassillis¹.]

ᵃ In the former session of parliament the acknowledging
the king's supremacy in ecclesiastical matters was added to
the oath of allegiance, and not kept a distinct oath by itself
as it is in England; upon which the earl of Cassillis, when it
was tendered to him, desired to have leave to offer an explanation of it, which should be no other than that which was
established by law in England. Middleton was willing to
let him say what he pleased, but would not suffer him to put
it in writing. He said he could not swear it except he were
suffered to make the one as lasting and as public as the other
was, so he rose and left the parliament, and went and resigned
his places to the king, ᵇ but gave [him?] positive assurances
of his constant fidelity, and so got under his hand an order that
no oaths should be put to him; and he, perceiving the change
that was like to be made in the church, got likewise licence to
keep what chaplain he [*f.* 11 (*b*)] pleased for himself and his
own family.

[The act explanatory rejected.]

Cf. *Hist.* i. 145-6 ('The ministers to whom . . . denied allegiance to the
king,' *omitting end of paragraph*).

Om. 'This was the first time that.'

Om. 'He said the land . . . taken.'

For 'and he thought . . . offenders for a word' *read* 'he thought that this
nation, as they took the expressions from England, so ought to shew rather
more tenderness on this occasion than had been shewed to papists in England.'

Om. 'it ill became . . . all his party'; *and for* 'for they designed' *read* 'for
he designed.'

Om. 'So the ministers' . . . sense upon it.'

After 'king' *add* 'though they declared they were ready to swear that part
of it which concerned their allegiance.'

Some passages relating to the lord Balmerino's trial.

Cf. *Hist.* i. 21-5.

Begin 'Upon this invidious mixing things of different natures together
I will set down a long story, which I had from the duke of Lauderdale², who

ᵃ Cf. *Hist.* i. 144-5.   ᵇ *Ibid.* 227.

---

¹ Cassillis, it will be remembered,
was the father of Burnet's first wife,
Lady Margaret Kennedy.

² In the printed *History*, i. 25, the
story is said to be derived from Burnet's father (to whom the above saying

assured me that there was not any one thing that had a greater influence on the disposing people's minds to the late wars than it had. When the late king was in Scotland in the year [16]33 an act of parliament was brought in from [the lords of] the articles,' &c.

Before 'the royal prerogative' *insert* 'several branches of'; *om.* 'as it had been . . . 1606,' *and* 'passed in the year 1609,' *and* 'with their own consent.'

After 'thing to king James' *om. to* 'drawn into one'; *and read* 'and was now declared to be perpetually inherent in the crown, so all the puritan party resolved to oppose it.'

After 'Rothes, who' *read* 'spake first when it came to his turn to give his vote, and said he voted to the act in all its points, except the last, which he thought belonged to the church; and so he desired it might be divided from the rest, and put in an act by itself, for otherwise it would be given out that those who voted against the act were enemies to the prerogative, though it was only upon the account of that single clause [*f.* 12 (*a*)] that they were against it; but the king himself answered him that it was all but one act, and he must either give his consent to it or deny it as it stood; so after some hot words had passed about it, he declared that though he voted against it, it was only upon the account of that addition.'

After 'Some few lords' *add* 'of that party.'

For 'Almost . . . negative' *read* 'So then all the puritans voted against it; they were inferior in number till it came to the gentry and burgesses, but it was carried in the negative.'

After 'Rothes' *add* 'who had also taken notes'; *and after* 'negative' *add* 'and desired a second scrutiny.'

After 'venture on that' *add* 'for if upon a second calling of the roll any had retracted their votes, and given them otherwise than they had done before, then he was gone.'

After 'was published' *read* 'and it was given out that all the puritans had voted against the prerogative'; *and om.* 'The king . . . opposition.'

After 'the lords' *add* 'and other heads of the puritan party.'

For 'if the clerk of register might declare' *read* 'if it was in the clerk of register's power to make an act of parliament by declaring'; *and om.* 'and that no scrutiny was allowed.'

For 'a zealous . . . party' *read* 'a great puritan.'

For 'setting forth . . . redress' *read* 'representing to the king all the hard and illegal things that he had been put on [*sic*] against them, and all the patience and duty with which they had borne them; and concluded with a prayer that he would rightly consider what their laws were, and not suffer himself to be wrought on by the ill advices of wicked men.'

---

is ascribed) in consequence of his intimacy with the father of Duke Lauderdale; Dr. Burnet having at the time when he rewrote his *History* no desire to lay stress on his own intercourse with the duke. It is also clear, from a comparison of the narrative as it appears in Harl. MSS. 6584, in the ordinary text of Burnet's *History*, and in the textual notes to Mr. Airy's edition respectively, that Burnet revised the whole on obtaining, after the second version had been written, the copy of the original record (*Hist.* i. 26). The great difference in detail between the three versions and the greater vividness of the present narrative render it of interest.

For from 'he shewed this' *to* 'from whom he had it' (p. 23) *read only* 'he put it in the lord Balmerino's hands, who gave it to the earl of Rothes, [*f.* 12 (*b*)] and he shewed it to the king, but after the king had read a few lines in it he flung it away. The party were resolved not to let it go so, and intended to get many hands to it, and so to send it after the king ; yet the thing cooled, and perhaps would have gone no further ; but the next winter, Balmerino being in his own house, a neighbour of his,' *&c.*, *as in Mr. Airy's edition,* i. 34, *note* b, *with these variations* : *for* 'kindly received by him' *read* 'entertained without any witness of him' ; *om.* 'not suspecting . . . neighbour' ; *for* 'The Petition . . . Act' *read* 'A petition to the king' ; *for* 'and the other . . . fair' *read* 'and made haste to be gone.'

After 'St. Andrews' *add* 'who hated Balmerino' ; *and om.* 'who . . . alarmed at it, and' ; *also* 'beginning . . . within this act.'

Om. 'so it was thought . . . parliament.'

After 'In Scotland' *add* 'a peer is tried as a commoner ; only.'

Om. 'At this time . . . the lord Balmerino's trial.'

Om. 'The court was created . . . poor.'

After 'jury' *add* 'there lie challenges in that kingdom against all, peers as well as commoners, but the prisoner must give the reason of every challenge, and must prove it instantly ; so a list was made of such peers as they thought would be very pliant, but because he might give reasons for his challenging some, the old earl of Lauderdale was a peer that they had in reserve to be one of the jury, since' ; *and om.* 'in which so great . . . of that title' ; *and after* 'yet' *add* 'after he had challenged some and got them cast.'

After 'exceptione major' *add* 'As for the seven gentlemen, they were so chosen that he had nothing in particular to object to them.'

Om. 'It was long considered . . . counsel.'

For 'So it was settled . . . insist only on this' *read* 'In his indictment it was set out.'

For 'The court . . . was clear' *read* 'And the lord Balmerino was either the contriver, or assistant in the contrivance, or was the divulger, or was the concealer of it, and which of these soever were true he was guilty of death; but [Haig's confession considered] there was no proof of the first of the branches of the crime ; upon which the king's advocate fixed on the last.'

After 'discover him' *add* 'since he ought to have brought it to some privy councillor or magistrate' ; *and for* 'He pleaded . . . court gave it in their favour' *read only* 'He answered he had delivered it to Rothes, who was by inheritance sheriff of that county, and that he had shewed it to the king; but this was not admitted, because it ought to have been brought to some legal magistrate. There was also great arguing upon the substance of the paper to prove that it did not fall within those statutes ; but all [*f.* 13 (*a*)] that was overruled by the court.'

For 'forty-three years before' *read* 'in his youth' ; *for* 'in the murder . . . Murray' *read* 'the marquis of Huntly in the burning of Dunnibrissel, where the earl of Murray was killed.'

For 'in being' *read* 'that so mean a man should be.'

For 'and they would feel . . . lived' *read* 'and therefore he must tell them what the horror was that followed innocent blood.'

Before 'blood' *add* 'innocent.'

For 'but it cost . . . day and night' *read* 'yet the terror of that pursued him continually.'

After 'Traquair' *add* 'who was then treasurer and was one of the jury, though it was known that he had undertaken to get Balmerino condemned.'

After 'argument' *read* 'vehemently; [though?] the proof was one single testimony of a base man that had found it on his table, and that the paper looked like his hand'; *and om.* 'and said . . . paper or not.'

After 'argument against him' *add* 'and though he had then a business of great consequence lying before the king, yet he resolved rather to put all to hazard than be wanting to his duty'; and *om.* 'and urged . . . Upon those heads.'

[*f.* 13 (*b*)] *Om.* 'some undertaking . . . houses.

After 'pardon' *add* 'after a while's imprisonment'; *om.* 'with which . . . ingratitude'; *and for* 'but he thought . . . account' *read* 'but he never considered the king's pardon as either mercy or kindness to him, but as done to preserve his own party; for there were no guards then in Scotland, and the nobility was still powerful.'

For 'My father . . . curious matter' *read* 'This is the true account of that matter as I had it, and I hope this is neither an impertinent nor unpleasant digression.'

The act of indemnity.

Cf. *Hist.* i. 146 ('The main business' *to* p. 147, *end of paragraph*).

Begin 'But I now return to the parliament of Scotland. All that now remained was to pass,' *&c.*

For 'or to other punishments . . . life' *read* 'and so to clog the indemnity with it. Lauderdale understood the meaning of this well enough, that,' *&c.*

For 'This matter was debated . . . argued against it. They' *read* 'so he opposed it much in council, and one day, he being sick, the debate lay upon Crawford. It was.'

For 'that had . . . suffered much for it' *read* '[that] had been beforehand with England in redeeming all past offences; they had sent an army in [16]48, for the delivering the late king; they had called home the present king, and had lost two armies for him at Dunbar and Worcester, and had been enslaved ten years; they had all as one joined with Monk in hopes that he would declare for the king.'

Om. 'since made lord Tarbot.'

For 'vivacity of parts' *read* 'quickness of apprehension and of extraordinary parts.'

For 'who has had the art . . . fifty years' *read* 'and set on raising himself by all [*f.* 14 (*a*)] means possible. He has talked often to me as if.'

For 'but they are only . . . at all times' *read* 'but whenever they are put to any trial it appears that interest is above all things with him. He was considered by Middleton as the most extraordinary man of Scotland, and.'

After 'cautious' *add* 'and not being able to drink hard he could not preserve his interest'; *om. remainder of paragraph and first sentence of next.*

It was desired that some might be incapacitated.

Mackenzie [a] proposed to Middleton to send up another draft of an act of indemnity, in which, besides the fining of many, a clause was put of incapacitating twelve from public trust; [b] so two drafts were made; the one, according to the king's instructions, containing exceptions only of persons to be fined; the other had the additional clause for incapacitating. They were both carried up by Mackenzie, and laid before the king as the drafts agreed to by the parliament; and when Lauderdale objected the difference between them, Mackenzie said the parliament would be satisfied with the one, which was all that Middleton had power to grant, but they desired the other, to which Middleton could not give way till he knew the king's pleasure in it. So Lauderdale, never imagining that it was designed against himself, neither objected against it nor proposed any restrictions to it; but in general drew an instruction allowing Middleton to consent to the incapacitating of twelve [b]. Mackenzie told me afterwards that he was surprised to see Lauderdale pass that so carelessly and without any limitations; and said to the English chancellor (then present) that he wondered to see him consent to so large an instruction who had so much provoked the parliament of Scotland. But in this Middleton and Mackenzie committed a strange error; for there had been no such desire made by the parliament, which yet was so entirely in their hands that they could have procured it for a word. [c] Middleton afterwards pretended that many members of parliament had made that desire to him in private [c], and yet when that came to be examined he could find but twelve that would own it. [d] Mackenzie was at that time much considered at court, for Lauderdale was much hated, and everybody looked on him as one that was come to accuse him, and indeed Lauderdale's interest then was so

[a] Cf. *Hist.* i. 147.   [b] *Ibid.* 148.   [c] *Ibid. supra.*   [d] *Ibid. infra.*

low, and he had so few friends, that nothing but the method Middleton took afterwards to ruin him could have preserved him.

Om. from 'So lord Tarbot' *to* 'reputation.'

[*Condemnation of lord Lorn.*]

Hist. i. 148–9 (*to* 'though he had no instruction for it').

For 'One instance of unusual severity was . . . parliament, and complained of as' *read* 'While Middleton was gone from the court, Lorn thought it was now a fit time to reckon his own pretensions, so he took care to find out by what means he could get chancellor Hyde to be his friend, or at least not to be his enemy. The earl of Berkshire, who was poor and made great court to the chancellor, [*f.* 14 (*b*)] undertook to soften him; for which he was to have a thousand pound. Upon this Lorn, being pressed by some of his friends in Scotland to let them know the state of his affairs, writ a very indiscreet letter, full of reflections on his enemies, and said he had already convinced the king of many of their lies, and hoped to. do it more effectually now that he had gained him upon whom the chief of them depended. This letter was intercepted and complained of in parliament as,' *&c.*

Om. 'since . . . to the king.'

After 'tried upon it' *read* 'and sent up the copy of his letter to court. When Mackenzie brought it to the king.'

After 'parole' *add* '(and, as I remember, Lauderdale was bound for him).'

For 'the execution . . . against him' *read* 'execution, as he would be answerable for it.'

For 'upon his appearance . . . prisoner' *read* 'came to Edinburgh, some days within the time assigned him, and entered [? rendered] himself a prisoner.'

After 'leasing-making' *add* 'and his letters (I think that were intercepted) were brought for evidence.'

After 'speech' *add* 'which he showed me.'

After 'provocation' *add* 'and much affliction.'

Before 'printed' *add* 'writ and some.'

Om. 'some of these . . . the king's own hands.'

Om. 'passed on him . . . tragical conclusion[1].'

For 'in this age' *read* 'that ever was.' *Om.* 'or rather of the mockery'; *and after* 'justice' *add* 'I never spoke with any of those that judged him, but such as abhorred it.' *For* 'All that was said . . . proceeding' *read* 'That with which they covered themselves.'

[*f.* 15 (*a*)] *After* 'news' *add* 'if the particulars in it proved not to be true. Lauderdale took advantages against Middleton for suffering the day of execution to be left to him; whereas it ought to have been left to the king. Yet in this

---

[1] Argyll, be it remembered, at the date when Burnet first wrote was alive, though an exile.

he aggravated the matter too much, for the leaving it to him, as the king's commissioner, was upon this matter the leaving it to the king.'

After 'attainted' *for* 'by parliament . . . unheard-of' *read* 'this gave Lauderdale another advantage against Middleton, since it was the laying'; *and om.* 'This the earl . . . extend to life.'

[*Further proceedings concerning the indemnity.*]

Cf. *Hist.* i. 149 (*from* 'A committee' *to end of* p. 150, 'in this form').

For 'A committee . . . fines' *read* 'The act of indemnity came in the last place to be finished, in which there was an exception put both for the persons that were to be fined, and for those that were to be incapacitated, which was to pass in two different acts. For the former.'

For 'had been abroad' *read* 'were men of known loyalty.'

Om. 'for the meaning . . . paid the fine,' *and* 'which [*or* that] was . . . hurry.'

For 'carried further . . . designed it' *read* 'tenderer'; *and then insert* (cf. p. 148) 'The duke of Richmond and the earl of Newburgh came down during that session, and never was there seen a time of more extravagant madness and drinking; every night produced some new disorder or other; but the turn that was to be served by them was the possessing of all people with an opinion that the king was weary,' *&c., as on* p. 150.

For 'falling upon a minister' *read* 'tearing a minister from him without a trial or any sort of form.'

After 'expedients' *add* 'and indeed his strength lies in the finding out dexterous methods.'

For 'by ballot' *read* 'in a billet.'

[*f.* 15 (*b*)] *After* 'in a paper; and that' *add* 'all those being gathered in a box'; *and for* 'three' *read* 'two[1]'; *and for* 'and that they, without making . . . indemnity' *read only* 'and to draw out of them the names of those upon whom most votes should fall.'

After 'any one had voted' *add* 'I was told some of the billets were not unpleasant; no man was required to sign his billet, nor to show it; so some put in white paper, others disguising their hands excepted twelve of the bishops, others were for incapacitating Middleton and twelve of his chief friends.'

Om. 'By this means . . . list, that so'; *also* 'might be three . . . majority they.'

For 'The earl of Middleton . . . form' *read* 'and with [the above proviso] Middleton thought he would be in no danger by giving the royal assent to it, and it was done, and upon that the parliament was adjourned for some months.' *Then add* (cf. *Hist.* i. 146, *paragraph on the subject*) 'Another act passed for a test or declaration (to be signed by all that were in any public trust) for renouncing both the national covenant and the league and covenant, and the doctrine[2] of the lawfulness of resistance. This was particularly levelled against Crawford for the turning him out of the treasury, in case the act for incapacitating should miscarry.'

---

[1] 'Two' is the reading also of Mr. Airy's edition.
[2] See *infra*, p. 32, note 2.

The king was displeased with the incapacitating act.

Cf. *Hist.* i. *from beginning of* p. 151 *to* p. 152 ('of all [that] he had done ').

For ' for they reckoned . . . or his party. So they' *read only* ' so that Lauderdale's friends could not give him notice of it so early as was to be wished. And Middleton.'

For ' sent one . . . Durhâm' *read only* ' got one to provide himself of a very good horse, that held out with him till he got into Yorkshire, and then he took post'; *and om.* ' three days.'

After ' court' *add* ' to give the king an account of the business and to put the act of incapacity in his hands. [*f.* 16 (*a*)] They carried up likewise a letter signed by ten of the bishops' (*see* p. 151, *infra*; *only for* ' and his care of them all' *read* ' both in what he had already done, and in what he was then going about to do'; *and after* ' minister' *add* ' for Middleton saw the step he made was so bold that it must either ruin Lauderdale, or turn upon himself and be his own ruin'; *then return supra to where the narrative broke off at* ' got to court ').

For ' He carried it presently to the king, who' *read* ' As soon as Lauderdale got the news he was surprised, and the king having gone that day to dine at a house of the earl of St. Albans some miles from London, he took sir Robert Moray with him and went to find him out, and taking him aside after dinner, he gave him an account of what had passed in Scotland. The king at first.'

After ' Middleton' *add* ' for Lauderdale, reckoning himself safe, saw this was the best opportunity he could ever expect of ruining his enemy, and in that he was never cold nor slack.'

For ' From him, by his orders, he' *read* ' In conclusion the king ordered him to give an account of it to the chancellor, and to bring him his sense of it; so Lauderdale returned in a much easier temper than he was in when he went out. Chancellor Hyde was then out of town, and came not in for two days. As soon as he came Lauderdale.'

For ' was amazed . . . and said' *read* ' at first said it was not possible; then he said pleasantly.'

For ' he was sure' *read* ' he hoped'; *and for* ' otherwise no man could serve him' *read* ' and all his ministers must agree in it'; *and after* ' suffer him' *add* [*f.* 16 (*b*)] ' So far had Lauderdale engaged Hyde. That very night the duke of Richmond and Mackenzie came to London. As soon as Hyde saw them he asked them if they were mad, and plainly told them that they had changed the scene now, and that instead of attacking Lauderdale they must now betake themselves to a defensive; for all that could now be done was to set out Middleton's zeal and services so advantageously as to obtain a pardon for this last error; but they had now established Lauderdale; so with this melancholy prospect of ill success they came to wait on the king. He received them,' *&c., as in concluding sentences of* p. 151, *whence continue.*

After ' incapacity' *add* ' sealed'; *and after* ' he' *add* ' laid it down, and.'

Om. ' both,' *also* ' safety and his,' *and* ' the incapacity act . . . judgement'; *and read after* ' honour' ' The king's way is not to speak much upon such occasions; [so because],' *and om.* ' and, without . . . dismissed them'; *and for* ' they hoped' *read* ' Mackenzie thought'; *and after* ' mollified him' *add* ' but he quickly found that he was mistaken.'

Om. 'the earl of Middleton and.'

For 'even the Athenians were ashamed of it' *read* 'and it appeared what a way of proceeding it was'; *and om.* 'and they . . . after.'

For 'studied' *read* 'took another way.'

Before 'The change' *read* 'He laid before the king [that].'

[*Primrose advises Middleton.*]

[*f.* 17 (*a*)] Primrose told me that he advised Middleton to go up immediately and to attack Lauderdale with courage and force, and he drew up for him an accusation, of which he told me the heads. The preamble was reflecting on his family, particularly his uncle, secretary Maitland; who was not only attainted, but the very name Maitland was condemned in an unprinted act of parliament that passed during the minority of king James. Then followed an enumeration of all the violences he had been guilty of during the rebellion [1], with this conclusion, that his turning to the king was not an effect of loyalty, but of resentment for an affront put on him by some independents in the army. From that it went to shew his enmity to all the king's friends, and his protecting his enemies ever since his restoration. But when Mackenzie came down they were forced to lay all these thoughts aside; and Middleton was advised to stay in Scotland as long as he could; and though Lauderdale got [a] the king to write to him to come up, and give an account of affairs there, yet he found new excuses still for delaying his journey; and it was hoped that a little time would serve to weather this storm [a]. So he continued in Scotland some months; but at last he went up about Christmas.

A general character of the presbyterian ministers and an account of their ruin in Scotland [2].

Cf. *Hist.* i. 152 (*from* 'One act' *to near end of* p. 155, 'and in good repair').

Begin 'I am next to tell what all this service was for the church in which he was now so much employed; for opening which I must let the reader know that the presbyterians were great enemies to all lay patronages, but the

[a] Cf. *Hist.* i. 152.

---

[1] See *Lauderdale Papers*, i. 125, 127; also *Hist.*, Mr. Airy's edition, i. 359, note 2.

[2] The marginal heading in the *History* runs: 'The presbyterian ministers silenced.'

nobility and gentry were so much concerned in them that, till the parliament in the year [16]49 came, they could not obtain their desire of having them put down, and then was the election of ministers put,' &c.

Om. ' only it . . . past,' *and* ' who was obliged . . . demanded.'

For ' One clause . . . declared' *read* ' In this last sessions of Parliament an act passed declaring.'

[*f.* 17 (*b*)] *Om.* ' This took . . . hot men : so,' *and* ' had many . . . in which they.'

Om. ' whereas . . . part were ' ; *and om.* ' main body of the.'

For ' and to look on, and' *read* ' and all men were in expectation to.'

For ' and that was heightened . . . law' *read* ' and it was the great argument now used for his preservation at court, that he was carrying on the service of the church with such zeal (for that is always the name that every party bestows on the violence of those that support it) ; this it is likely sharpened him more at that time.'

Om. ' and all about him,' *and put rest of sentence in singular.*

For ' the heads of the presbyterians ' *read* ' Douglas, and the other heads of the party at Edinburgh.'

Om. ' if there were such . . . service in it.'

Om. ' all the wiser of.'

For ' was, that the bishops . . . room' *read* ' as the more dangerous method, was that some few eminent men would be silenced, and that the state would go on by degrees still singling out a few.'

Retain the reading ' insensible,' *and add* ' [and] which would have been the surer way,' *omitting rest of sentence.*

Om. ' and do their duty . . . connived at.'

For ' and according . . . received ' *read* ' and the nobility and gentry that were well affected to them gathered such companies as they could bring together about them, to give them public receptions, of which they were generally very fond.'

Om. ' before Michaelmas ' ; *after* ' privy council' *add* ' at Glasgow.'

Om. ' or serving . . . immediately.'

For ' This was opposed . . . William Lockhart' *read* ' Duke Hamilton and sir James Lockhart, father to the famous sir William Lockhart, who was a judge and a privy councillor, and had, especially in his old age, [*f.* 18 (*a*)] great inclinations to that party, opposed this much.'

For ' had come . . . [16]49 ' *read* ' fell within the act.'

For ' but the immediate . . . law ' *read* ' but the law, and the meritoriousness of a zealous execution of it.'

For ' So the proclamation . . . out ' *read* ' So it was carried, and next day it was printed.'

After ' turned out' *add* ' on another act.'

Om. ' considering the consequence of it, or.'

After ' Sharp said' *add* ' often.'

After ' print' *add* ' and said he was struck with it ; and he used always to lay the load of all the disorders that followed afterwards upon that rash act ; but I ever thought that was only because.'

Om. ' and all that sort of people.'

After ' honour' *add* ' So that I could never see why that law might not have been executed as well as others; and I make no doubt, but if he had been present that council day, he had not only concurred in this act, but had set it on ' ; *and for* 'The earl . . . submission of the presbyterians' *read* 'The obedience given to this act put Middleton to new measures.'

Om. 'and that some . . . preserve the church.'

After 'shewed' *add* 'about a month before.'

After 'executed' *add* 'but that he undertook to fill the churches of London better than ever' (cf. *Hist.* i. 192).

For 'From thence . . . at nothing' *read* 'So they resolved to follow that pattern.'

Om. (*for the moment*) 'and among others . . . protection.'

For 'well endowed' *read* 'of the value of £60 a year.'

[*Personal fortunes of Burnet*, 1662-3.]

[a] At that time Glencairn sent for me, and obliged me to be oft with him; he also made me acquainted with Mackenzie[a] (known best in Scotland by the title of lord Tarbot, for he was a judge, or, as we call them, a lord of the session). He was a man of fine notions, and had the beginnings of very valuable parts of learning; so I delighted much in his company; but I soon grew weary of Glencairn, [b] for he was dull and haughty. [c] They both pressed me much to have accepted [*f.* 18 (*b*)] a benefice in the west[c]; but I thank God that preserved me from it, the reasons of which will appear afterwards.

Now I began to be known to great men, and have ever since been much in their company, which has brought much envy and censure on me from other clergymen, who fancied that I used odd arts to compass it. But I can give no other account of that matter but this; I never sought the acquaintance of a great man in my whole life, but have often declined it; many loved me for my father's sake; and I had a facetiousness and easiness in conversation that was entertaining; I had read a variety of things, and could dress them in easy words, so that many liked my company. I never imposed it on any; but I do not deny that I had great vanity in finding my company so much desired; I talked much, and was in many things very foolish and very faulty; yet I began early to set myself to serve all people that were low or in affliction. I waited often

[a] Cf. *Hist.* i. 155.   [b] See *ibid.* 58.   [c] *Ibid.* 155.

on Lorn[1] this winter [1662–3] in the castle of Edinburgh, and conversed much both with him and Swinton[2]; that which carried me into Lorn's acquaintance was a friendship into which the countess of Balcarres received me, who was then a widow[3]; both her lord and she had a great value for my father; and she, having heard no ill things of me, sent for me, and we grew soon acquainted. I found her a woman of great piety and worth[4]; she was not bigoted to presbytery, though she liked it better than episcopacy; she has a fine understanding, a pleasant temper, and having lived almost ten year in the court[5], she could talk of many things that were quite new to me. In short, though I have found since that she was mistaken in many things, yet the great conversation I had with her this winter was a very good preparation for my journey to London next year. From an acquaintance we entered into a very great friendship (if this is not too proud and too levelling a word); and it continues to this day very great, though she has thought fit sometimes to let it fall; yet whenever we meet it is the same it was; and it would be greater now than ever it was, both because she is now in affliction[6], and in her last troubles by the attainder of the earl of Argyll

---

[1] Lord Lorn (condemned to death Aug. 26, 1662) was not released from prison till June 4, 1663. In October, 1663, he was restored to the family title as ninth Earl of Argyll.

[2] See *Lauderdale Papers*, i. 64; and Mr. Airy's notes to i. 194, 229 of the *Hist.* in his edition.

[3] Anna Mackenzie, daughter of Colin Earl of Seaforth, married first Alexander second Lord Lindsay, afterwards first Earl of Balcarres; and secondly, in 1670, two years after the death of his first wife, that Earl of Argyll to whom, as Lord Lorn, she had introduced Burnet. At the time we are now considering, she had just settled as a widow of a little over forty at Balcarres; her first husband, a moderate Presbyterian, or 'Resolutioner' loyalist, having died in 1659 in exile. She was related by birth or marriage to the leading Scottish nobility of the day; being very intimate with Sir Robert Moray (who had married her husband's sister), as well as with Baxter, Cowley, &c. How well she deserved the esteem accorded to her by these distinguished men is shown in Lord Lindsay's charming *Memoir of Lady Anna Mackenzie*. See also *Lauderdale Papers*, i. 28, Mr. Airy's note; *Hist.*, Mr. Airy's edition, i. 104, note.

[4] Baxter says 'her great wisdom, modesty, piety, and sincerity made her accounted the saint at the Court'(quoted in Lord Lindsay's *Memoir*, pp. 52–3).

[5] From 1653, when, with her husband, she joined the exiled Court, to 1662, when she left London, whither she had returned on the Restoration pp. 32, 59 (*ibid.*).

[6] The second attainder of Argyll, in 1681, reduced her and her children almost to starvation; and in Dec. 1683 she was questioned before the Privy Council for corresponding with her husband (*ibid.* p. 124).

(whose wife she is now) I interposed to serve her with much zeal, though not with equal success [1]. Her friendship not only led me into Lorn's acquaintance, but likewise opened a way for me to some very useful friendships when I went to England. [a] But that which of all my other friendships has proved the greatest blessing of my life, was begun this summer with bishop Leighton [a]. I had heard him preach and was ravished with him ; it was beyond all that I had ever heard, so I found a way to be admitted into his [*f.* 19 (*a*)] acquaintance, and I can truly say it, I never was with him but [b] I felt within me a commentary on these words, ' Did not our hearts burn within us, while he talked with us? [b] ' He led me into higher thoughts than I had formerly known, both of a more total deadness to the world, and of a more entire dedication of my whole life to the service of God and to the good of souls ; he quite emancipated me from the servility I was yet somewhat in to systems and received opinions, and spoke always of religion as a thing above opinions and parties, and that these things were of no great consequence. He also spake much to me of humility, of abasement, of being nothing in one's eyes, and of being willing to be nothing in the eyes of all the world ; these discourses of his, and the sad scene that the country presented by the revolutions of affairs in it, filled me with many serious thoughts. I had some uneasiness at home, for my mother and all our family (being highly and indiscreetly presbyterian) were much troubled to see me episcopal, though I did not make haste to declare myself; all these things cast me into a deep melancholy. I spent whole days in silence and devotion, and the nights were tedious to me. I set myself to study mathematics that winter, and made a considerable progress with the help of George Keith [2] that is now a quaker ; he is a great mathema-

[a] Cf. *Hist.* i. 138.   [b] *Ibid.* 135.

[1] *Hist.* i. 520-1.

[2] Keith, who had been a class-fellow of Burnet's at Aberdeen between 1653 and 1657, had distinguished himself there by his attainments in mathe-matical and oriental learning. De-signed for the Presbyterian ministry, he became a Quaker between 1662 and 1664, but in 1700 finally seceded to Anglicanism, and, becoming a mis-

tician, and a very extraordinary man, only too fanciful and enthusiastical.   He was then a presbyterian, and I took him off from that, but he never settled to anything till he turned quaker, yet in many things he differs from them.

[*The presbyterian ministers described.*]

But now I return to the public. ª The presbyterian ministers were now turned out; they¹ were generally a grave and sober sort of men ; ᵇ they had little learning among them ᶜ but that of systems, commentaries ᶜ, and the Aristotelian philosophy ; the reformers were the ancientest authors they read.   ᵈ They had much of the Scripture by heart ᵈ; and their sermons were full of quotations out of them, though they were seldom critical in the application of them ; their ᵉ way of preaching was plain and intelligible, but very dull; it went generally on [?] doctrine, reason and use, only those of a more exalted form ran out much into subtilties, about scruples which they called cases of conscience ᵉ. They prayed long and with much fervour; they preached twice on Sunday, and for most part once on a week-day ; they catechised all their people at least once a year before their communions, ᶠand they used to visit the families in their parishes oft, and to pray to them, and exhort them in secret.   They had also frequent private meetings where those that were of a higher dispensation than the rest .[*f.* 19 (*b*)] met, sometimes without the minister and sometimes with him, and used to propose their cases and discourse about them, and pray concerning them; and by these means the people (especially in the west where those practices were frequenter) grew to that readiness both in discoursing about sacred things and in praying that it has astonished me oft to

ª Cf. *Hist.* i. 156.   ᵇ *Ibid.* 157.   ᶜ *Ibid.* 34.   ᵈ *Ibid.* 156.   ᵉ *Ibid.* 156 and 34.   ᶠ *Ibid.* 156.

---

sionary of the S. P. G., died in 1716, almost his latest published work bearing upon mathematical subjects (Rev. Al. Gordon in *Dict. Nat. Biog.* xxx. 318–21 ; *Hist.* ii. 248–9).
¹ With this passage should be compared pp. 12–29 of Burnet's youthful

but able work, *A modest and free Conference betwixt a Conformist and a Nonconformist about the present distempers of Scotland*, published by him anonymously in 1669 at the age of twenty-six. This early estimate is of course far less judicial in tone.

overhear them at these exercises; not but that they had many impertinences among them, yet it was a wonderful thing to me, and perhaps not to be paralleled anywhere, that the generality of the commons should have been able to pray extempore sometimes for a whole hour together. [a] Besides this there was great severity in punishing some sins, such as whoredoms, drunkenness, swearing, and breach of sabbath; and the church session and the pillar of repentance were great terrors. For fornication one was to make public profession of repentance for three several Lord's days [a], and this was executed on all without respect of persons; the present duke Hamilton submitted to it before his marriage. [b] They were held in great esteem with the people; they were likewise for [the] most part men either of birth themselves, or had married with gentlemen's families; and they lived very decently in the country. By all these things they had so great an interest both with the gentry and commonalty, [c] that it was no wonder if the turning out so many all at once made great impressions on them. [d] Their faults and defects were not so conspicuous; they were generally little men that had narrow souls and low notions; many of them were fawning and servile, especially to the ladies that were much esteemed for piety [1]; they were affected in their behaviour, and extremely apt to censure all that differed from them, and to believe and report everything they heard to their prejudice, and were a sour and supercilious sort of people.

Their opinions concerning civil governments [2].

[e] The greatest part of them had very ill principles as to civil government [e], of which there were two classes. The one was of those that thought the people had an unalienable right to them to assert their liberty and religion, in opposition

---

[a] Cf. *Hist.* i. 157.   [b] *Ibid.* 156.   [c] *Ibid.* 158.   [d] *Ibid.* 157.   [e] *Ibid.* 157-8.

---

[1] This clause was omitted in the final revision only; see Mr. Airy's edition, i. 273, note a.
[2] Burnet's views on non-resistance.

A note on this subject, too long to be inserted here, will be found among the Appendices to this volume.

both to king and parliament, and to all the laws that could be made ; and ever after the rising of the western counties in the year [16]48 against the parliament and their committee all the high men amongst them have been forced, in order to the justifying of that, [*f.* 20 (*a*)] to assert this principle, which seemed ever to me the most destructive to the peace of mankind that could be. For if such a number of people as find themselves in a capacity to resist the government may lawfully do it then all governments are left to an eternal danger ; since it is not possible to govern so, but very many will be dissatisfied ; and these will think the ends of government are broken by every ill administration. And as for religion (that is of a spiritual nature, in which we are to expect only such rewards as are in this life internal and spiritual and that will be eternal hereafter), it is certain we are to cast that care on Him whose providence governs all human affairs, and are to think it enough if we are truly religious ourselves, and diffuse it among such as are about us; but there being such a vast difference of opinion concerning religion it is certainly inconsistent with the peace of mankind (the preserving which must be a great part of religion) that men should raise commotions on that account. And this is yet much clearer in the Christian religion ; in which, as we have the declaration of our Saviour that his kingdom was not of this world (for otherwise his servants would have fought for him), and his practice likewise in reproving St. Peter when he drew his sword in his defence, so it is also plain (both from St. Paul's Epistle to the Romans and St. Peter's first Epistle) that the Apostles condemned all resistance ; for indeed words can scarce be found out that are more express and plain than theirs are upon the subject. The nature of the Christian religion proves this yet more fully than any particular text can do ; it is a doctrine of faith, patience, humility, self-denial, contempt of the world, and resignation to the will of God ; we are called in it to bear crosses, to suffer persecution, and to be ready to offer up our lives with joy for it; so that I much less wonder to find men that are very serious Christians to be against all wars whatsoever than to see them led into opinions about the lawfulness of resistance on that account.

It is also clear from the practice of all nations and from what is set down both in the Old and New Testaments that a state of slavery is neither contrary to laws of nature, nor religion, nor to the Christian doctrine; for in the New Testament masters are nowhere charged to [manumit][1] their servants but only to use them well, and St. Paul thought himself obliged to send Onesimus back to Philemon, for a servant having by a fair bargain given up his liberty was ever thereafter subject to his master; and by a greater congruity of reason, if a nation had chosen representatives who had consented to laws that gave away their liberty in the matter of resistance [*f.* 20 (*b*)] the thing is done, and can never be reversed but by the same authority that established it. So far I have given my sense of this very dangerous opinion that many of them hold.

A .digression concerning government.

The second opinion was that the king and the law were never to be resisted—that is, the king [and][2] parliament, or the king governing according to law—but that laws were the measures of subjects' submission as well as of their obedience, and that the king was as much bound to his people by his coronation oath, as they were bound to him by the oath of allegiance; and therefore when he brake the one they were absolved from the other and might defend themselves, particularly if there were any provisos in the law that seemed to reserve this right to them. This becomes a question of law: Whether the king is the head of the government or is only trusted with it as the chief minister in it. In our case this seemed to me to be out of doubt; for a king among us has his full power before he is crowned, so that, whatever coronations might have been anciently, they are now only the

---

[1] 'Emancipate' is the original reading; corrected by Burnet to 'manumit.'
[2] This seems preferable to the 'or' of the MS.

pompous declarations of his power and not the investitures by which he receives it; and therefore his oath is only an obligation on himself to God. And since by plain and express laws all the power of the militia is vested singly in the king (with as positive exclusions of the subjects using force against him as can be contrived in words) all this falls to the ground; and whatever power of self-preservation may be supposed to be in men before such laws were made, yet, these being once made, all that ceases and the liberty of the subject is in so far given up. This has been always my opinion in this matter; yet I do not deny, but the thing will bear a great debate from the nature and ends of government, in cases where they are visibly violated by high degrees of rage and cruelty. But all I can say in that case is, that it is certain a madman ceases to be a man and naturally falls under guardians and tutors, and every man has a right to stop him, if he runs about to do mischief; so the rage of a monstrous tyrant may be presumed to be really phrensy, and in that case he may be restrained and the next heir is guardian; not so much because his people cease to be subjects as because he ceases to be a man. But this falls out so seldom that it signifies nothing to the debate as it is stated amongst us. I will go a little further on this head because I studied it much with Mr. Nair[n?] [*f.* 21 (*a*)] at this time and have since that time applied my thoughts so much to it that if I am able to search any one thing to the bottom, I have done it in this matter; and indeed my aversion to the ill conduct of affairs, and somewhat of natural heat and carelessness in my temper, has given me the bias rather in favour of resistance than against it; so that nothing but the force of reason and conscience has determined me against it. I confess I could never understand what they meant who settled monarchy or the power of princes upon a divine right. Indeed, under the Mosaical dispensation (in which the Jews had the land of Canaan by an immediate grant from Heaven) God did reserve the supreme civil government to himself, and by prophets (solemnly authorized) he declared on whom he would have it fall. So it was done

in the cases of Saul, David, Jeroboam, and Jehu; therefore
all that is in the Old Testament concerning civil government
belonged only to the policy of the Jews and signifies nothing
to the present matter. But in the New Testament there are
no particular forms of government prescribed, only general
rules both for governors and subjects are given. The Roman
government was then in one person, not only by conquest,
but by the surrender the senate had made to Augustus, which
gave him and his family a good title. I was for sometimes
[*sic*] pleased with Dr. Hammond's notion[1], that the power of
the sword must be from God since the people could never
devolve it, for no man can give that which he has not; since
then no man has a right either to kill himself, or to kill
another, the right of killing can only come from God. This
looked fine and plausible, but I thought it too fine and at
last found the flaw in it. In order to the opening this, I shall
give the best account I can of the beginning and nature of
government. Certainly every father had an absolute power
over his children, but upon his death they were all free; for
primogeniture cannot be supposed by the law of nature to
give the elder brother any sort of authority over his younger
brethren. So upon the multiplication of mankind (their first
seats growing too narrow for them) we cannot but suppose
that they hived [*sic*] out to the next fields, and countries;
and the first possession gave a man as much right to any
fields as he that came first could employ or manage; and he
that came next had a right to sit down at a competent distance from him. Now self-preservation being a part of the
law of nature, every man has it entire that is a free man; and
such were all men upon the death of their father. There are
two branches in self-preservation; the one is a right [*f.* 21 (*b*)]
to beat off a violent and unjust aggressor; the other is a
right to take reparation of any sudden or violent invasion;
and without the second the first cannot effect its end (which

---

[1] The allusion is probably to the
famous *Practical Catechism*, Book II,
sect. v. There is, however, also a
tract by Hammond, *Of resisting the
lawful magistrate under colour of religion*, published at Oxford in 1644.

is self-preservation); and a man's whole property comes under the general notion of himself. Every man likewise owes his neighbour assistance in the case of invasion, both as it is an act of humanity to another and as it is a mean to cover himself; for he cannot expect that another should assist him but as he is ready likewise to give him assistance when he needs it. Now, government or civil society is nothing, but a compromise for the use of this second branch of self-preservation (that is the taking just revenge, or reparation) in which men reserve the first part entire still of covering themselves from an unjust aggressor (for that will not admit of delays nor stay for forms); but they resign up the other. Therefore I think, with reverence to Dr. Hammond (whose memory I highly honour [1]), that every man had a right to the sword against his neighbour that invaded him, both for self-defence and for just revenge; and that government is the resigning up the second of these to be managed in such a method as shall be agreed on. Now the first occasion of these compacts seems to have risen from the loose companies of robbers who lived on spoil and entered into combinations for the managing their designs and dividing the spoil; and as they prevailed over the weaker and more industrious part of mankind, that gave themselves to agriculture, so conquest and absolute monarchies did grow and spread itself [*sic*] by those troops of successful robbers; and the combination[s] of the more industrious seem to have given the beginnings to common-wealths which [oft times *or* at times [2]] were eaten up by conquerors. Another beginning of governments seems to have risen out of the industry and success of some and the laziness and unsuccessfulness of others, who were thereby reduced to such extremities, as to sell themselves to the others; and by this means a rich man like Abraham came to have a great family, and with his 318 males he must have grown up quickly to a vast empire, since we see to what a number seventy-two souls

---

[1] For Burnet's high sense of Hammond's virtues see *Hist.* i. 177.

[2] The phrase in brackets is insert-ed by Burnet, in correction of the words 'at time' written by the transcriber.

increased in Egypt in 400 years' time. So it is probable that those masters of numerous families took large countries and gave their servants a great deal of their liberty again; but retained still a dominion over their properties or lives though they did not always use it; and out of this the more regular and lasting monarchies seem to have risen. [*f.* 22 (*a*)] But upon the whole matter, since property and liberty are things alienable, we are not now to examine what were the first fountains or beginnings of this power, but must take things as we now find them. Those who assert a divine right had best shew where God has declared it, how it has come into such a family, how it comes to go in some governments to the heir general, and in others only to the heir male, besides many other vast diversities that are in government; and how to derive all these from God, is that which I could never conceive. But on the other hand, though I do not derive my property to my goods from the law of God but hold it only by the law of the land where I live, yet having this property once vested in me, the law of God sets a fence about it and binds up all men's consciences, so that they cannot break in upon this property without sinning against God. So likewise though I can see no divine right on which the king can found his title (there being no declaration made by God—unless it be in his supernatural curing the king's evil on which I believe he would not willingly ground his title—) yet he has otherwise a very good right. First, a long and immemorial possession which is the first title to any property; this has been often confirmed in his ancestors and in himself by plain and express laws, and is more particularly bound upon the consciences of his people by the oath of allegiance, all which are indeed human titles, but they vest in him the same right to the crown, and to all the prerogatives of it, and in particular to that of the militia, that any other man has in his property; and as the law of God secures every man in his property so that it is theft or robbery for another to invade it, so the same rule secures the king in his, so that it is usurpation and rebellion to invade any part of it. And thus I have taken occasion to give this full and plain account of my opinion as to civil government and all rebellion against it; which I have so openly and frequently declared both in books, in sermons, and in familiar discourses, that if I had not seen too much of the injustice and baseness of the world to wonder at anything I should wonder much to find myself aspersed as a favourer of rebellion; whereas I think there is no man living whose principles determine him more steadily against it. But I leave this digression and return to the change now made in Scotland.

[*Prejudices infused against episcopacy.*]

Cf. *Hist.* i. 158 ('The people were much troubled . . . before he died').

For 'infusing . . . both in public and private' *read* 'preaching to the people.'

For 'was to destroy . . . vice' *read* 'flowed from an enmity to Christ and to the power of religion.

[*f.* 22 (*b*)] *For* 'aimed . . . immoral' *read* 'were to be raised above their brethren; and so they made their hearers believe that all zeal and strictness in religion was [*sic*] to be borne down among them.

After 'northern parts' *add* 'such as had only taught schools there, and many of them could not get so high.'

Om. 'the most concerned'; *and from* 'I have thus opened' *to end of paragraph.*

[*Burnet's own conduct (winter of* 1662-3).]

I was all this winter at Edinburgh, and went very little abroad; I read besides mathematics[1] several of the fathers, and went through the tomes of the Councils in a series, till I came down to the second Nicene Council; and out of the canons that I found there I formed an idea of church government that quite spoiled me as to all preferment. I made a large abstract of what I liked best in all those ages, and I took up then such notions as I could never since that time lay down. I grew to hate all opinions that tended to raise the wealth and the secular power of the clergy, and insensibly came to love a monastic state of life. I hated our contentions at home, and my melancholy prevailed so upon me, that nothing but clear and strong principles could have preserved me from going over to the church of Rome, and

---

[1] See *ante*, p. 30.

entering into a religious order.   I writ an unsubscribed[1] letter to Sharp, setting before him the miserable state [*f.* 23 (*a*)] in which we were falling, and begged him to think on somewhat to heal our breaches, and to settle us again.   I sent it by my man, who did not come away so quick but he was examined and owned that he came from me.   Sharp bid him tell me that he would be glad to speak with me, so two days after I went to him.   I had never seen him before; I kneeled for his blessing, so by that he saw I was episcopal.   He treated me roughly, and asked me what I had to propose for the settlement of the government or church.   I told him remedies could be easily found out, if there were once a disposition to seek for them; but being pressed by him to offer somewhat, I proposed the suffering all the presbyterians to return to such churches as were not yet planted, and then seeking expedients for keeping matters in some unity till they should die out, and in the meanwhile to be taking care of a good breed[2].   He grew a little calm at last, and told me that young men understood not government and ought not to meddle in it; he believed I had good intentions, but charged me not to talk of that that passed between us to any person; and so dismissed me with some civilities.   I confess a disease had now got into my mind which held me above ten years.   It was an opinion that I had that mankind was capable of amendment, and that churches and churchmen could be reformed, and that abuses might be so laid open that they should grow generally odious to all the world.   With these things I pleased as well as I vexed myself very long, and I made it my chief business in the study of antiquity to pick up everything that might fortify these notions; and I have had many discourses with bishop Leighton concerning

---

[1] This 'letter' which was 'unsubscribed' and written before Burnet's introduction to Sharp (see f. 23 (*a*) *infra*) must not be confounded with the signed 'Memorial' sent by Burnet in 1666 to all the bishops of Burnet's acquaintance (see *Hist.* i. 217, and Mr. Airy's note *in loco*, i. e. vol. i. p. 387 of his edition).   A copy of the latter, which was not known to exist, has been found among the Burnet MSS. in the Bodleian (Add. MSS. D. 23, ff. 103-10), and will be published by the Scottish Historical Society in their next *Miscellany*.

[2] This was Leighton's scheme; see *supra*, p. 16; and *Hist.* i. 274-6.

them, who had heat enough that way. [a] Mr. Charteris had always the true notion of this matter, that it was a vain thing to dream of mending the world [a] (and chiefly that which is generally the worst part of it, I mean churchmen) ; so that all that a wise or good man ought to do was to possess his own mind with good notions and to infuse them in some few individuals that were prepared for them, or were capable of them ; and that it was a fruitless labour to hope to propagate them to the world, or to do any good on great numbers. But these things did not cool me ; time and experience have at last done it ; for I have now for many years laid down all these thoughts upon which I had formerly raised many schemes and formed many models.

In the beginning of the next year 1663 [b] a plot was discovered in London, and one that was taken for it said to the king that if he would save his life he would tell him where the lord Warriston was ; upon which it being found that he was at Rouen, one was sent to the court of France for a warrant to seize him ; and that being granted, he was taken and brought over to [*f.* 23 (*b*)] the Tower of London [b]. When the news of this came to Scotland my mother (who loved her brother to a very high degree) desired me to go to London to be assistant to his lady, hoping that I might have easy access to Lauderdale ; so I went thither.   It fell in an ill time ; for Lauderdale, being then in his struggle for mastery with Middleton, would not meddle in any sort to do us any service. We solicited all the hungry courtiers ; many that had a great mind to our money tried what could be done ; but they all found it was a thing too big for them to meddle with ; so after five months' fruitless attendance [c] he was sent down to Scotland, but the end of his business shall be told in its proper place [c].

Middleton disgraced.

Cf. *Hist.* i. 200 (*from* ' But now I return ' *to* p. 203, ' for all his high character ').

For ' But now I return . . . received by the king ' *read* ' At this time several papers passed between Lauderdale and Middleton, for as soon as the latter came up.'

For ' The lord Clarendon . . . fortnight ' *read only* ' which was done about a fortnight after.'

[a] Cf. *Hist.* i. 248.   [b] *Ibid.* 198.   [c] *Ibid.*

After 'writing' *add* 'that so he might prepare an answer for them. Lauderdale sent his paper to him within two days.'

For 'all on design . . . they had done' *read* 'Clarendon advised his delaying it as long as could be.'

For 'Sheldon . . . errors' *read* 'both Sheldon, who was then in high favour, and Monk were set on the king, to mitigate his displeasure against Middleton.'

For 'who knew Scotland . . . service' *read* 'said it would discontent all the cavalier interest.'

Om. (*for the time*) 'And to support all this . . . go up'; *reading only* 'During this contest, Sharp came up.'

Om. 'and that he would lay . . . advice sent to him.'

For 'When he reproached . . . denied all' *read* 'He protested to him he had opposed the billeting[1], and had put in a billet of white paper.'

After 'shewed it to Sharp' *add* 'written all with his own hand, and signed by him and nine other bishops.'

For 'in a most abject manner' *read* 'like a child that was to be whipped.'

After 'power' *add* 'and they that were not yet well settled and knew they had so many enemies durst not provoke him and his friends, which was all the party they had.'

Om. 'would forgive . . . past, and'; *also* 'So Sharp . . . wholly his.'

[*f.* 24 (*a*)] *After* 'the next day' *insert* 'for he grew very soon to put some confidence in me, and to speak to me of public affairs.'

For 'Sharp . . . well' *read* 'So that Sharp began to think it might be more for their interest to have Middleton changed than continued; he found.'

Om. 'which he was uneasy . . . resist it'; *and* 'for the lord Lauderdale . . . readily do.'

Om. 'desiring him . . . kept down.'

After 'king's hand' *add* 'and signet.'

After 'mind in the matter' *add* 'Lauderdale represented this to the king as a strange piece of insolence.'

Om. 'when his head . . . mind it;' *and for* 'bid him . . . master of himself' *read* 'said somewhat, which he fancied amounted to a warrant to recall his letter.'

Om. 'The queen-mother . . . end of May' *and substitute* 'Middleton gave in his answer [cf. *Hist.* i. 200] in which he laid all upon the parliament, and said he thought he had taken the safest way, by which, as he gratified so loyal a parliament, so he kept the thing entire to the king to do with it what he pleased. Within two or three days after he had given in his answer [*f.* 24 (*b*)] Lauderdale had a reply ready, which was soon put in his hands; and he took as much time to answer that, as he did for the former. In the meantime many letters came from Scotland [cf. *ibid. infra*] of the insolencies of the presbyterian party, and that the churchmen who built all their expectations on Middleton's zeal and steadiness were quite discouraged; all the cavaliers and the clergy about the court had this in their mouths perpetually, and Lauderdale expostulated with Sharp, as giving the credit, if not the being, to these discourses; and he knew him too well to believe his protestations to the contrary for his own vindication. At last, in the beginning of May, Middleton

---

[1] Cf. *Lauderdale Papers*, i. 112 3.

gave in his second paper of answers, and so they both left the matter before the king, and on the 22nd of May.'

After 'trust' *add* 'in which Monk spake the most.'

Om. 'Yet he promised . . . honest man.'

After 'after that' *add* 'on the 29th of May.'

For 'after a sort . . . injustice' *read* '[his] greatness overset him.'

Om. 'He and his company . . . anything like it, so.'

For 'great magnificence . . . many' *read* 'the highest magnificence of any commissioner I ever saw in Scotland.'

Om. 'and he was a firm ᵢ . . enemy.'

For 'trust him' *read* 'trust him too much ;' *and for* 'and kept . . . high character' *read* 'for holding another session of parliament. Crawford also resigned up the treasury, and Rothes was made treasurer. Sir Robert Moray was appointed to officiate as secretary in Lauderdale's absence [1].'

[Burnet in England, 1663[2].]

But now I shall give some account of myself during my stay at London. I contracted two friendships that proved of great use to me ; ᵃone was with sir Robert Morayᵃ and the other with Mr. Drummond, and they were both of that importance that in the daily enumeration I make in my thanksgivings to God for the signal blessings of my life I never forgot [*sic*] them. Sir Robert Moray[3] was a wonderful composition [*f.* 25 (*a*)] of a man ; there was nothing of art or form in him, all was simple and natural. ᵇHe had a great strength of apprehension and vivacity of mindᵇ in pursuing lively notions ; he knew mankind well, and though he never spake hardly of any man, yet when he gave characters of men to a friend, it appeared he did it with great judgement. He was not imposed upon by vulgar opinions or prejudices, but had a most unclouded clearness of mind. ᶜHe had studied Epictetus much and had wrought up his mind to all his maxims, so that things without him seemed to make no impressions on him, and he was ever the same, so well poised that I never saw him in different tempersᶜ. He could pass from business to learning, from that to pious discourses,

ᵃ Cf. Life (*Hist.* ii), p. 676.   ᵇ Cf. *Hist.* i. 59.   ᶜ *Ibid. supra.*

[1] See Mr. Airy's notes, *Hist. in loco.*

[2] For this episode see *ante*, p. 41 ; Autobiography, *infra*, ff. 199, 200 ; the Life by Thomas Burnet (appended to *Hist.* ii), p. 676 ; *Hist.* i. 200, and Routh's note.

[3] The reader should compare the characters of Moray given in *Hist.* i. 59 ; Life (*Hist.* ii), p. 676 ; Auto. *infra*, f. 200 ; and *Scottish Review*, Jan., 1885 (Mr. Airy).

and then go into familiar prating, and go round again, with that easiness that it was visible nothing went deeper into his thoughts than as he had a mind it should go. [a] He had noble and generous thoughts of God and religion [a]. The chief exercise of his devotion was every night to review what he had seen that day, with acts of adoration, celebrating such of the divine attributes as appeared to him in the new occurrences of providence ; and this he did commonly in an audible discourse which he said heated his fancy and fixed his thoughts. He had some favourable characters written to him of me by the countess of Balcarres [1], and after a whiles general conversation, he took me into his bosom, and carried me always about with him ; so that I spent the half of the day in his company ; and he gave me more good rules for human life than I had ever heard before. One thing in him was quite new to me, which was the receiving all that came to him with an open and cheerful visage as if he had known them long, and his talking of indifferent things frankly to them ; this was very obliging, and took off that restraint of bashfulness that is on modest men. [b] His greatest act of kindness was to me in reproving what he saw amiss in me [b]; which was, too much talk, and a bold way of speaking ; a readiness to censure others, and to set a value on myself, and to affect to talk eloquently [2] ; of this last he cured me quite, and shewed me how far plain simple reason was beyond all laboured stuff; but my other faults were too deeply rooted to be soon cured. My other friend was Mr. Drummond [3], who had lived above ten year in London, and had done great services to many of his countrymen

[a] Cf. *Hist*. i. 59.   [b] *Ibid*. and Life (*Hist*. ii), p. 676.

---

[1] See *ante*, p. 29, note 3.

[2] Cf. with this frank self-condemnation the very amusing and garrulous reminiscences of Cockburn, who had known Burnet in early youth, and speaks much of his self-conceit (*A specimen of some free and impartial remarks . . . occasioned by Dr. Burnet's 'History,'* Remark II, pp. 27-30).

[3] i. e. Mr. Patrick Drummond, the correspondent of Sharp (see *Lauderdale Papers*, i. 3, 36, 41-56, 60, 64-90, 93, 94). A Presbyterian minister living in London, he had acted as a channel between Sharp, before his defection, and the English Presbyterians ; and also served occasionally as the intermediary between Sharp in Scotland and Lauderdale in England (*ibid*. 79, 88, 90, and see Auto. *infra*, f. 200).

(especially to Lauderdale and Crawford in their imprisonment) and had been Sharp's particular friend and confidant.
He lived then in sir Thomas Viner's house [1] as his friend,
and was very low in a consumption; it was believed he had
an ulcer in his lungs, and it was not thought he could have
lived a month to an end; but [*f.* 25 (*b*)] a chemical medicine
had a wonderful effect on him, for it recovered him so that he
lived ten years after, but he had never perfect health. He
was a generous and worthy man, and set himself much to
do good; his heart was full of religion; he was free of all
superstition and bigotry, and saw through the errors and
follies of all parties. He was a man of great understanding
and of a true judgement. He likewise took me to task, for he
was morose and used to chide me for my faults a little too
much; but between him and sir Robert Moray I had many
a severe chiding; and though I mended but slowly upon it,
yet they found I took all in such good part that they were
much encouraged to go on with me; and indeed they both
took as much pains on me to form me right as if I had been
their brother, which was an invaluable blessing to me. For
now I was all in a fermentation; my devotion was much
rubbed off, and I was swelled up with pride and vanity; so
mercifully did God deal with me in providing me with two
such faithful friends and prudent monitors. I made at this
time great acquaintance among all sorts of people. I resolved
to know some of the more select of all parties, as Thurscrosse [2]
and Thorndike [3] among the high episcopal men; [a] Wilkins [4],

[a] Cf. Life (*Hist.* ii), p. 676.

---

[1] One of Sharp's letters is addressed
to him 'at Mr. Thomas Viner, his
shop in Lombard Street, London.'

[2] Dr. Timothy Thurscrosse (or Thirst-
crosse), a fellow of Magdalen College,
is mentioned in the *Life of Barwick* as
a person of great piety, who in 1660
was living in Westminster. He subsequently (?) became Prebendary of
York, and is said to have had some connexion with the Charterhouse; in
1670 he was a fellow of Eton (note
communicated by Mr. Doble, from
Fasti Oxonienses, ed. Bliss, col. 408,

note; see also Auto. *infra*, f. 199).

[3] Herbert Thorndike (1598–1672),
the distinguished scholar and divine
(whose works have been republished in
the Library of Anglo-Catholic Theology,
and whose views on the Eucharist
were regarded by Newman, after his
secession, as essentially orthodox), was
a fellow of Trinity, Cambridge, and
spent the years 1662–6 in the University (see *Dict. Nat. Biog.* and
Auto. *infra*, f. 199).

[4] John Wilkins (1614–72), who
under the Commonwealth had been

Whitchcot [1], Tillotson [2], and Stillingfleet [3] among the moderate
episcopal men, [a] who were then called Latitudinarians [a] ; and
Baxter [4] and Manton [5] among the presbyterians ; [b] and I went
to both universities. At Cambridge I conversed most with
Dr. More [6], whose candour and philosophic temper charmed
me much [b] ; I went also to Dr. Gunning [7], but could not bear
with his disputations and scholastical way. The new philosophy was then much in all people's discourse and the Royal
Society was much talked of, and I knew enough of those
matters to make some appearance [8] ; and indeed I concealed
nothing I knew.   [c] At Oxford I found ecclesiastical learning

[a] Cf. *Hist.* i. 188.   [b] Cf. *Life* (*Hist.* ii), p. 676.   [c] Cf. *ibid.*

successively Warden of Wadham and
Master of Trinity, Cambridge, had
been deprived of the latter office at
the Restoration ; and was at this
time Secretary of the Royal Society
(incorporated, principally at his instance, a few months earlier). About
four years after this date he became
Vicar of St. Lawrence, Jewry, and
shortly after was raised to the See
of Chester (*Dict. Nat. Biog.*; *Hist.* i.
186-7, and Mr. Airy's note; Auto.*infra*,
f. 199).

[1] Benjamin Whichcote (1609-83),
distinguished under the Commonwealth (as Vice-chancellor of Cambridge and Provost of King's) for his
moderate conduct and 'Rational'
theology, had been ejected on the
Restoration ; but on complying with
the Act of Uniformity he had been
appointed, a few months before this
date, to the cure of St. Anne's, Black-
friars (*Dict. Nat. Biog.* ; *Hist.* i. 186-7,
and Mr. Airy's note ; and Auto. *infra*,
f. 199).

[2] John Tillotson (1630-94), subsequently Archbishop of Canterbury,
had been ejected in 1660 (in favour of
Gunning, who is said to have been
himself previously ejected) from a
fellowship at Clare Hall, Cambridge.
He then took orders, and conformed,
and was at this date Rector of Ke-
dington, Suffolk (*Dict. Nat. Biog.* ;
Hist. i. 189, and Mr. Airy's note ; Auto.
infra, f. 199).

[3] Edward Stillingfleet (1635-99),
at this time Rector of Sutton

and subsequently Bishop of Worcester, was already, despite his
youth, known on account of his *Ireni-
cum* (1659) and *Origines* (1662) as
a man of learning and original ability
(*Dict. Nat. Biog.*; *Hist.* i. 189, and Mr.
Airy's note ; Auto. *infra*, f. 199).

[4] Richard Baxter (having been driven
from the Church by the Act of Uniformity) was at this time living in
retirement at Acton, Middlesex (*Dict.
Nat. Biog.*, and Auto. *infra*, f. 199).

[5] Thomas Manton (1620-77), the
' Prelate of the Presbyterians,' had
left the living of St. Paul's, Covent
Garden, rather than conform ; and had
apparently by this time opened a conventicle (*Dict. Nat. Biog.* ; *Hist.* i.
259, 308 ; Auto. *infra*, f. 199).

[6] Henry More, the famous 'Christian
Platonist' (1614-87), was a fellow of
Christ's, Cambridge (*Dict. Nat. Biog.*;
Hist. i. 187-8, and Mr. Airy's note ;
Auto. *infra*, f. 199).

[7] For Peter Gunning (1614-84),
afterwards Bishop of Ely, see *Hist.*
i. 181, 436 (and Mr. Airy's notes *in
locis*), 590. He was at this time head
of St. John's, Cambridge, and Regius
Professor of Divinity. His high
Royalist and Anglican views, and his
opposition to Baxter at the Savoy
conference, are well known (*Dict.
Nat. Biog.*; Auto. *infra*, f. 199).

[8] Cf. *A Discourse on the Memory
of . . . Sir Robert Fletcher of Saltoun
. . .* 1665, p. 65 ; *Hist.* i. 500 ; Life
by Thomas Burnet, appended to *Hist.*
ii. 690, and the Auto. *infra*, f. 209.

more in request; and there my study of antiquity (I being then so young) did me some service[a], or rather it advanced my vanity. I was much delighted with the spirit I saw in Dr. Fell[1] and Dr. Allestry[2], who were two of the devoutest men I saw in England; they were much mortified to the world and fasted and prayed much; only they were too hot as I thought in some little matters. My declaring for Lauderdale and [b] my being much with Dr. Wallis[b] (to whom sir Robert Moray recommended me) made me pass for a presbyterian[3] with them; so they were reserved to me [*f.* 26 (*a*)]; or perhaps they looked on me as a vain confident boy, who had a little knowledge and a vast deal of pride. [c] From the universities I returned to London[c], where I needed some of the mortifications that my two friends there gave me. [d] But now I came to understand a little the state of the court and church of England, and I shall give a true account of it all, [e] in which the reader is not to expect things so punctual as he found concerning Scotland[e].

I begin with a character of the king and the duke, but I must give these at present very imperfect, otherwise what I write may happen to be seized on, and I know not what may be made of that[4]; but I will venture on a good deal now, and if ever I outlive them I will say the rest then when it will be more safe.

[a] Cf. Life (*Hist.* ii), p. 676.   [b] Cf. *ibid.*   [c] Cf. *ibid.*   [d] Cf. *Hist.* i. 159, 200.   [e] *Ibid.* 91.

[1] John Fell (1625-86), expelled as a student from Oxford for his fervent royalism, had taken orders in 1647 and with Dolben, Allestree, &c. kept up the Anglican tradition at Oxford. At the Restoration he became Canon and Dean of Christ Church and chaplain to the king; and was Bishop of Oxford 1675-86 (*Dict. Nat. Biog.*; *Hist.* i. 601, 694-5; Auto. *infra*, f. 199).
[2] The learned Richard Allestree (1619-81), a friend and associate of Fell's, became on the Restoration Canon of Christ Church and Regius Professor. He was subsequently Provost of Eton; and has been now identified with the anonymous author of the *Whole*

Duty of Man (see *Dict. Nat. Biog.*, and Mr. Doble in *Academy* for Nov. 1884; *Hist.* ii.644; Auto. *infra*, f. 199).
[3] John Wallis (1616-1703), the celebrated mathematician, Savilian Professor of Geometry at Oxford from 1649, and a founder of the Royal Society, had been ordained in 1640, had held livings under the Common-wealth, had acted as secretary to the Westminster Assembly, and bore the title of D.D. (*Dict. Nat. Biog.*, and Auto. *infra*, f. 199).
[4] He evidently alludes to the possibility of his own arrest, in consequence of his connexion with Russell some weeks before; there can be no

The king's character [1].

[a] The king is certainly the best bred man in the world [a]; for the queen-mother observed often the great defects of the late king's breeding and the stiff roughness that was in him, by which he disobliged very many and did often prejudice his affairs very much; so she gave strict orders that the young princes should be bred to a wonderful civility. [b] The king is civil rather to an excess and has a softness and gentleness with him, both in his air and expressions, that has a charm in it. [c] The duke would also pass for an extraordinary civil and sweet tempered man if the king were not much above him in it [c], who is more naturally and universally civil than the duke. The king has a vast deal of wit (indeed no man has more), and a great deal of judgement when he thinks fit to employ it; he has strange command of himself, he can pass from business to pleasure and from pleasure to business in so easy a manner that all things seem alike to him; he has the greatest art of concealing himself of any man alive, so that those about him cannot tell when he is ill or well pleased, and in private discourse he will hear all sorts of things in such a manner that a man cannot know whether he hears them or not, or whether he is well or ill pleased at them. [d] He is very affable not only in public but in private, only [e] he talks too much and runs out too long and too far. He has a very ill opinion both of men and women, and so is infinitely distrustful; he thinks the world is governed wholly by interest [e], and indeed he has known so much of the baseness of mankind that no wonder if he has hard thoughts of them; but when he is satisfied that his interests are likewise become the interests of

[a] Cf. *Hist.* i. 612; ii. 661.   [b] *Ibid.* and i. 93.   [c] Cf. *ibid.* ii. 661.
[d] *Ibid.* i. 93.   [e] *Ibid.* 94 and 612-3.

---

specific reference to the papers of Algernon Sidney, unless this passage was added after his trial in Nov., 1683.
[1] Printed previously by Von Ranke, *Englische Geschichte*, ed. Leipzig, 1868,

vol. vii, Appendix II, p. 189. The reader should compare, not only the portraits mentioned by Mr. Airy in his note to *Hist.* i. p. 166 of his edition, but the admirable character of Charles II by the Marquis of Halifax.

his ministers then he delivers [*f.* 26 (*b*)] himself up to them in all their humours and revenges : for excusing this he has often said, that he must oblige his ministers and support their credit as necessary for his service ; yet he has often kept up differences amongst his ministers and has balanced his favours pretty equally among them, which (considering his temper) must be uneasy to him, except it be that there is art necessary and he naturally inclines to refinings and loves an intrigue. ᵃ His love of pleasure and his vast expense with his womenᵃ, together with the great influence they have had in all his affairs both at home and abroad, is the chief load that will lay on him ; for not only the women themselves have great power, but his court is full of pimps and bawds, and all matters in which one desires to succeed must be put in their hands. ᵇ He has very merciful inclinationsᵇ when one submits wholly to him, but is severe enough on those that oppose him, and speaks of all people with a sharpness that is not suitable to the greatness of a prince. He is apt to believe what is told him, so that the first impression goes deepest, for he thinks all apologies are lies. ᶜ He has knowledge in many things, chiefly in all naval affairs ; even in the architecture of ships he judges as critically as any of the trade can do, and knows the smallest things belonging to it ; he understands much natural philosophy and is a good chymist ; he knows many mechanical things and the inferior parts of the mathematics, but not the demonstrative ; ᵈ he is very little conversant in books, and, young and old, he could never apply himself to literatureᵈ. He is very kind to those he loves, but never thinks of doing anything for them, so that if they can find things for themselves he will easily enough grant them, but he never sets himself to find out anything for them ; and I never heard of above three or four instances of any places that he gave of his own motion, so that those who have received most of his bounty think they owe the thanks more to their instruments than to himself. ᵉ He never enters upon business with any himself, but if his

---

ᵃ Cf. *Hist.* i. 94. ᵇ *Ibid.* 612 contradicts this. ᶜ *Ibid.* 94. ᵈ Cf.
ibid. and 611. ᵉ Cf. *ibid* 94.

ministers can once draw him into business, they may hold him at it as long as they will. ^a He loves his ease so much, that the great secret of all his ministers is to find out his temper exactly and to be easy to him. ^b He has many odd opinions about religion and morality ; he thinks an implicitness in religion is necessary for the safety of government, and he looks [*f.* 27 (*a*)] upon all inquisitiveness into those things as mischievous to the state ; ^c he thinks all appetites are free and that God will never damn a man for allowing himself a little pleasure ^c, and on this he has so fixed his thoughts that no disorders of any kind have ever been seen to give him any trouble when they were over, and in sickness (except in his ague in [16]79¹) he seemed to have no concern on his mind. ^d And yet I believe he is no atheist ^d, but that rather he has formed an odd idea of the goodness of God in his mind ; ^e he thinks, to be wicked and to design mischief, is the only thing that God hates, and has said to me often, that he was sure he was not guilty of that ^e. I think I have gone pretty far, and scarce know how I should scape under the present chief justice ², if this should happen to be seized on.

The duke's character[3].

I go next to the duke ; he has not the king's wit nor quickness, but that is made up by great application and industry, ^f insomuch that he keeps a journal of all that passes, of which he shewed me once a great deal, and he had employed the late duchess to write it out in the style of a history, for she writ very correctly, and he intended to have made me prosecute what she had begun, which he shewed me. ^g He has naturally a candour and a justice in his temper very great, and is a firm

---

^a Cf. *Hist.* i. 93.   ^b *Ibid.*   ^c *Ibid.*   ^d *Ibid.*   ^e *Ibid.* 438.
^f *Ibid.* 168, 170.   ^g *Ibid.* 168-9 and ii. 292-3.

---

¹ See *Hist.* i. 474.
² Qu. Pemberton, C.J. Common Pleas, who had sentenced Russell, or Jeffreys ? The King's Bench was vacant from June 19, 1683, till Jeffreys' appointment, Sept. 29, 1683.
³ Printed by Von Ranke, vii, Appendix II. p. 191.

friend, but a heavy enemy, and will keep things long in his mind and wait for a fit opportunity. [a] He has a strange notion of government, that everything is to be carried on in a high way and that no regard is to be had to the pleasing the people; and he has an ill opinion of any that proposes soft methods, and thinks that is popularity [a] ; but at the same time he always talks of law and justice. He is apt enough to receive an enemy upon an absolute submission, but [b] he will strain hard to ruin an enemy that stands out, and when I knew him he scorned to use arts to take them off (as the phrase at court was of bringing over leading men in the house of commons to their party [b]), nor will he receive any upon half submissions, and [c] he thinks that all who oppose the king in parliament are rebels [c]. He understands business better than is generally believed, for [d] though he is not a man of wit nor fancy, yet he generally judges well when things are laid before him, except when the violence of his spirit gives him a bias, which it does too often. [e] He is a prince of great courage [e] and very serene in action, and naturally hates a coward, unless it be to make use of him in the conduct of his amours; he abhors drunkenness, he never swears nor talks [*f.* 27 (*b*)] irreligiously; [f] he has pursued many secret pleasures, but never with an open avowing them, and he does condemn himself for it, but yet he is ever going on from one intrigue to another, [g] though it is generally thought that these have been very fatal to him and that the death of so many of his children is owing to that. [h] He is a zealous and hearty papist, of which he gave me this account: when he was in Flanders, being in a nunnery, a nun pressed him much about religion, and begged him to use this prayer every day to God, that if he was not in the right way he would bring him to it; which he said sunk deep in his mind and raised scruples in him [h]. I asked him, if he was in love with the nun, but he assured me, she was no tempting object. He was reconciled to the church of Rome [i] while he was in

---

[a] Cf. *Hist.* i. 169, 360. [b] *Ibid.* 169. [c] *Ibid.* 360. [d] Cf. *Hist.* ii. 292.
[e] Cf. *ibid.* i. 168 ; ii. 292. [f] *Ibid.* ii. 293 ; i. 169, 228. [g] *Ibid.* i. 228.
[h] *Ibid.* 169. [i] This conflicts with *Hist.* i. 169.

Flanders, [a] but he dissembled the matter long after that. [b] The truth was, he had some tinctures in his education that disposed him the more to this ; he was bred to believe a mysterious sort of real presence in the sacrament, so that he thought he made no great step, when he believed transubstantiation, and there was infused in him very early a great reverence for the church and a great submission to it [b] ; this was done on design to possess him with prejudices against presbytery (for that was the thing of which the clergy was then most afraid), but it had this ill effect, that [c] he came to think, if a church was to be sub-mitted to, it was more reasonable that it should be the church of Rome than the church of England. He is very firm in his persuasion, but he has not inquired much into it and is very much devoted to his priests, [d] yet when I knew him he seemed very positive in his opinion against all persecution for con-science sake, but I looked on that only as a thing put in his mouth by his priests, for certainly he must be of another mind, if he comes to have power in his hands [d] ; yet I have wondered much at one thing, that being so firm as he is in his religion, he left his daughters so entirely in the hands of the divines of the church of England that he never made any attempt on them to persuade them to change, of which the princess of Orange assured Dr. Lloyd when he waited on her over into Holland. It is very hard to reconcile this with so much zeal as he has expressed for that religion. [e] He had indeed an answer ready to another thing, which I took the freedom to object to him, which was, that the rest of his life was not so exact that so high a zeal as he has shewed in his religion could be believed to flow from an inward sense of his duty to God, otherwise that would appear in [*f.* 28 (*a*)] other things. His answer was, that a man might have a per-suasion of his duty to God so as to restrain him from dis-sembling with God and man in professing himself to be of another religion than that which he believed was true, though it did not yet restrain all his appetites. He was so far from

---

[a] Cf. *Hist.* i. 170.   [b] *Ibid.* 169.   [c] *Ibid.*   [d] *Ibid.* 179, 359.
[e] Cf. *ibid.* 360.

being displeased with me for the freedom of speaking to him upon so tender a point, that he not only seemed to take it well from me but he has spoken very kindly of me to many others upon that very account.

Monk's character [1].

[a] As for Monk he deserves not a character so much for his own merit, as for the luck he had, to be so great an instrument in the bringing home the king [a]. He was a good officer, had much desperate courage, but was an illiterate and injudicious man, and was neither a man of religion nor strict virtue ; [b] he was by force put on a glorious action after he saw there was nothing else to be done, for the stream run so strong for bringing home the king, that it could not be resisted [b], so sir Tho. Clarges and his wife [2] put him on to that noble resolution [c] which brought so much wealth and honour on him while alive, and has left so much fame on his name. The king carried himself always with great respect to him, but he had no value for him in his heart.

The earl of Clarendon's character [3].

[d] The great man with the king was chancellor Hyde, afterwards made earl of Clarendon [d]. He had been in the beginning of the long parliament very high against the judges upon the account of the ship-money and became then a considerable man ; he spake well, his style had no flaw in it, but had a just mixture of wit and sense, only he spoke too copiously ; he had a great pleasantness in his spirit, which carried him sometimes too far into raillery, in which [e] he sometimes shewed more wit than discretion. [f] He went over to the court party when the war was like to break out, and was much in the late king's councils and confidence during the war [f]; though he was always

[a] Cf. *Hist.* i. 89.   [b] *Ibid.*   [c] *Ibid.* 98.   [d] *Ibid.* 94.   [e] *Ibid.* 95.   [f] *Ibid.* 94.

---

[1] Printed by Von Ranke, vii, App. II. p. 193.

[2] But see *Hist.* i. 99, where this advice is ascribed to Morrice.

[3] Printed by Von Ranke, vii, App. II. p. 193. It should be remembered that in the interval between the date when Burnet first composed this character (1683) and that at which he revised it (1705) Clarendon's own *History* had appeared (1702).

of the party that pressed the king to treat, and so was not in good terms with the queen. The late king recommended him to this king as the person on whose advices he wished him to rely most, and [a] he was about the king all the while that he was beyond sea [a], except a little that he was ambassador in Spain ; he managed all the king's correspondences in England, both in the little designs that the cavaliers were sometimes engaged in, and chiefly in procuring money for the king's subsistence, in which Dr. Sheldon was very active ; he had nothing so much before his eyes as the king's service and doated on him beyond expression: he had been a sort of governor to him and had given him many lectures on the politics [b] and was thought to assume and dictate too much [b]. He was in ill terms with the duke in Flanders [*f.* 28 (*b*)], but the duke's marrying his daughter took all that away ; [c] he seemed to be wholly a stranger to all that affair, when it broke out [c], though that was not generally believed ; but after that was done it was a great error in him to have any meddling in the matter of the king's marriage, and it being easy to persuade the world that men do those things on design that turn to be much for their interest, [d] it was generally cast on him that he made the king's match upon some informations he had that the queen was not like to bring any children, yet that must be false [d], for Dr. Willis said to a friend of mine that the queen had no visible cause of barrenness about her, and that all the stories that were spread of her person were false ; [e] he also told Dr. Lloyd that the queen once miscarried of a child that was so far formed that if it had been carefully handled the sex might have been distinguished, [f] and I saw a letter that the king writ the day after their marriage to Clarendon, in which he seemed wonderfully well pleased with her and by which it appeared that the marriage was consummated [f]. But to pursue Clarendon's character: he was a man that knew England well, and was [g] lawyer good enough to be an able chancellor, and was certainly a very incorrupt man. In all the king's

[a] Cf. *Hist.* i. 94.   [b] *Ibid.*   [c] *Ibid.* 168.   [d] *Ibid.* 251.   [e] *Ibid.* 174.
[f] *Ibid. supra.*   [g] *Ibid.* 95.

foreign negotiations he meddled too much, for I have been
told that he had not a right notion of foreign mattèrs, ^a but he
could not be gained to serve the interests of other princes [1].
Mr. Fouquet sent him over a present of 10,000 pounds after
the king's restoration and assured him he would renew that
every year, but though both the king and the duke advised him
to take it he very worthily refused it ^a. He took too much upon
him and meddled in everything, which was his greatest error.
^b He fell under the hatred of most of the cavaliers upon two
accounts. The one was the act of indemnity which cut off all
their hopes of repairing themselves of the estates of those that
had been in the rebellion, but he said it was the offer of the
indemnity that brought in the king and it was the observing
of it that must keep him in, so he would never let that be
touched, ^c and many that had been deeply engaged in the late
times having expiated it by their zeal of bringing home the
king were promoted by his means, such as Manchester,
Anglesey, Orrery, Ashley, Holles, and several others. ^d The
other thing was that, there being an infinite number of pre-
tenders to employments and rewards for their services and
sufferings, so that the king could only satisfy some few of
them, ^e he upon that, to stand between the king and the displeasure which those disappointments had given, spoke slightly
of many of them ^e and took it upon him that their petitions
[*f.* 29 (*a*)] were not granted; and some of them having procured
several warrants from the secretaries for the same thing (the
secretaries considering nothing but their fees), he who knew
on whom the king intended that the grant should fall, took all
upon him, so that those who were disappointed laid the blame

^a Cf. *Hist.* i. 167. ^b *Ibid.* 165. ^c *Ibid.* 98. ^d *Ibid.* 164.
^e *Ibid.* 165 and 95.

[1] 'The description given in the
printed text is nothing but an ill-
natured excerpt from this; it runs thus :
"he never seemed to understand
foreign affairs well, and yet he meddled
too much in them." (The "meddled" of
the original refers to his interference in
personal matters.) "He had too much
levity in his wit, and did not always
observe the decorum of his post." I
think the original is much better in this
case also. The really instructive part
is dropped in the later form' (note
translated from Von Ranke, vii, App. II.
p. 194).

chiefly if not wholly upon him. [a] He was apt to talk very imperiously and unmercifully, so that his manner of dealing with people was as provoking as the hard things themselves were [a]; but upon the whole matter he was a true Englishman and a sincere protestant, and what has passed at court since his disgrace has sufficiently vindicated him from all ill designs. In one thing it appeared that he had changed his mind much; he penned the declaration at Breda, in which the king promised indulgence and ease to tender consciences, and pursuant to that [b] he penned a long declaration concerning ecclesiastical affairs after the king was restored, which was drawn up with that prudence and temper, that by all appearance, if the king had stuck to it, both church and state had been very quickly happy; but it was observed that immediately after the duke's marriage broke out Clarendon changed his measures, and set on his own creatures to arraign that declaration in the house of commons, of which this account was given me: the bishops had stuck to him in the matter of that marriage, by letting the king know, that it could not be broken neither by the laws of God nor man, that he thereupon delivered himself up to their counsels in the affairs of the church and so did whatever they had mind to do. This gave his friend the earl of Southampton much trouble [b], whose character I shall next give.

The earl of Southampton's character [1].

He was a high assertor of the rights of his country in the business of the ship-money, and in the beginning of the long parliament was a leading man in the house of lords, but after the king had passed the bill for triennial parliaments (together with some other things), he with a great many more peers turned about and declared as highly for the king as they had done before for their country. [c] When the war brake out he followed the king to the last [c] without making one false

[a] Cf. *Hist.* i. 94.   [b] *Ibid.* 178.   [c] *Ibid.* 95.

[1] Printed by Von Ranke, vii, App. II. p. 195.

step, and was always one of those (or rather the head of them)
that were driving on a treaty. He was with the king in the
Isle of Wight, and was one of those that after the dismal
murder of that blessed prince waited on his body and saw it
buried at Windsor. He lived private during the usurpation,
but [a] was still sending over large supplies to the king beyond
sea; so his great parts together with his great merit made
him be now considered as one of the first men of England.
He was made treasurer [a], and Clarendon was proud of his
friendship and valued himself upon it. [b] He scorned to make
those advantages of his place that others had done, and so
came to an agreement with the king, that he should [*f.* 29 (*b*)]
have £8,000 a year for the place, and that all the offices that
used to be given, or to speak plain, that were sold by the
treasurer, which was the chief advantage of that place, should
be given by the king; this he observed during his life, but
since that time the treasurers or commissioners have both
£8,000 and likewise do really dispose of these places, though
they pass through the king's hands. [c] He quickly grew disgusted of the way in which he saw matters were carried at
court, and scarce minded business, [d] but turned over the affairs
of the treasury on his secretary sir Philip Warwick, who, though
he was a weak man and by being a pretender to wit[1] he
appeared much weaker than he would have otherwise been
thought, yet was a generous and worthy man, and in the seven
years in which he governed the treasury, though it was then
very full of money, he made not so much advantage as others
have done since that time in one year. [e] Southampton was
for healing the church by concessions [e] on both hands, but when
he saw that all that affair was put in Sheldon's hands, he withdrew from the meetings that were held about it and declared
against their methods. The bishops laid the blame of this
on the great ascendant that Ashley was observed to have over

[a] Cf. *Hist.* i. 95.   [b] *Ibid.* 96.   [c] *Ibid.* 95.   [d] *Ibid.* 96.   [e] *Ibid.* 178.

[1] Notice the absence of an allusion
to Warwick's memoirs (printed in
1701, see Mr. Airy's note *in loco*)
subsequently inserted in the *History*
when revised.

him, and were much troubled to see so unexceptionable a man as he was displeased with their maxims.   I have heard it also said that [a] he was sorry when he saw the king raise so many guards [b] and that the parliament was pouring all things into the hands of the court, [a] and that if he had not prevailed with Clarendon not to set on these things further, he would have openly stood up for the interests of his country.   [c] But he withdrew himself much from affairs, for which he had too visible an excuse, for he fell under most terrible pains by a confirmed stone in his bladder, [d] of which he died afterwards [d].

The earl of Shaftesbury's character [1].

But since I have named [e] the lord Ashley, afterwards the earl of Shaftesbury (that had married his niece and was much in his favour), and since he has made such a figure in the world, I shall enlarge more on his character ; because I knew him well [e] and so build not on what I have heard from others, as I did in the former ones.   He was a man of much wit, and [f] as long as the conversation run in a general ramble he was very entertaining company.   [g] He knew England well and all the interests in it [g], and had a competent skill in law, [h] but as to all matters of knowledge the quickness of his thoughts was such, that he never went to the bottom of anything, but snatched at some hints, which he improved by his fancy, and so he committed vast errors when he talked of matters of learning.   [i] As to religion he was a deist [i], and seemed to believe [*f*.30 (*a*)] nothing of Christianity, but only that it contained good morals ; he was against bringing in religion to the state or imposing it on any ; he had odd notions of a future state [k] and thought that our souls went into stars and animated them. He would have talked pleasantly of those things but without any strength of reason, for he never spake closely to anything,

---

[a] Cf. *Hist.* i. 161.   [b] *Ibid.* 89.   [c] *Ibid.* 95.   [d] *Ibid.* 249.   [e] *Ibid.* 96.
[f] *Ibid.* 97.   [g] *Ibid. infra.*   [h] *Ibid. supra.*   [i] *Ibid.* 96.   [k] *Ibid.* 97.

---

[1] Printed by Von Ranke, vii, App. II. p. 197.   At the time this character was written Shaftesbury had been dead about six months.

but always shifted that and got into a loose ramble. His
morals were of a piece with his religion. ª He was esteemed
a very corrupt man and false to all degrees, and that he had
no regard to anything but his own interest or rather his
vanity ª, which was the most fulsome thing I ever saw ; he
turned the discourse almost always to the magnifying of himself, which he did in so gross and coarse a manner that it
shewed his great want of judgement ; he told so many incredible things of himself that it put me often out of patience ;
he was mightily overcome with flattery; and that and his
private interests were the only things that could hold or turn
him. ᵇ He had likewise a great dexterity of engaging plain
and well meaning men that had no depth of understanding to
admire him and to depend on him, ᶜ but even these were often
disgusted with his vanity and indiscretion. He had turned
often, but done it with dexterity and success and was proud
of that, so that he would often set out the art that he had
shewed in it and never seemed to be ashamed of the meanness or levity of shifting sides so often ᶜ ; he pretended, that
ᵈ in the beginning of the civil wars he had offered to do great
service to the late king and to put two counties wholly in his
hands, and that he was going about it, but prince Maurice not
observing articles he went over upon that to the parliament ᵈ ;
then he was much courted by Cromwell and said he did him
great service in some of his parliaments, insomuch that he
told some ᵉ that Cromwell offered once to make him king ᵉ,
but he never offered to impose so gross a thing on me ; he
pretended he had a main hand in all the confusions that
followed after Cromwell's death, for he knew these frequent
revolutions must end in restoring the king, and he always
assumed to himself and the lord Holles the merit of forcing
Monk to declare himself[1]. He was certainly very active in
bringing home the king, and he made him an early present
of money, and that, together with his parts and Southampton's

ª Cf. *Hist.* i. 97.   ᵇ *Ibid.* 96.   ᶜ *Ibid.* 97.   ᵈ *Ibid.* 96.   ᵉ *Ibid.* 97.

[1] See *Hist.* i. 85, 98.

kindness to him, was to be considered ; he was made a baron
and chancellor of the exchequer, and that put him in the
way to all that followed.   He lived too long, for he lost that
only part of reputation of which he was fond, which was the
being a man of interest and understanding ; ᵃ but he died in
good time for his family, ᵇ in which astrology deceived him,
[*f.* 30 (*b*)] if he told me true, for he depended much on what
a drunken physician ¹ had predicted, and said it had held
exactly true through the former parts of his life ᵇ ; he did not
tell me what was to befall him at last, but ᶜ he believed he
should be yet a greater man than he had ever been ᶜ.   So
much I have said of him in this place, but I shall hereafter
have occasion to name him often.

The duke of Ormond's character ².

As Clarendon and Southampton were the great men in
England, so the duke of Ormond was the only man in Ireland
and had likewise a large share of the affairs in England.   He
was one on whose friendship Clarendon likewise valued himself as having been all along so faithfully and eminently
employed in the king's affairs.   ᵈ He is a man of a pleasant
conversation and has ever lived high and at a vast expense ᵈ ;
he writes the best of any man that has no learning that I ever
knew.   His friends have all of them complained much of him,
that he is a very cold friend and will neither put himself in
danger nor to trouble for them, and that he thinks it enough
to be civil and kind to them himself ; and it has been said by
many, that in the government of Ireland he has considered
the public good very little ; so that many have complained
that he was neither generous nor grateful.   ᵉ The affairs of
Ireland were very unsuccessful in his hands during the wars
ever after he began to treat with the Irish ᵉ, and both sides
complained much of him ; though it is generally a very good
argument for a man, when both extremes are displeased at

ᵃ *Hist.* i. 97.   ᵇ *Ibid.* 96.   ᶜ *Ibid.* 97.   ᵈ *Ibid.* 95.   ᵉ *Ibid.*

¹ The *History* says 'a Dutch doctor' ;   'and to espouse the English' only)
see Christie's *Shaftesbury*, i. 19–20.   has been printed by Von Ranke, vii,
² This character (as far as the words   App. II. pp. 198, 199.

him. [a] The Irish complain that he has broke his faith to them, for when they treated with the king through his hands many articles were granted them about their religion and estates and the government of Ireland, upon which they performed their parts and put themselves in his hands and raised a great army, which was so unexpectedly dispersed; now they have said upon the king's restoration those articles ought to have been made good to them [a], for though they were beaten they could not answer for success, but they had lost their lives and estates on the king's account and had been kept under great slavery for twelve years. [b] They had likewise another thing to depend on when they treated with Ormond: the king was then a prisoner, so that he could not ratify the articles that were granted them; upon that the queen, being then at Paris, got the crown of France to interpose and give their faith for the performance of the treaty, upon which they build their hopes to this day [b], and this will furnish that crown with a good colour for invading Ireland whenever they are on other accounts resolved on it [1]; [c] but the king was bound by his declaration from Breda to make [*f.* 31 (*a*)] good the present settlement of Ireland, and the earls of Anglesey, Orrery, and some others engaged the duke of Ormond to desert the Irish interest and to espouse the English [2]. For which this was all that he had to say for himself, that the popish bishops in Ireland broke all terms with him and at last excommunicated all that adhered to him, upon which he was forced to leave Ireland; so that the treaty failing on their side the king could not be bound by it [c]; and for their blood that was spilt, and the miseries that came upon the nation, that did not follow upon their adhering to the king, but on the first rebellion and massacre. Thus did Ormond justify his forsaking the Irish, of which they made great complaints, and said plainly that he had sold them; yet on the other hand the care he took to preserve some particular families of the

[a] Cf. *Hist.* i. 175, 95.   [b] *Ibid.* 175.   [c] *Ibid.*

[1] See *Hist.* i. 250.
[2] Here the extracts of Von Ranke abruptly conclude.

Irish has made the English likewise displeased at him. I have conversed more with his enemies than his friends, so perhaps this may be too severe a character of him, for I have very little acquaintance with him myself, and it never went further than very general civilities. He was very happy and very unhappy, first in having and at last in losing such a son as the earl of Ossory was, who had indeed no extraordinary parts, and was too much set on some forbidden pleasures, but was in all other respects [a] the bravest man and the generousest friend that was at court; and was indeed a great pattern both of honour and worth [a], and was beginning in the last year of his life to have deep reflections on religion, which seemed strongly rooted in him during his sickness, so that it is very likely if he had recovered he would have been a very good Christian, and then he would have been one of the greatest men in the nation.

The earl of Anglesey's character.

I have named the earl of Anglesey, and so shall say somewhat of him; [b] he is a man of great knowledge, he understands all the parts of the law and the government of this nation beyond any man of quality I know, and has great quickness of apprehension, and a faculty of speaking indefatigably, but he speaks very ungracefully, and loves to rally often, but does it in such a manner that it is insupportably odious and dull, for raillery is a sort of poetry, and must either be very fine or it is intolerable. He is looked upon as a very corrupt man, as one that sticks at nothing and is ashamed of nothing [b], and that will turn from one side to another so nimbly, that he has often begun a speech in parliament all one way, and (upon some secret look that wrought upon him) has changed his note quite and concluded totally different from his beginning. [c] He was very active in bringing home the king, [d] and has gone through very eminent employments since that time, but I never saw any one man that either loved him or trusted him.

[a] Cf. *Hist.* i. 334.　　[b] *Ibid.* 97 and 176.　　[c] *Ibid.* 98.　　[d] *Ibid.* 97.

Orrery's character.

[*f.* 31 *(b)*] Orrery pretended to knowledge, but was very ignorant, and to wit, but it was very luscious; to eloquence, but had the worst style in the world; and to religion, but ᵃ was thought a very fickle and false man, and was vain ᵃ to the pitch of the earl of Shaftesbury.

Holles' character.

ᵇ Holles was a man of great courage and a high spirit; he had much knowledge and was very well acquainted with all parliamentary records; he had a sound judgement and a noble sense of honour and gratitude; he was a kind friend, and was one of the sincerest and steadiest men in the nation; but he had with this a vast pride and could not bear contradiction, so that he was not a fair arguer, and his friends knew it. He never changed his principles for above sixty years, in which he made a considerable figure in the world, and had the soul of an old stubborn Roman in him; and as far as was consistent with that temper he was a very sincere and devout Christian, allowing somewhat for pride and passion.

The duke of Buckingham's character.

ᶜ And now I have done with the men of business of that time I will speak somewhat of some others that were Clarendon's great enemies. The first of these that occurs to my thoughts is the duke of Buckingham, a man of noble presence and that has an air that at first strikes all that see him; he has a flame in his wit that is inimitable; he has no manner of literature, and all he knows is in chemistry, for he has sought long for the philosopher's stone and with the ordinary fate of all that have pursued it, for he has often thought he was very near the finding it out, but has been as often deceived. He has no sort of principle either about religion, virtue, or friendship; pleasure, wit, and mirth is all that he has ever laid to heart; he had a great ascendant over the king, but has provoked

---

ᵃ Cf. *Hist.* i. 266 and 176.   ᵇ *Ibid.* 98.   ᶜ *Ibid.* 100.

him out of measure by talking in a style of him that has
shewed equal degrees of contempt and hatred, and he is not
to be trusted with any secret [a], for if he meets with a man that
happens to heat his fancy and seems to have the same notions
that he has he will pour out everything to him. [b] He was
never true either to things or persons, but forsakes every man
and departs from every maxim, sometimes out of levity and
an unsettledness of fancy and sometimes out [of] downright
falsehood ; he could never fix himself to business, but has
a [*f.* 32 (*a*)] perpetual unsteadiness about him [b]. He is revengeful to all degrees, and is, I think, one of the worst men alive,
both as to his personal deportment and as to the public.
He had conceived a mighty contempt of Clarendon, but he
was then so low in the king's thoughts that he could not
hurt him.

The earl of Bristol's character.

[c] Another of Clarendon's enemies was the earl of Bristol,
a man of great courage and considerably learned ; he had
much more wit than judgement ; he was too fine a speaker,
and abounded too much both in words and fancy, which is an
odious thing in public councils. He was a papist after a form
of his own and so was incapable of business, but was ever
forming projects ; he was a great dealer in astrology, and
had a great measure of other knowledge ; he intended to
make himself considered as the head of the popish party,
and was much the best speaker they had in parliament, but
was an inconsistent man and had too great a levity in his
thoughts. He had been in ill terms with Clarendon at Oxford
(being then the chief man of the queen's party) and was now
forming many cabals against him.

The duchess of Cleveland's character [with the earl of Falmouth's].

[d] But the strength of the opposition that was made to
Clarendon lay in mistress Palmer, since that time made first
countess of Castlemaine and then duchess of Cleveland [d].

[a] *Hist.* i. 100.   [b] *Ibid.*   [c] *Ibid.* 100-1.   [d] *Ibid.* 100, 165.

I love not to give characters of women, especially when there
is nothing that is good to be said of them, as indeed I never
heard any commend her but for [a] her beauty, which was very
extraordinary and has been now of long continuance. In
short, she was a woman of pleasure, and stuck at nothing that
would either serve her appetites or her passions; she was
vastly expensive, and by consequence very covetous; she
was weak, and so was easily managed. [b] He that had the
secret of this business was a young man of no extraordinary
parts, but of a generous and noble disposition; he was the
second son to sir Charles Berkeley (afterwards made viscount
Fitzharding); he grew mightily into the king's favour, was
made earl of Falmouth [b], and was upon the point of being made
a duke and declared the favourite, when he [c] was lost at sea;
[d] he had the luck to be almost equally dear both to the king
and duke [d], and those that knew him well told me that they
believed he would have proved one of the best favourites that
ever was, that he would have promoted men of merit and have
[d] set the king on to great and worthy things [d], and that he
would not have been insolent nor assumed much to himself,
but that he knew his own defects, and would have depended
on wiser men's counsels.

[*Conduct of Clarendon and Southampton.*]

[*f.* 32 (*b*)] Clarendon and Southampton were much
troubled to see the king so possessed by this fair mistress,
but [e] resolved never to make application to her nor to let anything pass in which her name was mentioned [e]; so that when
she resolved to have a title of honour she was forced to get
her husband to be made an earl in Ireland, which was a
device of Orrery's (as this earl of Clarendon has told me);
[e] nor was there ever a precept brought to the treasury in her
name during Southampton's life [e], so that all the money that
she got from the king was out of the privy purse. This was
noble in both these lords, but it was a greater thing in
Clarendon; for Southampton was not much concerned whether

---

[a] Cf. *Hist.* i. 94.   [b] *Ibid.* 100.   [c] *Ibid.* 219.   [d] *Ibid.* 100.   [e] *Ibid.* 165.

he lost his white staff or not, nor had he such powerful enemies; but Clarendon was both more pushed at and was more concerned to preserve himself, so that his firmness in that matter was truly heroical.

[*Characters of Nicholas and Morrice.*]

[a] Nicholas and Morrice were secretaries of state, both virtuous men but very weak; and it may be gathered from this one saying what a judgement Monk had in those matters, when, being told that the court was weary of his cousin Morrice and thought him not able enough for his office, he said he did not know what they required in a secretary, but his cousin could both speak French and write shorthand [a] I have observed that the court can bear with one indifferent secretary, and seem to be pleased to have one that is weak and tractable (which will appear to every one that considers what men Morrice, Williamson, and Jenkins have been); but they hardly bear two very weak ones at a time; though it seems when they were served by Jenkins and Conway at once that this rule admits of an exception.

The earl of Arlington's character.

[b] But at this time one was to be changed, and since Monk was too great to let it fall on his kinsman Nicholas was removed, and sir Henry Bennet (since made earl of Arlington) was put in his room ; that was brought about by the interest of the popish party, for he has been much suspected in his religion. He is no quick man, but has great knowledge of the affairs of Europe, and was ever cautious and fearful ; he quickly found out the king's temper and has been observed to be very dexterous in managing it ; he is proud and insolent, yet he has been generally firm to his friends, and so they have stuck very firmly to him ; he has been a man of great vanity and vast expense. He quickly took up this maxim, [*f.* 33 (*a*)] that the king ought not to shew any favour to

[a] Cf. *Hist.* i. 99.   [b] *Ibid.*

popery and that nothing would spoil all his other affairs so
much as that would do; so that he soon lost the popish
party, and has been considered by them an apostate and
as a betrayer of their interests.

The characters of Sheldon and Morley.

There were two churchmen so considerable at this time that
I shall add somewhat of them. The one was ᵃ Sheldon, made
at first bishop of London, that had the greatest hand in all
that passed concerning the church; for ᵇ Juxon, archbishop of
Canterbury (to whom he succeeded in that see), was super-
annuated. ᶜ Sheldon was a man of great pleasantness of
conversation and cheerful rather to excess, considering his
character; he had much wit, and was very well turned for
a court, if not too well; he had great quickness of apprehension and strength of judgement; he was considerably learned
before the wars and perfectly understood all he pretended to,
but the politics had worn learning out of his thoughts. He
was a generous and charitable man, he lived splendidly, and
had an art peculiar to himself of treating every one that came
to him with some particular and distinguishing civilities;
but he seemed to have no great sense of religion, nor of the
true concerns of the church, of which he spoke commonly
rather as of a matter of policy than of conscience, and he was
thought to have allowed himself in many indecent liberties;
he was civil to all, but friendly to very few. The other bishop
was Morley, made at first bishop of Worcester, and soon
after (upon Duppa's death) translated to Winchester. He is
a man of a lively wit and great openness of heart, and is both
a learned and devout man, and is now perhaps one of the
perfectest men of his age in the world. He was at first
known to the world in Falkland's company, and was thought
favourable to the puritans before the wars; but he has given
such demonstrations to the contrary that, though he is a
Calvinist in the matter of decrees and grace, yet no man is
more zealous for the church of England than he is. He is

ᵃ Cf. *Hist.* i. 177.   ᵇ *Ibid.* 176.   ᶜ *Ibid.* 177.

a very bountiful and generous man, and has no other fault but that he is too credulous and too passionate, and will be soon possessed with prejudices which cannot be easily rooted out. He was more particularly in Clarendon's favour, having been his chaplain, but Sheldon was thought the abler man [a].

The settlement of ecclesiastical matters in England.

[*f.* 33 (*b*)] The first thing proposed after the king's restoration was the settlement of the church. This was not to be ventured on till that parliament that had called home the king was dissolved, for they were for [the] most part presbyterians; and there was a particular reason given why that parliament ought to be dissolved, for it was said that the essential nullity of their being without the king's writ was such a defect, that neither their merit in bringing home the king nor his ratifying their actions could remove it, so that it was necessary to have a parliament legally called; upon which that was dissolved, and [b] a new one was summoned to which scarce any but those that were cavaliers or the sons of cavaliers (this was the distinguishing name of all that had been of the king's party) were chosen, so it was resolved to procure from this an act of uniformity. But to prepare matters for this [c] a conference was appointed to be held at the Savoy, between some of the chief divines of both persuasions (I think they were six of a side) in the presence of some privy councillors. [d] There were unhappily two men of that number who were much better fitted to widen old differences and create new ones than to find out a temper in them; these were doctor Gunning, now [1] bishop of Ely, on the one side, and Mr. Baxter on the other; [e] men of such metaphysical heads and so very disputatious that they were the best to spoil so good a design of any I ever knew, [f] and they spent often whole days in their disputes, as if the whole business in hand had been to try their skill at that fencing work [f]. It appeared plain enough

[a] Cf. *Hist.* i. 177.   [b] *Ibid.* 178-9.   [c] *Ibid.* 179.   [d] *Ibid.* 181.
[e] *Ibid.* 180-1.   [f] *Ibid.* 181.

---

[1] He died July 6, 1684 (Mr. Airy's note).

that the presbyterians had a great mind to have conformed, ·
for [a] they generally excepted more to the expediency than
to the lawfulness of the terms of communion with the
church of England, and [b] if the terms in the king's first
declaration concerning ecclesiastical affairs had been adhered
to it is very probable that not a fifth part of those that were
turned out would have left their livings. [c] But I have been
told that Sheldon[1] was afraid of nothing more than their
conformity upon two reasons.

They were possessed of most of the great livings in England,
and though all those that had taken the sequestered livings
of such as had been turned out for adhering to the king
during the late wars were thrown out, as having no titles in
law to them, yet many other benefices were still in their
hands, chiefly the pulpits of London, [*f.* 34 (*a*)] they had many
headships in the universities, and most of the corporations
were stocked with them, so Sheldon thought it necessary to
have all these turned out.   Those of London had likewise
merited so much in the matter of the king's restoration that
if they had conformed they must have been rewarded with
dignities, so in hatred to them [d] he thought that instead of
finding ways to bring them into the church, ways were to be
contrived for throwing them out of it [d].

His other reason, which I have perceived was likewise
Dr. Morley's, was that nothing had ruined the church [e] in the
late times so much as the lecturers and other churchmen
that were only so far conformable that the law could not
reach them, and were by little indirect ways still alienating
the people from the church and making divisions everywhere [e],
so that Morley has set this up for a maxim that [f] it is better
to have a schism without the church than within it. [g] Therefore it was resolved not only not to abate anything of the
conformity that was required before the wars, but to add some

[a] Cf. *Hist.* i. 181.   [b] *Ibid.* 178, 185.   [c] *Ibid.* 178.   [d] *Ibid.* 179.
[e] *Ibid.* 178.   [f] *Ibid. supra.*   [g] *Ibid.* 182.

· The *History* lays the blame on 'the bishops and their party.'

new tests, that so none might be capable of any ecclesiastical preferment that was not hearty in everything. [a] It was made necessary that all ordained without bishops should come and receive orders from them. Of this the presbyterians have complained much, pretending that it had not been the practice of the church of England formerly, and that the English bishops had looked on the presbyterian ordinations in other churches as valid [a] ; but the answer to this was obvious and hinted at before [1], that great difference was to be made between imperfect churches that were under defects which they could not remedy, and a set of men that threw off their bishops and set up in a schismatical and rebellious way a new form of ordination, not only without any necessity, but against the laws then in being.

 [b] To this the bishops added another test in a declaration of an assent and consent to everything contained or prescribed in the book of common prayer and ordinations which every man in any office in the church was to read before the congregation. Upon this great objections were raised. It was said that many things might be submitted to for peace sake to which men could not assent or consent, for that seemed to import a previous approbation of those things. Others, again, understood this assent and consent as importing only an assent and consent to the law then made, so that it went no further than to profess a bare submission and obedience to it. To these another declaration was added [c] condemning all resisting of the king by arms, upon what pretence soever, as unlawful, together with a [*f.* 34 (*b*)] renunciation of the covenant as unlawful in itself as well as imposed against law, and asserting that there lay no obligation on any by virtue of that oath to endeavour any change or alteration in the government either in church or state ; but this concerning the covenant was only to continue for twenty years. This pressed the presbyterians [2] hard, for they, having not only sworn the covenant

[a] Cf. *Hist.* i. 183.   [b] *Ibid.* 182.   [c] *Ibid.* 182-3.

---

[1] See *Hist.* i. 140 ; and *ante*, p. 15.   [2] The *History* says 'the old men.'

themselves but having persuaded other people to it, were now required to renounce it openly before their congregations ª, which was a great exposing of them.   It was visible that the design of the bishops was to put the strongest bars that could be thought on in their way to hinder their conforming, against which ᵇ Southampton declared openly.   Clarendon was not pleased with it, yet he left it in Sheldon's hands. The king himself did not like it at first, and thought it would drive things too high, but I was told that Sheldon persuaded him to it by letting him see that, the house of commons being composed for the greatest part of citizens and burgesses, nothing had spoiled the late king's affairs so much as the credit that the factious lecturers had in all corporations, for this had so great an influence on their elections that he ascribed all the war to that half-conformity, and therefore he said ᶜ it was necessary in order to the having a good parliament that all the clergy should be hearty conformists ; and no wonder if this satisfied the king, for it was very plausible ¹.

ᵈ There were some small alterations made in the book of common prayer, together with some additions ; ᵉ the most important was that concerning the kneeling in the sacrament, which had been put in the second book of common prayer set out by Edward the 6th, but was left out by queen Elizabeth and was now, by bishop Gauden's means, put in at the end of the office of the communion ᵉ.   Sheldon opposed it, but Gauden was seconded by Southampton and Morley.   ᶠ The duke complained of this much to me as a puritanical thing ᶠ, and spake severely of Gauden as a popular man for his procuring it to be added (though I have been told that it was used in king James's time).   ᵍ Another addition has occasioned much raillery ᵍ, and I have also heard that the king has often wished it had never

---

ª Cf. *Hist.* i. 183.   ᵇ *Ibid.* 178.   ᶜ *Ibid.* 178–9.   ᵈ *Ibid.* 183.
ᵉ *Ibid. infra.*   ᶠ *Ibid.*   ᵍ *Ibid. supra.*

---

¹ Burnet subsequently made large additions to his account of these matters, to some extent no doubt on the authority of Baxter's *Reliquiae*, which appeared in 1696, and Calamy's *Abridgment* (1702). See Mr. Airy's note to vol. i. p. 322 in his edition.

been made ^a in the collect during a session of parliament. The king is prayed for by the title of our religious king, which had not been used in the former king's time ; now how this addition should have fallen on this king is too liable to censure, [*f.* 35 (*a*)] and he has heard enough of it by those of his bedchamber that have taken the liberty to be merry with him. Thus was ^b the act of uniformity prepared for the parliament ^b. The book of common prayer was ordered to be read over in the house of commons, but they resolved to debate no part of it [1], but to take it in the lump as it had been prepared by the clergy ; only it was thought too implicit to pass it without reading it, so it was read over for form's sake ; but what opposition it met with in either house I do not know, for I have never taken the pains to go over the journals of parliament, not intending to write an exact and particular history, but only to give such general views of things as I have laid up in my own thoughts, and which may perhaps be useful to others and will give some light to a more particular history.

The designs of the popish party.

Cf. *Hist.* i. 195-6 (*confidences of Peter Walsh, from* 'I knew all this' *to end of paragraph*) ; *ibid.* 193-5 (*intrigues of Bristol*) ; *ibid.* 174-5 (*intervention of Lady Castlemaine*) ; *ibid.* 197 (*action of the Parliament*) ; *ibid.* 196-7 (*mad schemes of Bristol*).

For 'I knew all this' *read* 'One secret I must add here that I had.'

For 'who was the honestest . . . Franciscan order' *read* 'well known by many books that he has published.' (*This occurs later, on f.* 35 (*b*)).

Om. 'and he said . . . come over.'

Om. 'and knew well . . . missionaries.'

For 'and that the more . . . them the less' *read* 'and likewise they hoped that if the terms of our communion were made narrow then there would be many dividers from it, and upon this they thought it would be plausible to plead for indulgence and toleration and so they might be covered from any persecution [cf. *Hist.* i. 179], and that might pass under the pretence of granting some liberty to tender consciences. This agreed exactly with what I heard oft from the duke, who was always much for a toleration [*ibid.* 359] but could not speak with any patience of comprehending the dissenters [*ibid.* 179]. That same priest upon that told me that.'

^a Cf. *Hist.* i. 183.   ^b *Ibid.* 184.

---

[1] See Speaker Onslow's note to *Hist.* i. 184.

Om. 'prosecution . . . harsh word of.'

After 'persecution' *add* 'as the likeliest way to procure the other.'

For 'that censures . . . at Rome' *read* 'that the Jesuits, finding themselves shut out by such a test, would easily have procured censures from Rome.'

[*f.* 35 (*b*)] *Om.* 'But he found . . . at court.' *Then return to* p. 193, 'After St. Bartholomew's day,' *substituting for opening sentence* 'Upon the passing the act of uniformity and the turning out near 2,000 ministers by St. Bartholomew's day in the year [16]62 it began to appear how great the party of the dissenters was like to prove, particularly in the city of London, where many,' &c.

Om. 'and settling . . . plantations.'

For 'a meeting' *read* 'some meetings.'

After 'secrecy' *add* '(as the lord Stafford told me in the Tower).'

For 'seconded the motion' *read* 'did great service in this matter.'

Om. 'He said, it was so visibly . . . the design.'

For 'Bennet . . . meddling' *read only* 'and Bennet set it likewise forward.'

Om. 'but it had a deeper root . . . king himself.'

Om. from 'The wiser of the nonconformists' *to* p. 195, 'proposed in council.'

For 'But there was nothing . . . passed' *read* '[it] was the first public discovery that was made of the court's kindness to papists.'

After 'victory' *insert* 'and reckoned that Clarendon would certainly fall upon it. Stafford told me he saw it was an intrigue of Bristol's to raise himself as the head of their party, and said that he and many others thought if it miscarried it might draw a storm on them, who were then easy and in no danger except they brought it on themselves; so they left him.' (*Vide* p. 194.)

Om. 'But the poor priests . . . betray them.'

Then return to pp. 174-5 (*Lady Castlemain's affairs*), *from* 'For some time' *to* 'solemn manner,' *reading instead of that passage* [*f.* 36 (*a*)] 'My lady Castlemaine was now become very insolent, for though upon the queen's first coming over, the king's courtship of her was carried very secretly, yet she would not rest satisfied unless she were publicly owned. So that was done this winter, and she, finding that Clarendon would not so much as be civil to her, much less depend on her, was easily persuaded to set forward everything that might ruin him or Southampton.'

Then proceed to p. 197, 'The parliament expressed . . . uniformity'; *and* 'The parliament did pass' *to end of paragraph; reading instead of these passages* 'But in the next session of parliament the members being still high for the church, as they obliged the king by the repeal of the act of triennial parliaments, which had lodged a vast power in the people of choosing a parliament every third year in case the king should not call one, so they broke all those designs for toleration.' (*Cf. with this also* p. 196, 'The church party . . . pointed at.')

Then revert to p. 196 (*Bristol's wild schemes*), *from* 'He had great skill,' *beginning thus*: 'Here a passage has been told me which perhaps is of too great importance to be put in writing, nor is the conveyance of it to me so sure that I can depend much on it, for the earl of Rochester said (but not in his latest and best days) that he had it from the duke of Buckingham, and they were men that stuck so little at telling a made story that pleased them, whether true or false, that nothing is to be much built on what comes by such a conveyance. The story was this : Bristol dealt much in astrology,' &c.

For 'opinion of it' *read* 'opinion of his skill in that art, of which many instances have been told me.'

For 'he was to fall' *read* 'he was in great danger of falling,' *and om.* ' means, if not by his.'

After 'provoke him' *add* 'and so would be more governed by him and his father-in-law than ever.'

Om. 'and the duke of Buckingham . . . carried it to the king,' *reading* 'I tell this story as I had it, though I give no credit to it. When the parliament met in the year [16]63, Bristol and his party found the king intended to leave them, so he acted a mad part, he expostulated very insolently with the king.'

For 'forsook him' *read* 'forsook them.'

For 'who said . . . room' *read* 'thought that he was mad, and once intended to have sent him to the Tower, but he turned away from him.'

Om. 'It is very probable . . . fearful.'

For 'a very mixed nature . . . lords, in which' *read* [*f.* 36 (*b*)] 'a very extravagant crime to be cast on him by a papist, that he was engaged in a design to introduce popery, and had sent one sir Richard Bellings[1] to Rome upon that negotiation [and].'

For 'Proclamations. . . over' *read* 'I left England while this was in agitation, so I must leave this matter, for I know no more of it, but that it came to nothing, and the earl of Bristol absconded for some time.'

The king was married by Aubigny.

Cf. *Hist.* i. 174 (*from* 'When the queen' *to* 'witnesses to prove it').

Begin 'But since I have sometimes named Aubigny, I shall tell one secret of him. When the queen,' *&c.*

Om. 'The king . . . 1662.'

Before 'bigoted' *insert* 'then.'

For 'Upon this . . . given. But' *read* 'All this did not satisfy her, for she would needs be married according to the Roman ritual, and the king was not so scrupulous in this matter as she was. So.'

After 'told me' *add* 'as a great secret, when I was talking to him concerning the design of putting away the queen, for which this was one main thing pretended, that the king and she were never lawfully married.'

For 'before he told me this' *read* 'before I spake of this to him.'

Om. at this place all after 'witnesses to prove it.'

[*Deaths in the royal family.*]

Cf. *Hist.* i. 170 ('The king's third brother' *to end of paragraph*).

Begin 'But now that the queen brought no children, a great change appeared in all the court, for the duke was much looked at.

---

[1] See Mr. Airy's note to i. 303 of his edition, 307 same edition ; Christie's *Shaftesbury*, ii. 16–9, and the curious Italian publication there quoted.

'What are all the most promising hopes of a very flourishing family? This has appeared very signally in the elector of Palatine's family, where of six brothers (all graceful and personable men) there is no succession sprung but the present elector, who has no children[1]. So here in England what hopes had we of spreading a family when we had three such young princes and two princesses, that in the world the like was not to be seen [cf. *Hist.* i. 171]. The duke of Gloucester died soon after the king's coming over of the small-pox.'

For 'The king's third . . . acceptable' *read only* 'He was a prince of great parts.'

After 'the duke of York' *add* 'but had he lived the court had very likely been broken into great factions, for he,' *&c.*

For 'But he told him . . . by the king who' *read only* 'and Clarendon had much ado to divert him from it. His spirit was restless; [*f.* 37 (*a*)] so that after the entertainments and jollities that followed upon the king's coming in had been over, it was expected that he would be earnest for somewhat, but he died very soon after, and the king.'

Om. 'Those who would not . . . balance him.'

For 'died likewise . . . lamented' *read only* 'came over.'

Om. 'who had the art . . . queen-mother of France.'

For 'On that . . . lived in' *read* 'That journey, and many unhappy accidents in it, as it run her out of all her estate, so it engaged her in some things that did not please the king, so when she came to die, he bore it very easily.' *Om. remainder of paragraph.*

[*State of the succession in* 1683.]

[a] Thus were two branches of this family cut off, and only the prince of Orange left by the princess royal. The king has no issue by the queen. The duke has had many children [a], but has buried nine or ten, of whom five were sons, so that two only live. The eldest has been now almost six years married to the prince of Orange[2], and no issue is come yet. The second is just now married to prince George of Denmark[3], by whom I pray God send us issue, for it is a melancholy

[a] Cf. *Hist.* i. 170.

---

[1] By his marriage with Elisabeth of England, Frederic V, Elector Palatine and King of Bohemia, had six sons, of whom four (Frederic Henry, Rupert, Maurice, and Philip) died unmarried before the end of 1682. The two exceptions were, (1) Charles Lewis, who died in 1680, leaving a son and successor (see note 3, p. 76, *infra*) and a daughter Charlotte Elisabeth (see note 4, p. 76, *infra*); (2) Edward, who died in 1663, leaving three daughters (see note 5, p. 76, *infra*). Of the King and Queen of Bohemia's five daughters, moreover, four were childless; the only one who bore issue being (the Electress) Sophia, for whom see note 6, p. 76, *infra*.

[2] The Princess Mary was married to the Prince of Orange, Nov. 15, 1677.

[3] The Princess Anne espoused Prince George of Denmark, July 28, 1683.

thing to think that our crown should go to the queen of Spain, that is the eldest daughter of the princess Henrietta, the king's younger sister, that was married to the duke of Orleans; but though she has been five years [1] married there is no issue by her. [a] Her younger and only sister is, as it is thought, to be married [2] to the duke of Savoy [a]. After these comes the prince elector [3] as the next heir; and if he has no issue, then his sister that is now duchess of Orleans [4] and her son must succeed, and after them comes prince Edward's daughters [5], and after them the family of Lunenburgh Hanover [6]. So far have I run out in a melancholy speculation of the witherings of this family that put forth so fair and promising a blossom.

The king lost the hearts of his subjects.

[b] But now I shall give some account of the civil part of the government as far as I understand it. When the king came first over there was a springtide of joy in all people's hearts, and in that first run out of it the court might have had what they had asked either as to revenue or power; [c] but £1,200,000 a year was thought enough for revenue. [d] Soon after that the mad rising of Venner and his followers broke out, [e] upon which

[a] Cf. *Hist.* i. 171.   [b] *Ibid.* 159.   [c] *Ibid.* 160.   [d] *Ibid. infra.*
[e] *Ibid.* 161.

---

[1] Burnet is in error by a year; Marie Louise, elder daughter of Philip Duke of Orleans and his first wife Henrietta of England, had become the first wife of Charles II of Spain in the summer of 1679, and had thus been married, by the summer of 1683, four years. She died childless in 1689.

[2] The marriage of Anne Marie (younger sister of the above) with Victor Amadeus II, Duke of Savoy, actually took place April 10, 1684.

[3] i.e. Charles, son of Charles Lewis (see note 1, p. 75, *supra*); he died s. p. in 1685.

[4] Charlotte Elisabeth, daughter of Charles Lewis, Elector Palatine (note 1, p. 75), had become a Roman Catholic in 1671, when she married, as his second wife, Philip, Duke of Orleans; her son was the Regent Orleans.

[5] Edward, Count Palatine (for whom see note 1, p. 75, *supra*), became a Roman Catholic, died in 1663, and left three daughters, who became respectively Princess of Salms, Princess of Condé, and Duchess of Brunswick Lunenburg (by marriage with John-Frederick, brother of Ernest Augustus, and a Roman Catholic). In consequence of their faith, they were eventually excluded from the succession.

[6] Sophia, daughter of Frederic V, Elector Palatine, and his wife Elisabeth, married in 1658 Ernest Augustus, Duke of Brunswick, and subsequently Elector of Hanover; by whom she was mother of George I.

the king begun to form troops of guards[a]. This passed then
well enough; only some men of greater spirit begun to object
against it that it was a new thing and looked like the distrust
of the nation, and that the guards which they raised were
enough to give jealousy, but not enough to give security.
He that spake the most of this strain was the old earl of
Northumberland[1], who was a man of a great spirit [*f. 37 (b)*]
and of a high sense of honour, that lived with all the greatness
of the ancient nobility, and under much form and high civilities
kept himself on the reserve with all people. He was not a man
of much knowledge, but he had the luck to have a great
friend that was one of the knowingest men of the nation,
Mr. Pierpoint[2], who knew the laws and understood the interests
and constitution of this nation beyond most I ever knew. He
was likewise a man of great form and method, and as to the
discreet and cautious part of wisdom I thought him one of
the most extraordinary men I ever saw, if he was not too full
of jealousy and foresight; he indeed thought that nothing
was to be done for mending matters, for the nation could not
be ripe for that in a whole age, so all that he thought on was
how to stop the progress that the crown was like to make at
that time. But to return to Northumberland: he had a cloud
now upon him, for the late king had taken all possible ways
to gain him, and had made him both admiral and general;
but he went in to the parliament's side, which the court called
high ingratitude, but he pretended it was love to his country,
for he had a high sense both of public liberty and of the

[a] Cf. *Hist.* i. 161.

---

[1] Algernon Percy, tenth Earl of
Northumberland, is never described at
length in the printed *History*; but is
cursorily mentioned on pp. 40, 41, 169,
242.

[2] William Pierpoint ('wise William'), 1607 (?)–1678, second son of
the Earl of Kingston, the distinguished
Parliamentarian described by Mrs.
Hutchinson as 'one of the wisest coun-
sellors and most excellent speakers in
the House,' by Cromwell as ' my wise
friend,' by Whitelocke as being of

'deep foresight and prudence.' For
the career of this remarkable man,
whose character does not appear in
the printed *History*, but whose name
occurs incidentally on pp. 16, 44, 267
of vol. i, the reader is referred to
Mr. Firth's article in the *Dictionary
Nat. Biog.* His daughter Gertrude
married George, Viscount and afterwards Earl and Marquis of Halifax,
who had been associated with Pierpoint on the 'Brook House' Commission of 1667.

dignity of peers. He had merited much at the duke's hands,
[a] by the care he had of him when he was put under his government by order of parliament, for he had treated him with all
the nobleness and greatness that was due to his birth [a] ; but
though he was not in such terms with the court as to be admitted into the secret of their councils, yet they used him with
a respect beyond what they gave to any of the nobility, and
he distinguished himself in his manner as much from the rest
as his birth set him above them. He was one of the first that
began to complain of the guards, and [b] used to say it was good
for the nation that the luxury of the court increased; for it
was better to have the treasure melt away, than to see the
king raise and pay a military force with it. [c] Southampton
looked on when the first guards were raised with more indifferency, and thought it was only a piece of state and for
the king's personal safety ; but when he saw the growth
of that force he begun to apprehend it much and complained of it severely to Clarendon, and told him plainly
that a white staff could not corrupt him and make him serve
in designs that tended to the subduing his country and the
governing it by a military power [c] ; and asked Clarendon, what
did he think that he or the law would signify if these guards
should increase into an army. Upon this it is said that
[d] Clarendon made a stop, and did not set on the designs of
increasing the king's revenue and power so much as he might
have done, for the house of commons was then so well disposed, that there was scarce anything that the court could
[*f.* 38 (*a*)] have asked which might not have been obtained.

[*The sale of Dunkirk.*]

Cf. *Hist.* i. 172-3.

Postpone opening passage (*see infra*, p. 79) *and begin* 'One of the first public
things that was much cried out on was the sale of Dunkirk. The Spaniards
pretended,' &c.

Om. 'The king was in no sort . . . or sold?'

For 'who were believed . . . France' *read only* 'that were there.'

After 'Clarendon' *add* 'as his son has told me.'

For 'To make . . . easier' *read* 'and that the rather because.'

[a] Cf. *Hist.* i. 169.   [b] *Ibid.* 242.   [c] *Ibid.* 161.   [d] *Ibid.* 160-1.

After ' occasions' *add* 'and was, if I remember right, to be made the foundation of a bank '; *then go straight to* 'it was sold.'

Om. 'among . . . venal.'

Om. 'though . . . entirely.'

Then insert those parts of the paragraph relating to Schomberg, which seem to have been a subsequent addition; since the passage begins with the words 'The marshal de Schomberg told me when I was with him last at Paris that,' *and concludes with the sentence* 'This is added by me after my return from France' (*i.e. after the visit Burnet paid to that country towards the end of* 1683). *The variations are as follows:*—

For 'As the treaty . . . from England' *read only* 'he waited of the king in his way to Portugal, not long after his restoration, and had much free discourse with him about Dunkirk and several other things.'

After ' Paris ' *add* ' during the king's exile, where they had been mutual confidants in some of their loose amours'; *and omitting* ' but had so great . . . general they had,' *continue* ' so he now used great freedom with the king.'

Om. ' It would keep . . . affairs.'

Before ' wild ' *read* ' raw.'

After ' Dunkirk ' *proceed to* ' Schomberg advised.'

After ' thoughts of it ' *add* ' and when I objected what I have heard some military men say concerning the place's not being tenable, he assured me that those were but made stories to cover the infamy of that action, that.'

For ' could never be taken ' *read* ' would never have been besieged, much less taken.'

For ' But he was singular in that opinion ' *read* [*f.* 38 (*b*)] 'and [he] told me that the king's selling it was the first thing that made his reputation sink all Europe over. He was also very free with the king as to his pleasures, not that he talked to him as a divine on that head, in which he has been too much a libertine himself[1], but he was troubled to see that these things possessed the king's spirit too much.'

[*Tangier.*]

The Spaniards were highly dissatisfied with the court, both for this and for the king's marrying the infanta of Portugal, but Clarendon thought that[a] Tangier, which was given as a part of the queen's portion, would wash off the blot of Dunkirk ; and considering more its general situation as it lies in the map than the true value of the place, either as it might be a station for ships or a foundation for subduing as much territory as might defray the cost of keeping it, he set the king on a vast charge about it, and for building a mole for

---

[a] Cf. *Hist.* i. 173.

[1] See note b to p. 4, vol. ii. of *History* (in Mr. Airy's edition).

ships before it. It has hitherto been a great and constant charge, and has involved the king in some little wars with the Moors, but has not yet turned to any account, nor is there any probability that it can ever be made an important place. Yet I remember, when I knew the court first, it was talked of at a mighty rate as the foundation of a new empire, and he would have been a very hardy man that would have ventured to have spoke slightly of it; but men have been more liberal of their discourse since that time, and it is generally believed that, after near two millions of charge, [a] the king is now resolved [1] on blowing it up and bringing over his garrison [a]. And thus I have given a very copious account of all that I learnt of the state of the court at that time. I understood not all this then, but have picked up much of it since that time. I will not say but in many things (especially in the characters that I have given upon hearsay) I may have been mistaken, but I think I have writ of all men and things with a due caution and exactness.

A session of parliament in Scotland; [death of Warriston].

I went down to Scotland in summer [16]63, where [b] one of the first things that was done was the execution of my unfortunate uncle. He was much disordered both in body and mind [b], and he shewed it too much before the parliament; his head was much turned, for by unskilful physicians and excessive bleeding he was brought so low [*f.* 39 (*a*)] that [c] he had lost his memory and sense, so that he did not so much as know his own [2] children [c]. I heard his speech, with great confusion [3];

[a] Cf. *Hist.* i. 174.   [b] *Ibid.* 203.   [c] *Ibid.*

---

[1] Secret instructions for its abandonment had been actually signed (July 2, 1683) about a month before this was written, but Lord Dartmouth, sent to execute them, did not return till April, 1684; cf. *Hist.*, Airy's edition, i. 306, note 1; ii. 437, with note 2; and Reresby, *Memoirs*, April 15, 1684.

[2] *Lauderdale Papers*, i. 135, 144.

[3] Lauderdale says, 'The prisoner was bro[u]ght; he was commanded to kneel at the hearing his sentence, which he did, and I must confess I never saw so miserable a spectacle. I have often heard of a man feared out of his wits, but never saw it before; yet, what he said was sense good enough, but he roared and cryed and exprest more feare than ever I saw' (*Lauderdale Papers*, i. 145. See also *ibid.* 155, 163, 175; and *Hist.*, Mr. Airy's edition, i. 364, notes).

[a] there.was a visible disorder in him, but he set it out with so much passion that no wonder if it was not much believed nor considered. So he was sentenced to die. Many presbyterians came about him, and prayed for him in a style, as if he had merited strangely at God's hands, and as if he had been a martyr. He was very unequal in his deportment; sometimes it was composed and at other times he was much out of order, yet when the day of his execution came he was very serene[a]. In Scotland the executions are after dinner. I dined with him that day; he eat cheerfully, and I remember he called upon me twice to eat. I stayed with him, and was now and then leaving him and returning after short intervals. One thing I thought strange; when I cited some passage of scripture for his meditation not a quarter of an hour before he was led out, he would know the chapter and verse and turn to it, which he needed not to have done had he been entire, for he had the whole scriptures almost by heart. I walked with him to the scaffold (for all go to their execution on foot in Scotland). [b] He read his speech twice, which I am sure was all of his own composing[b]; then he prayed long, and after being twice or thrice in his private devotions he was executed[1]. I have already given his character[2]; I shall add nothing here; but by this relation the reader will see that I am not biassed much by kindred. I am afraid friendship may mislead me more, yet I shall watch over myself the best I can even in that.

[*The session continued; Nisbet's character.*]

Cf. *Hist.* i. 203 ('The business of the parliament' *to* p. 205, 'the effects they might have') *and* p. 279 (*Nisbet's character*).

After 'laid open' *read* 'Mackenzie laid it all upon Middleton.'

After 'the putting' *insert* 'Mackenzie and Fletcher and'; *and for* 'all' *read* 'most of.'

[a] Cf. *Hist.* i. 203.   [b] *Ibid.*

Burnet had 'forced' Lauderdale to write a few lines in his favour (*Lauderdale Papers*, i. 156), and Lady Margaret Kennedy, whom Burnet eventually married, pleaded earnestly with the Secretary for the material interests of the unfortunate man's family, which Burnet was safe-guarding (*Letters from Lady Margaret Burnet*, Bannatyne Club, 1828, p. 31).

[1] See Morison's *Warriston*, pp. 148–9.
[2] See *Hist.* i. 28; and cf. Autobiography, *infra*, f. 197.

After 'employments' *insert Sir John Nisbet's character (Hist.* i. 279) ; *reading thus* : 'Sir John Nisbet was made king's advocate ; he was a man of a slow apprehension, but of a deep judgement ; and very learned, not only in the law, but in all the other parts of learning, particularly in the Latin and Greek tongues, and was a great lover of justice ; he had been always of the king's side, yet his great love of money (which is his only blemish) has so entangled him that he will never put much to hazard. But this change fell .out some months after this' ; *then revert to* p. 204, 'So an act,' *omitting all about English Conventicle Act.*

[*f.* 39 (*b*)] *For* 'So an act . . . terms' *read* 'In parliament there were two acts passed that related to the church ; by one of them the government by bishops was more fully confirmed, and all the subjects were required to keep their parish churches, and fines were set upon transgressors.'

For 'zeal for the church' *read* 'zeal for episcopacy ; but this did not work much on the bishops, who thought that all this was only a little court artifice.'

Om. 'There was some . . . majority.'   *Om.* 'of all deans.'

After 'Trent' *add* 'so that things could not be so much as complained of without leave from the king, and in cases of heresy, or any disorder whatsoever, that might at any time be supported by the court, the church's hands were bound up.'

After 'irregular' *add* 'Sharp's taking it to himself was thought very insolent.'

After 'told him of it' *add* 'two or three days after[1].'

For 'The inferior . . . a person' *read* 'Others also said that there was no shadow of liberty left to this national synod, since the one half of the commissioners was to be.'

Om. 'The act . . . constituted'; *and after* 'Two other' *add* 'considerable.'

For 'and not having . . . goods as might' *read* 'it [being] thought necessary to do somewhat in Scotland for excluding the English commodities till they had repealed that act, and (so).'

After 'to him[2]' *add* 'by which the trade of that kingdom, and the customs arising out of it, are now wholly in the crown.'

Om. 'and so it passed . . . opposition.'

[*f.* 40 (*a*)] *For* 'Nobody dreamt . . . of this' *read* 'Nobody dreamt ever how to raise, to march, or to command this army.'

Om. 'to let the king . . . England.'

For 'they had not much treasure to offer him . . . good army' *read* 'which he said was neither by their treasure, nor good government, but by the threatening of an army.'

Om. 'And of this . . . ends.'

[*Conduct of Glencairn.*]

[a] When the business of the parliament was over, it was dissolved [a]. Rothes dismissed them with a dull speech that was penned by Sharp and had figures in it that looked like

[a] Cf. *Hist.* i. 205.

---

[1] Lauderdale was at Edinburgh.   [2] Mr. Airy's ed. reads 'to the king.'

a schoolmaster; the chief thing he recommended to their care was the executing those laws to which themselves had consented that related to the church. When Rothes and Lauderdale went back to court to give an account of affairs, ᵃ the government of Scotland was left chiefly in Glencairn's hands ᵃ; he was too proud to stoop to Lauderdale [1], but on the other hand it was not easy to find matter to turn him out; yet he expected it, and both Primrose and he apprehending that they would be turned out of their places, set themselves much to recover the favour of the people, which they had formerly lost so much. The first thing in which Glencairn shewed these inclinations was in my uncle Warriston's concern; for though he hated him out of measure, yet he was very friendly to him and procured him the favour of much time, and put it on the parliament as much as decently he could to recommend him to the king's mercy; and after the dissolution of the parliament ᵇ he was always moving in council for the moderating of Sharp's violent conditions and propositions.

Argyll restored.

While the parliament of Scotland was almost at an end, Lorn's business was despatched at court ᵇ; he was set at liberty before Lauderdale came to Scotland, and went up to court with very earnest recommendations both from Rothes and Lauderdale; and (that summer happening to be a time of little business at court) sir Robert Moray [2] laid hold of the conjuncture and pressed the king so in it that ᶜ he restored him to his grandfather's title ᶜ; so that he was the first earl of Scotland, and by not being made a marquis he only lost the precedence of Montrose. ᵈ The king also gave him 1,500 pounds sterling a year clear out of the estate ᵈ, and gave to his brother and sisters all that their father had settled on them; and for the rest of the estate he ordered it to be first charged with that debt in which Lorn had been bound with his father

ᵃ Cf. *Hist.* i. 205.　　ᵇ *Ibid.*　　ᶜ *Ibid.*　　ᵈ *Ibid.*

---

[1] *Lauderdale Papers*, i. 166.
[2] Who acted as Secretary this year during Lauderdale's absence.

(for if that had not been done all the king's favour to him would have signified little, for he was liable to so much debt as must have eat up his estate). [*f.* 40 (*b*)] And when that was done [a] the overplus of the estate was ordered to be divided for the payment of all the other debts proportionally; but that was so little that presently a great outcry was raised, which has pursued Argyll ever since [a1]; it being said that he was restored to his father's estate without paying his debts, so that really the attainder has fallen on the creditors; but this was occasioned by the restoring Huntly without making him liable for his just debts. So the affairs of this year are at an end. Now I return to my own private ones.

My own concerns.

I was not a little lifted up this summer with the civilities that Lauderdale shewed me, and I waited on him perpetually, so there I began to have a great acquaintance with our nobility and gentry; and when he was one day sick (a great court of ladies being about him), I was first acquainted with her whom I have since married [2]. She was his great friend, a zealous presbyterian, and a woman of so great intrigue that though I was nearly related to her and had been invited to her acquaintance by several obliging messages from her, yet I had still declined it. For I dislike all meddling women;

[a] Cf. *Hist.* i. 205.

---

[1] See *supra*, pp. 5-7; and *infra*, p. 158.

[2] For Lady Margaret Burnet see Mr. Airy's article (under her married designation) in *Dict. Nat. Biog.*; his note to *Hist.* in his edition, i. 196; Burnet's own account of their marriage and her death, *infra*, Autobiography, ff. 206, 208, and Harl. MSS. 6584, f. 118 (*a*); Cockburn, *A specimen of some free and impartial remarks*, pp. 46-7; and last, but not least, the valuable collection of her letters to Lauderdale (published in 1828 by the Bannatyne Club, and edited by Mr. Airy) with the Introduction. These last entirely confirm Burnet's character of her and give an attractive presentment of the high-minded, high-spirited, witty, and accomplished woman, with affections as strong as her intelligence; who, when reproached by her friends for an unconventional intimacy with Lauderdale, her own cousin-germane (whose coldness towards his own wife was notorious), gave 'no other answer, than that her virtue was above suspicion; as really it was' (adds our informant Mackenzie), 'she being a person whose religion exceeded as far her wit, as her parts exceeded others of her sex' (Mackenzie's *Memoirs*, p. 165, quoted in p. ii of the Preface to her *Letters*).

upon which I said once to the duchess of Lauderdale [somewhat?] that was not ill-turned: I thought there were two sorts of persons that ought not to meddle in affairs, though upon very different accounts, these were churchmen and women; we ought to be above it [1], and women were below it. But from a general acquaintance with my wife there grew a great friendship between us. She was a woman of much knowledge, had read vastly; she understood both French, Italian, and Spanish; she knew the old Roman and Greek authors well in the translations; she was an excellent historian and knew all our late affairs exactly well, and had many things in her to furnish out much conversation. She was generous to a high degree, and was a noble friend and a very tender-hearted woman to all in misery [2], and sincere even to a nicety. In a word she had many rare qualities, but she had some bad ones; she was apt to mistake little things, and to fancy that her friends neglected her, and upon these jealousies she was peevish and bitter; but it was long before I observed these defects in her.

At this time I grew acquainted with Mr. Scougall [3], afterwards the pious and worthy bishop of Aberdeen; he took a great liking to me, and as I was one day standing with him on the streets of Edinburgh, a gentleman of a pale countenance and in a very plain garb came to us and made me a great compliment [a] in acknowledgement of the kindness he had received from my father at Paris [a]. I thought he was some ordinary man, and did not much mind his compliment, but we went on in our discourse, [*f.* 41 (*a*)] and he happened to say some things that discovered both great learning and much sense. So I asked who it was, and found it was sir Robert Fletcher [4];

[a] Cf. Life (*Hist.* ii), p. 676.

---

[1] The ludicrous discrepancy between Burnet's doctrine and practice on this point furnished a not unfair topic for the bitter sarcasms of Hickes (*Some Discourses*, p. 4).

[2] Her letters to Lauderdale consist largely of urgent appeals in favour of persons in distress.

[3] See *Hist.* (Airy's ed.), i. 387-8; *Dict. Nat. Biog.*; and *Specimen*, &c., by Cockburn (Scougall's nephew), who gives a most amusing account of Scougall's sentiments concerning Burnet, both at this date and as subsequently developed (pp. 28-43, 59-63).

[4] See Burnet's anonymous *Dis-*

thus did I stumble on my first patron. We had a great deal of discourse, and I had the luck to please him; at which I wonder much, for he was one of the humblest and modestest men in the world, and I was then one of the vainest and insolentest. His genius lay to mathematics and philosophy, and he wanted a friend and companion in study, so he began to resolve on having me about him. I was at this time very uneasy at home; for my mother and the rest of our family were much troubled to find that I was resolved to conform to episcopacy. So I had many sad [hard?] things said to me on that subject; and my mother laid it so to heart that it put her into fits so that we thought she would have died of them; therefore to give her some content I promised not to take orders yet for a year, and so we were more at ease.

The story of Thauler's conversion had a great effect on me.

At Christmas I went to the earl of Tweeddale's house in the country, where I had much conversation with Mr. Charteris that was his minister, and Mr. Nairn, that had retired to a living in the country that was in Lauderdale's gift. I preached there, and it was the first time that Mr. Charteris had ever heard me. He is a very modest man, and was sorry to find that some good things which he fancied he saw in me were like to be spoilt with pride and arrogance; and being resolved to say something to me and yet being restrained by his modesty, he did it in a more effectual way by telling me the story of Thauler's[1] conversion, which I heard with such attention that I think I remember yet the very words he used. The stops he made, his looks to me and gesture are yet fresh in my thoughts; and it had such an effect on me that I must say there was never any one thing befell me in my whole life that touched me more. And because this may be read by such as cannot find Thauler's life[2], I shall set it down in

---

course on the memory of this excellent man; Cockburn's *Specimen*, pp. 30, 32, and *infra*, Autobiography, pp. 200, 202.

[1] J. Tauler, the Mystic.

[2] A life which Burnet may have seen is the *D. Ioannes Thauleri ... sermones ... Historia et ennarratio vitae ... D. Ioannes Thauleri*, Coloniae, 1603.

a few words. Thauler was the most celebrated preacher in
his time, and many came from divers places to Cologne to hear
him preach. Among others a country boor came once and
desired him to preach a sermon of perfection, which he did ;
and when the boor gave him thanks for his sermon he seemed
to be much pleased with it. So the boor told him though he
preached of perfection to others he was far from it himself,
otherwise he would not be so delighted with the praises he
gave him ; at which, when Thauler grew angry, he told him
that was a further proof how little he [*f.* 41 (*b*)] had attained
to perfection, otherwise he would not be much concerned in
his opinion of him nor be displeased if he thought ill of him.
He further told him he had lewd thoughts in his mind at the
time of his sermon ; with this Thauler was struck, and said he
looked on him as sent to him of God and so surrendered
himself up to his conduct. The boor told him he must give
over preaching till he had mortified the vain temper in himself; upon which he gave himself wholly to devotion and
fasting and to everything that might mortify his vanity ; and
after some time his boor desired him to try how preaching
would do. So he went to the bishop's vicar and asked leave
to preach, which was granted, and a great assembly was
gathered in the cathedral upon the expectation of him ; but
as he went up to the pulpit he found his old vanity returning
upon him ; so (being resolved never to preach while he was
under the dominion of that temper) he wept and came down,
saying only a few words tending to the abasing himself.
Upon this he was generally looked on as an hypochondriacal
man ; but his boor was well pleased with what he had done, and
after some more time was spent by him in that course of intro-
version (as the mystics express it), the boor called on him to
preach again ; but the vicar would not suffer him to preach in
public till he heard how he performed in a private chapel. So
he preached in the Dominicans' chapel (being himself one of
that order), but it was not so privately carried, but that many
of the town heard of it, and came thither. His text was,
' Behold, the Bridegroom cometh, go ye out to meet him ' ; he

turned the words to a mystical sense, and preached in such a manner that all who heard him were so struck with the impressions that his sermon made on them, that they seemed ravished, and one died in a transport; and so his boor told him he saw what effects his preaching had when he set about it with a right spirit. This story went to my heart, and I have been often since that time at the point of coming down out of the pulpit or of breaking off in the middle when I have felt violent temptations to vanity seize on me; and I have seldom preached on extraordinary occasions before which I have not very heartily prayed that if the rubbing shame on me by my miscarriage in it might contribute more to the honour of God than my performing well, that God's will might be done. I confess I have had another notion of preaching ever since that time than I had before; till then I had only thought on a laboured and adorned discourse for which I might [*f.* 42 (*a*)] be much applauded, but from henceforth I have conceived that the true end of preaching was to give men plain and easy notions of religion and to beget in them tender and warm affections. And I went on in my former method of accustoming myself to an extemporary way of preaching. While I was at the earl of Tweeddale's sir Robert Fletcher (that lived but four miles from him) came over to see him; and finding me there, [a] he invited me to come see him at his house before I went out of the country. So I waited on him; and a Sunday falling to be in the time of my visit he heard me preach twice, and then determined to present me to his church[a]. When he promised it first to me, I was much surprised at it[1]. It was one of the best benefices of those parts (but that had never great weight with me); the parsonage house was not only convenient but noble; it was near all my friends; but the gentleman's own conversation was more than all these. He was an humble, good, and worthy man; he had a great love of learning, and

---

[a] Cf. Life (*Hist.* ii), p. 676.

---

[1] See Cockburn, p. 30.

had made considerable progress in it; and his two eldest sons[1] were then under a very exact education and in the years most capable of it, so he intended that I should live in the house with him, and assist both himself in his own studies and his sons' tutor in instructing them. But that which seemed to me the most considerable thing in that matter was that which I ever endeavoured to follow as the safest rule for the conduct of one's life; and it was that from first to last it seemed to be carried on by a series of providences. No person had ever proposed it to the patron; on the contrary, I had moved the earl of Tweeddale to propose Mr. Nairn to him, and then I resolved to have come in Mr. Nairn's living; but he declined the notion; at which Tweeddale was amazed, for there was not such another as Nairn to be found. The excuse he made was he knew Mr. Nairn would be quickly pulled from him, so that he should be put to choose again; but he did not at first speak of me (for he had not then heard me preach); and when I pressed him further for Nairn, he repeated what he had told Tweeddale, and added that my inclinations to philosophy[2] and mathematics made him prefer me. [a] I told him I intended to travel; he said it was so much the better; I would be the more improved by it, and bishop Scougall was not yet to remove for six months, so I might accomplish it [a]. I had designed this year a short ramble over Holland, Flanders, and France; [*f.* 42 (*b*)] and on [? in] February I went to London, where I was received by sir Robert Moray with more kindness than formerly. I grew likewise to be engaged into great intimacies both with Argyll and Tweeddale; [b] and then I was carried by sir Robert to the Royal Society and chosen a fellow[3] of it [b]; which was a new increase to my vanity that indeed needed no addition.

[a] Life (*Hist.* ii), p. 677.   [b] *Ibid.*

[1] One of whom was afterwards famous as Andrew Fletcher of Saltoun (*Hist.* i. 630-1, 642, and, *infra* p. 161).

[2] i.e. the New or Experimental Philosophy of which both Burnet and Fletcher were devotees. See the memorial *Discourse* on Fletcher, p. 65; *Hist.* i. 500; *infra*, Autobiography, f. 202, where he gives some account of the mathematical studies he undertook with Sir Robert Fletcher, and their fatal results.

[3] Mr. Burnet's *Life* of his father states (following the Autobiography, on

The ill state of the church in Scotland.

Hist. i. 206-7 ('He moved that a letter' *to* 'given him very easily').

Begin 'Lauderdale spake then more freely of the affairs of the church to me than he had done formerly; he told me all Sharp's past life,' *&c.*

Om. 'for he had not . . . stop him.'

Om. 'Things would run to a height . . . jealous of me,' *and revert to* '[Sharp] moved that a letter might be writ,' *&c.*

For 'for in Scotland . . . person' *read* 'in the procuring of which Lauderdale confessed he was not backward, for he knew they would fall out about it.'

After 'church' *add* 'He said the privy council was very remiss in looking to these things, so that it was necessary to lodge it with a commission for whose zeal he could be answerable.'

Om. 'though much . . . ruin them'; *and proceed to* 'Fairfoul.'

For 'near kinsman' *read* 'cousin-germane'; *for* 'lord Rutherford' *read* 'earl of Teviot' (*see Airy's note* a, *in loco*).

For 'who, from being . . . Moors' *read only* 'who was soon after killed by the Moors at Tangier.'

Om. 'and knew . . . Scotland' *and* 'but was . . . genius.'

Om. 'I was much . . . principles.'

[*Burnet and his namesake.*]

He and I, though of the same name, were not akin, and were not at all of a temper; for he yielded to everybody, and I had it always in my nature to oppose everything that was uppermost. The truth is, I never saw any in power but they abused [*f.* 43 (*a*)] it to such a degree that a man who exercised a due freedom in the conduct of himself (and that did not consult his interests in the judgements that he made of them) could not comply with them or approve of them. So much of our Scottish affairs.

My stay in Holland.

[a] Now I went beyond sea [a]; and after I was surfeited with the intolerable peevishness and ill-nature that I saw among our exiles[1] at Rotterdam, and [b] had run through Holland, I settled

---

[a] Cf. *Hist.* i. 207; Life, by Thomas Burnet, in *Hist.* ii. 677; and Autobiography, *infra*, f. 200.   [b] Life (*Hist.* ii), p. 677.

---

which it is founded) that the election took place on his *return* from the continent.

[1] For these exiles see *Hist.* i. 214, 226, 227, 340; and more especially 117, with Mr. Airy's note (i. 213 in his edition).

for six weeks at Amsterdam [a]. Many wondered what I meant
by my stay there. The truth was I did not admire the learning of Holland; I found little spirit among the professors at
Leyden. I could not bear the peevishness of Voet[1] and his party
at Utrecht; and though I liked Des Mares[2] at Groningen better
than any of them, yet I did not admire him. There was some
philological and rabbinical learning among them, but that
made but a dull conversation. A few Cartesian philosophers
were more entertaining ; [b] but my chief business at Amsterdam
was to be well acquainted with all the several religions there.
I conversed much with the Jews, and was two hours a day
with a master there [b], and had much discourse with Ahoab and
Musaphia [? Mustapha], that were esteemed very learned ;
but I could not converse with Ahoab except by an interpreter,
for he understood not Latin. I heard him preach, and had an
interpreter sit by me that explained the remarkablest passages
of his sermon. I shall never forget one thought which was
indeed a noble one: he was preaching on our conformity
to the nature of God, and said that God made man after
his own image, or to be a shadow to himself (according to
the Hebrew word) ; now a shadow had no substance in itself,
and was only a ruder draught of the body whose shadow it
was, and moved always as the body moved. So he applied
it thus: that a man was to have no will of his own, but that
in all things he ought to follow God, and be a sort of a representation (though but a rude one) of his perfections. [c] I was
well acquainted with the Lutherans there [c]; some of them were

[a] Cf. Life (*Hist.* ii), p. 677.　　　[b] *Ibid.*　　　[c] *Ibid.*

---

[1] Gisbert Voet (1588–1676), professor of theology and oriental languages at Utrecht from 1634 ; head of
the Calvinists at the synod of Dort ;
the persecutor of Descartes, and the
fierce opponent of Cocceius, with
whose followers his disciples for a
hundred years disputed theologic
pre-eminence in Holland. He was a
voluminous writer (*Biog. Universelle* ;
Van der Aa, *Biographisch Woordenboek
der Nederlanden*, xix. 296–303).

[2] Samuel des Marèts (Maresius)
(1599–1673), a Frenchman, settled at
Groningen in 1643, where he held a
theologic chair till his death thirty years
later. Bayle admired him ; Burmann
described him as a man of keen intelligence and profound learning, but
of a violent and arrogant temper. He
left more than a hundred works (*Biog.
Universelle* ; Paquot, *Hist. Litt. des
Pays-Bas*, i. 274–283 ; Van der Aa, xii.
198–212).

fierce and untractable, but one of them, Hoppius[1], was one
of Calixtus's disciples[2], and was both moderate in his opinions
and had truly elevated thoughts of God and religion. For I
made ever this observation, that [*f.* 43 (*b*)] the moderate men
had larger and nobler thoughts of God and of the design of
the Christian religion than the zealots have ; who are often
strict indeed in their lives, and very exact to a superstition
in all outward performances, but they seem still to serve God
rather as a severe master than as a merciful Father.   [a] I was
well acquainted with the Remonstrants[a], particularly with
Poelenburgh[3] ; their professors [. . . . [4]].   They were the
men I saw in all Holland of the clearest heads and the best
tempers ; they had an excellent sense of the practical parts of
religion (particularly of love and peace), and expressed great
readiness to reunite with the Calvinists whenever they should
come to cease from their imposing of their doctrines upon
them ; and thought that in these and many other points there
ought to be more mutual forbearance.   This they extended
even to the Socinians ; but they assured me they were not
Socinians themselves, yet they did not like the subtleties of
the fathers and schoolmen in mysterious points.   [b] I was
likewise acquainted[5] with the Socinians[b], in particular
with Zuicker[6], the author of *Irenicon Irenicorum* ; he was

[a] Cf. Life (*Hist.* ii), p. 677.   [b] *Ibid.*

----

[1] Evidently the 'C. Hoppe' whose
works on the 'Sacrament des Avond-
maels' (1667) and on 'de Heylige
Doop' (1669) are in the Library of the
'Evangelisch-Luthersch Seminarium'
at Amsterdam (Catal., 1876, p. 139).

[2] George Calixtus (1586-1656), professor of theology at Helmstadt, 'gave
his name to a sect of Lutherans, who
imagined they could reconcile the
various sects of this faith, and bore
also the title of Syncretists.'

[3] Arnold Poelenburg (1628-66),
minister successively at Horne (1653),
Rotterdam (1653), Amsterdam (1659),
was a copious writer of the Arminian or
Remonstrant party, with a reputation
for learning (Paquot, ed. 1770, iii,

page following p. 56 and numbered
53-4 ; Van der AA, xv. 370-1.)

[4] Something is here missing.

[5] Dr. Cockburn (p. 59) says Burnet's
intimacy with Socinians in Holland
gave great offence to the orthodox
divines, both Dutch and English ; it
explains the subsequent charge of
Socinianism brought against Burnet.

[6] Daniel Zwicker (1612-78).   A
physician, he soon plunged into
theological investigations, with the
object of reconciling the various
Christian sects.   He is said to have
become successively a Socinian, an
Arminian, and a Moravian ; and died
disappointed, and in estrangement
from all recognized bodies.   The

a man of clear thoughts and very composed, and was indeed by far the devoutest man I saw in Holland. He was much for a community of goods and for reducing Christianity in all things to what it was in the Apostles' days; he said it was not a religion that could bear great multitudes, and thought that whole nations turning Christians by the lump had made that there were no true Christians almost left now in the world. He was against the doctrine of the Trinity, but did believe that Christ's death was a sacrifice for our sins. [a] I knew likewise the Brownists, and Menonists or Anabaptists[a], who were subdivided into many little fractions[1]; they were very strict in their lives, but had narrow thoughts. The city ministers were good, plain men. Langelius was a strain above them all in my opinion; they made great use of the English practical books in their sermons, which were very methodical and dull. [b] One thing I drank in at Amsterdam (which sticks still with me and is not like to leave me), which is never to form a prejudice in my mind against any man because he is of this or that persuasion; for I saw so many men of all persuasions that were, as far as I could perceive, so truly religious that I never think the worse of [*f.* 44 (*a*)] a man for his opinions[b]. Education is all, to men of weak heads; they never examine the first principles that were infused in them, nor were it fit to put them upon it; for they, believing all alike, if they began to doubt of some things, that would carry them to doubt of others, and so they would not stop perhaps till they might run too far. [c] I became likewise much in love with toleration by what I saw in Holland, for there was only a difference of opinion among them, but no heat nor anger raised by it, every one enjoying his own conscience without disturbance[c]; and this has ever since given me a great

[a] Cf. Life (*Hist.* ii), p. 677.   [b] *Ibid.*   [c] Cf. *Hist.* i. 207; and Life as above.

Irenicon was written in 1658; his *Irenomastix Victus* in 1661 (*Biog. Univ.*; Van der Aa, xxi. 86).
[1] Was it not among the Amsterdam Anabaptists that Leighton found the supreme instance of the spirit of sectarianism?

bias for toleration, for real arguments are to me much stronger than speculative motions [? notions] can be.

After this I ran round all the provinces except Zealand, and stayed some time both at Leyden and the Hague, and (being set on it by sir Robert Fletcher) I observed all their mechanical arts and the peculiar engines and instruments they made use of, and took notes of all these things, which has since furnished me with a great deal of forwardness in discourse, and has helped me to much idle talk. I also looked into as much of their government as I could observe, and I do not deny but it gave me some tincture of a commonwealth; yet when I understood the English constitution right I thought it was a much perfecter one, where there is as much both of monarchy and commonwealth mixed as may give all the advantages together which are to be found in either of these governments apart; only the danger of a jealousy and struggle may give us disquiet, as it has done now for some years[1]. But of all the parts of the Dutch government there was nothing that delighted me so much as the care that was taken of the poor in so liberal and plentiful a manner, and the method in which this was managed, without partiality or regard to men's religions. In fine[2], I liked many things that I saw among them; but the rudeness of their behaviour, particularly to strangers (even their learned men and clergymen not excepted), was a very odious thing. Golius, the Arabic professor at Leyden[3], was the only civil man I met with, for travelling had polished him. Their divines did generally dictate, and did not easily bear contradiction; and they laid great stress upon very inconsiderable things. The way of private colleges

---

[1] This passage bears a curious resemblance to a passage in the character of a 'Trimmer' (written about a year later), and is probably derived from conversations with Halifax.

[2] Transcriber wrote 'some,' Burnet corrects to 'sum or fin.'

[3] James Golius (1596–1667), pupil in Arabic of Erpenius, travelled first in France, and then, as interpreter to a Dutch embassy, in Morocco (1622). There he collected valuable Arabic MSS.; became on his return Arabic professor at Leyden; during 1625 travelled again in the Levant, and died at Leyden as professor of mathematics. His works, highly esteemed during his own age, are said to be still in repute (*Biog. Universelle*; Van der Aa, vii. 270-3).

in their universities is an excellent method for giving an introduction to learning, [*f.* 44 (*b*)] or for a superficial view of things;
in which, for an hour a day, in one or two months' time, the
professor gives (to such as come by an appointment together
to his chamber) a general idea and short system of his science,
or of any part of it in which they desire to be informed. So
much of my travels in Holland.

My journey to France.

ᵃ I went from thence through Flanders to France ᵃ. I only
saw things, but knew no considerable persons, in Flanders;
and I was under a great constraint by reason of the company
of many Scotchmen that travelled with me from Holland to
Paris, and I was afraid that they might have made stories in
Scotland if I had conversed much, or freely, with any papists
as we passed through Flanders. But at Paris I was more at
liberty. I was recommended very particularly by sir Robert
Moray to Mr. Morus [1], and he made me ᵇ acquainted with
the lord Holles (then ambassador at Paris), who used me
kindly and continued to be a faithful and useful friend to me
to his death. He stood too much upon the points of an
ambassador, and considered more what an ambassador ought
to be than what this age can bear or that court did like ᵇ; so
he was looked on there as a sort of a stubborn hero, but
as a very ill courtier. He gave me many good directions
and charged me to come oft to him. ᶜ I was once a day with
Mr. Morus ᶜ, who was a man of a great vivacity of spirit, and
had life in his conversation; but I thought he had not deep

ᵃ Cf. *Hist.* i. 207; Life (*Hist.* ii), p. 677; and *infra*, Autobiography.   ᵇ Cf.
Hist. i. 207; and Life as above.   ᶜ Cf. Life as above.

---

[1] Alexander Morus (1616-79), born
in Languedoc of Scotch parentage, held
various theologic chairs, and died
minister of Charenton; where his
sermons attracted crowds, less on
account of their eloquence than of the
sarcasms and witticisms interspersed.
His orthodoxy was much questioned;
and Bayle says: ' M. de Morus a beau-
coup d'érudition et d'esprit, peu de
religion et de jugement. Il est mal-
propre, ambitieux, inquiet, changeant,
hardi, présomptueux, et irrésolu. Il
sait le latin, le grec, l'hébreu, l'arabe;
et ne sait pas vivre.' He was engaged
in acrimonious controversy with Milton
(*Biog. Universelle*). See also *Lauderdale Papers*, i. 28.

impressions of religion, and we were often of different minds. He said I was too enthusiastical and would turn hypochondriacal; and I was afraid that he had too much levity in his mind and was too near a libertine. Mr. Daillié [1] and he were then in ill terms, which perhaps made Daillié less civil to me, for I had but one long [a] conversation with him. I saw in him a great genius [a], but too much heat in the matter of Morus, who was certainly a very indiscreet man; but I believe he was very innocent of those things that were laid to his charge. I heard him preach twice; [b] he was much admired for the fire and spirit with which he adorned and expressed his matter, but his sermons, when stripped of that garniture, would have appeared to be very ordinary things [b]. The truth was, the great thing that made sir Robert Moray put me so much on going to France as he did was that I might observe their way of preaching and learn to speak my sermons with more advantage; for he thought if our English sermons were pronounced as the French did theirs, the business of preaching would be at great perfection [*f.* 45 *(a)*] among us; and I observed this carefully. I heard many sermons of the popish clergy; I did not like the way of the Jesuits and the friars, and thought it had too much of the stage in it; too much art and too much acting spoiled it; but the secular priests pleased me more, who preached more staidly and more like men that were all the while thinking of what they were saying. I took a good tincture of their way—indeed more than Scotland could well bear and much more than England could endure; but I have worn off some gestures that looked too like acting, and yet the way of preaching in which I still hold is (as some that have observed it well have told me) very like the way of the secular clergy of the Port Royal.

While I was at Paris I could not get into the acquaintance of any of the Jansenists; they were then run down, and were very reserved, so that it was not easy to get into any

[a] Life (*Hist.* ii), p. 677.   [b] *Ibid.*

---

[1] Jean Daillé (1594-1670), minister at Saumur (1625) and Charenton (1626).

familiarity with them. I confess I thought the French protestants had no great sense of devotion, and did not imagine
that they would have stuck much to their religion. I made
some acquaintance in many religious houses, for I had then
a great inclination to that state of life ; but their worship
appeared to me to be so plainly idolatrous in many parts, and
superstitious in most other parts, that I could not bring myself
so much as to endure it, though I thought very well of those
who, by their education, were blindfold engaged in their
church. I did not at all like the Jesuits, but I admired the
methods of their order and their way of training up youth,
which has ever since run much in my mind. For themselves,
I knew indeed but few of them ; yet I saw a vast pride and
vanity among them, and a most horrid rage against all that
they looked on as enemies of their order. I saw nothing
among the Carthusians but dulness and stupidity. They were
overgrown with fat ; some were full of phlegm, and others
were hypochondriacal ; and no wonder, considering what
a violence it is to a Frenchman's nature to be in perpetual
silence. The Benedictines seemed a plain, honest sort of
people. They were very rich, and much despised ; but they
spoke of all orders with great contempt in comparison of their
own. The unreformed Cordeliers seemed to have no sense of
religion. I was not acquainted with any of the Recollets, but
knew many Capuchins, who were much better than the unreformed Franciscans, but they had much wild-fire among
them. In short, the two points that most of all the [*f.* 45 (*b*)]
disputing men insisted on with me were the two least things
like to have wrought on me, which were the authority of the
church and the presence in the host. The notion I had of
Christianity made me incapable of admitting the one, and I
was too much a philosopher ever to let the possibility of the
other enter into me. But I looked often to find out some
that understood the mystical divinity, and that followed the
rules of it ; but I could never fall on any. I was told they
were persons who would not be seen ; so whether this was
only an excuse, or if there were really any such among them,

I do not know. I had also much conversation [with] several nuns at grates, particularly with my lady Balcarres' daughter [1], who I found had more of the mystical notions than any I spoke with; but I saw she was very weary of the house in which she lived. There were many boarders in it, by which the abbess made great advantages; and she being concerned to raise her nephew was so much set on that matter that she looked very little after the strict government of the house; and upon that a faction was formed against her, of which my friend was said to be the chief, and was much complained of as very seditious. She had a warm fancy, and was enticed to go over to them as thinking a nun's life was but a little lower than an angel's, and was very uneasy when she found it not so. The abbess was so severe to her that she laid many projects to get out to leave that house; not that she intended to change her religion, but she was weary of her prison and of her jailor; but none of her projects could take effect. At last she thought of an escape. I was to have assisted her in it, but that could not be compassed neither.

[a] After six weeks' stay in Paris [2] I came back to England [a]; and as I had made some improvement by this short ramble, so I did not stick to talk of it enough to weary those that fell in my way. I stayed three months longer in England. I saw the war with Holland was going on, at which Lauderdale was very glad, for he hoped it would ruin chancellor Hyde, who he believed did not understand foreign affairs. But (that he

[a] Cf. *Hist.* i. 208; Life (in *Hist.* ii), p. 677.

---

[1] Lady Anne Lindsay, converted to Romanism by Jesuits about the English Court during the close of the year 1660, at the age of sixteen, and in the absence of her mother, was a few weeks later 'stolen away secretly from her mother in a coach,' carried to France, and placed in a nunnery, where before the end of the year she took the veil, under the name of Sister Anna Maria. Her mother retained to the last a pathetic conviction of her daughter's sincerity, and thankfully recorded the testimony of a Scots minister (who had seen her?) that 'she was' (still) 'a knowing and virtuous person, and had retained the saving principles of our religion' (*Memoir of Lady Anna Mackenzie*, pp. 53-6 (quoting Baxter), 139-40).

[2] Notice that three passages on p. 207 of the printed *History* ('I was much ... principles,' 'an universal industry ... satisfaction in that matter,' and 'This established ... absolute power') are later additions.

himself might have some secret advices to give the king) he sent over to Holland for doctor Macdonal[1] (a Scotch physician then in good employment there) and promised him great matters. [Here the fragment ends abruptly with the folio, 'desunt' being written in a hand which resembles that of *f.* 2.]

[CONNECTING NOTE.

The first fragment of the Harleian MS. ending thus abruptly at this point, a very large portion of Burnet's early narrative (corresponding on a general estimate to pp. 208–310 and 333–543 of Burnet's first volume, and including the events of the years 1665–82) is unfortunately missing; with the exception only of the few fragmentary passages relating to the years 1679–81, preserved by Leslie and Elliot, as explained at length in the preface. These are here given entire. See also *infra*, Autobiography, ff. 202–7.]

THE ELLIOT-LESLIE EXTRACTS, 1679–81

[EXTRACT I : *The exclusion intrigues* (1679-81[2]).]

[a] He doth acknowledge himself to have been for the bill of exclusion, and writes, that he travelled much among noble-men in negotiating this affair. [b] And here he shews that the country party . . .[3] was broken in pieces; for nothing less would satisfy Shaftesbury than a total exclusion. Halifax would not hear of this, but was as tenacious for a limited power as the other was for exclusion; so the party was divided. [c] Burnet shews us that he endeavoured much to reconcile them, and

---

[a] Cf. *Hist.* i. 459 and 481.   [b] *Ibid.* 455–9.   [c] *Ibid.* 459, 481.

---

[1] Jan. 21 [166⅘], Rothes writing to Lauderdale says he has shown to Argyll the 'double' (duplicate or copy) of Mackdonnill's letters (*Laud. Pap.* i. 207). Q. is this the man? or it may be 'my lord MacDonald' (*Ibid.* 201).

[2] Elliot, pp. 13–4. For comments see *ibid.* pp. 45–6; and [Leslie in] *New Association*, ii. 23; *Cassandra*, ii. 22–4, where [Leslie] makes the curious assertion that 'the author of the *New Association*' [himself] has recently discovered 'the author of the *Secret History*' to have been 'so far against the bill for excluding the duke

of York that he found means of in-forming his royal highness very early of that design in agitation against him; and thereby came into his good graces, though it is at the same time 'apparent from his history 'that he drove on with the faction against him'; and [adds Leslie] 'If he has forgot . . . sir. J. B. can refresh his memory.'

[3] 'For so he frequently distinguishes between the king and his loyal sub-jects, for the one party, and the factious plotters against the king and government for the other; calling the first the court party, and the other the country party' [Elliot].

particularly that he took pains upon Halifax to make him comply with Shaftesbury's designs, but in vain. In the end, [a] he tells us the project that he fell upon, which he thought might please both parties, and this was a guardian-regent to be set over the king in case he were a Roman Catholic. This project of his, as he writes, was generally applauded [a] by the whole party ; wherewith he seems to be so well pleased that he falls in love with himself, and doth commend and admire himself for this, as if he had found heaven upon earth. [b] But the mischief on't was, these castles in the air of his were soon blown down [b] ; for when this project of his came to be proposed by the whole party to the king and parliament, the king very briskly crushed it in the head, would not hear of it, and so sent it packing out of doors [1].

*   *   *   *   *   *   *   *   *   *   *

[EXTRACT II : *Action of the clergy in* 1679.

Upon the earl of Danby's trial Burnet explains that] [c] " Many books came out likewise against the church of England. This alarmed the bishops and clergy much, so they [Leslie reads " so that they "] set up to preach against rebellion and the late times in such a strain that it was visible they meant a parallel between those and the present times [Leslie reads " these . . . present times "] ; and this produced at last that heat and rage into which the clergy has ran [c] so far that it

....

[a] Cf. *Hist.* i. 496.   [b] *Ibid.* 498.   [c] *Ibid.* 461.

---

[1] The *reverse* of this is insinuated in *Hist.* i. 496, 498. Elliot probably misunderstood the passage.

[2] Given verbatim by Elliot, pp. 10–1. Quoted previously in [Leslie's] *Cassandra*, No. ii, published 1704, pp. 26–7 ; and (down to the words ' are in the nation' only) on the title-page of *Speculum Sarisburianum*, by ' Philoclerus,' published in 1714 (by the latter of which it is ascribed to a ' MS. History representing the affairs of Church and State within Britain and Ireland in the author's

time '). For the furious indignation excited by these and similar strictures upon the clergy, see Elliot, pp. 30–8 ; *Cassandra*, ii. 27 ; and *Speculum Sarisburianum*, pp. 13, 17 (' This author . . . by his intemperate and contemptuous expressions for a long time, but more especially of late, *universo clero bellum indixerit*'). That these animadversions had some effect on Burnet may be concluded from the transformation which the passage has undergone in the printed version ; and from *Hist.* i. 3 (*bis*).

is like to end very fatally. They on their part should have shewn more temper, and more of the spirit of the gospel; whereas, for the greatest part, they are the worst natured, the fiercest, indiscreetest, and most persecuting sort of people that are in the nation. There is ᵃa sort of them do so aspire to preferment, that there is nothing so mean and indecent that they will not do to compass itᵃ; and when they have got into preferments, they take no care either of themselves or of their flocks committed to their charge, but do generally neglect their parishes. If they are rich [Leslie reads " rich enough "] they hire some pitiful curate at as low a price as they can, and turn all over on him; or, if their income will not bear out that, they perform the public offices in the slightest manner they can, but take no care of the [Leslie reads " their "] people in the way of private instruction or admonition, and so do nothing to justify the character of pastors or watchmen that feed the souls of the [Leslie reads " their "] people, or watch over [th]em; and they allow themselves many indecent liberties of going to taverns and alehouses, and of railing scurrilously against all that differ from them; and they cherish the profaneness of their people if they but come to church, and rail with them against dissenters, and are implacably set on the ruin of all that separate from them if the course of their lives were otherwise never [Leslie " ever"] so good and unblamable. In a word, many of them are a reproach to Christianity and to their profession, and are now perhaps one of the most corrupt bodies of men in the nation.'

.   .   .   .

[EXTRACT III: *On bishops voting upon capital cases*[1].

ᵇ Upon the debate on Danby's trial, Whether the bishops ought to sit in parliament to vote in trials of life and death?]

ᵃ *Hist.* i. 462.   ᵇ Cf. *ibid.* 462-3.

---

[1] Given verbatim by Elliot, pp. 11-3. [Leslie, in] *New Association*, ii (1703), 23, refers to the passage; which (from 'Their unacquaintedness ' to 'act against it' only) is also cited verbally at p. 27 of the same work.

[a] ' Thus was the matter argued on both sides, and upon this occasion doctor Stillingfleet gave an astonishing proof of his great capacity and how he can make himself master of any argument; for, after the lawyers and others versed in parliamentary records had writ of these matters, he undertook it, and shewed so much more skill and exactness in searching and judging of records than all the rest that had meddled with it had done, that he indeed put an end to the controversy in the opinion of all wise and impartial men. He was for the right of the bishops, and made it out, in my opinion, beyond contradiction from the ground of the laws of England [a].

' But to give my sense upon the matter, separated from the particular constitution of this government : I cannot but look upon the bishops' meddling in all parliamentary matters (except when the consultations of religion are on foot) as a thing very unsuitable to their profession, so that I wish they only sat in the house of lords as the judges do, who only give their opinion in matters of law when they are asked. So if bishops had no other share in those consultations, it would be better both for themselves and the church ; for they are considered as so many sure votes to the court, which must always go as the king would have them ; and being generally men of weak minds, they do very probably comply with the king's solicitations often against their own reasons. [b] Their unacquaintedness with the law, and the wrong notion they generally have of civil society [b], make them very unfit for those consultations ; and their voting as they commonly do, creates a very ill opinion of all clergymen, which fortifies atheism mightily, and gives all, that are concerned for public

[a] Cf. *Hist.* i. 463-4.   [b] Cf. Life (in *Hist.* ii), p. 673.

Comments on the sentiments expressed will be found in Elliot, pp. 42-5, who makes considerable capital out of Burnet's own Parliamentary activity in his episcopal capacity ; with special reference to his conduct in the matter of Sir John Fenwick, 1697 (consult here *Hist.* ii. 193 and notes). For the charge of inconsistency levelled against Burnet, with respect to the vexed question of clerical interference in general politics, see Hickes, *Some discourses upon Dr. Burnet*, &c., p. 4 ; Harl. MSS. 6584, f. 40 (*b*), *ante* ; *Hist.* i. 380.

liberty, an aversion to them as a set of men that will ever vote and act against it.

' And indeed, when I consider the general corruption of the clergy that has been now for many ages over all Christendom, I know not where to lay the first source and spring of it.' [1] The source and spring which he fixeth as the common cause of the corruption of the clergy is too great livings; he wishes they had a more precarious dependence upon their people, and that they were only to have their gratuities and benevolences instead of a settled living. This, says he, would make them more strict in their lives, and more diligent in the exercise of their ministerial function and office.

[EXTRACT IV: *Murder of archbishop Sharp, May* 3, 1679 [2].]

' But now they began with a man of another figure; they looked on Sharp as the man that set on all the hard things that were done against them : so some of them lay in his way [a] as he passed through a moor within two miles of St. Andrews. [b] The company that were with him had rid before to order dinner; others were sent about by him with some civil messages to some persons of quality, near whose houses he had passed; so that he was alone, without any to defend the coach, when six or seven assassinates espied the coach and stopped it. One of them fired a pistol at him, which burnt his coat and gown, but the shot did not go into his body; upon which a report was afterwards spread that he had purchased a magical secret for securing him against shot [b]. [3]And his murderers gave

[a] Cf. *Hist.* i. 470.   [b] *Ibid.* 471.

---

[1] Elliot, p. 13. It seems to be an abstracted continuation of the preceding verbatim passage.

[2] Elliot, pp. 9-10; it had been previously quoted [by Leslie] in *Cassandra*, No. ii. (1704), pp. 33-6. For vituperative comments on it, see Elliot, pp. 17-30. He suggests that Burnet may have obtained his materials from 'Mess. John Welsh' (who after Bothwell-Bridge lived principally with Shaftesbury). See too *Cassandra*, ii.

33-6, which refers to *The Spirit of Popery speaking out of the mouths of fanatical Protestants* . . . 1680 (p. 58), the Presbyterian *Narrative* of the occurrence, in which Burnet would seem to have been mentioned; and eulogizes the *True Account* (1679) of the murder, and the *Narrative* appended to the above *Spirit of Popery*.

[3] The following sentence is probably the 'line' referred to by Airy, *Hist. in loco*, note a.

out that there were very suspicious things found in a purse about him. But it was no wonder to find those that murdered his person endeavour to blacken his reputation. He begged his life[1] in a very abject manner of them, and was in great disorder: [a]they murdered him very barbarously, and repeated their strokes till it was sure he was dead, and so rid away[a]. Some of them have since given it out that they had not resolved on doing this any time before that; [b]but, seeing his coach appear alone on the moor, they took their resolution all on a sudden. And this was the fate of that unhappy man[b], who certainly needed a little more time to have fitted him for an unchangeable state[2]. But I would fain hope that he had all his punishment in that terrible conclusion of his life[3].'

. . . .

[Extract V : *Godolphin in* 1679; *general character of the clergy*[4].]

[c]'And now the governing men were Sunderland, Hyde, and Godolphin. The last of these is a very silent man; he has a great deal of wit and sense, and is esteemed a virtuous man[c], but I know him not. I have heard different characters of him; but I always believe well of laymen till I see cause to change my mind; though as to churchmen, it is quite otherwise with me, for I have seen so much amiss in that

[a] Cf. *Hist.* i. 471.   [b] *Ibid.* 470-1.   [c] *Ibid.* 478-9.

---

[1] [Leslie in] *Cassandra* denies this on the authority of the official *Narrative*, and says the archbishop died with 'Christian courage and resolution. . . . No history since St. Stephen can shew a greater example of composure of mind.'

[2] This clause was only expunged in the final revision; see Airy, *Hist.*, note c, *in loco*.

[3] This sentence probably answers to Airy's illegible line referring to Burnet himself in the Bodleian autograph of the *History*.

[4] Elliot, p. 11. The sentences from ' I always believe well' to end of extract had been previously quoted in *The New Association*, ii (1703), 23 ; and in the Preface to *Three Short Treatises now again published by Dr. George Hickes . . .* 1709, from one of which we may no doubt derive the paraphrase given by Swift, *Works*, ed. 1824, iv. 167, as a notorious saying of Burnet's. For comments see Elliot, pp. 34-41 ; the other tract mentioned *loc. cit.*

profession that I am always inclined to think ill of them till I see cause to think otherwise.'

*   *   *   *   *   *   *   *   *   *   *

[EXTRACT VI : *The prince of Orange and the exclusion bill in* 1680[1].]

Of the prince of Orange he writes : [a] That minheer Fagel, to the best of my remembrance, who was sent over from the States of Holland to the king at that time, when the bill of exclusion was in agitation, had particular instructions from the prince of Orange to deal with the leading members of the house of commons to promote the passing of that bill.

[EXTRACT VII : *Reception of his History of the Reformation[2].*]

Upon his finishing his *History of the Reformation of the Church of England* [vol. i] he informs us : [b] That he had such thanks returned in a compliment from the parliament of England [b], that never any had the like in such a case bestowed upon them.

[EXTRACT VIII : *Reception of his sermon and Dr. Sprat's before the house of commons[3].*]

[c] Upon Dr. Sprat's sermon and his, before the house of commons, he says : That his sermon had both the applause and thanks of the house. But of Dr. Sprat's sermon he gives this account : That it was indeed the worst sermon that ever

[a] Cf. *Hist.* i. 482.   [b] *Ibid.* 483.   [c] *Ibid.*

---

[1] Elliot, p. 17 ; previously quoted in *Cassandra*, ii. 40. For comments, see Elliot, p. 61, who not only speaks of Burnet as privy to this 'early plot,' this 'great secret' of the prince's, but adds the scurrilous suggestion that he was also privy to the murder plot of the 'Rye House'; and *Cassandra* (as above), whence the sinister suggestion originally emanates. Leslie lays great stress on this 'underhand attempt' of the prince 'against his father'; and maliciously insinuates,

that Burnet had perhaps 'blabbed' the secret, because, despite his great services, he was postponed to Tillotson and another at the Revolution. For the history of this episode the editor may be permitted a reference to the *Life of Halifax*, i. 235, 237, 264-5, 267, 285-6, 306-9.

[2] Elliot, p. 15 ; for his comments see *ibid.* 47-8.

[3] Elliot, p. 14 ; previously cited in *Cassandra*, ii. 24, where Sprat's name is suppressed in favour of the de-

he heard him preach [a] ; and adds this character of the doctor,
That he is a man that has little knowledge of divinity, and as
little sense of it, and [b] describes him to be a man that is much
addicted to pleasures.

[EXTRACT IX: *Dissolution of the Oxford parliament;
a declaration; and addresses* [1].]

[c] He writes of the king, at the dissolution of the Oxford
parliament : That he came to the parliament house in a very
indecent manner, being carried in a chair to the house of
lords, with the crown between his legs ; and having sent for
the house of commons, he pulled it out from thence—i. e. from
his codpiece, as the factious party made the story pass—and
put it on his head, and so dissolved the parliament.

[d] After the dissolution of the Oxford parliament, the king emits
a declaration, in which he endeavours to satisfy all his subjects
with his proceedings, and shews how insolent the parliament
had been in their doings ; and withal signifies to all his subjects that he would ever adhere to and defend the protestant
religion, and would call parliament as often as his subjects
could desire, when he found them inclined to make a right use
of them.

The archbishop of Canterbury advised in council that this
declaration or manifesto of the king's should be read by the
clergy from their pulpits upon a Sunday ; whereupon Burnet
reflects severely upon the archbishop for giving this advice,
and the clergy for reading this declaration, as a thing whereby
they became heralds to the king, which was unsuitable to their
office : and as if it had been some horrible wickedness, or at
least some disorderly practice, he would fain persuade us that
such a thing was never done before.   He says the declaration

---

[a] Cf. *Hist.* i. 483.   [b] *Ibid.*   [c] *Ibid.* 499.   [d] *Ibid.* 500.

cription 'a reverend and learned
divine of the first figure, now living,
. . . who has the reputation of as
ingenious a man as any in England.'
For comments see Elliot, pp. 46-7,
who gives the further detail, that
Charles II recompensed Dr. Sprat's
sermon, which was full of loyalty, with

a good living; 'which the king said was
as good as thanks of the house of
commons.'

[1] Elliot, pp. 15-6 ; see his comments,
pp. 49-55. It was previously quoted,
with comments, [by Leslie] in *Cassandra*, ii. 37.

had that effect, that the whole people of England addressed the king from all places, signifying their resolution to stand by the king and the hereditary succession in the true line.

[a] These addresses he calls fulsome, and again flies in the face of the clergy, [b] as being the contrivers or penmen of these addresses ; and takes occasion often to renew his repeated accusations against the clergy [b], saying they were men of loose lives, going to taverns, and their business there was [c] to drink the duke's health, and confusion to his enemies.

[EXTRACT X : *Burnet's retirement from politics in* 1681 [1].]

[d] He writes of himself that, after the dissolution of the Oxford parliament, he did betake himself to a more strict course of life [d] than he had formerly accustomed himself to ; he had formerly been too much elevated and carried away by the applause of men, and had been given to a looseness in his life ; and though he does not particularly mention what his crime was, yet in general terms he does acknowledge himself to have been an ill man, and guilty of such things as he should for the time to come remember with sorrow of heart, as he expressly words it. [e] He writes that now he gave himself to fasting and prayer [e], and he doubts not but the fruits of it will ever remain with him. It has made him more humble, more watchful, more charitable to the failings of others, and many such like words to this purpose.

[EXTRACT XI: *He declines preferment* [2].]

[f] He says that he might several times have been preferred

---

[a] Cf. *Hist.* i. 500–1, 509.   [b] Cf. *ibid.* 501, 509.   [c] Cf. *ibid.* 509.   [d] Cf. *ibid.* 500.   [e] *Ibid.*   [f] *Ibid.* 507.

[1] Elliot, pp. 16–7 ; previously cited, with comments, [by Leslie] in the *New Association*, ii. 24 ; *Cassandra*, ii. 27. Elliot's own remarks (pp. 55–60) are peculiarly virulent, and the disgraceful manner in which he distorts a general confession of penitence into an admission of concealed infamy, of 'some extraordinary lewdness or wickedness in his private conversation,' with the disgusting insinuation on p. 55, seem specially discreditable in a man of Elliot's profession. It must however be admitted that Elliot is not the only offender in this respect.

[2] Elliot, p. 15 ; previously quoted [by Leslie] in *Cassandra*, ii. p. 28. The comments of Elliot are on pp. 48–9 of his tract ; those of *Cassandra (in loco)* are rather pertinent. He asks, for instance, why the Temple should lie less heavy on Burnet's conscience than any other cure ; have lawyers no souls ?

to considerable [1] livings [a], and in particular that the dean and chapter of St. Paul's offered him a living within the City of £500 per ann., but he would not embrace it, because he could not in conscience exoner himself of the vast charge which did belong to it [2]. [b] But the Temple, in appearance, being to fall vacant at that time, he was rather desirous of that [b]; and so much the rather, because he was averse to mingle himself with the church and clergy.

[EXTRACT XII : *Burnet reflects on the Maitlands* [3].]

[c] He reflects severely upon the duke of Lauderdale, and scribbles much of his insolencies [d] and the brutalities of Hatton; so he is pleased to express the actions of that lord, who was brother-germane to duke Lauderdale.

CONNECTING NOTE.

[The next fragment of the original version preserved in the Harleian MS. relates to the ' Rye House' conspiracy, and was composed (to judge by internal evidence) between June 20, 1684, when Sir Thomas Armstrong was executed (see *infra*, f. 97 (*a*)), and Dec. 23 in the same year, when Baillie (Jerviswood) suffered (see f. 95 (*b*)). It occupies ff. 93–106 of the MS. and represents ' No. 3 ' in Dr. Gifford's arrangement. Though in a different hand from the first fragment, it evidently formed part of the same transcript; the paper employed bears a close resemblance to that in use for the former specimen; and both have been corrected by Dr. Burnet himself. On f. 92 we find a few notes by Dr. Gifford, relative to the principal divergences between the MS. and the printed version; and at the bottom of the first and last sheets, in a writing which resembles that of f. 2, 'Desunt' (which has been erroneously entered, and then obliterated at several other points) is inscribed. On f. 93 is pasted a minute scrap of paper, apparently employed as a marker; it bears a few words in the same hand, of which ' Russel's tryal ' are alone decipherable. As the fragment begins abruptly, and as the opening sentence corresponds with nothing in the printed *History*, an introductory heading is conjecturally supplied, on the strength of James Ferguson's *Ferguson the Plotter*, pp. 422–37; Sprat's *Rye House Plot*, Appendix, p. 42.]

[a] Cf. *Hist.* i. 507.   [b] *Ibid.*   [c] *Ibid.* 472.   [d] *Ibid.* 523.

---

[1] See Life (in *Hist.* ii), p. 691 ; *Life of Halifax*, i. 230, note 4.

[2] Leslie's paraphrase in *Cassandra* runs, ' taken upon him so great a cure of souls.'

[3] Elliot, p. 17. His remarks, pp. 62–6, are sufficiently vituperative and revive all the old scandals of Burnet's early intimacy with Lauderdale. Hatton he is said to have hated as being ' a true friend to the episcopal church of Scotland.' The context of Burnet's disparaging remarks is of course merely conjectural ; he gives a very unfavourable view of Hatton, *Hist.* i. 299.

HARL. MSS. 6584; SECOND FRAGMENT:
THE 'RYE HOUSE PLOT'[1]

[The duke of Monmouth and the king's murder?]

[*f.* 93 (*a*)] Some had offered to him to do it, but he seemed to abhor it, as Essex did extremely. [a] West and Rumsey did speak often of it, as both Walcot and Holloway have confessed at their deaths; [b] some indeed talked of killing the king, and not the duke, and spoke to Hone to engage him in it [b], but it is hard to know what to make of this unless they were disguised papists. [c] Others, as is said, and with more probability, were for killing the duke, and it is not unlike that Rumbold might have proposed his house, as a fit place for executing so black a design, but I cannot think that it was ever laid [c], much less that it was so near as has been given out.

Keeling discovers all.

Cf. *from beginning of Hist.* i. 544 *to* ' contradict one another.'

For ' who was sinking . . . better trade ' *read* ' who was broken in his fortune; he was become desperate and run in with great fury into all the violent things that could be proposed to him.'

. *For* ' often to try . . . brothers ' *read* ' he was engaged in these designs of inflaming the city, but he found the turning a witness was like to be a safer and more profitable operation.'

For ' Legge made . . . witnesses ' *read* ' At first there was no great account had of him and his story; he had no other witnesses to make it out, and none appearing to be engaged in it but a mean sort of persons, it was not much considered; yet he was encouraged, and bid to lay the matter so as to be sure of another witness.'

For ' So Goodenough . . . would do ' *read* ' and then Goodenough, not being distrustful of him, talked freely to him . . . of seizing the Tower and many other extravagant wicked things, which struck a horror in this other Keeling, that had never heard such discourse in his whole life.'

[*f.* 93 (*b*)] *Om.* (*at this point*) ' but stopped at Whitehall '; *and for* ' drew him on and ' *read* ' engaged him, so that he could not easily get away from him; he stopped the hackney coach in which they went at Whitehall gate, and pretending business with one there.'

[a] Cf. *Hist.* i. 558-9, 576.   [b] *Ibid.* 559.   [c] *Ibid.* 543.

[1] It has been thought advisable in this section to record even slight variations of expression, where these appear at all significant; the general tenor of the language in the earlier version being decidedly more compatible than the modified wording of the final rendering with a distinct, if restricted, belief in the existence of an important conspiracy; though not in the justice of all the convictions, or in the complete veracity of the witnesses.

For 'His brother . . . heard' *read* 'So the secretary took his deposition. Upon this the secretary ought either to have kept up the witnesses, or have sent to seize on Goodenough and the others against whom Keeling swore treason. But.'

Before 'phlegmatic' *read* 'cold and'; *and for* 'such a work' *read* 'such quick work as the discovery of a conspiracy.'

For 'and all . . . way' *read* 'and he both withdrew himself, and some others went from their houses, upon advices given as is most likely by him.'

For 'and apprehending . . . contradict one another,' *read only* 'and so had the conveniency of laying their story; and they both went away.'

[*Discourse on the subject.*]

[a] Within three days the plot broke out, and was the whole discourse of the town : there were many examinations taken [a]; but people had become so much accustomed to discourses of sham plots and false witnesses, that there was no great regard had to it. [b] Some came to me and assured me there was a reality in it. [*f.* 94 (*a*)] Col. Fitzpatrick [1] and Mr. Brisbane [2] told me the evidence was clear and undeniable. Among others, Howard came to see me the next day, and talked of it so much in his spiteful way of raillery that he possessed me really with a belief that he knew nothing of it. He said now that the court had got sheriffs of London and, by consequence, juries in their hands, we would not be long without false witnesses ; and he believed many honest men would be taken off. He wished himself beyond seas, and spake terribly of the duke as one that would not be only worse than queen Mary, but worse than Nero [b]. But I was so full of the impressions that were given me of the truth of the plot, that I said I should be very sorry if there had been anything of that sort among any of them ; for I believed it would tend more to the bringing in of popery among us than all things else whatsoever. [c] So he lifted up his hands and eyes to heaven, and vowed to me that he knew of no plot, and that he believed nothing of it. Two days after that a proclamation came out for the discovery of the conspirators who had left their houses, and Rumsey and

[a] Cf. *Hist.* i. 546.   [b] Cf. *ibid. infra.*   [c] *Ibid.*

[1] *Hist.* i. 266; Dalrymple, ed. 1790, part i. bk. v, App. p. 66; *Portland MSS.* (H. M. C.), iii. 553 sq.; *Life of Halifax*, ii. 209.

[2] See *Life of Halifax*, i. 178; *Hist.*, ed. Airy, ii. 153, note.

West were named among them ; but that very night West rendered himself, and Rumsey came in next day. ªAnd then they told a long story of an insurrection that Shaftesbury had been managing, and that had been carried on so far after he went out of England that they came to debate whether it should begin on the seventeenth day of November, the day of queen Elizabeth's coming to the crown, ᵇor the Sunday thereafter. ᶜRumsey also told of that meeting at Shepherd's, ᵈand both of them related a long story of the design of assassinating the king and duke at Rye. ᵉThey had likewise got a hint of the meetings of the six persons formerly named, and of a treaty in which they were engaged with the Scotsᵉ. It is not yet understood how they came to know anything of this, whether it was [*f.* 94 (*b*)] by the Scottish men that Ferguson knew it, and that he trusted it to them ; or whether Monmouth had trusted it to Armstrong, and he had trusted it to Rumsey and Ferguson ; ᶠbut all that they knew of this was only from second-hand ᶠand upon report, so that the discourse at Shepherd's was all that affected any of the lords. ᵍThis gave the greatest advantage to the duke and his party that was possible, for now they twisted the design of murdering the king with the other consultations that were among the lords, and made it all appear as one complicated thing, and so the matter went over England and over all Europe.

[*Various arrests.*]

Cf. *Hist.* i. 547 (*from* 'When the council found' *to* p. 548, 'his life was a burden to him ').

After 'lord Russell' *add* 'and Grey.'

For 'They would not . . . leave' *read* 'The king's tenderness for Monmouth was the cause of this, for they would not seize on him till they knew the king's mind.'

After ' go out' *read* 'but he was ordered not to go into the house.'

For 'He heard that Rumsey . . . his own mind' *read* 'but though there was a great difference among his friends concerning his stay or his going, yet he was positive himself in his resolution of staying. He knew he had never trusted Rumsey with any secrets ; he thought that discourse at Shepherd's was

---

ª Cf. *Hist.* i. 544, 536–7.   ᵇ *Ibid.* 545.   ᶜ *Ibid.* 547.   ᵈ *Ib.d.* 54;.
ᵉ *Ibid.* 547.   ᶠ *Ibid.*   ᵍ Cf. *Hist.* i, end of p. 559 and beginning of p. 560.

so honest and well-meant, that it could be no more at worst than a conceal-ment. So.'

For 'till the king was come : and then' *read* 'and as he was at dinner.'

[*f.* 95 (*a*)] *After* 'examined' *add* 'only.'

Om. from 'and said to the last' *to* 'prisoner to the Tower.'

For 'but his examination . . . maxim' *read only* 'who in his rough way refused to answer the questions that the lord keeper put to him.'

For 'There was at that time . . . against law' *read* 'By what has appeared since it seems his imprisonment was illegal, for unless the lord Howard had at that time secretly made oath against him nobody else had done it except from second-hand. Now though a man may be examined and keeped in a messenger's hands upon such a remote evidence, yet no man can be imprisoned according to the law but upon a positive evidence against him.'

For 'while the town . . . fermentation' *read* 'often and kept much out of the way.'

For 'examined them' *read* 'took a subtle method in examining them.'

After 'his person' *add* 'in which he believed they had no share.'

Om. 'or others in England.'

After 'Scotland' *add* 'and concerning their commerce with Argyll.'

[*f.* 95 (*b*)] *After* 'answers' *add* 'against himself or others.'

For 'and he seemed . . . against him' *read* 'and he shewed too rough a neglect of all that could be done to himself, and acted the part of a philosopher rather than of a prudent man.'

Before 'Baillie was loaded' *insert* 'Upon this occasion the king told him he would order garters for his legs, which was carried about as if the king had threatened him with the boots ; but that was false ; yet upon it.'

After 'burden to him' *add* 'But the ill usage he met with, though it brought diseases upon him, of which he is now dying in Scotland, yet could draw nothing from him.'

[*Fate of others implicated.*]

[a] Sir.John Cochrane had spoken too liberally of the duke's government in Scotland, in the hearing of some who carried it to court; so the king bid the secretary for Scotland write to him to come to court, and it was intended to have given him a reprimand, and to have ordered him to go presently to Scotland. But he, knowing that this was coming to him, left his lodging [a], and so the letter did not find him. I, in the sim-plicity of my heart, sent and advised him to go to court, and to ask pardon if he had spoken anything indecently ; for I thought the king's ordering him to be thus writ for looked as if he had been in no danger ; but I did not know that he had been engaged in more dangerous intrigues. He hid himself for some time in London, [b] and got beyond sea [b] before the ports

[a] Cf. *Hist.* i. 548.   [b] *Ibid.* 549.

were stopped upon the breaking out of the plot, and so he escaped a long imprisonment and the boots perhaps by this time. Munro[1] had been sick all the while, so he had no meetings with any English men ; only he was once with Shepherd, which has brought him into a great deal of trouble. Shepherd (being named by Rumsey) was seized on, but some of his friends undertook he should tell all he knew, and so he was let go again in a [*f.* 96 (*a*)] few days.

[a] Major Wildman was also seized on. He is a great commonwealth's man, and as both Sidney and he had appeared very resolutely against Cromwell when he began to set up for himself, so he was kept in prison many years after the king's restoration. He is very learned both in law and physic[a], and has a great quickness of apprehension, but has a heat in his temper, and though it is a more governable thing than Sidney's was yet [it] is very apt to break out. [b] In one of his cellars there was two small guns found that had belonged to the earl of Northumberland and were left by him in York house when he removed out of it ; so the duke of Buckingham, that was the owner of that house, kept them and put them in Wildman's hand, who had laid them on wooden carriages to save them from spoiling on the ground ; but as they were too small for service, so the carriages, not being fortified with iron, were only fit to bear them but not to draw them. Yet it was said, here was cannon found on new carriages ; and so they were let stand some days in the court of Whitehall to affect the unthinking multitudes that ran thither to see them ; and while others laughed at this, the rabble looked on it as an undeniable evidence of the plot.

[c] As soon as the council rose after Russell had been sent to the Tower the king went to the duchess of Monmouth[c], and was an hour with her ; and immediately after that the duke of Monmouth left his house, so those who came to seize on him looked for him in vain ; but all people believed this was

[a] Cf. *Hist.* i. 546.   [b] *Ibid.*   [c] *Ibid.* 549.

---

[1] Munro is the 'Commissary Monro' of Sprat's *Rye House Plot*, p. 73 (List of the Scotch Plotters), and Appendix, p. 125, Carstares' confession.

done by the king's direction, for Rumsey had accused him the day before, so it had been easy to have taken him had not the king resolved to preserve him. [a] Yet Monmouth himself told Mr. Cutts a strange passage relating to his escape, which Cutts told me. The king said to the duchess of Monmouth that, though some were to come and search her house, he should give them a strict order not to search her apartment, and so encouraged her to conceal him in her chamber ; but Monmouth said he knew him too well to [*f.* 96 (*b*)] trust him, so he went out of the house : and it seems he judged right, for when those came who were ordered to search for him, the first place they searched for him was the duchess' own rooms [a]. So that he had certainly been taken had he trusted to what the king promised to his wife ; and indeed this is one of the most unaccountable passages of the king's life, since, notwithstanding all the love he bore Monmouth, yet he laid a snare for catching him [1]. [b] This gave Monmouth the justest grounds possible of suspecting him ever afterwards in everything that he either did or said ; since, if this is true, it was one of the foulest things that could be. An order was sent to bring up the lord Grey, which found him on the way coming up to town ; he might have gone away easily if he had intended it ; yet he came along with the messenger, and carried himself with great presence of mind before the council, but he was sent to the Tower. It was too late to get in when he was sent away, so the messenger was to keep him all night and to deliver him next morning to the lieutenant of the Tower. In the night he sent for some of his friends, and furnished the messenger so liberally with wine that he was dead drunk, so that he could have got out of his hands for four hours together in which he lay fast asleep, but he would not do it. Next morning by six o'clock the messenger and he went alone in

[a] Cf. *Hist.* i. 549.   [b] *Ibid.*

---

[1] In all probability the king, having arranged with the duchess that the duke should abscond, promised her that her rooms should not be disturbed during the formal search which was inevitable ; by mistake his orders may have been ignored ; and the duke misinterpreted the incident.

a hackney coach to the Tower. The messenger fell again asleep ; so when they came to the Tower, Grey went out of the coach, leaving the other asleep in it, and knocked at the gate and bid the sentinel within call the lieutenant to come and receive a prisoner ; but then he bethought himself of his danger. There was already one witness against him, and another would do the business, so he stept down to the water-stairs and called a boat. A soldier walking a little way off spied it and followed him, but he called him to him and took him into his service ; and so they went away together, and when the Tower gate was opened they found none but the messenger drunk [1] and asleep [a]. Armstrong went out of the way, and when all places came to be [*f.* 97 (*a*)] strictly searched he was lodged some days in Southampton house [2], and was then so oppressed with fear that those who saw him at that time did not think that he could have met death with so much courage as he has done since. Walcot was shifting about, and wrote a letter to secretary Jenkins, in which he promised a great discovery if he might have his pardon [3], but he was taken some days after that ; he suspected that Shepherd had betrayed him, but I have been told that in that particular he was in the wrong to him. Mr. Booth, now lord Delamere, was also brought up and accused of a design to raise Cheshire, and one had sworn that he was to be a captain ; but that was so far below his quality that it made the other story look ridiculous. The lord Brandon, son to the earl of Maccles-field, was clapt up upon the same suggestions. Major Bremen [4], of Chichester, that was an officer in the civil wars and retained his inclinations to a commonwealth, and had been a parliament man of late, was also put in the Tower.   [b] Warrants were sent

[a] Cf. *Hist.* i. 549.   [b] *Ibid.*

[1] The reader cannot fail to remark how considerably Burnet's omissions in the printed version have impaired the force and coherence of this dramatic episode. See Swift's note, *Hist. in loco.*

[2] Lord Russell's town house, part of his wife's dower as coheiress of the Southampton estate.

[3] See Sprat's *Rye House Plot*, Appendix, pp. 86-7.

[4] See *ibid.* p. 73, and Appendix, p. 68. He was acquitted.

out for some others who went out of the way[a]. Charlton[1], with the wooden leg (who is a great enemy to the court and was devoted to Shaftesbury, and is a hot, indiscreet talker), after he had kept out of the way for some weeks, delivered himself; it was given out that he had confessed all and made great discoveries, but on the contrary he denied everything.

There were at that time some letters of Argyle taken in the post-house, but nothing could be made of them. The witnesses were Keeling, Rumsey, West, and one Lee that pretended he was also engaged by Goodenough in the design; he chiefly accused one Rouse that had belonged to sir Thomas Player, chamberlain of London.

[b] In the examinations of those that were seized on, and of the witnesses, the king valued himself much upon the method he took; for as the witnesses were kept from coming at one another, so the king had led them into no accusations by previous [*f.* 97 (*b*)] questions, but bid them tell on their story; and also he told them he would not have a growing evidence (as he said Oates' had been), so he bid them say at once all that they had to say, for he would hear no new stories. He only asked if Oates was in their business, but they said they all looked on him as such a rogue that they would not trust him. The king also said that he found Howard was not trusted with it on the same account[b]; and he said the same of Mr. Montagu, now lord Montagu by his father's death. [c] But there are many particulars (besides those set down in the trials) in West's Narrative, which has never yet been printed, and it is certain with all fair readers it will rather destroy the belief of the plot than establish it[c].

As soon as Russell was put in the Tower I went to his lady and offered my service to her; for as I loved her lord much, so I was particularly obliged by him[2]. Before this time I

---

[a] Cf. *Hist.* i. 549.   [b] *Ibid.*   [c] *Ibid.* 549-50.

[1] Mr. Charleton of Totteridge, a cousin of Lord Shaftesbury (*Ferguson the Plotter*, pp. 422-3). Taken in disguise but acquitted (Sprat, p. 73). His wooden leg is mentioned, *ibid.* Appendix, p. 49. See also *ibid.* Appendix, pp. 72, 74, 85, 133.

[2] *Life of Halifax*, i. 230, note 4.

knew his lady so well as the general conversation at table amounted to, but now I came to understand her better ; and indeed she has acted so noble a part in this matter, and has earned so great a character, that I will stop to give a particular account of her [1].

The lady Russell's character.

She is a mixture between English and French, for her mother was Mr. de Rouvigny's sister [2], and the earl of Southampton was her father. In her the vivacity of the French temper and the solidity of the English have produced a very rare mixture, for as she has a quickness of thought that makes her see very soon through things, so she is corrected with a true judgement. Her thoughts furnish so fast for her in discourse that she is sometimes as it were choked with them, and can scarce fetch them all out ; but her style in writing is extraordinary, and if she had all the little rules of grammar as well as her thoughts are great and beautifully expressed, her writing would be one of the perfectest things I know [3]. The whole course of her life has been very exemplary ; she has been always of the church of England, but has much charity for the dissenters, [*f.* 98 (*a*)] and has her father's notions both of that matter and of the business of civil government. She has naturally a great edge upon her temper [4], but better principles have softened that much ; yet though the fire of her passions is much extinguished, the heat and tenderness of them is still such that, as it has made her one of the best wives I ever knew, so it has sunk her into an extreme sorrow upon her lord's death ; which yet she governs so, that though it must appear much to her friends, she sets it off with no affectation to

---

[1] This charming portrait was no doubt eventually omitted out of deference to the feelings of Lady Russell, who survived Burnet, dying in Sept. 1723, at the age of eighty-six ; having remained Lord Russell's widow for a period of forty years. For her correspondence with Burnet, see the first collection of her letters.

[2] *Strafford Correspondence*, i. 337.

[3] Cf. *Letters*, seventh ed. (1809), p. 17 (Burnet to Lady Russell, Feb. 2, 168¾). Her letters in that collection have been slightly revised, as regards grammar and punctuation ; those subsequently published by Miss Berry answer to Burnet's description.

[4] ' Some account . . . of Rachel . . . Lady Russell ' (prefixed to a collection of her letters by Miss Berry), ed. 1819, p. 148.

others, and indeed I have scarce seen one freer of all the exterior parts of pride than she is. So that I account her among the perfectest pieces of her sex.

[*Lord Russell in prison; Howard turns king's evidence; arrest and suicide of Essex.*]

Cf. *Hist.* i. 550 (*to* p. 553, ' *aspera arteria* must have been cut ').

After ' another world ' *add* ' and spoke of it with so much composure that all who saw him were struck with it.'

For ' and said . . . objected to him ' *read* ' and in general terms.'

After ' nothing from him ' *add* ' till he were brought to his trial.'

After ' well assured ' *add* ' that though this is a common artifice to draw out confessions, yet he thought some Scottish men were engaged to come and witness against him. So.'

For ' but this appeared . . . was gone ' *read* ' I met with Munro, who had been taken up but was let go (though he has been taken up again upon Shepherd's evidence) ; I asked him only with relation to my cousin Baillie ; and he told me sir John Cochrane was out of England ; he also assured me [*f.* 98 (*b*)] that it would be found there had been no treasonable consultations among them.'

Om. ' and Baillie . . . admitted to him.'

For ' prison ' *read* ' Gatehouse, where my cousin was kept.'

For ' I also . . . done by ' *read* ' In this some thought I was too bold, but the doing to others what I would have others do to me was my rule. I sent him some books to entertain him ; but when he was threatened with a trial he sent me word to come and stand by him in it ; I thought that was not decent for one of my profession ; so I excused it.'

Om. ' From what I found . . . friends ' ; *and read instead* ' All this while it was given out that there was a witness that would appear against Russell that was beyond exception, which gave occasion for many suspicions.'

After ' knew of none ' *add* ' He did it solemnly at the earl of Bedford's to the earl of Anglesey ; he did it also to the earl of Clare, the lord Paget, and to two brothers of the earl of Berkshire [1].'

After ' as with any man ' *add* ' so that Russell believed he was possibly engaged in the design of killing the king, and to save himself he had discovered all he knew of others ; which he made up, with a good many additions of his own.'

After ' that might happen [2] to him ' *insert* ' It has been since thought that he was then secretly at court giving information, but I do not believe that, for.'

After ' spoke of him ' *add* ' as Arran told me.'

[*f.* 99 (*a*)] *After* ' the court ' *add* ' otherwise he would not have blasted his credit so much as he did.'

Om. ' as he said,' *and after* ' all he knew ' *insert* ' I incline always to judge as fairly as I can, so the true account of this matter as I believe was this.'

For ' West and Rumsey . . . some things ' *read* ' West in his evidence had spoken of all persons except the lower sort of people very sparingly, and thought that the story of the Rye plot would have served their turn at court.

---

[1] *Vide* trials of Russell and Sydney. [2] Airy reads ' come.'

But the court looked for greater game ; and a contradiction was found between him and Rumsey.'

For 'and perhaps more than he knew . . . very credible' *read* 'and amongst others he accused Howard ; for in his written Narrative he plainly says.'

For 'As if it had been . . . a service' *read* 'So this agrees with Russell's conjecture.'

After 'design' *insert* '(or rather his folly).'

After 'the city' *add* 'and of the misunderstanding between him and Monmouth and his own being employed to take it up.'

For 'but he knew of nobody . . . more home was, that' *read* 'which was a ridiculously made story, for nothing can be so near that it comes under debate on what day it is to be executed, till great numbers are engaged, and that there are great preparations made both of horses, arms, and ammunition, [*f.* 99 (*b*)] and that officers are named ; and if any such thing had been, it is not to be imagined but many more witnesses would have come in.'

After 'Aaron Smith' *insert* 'a hot and factious solicitor[1].'

Om. 'and more of that matter . . . saw him very little.'

For 'when examined' *read* 'answered the king very decently, but.'

For 'did not imagine . . . would not stir' *read* 'to whom he had communicated nothing of the whole affair, believed there was nothing in it. He both eat, and slept, and entertained himself in his ordinary manner ; and when a neighbour of his advised him to go out of the way, he refused to do it.'

For 'His tenderness . . . care of himself' *read* 'The reason of this tenderness both in him and Mr. Hampden (after they knew that the court had got hints of their meddling with the Scots) was their care to preserve Russell, for whose trial the day was now set ; for they thought that if they had gone out of the way, it would have been made use of to possess the jury against him ; and I believe if his trial had been over, they would have withdrawn themselves. But it seems Essex had ill spies in London ; for he might have had the news of Howard's being taken, and his confessing all he knew, many hours before the party came to take him.'

[*f.* 100 (*a*)] *For* 'he was in much confusion' *read* 'he expressed no presence of mind ; yet the natural coldness of his temper made that to be the less regarded.'

After 'the Tower' *add* 'next morning.'

After 'with more violence' *add* 'He had some notions [cf. *Hist.* i. 570] of the lawfulness of a man's delivering himself a little sooner when he saw death was inevitable ; he spake of this once to me, but it was in case a man was to die a cruel lingering death ; and perhaps the remembrance of his wife's great-grandfather, who, to preserve his family, shot himself dead in the Tower in queen Elizabeth's time, might have come fatally into his thoughts.'

For 'He sent by a servant . . . sent back the servant' *read only* 'His lady understood he was much cast down, and that the greatest part of his trouble was for the ruin that would come on her and on her children ; so she writ twice to him.'

---

[1] After the Revolution he was solicitor to the Treasury from April 9, 1689, to July, 1696, when he was dismissed on a charge of peculation. He acted as public prosecutor, and seems to have deserved Mr. Seccombe's epithet of 'disreputable' (*Dict. Nat. Biog.* liii. 1).

For 'and desired him . . . come to him' *read* 'and to get through his present trouble, of which she gave him good hopes ; his servants were suffered to be about him.'

After 'day' or two' *add* 'for which she was constantly soliciting at court. He sent a message to Bedford, to assure him that he was in no less concern about his son than he himself could be, and I believe that went much to his heart ; for he had imposed Howard upon Russell much against his mind.' (Cf. Burnet's Diary in Russell's *Russell,* 3rd ed., ii. 263.)

After 'message' *add* 'having obtained leave from the king.'

After 'council' *add* 'concerning Walcot, that lived in Ireland when he was there.'

[*f.* 100 (*b*)] *After* 'told me' *add* 'and had no apprehension of that which followed next morning, which was the day of Russell's trial.'

Om. 'His lady . . . other things.'

Om. 'very nicely . . . amusement.'

After 'as well' *add* 'and went into the closet within his chamber, and there cut his throat.'

For 'as was given out . . . ordnance' *read* 'upon another occasion.'

For 'said he looked . . . dead' *read* 'came to look to him and was struck when he saw the blood.'

For 'he was found dead' *read* 'he called out ; upon which many came to look on so astonishing an object.'

Om. 'I shall afterwards . . . himself.'

After 'must have been cut' *add* 'and that part of his thumb with which he held the razor was also cut, which shewed clearly he had done it himself ; his sending so oft for the penknife, the great oppression of his spirits, and some other more certain indications, which are not yet publicly known, made it but too evident that it was his own act.'

Om. 'But to go on . . . world.'

[*The rumour that Essex had been murdered.*]

His lady was terribly struck with this, as may be easily imagined ; it put her into such rages of sorrow at first, and has since so sunk into her mind, that it will press her down as long as she lives. The king sent back all his cabinets and papers ; and whereas by this fact all his personal estate was forfeited (which was very considerable), the king ordered a grant to be made of it to his lady ; but she refused to take anything but what her lord had given her by his will, which was not the tenth [*f.* 101 (*a*)] part of the whole. So she obtained a grant in the same terms in which he had made his will.

But while she lay under this burden another storm rose against her ; some stories came to be set about that her lord's throat was cut by others. [a] A boy and a girl who had been that morning in the Tower to see the king came down and reported to the families to which they belonged that they had heard cries at Essex's lodgings, and that they saw a bloody razor cast out at the window, and that a woman came out from the house to take it up. The boy was son to a waiter at the custom house, and as he was the first person that gave the rise to all the discourse, so he has since that time gone often backward and forward in his story ; he is about ten or twelve years old. What his qualities are I do not know, only I have been told that he is a notorious liar. When the matter was brought to a trial, he denied it in full court ; but the girl, which is also about his age, affirms it still. They differed in some circumstances but agreed in the main parts of the story, and their age made many inclined to believe that what they said must have some truth in it [a] ; for though a man may trust himself to another man and hire him to swear falsehoods, yet none will employ or trust a child. I indeed think the children made the story themselves ; but they having once made it, the thing took some wind, and was presently set about and taken up by the whole party. Some weeks passed before the countess of Essex was let know anything concerning it. At last I writ of it to her, and [b] she ordered presently a strict enquiry to be made into every particular, and sent me all the account she could gather together ; which was so slight that I was positively of opinion that there was nothing in it to justify her engaging into any prosecution of it [b]. And indeed the certainty she had was such, that no person that made conscience of what they did could pursue a matter of which she knew the [*f.* 101 (*b*)] falsehood but too evidently, so she was advised to sit still and be quiet. This raised a great clamour against her from the party, who thought her too remiss in prosecuting her husband's blood ; and it was said the king's kindness in the grant of the personal estate had taken her off. But they knew her little who said this of her, for [c] if she had seen anything on which she could have fastened a legal prose-

---

[a] Cf. *Hist.* i. 569.   [b] *Ibid.*   [c] *Ibid.*

cution, she would have ventured [a] not only the personal estate
but her life, rather than have failed in so essential a point of
her duty. But as she preferred the following her conscience
before the humouring a party, so she resolved to bear all their
censures rather than own those secret grounds that determined
her belief of her lord's sad fate (since that could not be done
[b] without bringing a prejudice upon some other persons [b]); so
she resolved to bear all that could be said of her, and commits
herself to God, who knows how unjustly she was censured,
and she has endured it all with a patience and silence that
cannot be enough commended, especially considering her
temper, that is perhaps too tender in such points ; and indeed
the censure is so foul that any person whatsoever would be
very uneasy under it.

[c] There was one Braddon, whom I have known for some
time, that heard of the discourses of these children, and he
(either being set on by others or from an enthusiastical heat
in his own temper, to which I am more inclined to impute it)
went in very warmly and officiously to enquire into this matter [c].
He came to me about it, and shewed me the examinations he
had taken of those who had heard the children report their
story, which they had done several days before he meddled in
it or so much as knew of it. I read them and wondered much
at it ; I wished him not to meddle in it, for I was persuaded
there was no truth in it ; and when I found that he was resolved
to go [*f.* 102 (*a*)] on, of which he spake very enthusiastically to
me, [d] I desired he would come at me no more [d]. But he had
heard some reports of discourses that had been made in the
country concerning Essex's death before it was possible for
them that reported it to know it from London, upon which
he inferred that it had been laid some time before ; and so he
went to hunt after these stories, and carried a letter from one
Speke, recommending him to sir Robert Atkins, a great
lawyer that had been a judge and was turned out, since
which time he has set up in a high opposition to the court.
He is a very learned man, but he is very hot and indiscreet.

[a] Cf. *Hist.* i. 569.   [b] *Ibid.* 570 ('suppressed passage').   [c] *Ibid.* 570.   [d] *Ibid.*

While Braddon was in pursuit after these stories, and before he had delivered his letter, [a] he was taken up [a] by order from the council; and both he and Speke have been prosecuted [1] for the endeavouring to spread false news, and to practise with witnesses; and to end all this matter at once, they have been both tried.   There was nothing against Speke but his letter, which imports only the spreading the news; but the matter was carried higher against Braddon. [b] He brought the boy and the girl into the court, who both confessed what they had reported; only the boy said he had lied, and the girl stood still to it.   Braddon proved that he knew not of it for several days after they had told it, and that when he came to enquire into it he charged the boy as well as the girl not to lie, and cited passages of scripture to shew God's judgements against liars; and then, when they had repeated their stories to him, he pressed the boy to sign a written relation of it [b].   It was on this last point that hold was laid against him, as if he had suborned the boy; though he instructed him in no part of that which he was to say, but only pressed him to set his hand to that which he had reported by word of mouth, which though it is against the civil law, yet it is an ordinary thing in England; for witnesses are got to make affidavits of the particulars that they are afterwards to swear in judgement when there is occasion for it. [c] Yet this officiousness of his was [*f.* 102 (*b*)] called a subornation, and so he was judged and fined in 2,000 lib.[c], and Speke in one, for which they both lie prisoners [2].   But I now return to trials of another nature.

[*Trials of the Rye House plotters.*]

At the sessions in the Old Bailey, [d] Walcot was first tried. Rumsey and West swore full against him, and his letter to the secretary was likewise very clear [d].   He made a very slight defence to prove he was ill of the gout at those times in which

---

[a] Cf. *Hist.* i. 570.   [b] *Ibid.*   [c] *Ibid.*   [d] *Ibid.* 559.

[1] Hilary Term, 1683–4.
[2] For these events see the report of the trials (*State Trials*, ed. Cobbett, ix; see also *Dict. Nat. Biog.* art. Speke). Sentence had been given in Feb. 168$\frac{3}{4}$.

Speke was afterwards notorious as the author of the 'forged' Third Declaration published after the landing of the Prince of Orange.

they said he met with them, [a] so he was cast. Hone was tried
next morning, and was cast upon the same evidence, Lee
coming also in against him. Rouse was tried next; Lee and
Keeling swore against him [a]. Lee also swore against one captain Blage [1] that he was in a design of seizing on the Tower;
but said he had only talked of the weakness of the Tower,
and how easy a thing it might be to seize on it. There was
but one witness against him, so he was acquitted; [b] but the
other was cast, and a week after they all suffered together.
Walcot positively denied that he had been in any design of
cutting off the king; and whereas the witnesses had sworn
that he had declined to kill the king or the duke but had
undertaken to fight the guards, he positively denied that,
and said he looked on that as the same thing with the other.
He said, indeed, that West had often said to him that he
thought the surest way was the lopping, but that he had
always said he would not meddle in that, it was so infamous
a thing, and that he was confident the duke of Monmouth
would revenge his father's blood [b]; so that, as he confessed
he knew of West's wicked designs, it is plain he rather disapproved of the assassinating of the king as being a mean
and a dangerous thing than that he any way abhorred it;
and it seems he would not have been ill-pleased if others had
done it, so he had not been engaged in it. Now when a man
confesses so ill a thing of himself, it is reasonable to believe
that he tells all; for if he made no conscience of lying, it were
as easy to deny the whole as deny any part; and the sin is
the same. I should not indeed be determined by a man's
positive denial of the whole matter laid to his charge, because
either some false [*f.* 103 (*a*)] principles of religion or the being
so atheistical as to be raised above all checks or remorse, may
carry a man to a simple denial to cover his party or to raise
a reputation to himself after death, of which some men retain
their fondness to the last minute of their lives. Yet when

[a] Cf. *Hist.* i. 559.   [b] *Ibid.*

---

[1] For Captain William Blague, see Cobbett's *State Trials*, vol. ix, cols. 653-6.

a man confesses some foul and ill things, and stops there, and
denies all the rest, I am very much inclined to believe him to
be sincere in it. So that Walcot's confessing so much as he
did, and denying the rest, did in my opinion very much overthrow the credit of the witnesses. There was one particular
in Walcot's paper on which the scribblers at that time laid
great hold. He said the plot was laid deep, and many were
concerned in it; and so he over and over again wished that
the king might grant an act of indemnity. It is probable
he meant this of the numbers of those who were malcontented,
and might have talked of making resistance, of whom no doubt
there are great numbers; but it is not like there were such
numbers concerned in this plot. That part of his paper that
concerns religion was writ in such a canting strain that it was
not easy to find out his meaning in it. [a] Hone died confessing
that he had been spoke to in general to assist in a design of
killing the king and the duke, but there was no particular
time marked out, so he knew nothing more of the plot [a]. He
said at the place of execution (when this was drawn out of
him not very decently by Dr. Cartwright, dean of Ripon, who
expected a bishopric by this excessive zeal of his) that [b] they
thought there was less danger from the duke, who was a known
papist, than from the king. The third seemed to be more
affected with the sense of those courses than the other two
were; he said he was never in any design against the king's
life, but the witnesses against him had let fall many wicked
things to him, and he was resolved to have discovered them,
and was only waiting till he might find out the bottom of the
design and have a consisting story to carry with him to
[*f.* 104 (*a*) [1]] Whitehall; but they had prevented him. He
vindicated all his other acquaintances [b], and in particular sir
Thomas Player, and wished that all men would give over
factious and seditious discourses and study to be more quiet
and more dutiful to the king, for whom he prayed very

[a] Cf. *Hist.* i. 559.   [b] *Ibid.*

---

[1] f. 103 (*b*) is a blank.

earnestly. [a] These executions did so much disgrace the witnesses that there has been no further use made of them [a]; for it appeared that as they had drawn others into those treasonable discourses, so they had swelled them in evidence that they gave much above the truth.

[*Lord Russell's trial.*]

Cf. *Hist.* i. 553 (*to* p. 556, 'than that of his execution would be ').

For ' was fixed for that day' *read* ' was a more important thing.'

For ' They were picked . . . of that side' *read* '[being] men that, as was generally believed, were resolved to give a very implicit obedience to all that the king's counsel should dictate to them.'

For ' to the seizing on the guards' *read* ' to that which was proposed at the meeting'; *and om.* ' so that here . . . treason only.'

Before ' As lord Howard' *insert* ' Howard delivered his evidence with much artificial malice ; for.'

After ' defended himself' *add* ' chiefly ' ; *and after* ' designs ' *add* [*f.* 104 (*b*)] ' but there was no great force in this ; for if a man has an opinion of the lawfulness of resistance, his entering into such consultations was not contrary to that character in which he was held.'

For ' Some others . . . testified ' *read* ' There was more force in what Anglesey, Mr. Edward Howard, and I declared.'

After ' at first' *add* ' and all witnesses in plots might be thus discredited.'

After ' of less moment' *read* ' for then it might have been said, that he only denied it to preserve himself and his friends.'

After ' offered' *add* ' (and [he] had in particular said he was confident there was nothing against Russell). This unnecessary lying.'

' *For* ' words to that effect: and' *read* ' since in trials for words witnesses must swear either to some determined words, or words to such effect, for a man's being present in a company does not prove that he hears all that is said in the conversation. I have been often myself so engaged in the pursuit of one thought that has been started, that for some time I have not known what was said about me ; though I have seemed to make general answers of smiles and half words ; and silent men, such as Russell was, are more apt to run out into such thoughtfulness, therefore.'

Om. ' They could not rely . . . discourses : so.'

[*f.* 105 (*a*)] *After* ' and Hale' *add* ' and many other great lawyers' ; *and for* ' and gave . . . for it' *read* ' and the reason given for it is plain ; the law makes actions criminal according to the danger that may be in them: now, since it is in any one man's power to murder the king, therefore it is reasonable to make every step towards it treason, but a war not being so easily levied, every discourse concerning it is not of such dangerous consequence.'

After ' during that reign' *add* ' so they are prosecuted within six months.'

Om. ' None of the witnesses . . . king's person.'

For ' So that' *read* ' Here was only a constructive treason brought against him' ; *and om.* ' the court . . . in their way.'

[a] Cf. *Hist.* i. 559.

[*f.* 105 (*b*)] *Om.* 'as the witnesses had sworn it.'

After 'of treason' *add* '(the punishment of which is a praemunire).'

After 'distinguished' *add* '(and I believe they were in the right).'

After 'suggested to him' *add* 'He also shewed how unlikely it was that any man could now raise a country; for so great an interest as was now requisite for that was now fallen with the greatness of the nobility, and was no more known in England [1].'

Om. 'shew his zeal and'; *and for* 'but it was only . . . invectives' *read* 'and aggravated matters with much insolence and spleen.'

After 'soon after' *add* 'Russell was cast, and received sentence the next day.'

For 'Lord Russell's behaviour . . . of the matter' *read* 'During his whole trial he had expressed so just an indifference, that as there was no affectation in his behaviour, so those who only saw him could not have imagined from anything that [*f.* 106 (*a*)] appeared in him, that he was the person concerned.'

For 'He was a man . . . fact; for' *read* 'He spake indeed but little; his talent lay not in a quickness of thought, much less in a readiness of speaking; and he was a man of such unblemished candour.'

For 'so he left . . . He said' *read* 'He reckoned the conclusion of his business was resolved on before it was begun, so that he gave his thoughts very little trouble about it; though he told me.'

[*The last days of lord Russell.*]

[a] After sentence, both his lady and father set on foot all possible methods for mollifying the king and duke. All that had interest with either of them were tried, and if money could have done it there was nothing that could have been asked that would not have been laid down. At first it was said that nothing could be hoped for unless as he petitioned the king he would likewise write to the duke [a]. He was averse to anything of that kind, and nothing but his kindness to his wife and his submission to his father could have prevailed with him to have made any attempts for a pardon; yet he was overcome to write to the duke [2]. In his letter he acknowledged that he had appeared so much against his interest that he was out of countenance to ask any favour by his means; but he protested he had done nothing out of any personal ill-will to [? against] him. [b] He offered to give his faith, that in case

[a] *Hist.* i. 556.   [b] *Ibid.*

---

[1] This passage is very curious. In the reports of Russell's trial occurs a condensed version of it; which Dalrymple (always, as Lord [John] Russell, *Life of William Lord Russell*, 3rd edition, ii. 60, happily observes,

'falling into blunders for the sake of effect') has amplified in melodramatic fashion (*Memoirs*, ed. 1790, pt. i. bk i. p. 44).

[2] Russell's *Russell*, 3rd ed., ii. 79, 262.

the king should think fit to pardon him, that he should live in any place beyond sea which the king should name, and never meddle any more in English affairs. This was also the sub-stance of his petition to the king[1], but all was to no purpose; for it was determined he should die the same day sennight after his sentence, and it is said that the duke moved that the place of his execution should be the square before his own house; but that was thought cruel, and I have been told that the king himself [*f.* 106 (*b*)] rejected that proposition as inhuman. So Lincoln's Inn Fields was named. [a]He only wished for two days' delay that he might have time enough to finish a paper that he was writing, but that was denied. This gave him some little trouble, but it went off in a moment, and he returned to his ordinary temper. [b]I waited upon him for a great part of the afternoon every day of that last week, and was with him the last night of his life, and went with him in his coach and saw the last part of this tragedy; but it was indeed a triumph over death. There was no vanity, nor affectation, nor sharpness, nor resentment in his discourses or deportment; on the contrary he was so serene and composed, and [c]upon occasions, as at table or when his friends came to see him, so decently cheerful, that it amazed me. There was a life in his thoughts and conversation that was very extraordinary. I was with him when the sheriff[s] came and shewed him the warrant for his execution; he read it as he would have done any other paper; and when they went away he said he thought it was not decent to be merry on such an occasion, otherwise he would have said to sheriff Rich (who had been a member of the last parliament, and had given his vote for the bill of exclusion, but was now turned about) that they would never sit again in a house of commons to vote on that bill any more. The day before his death he was taken twice with a bleeding at his nose, upon which he said to me, smiling, 'I shall not need to let blood, that will be done to-

---

[a] Cf. Burnet's Diary, Russell's *Russell*, ii. 270.   [b] Cf. *Hist.* i. 556.   [c] *Ibid.* 557.

---

[1] Russell's *Russell*, 3rd ed., ii. 78.

morrow'; and at supper it rained hard, upon which he said if that rain continued it would spoil a sight to-morrow, for a show in a rainy day was a very dull thing. [a] He composed himself to die [a] with the devotion of a serious Christian, as well as with the courage of a great man. He had lived for many years under a great sense of religion, and in a very innocent course of life. . [b] He said the sins of his youth lay heavy upon his thoughts ; but he hoped God had forgiven them, for he was sure he had forsaken them. He had acted with relation to the public very sincerely, and had neither private designs nor resentments to prompt him. It was his zeal for the protestant religion and his love to his country (which he valued much above his own life) that had act[uat]ed him. He had done nothing for which his conscience reproached [*f.* 107 (*a*)] him, for he thought that, as the king was limited by law, so when that was broke in upon the subjects might restrain him [b]. He had lived out the best part of his life, being then forty-four, [c] and he looked upon this death that was before him as a much easier thing than the dying of a colic or some other painful disease. He found himself now in a good temper, whereas he was much sunk with sickness, so that [d] he thought this the more eligible way of dying: it was but to be exposed for a while to be gazed at, and to endure a moment's pain, which was not so great as the drawing of a tooth. [e] And then he comforted himself with the hope that was before him. He said often, 'What a sort of change is this!' He had been told how some that were born blind were ravished when (by the couching their cataracts) their sight was given to them ; but he thought how much greater would the transport be if the first object that one saw was the rising sun [e]. He had a very firm assurance of his happiness in the next state, though [f] he said he had none of those transports that perhaps others had. He was much concerned at the cloud that seemed set over his country, but he hoped his death should do more service to the public than his life could have done.

Cf. *Hist.* i. 556. [b] *Ibid.* 557. [c] Cf. Burnet's Diary, Russell's *Russell*, ii. 264–5. [d] Cf. *Hist.* i. 557. [e] Cf. Diary (as above), ii. 274. [f] Cf. *Hist.* i. 557.

This was the substance of his discourses both with me and with the dean of Canterbury, Tillotson, who had been his friend formerly, and was much with him that week[a]. As to the public, he said often that, as he would wrong no man by discovering the freedoms they had used with him, for which some that then were in very great favour with the duke owed him more thanks than perhaps most others did (by which it was plain that Sunderland[1] was the person he meant), yet[b] he assured me there was never anything among them but embryos of things that never came to anything nor were like to come to anything, and had then no sort of being. [c] He said Howard had sworn falsely in several particulars[c]. But as to those affairs, I not only led him into no discourse concerning them, but I avoided it and desired his lady to tell him not to engage into freedom in those matters with me; for I was not willing to have the load of such a concealment upon my conscience, so I desired to decline the temptation to lying which the knowledge of their secrets and the questions that afterwards might [*f.* 107 (*b*)] be put to me would draw upon me. [d] Both Tillotson and I took much pains on him to persuade him of the unlawfulness of taking arms against the king[d] in any case[2]; but though we shook him a little, we could carry him no further than to say if it was a sin that he prayed God to forgive him for it; and so he put somewhat in his paper to that purpose, but it was so cold, and seemed put in only to justify us, that Tillotson thought it better to leave out that part, which he did. As for the paper that he left behind him, [e] he told me, at my first being with him, the substance of

[a] Cf. *Hist.* i. 557.   [b] *Ibid.*   [c] Cf. Diary, Russell's *Russell*, ii. 263,
[d] *Hist.* i. 557.   [e] Diary, p. 266.

[1] This curious charge must refer to some proposition made by Sunderland during his alliance with the Exclusionists in 1680-1; at least, it is hardly possible to suppose that Sunderland, after his reconciliation with the Court in July, 1682, should have committed himself to any treasonable intrigue; see however the strange story of Monmouth's confession in 1685, with the authorities quoted, in the *Life of Halifax*, i. 446, note 3.

[2] The reader will notice the significant alteration in the printed version; see also *infra*, App. I; Ranke, vii. App. II. 166.

it; for he had turned it much in his thoughts, expecting from
the first day of his imprisonment that it would have this conclusion, for he did not doubt but the sheriffs would pack a jury
for him. ªHe desired me to lay his matter in a method, for
he was not so well acquainted with forms; so I laid before him
the scheme of the heads that he had named in their right orderª;
only I suggested one particular to him ᵇconcerning the subornation of witnesses in the matter of the popish plot, from which
he cleared himself, not only of any accession to it, but of any
suspicion of it. ᶜHe set himself to write Wednesday and
Thursday morning, for ᵈhe desired to see no company before
one o'clockᵈ. In writing it he went on with the plain parts of
it quite through as it is printed, but when he came to the
tenderer points (such as that concerning the bill of exclusion,
the part that related to the dissenters, and two or three other
particulars) ᵉhe writ on other pieces of paper that which he
intended to say concerning them, and shewed them to me
before he filled up the void spaces that he had left for them ᵉ.
In some particulars I had different apprehensions from him,
but h[e] was settled in his thoughts, so that though he was
wrought to soften some expressions[1] he could be carried no
further. ᶠHis lady saw his paper as it grew under his pen, and
the void spaces, toge[ther] with the blotted draughts of that
with which he afterw[ards] filled . . . [*End of folio and
fragment*].

.   .   .   .

CONNECTING NOTE.

[At this point there is another gap in the narrative, of which the portion
containing events from July, 1683, to Oct., 1684, and corresponding to
the remainder of pp. 558 and 560-98 in Burnet's first published volume,
is missing. From Oct. 1684, however, to the beginning of 1696 (vol. i.
p. 598 to vol. ii. p. 163 in the printed *History*) the original narrative
remains unbroken; certain parts being preserved in duplicate, while
others are extant only among the fragments of one or other transcript. The
scheme placed at the beginning of the present volume gives a complete view

---

ª *Hist.* i. 558.   ᵇ Cf. *ibid.* 561.   ᶜ Cf. *ibid.* 558.   ᵈ Cf.
ibid. 556.   ᵉ *Ibid.* 558.   ᶠ *Ibid.*

---

[1] 'But' is here erroneously inserted by Burnet himself.

of these details and of the dates at which the various portions were written. Here it will suffice to say, that the part which contains the account of events from Oct., 1684, to the end of the reign of Charles II was written before the close of the year 1686 (see note, p. 141, *infra*) ; while the events of the reign of James II till the conclusion of 1687 were chronicled at intervals before Dec. 27 in the latter year. They are thus preserved ; Oct., 1684–Sept., 1686 in ff. 109–46 (Transcript A), ff. 148–218 (Transcript B) ; Sept., 1686–Dec., 1687 in ff. 219–46 (Transcript B only). As stated in the preface the pagination of Transcript A is alone quoted in duplicate passages. On ff. 108, 170 (*a*), 211, 263 are a few remarks by Dr. Gifford.]

[*Fragment concerning Roswell's trial.*]

[*f.* 109 (*a*)] Cf. *Hist.* i. 598-9 (*from* ' could remember so long a period ').

For ' I set down . . . such a defence' *read* ' Here [or there] was too much evidence to overthrow their testimony,' *and om.* ' urged . . . vehemence. He.'

For ' And there was a shameful rejoicing upon this' *read* ' And many of our clergy were both so wicked and so foolish as to rejoice at this, because.'

For ' since . . . might be ' *read* ' and they did not see that here a precedent was made, that might quite ruin the church, when infamous persons were received as sufficient evidence over against all the contrary proofs that were brought [cf. *Hist.* i. 599]. Yet the court was ashamed of the thing, though Jeffreys had a great mind to have him hanged.'

Om. ' though that . . . censured.'

Om. ' The impudence . . . clergy.

[*Hayes' trial.*]

Cf. *Hist.* i. 599.

For ' The other trial was' *read* ' The day after this there was another trial.'

For ' that whole cabal of men, that, it seemed ' *read* ' the club-men [1], that.'

Before ' and they hoped' *add* ' for it was taken for granted that all went through his hands.'

After ' Armstrong' *for* ' but to another . . . had it ' *read* ' by his own name, but by another name. So he said if it were his (which he still denied) yet it was addressed to [*f.* 109 (*b*)] an innocent person, and if that person had given it to Armstrong, so that it was found in his pocket, that was no proof against him. But his main defence was that there was no entry,' *&c.*

After ' in upon it ' *add* ' which shewed that this letter could not be imputed to him ' ; *and for* ' But . . . defence was' *read* ' And in fine he said.'

After ' as they were desired ' *add* ' All that was urged by the king's counsel was that in the letter he had writ advising Armstrong not to spend too lavishly, which was more than a simple letter of credit ' ; and *om.* ' The little difference . . . more guilty.'

For ' which mortified' *read* ' [Hayes] behaved himself so well, both in his imprisonment and at his trial, that this raised him as much as it mortified' ; *and om.* ' for they had reckoned . . . directed.'

---

[1] i. e. the members of the King's Head or Green-Ribbon Club, of which the Rye conspirators were all mem-bers. See *Life of Halifax*, i. 389, note 2 ; Sitwell's *First Whig*, pp. 74-93, 123-7, 197-203.

A new intrigue with the duchess of Portsmouth.

[a] There was this winter a new intrigue carried on at the duchess of Portsmouth's, to which it was believed that none was admitted but Barillon and Sunderland[1]. The duke of Monmouth came over secretly, and though he saw not the king, yet he went away extremely well satisfied with his journey [a]. [Whether][2] he engaged in this intrigue at the duchess of Portsmouth's or not I cannot tell, but it is certain the duke was shut out of it. Halifax saw it go on, but he told me [b]he knew nothing[3] of it. [c]The king was pressing the duke to make haste in his journey to Scotland, and when the duke answered how that affairs there did not require it so much, the king said to him that either he must go or he himself would go [c]. The queen seemed to re[s]ent[4] highly the dependence that was upon the duke, and the general forsaking of the king; for [d]often in the king's bedchamber there were not above three or four persons besides those that were in waiting; and even the duke's antechamber was crowded [d]. On several occasions the queen seemed concerned in the duke of Monmouth and in all his friends; so that there was a visible coldness between her and the duke. Now though she was not considerable enough by her interest in the king to give any apprehensions, yet she could still deliver him letters, and procure secret audiences[5].

The affairs of Ireland.

Cf. *Hist.* i. 601 ('The earl of Rochester' *to* p. 602, 'afflicted him so much '). *For* 'The earl of Rochester . . . method in the government of Ireland' *read*

[a] *Hist.* i. 604.   [b] *Ibid.* 605.   [c] *Ibid. infra.*   [d] Cf. *ibid.* 583.

---

[1] The *History* also mentions Godolphin.

[2] The 'whatever' of both transcripts is an obvious error.

[3] The reader is referred to the *Life of Halifax*, i. 422-7, for the reasons which suggest that Burnet was exceptionally ill-informed on this point, and that Lord Halifax was unwilling to confide in him.

[4] The original has 'repent'; an obvious error.

[5] The whole of this curious passage concerning the queen has been printed by Miss Strickland, *Queens of England*, ed. 1851-2, v. 667. See also *Life of Halifax*, i. 423; *Longman's Magazine*, March, 1899, pp. 435-438. The queen, though she had bitterly opposed the recognition of the boy, showed 'invariable kindness' to him (Strickland, ed. 1851-2, v. 545, quoting Brit Mus. Lans. MSS. 1236 (77), f. 119).

' Rochester was every day [sinking in] [1] favour, and was to go to Ireland more limited than any lord lieutenant had ever done.'

[*f.* 110 (*a*)] *For* ' as well . . . kingdom' *read* ' and they gave all the commissions. It is true they gave all considerable employments, according to the directions they had from the king ; but still.'

After ' secretaries' *add* ' In short, the disposing of the places in the army was the best perquisite of the lord lieutenant's place.'

For ' and therefore he proposed . . . check upon him' *read* ' and that therefore it were better to keep the army in an immediate dependence on himself.'

Before ' When there were' *add* ' In this Sunderland was in the right ; for it was too great a trust to put a whole kingdom in one man's hands ; and though anciently.'

Before ' In this the earl of Sunderland's' *add* ' But' ; *and after* ' himself' *add* ' and the profits of those commissions [2].'

For ' Yet little regard . . . so much' *read* ' Yet in this, as in everything else that was proposed by him, the king seemed to take a pleasure in humbling him ; and everybody concluded that he would be no sooner in Ireland than he would be disgraced.'

[*The treasury books.*]

Cf. *Hist.* i. 605 (' He complained . . . turned out of all ').

Begin ' But his misfortunes grew upon him ; for a discovery was made to Halifax.'

After ' of those books' *add* ' and these were in matters of great consequence.'

Om. ' if not . . . way' ; *and read only* ' but the king's illness took him that day, and so this was prevented.'

[*The affair of col. Maccarty.*]

Cf. *Hist.* i. 602 (*from* ' The first instance') ; and *ibid.* 600-1 (*marriage of lord Clancarty*).

For ' The first instance . . . acceptable ; for it was that' *read* ' Sunderland began to shew the world how he intended to model the Irish army. It was raised as a security to the English protestants, and paid out of funds given by the parliament of Ireland for that intent, to secure the nation from the insurrections of the Irish papists. Yet now it was resolved on to put Irish papists in command.'

For ' in which . . . at an end' *read* ' [he] was now pitched on for the first person in whose favour the law was to be broke. And he, to insinuate himself into Sunderland's favours, undertook to make a match between Sunderland's daughter and his nephew, whom his mother had put in the bishop of Oxford's hands to breed a protestant, all his family before him having been papists. So the king writ by Maccarty to the bishop,' *&c. as in* p. 601.

For ' at [of] the age of consent' *read* ' but sixteen.'

---

[1] Transcript A has originally ' speaking in,' corrected by Burnet to ' speaking for' : the above is no doubt the real reading.

[2] i. e. of the commissions issued direct from the king, through the Secretary of State's Office.

Om. 'and so . . . papist'; *and for* 'Thus' *read* 'This was strangely cried out [*f.* 110 (*b*)] on, when.'

After 'very effectually' *return to* p. 602, 'The king intended.'

After 'Halifax' *add* 'and told him that since Maccarty had lost a good post on his account, he was resolved to make it up to him in Ireland; but Halifax told him that might be made up by pensions without breaking of a law' (cf. *Hist.* i. 602 *infra*); *and om.* 'and he . . . according to law.'

Om. 'he said . . . interest.'

Om. 'Lord Halifax replied . . . jealousy.'

For 'who came' *read* 'So that Maccarty (who had married Halifax's cousin-germane[1]) came.'

After 'lord' *add* 'for opposing his preferment.'

Om. 'when he crossed . . . inclinations.'

[*Conduct of the duchess of Portsmouth.*]

[a] The secret at the duchess of Portsmouth's went still on; [b] the king seemed fonder of her than ever [2], though an intrigue had been discovered between the grand prior of France and her, in which it was said that the king (coming himself in a little abruptly on them, where they were together in her closet) saw more than he himself had a mind to see. Upon that the king ordered the grand prior to go out of England immediately [h]; but he, that had all the insolence of his country about him (without the spirit that generally accompanies it), began to pretend that by the laws of England the king could banish nobody, and that therefore he would not obey his order. But the king let him understand that the laws of England could only be claimed by Englishmen, and so, if he did not obey his orders in twenty-four hours' time, he would make him feel what he could do to him. Upon this he went away [3]; but this, instead of diminishing the king's kindness for the duchess of Portsmouth, as everybody expected it would have done, increased it to that pitch, that [c] after this the king kissed her often before all the world, which he was never observed to do before this time [c].

[a] Cf. *Hist.* i. 605.   [b] *Ibid. supra.*   [c] *Ibid.*

[1] Lady Arabella Wentworth, dau. of the first Earl of Strafford, and consequently cousin-germane to the father of Lord Halifax (Sir William Savile, son of Sir George Savile and Anne Wentworth, sister of Lord Strafford).

[2] Lord Ailesbury, in his *Memoirs*, traverses this (p. 86).

[3] See Routh, *Hist. in loco*; Klopp, ii.

The duchess of Portsmouth's medal; [and her political intrigues.]

And there was a medal struck for her; her face was on the one side, with 'Lucia Duchessa Portsmouthensis' about it; and on the reverse a Cupid was sitting on a globe and about him 'Omnia Vincit [1].' This was insolent to all degrees, the medals being exposed to sale by the goldsmiths. One that happened to go by a goldsmith's shop bought one of them for me, which I happened to shew that evening to some of the court that came to see me; with those reflections upon it that such an affront done the king drew from me. Whether this was told again or not I cannot tell, but the very next day all the medals were called in and were never seen any more; so that I never saw any of them but my own, which is in silver and of the size of half a crown. This I thought deserved to be put in history to shew how far [*f.* 111 (*a*)] the insolence of a whore can rise. But what the design between her and the French ambassador was at this time is not yet perfectly known; yet it may be guessed at by this, which I go to set down: that was told me by my lord Montagu, with whom I conversed much at Paris in summer [16]85. [a] He made me first understand the secret of her being so much for the bill of exclusion; and he told it to me so particularly, that I believe he himself had a particular hand in it.

Her design in the business of exclusion.

It was then proposed to the earl of Sunderland and her in the year [16]80, that if the king would agree to the exclusion, an

---

[a] *Hist.* i. 487.

422, 483; *Hist. MSS. Com. Rep.* vii. 368a; *Life of Halifax,* i. 409; Forneron, *Louise de Kéroualle,* 208-15.

[1] The British Museum has both bronze and silver specimens of this rare medal, which is by George Bower, appointed in 1664 one of the engravers of the Royal Mint and embosser in ordinary. Bower, who died before March, 1689-90, worked indiscriminately for Court and Opposition, having executed the famous ' Shaftesbury' medal in 1681, two medals in honour of the Seven Bishops, &c., as well as a large number of official commissions, including a satirical memento of the *Rye House Plot.* We can see however no reason for the supposition (advanced in the *Medallic Illustrations of the History of Great Britain and Ireland,* Hawkins, ed. Franks and Grueber, 1885, vol. i. p. 554) that the intention of the medal is sarcastic.

act might be obtained like that which had been granted to
Henry the Eighth, by which the nomination of the successor
should be left to the king; and this would extremely raise
the king's reputation and authority and oblige all that could
pretend to it to depend on him, and even the prince of Orange [a]
would not be made desperate, since the king, who was so
good at promising as he was bad in performing, would not
have been wanting to give him all the assurance that words
could contain.   Now the duchess of Portsmouth was made
to apprehend that [b] the duke of Monmouth would certainly
set on such an act by all possible means, since it was only on
such a bottom that he could found his hopes; and he would
no doubt assure himself that if the nomination were left to
the king, he would certainly be the person.   And the
duchess of Portsmouth made herself believe that she was
so far master of the king's spirit as to engage him to name
her son.   Thus the duke of Monmouth and she went into the
same game, but with very different prospects, both of them
hoping that they should have outwitted one another.   And
it was thought that her journey over to France the year
following was chiefly intended to engage that court in her
interests, and to make a match between her son and
a daughter of the king's by madame de Montespan that
is now duchess of Enghien.   But Montagu added to this,
that she had brought the king so far on in the exclusion,
that she herself told him the king would pass it if the
house of commons would have given 600,000*l.* for it [b]; but
if they would have raised it up to 800,000*l.* the king would
be so well pleased that they might promise themselves everything that they could desire from him upon it.   The same
was confirmed to me by c[olonel] Titus; but they both said
to me, that [c] the distrust of the king was then so great [c] and
the jealousy of some of the members going into the court
to make bargains for themselves grew to be so universal, [d] that
none of those who led the party durst move for money,
fearing that upon that they should lose their credit [d].   There-

---

[a] Cf. *Hist.* i. 487.　　　[b] *Ibid.*　　　[c] *Ibid.*　　　[d] *Ibid.*

fore they pressed the duchess of Portsmouth to prevail with
the king once to pass the bill and after he might have as
much money as he would desire ; ªbut the king would not
trust them.   And so that business fell when it was brought
so near a pointª ; so great a transaction having failed only
upon the distrust that the king and the parliament had one
of another.   Whether something like this was now again on
foot or not is that which I cannot affirm.

The state of the king's health.

Cf. *Hist.* i. 606 ('All this winter . . . hold up with him ').

Discourses of his being a papist.

Cf. *Hist.* i. 603-4.

[*f.* 111 (*b*)] *For* 'There was a great . . . of France' *read* 'There were many
discourses fell out this winter.'

For 'They did not . . . from Paris' *read* 'and one was more remarkable
because.'

For 'The occasion . . . better known' *read* 'No doubt the duke set this on
all he could, that so the king and he might be more inseparably united in their
interests.'

For 'one of the missionaries of Siam' *read* 'a secular priest from Siam.'

For 'who was a man . . . talked of his having' *read* 'who had, as was given out.'

For 'He was well received . . . desired' *read* 'He had much heat in him ;
and he [was] admitted to the king in.'

After 'in which' *add* 'as was said.'

For 'The confessor . . . convert him' *read* 'But that priest unhappily exposed
himself so that he was quickly sent out of England.   He went to see Halifax.'

Om. 'he was so vain . . . man'; 'such' (*before* 'simple '); *and* 'as furnished
. . . men.'

After 'thigh ' *add* ' (and) he had greater occasions to use his leg.'

[*f.* 112 (*a*)] *For* 'a miracle' *read* 'the half of a miracle.'

For 'and lord Halifax. . . contempt that' *read* ' which Halifax carried further;
for he not only told it to the king, but told it to the duke in the king's presence
before a great company, [so].'   *Om.* 'and the priest . . . no more.'

Halifax discovered the king's inclinations to popery so
plainly that I saw he was in great apprehensions.   Many
but little things began to break out which gave great
suspicion [1].   One ᵇsir Allan Brodrick, who had been brought
up by chancellor Hyde and was much trusted and much
employed by him, became the two last years of his life

ª *Hist.* i. 488.   ᵇ Cf. *ibid.* 74.

[1] Cf. the remarks of Halifax in his 'Character of Charles II,' *Life and Works,* ii. 347.

a strict and a religious person : he had been very atheistical
and vicious, but was as great an example as ever I knew of
an eminent conversion before his death[a]. He had opposed
the court much in parliament, which was generally imputed
to his revenge because of his patron's disgrace; yet, coming
to die some time before the king, [b]he told to one or two the
secret of the king's religion on his deathbed ; and I had it
from one of them. He said that both the brothers changed
when they were in Paris ; that [c]cardinal de Retz reconciled
them to the church of Rome [d]at Fountainebleau[d], and that after
that the king gave assurances to both the crowns at the time
of the treaty of the Pyrenees that he would declare himself
openly a catholic. He added that [e]chancellor Hyde knew
this[e] and did what he could to divert the king from it, but
that the king always denied it to him and hid it from him ;
[f]yet after the king's restoration the c[ardinal de] Retz
came over incognito and pressed the king to declare himself,
and that upon all these considerations the chancellor got
that act of parliament to pass by which it was declared
capital[1] for any to say that the king was a papist[f]. And
that in doing this he had two ends; the one was to restrain
all who might either know or suspect the secret from talking
of it (for he saw well how hurtful such jealousies and discourses would be to the public peace); but [g]his main end
was to let the king see the aversion that his best friends
had to popery when they made so severe a law against such
discourses. For it was at least to infer that they who could
not bear the discourses of the king's being a papist could
less bear the thing itself[g]. This act indeed had all the effect
that Clarendon designed by it ; for as the king would never
declare himself, so all people were very shy of talking of this
matter ; yet the priests beyond sea talked so freely of it in all
other places that such as travelled in foreign parts came home
very full of suspicions.

[a] *Hist.* i. 74.   [b] *Ibid.*   [c] *Ibid.* 73.   [d] *Ibid.* 74.   [e] *Ibid.* 194.
[f] *Ibid.*   [g] *Ibid.*

---

[1] Cf. Mr. Airy's edition, i. 347, note a.

The king's readiness to pardon murders.

Cf. *Hist.* i. 600 (*from* ' A trial in a matter ' *to end of paragraph.*)

For 'A trial . . . after this' *read* 'The last act[1] of the king's reign was of a piece with all that had gone before it.'

[*f.* 112 (*b*)] *After* 'appearing' *add* 'they having gone in friends to eat together.'

After ' prevailed on ' *add* 'by some of the court.'

After ' do so ' *add* ' and only submitted himself to the king's mercy.'

After ' defence' *add* ' So he followed this advice rather than that which was given him by his friends.'

Om. 'It was rich . . . court. So.'

After ' cost him' *add* ' as I was assured by those of the family'; *and after* ' of which' *add* ' I was told.'

Om. ' the other half . . . favour.'

For 'which cries for vengeance . . . criminal' *read* ' for thereby the prince draws still upon himself the guilt of the unrevenged blood ; yet, on the other hand, the importunities of courtiers and ladies are such things to a tender-hearted prince, that there will be no quiet in a court unless a prince declares it ill if any speaks to him on such a subject. And indeed pardons for murders ought never to be granted, unless the judge that tried the cause make such a report of the case that it appears by the circumstances that there is room for mercy without going too much against justice.'

For ' and that not . . . innocent[2]' *read* 'The king, that was very ready [cf. *Hist.* i. 612] to pardon all other crimes, was inexorable in matters of treason, though, these being against himself, he was more at liberty in them than in any other. The king [cf. *Hist.* i. 609] had by some such methods got a little secret treasure of about 80,000 guineas, in the disposing of which he was so shy, that even his mistress never knew anything of it.'

The king's sickness.

Cf. *Hist.* i. 606-9.

Begin 'Thus matters went on at court till,' *and proceed as in Hist. from* 'On the first of February.'

Om. ' he eat little . . . little of it, and.'

For ' a physician' *read* ' who was now become a very good.'

After ' wait on him' *add* 'The king was at this time carrying on a progress [*sic*] in his laboratory for the fixing of mercury [cf. *Hist.* i. 606, *supra*], and it was believed that this was the occasion of his sending for Dr. King.'

For 'All the king's . . . amazed at this' *read* ' who found him in so much disorder, that he did not seem neither to know what he said himself, nor what the doctor answered him. The doctor.'

For ' humour . . . staring' *read only* ' confusion.'

For ' fell down . . . sudden in ' *read* ' sat down, and fell immediately into.'

For ' like' *read* ' of '; *and after* 'head' *add* ' and the veins of his head swelled.'

After ' and so' *add* ' having a lancet in his pocket.'

After ' blood' *add* ' All the court ran together presently upon this alarm.'

[*f.* 113 (*a*)] *For* ' and that it would . . . off; so they' *read* ' It was indeed

---

[1] See Mr. Airy's note *in loco.* [2] Or ' accounts ' (Airy's ed.).

given out and printed by order of council that he was out of danger, yet those who understood better.'

Om. 'partly . . . partly' *and* 'as too busy . . . popery.'

Om. 'that had a great hand . . . against priests.'

For 'the lodgings . . . bedchamber' *read* 'Mr. Chiffin[ch]'s lodgings'; *and om.* 'and when he was told . . . with fear.'

For 'according to the relation . . . superficially' *read* 'went over some devòtions with the king, and then gave him all the sacraments; so it seems the king's confession was very general and short[1].'

Om. 'It was given out . . . suffered to come in.'

For 'and knew . . . effect of that' *read* 'and·it made some conclude that there was a great charm in what had passed between the priest and him, since it gave him so much quiet; which was very extraordinary after a life led as his had been: and it was unaccountable how a man of the king's understanding could satisfy himself with so slight a matter. It was given out that the turning all out of the bedchamber was in order to the king's signing his testament; and after that appeared to be false, then it was said he had then signed a farm of the excise for three years; and there were such numbers over England that seemed resolved not to believe him a papist that this was generally received as the occasion of that putting out the company. When the door was opened that the company was suffered to come in.'

Om. 'with a great . . . expression' *and* 'as those . . . told me,' *and* 'who seemed . . . answers to it.'

[*f.* 113 (*b*)] *For* 'nor any purpose . . . said to him' *read* '[so] that this looked like the casting of pearls before swine.'

For 'some that were in the room' *read* 'some abject flatterers.'

For 'which was the only word . . . attention' *read* 'After this he spoke pretty long to the duke; all hearkened when he came to this, and fancied he would have spoke of religion to him, and that he would have recommended his people or his friends and servants to him, or that he would have spoke of the payment of his debts, or that he would have told somewhat of his own ill-life; but there was nothing of all this in his discourse.'

After 'of the queen' *add* 'though she had expressed a most violent concern for him,' *and om. remainder of paragraph.*

His death and character[2].

Cf. *Hist.* i. 609; 611–2 (*to* 'at his restoration'); 613 ('His person . . . made for him'); 614 ('No part . . . parts of his').

Om. (*at this place*) *from* 'There were many very apparent suspicions of his being poisoned' *to the end of* p. 610.

p. 611. *Om.* 'did not only . . . digestion, but' *and* 'though a feeble one.'

[*f.* 114 (*a*)] *For* 'a good round pension' *read* 'a pension of £100,000 a year.'

Om. 'He spent little . . . thinking.'

---

[1] The mention of Howard's information in the original narrative proves that this part cannot have been composed till after the autumn of 1685, when Burnet was in Italy.

[2] Cf. this posthumous character, written abroad 1686 (*Hist.* ed. Airy, ii. 474), with that written in England 1683, ere the king's death (*supra*, pp. 47–50); noting p. 47, ll. 19–24, p. 50, ll. 18–21.

For 'and he had so ill . . . mistrustful of him' *read* 'and he took no greater pleasure in anything than in the deceiving of people.'

For 'scarce any virtues' *read* 'no virtues [1].'

After 'laws, yet' *insert* 'he was both lazy and fearful, so that.'

For 'but he seemed . . . became' *read* 'but was really very'; *and om.* 'He was apt . . . itself yet' *and* 'after his first . . . mercy.'

For 'even from the consideration . . . pursued by him' *read* 'and it was believed that the nearest relations in blood, even that of a daughter, made no difference in his esteem, who allowed of all appetites to all women; and even a modest whore was unacceptable to him, for studied brutalities were the only things that recommended women long to him.'

Om. 'as he was certainly . . . age.'

Om. 'He loved to talk over . . . condescension in a king [1].'

[*f.* 114 (*b*)] *After* 'Borghese' *add* '[who] took me with him to see those statues.'

Om. 'Few things ever went' *to* p. 614, 'insolent subjects,'

For 'as well as meaner than that he was' *read* '[than] the end [of it]; for to see a man.'

Om. 'expressing both . . . affection to it' *and* 'thus mocking . . . prevarication.'

Om. from 'The two papers . . . be forgotten' (*at this place*), *and the remainder of* p. 615 *altogether.*

[*Reign of James II.*]   *The new king proclaimed.*

Cf. *Hist.* i. 620 (*to* 'never yet broken').

Begin 'The duke was presently proclaimed king with the heaviest solemnity that ever was.'

Om. 'and much liked' *and* 'to his parliament and.'

After 'occasions' *add* 'I have it not now by me, otherwise I would insert it here.'

For 'but with that he promised' *read* 'but he used more caution in the promise he made.'

[*Addresses presented; Burnet's forebodings.*]

[a] And upon this there came up a set of addresses from all the parts of England, in which the highest praises that could possibly be set forth in words were offered up to the memory of the dead king, and the new king had assurances of obedience given him [a], in such excessive terms, that I have often wondered that the papists have not made more use of these to reproach the church of England with them; chiefly of [b] that from the university of Oxford, in which they promised to obey the king without restrictions and limita-

[a] Cf. *Hist.* i. 620.   [b] *Ibid.*

---

[1] See Mr. Airy's note c *in loco.*

tions. Some magnified the king's promise as if it had been
the freest concession that ever prince made ; and they were
thought ill courtiers who put in their addresses these words,
'our religion established by law' ; as if these had pretended
that the king was bound by law to maintain the established
religion[a]. I, that knew the king looked upon queen Elizabeth
as an usurper that had no more authority than Oliver Cromwell (which he had once said to myself), saw well enough how
far [*f.* 115 (*a*)] the king thought himself obliged by his promise ;
for he looked on all these laws that established our religion
as null and void of themselves, since they were made by one
that was an usurper, in his saying. So I knew well enough
how little hold was to be laid on this general promise, with
which the nation and the church of England were then so
lifted up ; but as this was an effect of the king's confidence
in me, that he spoke so freely to me, so that I could not
decently talk of it ; so (though I had spoken of it) it would
not have signified much ; for all people took up this for
a maxim that they must trust the king, and they resolved
to go in headlong, and to give him the revenue for life, and
everything else that he could ask, in the confidence that they
had of his keeping his word.

The late king's funeral.

The body of the late king was quickly buried. The king
ordered his body to be [b]opened in the presence of many
physicians[b]. I saw Dr. Lower that night, who was excessively
dissatisfied with the court, and seemed to have some jealousies
during the king's illness ; but he told me that all was so
sound within that not only there appeared no marks of any
poison in any of his vitals, but that if he had let blood in
time, he might very probably have lived to a great age.
It is true [c]the veins that had broke in his head had put
his brain into such a disorder, that he could make no judgement of it ; and it was upon this that some have since that
time grafted a suspicion that the king, who took much snuff,

[a] Cf. *Hist.* i. 620.   [b] *Ibid.* 609.   [c] *Ibid.* 610.

had poison given him that way [a]. This was said by those who were resolved to say somewhat, and they said this because this was all that could be said; for they first believe that the king was poisoned, and therefore they fastened it upon his snuff; but all this seemed to me to be mere malice. [b] The king's inwards were looked after with too little care, and some parcels of fat were left in the water in which they were washed, with great parcels of his entrails, all which were so much neglected, that the water being poured out at a scullery hole that went to a drain, in the mouth of which a grate lay, these were seen for many days lying upon the grates; and it was thought somewhat extraordinary to see so little care taken about the body of so great a king. His funeral was also extremely mean; he did not lie in state and no mournings were given [b]. The rooms in Westminster where his body lay for a week were furnished only with coarse cloth, and the candles that burned about him were of tallow. So that his funeral, as was believed, did not cost £100. Those that were sharp upon his memory, said it was such as he deserved; others [c] reflected on his brother's ingratitude for doing so little honour to his dead body [c]. But now I return to the new king.

The employments given by the king.

[d] All employments being ended of course with the king's life, the present king renewed them all, excepting those employments that he had about himself as duke of York; for his master of the horse, groom of the stole, and the rest of his family held now the same places about him as king. Halifax had a secret audience three days after he came to the crown; in which he made some excuses to the king for the distance in which he had [*f.* 115 (*b*)] lived with him of late; which the king put by handsomely enough, telling him that he would remember nothing that was past, except his behaviour in the business of the exclusion [d]. To this Halifax replied that the king knew upon what bottom

[a] Cf. *Hist.* i. 610.   [b] *Ibid.*   [c] *Ibid.*   [d] *Ibid.* 621.

he stood ; and that as long as the king exacted no other service of him than that which was consistent with the law no man should serve him with more zeal. [a] The king prepared him for the exaltation of Rochester, and told him that since he had suffered on his account he must consider him ; and the next day he declared him treasurer ; and his brother Clarendon was made privy seal, and Halifax was made president [a]. So his own jest was now turned upon himself ; for [b] when Rochester was turned out of the treasury and made lord president of the council (which was a higher place as to precedence, but much lower as to interest) he had said he had known many kicked down stairs, but he never knew any kicked up stairs before [b] ; so now this returned upon himself, since he was raised from being privy seal to be president. Rochester was considered as the favourite, and carried himself like one, for [c] he was insolent to all degrees [c]. Sunderland was looked on as a man lost at court, but [c] he found a way to engage [c] both France and [c] the queen [c] so entirely in his interests, that he was quickly more in favour than ever. It is said that he had promised to change his religion, but he delays this as much as is possible.

[*Reception of the Whigs ; king's attitude towards France.*]

Cf. *Hist.* i. 622 ('Persons of all ranks' *to* p. 623, 'with the prince of Orange').
Om. 'in such crowds' *and* 'that it was not easy . . . all.'
For 'the Whigs' *read* 'those that were called Whigs.'
For 'some . . . access' *read* 'some of them he would not see ; to others he spoke so sharply that they wished rather that he had refused to see them.'
After 'to say' *add* '[to] many of the family and others that were in employments.'
For 'though it proved . . . done formerly' *read* 'for he seemed to be animated against the French.'
For 'of another spirit . . . had done' *read* 'that the king would not give himself up to the French councils as his brother had done.'
After 'prince of Orange' *om.* 'and the States of Holland.'

[*The prince of Orange dismisses Monmouth.*]

[d] So soon as the news of the king's death came to the Hague, the prince saw the necessity of dismissing the duke of Monmouth, and so he resolved to prevent the king's

[a] Cf. *Hist.* i. 621.   [b] *Ibid.* 592.   [c] *Ibid.* 621.   [d] *Ibid.* 624.

asking it [a]. He had a long conversation with him, upon which they parted; I have not yet asked in what terms they parted; but a friend of Monmouth's complained highly to me of the prince's abandoning him; and [b] pretended to justify all that Monmouth did after that against the prince's right, since he said the prince brake first to him. [*f.* 116 (*a*)] But it is certain [c] the prince must either have done it thus of himself or he would have presently been so pressed by the king that he must have broke upon it [c]; and in all this the world would have condemned the prince, as wanting both in duty to the king and in prudence, if he had given the king, who he knew sought advantages against him, so just a one as this would have been of not dismissing him. But I do not yet know how the prince gilded this pill to Monmouth, who [d] went presently to Brussels; but he was quickly made to understand that as soon as the return of a courier could come from Spain he would be ordered to leave that place [d]; so that he did not know whither to go, since the expectations and apprehensions that all Europe had of the king made that few princes would have willingly received him.

[*The king's course of life.*]

Cf. *Hist.* i. 624 ('The courtiers now said everywhere . . . fair appearances ').

For 'who would bring . . . court' *read* '[who] would not go into that dependence on France which had been the reproach of the former reign.'

Om. 'the queen and his priests.'

For '(by whom . . . children)' *read* 'whom he has since made countess of Dorchester.'

After 'orders were' *add* ' publicly.'

For 'yet the king' *read* ' yet I knew, for all that, he.'

[*Relations with Spain and the States.*]

[e] He gave also very good words to the Spanish ambassador, and writ very kindly to the prince of Orange, [f] though he imposed a hard thing upon him, which was the cashiering some of the English and Scotch officers, that were suspected

---

[a] Cf. *Hist.* i. 624. [b] *Ibid. infra.* [c] *Ibid. supra.* [d] *Ibid.*
[e] *Ibid.* 623. [f] *Ibid.* 627.

to be in Monmouth's interests[a], though they had never
declared it, and the suspicion was only founded on some
malicious suggestions of Mr. Chudleigh, that had been
envoy in Holland. These officers had served the States
well during the wars, and the cashiering of brave men upon
little stories was a hard thing. The prince saw well that
this would bring the regiments under a great dependence
on the English envoys, if he should cashier the officers upon
every tattle that they writ over to the king. [b]Yet he resolved
for once to gratify the king, and to recompense the hurt that
was done to those officers[b] by secret favours, for it was not
advisable for him, neither in his own particular nor as he was
at the head of the government of the States, to give the king
a colour to complain of him; [c]with all which the king was
so well pleased, that he said to the bishop of Ely, who was
then in great favour, that it was absolutely necessary upon all
accounts for him to be extremely well with the prince, and
therefore he refused to do an indiscreet thing that the bishop
proposed to him, because he said he knew it would offend the
prince. This was set about[c] as one of those secrets that are
intended to be made known to all the world, and the clergy
were so lifted up with hopes, that the king gave them, of his
supporting them, [*f.* 116 (*b*)] and his bearing down the dissenters, that I never saw a tide go so high. It was not safe
to express the least fear or distrust, though there appeared
very quickly grounds for jealousies.

[*Customs and excise levied.*]

Cf. *Hist.* i. 621–2 (*from* 'But before' *to* 'talk of those matters').

For 'But before the earl of Rochester . . . passed upon it' *read* 'The parliament had, as in all former times, granted the custom to the late king for life.'

For 'Yet the king . . . excuse for it, that' *read only* 'For.'

For 'But in answer . . . pass' *return to* 'Yet the king declared . . . new
grant' (*on* p. 622, *supra*).

After 'Endeavours were used' *add* '[by] the party that opposed the
court.'

Om. 'The earl . . . others.'

For 'Such beginnings . . . matters' *read only* 'and it did not look like a
prince that intended to govern by law.'

[a] Cf. *Hist.* i. 627.   [b] *Ibid.*   [c] *Ibid.*

[Practices in elections.]

Cf. *Hist.* i. 625 (*from* 'At the same time' *to* p. 626, 'on all occasions ').

Begin 'But that which came next was beyond all the rest.   For.'

After 'neglected' *insert* 'In above three parts of four of the boroughs of England, the elections had been always made by the whole inhabitants, but.'

After 'corporation men' *add* 'these were all named by the king in the new charters.'

After 'in some of these' *add* 'where even these could not be found.'

For 'by the earl of Bath' *read* 'by the treachery of the earl of Bath.'

[Fate of the earl of Bath; reflections.]

[*f.* 117 (*a*)] And yet though he did what in him lay to betray his country, he lost his place; for Peterborough, that had been in that place about the king while he was duke, carried it from him, at which all people were glad, not so much out of their love to the one, as out of their hatred to the other. [a] Now this method of choosing parliament struck at the whole constitution and liberty of England ; for the house of commons being the fence of liberty the freedom of elections is that upon which all depends.   And if the king can by his charter take away the right of elections from the body of a town, and put it in a smaller number of one and twenty, who are all named by himself, it is plain that a parliament so made up is rather made by the king than chosen by the people.   All the inhabitants of the towns were extremely troubled when they saw their birthright thus taken from them ; for this to them was not only a point of honour and of liberty, but was really a main point of interest ; since all the gentry that lay about these towns, and that courted them that they might be favoured by them when elections to parliament came about, and that feasted them after, and made constant presents to them, would now give over all that courtship, so that they saw that hereafter there would be no difference between parliament boroughs and every market town.   Upon this the discontent was very universal ; yet in the beginning of a reign that was like to be severe, nobody durst speak out that which he had in his heart upon this occasion [a].   But the court was mightily lifted up with

[a] Cf. *Hist.* i. 626.

their success in carrying the elections as they had a mind
to it.   [a] The king said there were not above forty men here
chosen other than as he had wished for; and that which gave
the saddest view of this whole matter was that the members
that were chosen were neither men of parts nor of estates;
so that it was not easy either to convince their understandings
or to make them see their interest, since they had none unless
it were to recommend themselves to the king.   [b] Thus all
thinking men looked on England as lost, and believed that
this parliament would certainly be the ruin of the nation.
[c] For it was expected that they would not only give the king
the whole revenue for life, and not from three years to three
years [v] (which wise men had projected, and were resolved to
move if the elections had given any good prospect), but that
which was yet more apprehended was that [d] they would confirm
all their own elections; for since the member that is returned
sits till his election is questioned, then it was not to be
doubted but upon the first questioned election, all the other
questionable members, who were much more than the
majority, would have voted in favour of the elections, since
that indeed was to vote for themselves; and if the house
had once confirmed this method of restraining elections by
new charters, this was the sacrificing of all the liberties of
England.   [e] So that men began to be very sad; for a blow
given to the constitution of the government by a parliament
cannot be recovered but[1] by a rebellion [v], and a disease is
justly accounted desperate when the remedies are likewise
such.

[*Opinions of Halifax.*]

Halifax told me[2] there were two things which only could
save us.   The one was [f] that perhaps the king would declare

[a] *Hist.* i. 626.   [b] *Ibid.*   [c] *Ibid.*   [d] *Ibid.* 627.   [e] *Ibid.* 626.
[f] *Ibid.* 627.

---

[1] This we see was written between
the summer of 1686 and the end of 1687.
[2] It is difficult to see why Burnet
in his printed *History* deprives Lord
Halifax of the credit of these sagacious

forecasts. We notice, however, that,
in the interval between 1686 and the
death of the marquis in 1695, relations
between Burnet and Halifax had
become strained.

himself against France, and for bringing the state of Europe to a righter balance.   He told me that [*f.* 117 (*b*)] both the court of Spain and the States would certainly make such addresses to the king that he would have all the offers made him that were possible, if he would depart from the French interest, [a] and by this we would be quickly able to judge whether bigotry or a desire of glory wrought most powerfully on the king.

[*Same subject continued.*]

Cf. *Hist.* i. 627 (*from* ' since if he did not' *to* p. 628, ' judge of any election ').

For ' The season . . . short' *read* ' The other was that he hoped . . . since it was to be in summer.'

Om. ' but that . . . winter session.'

For ' they might come . . . and either see' *read* ' there would still be hopes ; since after members had been once together and they begin to see.'

For ' and so ' *read* ' they would be the more easily prevailed on at least to.'

For ' sparing' *read* ' so sparing' ; *and after* ' bounty' *add* ' that the court might have frequent occasions of bringing them together.'

Om. ' which they had learned . . . setting out.'

For ' resolved' *read* ' generally resolved.'

For ' but to keep . . . parties' *read* ' but the giving the revenue entirely to the king for life was so sure, that it was not safe to oppose it.'

[*The coronation.*]

When the elections were over, [b] the next care of the court was to order the coronation ; for both king and queen were to be crowned, and so the peeresses as well as the peers were to bear a share in the solemnity.   This was done with great order and magnificence[1], and the court was so possessed with this matter[b], that it lessened the king in many people's thoughts, who saw him more intent upon the ceremony of the splendour of that day than became a man of his age.   [c] Yet the crown was so ill fitted to his head, that it hung over his face, so that he made but an ill figure that day ; and that very morning his son by Mrs. Sedley died, the pall that was carried over his head broke, and some other small accidents happened from which foolish people that looked at those trifles drew ill auguries.

[a] *Hist.* i. 627, *infra.*   [b] *Ibid.* 625.   [c] *Ibid.* 628.

[1] See Strickland, *Queens of Eng.*, ed. 1851-2, vi. 164-5.

[*Burnet goes abroad; a rebellion projected.*]

ᵃ But the discontent that was over England made some
hot men in London, such as major Wildman and Charleton,
fancy that it might be a fit time now for the duke of Monmouth to raise a rebellion ᵃ. I knew they met often together,
and were often shut up in little cabals; ᵇ some of them came
to see me, and talked in general ᵇ of what might be expected
from this parliament; for ᶜ the king had put me in great
credit with them; since Halifax desired leave to present me
to the king, that I might kiss his hand, which all people did.
The king not only refused it, but spake sharply of me. Upon
which I desired Halifax to ask the king's leave for me to go
beyond sea; which the king said he agreed to ᶜ with all his
heart. Yet I could not execute this as soon as I intended,
for my wife was languishing and likely to die every day[1]; so
that I stayed two months longer than I intended. Yet seeing
the parliament draw near, I satisfied her friends in Scotland
[*f.* 118 (*a*)] so well, with the method I had settled for looking
after her, that they all consented to my leaving her. So I
resolved to go out of England in the beginning of May, and
she died about the end of the month. ᵈ Thus I was in great
credit with all the party that were against the court ᵈ; but
they were in no credit with me, for I knew that all the men
that were for the duke of Monmouth were factious and
wicked people. So I would have nothing to do with them.
I was afraid they would have insinuated themselves into my
lady Russell, who as she had great resentments for her
husband's death, so was mistress of a great estate, and by
that means could raise much money, which was the thing
they wanted most; but I prevailed so effectually with her,
that she resolved not to enter into any communication with
them; and this reservedness of hers was imputed to me, and

ᵃ Cf. *Hist.* i. 626, 625.   ᵇ *Ibid.* 625, 628.   ᶜ *Ibid.* 628-9.   ᵈ *Ibid.*
629.

---

[1] See Autobiography, *infra*, ff. 208–9.

I was severely railed at for it by these men[1]; we see clearly that there was somewhat among them. [a] I spoke earnestly to my lord Delamere to keep himself from all designs of that kind, and he assured me he was resolved not to embark in them; yet I suspected him extremely. Mr. Hampden gave me also the same assurances. [b] That which I proposed to them was that I did not yet think the king had done enough to justify any such extreme counsels; a raw rebellion would be either presently crushed, and so raise the power of the court and give them a colour for keeping up a standing army, or, on the other hand, if it grew strong it would throw us into a commonwealth or lasting civil wars, and either of these would be the ruin of the nation, and would drive the king to bring over a French army. [c] Yet I saw many consider the nation as already undone by this election of parliament-men, so that they were disposed to put all to hazard; but nobody that I saw thought it was near [c]. And the king repeated so frequently the assurances that he had given concerning religion, that even those who did not depend much upon his word yet fancied that the impossibility of the thing might perhaps keep him from attempting that in which he was not like to succeed; and the church of England had done him so great service not only during the business of the exclusion, but now in the procuring the elections of parliament to go everywhere as the court desired, in which they had behaved themselves like men that had neither any regard to public liberty, nor any sort of distrust of the king. All this concurring, many flattered themselves with hopes that at least some considerable time would pass before such things could be forgotten; and time was all unless the king had sons, or could prevail on the princess of Denmark to change her religion. For the former, [d] the queen was not like to bring more children; [e] but her very

---

[a] *Hist.* i. 629.   [b] *Ibid.*, and 625.   [c] *Ibid.* 629.   [d] *Ibid.* 683.   [e] *Ibid.* 682.

---

[1] For Lady Russell's expressed sentiments on Monmouth's rebellion, see her letter of July 21, 1685, to Doctor Fitzwilliam, *Letters* (First Collection, seventh ed., 1809), pp. 74-5.

ill-health made many fear she could not be long-lived; yet she recovered out of a languishing which almost all people thought would be fatal to her. But if she recovered her health, [a] she quickly came to lose the esteem and love of the nation, which she had possessed hitherto to a high degree[a]. She began to grow so very haughty and ill-natured and so bigoted and fierce in matters of religion that she is as much hated since she was queen, as she was beloved whilst she was duchess; [*f.* 118 (*b*)] yet she lives still, and by that she does the protestant interest more service[1] than all her ill-affects can do it a prejudice. [b] She has had many little quarrels with the king about his amours, which, as some say, have been carried by her to great excesses. [c] But if the king doth her wrong one way, he doth all he can to make it up another way; for he treats her with great respect, so that it is believed she has a great stroke in the councils[c]. She has gone in wholly into the French interests, and has espoused all the concerns of her religion with a violence that very ill becomes her sex. As for the princess of Denmark, she has disappointed all the people as much the other way; for it was generally thought that she would be so complaisant to the king as to let herself be instructed in her religion; yet as she has begun very early to declare to the bishops and several others that she was resolved never to change, so [d] she seemed to apply herself more to devotion, and to be more serious in receiving the sacrament than formerly, and has ever since that time behaved herself so worthily in all respects[d] that now all people trust as much to her as ever they were afraid of her; and this in her is so much the greater virtue, that no doubt a thing which is obvious has been suggested to her, that if she would turn she should be put in a condition to succeed even in a preference in her elder sister. For she being upon the place,

[a] *Hist.* i. 368, 618.　　[b] *Ibid.* 682.　　[c] *Ibid.* 748.　　[d] *Ibid.* 720.

---

[1] This phrase shews that the whole of the passage was written before the first report of the queen's pregnancy, in the winter of 1687; and is therefore full proof of a contemporary belief in the probability of her continued childlessness. Miss Strickland (*op. cit.,* 1851–2, vi. 161), quoting Fox, gives a very bad account of her health in 1685.

if her creatures were all over put in the government, this, together with the assistance of France, might make a dangerous competition between her and her eldest sister. But it is visible she hearkens to none of those things. So that we are now out of that danger which I confess I apprehended more than all other when I came out of England.

The affairs of Scotland.

A few days before I left London [a] the marquis of Queensberry and the earl of Perth came up from Scotland; the former was made a duke, [b] and the king declared him his commissioner for the parliament that was summoned in Scotland; but upon this, Queensberry told the king that if he had any thoughts of changing the religion, he himself could not make one step in that project, and therefore the king would do better to employ another. The king received it so well from him, and gave him such ample assurances in his speech to the parliament of the king's resolutions to maintain the established religion [. . .][1]; but he got likewise instructions to enact what laws might be necessary for the further securing of it; [c] and because the law concerning the test was [. . .][1] not only in order to having of public employments but whensoever it should be presented to them by order of council, and that under the pain of treason. He had also instructions for many other severe laws, by which he, who was naturally violent and imperious, thought to make his court so dexterously to the king that even his firmness to the protestant religion should not do him hurt. But he found afterwards that he reckoned wrong[c]; the king made use of him to get the revenue confirmed, and to do some other odious things; [d] but what has fallen out since that time has showed that the king has been strangely prevailed on by his priests[d] to do the things that are the most contrary to his disposition. For there is scarce any virtue more rooted in the king's nature [*f.* 119 (*a*)] than sincerity; and yet by the many promises that the king made then, and his strange way of

[a] *Hist.* i. 634.   [b] *Ibid.* 635.   [c] *Ibid. infra.*   [d] *Ibid. supra.*

[1] Some words have evidently dropped out here. See *Hist. in loco.*

observing them since that time, it must be acknowledged that
either he then made promises with an intention to break
them, or that having found a favourable conjuncture since
that time, he has thought it below him to be a slave to his
word; and either of these two is so bad, that it is hard to
tell which of them is the worst, and the least suitable to so
sublime a dignity.   I went out of England in the beginning
of May, so that I cannot since that time prosecute matters
so particularly, as I have hitherto done; yet I shall give so
distinct a view of the state of affairs as shall still let my readers
see the errors that have been made of all hands, both by the
people on the one side and by the government on the other.

Argyll's rebellion in Scotland.

[a] Argyll had lived near two years secretly in Friesland;
but he came often over into Amsterdam, and met there with
the rest of the Scotch exiles, the chief of whom were sir
Jo[hn] Cochrane and sir Patrick Hume [a].   They all knew how
odious the king's person, as well as his religion, was in
Scotland; and they reckoned that those who had felt his
severity so much when he was only a subject would very
probably apprehend it much more now that he was a king.
[b] Argyll believed that if he had but money to buy a stock of
arms and ammunition he might venture into Scotland without
taking any precaution for the preparing people to it; he
thought his own interest would bring all his Highlanders
together, and he fancied the western and southern counties
were under such apprehensions, both for religion and liberty,
that they wanted nothing but arms and a head.   And a rich
[1] widow in Amsterdam [b], who was a zealous lover both of

----

[a] Cf. *Hist.* i. 629.   [b] *Ibid.*

[1] In Transcript B, f. 164(*a*), 'English'
is inserted before 'widow.'   In the
margin opposite are two notes: (*a*)
one in the same hand as that of f. 2
(see Preface), 'Her name was Smith.
She had a share in a sugar House [?].
She was of an Anabaptist congregation.
She lent money [?] to l[o]rd Melville'; (*b*) and the second, in the
hand of Dr. Gifford, in these words,
'I knew her well—A. G.' [Dr. Andrew
Gifford (Baptist minister, numisma-
tist, and assistant librarian at the
British Museum from 1757 to his
death in 1784), born August 17, 1700,
the son and grandson of Baptist
ministers at Bristol (*Dict. Nat. Biog.*)].

presbytery and of a commonwealth, [a] hearing that it was believed ten thousand pound sterling might compass this great design, laid down the money [a]. Argyll now fancied Scotland was his own, and was very insolent in all his discourses with the other gentlemen, who really thought his brain turned. Hume [1] knew the state of the southern and western counties much better than he did, for many had that opinion of Argyll that if at any time the king had offered him his estate again he would have made his own peace and have betrayed all his friends ; but they had trusted themselves to Hume, so that he was sure of above 4,000 persons, and they had engaged above the half of the garrison that was in the castle of Edinburgh ; so that here would have been a formidable rebellion if Argyll could have managed it. [b] He went about the business of buying arms and his vessel to carry them over with so much dexterity that this passed as if it had been for the service of the Venetians. But when he and the rest came to reason about the methods of carrying on their business they differed in every point. Hume was for the shortest passage, and for landing in the south. But Argyll thought the fastnesses of his own country made that it would be properest, since he reckoned the country would gather to him safer there, and in short he rather dictated to the rest than [*f.* 119 (*b*)] advised with them [b]. Hume thought often to have left him, and would never trust him with the secrets of those who he knew were waiting for a fit opportunity ; nor would he trust it to Cochrane. Monmouth hearing of all this came to them, and though he did not like the business and thought it was too early, yet [c] he studied to make them all friends, and shewed great temper in his way of managing them. He had such inclinations to have set himself at the head

[a] Cf. *Hist.* i 629-30.   [b] *Ibid.* 630.   [c] *Ibid.*

[1] On comparing Burnet's eventual account of Argyll's rising with that printed above it is difficult to avoid the conclusion that his original version is founded entirely upon the verbal reports of Sir Patrick Hume, who, as is well known, escaped to Holland after the failure of the expedition. If so, however, Burnet's record is in some respects mistaken ; compare his account of Ayloffe's capture, *infra,* p. 158, with Hume's own narrative printed in Rose's *Observations,* pp. 1-67, and in the *Marchmont Papers,* iii. 1-66.

of them, that if Argyll had offered it to him, he seemed ready to have accepted of the command [a]. But Argyll was strangely blown up, and, as it appeared afterwards, he seemed guilty of the folly of fancying that he could make himself king of Scotland. He had provided all things with so much secrecy that [b] the king had not the least suspicion of him, till he heard he had set sail; which he knew the day before I left London, for Arran, that came to see me in the night, told me this, and said he had it from the king's own mouth; so that I saw it was time for me to be gone, since if risings were once begun I had all reason to expect that I should be used as a suspected person [b]; and if Argyll was gone to Scotland, it was reasonable enough to imagine that the duke of Monmouth would be quickly in England. [c] I went first to France, because I knew that if I had gone to Holland some of the duke of Monmouth's party would have perhaps found me out, and have either made me guilty by communicating somewhat to me [c], or at least have made me seem guilty by their having been with me; and as things were then between the prince of Orange and the king I could not expect to have any countenance from him. [d] So France was at first my safest retreat, and Mr. Barillon told me that I might assure myself I should be safe there; for he had asked the king if he was satisfied with my going out of England and with my going to him in France, and the king told him he was. Mr. Barillon gave me else all the assurances that I could expect of an ambassador, that as soon as he perceived that the king had any design to demand me from the court of France he should presently give me notice of it, that so I might have time to retire myself from thence. So I went to Paris; where, that I might be quiet and less suspected, I took a house and lived by myself [d]. But before I enter upon the secrets that I have discovered beyond sea I will carry on the recital of English affairs, which I have gathered partly out of the letters that have been writ me and partly from the persons whom I have seen.

[a] Cf. *Hist.* i. 630.   [b] *Ibid.* 631.   [c] *Ibid.* 655.   [d] *Ibid.*

[Argyll's expedition.]

Cf. *Hist.* i. 631 (*from* 'Argyll had' *to* p. 632, 'by more of his Highlanders ').

After 'voyage' *add* 'and some few English went with him [*see* p. 632], in particular Mr. Ayloffe and one Mr. Rumbold' (*and then continue as on* p. 633, *from* 'that dwelt' *to* 'present king').

For 'this had no effect . . . sail away and' *read* 'but went away in such haste [as to],' *and for* 'to mercy' *read* 'to be made prisoners.'

After 'very few days' *add* 'after he sailed from Holland.'

For 'Hume' *read* 'the other Scotch gentleman.'

[*f.* 120 (*a*)] *Om.* 'who were setting . . . liberty.'

For 'he found that the early notice . . . got above' *read* 'he was much surprised to find that almost all of the gentry of the country had been called to Edinburgh ; for the king sent the advertisement that he had received from Holland with all haste to Scotland, upon which the privy council had sent for all the most considerable gentlemen of his country. He had not behaved himself in his prosperity like a man that thought he might at some time or another need the affections of his people ; and he felt that now, for though he always reckoned that he was sure he could raise 5,000 men in his country, yet he could not bring together.'

For 'at last . . . sea and' *read* 'And when at last he should have crossed the arm of the sea, and come to the western counties, instead of landing in them, he.'

After 'Bute' *add* 'a poor little island.'

[Conclusion of the attempt.]

[a] He had also left his arms behind him in a castle, with a body of men to guard it ; who were routed by a party of the king's[a] and run away. So all his arms were taken, and then his design was lost ; and in the whole progress of the matter it appeared that [b] he had lost both head and heart[b]. His men were now got out of the island, but a rebellion that begins to go backward is quickly at an end ; [c] he put himself in a poor man's habit, and had almost got out of their hands ; but at last he was shamefully taken. Yet a body of his men stuck together and fought, so that though in that feeble opposition which the king's troops gave them some were wounded, others taken (amongst these were Cochrane, Ayloffe, and Rumbold)[c], sir Patrick Hume with [d] several others fought out their way[d] and got clear of their enemies. But now all those in the western and southern counties who had re-solved to rise were still in the same mind, and upon the first news of the duke of Monmouth's success there would have been a second and much more considerable rising. So they lay in the way where the packets passed from London to

[a] Cf. *Hist.* i. 633.   [b] *Ibid.*   [c] *Ibid.*   [d] *Ibid.*

Edinburgh and took two or three of them, which gave those at the council at Edinburgh no small disorder, since there passed so many days without their hearing any news from England.

[Fate of the prisoners.]

Cf. *Hist.* i. 632 (*from* 'Argyll was' *to* p. 634, 'suffered with the rest') (*the order differs, but is immaterial*).

After 'Edinburgh' *add* 'so were the other prisoners.'

Om. 'he expressed . . . misfortunes.'

[*f.* 120 (*b*)] *For* 'so it was justice . . . taken from him' *read* 'so that he thought all that he did was but a just revenge.'

After 'the oath' *add* 'to defend the protestant religion.'

After 'dignity' *add* 'by which he concluded that a papist who could not take the oath could not be the legal king of Scotland. He expressed a great zeal for the protestant religion, and a very serene constancy of mind at his execution.'

Om. 'He desired . . . firmness [1].'

For 'He said, he had not laid . . . administration' *read* 'He discovered the whole secret of his affair, and how he had got his money with which he bought the arms, so he died generally pitied of all men, but esteemed by few.'

Om. 'When the day . . . serenity.'

Om. from 'at parting' *to* 'designs of this kind.'

For 'several stabs' *read* '6 or 7'; *and om.* 'it being believed . . . discoveries.'

For 'was he that dwelt . . . king' *read* 'suffered next; he shewed a wonderful resolution.'

For 'the truth of that conspiracy' *read* 'absolutely the Rye conspiracy,' *and om.* 'He did not deny . . . resolved on.'

After 'Cochrane' *insert* 'was to go next, but.'

After 'made. But' *insert* 'because it would look a little odd to suspect [? see such] an eminent rebel pardoned.'

After 'pardoned him' *insert* 'Everybody expected to see him set up for an evidence to hang other people, but when nothing of that appeared, then.'

After 'negotiations with' *add* 'foreign princes in particular with.'

For 'The secret . . . after' *read* 'I have since understood the true secret of this matter.'

Om. 'but could draw . . . repartee.'

For 'nephew . . . children' *read* 'cousin-germane to the duchess.'

For 'which would . . . with the rest' *read* '[but] he suffered at Tyburn [2].'

[Few suffer in Scotland; insinuation against Argyll.]

[*f.* 121 (*a*)] [a] And thus was the rebellion in Scotland dissipated with the effusion of very little blood either in the field or on the scaffold. The greatest number of those who joined

[a] *Hist.* i. 632.

---

[1] As Charteris did not die till 1700 (*Hist.* i. 216), it is probable that Burnet after his return from Holland obtained from him the account of Argyll's last hours.

[2] Original note (qu. in hand of f. 2 ?), 'Mistake, it was over against the Temple' (Transcript B, f. 167 (*a*)).

with Argyll were Highlanders, whose following their lord
was so suitable to their way of living that the government
thought it fit to be gentle to them[a]. And for the other
gentlemen, they had got away, so that none were taken that
could make any great discoveries. And the truth was the
council fancied that Argyll must needs know all. And so
when they saw by him that he had no correspondence with
any in Scotland upon that matter, they concluded that there
was nothing in it; so that many men's lives and estates were
saved who would have been very probably ruined if Argyll
had drawn all Hume's secrets out of him.

A parliament in Scotland.

Cf. *Hist.* 636–7 (*from* 'The parliament' *to end of paragraph*).

Om. 'no opposition was made' *and* 'and was looked on . . . church of Rome.'

For 'This put men . . . pleased' *read* 'by which any man may be taken up
and examined upon oath to any matters of which he may be suspected.'

After 'Campbell' *add* 'of Cesnock'; *and after* 'Melfort' *add* 'Perth's brother.'

Om. 'of about £1,000 a year.'

For 'any of the' *read* 'two [of the].'

After 'attainted' *add* 'without any further process.'

For 'four' *read* 'two.'

After 'Carstares' deposition' *add* '(though it was not mentioned).'

For 'Upon this . . . executed' *read only* 'Upon this they were both condemned but not executed, for'; *and om.* 'then near eighty,' 'and that he
was condemned . . . manner,' *and* 'upon this . . . upon all this.'

[*f.* 121 (*b*)] *For* 'So it was pretended . . . pardoned' *read* 'Upon his confession he had his life and liberty.'

For 'and very probably . . . conclusion of' *read* 'which was certainly precipitated by his long and hard imprisonment.'

For 'which was so universally . . . believe it possible' *read* 'A man must
be presented with a very hard opinion of a government before he can believe
it capable of such acts of tyranny. An agreement is made with a man in torture
to persuade him to tell all he knows, and one part of it is that he shall never be
brought to be a witness against any person. And yet so barbarous an act of
parliament is made to bring about that under the colour of law, which is so
plainly contrary to all law. And thus a noble family and one of the ancientest
and worthiest gentlemen of Scotland was destroyed, though he was not
executed upon it.' (*This passage, as it precedes the two last, will be found on
f.* 121 (*a*).)

The duke of Monmouth's rebellion. [1. His preparations.]

Cf. *Hist.* i. 640 ('As soon as lord Argyll . . . ill-designed invasion'), *reading
for this* [*f.* 121 (*b*)], 'But now I return to the affairs of England, and to the
duke of Monmouth's business. As soon as Argyll was gone he set about his

[a] Cf. *Hist.* i. 632.

voyage with all the haste possible; he wanted money extremely, and none was remitted to him out of England, from which some about him endeavoured to convince him that things could not be so ripe as some hot people that came over studied to persuade him.'

Then return to Hist. i. 630 ('He had been indeed much pressed' *to* p. 631, 'freighted for Spain') [1].

For 'He had been indeed much pressed ... to venture' *read* 'The lord Grey, Mr. Wade [2], and Ferguson pressed him vehemently to venture; and some others that were poor pushed him on.'

For 'He could not have two armies ... equal terms' *read* 'They reckoned that if the king sent forces against him, the city, being thus left to itself, would rise; and with these imaginations they pleased themselves; all which they enforced the more since Argyll and his friends were gone to try what could be done in Scotland; so that they thought it unworthy of the English nation to see such an attempt made by the Scotch without vying with them in the like gallantry.'

After 'Fletcher' *add* 'of Saltoun, a Scotch gentleman of great parts, but very hot and violent, and a most passionate and indiscreet assertor of public liberty [cf. *Hist.* i. 630, *supra*], was now much in his favour. I, that bred Fletcher [3], should have expected that he should have driven him on to the mad attempt he made, but I know the contrary.'

. *After* 'much against it' *add* 'both in private with Monmouth and in their little councils.'

After 'reason; but' *add* 'he told him'; *and om.* 'in his enthusiastical way.'

After 'subject' *add* 'So Fletcher told him he would run fortunes with him, though he could not hope for great matters.'

For 'But Argyll's ... Spain' *read* 'Then Monmouth pawned all his jewels, and raised a stock of about 10 or 12 thousand pounds. He bought his arms and provided himself of a ship.'

[2. *He sails.*]

Cf. *Hist.* i. 640 ('The whole company' *to* p. 641, 'brought from the Hague').

After 'eighty-two persons' *add* 'a small number to conquer a kingdom.'

For 'some spies ... arms' *read* 'yet Argyll's business had given such an alarm, that Skelton, the king's envoy in Holland, got some hint of this. He was a very insignificant minister, who, notwithstanding his long practice in foreign affairs, had as little capacity for them as he had either good judgement or probity.' (Cf. *Hist.* i. 623.)

[*f.* 122 (*a*)] *Om.* 'those on board ... favouring them'; *and for* 'got ... Texel' *read* 'sailed away.'

---

[1] The reader will observe how very carelessly Burnet's revision has been made at this point. A passage which should have been continuous is not only divided in the printed version, but in so hasty a manner that a passage concerning the sale of Monmouth's jewels and the purchase of arms appears both on p. 631 and p. 640.

[2] Nathaniel Wade's confession (Harl. MSS. 6845, ff. 260–74) is one of the best and most trustworthy contemporary versions of the affair. He was a lawyer, who had been implicated in the Rye House Plot and had fled to Holland.

[3] See p. 89, *supra*.

After ' Hague ' *add* ' Thus the ignorance of the king's minister exposed his master to all the danger that he run in this matter, which was much greater than could have been imagined.'

[3. *His first steps.*]

Cf. *Hist.* i. 641 (' Upon the duke of Monmouth's landing ' *to* p. 643, ' acknowledgement and kindness ').

For ' He had quickly . . . arms' *read* ' He found that if he had brought ten times so many arms as he had, he would have found men for them.   Many blamed him for not going straight to Exeter or Bristol, where he would have found much wealth [cf. *Hist.* i. 643], and if he had been master of those places he would very probably have been able to have made a war of it.'

Om. ' as lord lieutenant of Devonshire.'

After ' deserted ' *add* ' others went over to the enemy.'

For ' that he was master . . . possible' *read* ' and if it is certain he erred extremely in the main of his conduct yet the de[tail][1] was admirable.   He shewed much temper and a good judgement in all he did.'

After ' rigour' *add* ' and [what it was] to be alone, without officers, arms, ammunition, or bread ; and (which was the cause of all the rest) without money.'

Om. the greater part of p. 642, *from* ' Soon after their landing' *to* ' preserved for that time,' *being the episodes of Grey (given later) and Fletcher (omitted entirely).*

For ' enraged man, that affected . . . dry' *read only* ' enraged preacher.'

After ' error, was that' *insert* ' seeing so few of the gentry come in to him.'

For ' and then march . . . Lime' *read* ' and that he did not fight those that were gathering the militia against him, for the beating of them would give him a great reputation ; and being spread abroad might induce many to come to him that would not declare till they saw some probability.   He might well have ventured countrymen that had made themselves desperate against other country-men that were less zealous for their side than his men were.   His lingering ruined him ; for [by this means] the king,' *&c.*

Before ' English and Scotch' *add* ' six.'

For ' and offered . . . necessary' *add* ' [and] sent over Mr. Bentinck to offer his person, and everything that depended on him, to the king's service.'

[*The king's dilemma.*]

[a]And no doubt the king was then in great straits in his own thoughts ; for if Monmouth had got any advantage, so that it had gone to a formed war, the king must either have taken help from the prince of Orange or the French. If the former had once been at the head of his troops he would have been master of his councils, and been able to have set laws to him,

---

[a] Cf. *Hist.* i. 643.

---

[1] Both transcripts read, erroneously, ' debate.'

and in that case the French no doubt would have supported Monmouth. But on the other hand, though no doubt the king's heart lay more to take help from France, yet by doing so he would have lost the whole English nation. It was visible enough that the king was all this while in great disorders, for how high soever he affects the reputation of an extraordinary courage, all that have been about him in great dangers have assured me he [*f.* 122 (*b*)] was as fearful as other men.

[*Parliament in England.*]

Cf. *Hist.* i. 638 (*from* 'At last' *to* p. 640, 'certainly passed ').

For ' At last ' *read* ' Some weeks before Monmouth's landing.'

For ' term of years ' *read* ' from three years to three years.'

Om. ' the revenue was granted . . . public treasure.'

Om. ' and the tide . . . opposition.'

For ' and set up . . . commons' *read* ' and was in full hopes of succeeding the earl of Sunderland, whose disgrace was still looked for, resolved to merit the king's favour.'

For ' even . . . matters' *read* ' even for their religion, which was dearer to them than their lives.'

For ' court flatterers ' *read* ' other flatterers.'

For ' So in . . . to them ' *read* ' and the house went into it ; so that both the revenue that the late king had and some other additional revenues were given to the king [*vide Hist.* i. 638, *supra*], and no new law was asked for religion, the house in their address of thanks for his speech having declared that they would rely upon his word.'

For ' When this ' *read* ' When the main business.'

Om. ' He said, it concerned . . . would not do.'

For ' This had no effect . . . debate' *read* ' So here was a brave attempt made but spoiled in the management, so that it had no effect.'

For ' The courtiers . . . designs ' *read only* ' There were several other laws proposed.'

For ' by which words . . . modelled' *read* ' The main point was whether words should be made treason or not. L'Estrange, and all the violent men, pressed this most vehemently ; but.'

Om. ' and were apt . . . variation.'

For ' in drink ' *read* ' rashly.'

For ' therefore he hoped . . . intentions' *read* ' therefore nothing ought to be made high treason, but that in which a man's mind did evidently appear.'

After ' insisted' *add* ' that words discovered men's thoughts, and.'

For ' he brought . . . words' *read* ' he told them he would convince them more fully out of a book which perhaps these gentlemen did not much study, but yet it had a good authority in the world ; the title of it was, The New Testament ; in it they would find that by a very small alteration treason was made out of our Saviour's words ; when it was sworn that he had [*f.* 123 (*a*)] said.'

Om. ' pronouncing it . . . imperceptible.'

After ' criminal' *add* ' among the Jews,' *and om.* ' This made . . . time.'

For ' But if the duke of Monmouth . . . certainly passed' *read* ' But if the parliament had got time to sit, the act would have passed ; and as it was drawn it would have brought everything that any man had said against any of the king's proceedings within its compass.' (Cf. *Hist.* i. 639, *supra*.)

[*Proceedings relative to the popish plot.*]

Cf. *Hist.* i. 640 (' The most important . . . Stafford ').

For ' The most important . . . lords' *read* ' Another thing that was set on foot.'

After ' lord Stafford' *add* ' which was so prepared as to carry it in [? in it] a total discovery [? discrediting] of the whole popish plot. For Oates had been attainted,' &c., *as from Hist.* i. 637, ' Oates was convicted,' *to* p. 638, ' hanged for it.'

After ' formerly. So' *add* ' a most terrible sentence was laid upon him.'

Om. ' he was condemned . . . from him.'

After ' rigour' *add* ' the hangman being no doubt ordered to lash him to purpose.'

After ' guilty' *add* ' which I doubt [i. e. fear] he was.'

Om. ' and was illegal . . . a precedent.'

Om. ' that I may join . . . distance of time.'

After ' And the king' *add* ' resolved to shew an equality in his justice, for he.'

Revert to Hist. i. 640 (' It was said for it . . . session to a conclusion ').

For ' said for it ' *read* ' said.'

For ' house of lords ' *read* ' house of commons,' *and om.* ' that they might . . . house of commons.'

After ' liberty' *add* ' (so easily are great matters brought to a conclusion at one time which cannot be compassed at another).'

For ' the lords had no mind' *read* ' there were many in both houses would have been much troubled if they had been put.'

[*The duke of Monmouth's manifesto.*]

Cf. *Hist.* i. 641.

Om. ' which was both . . . fulsome' *and* ' that the king's religion . . . crown.'

Om. ' very odiously . . . of style.'

[*f.* 123 (*b*)] *Om.* ' both in temporals and spirituals.'

[*His attainder.*]

Ibid. supra.

Begin ' Upon this the parliament passed an act of attainder,' *and om.* ' both houses . . . one day.'

Om. ' Some small opposition . . . severe a sentence.'

For ' which was no small . . . hurt' *read* (and cf. *Hist.* i. 639-40) ' which was so great a happiness to the nation that some will ever reckon Monmouth's landing to have been our preservation ; for it was plain that in the first heats of the parliament's loyalty it would have been hard to have stemmed the tide for anything the king would have asked.'

[*The command of the army.*]

Cf. *Hist.* i. 643 ('Prince George . . . army lay divided').

Before 'Prince George' *read* 'In a few weeks' time the king had an army ready to send against Monmouth ; and he gave the command of it to the earl of Feversham.'

After 'neglect' *add* 'and indeed.'

Om. 'who was a Frenchman . . . conceived.'•

After 'service' *add* 'but the greatest of all was that when he was within a few hours of Monmouth,' *and om.* 'and was almost . . . disorder,' *reading only* 'so that the duke of Monmouth had almost,' *&c.*

Monmouth's defeat [*and death*].

Cf. *Hist.* i. 643 ('He now saw his error' *to* p. 646, 'and to favourites').

Begin 'I am not well enough informed to describe the particulars of the action, and I will never forget an advice which the maréchal de Schomberg,' *&c. as Hist.* i. 49. 'All that I will say is that the duke of Monmouth saw now his error,' *&c.*

For 'and to be so straitened that' *read* 'and so could not keep his men together long. Therefore.'

For 'and when he came near . . . ditch' *read* 'and he could not get his men to venture the passing of a very inconsiderable ditch.'

For 'that the officers . . . dressed' *read* 'otherwise by all appearance he had quite surprised the king's army and routed it ; but.'

For 'longer . . . expected' *read* 'long and fought well.'

For 'upon the first charge . . . Grey' *read* 'which some imputed to the lord Grey's treachery, and others to his ignorance and cowardice.'

Before 'About a thousand' *add* 'yet above.'

After 'prisoners' *add* 'the rest dispersed themselves.'

For 'between five . . . thousand' *read* 'about 5,000 foot and 1,000 horse' (*this sentence occurs further on upon f.* 124 (*b*)).

For 'a man of courage' *read* 'a man of his courage,' *and omit remainder of sentence.*

Om. 'whom . . . him.'

[*f.* 124 (*a*)] *After* 'posture' *add* 'This was a great fall from having a few days before suffered a foolish pageantry of a coronation made, and had assumed the title and state of a king.' (Cf. *Hist.* i. 644, *supra.*)

For 'and his mind . . . low, that' *read* 'and this perhaps made him sink so much in his courage, for.'

For 'The king's temper . . . letters' *read* 'It was a great weakness in him if he fancied his life was a thing that could not be attained, and it was as great a meanness in him to ask that which could not be expected. In the injurious manner in which he treated the king, and after the rebellion that he had raised, he had put himself beyond mercy, even though the king's inclinations had been more gentle than they were.'

Om. 'But he called . . . Tenison.'

After 'his mother. This' *add* 'when they desired him.'

For 'He shewed . . . duchess and' *read* 'It is not likely that he considered his wife much in anything that he did ; for as he had for some years lived in a scandalous familiarity with lady Henrietta Wentworth, the heiress of the lord Wentworth's family, so he and she had been long in ill terms ; and upon this occasion either'; *om.* ' her sex and'; *and after* 'circumstances' *add* 'or she was very careful to preserve herself.'

For 'would have witnesses to hear' *read* 'brought the earl of Clarendon along with her to be the witness of.'

For 'to justify . . . family' *read* 'She desired him likewise to declare if she had been anyways privy to the last attempt of his ; in this he vindicated her ; but since he saw she was more concerned [*f.* 124 (*b*)] in herself than in him, the conversation was soon at an end.'

For 'very coldly' *read* 'a little too indifferently on both hands.'

For 'They next charged him with ' *read* 'They fell upon another head that was no less unpleasant to him.'

After 'consent' *add* 'so he did not think himself tied by that marriage.'

After 'as they did ; for' *add* 'though we do not practise confession, yet after all.'

After 'as little in him' *read* 'for they refused to give him the sacrament, since he expressed so little repentance for two such heinous sins as rebellion and adultery ; but they prayed oft with him.'

Om. 'He was much better pleased . . . dying man.'

After 'begged' *add* 'them to move the king for.'

After 'that' *om.* 'as,' *and for* 'so it gave . . . anything' *read* 'and it was thought he owed so much to his brother as to oblige him to grant this small favour to one that had been so near and so dear to him.'

Om. 'He prayed . . . unknown.'

After 'nation' *add* 'He also said somewhat in justification of lady Henrietta.'

[*f.* 125 (*a*)] *For* 'and understood . . . too much given' *read* 'but if he had obtained what he aspired to he would have given himself up.'

[*Reflections on his fate.*]

If he had not been hurried on to this business by the lord Grey and Mr. Wade, and forced to it at this conjuncture by Argyll, so that he not only came to England unprovided of men, arms, and money, but came at a time when, by reason of a session of parliament and the term that was sitting, most of those who were inclined to run fortunes with him were at London, and so were clapt up (the court having good hints of his design both by what Argyll was doing in Scotland and by some other discoveries), this fire had not so easily been quenched. He also committed great errors ; ª his landing in daylight discovered the smallness of his company ª and made it contemptible, whereas if he had landed in the night, as his true number would not

ª Cf. *Hist.* i. 641.

have appeared, so fear and darkness, that multiply their objects, would have given the first impression of this matter with more advantage; "and if he had marched straight either to Exeter or Bristol he would have been soon out of those extremities that lay so heavy upon him". If he had fought the trained bands, or had his men pursued the advantage that they had at Philip's Norton, matters had gone much otherwise; but, above all, if he had not been so extremely deceived as he was in his opinion of the lord Grey, whom he took to be a man of courage, and ᵇto whom he gave the command of his horseᵇ, this flame had not been so easily extinguished as it was. ᶜHe sent out Grey with the first party that he ordered and composed of some horse and foot, but Grey ran away as soon as he saw the enemy, and was with the duke of Monmouth the first of all; he told him a false story, that their men were defeated and had run for it; but when it appeared afterwards that the foot had stood, and beat off the enemy, and that he only out of fear had run away, Monmouth was strangely confounded when he saw that he was such a cowardᶜ. Afterwards, in the engagement at Sedgemoor, he shewed that he had neither courage nor conduct, and not only lost the whole business, but came and persuaded Monmouth that all was gone, so that it was necessary for him to study to preserve himself, in which he prevailed upon the easy nature of the other; so that it was no wonder ᵈhe got his pardonᵈ, for his cowardice did the king more service than the courage of any of his own officers had done him.

The executions of prisoners.

Cf. *Hist.* i. 647 ('The king was now' *to* p. 648, 'into those indecencies').

For 'The king . . . beginnings' *read* 'Now the rebellion was subdued, and the court was so lifted up upon it, that by their way of managing the advantages that they now had they lost the hearts of the nation, and quite spoilt their design of changing their religion and subverting the government of England; for.'

For 'execution' *read* 'prosecution in the way of justice.'

For 'such persons as' *read* 'those few that.'

After 'examples' *add* 'while the thing was yet warm in the spirits of the nation.'

ᵃ Cf. *Hist.* i. 642.   ᵇ *Ibid.*   ᶜ *Ibid.*   ᵈ *Ibid.* 646.

For 'and if he had but covered . . . designs' *read* 'this had given such an impression of the king and of the counsels, that it might have produced very fatal effects to the nation.'

For 'But his own . . . him lose' *read only* 'But the king's temper appeared too visibly upon this occasion, so that he lost'; *and for* 'that were . . . recovered' *read* 'which it is not like he will [*f.* 125 (*b*)] ever recover.'

Om. 'The army . . . counties where'; *and for* 'lived as in' *read* 'committed such violences even upon those who were no way guilty as if they had been.'

For 'and treated . . . violence' *read* 'and no complaints were so much as heard that were carried to the superior officers.'

After 'of law' *add* 'I have been told they were above twenty whom he thus murdered ; and to add to the barbarity of this fact, which was never before practised in England, he did it at the door of the room in which he received an entertainment.'

For 'and they were so brutal . . . called for' *read only* 'and all the while that those miserable people were thus destroyed he was in riot within, and had his music about him.'

For 'And it was said' *read* 'Russell [1], that was once a bedchamber man to the king, assured me.'

After 'manner of it' *add* 'It is hard on the one hand to believe that the king should have given him such an order ; yet on the other hand it is no less hard to imagine how a chiding was all the displeasure that was expressed upon it, if it was done without any order.'

Om. '(Some particulars . . . mentioned by me.)'

After 'sent' *add* 'two months after.'

For 'His behaviour . . . nation' *read* '[He proceeded] in a way little less barbarous than Kirk's had been ; no judge behaved himself in such a manner.'

Om. 'liker a fury . . . judge.'

For 'he shewed no mercy' *read* '[he] threaten[ed] the juries [for not bringing prisoners in guilty] when they saw such clear proofs.'

After 'distinction' *read* '[These] were all originals, and things which posterity will hardly believe.'

Om. 'The impieties . . . treated them and' *and* 'that were well affected . . . prisoners.'

Om. 'England . . . reckoned up.'

For 'But that which . . . and he' *read* 'But that which brought this matter near home to the king, was that he.'

For 'that he wondered . . . indecencies' *read* 'to his great regret.'

Om. remainder of paragraph.

Two women executed.

Cf. *Hist.* i. 648-50.

For 'The king apprehended . . . those who had served' *read* 'The king had a great mind to catch some prisoners that had escaped, and in particular Ferguson and some other preachers who he thought might be able to make great discoveries of those that had correspondence with Monmouth ; for though the court had occasion enough to satiate [*f.* 126 (*a*)] themselves with a great

---

[1] Mr. Russell, afterwards admiral.

deal of blood, yet all this brought in no booty to them ; for there were no men of estates found to be engaged in it, yet it was thought the preachers could make great discoveries of some rich citizens.'

Om. 'He went about . . . king had said.'

For 'her maid . . . house' *read* '[there were] some other presumptions.'

Om. 'But though . . . criminal part.'

For 'as the law directs . . . treason' *read* 'but she was first strangled.'

Om. 'as well as faith . . . enemy.'

For 'And behaved . . . manner that' *read* '[and] he never saw so much compassion in the looks of the spectators as appeared upon that occasion for.'

Om. 'desperate' *and* 'hoping . . . fortune' *and* 'into France.'

For 'piety and charity' *read* 'charity, and by consequence much esteemed in her country, so' ; *for* 'Hickes . . . Nelthorp' *read* 'two that had been in the rebellion.'

For 'She knew Hickes . . . Monmouth' *read* 'One of them was a preacher ; their names were put in no proclamation, so she knew nothing of their guilt ; but after supper they ventured to talk of it indiscreetly.'

After 'begged it' *read* 'and because her husband's guilt was like to lie heavy upon her, proof was offered that she had expressed as great horror of the old king's murder as any in England had done' ; *and for* 'so' *read* 'yet.'

[*f.* 126 (*b*)] *Om.* 'and though . . . guilty yet.'

Before 'not guilty' *read* 'twice,' *and after add* 'because there was no evidence to prove that she knew anything of their crime' ; *for* 'But the judge . . . attaint of jury' *read only* 'upon which Jeffreys threatened the jury so heavily.'

[*The behaviour of others.*]

Cf. *Hist.* i. 650–1 (*to* 'impetuous and cruel temper').

For 'most of those' *read* 'And indeed all those many hundreds.'

Om. 'and such a zeal . . . danger.'

Om. 'who had been . . . sheriff,' *and after* 'Cornish' *add* 'that had been sheriff of London.'

Om. 'and also said that.'

After 'temper' *add* 'who soon after had that reward of it to which he had so long aspired ; for lord North, whose spirit as well as his credit at court was much sunk [cf. *Hist.* i. 665], died, and Jeffreys not only had the great seal, but was made both lord chancellor and a peer[1] of England [cf. *ibid.*], and this was the price of all the blood he had shed.'

Preparations for a new sessions of parliament.

Cf. *Hist.* i. 651 (*from* 'The king had raised' *to* p. 652, 'so the motion fell').

Begin 'But I must now turn from this dismal scene to give an account of the session of parliament that came on in November.'

For 'raised . . . and' *read* 'during the rebellion.'

[*f.* 127 (*a*)] *For from* 'the first' *to* p. 652, 'it was said to be,' *read only* 'that it was.'

---

[1] Original note on f. 181 (*b*) (in the same hand as f. 2 ?), 'A mistake ; he was a peer before [two words illegible].' See also Routh's *Burnet's James II*, p. 99, note.

After 'idolatrous' *add* 'these were the commonplaces of all the flatterers at court.'

Om. entirely 'On the other hand . . . much altered.'

For 'did move . . . or not' *read only* 'spake of it twice at the council board.'

Om. from 'so the motion' *to end of paragraph.*

[*Same subject continued.*]

Cf. *Hist.* i. 654 (*from* 'The king after he had declared' *to* p. 655, 'pursue them too far').

For 'called for the marquis . . . turned out' *read* 'and because Halifax was the man of the greatest weight that was like to be on the contrary side, the king pressed him to give assurances of his concurrence; and upon his refusing to do it, he was turned out; yet the king did it with as great a grace as the matter could bear, and assured him he would never forget his past services.'

Om. 'And the earl of Sunderland . . . isle of Britain.'

For 'The Irish . . . household' *read* 'It was expected that Ormond should be turned out next, but the recalling him out of Ireland was thought disgrace enough, so he continued still lord steward, and this was left him in consideration of his old age and his great services.'

For 'So sir Charles . . . pursue them too far' *read* 'And so one Porter, who had got into some practice in the chancery in England, and was a furious man for the court, was of a sudden made lord chancellor, and was generally looked upon as a person raised to this height on design to destroy the settlement of Ireland, in which he has since that time disappointed the expectations that were had of him. But at this time the king said he would maintain the settlement of Ireland; though his promises now began less to be built on than they had been formerly.'

The affairs of Scotland; [king Charles' papers].

And that all his three chancellors might be of a piece, [a] the chancellor of Scotland came up at this time; he had fallen out with Queensberry, who is indeed naturally very insolent, and they came both up together to complain of one another. It appeared clearly that Queensberry had the better in all the points upon which they had quarrelled [a]; but upon that Perth and his brother Melfort resolved to have the better of him in one point, by which they reckoned they would carry all the rest. [b] The king began now to shew two papers that he had found in his brother's strong box, [c] all writ with his own hand [c], in which the necessity of an infallible judge was argued upon the common topics, but in very few words and very well expressed. [d] It was plain enough to all that knew the late king that there was too much art and too much

---

[a] Cf. *Hist.* i. 652. [b] *Ibid.* [c] But see *ibid.* 615. [d] *Ibid.*

scripture in these to be of his production[a]; and they had not the natural [*f.* 127 (*b*)] nor lively way in them in which he used to express himself. [b] He had to myself in discourse mentioned several arguments that I find there almost in the same words[b]; he proposed them to me as objections to our doctrine, and he had seemed satisfied with the answers I had made to them. I fancy [c] either Bristol or Aubigny writ them, and that they prevailed with the king to copy them in order to his considering them well, since it might have been made a great crime if such a paper had been found about the king writ in any other man's hand. [d] But now the king began to shew them, and Perth and his brother resolved to shew a new strain of courtship, and seemed to be converted by the force of those papers, which drew a repartee from Halifax that became very public. It happened that at the same time he was falling in disgrace, and that Queensberry was found to have the better of Perth in their contest; so Perth, meeting Halifax, made him a compliment as if they two were like to suffer both at the same time; but Halifax answered him, 'No, my lord, your faith will make you whole,' and it proved so.

[*Fate of Queensberry.*]

Cf. *Hist.* i. 653 ('Before he declared . . . made him a sacrifice ').

For 'So well satisfied with' *read* 'more inclined to '; *om.* 'that he was resolved . . . dismiss him.'

Om. 'not to be too much . . . at once.'

For 'between . . . Melfort' *read only* '[with] Perth.'

After 'sacrifice' *for* 'This sudden hatred . . . relation to religion' *read* 'So far does the king depart from a branch of his brother's character, as Shaftesbury [1] expressed it in one of his speeches; that under him the unfortunate fell gently.'

[*Remarriage of the earl of Perth; a tumult at Edinburgh.*]

Cf. *Hist.* i. 678 (*from* 'The earl of Perth prevailed' *to* p. 679, 'as much detested ').

Begin 'Perth's lady died about this time'; *and for* 'The earl of Perth . . . dying to change' *read* 'And they forced from her, while she was in her last agonies, a declaration of her changing.'

For 'for many years' *read* 'they being both in a married state. [He] was resolved to legitimate that matter; for both were now in widowhood.'

Om. 'The pope said . . . such importance. So.'

[a] Cf. *Hist.* i. 615.   [b] *Ibid.*   [c] *Ibid.*   [d] *Ibid.* 653.

---

[1] Original note on *f.* 181 (*b*) (same hand as f. 2 ?), 'Anglesea, qu.'

[*f.* 128 (*a*)] *For* 'The earl of Perth set up ... alarmed at this. And' *read only* 'Some time after this Perth, being at mass, very publicly.'

For 'Mr. Macom ... weak man' *read* 'The minister is to my knowledge a very honest man, but, as it will appear by the management of this matter, he is a very weak man.'

[*A fatal year to the protestant religion.*]

Cf. *Hist.* i. 655 (*from* 'This year' *to* p. 656, 'fifth great crisis of the protestant religion').

Preface it thus: 'But here I leave the affairs of Scotland and return back to England; the parliament was now to be opened [cf. *Hist.* i. 663], and the popish party was so confident that I saw by some long letters writ to cardinal Howard, and which he shewed me, for I was then at Rome, that they reckoned the matter sure [cf. *ibid.* 661]. Yet a remarkable revolution fell out in France that contributed not a little to the bringing the English nation back to their wits again [*ibid.* 664].'

After 'of Nantes' *add* 'and began that terrible persecution which has made so much noise in the world.'

The several critical times for the protestant religion[1]. *The first.*

Cf. *Hist.* i. 310 ('The first crisis').

Begin 'And I hope the reader will pardon my digression if I lead him to look back on the former four.'

The second crisis[2].

Cf. *Hist.* i. 311 (*from the words* 'the third crisis' *to end of* p. 313).

[*f.* 128 (*b*)] *For* 'And Spain ... stead' *read* 'And the conquest of England was then looked on as assured. For the opening of this I will acquaint my reader with some very curious transactions relating both to Scotland and England. The house of Guise and the king of Spain both agreed in their design of destroying queen Elizabeth and of setting up the queen of Scots, who was niece to the great duke of Guise; and as queen Elizabeth gave the chief support both to the protestants in France and to the States, so it was equally the interest of the king of Spain and the house of Guise to destroy her, and to set up Mary of Scotland that was the heiress.'

After 'invincible armada' *insert the following:*—

[a] It was of great consequence to this design to engage the king of Scotland in it, so his cousin, whom he afterwards made duke of Lennox, was sent out of France to insinuate

[a] Cf. *Hist.* i. 6.

---

[1] It is a curious testimony to the carelessness of Burnet's revision, that while, on p. 656 of the first volume, Burnet's original computation is preserved, and the year 1685 represents the fifth crisis; yet in an earlier part of the work a different division is adopted; and on pp. 310, 321 the year 1672 begins the fifth crisis. Throughout this part of the *History* (Burnet being no authority with regard to it) slight differences of statement are here ignored.

[2] On p. 311 of the printed *History*, the *second* crisis is placed in the reign of Mary I of England; the *second* crisis of the original forming the *third* of the revised version.

himself into his favour and to engage him into the project. He and the French ambassador [a] were always representing to him the barbarous usage of his mother, and how much it was against nature for him to be in the interest that had first defamed and then dethroned her, and that kept her now for so many years a prisoner [a]; they offered to assist him not only with great pensions from France, but to engage his mother to receive him next to herself, both in the crown of Scotland and England; and by these things they prevailed so much upon him, that was always easy to favourites and flatterers, that I find the [b] court of England were very apprehensive of his being prevailed on at last; [c] and in a paper of Walsingham's I find they thought he was likely to turn papist or to fall into a contempt of all religion; upon which queen Elizabeth took very subtle methods to give him so much work at home that he should not be able to hurt her. She employed both instruments and pensions to alarm all the most zealous, both of the nobility and clergy, with the prospect of their danger. [d] So that all that insolence of the assemblies and ministers of Scotland which archbishop Spottiswood sets out as the effect of their violence flowed from queen Elizabeth's agents, and the great jealousies the king's conduct gave this nation, as if he had been going into the interests [*f.* 129 (*a*)] of the house of Guise, and gives another view of all that matter [d]. But queen Elizabeth was not satisfied with this. [e] There was one sir Rich[ard] Wigmore, an English gentleman that was a lover of hunting and a man of honour [? humour], so that it was likely he might insinuate himself into king James. He was neglected and ill-used by the queen, so that he, pretending discontent, went and lived in Scotland; but all this was artifice, for he was underhand sent by the queen and received a long paper of instructions from secretary Walsingham [e], of which I have a copy [1]; which are indeed liker a book for their length than a memorial of instructions, and in these all this

[a] Cf. *Hist.* i. 6, *supra.*   [b] *Ibid.* 7.   [c] *Ibid. infra.*   [d] *Ibid.* 8.   [e] *Ibid.* 7.

[1] It is among the Burnet Papers in the Bodleian, Add. MSS. D. 23, ff. 213-22. (For other copies, see Mr. Airy's note *in loco.*)

design is very plainly opened. I have also the copies[1] of
most of the French ambassador's letters (which it seems some
of the court of Scotland that were in pension to queen Elizabeth opened and copied for Walsingham); by these I see [a] the
court of France kept king James long from marrying [a]. Both
queen Elizabeth and his own subjects pressed his marriage,
hoping that if he married to some protestant this would fix
him the more to that interest. But the French, as they saw
they could not engage the king to take a wife of their nomination and religion, so they resolved to divert him as long
as they could from marrying, which was all that could be
done at that time. Yet the French were still distrustful of
the king, for he complied sometimes with so good a grace
with the creatures of the court of England that they thought
they had lost him, [b] of which the ambassador gives this instance
in one of his letters.

Here insert anecdote of Stewart, Hist. i. 312 ('king James sent ... bedchamber,'
omitting 'But in one . . . resolutions'); *and then revert to* p. 311 ('All Europe')
and proceed to 'fatal to the queen of Scots' [*f.* 129 (*b*)]; *and continue from* p. 312
('As for the pompous embassy') *to* 'he would do nothing upon it,' *and from*
'But the court of England' *to end of* p. 313; *with these alterations on* p. 313 :—

After 'so powerful a fleet' *add* 'though after all it was built with very little
judgement, since it was to be sent into these narrow seas; the ships being
extreme heavy, so that it was not possible to work them.'

After 'London' *add* 'who had a vast trade in Spain.'

For 'undertook it' *read* 'brought this about in so ingenious a manner that it
is a pity that his name is lost[2], which indeed deserves to be immortal.'

[*f.* 130 (*a*)] *For* 'with which the great designs of Spain fell to the ground'
read 'and established the liberty of the protestant religion; the duke of Parma
made no progress after this time, and prince Maurice, though but a very young
man when he was set at the head of the States, quickly changed the scene.'

[*The third crisis.*]

Cf. *Hist.* i. 314; *ibid.* 12, 13; *ibid.* 314; *ibid.* 48–9.

Begin from Hist. i. 314 'The 4th [3rd][3] crisis was from the battle of Prague

[a] Cf. *Hist.* i. 7.　　　[b] *Ibid.* 312.

---

[1] Copies of papers in the State
Paper Office relating to Queen Elizabeth's intrigues with Scotland are in
the Bodl. Add. MSS. D. 23, ff. 202–7.

[2] Routh, note to *Hist. in loco,* identi-
fies him with Thomas Sutton, founder
of the Charterhouse.

[3] See p. 172, note 1, *supra.*

to the year 1630,' *and then revert to the affairs of the elector palatine,* p. 12
('[King James] married his only daughter ') *to* p. 13, 'without any assistance ';
with these alterations :—

(p. 12) *Om.* 'one ... sincere[st, but] ' ; *retain Airy's* 'one of the weakest
... all.'

Om. 'The eldest branch ... joined to advance '; *and for* 'the son of Charles
... king' *read* 'usurped the crown without an election.'

Om. 'But his government ... protestants.'

(p. 13) *Om.* ' first to the duke ... and then.'

After ' elector palatine' *om.* 'who accepted of it ... establishment,' *and read*
' Never was any design better laid. The cause of the Bohemians was just in
itself, for they were an elective and free kingdom.—And at the same time and
almost upon the same reasons Hungary also revolted and chose the prince of
Transylvania their king. The elector palatine was son-in-law to the king of
England and nephew to the prince of Orange, who was then the greatest general
in the world, and had raised himself to a great height of power over the States.
—And the protestant cantons were very much in [the] interest [of the newly
elected king].' (*These sentences are not continuous in the MS.*)

Om. 'The English nation ... support it.'

For 'was so possessed ... dignity' *read only* ' hat[ed] anything that looked
like a rebellion.'

For ' The jealousy ... towards him' *read* 'The electors grew jealous of the
greatness of the palatine family, since it had now two voices in the election of
the emperor,' *and return* [*f.* 130 (*b*)] *to Hist.* i. 314 (' not only the elector palatine
fell ... Austrian yoke'); *om.* 'All attempts ... his people'; *and after*
'Breda was taken' *add* 'and the Rhine was in the hands of the Spaniards.
At the same time the war of the Rochelle broke out in France, upon which
I must make another digression.' *Then revert to Hist.* i. 48, *as follows* :

When the duke of Buckingham went over to France to end
the match for the queen of England, [a] he made his addresses
so secretly and successfully to the queen of France [a] that he
obtained all favours of her, of which I know some particulars
that are not modest enough for me to write. [b] This being discovered, he was not suffered to return again as he intended [b],
who, what out of vanity, what out of amour, had resolved to
continue that intrigue ; and though he was in the chief
ministry, and in high favour in England, yet he had a mind
to have returned into France, but the court of France would
not suffer it, and pretended some other reason for the refusal.
[c] This enraged him so much that he got all the queen of England's French servants to be sent away. But he resolved to

[a] *Hist.* i. 48.   [b] *Ibid.*   [c] *Ibid.*

carry his revenges further; he shewed the king of England how much it was his interest to make the town of Rochelle rebel[a], and to form itself into a commonwealth under the conduct of the duke of Rohan and the protection of England. It had anciently revolted from England to France, and so it was but just to try if it could be brought to revert again. This seemed easy to be effected; France had then no fleet, and if this could be done the king would have France open to him, and the whole protestants to depend upon him. The design was great, and might have been easily executed if the king of England had been a vigorous prince. [b] The duke of Rohan was sent to[b], who had all the qualities necessary for such an undertaking, being one of the greatest men of this age, both for the councils of peace and war; and all the protestants of France, who began to be ill-used, depended on him. So he, who was then living in his country house and dreamt of no such thing, was easily engaged by the messenger that the duke of Buckingham sent to him to go into so great a design; [c] but when the court of France saw this, cardinal de Richelieu, who was the master of the king's spirit, persuaded him to order the queen to write a cajoling letter to the duke of Buckingham, telling him that if he would let the business of the Rochelle fall, the court of France would enter into great confidences with him, and he should be suffered to come over[c] as oft as he pleased to the court of France. This letter had so powerful an effect on him that he not only suffered some of the king's best ships to be hired by the French, but [d] he went on so slowly and feebly that he did nothing considerable the first year; but finding that the cajolery of the court of France was intended only to deceive him, he resolved to have followed that design with more vigour next year, but was prevented from executing it [*f.* 131 (*a*)] by being stabbed at Portsmouth[d]; and so that business of the Rochelle miscarried, and they were forced to make the best terms they could with the crown of France, by which they not only lost their own liberties, but by this rash

[a] Cf. *Hist.* i. 48. [b] *Ibid.* [c] *Ibid.* [d] *Ibid.*

undertaking the whole protestant party was now so exposed
to the indignation of the court, as well as become destitute of
all means of defence, that it is very probable the matter would
have been carried further against them if the exaltation of
the house of Austria and their successes had not determined
cardinal Richelieu, who was no bigot, to settle all matters
in France by a new confirmation of the edict of Nantes,
that so he might apply himself wholly to the affairs of
Germany.   Thus it appears that there was at this time
a great crisis upon the reformation, but all this went off by
a hand whence it was least looked for : [a] the great Gustavus
came in [a] with a very small but very good army, and as he
had great successes (most of the German princes declaring for
him), so if his own unhappy fate had not cut him off while he
was in so triumphant a progress he would very likely have
given matters a great turn the other way ; yet he did enough
to break this whole storm, so this crisis went over very happily.
One great design did indeed miscarry by the king of England's feebleness.

Here give the episode of the Spanish Netherlands from p. 48, 'When Isabella
Clara Eugenia,' *to* p. 49, 'lost his head for it.' (*The details are a little different.*)
   For 'stolen from him' *read* 'stolen out of his pocket or cabinet (which befell
him often, and which I am apt to believe is the truth of the matter).'
   After 'head for it' *add* 'and the king of England's honour suffered extremely
in that matter ; and so far have I carried my reflections on the third crisis.'

[*The fourth crisis ; passage introductory to it.*[1]]

Cf. *Hist.* i. 321 ; 314-6 ; 14 ; 316-7 ; 15 ; 317-8.
   Begin 'I now come to the fourth, which was in the year 1672 [cf. *Hist.* i.
321], when the crowns of France and England were united for the destroying
the protestant religion [*f.* 131 (*b*)], first in Holland, and then both in France
and England : I have said[2] so many things concerning this formerly that I
may have seemed to have satisfied my reader about it ; yet I have still a
reserve of many particulars for a new digression : I will not run so far back as to
mention things so well known as the wars of Holland, and the character of

[a] *Hist.* i. 314.

---

[1] The fourth crisis of this version
(1672) is the first part of the fifth
crisis in the printed *History*, vol. i.
p. 321.   As material prefatory to
the fourth crisis, the original version
includes however much that was subsequently ranged under the fourth
crisis of the printed *History*, 1620-30.
   [2] i. e. *sub anno* 1672, in the lost
portion of the original narrative.

William, prince of Orange'; *and then revert to Hist.* i. 314 *and proceed from* 'All agree' *to* p. 316, 'predestination firmly,' *omitting* ' but as he left . . . popery.'

Om. 'It seems he designed . . . prince's hands.'

For 'This was much opposed . . . methods' *read* ' There is a strange thing in the spirit of churchmen of what side soever they may be, for they go always into violent and cruel methods [1].'

Om. 'Their ministers . . . write afterwards.'

For 'When the queen . . . Leicester' *read* ' So, since the earl of Leicester was so much in queen Elizabeth's favour that it even gave matter to censure, they offered him a new power which began and ended with him.'

Before 'he as . . . landed' *add* [*f.* 132 (*a*)] 'He came over; and though he was known to be a very atheistical man'; *om.* 'went . . . counsels, and'; *for* 'people' *read* '[ministers].'

After 'Holland and Zealand' *add* 'before [Leicester] got to the Hague. This was not inconsistent with the charge of supreme governor, though it was a great check upon it; and as Dudley was soon after as hateful as he was popular at first, so prince Maurice became the most celebrated captain of his age.'

Om. rest of paragraph and 'Prince Maurice was for . . . political views.'

For 'Prince Maurice in private . . . Arminians' *read* ' Prince Maurice, that leaned more to Arminianism, headed the Calvinists; at least he was as long a trying which of them upon the division was like to be the strongest, as the States had been in the beginning of their reformation in deliberating whether they should authorize the Calvinist or the Lutheran confession.' *Then revert to Hist.* i. 14 (*Fabricius' story, derived from Charles Lewis, elector palatine*).

Om. 'the wisest . . . among them.'

For 'This that elector . . . himself had' *read only* 'So little do most princes consider religion any other way, than as it may serve to advance their own ends.' *Then return to Hist.* i. 316, 'I will go no further,' *to end of* p. 318.

[*f.* 132 (*b*)] *For* 'He hated Barneveldt . . . hands,' *insert the whole story as given in Hist.* i. 15 ('The States having borrowed . . . wisdom [2]'); *in which for* ' Soon after . . . secret article, he' *read only* ' Barneveldt.'

For 'and he came over . . . proposition' *read* 'The sum and the interest of it was vast; and king James' courtiers were glad to have so much money to be dealt among them. But his councillors thought there was no danger in a civil offer of delivering up those places when the money should be ready, for they fancied it would not be possible for the States, that were so deep in debt, to raise it.'

For 'an action . . . wisdom [2]' *read* 'but as soon as ever king James found that this had drawn on him, not only the contempt of all foreign princes, but of all his own subjects' (*then return to* p. 317, 'according to the nature,' *&c.*).

After 'carry it much further' *add* ' whether it was because '; *after* 'horror' *for* 'He studied . . . free state' *read* ' or because the great business of Germany was overturned (for though he had an ascendant over his nephew the king of Bohemia in everything, yet he could neither infuse his own sense or his courage into him), or whether he really had no further designs, I cannot determine.'

---

[1] Airy's ed., i. 565, note a.
[2] Ed. 1833 gives last clause wrongly to Onslow.

Om. 'quickly settled . . . tenets. He,' *and* [*f.* 133 (*a*)] 'The States . . . rich.'
Om. 'much to the honour . . . myself have to it.'
For 'It was a common . . . his widow was' *read* 'which did not at all please
the princess royal, for she had no mind to make way for the widow.'
Om. 'and it struck his fancy . . . stadtholdership.'

[*Passage prefatory to the fourth crisis continued; John de Witt.*]

[a] Upon the prince's death, those who had been sent to
Loevestein had so great credit that the government fell into
their hands, and De Witt the father got [*f.* 133 (*b*)] his second
son John, who was then a young advocate of twenty-five years
of age, made at first pensioner of Dort, and after little more
than a year made pensioner of Holland [a], who continued for
twenty-two years in the ministry with the greatest applause,
but ended it with the greatest misfortunes possible.

De Witt's character.

I will give his character as I had it from Mr. Halewyn,
who knew him well and valued him highly. His being so
early brought into the government gave him not time for
making any great compass in learning, so that as he had not
travelled in his youth [b] he had never time enough to read
history [b], and even in his own profession he rather [c] knew the
practice of the law [c] than the principles and history of it; so
that as to all acquired dispositions for the chief ministry, he
was as ill furnished as ever man was. [d] His strength as to
learning lay in the mathematics, in which he was one of the
greatest men of the age, and made a progress in them which
astonishes all those who have been able to understand his
Elementa Curvarum [d], and his *Loca Geometrica*; for it passes
imagination to see a man in the midst of so many affairs
carry his thoughts so far into abstruse matters. But to
balance all his defects he had a vivacity of apprehension and
a strength of judgement that were indeed amazing ; [e] he made
himself quickly master of everything that was laid before
him, and scarce ever took things by the wrong handle; he
had much patience in hearing everything [e] that was said to

[a] Cf. *Hist.* i. 220.   [b] *Ibid.*   [c] *Ibid.*   [d] *Ibid.*   [e] *Ibid.*

him, and was neither guilty of pride, passion, nor revenge; he was not corruptible, neither by money nor other artifices; and he was a man of undaunted courage, even in military matters, which is not ordinary for a man of the robe. [a] He showed this in his going to sea in the year [16]65 and [16]66, where Mr. de Ruyter confessed[a] that he taught him many things in his own art[1], in particular a new method of drawing up the fleet in bataglia; and [b] as he had himself examined and sounded the sea near the Texel, he discovered so many new channels, that the ships could go out with many more winds than they thought they could have done formerly[b]. He laid the design of burning the English fleet at Chatham, in which he reckoned he was so sure, that in the orders that were to be opened at sea for executing it, the matter was not referred to a council of war. He was for many years as much the master of the government of Holland as any stadtholder had ever been, but he built his whole administration upon a very weak bottom.

[*His error.*]

Cf. Hist. i. 319 (*to* ' immediately to the States ').

[*f.* 134 (*a*)] *After* ' the States themselves ' *add* ' of whom the greater part does not understand them.'

[*Reflections on this topic.*]

Now this seems to be the most essential error in the whole Dutch constitution; for, as I have often seen it in a house of commons in England, [c] a great body is the most improper subject of power in their hands[c]; and the more numerous the body is the state is still the safer, there being less room for corruption in such an assembly; for our house of commons acts and deliberates wisely, when they examine the conduct of the ministry, and upon that enter into the consultations either of making laws, raising money, or of examining the grievances of the nation; but whensoever the king thought fit to ask their advice, it was apparent how poorly they consulted if they happened to descend to more particular propositions.

[a] Cf. *Hist.* i. 221.　　[b] *Ibid.*　　[c] *Ibid.* 319.

[1] See *Hist.* i. 229.

[*De Witt's errors resumed.*]

Cf. Hist. i. 319 ('It had been happy ... miscarriages on him ').
After ' of the courts' *add* ' of justice.'
For 'This raised ... hands' *read* 'Another great error in his ministry was that he engrossed the secret of all affairs, especially of foreign negotiations, wholly to himself.'
After 'miscarriages' *add* ' in [16]72.'

[*De Witt's character resumed.*]

There was no part of the ministry in which he was so exact as in the conduct of the revenue ; for ªhe had digested that into a little table-book, that he carried always about him, so. exactly that upon all emergencies he knew what the state could do ; and how far their revenue would carry them in any proposition that was made to him ª. Having given De Witt's character so largely I will not enter further into the particulars of his ministry, neither will ˙I say anything of the war with Cromwell, nor of the peace made upon it, nor ᵇ of the exclusion of the prince of Orange, and the perpetual edict made against having any more stadtholders ᵇ ; nor will I say anything more of ᶜthe war that he managed with the late king of England, in which he acquired so much reputation both as a statesman and as a commander, that the war ending with [*f.* 134 (*b*)] so much advantage and honour to the States, all this raised his credit extremely, which was then so much shaken by the factions that were formed against him ᵉ, that a misfortune in that war had certainly sunk him.

[*Neglect of the prince of Orange.*]

All the world was ᵈamazed to see the court of England take so little care of the prince of Orange's interests, as never to interpose for him : ᵉfor the Triple Alliance gave England a great credit in the Dutch counsels as long as our court was true to it ; and that the prince was then growing near his majority, yet no endeavours were used to open a way for his coming into the government of Holland. ᶠThe prince went over in person to try what could be hoped for from the court of England ; he had also a private business to solicit,

ª Cf. *Hist.* i. 220. ᵇ *Ibid.* 320. ᶜ *Ibid.* 319. ᵈ *Ibid.* 320. ᵉ *Ibid.* 321.
ᶠ *Ibid.* 273.

which was the payment of that great debt which the king owed him [a], which amounted to some millions; but he succeeded equally ill in both. It seemed very strange, to all that observed this coldness of the court of England in his concerns; for it was certainly very much the king's interest to raise one to the government of Holland, who, as might be naturally imagined, must needs continue still in a great dependence on him, and need his assistance very much; since this one thing must have raised the figure that the king made in the affairs of Europe more than all the other projects that he ever engaged in. I have often talked of this matter with those who were then in the ministry and could not wonder enough at the king's not seeing his own interest in this matter. I knew his majesty's temper too well to wonder at his want of natural affection to his nephew, or at his want of gratitude for all the obligations that had been put on him by the prince's father and mother during his exile; in such things the king had taken such care to let his nature be known, that nobody could be surprised with new discoveries of it. But here his interest lay so visibly that it was indeed strange to see him mind it so little; but all the answer that was made to me upon this question was that the king's recommending the prince to the States would rather have set him backward than forward; for if the States intended to bring him into the government, they would make it their own act, and have him beholden for it to them only, and not be contented that he should owe any part of the obligation to a foreign prince. This looked rather like an excuse than a reason; for though it is very probable that a public recommendation might have been a prejudice to him, yet secret and vigorous offers underhand could not have hurt him. But the true reason was that France, that still had its eye upon the conquest of Flanders, saw that nothing could oppose them in that but the exaltation of the prince of Orange, which would naturally put the land army of the States in another posture, and have animated them into a more martial disposition. And since it was the

[a] *Hist.* i. 273.

interest of France to have this so laid that it might not be an obstacle to their designs, our court resolved to sacrifice the interests of a nephew to so [*f.* 135 (*a*)] dear a friendship[1]. ᵃ Perhaps the prince's firmness to the protestant religion had a share in this aversion; ᵇfor he told me himself that when he was first in England, the king discovered very plainly to him that he was a papist, and insinuated to the prince his advice to him to be of the same religion, which surprised the prince extremely; and he has often wondered how the king came to trust so young a person with so important a secret ᵇ. As for his debts, our court, that was so lavish in all its expense, never troubled itself with such matters; for though a recommendation of that to the parliament for many years together would have easily procured a much greater sum, yet our court had still so much occasion for all the money that could be raised from a house of commons that they were never in a condition to do justice to any or to pay their debts ; so that the prince was abandoned by his uncle, and therefore he was to try how to insinuate himself into the hearts of the Dutch.

[*Youth of the prince of Orange.*]

Cf. *Hist.* i. 320 ('The prince was left much to himself' *to end of paragraph*).
For ' yet as his natural . . . recommended him much to ' *read* ' yet he behaved himself so discreetly in his youth that he gained great ground, especially with.'
For ' to raise . . . happy ' *read only* ' for the making a party to him.'

[*The fourth crisis ; elevation of the prince ; invasion of the provinces.*]

Cf. *Hist.* i. 320 (*from* ' When he was of full age ' *to* p. 322, ' Pomponne and Louvois ').
For ' When he was of full age ' *read* ' At last the wars with France came on, and then.'
Om. ' could only be meant . . . army ; but,' *and* ' The court of England . . . in their affairs.'
For ' cold . . . depend upon him ' *read* ' civil and cold ; so that he saw his friendship was no more to be depended on.'
After ' age ' *om.* ' and he believed . . . faithfully,' *and add* ' Soon after that followed the vast progress that the French made ; for whereas.'
[*f.* 135 (*b*)] *For* ' nor practice . . . spirit nor courage left ' *read only* ' and a long peace at land had put them out of all practice.'
After ' to be done ' *add* ' but their delivering themselves so shamefully as

ᵃ Cf. *Hist.* i. 273.   ᵇ *Ibid. supra.*

---

[1] His interests were not ignored in the Treaty of Dover.

they did brought not only infamy on themselves, but the greatest danger possible to the States, for all was set open to the king of France, who,' *&c..*

For 'the Dutch with so . . . up to him' *read* 'such a terror in the country, that their not being wrought on by that panic fear to deliver all up to him is one of the wonders of the age, and the driving back such a torrent looked like the effect of some happy star that was over the prince of Orange.'

For 'than to his own conduct' *read* 'than either [to] his own valour or conduct.'

For 'that, when that year . . . may be' *read* 'that I make no doubt to make it appear when I have memoirs to enable me to write more particularly of that matter.'

After 'preserve himself' *insert* ' If he had either followed the prince of Condé's or Mr. de Turenne's advice the thing had been sure ; but he would examine the matter rather with the ministers than with those two great captains. His army was indeed reduced to a small number by his keeping so many places which he ought to have dismantled' (cf. *Hist.* i. 332). *Insert capture of Noerden and Muyden* (cf. *Hist.* i. 323, 'The French,' *to* p. 324, 'preserved Amsterdam') ; *then return to* p. 322, 'When he came.'

For 'Pomponne and Louvois' *read* 'Louvois,' *and add* 'and the king was impatient to return to Versailles' (cf. *Hist.* i. 332 *to* 'preparing for him there ') ; *and proceed* 'He left behind him the brutalest man and the most unfit for softening the spirits of his newly conquered places that could be found, in Mr. de Luxembourg' (cf. *Hist.* i. 333).

[*Despair at the Hague; mission sent to England.*]

Cf. *Hist.* i. 323 ('It may easily be imagined' *to* p. 325, 'gained the court').

Om. 'The French possessed . . . extremities of despair' (*see supra*, ll. 16-7).

After 'garrisons in them' *add* 'so that they had not above 7,000 men left for their defence.'

Om. 'and the bishop . . . spirit was left.'

Before 'Montbas' *insert* '[It] gave some ground to [these] jealousies that.'

For 'married . . . sister' *read* '[was] brother-[*f.* 136 (*a*)] in-law to Mr. de Groot (or Grotius), who had been ambassador in France the former winter.'

Om. 'which was to defend . . . sanctuary,' *and for* 'and the States were so puzzled . . . and followed it' *read* 'and cried out for a peace ; and since it might be hoped that the setting up the prince would separate England from France, which was the only thing in which they could trust.'

Om. 'And the morning in which they were dispatched away.'

For 'the prince . . . stadtholder' *read* 'the raising the prince of Orange.'

Om. 'lord Arlington . . . doing it, that.'

After 'press that on them' *read* 'They were ordered to see what it was that would content the king ; but they had no power to conclude anything. Mr. de Witt, who did not take so much care as was necessary to have good intelligence, fancied that the court of England would insist on making the prince stadtholder.'

For 'When they came over . . . gained the court' *read* 'And when Boreel came first to them he seemed likewise assured of it ; but he quickly found his mistake ; and indeed the ambassadors were amazed when they found that the court of England was not concerned at the prince's interests, and that it was not possible to separate them from France.'

The States treat with France.

[a] So the States were forced to treat with the king of France ; but the debate falling out between Mr. Pomponne and Mr. de Louvois [a], the last carried it, very happily for the Dutch. The former proposed the danger of making the Dutch desperate, and of engaging all Europe and perhaps England at last in the war (since the people of England were against them, though the king was for them). He therefore [b] moved that the king should restore all that belonged to the seven provinces, and only ask the places that they had out of them [b]; that the States being brought so low, and without an army as well as without all places, they would no more provoke the king, who might by that means [c] easily make himself master of the Spanish Netherlands, and after that the States would be at mercy. If the king had followed this counsel it is not likely that the Dutch would have refused to comply with it [c], and it would have certainly turned to their utter ruin within a few years. But Mr. de Louvois drew up the most extravagant terms that could be imagined, in which he complied both with the bigotry and the vanity of the French king; for [d] besides the public exercise [1] that he asked for the popish religion, he moved that the States should send once a year an ambassador to the court of France with a great medal acknowledging the protection that they had received from thence. The extravagance of this [d] made both it and the king as ridiculous as the other articles were insupportable to the States: for they would not have been a people if they had accepted them. But now the aversion that the Dutch had to the De Witt family and their inclinations to the prince came to a crisis. For the populace began everywhere to make tumults and to complain of the government, and this at last produced that great change which has been so copiously set out that I can add nothing to that which is generally known concerning it.

[a] Cf. *Hist.* i. 322.   [b] *Ibid.*   [c] *Ibid.*   [d] *Ibid.*

---

[1] A glance at Mr. Airy's note, *Hist. in loco,* will shew that Burnet's original version is here more accurate than the revision.

The prince of Orange's exaltation.

Cf. *Hist.* i. 326 ('I need not relate . . . carry it any further').

For 'I need not relate . . . bound by it' *read* 'The government of the towns was changed, and the prince of Orange was declared stadtholder, and this dignity was to descend to his posterity by inheritance[1].'

After 'their town' *add* [*f.* 136 (*b*)] 'which was carried to him by Ho[o]ft; and no doubt it would have been followed by all the other towns.'

[*Return of the mission sent to England.*]

Cf. *Hist.* i. 325 ('The Dutch . . . agitation').

Begin 'The ambassadors that were sent to England, finding that they could not prevail with the court, returned[2]; but.'

For 'ran together . . . numbers' *read* 'above 200 men got together.'

For 'for they heard . . . Brill' *read* 'which had been infallibly executed.'

For 'the next day' *read* 'that very day.'

[*Murder of the De Witts.*]

Cf. *Hist.* i. 325-6 (*to* 'greatest horror possible').

Begin 'I love not . . . so often printed (*as on* p. 326); *then proceed* (*as on* p. 325) *to the accusation of Cornelius, for* 'At the same time . . . prince. There were' *reading* 'The barbarous[3] accusation against Cornelius de Witt had'; *for* 'which was supported . . . circumstances' *read* 'that I have heard many say'; *and for* 'Yet Cornelius . . . innocence' *read* 'though he was a violent obstinate man, who had neither his brother's abilities nor virtues.'

Revert to the attack on John de Witt (p. 325), *for* 'De Witt was once . . . spectators' *reading* 'The attempt made on his brother's person, who showed as much personal courage as presence of mind in defending himself from it, was too severely punished, for though the crime deserved death, yet De Witt ought to have considered better than he did what the time would bear; for the execution of that assassin inflamed the people more against him'; *then proceed to* 'De Witt's going' (p. 326).

For 'the prince spoke of it' *read* 'he speaks of it.'

Conduct of the preachers.

[a] Some of the ministers shewed upon this occasion that violence which belongs to their character[4]. Des Mares of Groningen[5] in some printed theses insinuated that the

[a] Cf. *Hist.* i. 326.

---

[1] This statement, erroneous as to date, was corrected in the final revision; see Airy, note a, *Hist. in loco.*

[2] The *History* says they were sent back.

[3] Qu. 'barber's'?

[4] i. e. their function; see *supra*, p. 178.

[5] This probably refers to the famous Samuel des Marèts of Groningen, who died there May 18, 1673. See *ante*, p. 91, note 2. He is said to have written a *Catechesis Publica* which appeared at Groningen in 1672, and a *Brevis Discursus*, dated August 23, 1672. Query if these are the works mentioned? As regards responsibility for the republication, Burnet clearly con-

judges had been corrupted who had not carried the judgement against Cornelius de Witt further, and spoke so in a sermon that he preached soon after at the Hague; he insulted upon their death, and compared them to Haman; and though it was too much to have said this at that time, yet he has carried [*f.* 137 (*a*)] this further, and has not struck out the virulent expression, but has printed it among his sermons a year ago.

[*Heroism of the prince.*]

Cf. *Hist.* i. 326 (*from* 'The prince's advancement put new life' *to* p. 327, *end of paragraph*).

For 'The prince's advancement' *read* 'The state of affairs in Holland took another ply; all that were in the former administrations had lost their credit with the people; but the great confidence that they all put in the prince.'

For 'tried to bring... very little' *read* 'were sent over to mediate the peace.'

After 'so high' *insert* 'and the English were so true to him.'

For 'That duke... as of his own' *read* 'Buckingham told a passage relating to the prince to a friend of mine that cannot be enough commended; he said that when he was once pressing him to come into the French project, by shewing him the advantages that he himself might find in it.'

For 'and he would never... of his own' *read* 'and he would only consider their concerns, and not make so infamous a bargain as to sell them for his own ends.'

After 'ditch' *add* 'This had indeed much of the hero in it. I will not carry this matter further, my design in all this digression having only been to shew how that by so unpromising a revolution as the exaltation of the prince of Orange this great crisis that was at that time upon the protestant religion went over.'

[*Excursus on*] the prince's marriage.

Cf. *Hist.* i. 408 '([Danby] got the prince of Orange' *to* p. 409, 'very ill consequences').

For 'He got... campaign' *read* 'But the affinity of the matter leads me to set down here the secret of the prince of Orange's marriage, since upon it the next probable revolution of Europe is like to turn; and it was told me in all its circumstances by Montagu, who was upon the secret of it [*see* p. 411]. After the campaign in the year 1677 broke up Danby advised the prince to offer to come over to satisfy his uncle of his conduct, who was highly dissatisfied with him for opposing the peace.'

After 'marriage' *add* 'and sent [*f.* 137 (*b*)] over an express to divert the king from it, at least to keep him to that of giving the prince the hopes of the marriage only after the peace was made.'

---

fuses Samuel with one of his sons, presumably Daniel, the younger, who was a preacher at the Hague 1662– 89, and a favourite of the Prince of Orange (see Van der Aa, xii. 212.)

Om. 'The campaign . . . over.'

For 'But they could not . . . left to him' *read* 'Danby had desired him never to move the marriage, but to leave that wholly to his care. The prince, after he had stayed some weeks in England, seeing no fruit of his journey neither as to public nor private concerns, began to grow impatient ; at last Danby took his opportunity.'

For 'after he had taken . . . directed' *read* 'he told the king that all his friends over England had signified to him that the king had now an occasion of getting out of all his troubles, and that if he let it slip out of his hands, he would hardly ever recover it again.'

For 'the king would lose . . . thanks of it' *read* 'the prince would owe the obligation to the parliament.'

For 'even . . . consequences' *read* 'it would give greater jealousies than were at present, and would spoil all the king's affairs.'

[*Danby urges an immediate marriage.*]

[a] In short he pressed this with so much force on the king, that he agreed to it [a]. Upon that Danby insisted, and shewed the king that if he intended to do it, the best and easiest way was to declare it immediately; otherwise both the court of France and his brother's priests would use all possible means to obstruct it. Now an easy way of doing a thing had always a charm in it to gain the king. Perhaps another consideration that Danby offered had great weight, because there was somewhat like art and artifice in it; he said that as the king's doing it before a session of parliament would prepare a way to compass all his other designs, so he added that he saw the prince was of a temper not to be wrought on by ill-usage; but if he used him kindly the king might gain such an ascendant over his spirit, as to govern him, and by that means he might govern all Europe. To all this the king yielded so frankly that he resolved to put an end to it before anybody thought that it was begun, so [b] he presently sent for the duke, and told him that the treasurer had proposed a matter to him that he saw was extremely for both their service, that therefore he expected that he would concur heartily with him in it, and that he would give him in this a mark of his friendship in agreeing with him. The duke, who did not know where all this would end, said that the

[a] Cf. *Hist.* i. 409.

king knew how ready he was to obey him in all things, so that he needed not use so much preamble with him; upon which the king named the marriage. Danby saw a concern in his looks; ᵃ yet he complied in words heartily enough how averse soever he might be inwardly to it. Upon this Danby ᵃ, who would not trust the king by himself till this was past recalling, since the miscarriage of it would have been infallibly his own ruin, ᵇ sent for the prince of Orange ᵇ, who was surprised at this proposition, which was now [*f.* 138 (*a*)] further advanced than he could have imagined. ᶜ Danby put the king further, and moved that an extraordinary council might be presently called, which was done; ᵈ and there the king declared his designs, and then carried the prince to St. James' and presented him to his niece.

[*French reception of the news.*]

Cf. *Hist.* i. 410 (*from* 'Barillon was amazed' *to* p. 411, 'above two hours').

For 'had ordered . . . husband' *read only* 'besieged him so that it was impossible.'

For 'when was the marriage . . . forsaken him' *read* 'If he had no news from England? And when Montagu told him he had none, the king told him the news.'

For 'on the duke's part' *read* 'of the duke's failing to him, and of his ingratitude.'

For 'The prince had no mind . . . satisfied with them' *read only* 'though the last was but a general compliment.'

Om. 'As he would have done . . . army; and.'

After 'two hours' *add* 'and so he told him how he managed it'; *and om. remainder of paragraph.*

[*Montagu accuses Danby.*]

A few months after that Montagu and Danby fell out most mortally[1]; and in an expostulation that they had together in the king's presence, Montagu thought to give Danby a severe blow by telling the king that he had not misrepresented himself worse to the king than he had done the king to himself; since he assumed to himself the whole praise of that marriage by which the king ought to have been

ᵃ Cf. *Hist.* i. 410. ᵇ *Ibid.* ᶜ *Ibid.* ᵈ *Ibid.*

---

[1] For this affair see *Hist.* i. 391, 422, 439, and Mr. Airy's notes *in locis.*

recommended to the affections of his people; but he told me the king was no more affected with it than if it had not at all concerned him. I have told this story more particularly than perhaps was necessary, but my design is to shew that the greatest affairs upon which the greatest consequences depend are sometimes brought about with less labour than perhaps would have been needful for the procuring the smallest office in the court. But having said so much of the prince of Orange, and it being likely that if I have long to continue this work ᵃ I may have occasion to say much more both of him and the princess ᵃ, I will here give their characters.

The character of the prince of Orange [1].

The prince has shewed by his conduct and action that notwithstanding all ᵇ the defects of his education ᵇ, and his total want of literature, nature is capable of producing great matters, even when she is not at all assisted by art. ᶜ He has a great application to affairs ᶜ, and turns them much in his thoughts, and indeed perhaps too much; for his slowness in coming to a resolution is much complained of; but if he is slow in taking up a resolution he is as firm in adhering to it. ᵈ He has a vast memory, and a true judgement ᵈ, for he [*f.* 138 (*b*)] sees presently the critical point of any matter that is proposed to him. ᵉ He is the closest man in the world ᵉ, so that it is not possible so much as to guess at his intentions, till he declares them: he is extreme calm both in council and actions, and hears very gently things that are said to him, even when he is not pleased with them [2];

ᵃ Cf. *Hist.* i. 691.   ᵇ *Ibid.* 689; and ii. 304.   ᶜ *Ibid.* i. 689.   ᵈ *Ibid.* ii. 304.   ᵉ *Ibid.*; and i. 689.

---

[1] This character, which from its date (1686 or 1687) is of particular value, should be compared not only with the two characters mentioned above, but with the additional passages quoted in Dr. Routh's *Burnet's History of James II*, p. 147 note. Those features were probably deleted, simply to avoid repetition, as they occur in the more elaborate character *sub anno* 1702.

[2] The reverse is asserted in *Hist.* ii. 304; the fact no doubt being that William after the Revolution openly resented Burnet's interference (see *infra*). Cunningham distorts this love of intermeddling into a restless 'pursuit of dignities,' and affirms that he blackened William's character in revenge (i 254).

but he has the haughtiness of a great mind [a]not to forget too soon injuries done him, but he has never been observed to affect revenges[a], only he does not easily return to confidences with those that have offended him. [b]His courage[b] is indeed greater than it ought to be, and though it was very fit for one that had the ambition of arriving at the reputation of his ancestors to hazard his person sometimes, that so it might appear that he was a soldier as well as a general, yet his great carelessness of all personal danger both in time of peace and war has been censured as excessive; for to [c]see him go about with a footman or two[c] when so much depends on his life has been called rather a tempting of providence than a trusting to it. This some have [d]ascribed to his belief of predestination, as if that pushed him on headlong in this confidence that all things will be as God will have them. But though [e]he is firmly persuaded of predestination[e], yet he said to me, he never reflected upon it in any of his counsels before things fall out; but he owned to me, when things fall out, the belief that God would have them so quieted his mind much, and has helped him to bear many misfortunes and disappointments very easily. This is his peculiar carriage and the nature of his courage, that it does not sink with misfortunes; for when things have miscarried in his hands, he has been observed to have the same calm equality that he had upon happier occasions. He understands the government of Holland exactly, and if he does stick in some things too close to his rights as he is stadtholder, yet he has often assured me that he has never gone beyond them. He has great virtues; he is temperate and sober; if [f]he has been guilty of any of the disorders[f] that are too common to princes, yet he has not practised them as some to whom he is nearly related have done, but [g]has endeavoured to cover [1] them[g]; though let princes be as secret as they will

[a] Cf. *Hist.* ii. 305.   [b] *Ibid.* 304.   [c] *Ibid.* i. 689.   [d] *Ibid. infra.*   [e] Cf. *ibid.* and ii. 305.   [f] Cf. *Hist.* i. 690.   [g] *Ibid.*

---

[1] Burnet's clumsy endeavour to soften this charge in the corresponding portion of the printed *History* has laid him open to the most sinister

in such matters, they are always known. But a sincerity and a round plainness is of all his virtues that upon which he values himself most; and that justly, for he is very eminent in it even for a private man; and this is so extraordinary a virtue in a prince, that it is the more singular in him, since he has very little of it round about him. [a] He seems to have a real sense of religion, and looks like a man that is in earnest when he is worshipping God[a]. He is a hearty enemy to popery, and in particular to the cruelty of it; for [b] he is a great enemy to persecution on the account of religion. [c] He thinks the church of England ought to be maintained, but softened a little both with relation to the nonconformists at home and to the foreign churches beyond sea[c]. He has a coldness in his way that damps a modest man extremely, for he hears things with a dry silence that shows too much of distrust of those to whom he speaks. He seems to have made it a maxim to be slow in everything of resolution he takes, and this he carries too far, that he makes those to whom he intends to shew favours wait on so long that the grace of giving them is much lost by the slowness; and he does not seem enough to consider the sourness of spirit under which men languish that are perplexed with incertainty and want. [d] He has a true notion [1] of government and liberty[d], and does not think that subjects were made to be [*f.* 139 (*a*)] slaves; but after the laws and foundations of government are overturned by those who ought to maintain them, he thinks the people may assert their freedom. He is a close manager of his affairs, and though [e] he spends much in building[e], yet he is not thought

[a] Cf. *Hist.* ii. 305.   [b] *Ibid.*   [c] Cf. *ibid.* i. 691.   [d] *Ibid.*
[e] Cf. *ibid.* ii. 305.

misconstructions. He has been supposed to insinuate a secret love of dram-drinking, while yet darker interpretations have been freely hazarded by political partisans (as for instance by Swift, ed. 1824, iv. 218; *A Short Review on. . . Burnet's History*, *by a Gentleman*, 1724, p. 35; Cunningham, i. 254). The context here however shews that he had in view the prince's intrigue with ElizabethVilliers. See Onslow's note to *Hist.* ii. 240.

[1] This seems to mark again a considerable alteration in Burnet's views since the year 1683; though it is not by any means so strong as Burnet's subsequent version of his own views at the time, *Hist.* i. 691.

so .free-hearted and generous as a great prince ought to be. His martial inclination will naturally carry him, when he comes [1] to the crown of England, ᵃ to bear down the greatness of France ᵃ ; and if he but hits the nature of the English nation right at first he will be able to give laws to all Europe ; for in this single point the greatness of England may appear, that not only it is full of wealth and people, but that in time of war the only expense to which the nation is put is the keeping a great fleet at sea, by which the money circulates within the kingdom ; but the defensive part costs the nation nothing, no garrisons nor strong places being necessary. So that a king of England that governs well at home may make war against all Europe together, and neither be exhausted nor endangered by it. But if the prince does not in many things change his way, he will hardly gain the hearts of the nation ; ᵇ his coldness ᵇ will look like contempt, and that ᶜ the English cannot bear ; and they are too impatient to digest that slowness ᶜ that is almost become natural to him in the most inconsiderable things ; and his silent way will pass for superciliousness. But that which ·is more important, he will be both the king of England and stadtholder ; the Dutch will perhaps think a king of England too great to be their stadtholder, and the English will hardly be brought to trust a prince that has an army of 30,000 men at his command so near them. If this matter is not settled upon the first opening his succession to the crown of England, there will arise a train of jealousies upon it, that being fomented (as they will certainly be) from France, may throw us into a mistrust that will perhaps never be healed. This and another particular, that is too tender to be put in writing [2], are the only things that can hinder him from being the greatest king that has been for many ages.

ᵃ Cf. *Hist.* ii. 305.   ᵇ *Ibid.* i. 690.   ᶜ *Ibid.*

---

[1] i.e. in due course, as husband of the heiress-presumptive.

[2] The allusion may be to the Villiers intrigue ; see p. 191 and note, *supra.*

The princess's character.

The princess was born with all the advantages of nature, [a] [? dignity] [1] and sweetness mixing almost equally in everything that she did or said. [b] She has a vivacity of thought, a liveliness of apprehension, and a correctness of judgment that surprise all that see her ; [c] she has all the cheerfulness in her that becomes her age [2], but tempered with such an exactness of decency [c] that those who had observed her deportment long, with a sort of malicious criticalness, wishing to find somewhat to censure, have protested they could never find it. [d] In her devotions there is a solemn gravity that edifies all that see her ; there is no sort of affectation in it, but yet there is an exactness both in her secret and chapel devotions and at sacrament that shows that she does not think the sublimity of her rank exempts her from the strictest duty of Christianity. [e] She has accomplished herself by reading a great variety of books, both in divinity, history, [f] and poetry, and she forgets very little of whatsoever she reads. [g] She has a modesty and humility in her that wants a name, and that gentleness with which she charms all people is of so peculiar a composition, that at the same time she seems to invite them to a familiarity, she inspires them with respects [g]. She is much animated against popery, [h] and seems to have a true notion of government, that the chief end of power ought to be the doing [*f.* 139 (*b*)] of good. [i] She is certainly in all respects the best wife that ever was [i], the most united to the prince in friendship, confidence, and affection, and if she governs as well as she obeys, her reign will be the happiest that ever was. In short, considering her age, her education, and the company that has been always about her (who have never been able to exalt her), she seems to be a person raised and

[a] Cf. *Hist.* i. 690.　　[b] Cf. *ibid.*; and *Essay on the . . . late Queen* (1695), pp. 71-3.　[c] *Essay*, 61.　[d] Cf. *ibid.* 97-9.　[e] *Hist.* i. 690 ; *Essay*, 73, 78, 79. [f] *Essay*, 79, 80.　[g] *Ibid.* 68-71.　[h] *Ibid.* 92.　[i] *Ibid.* 125.

[1] A word seems to have been omitted here.
[2] She was then about twenty-six. In an undated and unpublished letter to Dr. Fall, which must belong to 1686 -7, Burnet describes her as ' the most wonderful person that I ever knew ' (Bodl. Add. MSS. D. 23, f. 1).

prepared by God Almighty to make the nations happy; of which she herself thinks so little, that one [1] having [a] presumed to ask her if she knew her own mind so far as to apprehend how she could bear the king's having a son, she answered [2], she did not care to talk of these things, lest it might seem an affectation; but she believed she should be very little troubled at it, for in all these things the will of God was to be considered, and if it were not for the doing good to others, she said for her own particular it would be perhaps better for her to live and die what she was. [b] She is hearty to the church of England, but will never be drawn in to like the superstition and fierceness of some of our divines; for she thinks we have aggravated too much the matters of conformity [b]. All that I can possibly set against this character is that [c] she is the most reserved person alive, unto whose thoughts no creature can enter further than as she discovers them [c]; and that her goodness is too general without carrying her into the particularities of friendship with any person. Her closeness is the strangest thing that ever was seen in one of her age and sex, and gives some colour to fear there may be something under all this secrecy. Her engaging into no friendships may be justly enough resolved in this, that she has not yet had any ladies about her that were capable of it [3], otherwise it looks like a mind too much recollected within itself, when it does not flow out into some vigorous friendship. [d] I am sensible I have not set faults or defects [d] enough in opposition to all the princess's virtues; but I protest I have taken all the pains I could to seek for them; for I know the good I say of her would be the better believed if I had mixed more ill things with it, but it will appear almost incredible that one of her birth and way of breeding should have come into

[a] *Hist.* i. 754.   [b] Cf. *Essay*, 74.   [c] *Ibid.* 61.   [d] *Ibid.* 55-6, 89.

[1] Burnet himself: he ascribes the incident to the year 1686—at a time when the queen had no expectation of offspring (see *Hist.* i. 754).

[2] Compare *Lettres et Mémoires de Marie Reine d'Angleterre*, 1880, p. 62.

[3] Her principal ladies so far had included Elizabeth Villiers, her husband's mistress from 1680 onwards; and Jane Wroth, who became the mistress, and was at this time the wife, of Count Zulestein.

a strange country when she was but a little past fifteen, and that [a] during her ten years' stay in it she has never said nor done the least thing that has given any offence [a] to any one person whatsoever, and that neither the difference in religion nor the sorriness of the ministers or of some of the sects here, nor the factions that are against the prince, have produced the least censure of any of her actions. [b] When one talked once to her of this, she said it was a particular blessing of God to her, for she was confident there were many others that had fallen under much censure, that had as little deserved it [b]. I have been a little longer than ordinary on their characters, but the great figure that they are like to make in the world will well justify it. But to this I will add a short character of those who have the greatest share in the prince's confidence.

Bentinck's character.

Mr. Bentinck was bred about the prince, and he observed in him that application to business and those virtues that made him think fit to take him into [c] his particular confidence, and to employ him in the secretest of all his concerns [c] as well as the looking to all his private affairs. He is a man of a great probity [*f.* 140 (*a*)] and sincerity, and [d] is as close as his master is [d]. He bears his favour with great modesty, and has nothing of that haughtiness that seems to belong to all favourites. He is a virtuous and religious man, and I have heard instances of this that are very extraordinary, chiefly in a courtier. He has all the passion of a friend for the prince's person, as well as [e] the fidelity of a minister in his affairs [e], and makes up the defects of his education in a great application to business; and as he has a true and clear judgement, so the probity of his temper appears in all his counsels, which are just and moderate; and this is so well known, that though commonwealths can very ill bear any inequality of favour that is lodged in one person, yet I never heard any that are in the government of the towns of Holland complain of him; nor does he make those advantages of his favour which were ordinarily made by

[a] Cf. *Essay,* 122-4.   [b] *Ibid.* 87-8.   [c] *Hist.* i. 781; ii. 5, 306.   [d] *Ibid.* 306.   [e] *Ibid.*

those that have access to princes, by employing it for those
who pay them best.   I do not know him well enough to say
much concerning him; but though I naturally hate favourites,
because all those whom I have known hitherto have made
a very ill use of their greatness, yet by all I could ever
discern, the prince has shewed a very true judgement of
persons in placing so much of his confidence on him.

Fagel's character.

[a] The pensioner Mr. Fagel is profoundly learned in the law,
and has quick apprehensions of things, and dispatches
matters with great easiness [a] (which he had needs do, for he
has a great load of affairs on him, and is very ill furnished
with secretaries).   [b] He has a very copious, popular eloquence,
and is a very fit person for carrying matters before him in a
great assembly, which made Mr. de Witt take great notice of
him and bring him up from being pensioner of Haarlem to
be the greffier or secretary to the States General, which is
one of the best places in Holland.   He continued long in
a great confidence with him, and he concurred with great zeal
in the making the perpetual edict, for he negotiated that
business with those of Friesland, who opposed it most [b]; yet
he turned to the prince's interests, and has served him ever
since his elevation with great fidelity and zeal.   [c] He is a pious
and virtuous man, only he is thought too eager and violent [c],
and one that pushes matters with too much force.   He has
not great notions, nor has he studied to raise men of merit so
much as he ought to have done, but [d] he is too partial to his
family and kindred [d], who, being numerous, are raised up by
him to the best employments of the state.

Dyckveldt's character.

Cf. *Hist.* i. 328.

For 'Dyckveldt . . . interest lay' *read only* 'Mr. Dyckveldt was a man much
trusted by Mr. de Witt, but upon the French progress in the year [16]72 he.'

Before 'Upon the French' *insert* 'Yet after all that compliance lessened him
so much that'; *and for* 'left out' *read* 'turned out.'

After 'temper' *add* 'he being perhaps the smoothest man that ever was
bred in a commonwealth.'

[a] *Hist.* i. 327.   [b] *Ibid.*   [c] *Ibid.* 328.   [d] *Ibid.*

Om. 'and he had a great share . . . deserved it.'

After 'Europe' *add* 'and a long practice in the government at home.'

For 'and great practice . . . embassies' *read* 'He is very fit for embassies, and it is believed that he loves them.'

For 'He spoke . . . He was' *read* 'He speaks long and slow, but with great weight ; he is a man of a [*f.* 140 (*b*)] good understanding, and.'

Halewyn's character[1].

Cf. *Hist.* i. 328-9.

Om. 'a man . . . Dort, and.'

Place 'was the person . . . most' *in present tense and om.* 'and was next . . . confidence' ; *and continue in present tense.*

For 'but most particularly . . . authors' *read* 'and understands the state of Greek and Roman commonwealths beyond any man I ever knew, except Algernon Sidney ; so that the Roman authors, being equally dear to us both, have afforded us much matter of discourse.'

Om. 'He spoke . . . life.'

For 'the best models . . . authors' *read* 'the ancient Romans.'

After 'justice' *add* 'I believe his natural temper carries him to have quick resentments of auguries ; yet he governs this so, that I could never perceive it, though I have put him upon subjects to fish it out.'

After 'notions' *insert* 'of public liberty,' *and om.* 'Christian.'

After 'and went in' *insert* '[to] the common maxims of that time [and].'

After 'yet he' *insert* 'has told me that he' ; *and after* 'error' *insert* 'in their present constitution.'

After 'sovereign power' *insert* 'together with the whole legislative power.'

For 'must be' *read* 'can never be upon a sure bottom till it is.'

For 'He thought it' *read* 'And therefore he told me that it was.'

After 'affairs' *add* 'and his own unacquaintedness with them.'

After 'rank ; yet' *add* 'he told me.'

For 'He observed . . . always in' *read* 'He also told me that he came to observe in the prince's whole conduct that he was in.'

[*f.* 141 (*a*)] *After* 'themselves' *add* 'and therefore, though he was one of the latest that engaged in his interests, yet he seems to be the most convinced of all that I see, that the interests of the prince and the country are now the same.'

[Introduction to the character of Van Beuning]; the error committed by the town of Amsterdam.

[a] Mr. Van Beuning has appeared so oft in all the courts of Europe, and has been so long in England, that his character is much known. [b] He bore a great stroke in the affairs of Amsterdam for many years [b]; but before I speak of him, I will give some account of the interests and maxims of that great city, where the security of harbour and its being so uneasily come at has brought together an infinite wealth, which is generally

[a] Cf. *Hist.* i. 330.   [b] *Ibid. infra.*

---

[1] See p. 383, *infra.*

accompanied with much city pride, which is one of the haugh-
tiest and most ungovernable things that can be imagined. It
was their adhering so long to the Spanish interest in the first
formation of the States that had almost crushed them in their
first beginning. Since that time, as the vast disproportion of
their wealth to all the other towns must needs give them
a great share in the counsels, so their want of men who have
studied or travelled enough to be statesmen, and whose views
are wide enough for government and that are not measured
by the small regard to a present interest of saving of expense,
has been the cause of many great errors in the conduct of
affairs, of which I will mention some. The West India
company was one of the best stocks of Holland: they had
sixty good ships, and had procured a good establishment in
Brazil. All the towns of Holland had a considerable share in
this, but because the ruin of this company was the raising the
East India company, of which Amsterdam had the half, and
was the depressing of many other towns, they would not
concur in the preserving it when the Portuguese, upon their
revolt from the Spanish yoke, studied to recover Brazil and
to drive the Dutch out of it ; so ª the company, not being supported by the States, fell to nothingª, and Brazil was abandoned
in the year 1652, to the great prejudice of the States. After
the peace of Munster the town of Amsterdam forced the States
not only to an excessive diminution of their land forces, but
to such a neglect of the fleet that many of their men-of-war
were sold. After that, when the late king went to Scotland,
though it was visibly the interest of Holland to keep England
embroiled at that time, and not to suffer it to form itself into
a commonwealth ; yet they pressed that which is upon all
such occasions the worst counsel, which was a neutrality in
that quarrel, whereas it is plain that they should have either
entered into an alliance with the new commonwealth or they
should have openly supported the king against it, whereas they
did enough to provoke England, but not enough to depress or
weaken it. And upon this occasion I call to mind a severe

ª *Hist.* i. 221, 330.

passage that is in a letter of cardinal Mazarin's, of which Mr. Brisbane[1] shewed me the copy. It was writ from Bayonne when he was concluding the peace of the Pyrenees, and addressed to Mr. Dehorne. He tells him that he had held some conferences with the king of England and his ministers, for he had gone thither to get himself to be included in that peace. The cardinal writes that his ministers were a [*f.* 141 (*b*)] set of men who, if he had a kingdom, could well help him to lose it; but he saw none of them that had any views to help him to get it. Yet he adds that he was of opinion that it would be the interest of both crowns to concur in procuring his re-establishment, for if England could once form itself into a commonwealth it would soon draw all the trade and the wealth of the world to it, and therefore it was the interest of the crowns to take care to hinder that; and it seems he thought there would be no great danger of that if the king were put in possession. And according to this maxim it was the interest of the States above all others to hinder the forming of the commonwealth of England. But now I return to the errors that the managery of Amsterdam has made the States commit.

[*Error with regard to Munster.*]

Cf. *Hist.* i. 221, 'When the bishop . . . up to the States,' *omitting reference to Westphalia, and adding* 'so this was brought under debate'; *then revert to* p. 330, 'It was then demonstrated . . . many millions.'

For 'in Westphalia' *read* 'if they should happen to need them.'

[*Error with regard to the barrier.*]

Cf. *Hist.* i. 331 ('Another error . . . Amsterdam made to it').

Om. 'as Halewyn[2] . . . Holland over.'

Om. 'and have become . . . conduct.'

After 'made to it' *add* 'though the advantages of this to the States are too visible that they need to be insisted on.'

Error with regard to the English alliance.

And in [16]73 their haste to make a peace with England on any terms made that they would not insist on demanding a ratification from the parliament of England, which had been a thing often practised in the alliances that were

---

[1] See *ante*, note 2, p. 110.   [2] See Mr. Airy's note a *in loco*.

made between the crown of England and the house of Burgundy. This was much desired by all in England that wished well to the States, for if the king had been held to that of procuring a ratification from the parliament, so that the session of parliament had been continued a little longer, they had engaged him much further, and would have carried the king not only to a peace with the Dutch, but to an alliance with them against France. And after the peace of Nimeguen, when the court of England proposed a new alliance with the States, it was then moved that a ratification in parliament should be demanded, but those of Amsterdam would not concur in urging it. It must be confessed that the States had the more reason to insist on this, since the attempt made on the Smyrna fleet [1] had shewn them how little reason they had to depend on the king's word. It would have indeed been a great diminution to the king, and would have shewn too plain a distrust of him, since [though] the parliament did confirm our treaties anciently, yet it is near 200 years since the practice was discontinued ; but if a king will break his faith, it is [*f.* 142 (*a*)] no wonder if his neighbours ask a greater security than his own word. [a] But after all this it does not appear that those of Amsterdam have the ambition of making themselves the Rome or Venice of the country [a]. They do not seem to have such an elevated ambition ; and during De Witt's government, when several of the towns of the smallest interests and that had the fewest good heads among them were for diminishing the authority of the courts of the Hague, [b] they of Amsterdam were not at all guilty of it [b], though the depressing of those courts is the readiest way to make them the Venice of all the provinces. But I now return from all this digression to Van Beuning's character.

Van Beuning's character ; [conclusion of fourth crisis].

[c] He has great notions and talks perpetually. He can never be convinced by others, because he hears nobody speak but himself ; but at the same time there appears too much levity

[a] Cf. *Hist.* i. 221.   [b] *Ibid.*   [c] *Ibid.* 330.
_____
[1] See *Hist.* i. 307.

in all his own thoughts.   He has changed so often, and failed
in so many of his promises, that either it flows from a great
inconstancy of temper or [a] falsehood in his nature; though
I believe it flows rather from the former[a]; but by this he is
become now as much despised as he was once esteemed by his
countrymen.   I will go no further in the character of men in
Holland, but will now return to the thread of my history, from
which I have wandered so long upon the occasion that the
fourth crisis that befell the protestant religion gave, which was
when the king of France was at Utrecht, and that was so
happily dissipated by the exaltation of the prince of Orange.

The fifth crisis of the protestant religion; [*Ruvigny's errand,
persecution in France*].

I go next to the fifth, under which we are at present.   The
court of France was not sure which way the king of England
would turn him, with relation to the affairs of Europe.   Upon
which I will set down a great secret.   Mr. de Ruvigny had
been, as was told, in England for many years during the war,
and no doubt he had got all possible engagement from the
king, while he was duke, to be always true to the interests of
France; he had also penetrated so far into the duke's thoughts
that it was believed no man knew him better than he did.   So
the king of France intended to send him over; but he, who
at 82 years of age was the closest man in Europe, resolved
to manage this so artificially that the true design of his
journey could not at all appear.   [b]He writ to his niece the
lady Russell, and told her that, he having writ a letter of
congratulation to the king upon his coming to the crown, he
had received so obliging an answer that he saw the king
desired an occasion of shewing his kindness to him, and therefore he intended to come over in person to beg of him the
restitution of her son to his father's honour.   [c]Halifax presently
took the thing right, that this was only a blind art[c]; to come
over in person at that age and to ask a favour that required
no haste was such an extravagant piece of friendliness that

[a] *Hist.* i. 330.   [b] *Ibid.* 657.   [c] *Ibid.* 658.

he was persuaded there was a mystery in it. So I being
then going over, [a] the answer was referred to me. I pressed
Mr. de Ruvigny not to think of it; I told him that in such
a matter as her husband's life his niece had indeed begged
of him to undertake the journey, but that a title for her son
was too inconsiderable a thing for her to venture a life that
was so dear to her in order to the obtaining it. I pressed
this often on him, but found him always so fixed on it that
it was easy to discern there was somewhat under it [*f.* 142 (*b*)].
I knew he had an audience of the king of France of above
two hours before he went away, and in England he had some
very long audiences of the king. But though all the voyage
passed on the account of the lady Russell's son, yet a general
promise, without specifying the time when, was all that could
be obtained; upon which nothing has followed since that time.
So that the true secret of the matter was his searching into
the king's designs [1]; and immediately upon the assurances
that the king of France received of his adhering firmly to his
interests [a] he went to finish that great design which he had
been carrying on so vigorously for several years, but which
was not yet ready to be finished, if the affairs of England had
not seemed to offer so promising a conjuncture. [b] For several
months the dragoons had orders to go through Béarn and
Languedoc, and to live upon free quarters on those of the
Religion [b], committing all possible insolencies, till they should
force them to abjure their religion. This was so violent and
so unlooked-for a method that the surprise of it, as well as
the rages that the dragoons broke out into everywhere, [c] had
a terrible effect on all; [the] people, some few generous con-
fessors only excepted, complied. The court, animated by this
success [c], and set on always by the assurances that they had
from England, gave now the last blow and [d] repealed the edict
of Nantes, that had passed with so much solemnities that it
was made a perpetual and irrevocable edict [d], that the king had

[a] Cf. *Hist.* i. 658.   [b] *Ibid.*   [c] *Ibid.*   [d] *Ibid.* 659.

---

[1] The revised version of this incident, given in the *History*, was no
doubt obtained, after the Revolution,
from the Ruvigny's themselves.

sworn to maintain at his coronation, and that he confirmed in almost all the edicts that he put out against the Religion, which at the same time that they enacted the most visible infractions of that edict that were possible, yet contained plain and positive confirmations of it in clauses that were as formal and express as words could make them. This was done with a boldness of impudence that no former age had ever seen; and because that king will be an original in assurance, [a]there was a clause put in this new edict giving those that were of the Religion a positive promise that they should not be disturbed in the secret exercise of it[a], nor forced to any exercises that were contrary to it; [b]and yet at the same time troops were ordered to march into all the parts of France where any of the Religion were to be found, and to quarter upon them till they had eat them up[b]; and then they were to be thrown into prisons, where great numbers of them have continued ever since, firm under a course of miseries that cannot be matched in history.

[*Further cruelties.*]

Cf. *Hist.* i. 660 (*from* 'such as endeavoured' *to end of paragraph*).

Om. '(for guards . . . France).'

After 'monasteries' *add* 'and for such as had abjured they were required to assist oft at mass, and at the other functions of that religion; and when they were sick, they were required to receive the sacrament under the pain of death if they should recover.'

After 'bodies should be' *add* 'dragged through the towns and.'

For 'and it gave . . . let fall' *read* 'and is the maddest part of this whole persecution.'

For 'even with more . . . felt' *read only* 'with horror.'

For 'with a sort of contagion' *read* 'in all the parts of the kingdom.'

For 'seemed now to have laid . . . humanity' *read* 'received such directions from the court, and saw how much a rigorous diligence would recommend them, that all France seemed a scene of brutal and barbarous fury.'

For 'The great part . . . especially' *read only* 'The clergy.'

[*Burnet's own experience.*]

Cf. *Hist.* i. 660-1 (*to* 'journey together').

[*f.* 143 (*a*)] *Begin* 'I saw much of this myself; I stayed at Paris only till,' &c.

For 'Barillon . . . myself' *read* 'Mr. Barillon sent me three several advertisements during the duke of Monmouth's business, advising me to go from Paris.'

[a] Cf. *Hist.* i. 659.   [b] *Ibid.* 658.

For 'some . . . suspicion' *read* 'fall such suspicion'; *and after* 'business' *add* 'that he thought I would do well to look to myself.'

Before 'Whether' *insert* 'Whether this was sincerely meant or.'

For 'for in that time . . . managed. But' *read* 'Therefore I writ answer that.'

For 'of concealment' *read* 'in my thoughts, would do nothing that looked like guilty.'

For 'examined and tried' *read* 'taken, that so it might appear that I was afraid of no discoveries.'

For 'Stoupe, a brigadier . . . journey together' *read* 'I came by a secret way to know certainly that a persecution was coming on; so I was not unwilling to take an occasion of travelling into Italy with colonel Stoupe.'

[*Fate of the principality of Orange.*]

Cf. *Hist.* i. 663 (*from* 'And then I went through' *to* 'possession of the prince of Orange').

For 'And then' *read* 'And at my return.'

For 'I intended . . . neighbouring places' *read* 'That which was the strangest of all was that many that were in the neighbourhood of the principality of Orange.'

For 'who commanded . . . parts' *read* 'a colonel of dragoons.'

After 'into the town' *add* 'and [quartered them] upon all of both religions, but most heavily on the protestants.'

For 'and they plied . . . done' *read* 'and [they] were forced to abjure.'

[*Reflections on the same.*]

[a]This was not only a plain infraction of an article of the treaty of Nimeguen, in which the principality of Orange was comprehended, and for the observation of which the crown of England was guarantee[a], but it was such an indignity to the king to treat his son-in-law and his next heir in such a manner, that [b]many have concluded that the French would never have adventured on it without they had first obtained the king of England's leave[b]; and in this no doubt the French had a deeper design than barely to rob the prince of Orange and to ruin the principality. It is probable that they expected that the prince, finding that the king of England would not execute the treaty of Nimeguen in this article, would have made great complaints of it in all the courts of Europe, and that this might have made a breach between them, which it was their interest to promote by all means possible. But the prince proceeded more moderately, and behaved himself so prudently on this occasion, that if

[a] *Hist.* i. 663.   [b] *Ibid.*

a breach comes he will have this advantage in the dispute, that he can say he sacrificed his own concerns [*f.* 143 (*b*)] and made no complaints (but to the king himself) upon his abandoning him in his own particular. The king seemed to resent the thing, and ª ordered his envoy at Paris to give in a memorial complaining of the invasion of Orange ª, to which the answer that was given was that the French ambassador had orders to satisfy the king; but no satisfactory answer being made, the envoy had orders to put in ᵇ a second memorial, which was conceived in very high terms ᵇ and setting forth the importance of the invasion contrary to the peace of Nimeguen, which the French king was at so much pains to procure; and of which the king of England was guarantee, besides the near relation that was between him and the prince of Orange. This was like a memorial preparatory to a denouncing of war; but all the answer that was obtained was that the king of France had taken his measures in that matter which he could not alter, and with this the king of England was satisfied, and upon it ᶜ writ to his daughter that he could do no more in that matter, unless he could make a war upon it; and he did not think it of that importance ᶜ. And thus, after two threatening memorials, he quitted this matter so poorly that he laid himself open either to the suspicions of having consented to it at first, which was indeed a betraying of his son-in-law, or of a strange lowness of spirit in submitting to whatsoever France should impose upon him, which was an open declaration for the French interests as well as a partial injustice [query ' particular injury *or* injustice '?] to the prince.

[*The king's parsimonious treatment of the princess.*]

He committed another great error with relation to the prince; his brother had settled on him and his posterity for ever an estate that was now above £120,000 sterling a year; and if one brother took such care of another, it might have been expected that a father would not be less kind to his own children, but that he should have divided the estate

---

ª Cf. *Hist.* i. 663.   ᵇ *Ibid.*   ᶜ *Ibid.*

that he had as duke of York between his two daughters.
ᵃ Yet as he never set off any appanage for the princess of
Orange ᵃ, so the princess of Denmark has but thirty thousand
pounds a year, which is so exhausted by a great establishment
that she is really extreme poor for one of her rank. If the
king had settled good appointments for the princess of
Orange, as the kindness of it must have made some impression, so ᵇ it would have given the nation a great jealousy
of the prince, as if the king and he had still understood one
another; whereas the king looking on and seeing him robbed,
and assigning him nothing for supporting the princess's
dignity with more lustre, was an open declaration to the
world that the king had no regard to him ᵇ; which was
the worst of all the maxims that a king who was not like
to retain the affections of his people long could possibly take
up. For this naturally leads all his subjects to look to the
rising sun; and animated them with much more spirit than
they could have ever had, if the king had managed the prince
more artificially.

[Effect of the persecution on English opinion.]

ᶜ But to return to the parliament of England. The French
refugees were coming over in great multitudes for a month
together before the parliament met; which tended not a little
to alarm the nation ᶜ, and both to let them see what a standing
army was, and what account was to be made of all the oaths
and promises of a prince of the Roman religion, how soon
they were broken, and ᵈ how much violence and cruelty was
to be expected as soon as it should have [*f.* 144 (*a*)] the
upper hand: these were sensible arguments that could neither
be denied nor resisted.

A session of parliament.

Cf. *Hist.* i. 664 (*from* 'When it was opened' *to* p. 667, 'dissolved the
parliament').
    Om. 'how happy . . . appeared' *and* 'for all . . . security.'
    After 'commission' *add* 'who had not taken the tests.'
    Om. 'He told them . . . promised.'

    ᵃ Cf. *Hist.* i. 690.   ᵇ *Ibid.*   ᶜ *Ibid.* 663–4.   ᵈ *Ibid.* 664.

For 'pressed by the courtiers' *read* 'understood by some.'

Om. 'The lord Guilford . . . original in everything' (*for this see supra,* p. 169).

After 'told' *add* '[by] those who had procured the thanks only as a matter of respect.'

Om. 'with indignation . . . reason for it.'

Om. 'above all . . . incapacity' *and* 'the government . . . absolute' *and* 'that how furiously . . . tyrant, yet.'

For 'But as the scene . . . important' *read* 'In the house of commons they proceeded in the same method.'

Om. 'But to oppose . . . rebellion.'

Om. 'whereas others . . . court.'

Om. 'The reasoning . . . him and them.'

For 'So the whole house . . . vote for an' *read* 'And to this the whole house went in so unanimously that the court would [*f.* 144 (*b*)] not make a division, fearing that by this the weakness of their party should be too sensibly discovered; so it was carried to make an.'

Om. 'and were ready . . . give.'

For 'one Cook said' *read* 'one Cook studied to inflame them by telling them.'

For 'And now those . . . it was probable, they' *read* 'which were so laid open, that though it was the interest of the greatest part of the house to maintain them, yet they were resolved to.'

Om. 'By this means . . . voted out.'

For 'unless he would . . . place. So' *read* 'so within a few days.'

For 'had served . . . zeal' *read* 'were formerly most in favour, [and] had done him the best services in adhering most steadily to him.'

Om. 'upon which . . . tossed about,' *and* 'others, though . . . steady.'

[*Reflections on the dissolution.*]

[This] was much such a stroke in politics as his brother's dissolving the Long Parliament [1] had been. The surprises and violences used in the election of this had brought together such a pack of men that [a] it was scarce possible to name five hundred worse men in all England than they were. And when men so weak, so poor, so devoted to the court [a], so void of all religion as they were, could not be brought to agree with the court, it was not probable that the king should succeed so well in any new choice that could be made.

Lord Brandon tried.

Soon after the parliament was dissolved two famous trials were brought on: the one was of the lord Brandon's, [b] who was convicted by the testimony of the lord Grey [b] and Rumsey,

---

[a] Cf. *Hist.* i. 667.   [b] *Ibid.* 646.

---

[1] i. e. the parliament which sat from 1661 to 1678.

ᵃ with some others ᵃ, to have been in those consultations that the duke of Monmouth had two years ago ; but he had kissed the king's hand, all that was past had been [*f.* 145 (*a*)] forgiven him, and he had not at all meddled in this late business ; so, though ᵇ he was condemned ᵇ, and that for a great while it was doubted whether he should be pardoned or not, yet the court found that the nation was weary of the many executions it had seen ; he had his pardon, but was kept long in prison after that [1].

The lord Delamere's trial.

Cf. *Hist.* i. 668 (*from* 'Soon after the prorogation' *to end of page*).

Om. 'that he had designed . . . Monmouth.'

Om. 'The witness, to gain . . . destroyed the evidence.'

For 'pursuant . . . violent declamation' *read* 'made a very ill use of his eloquence.'

After 'acquit the lord' *add* 'and the witness was attainted of perjury and both set in the pillory and whipped.'

[*The law officers changed; the Hales trial.*]

Cf. *Hist.* i. 669–71 (*to* ' cause of course').

Om. 'So that trial . . . for it,' *and begin* '[Finch] had opposed the court in the business of the test in the house of commons [*see* p. 668], and was continued,' *&c.*

Om. 'and he acted . . . vehemence' *and* 'who was . . . ill-natured man.'

For 'Now the posts . . . year began' *read* 'And now the judges began to be examined, that so they might by a judgement declare in favour of the king's power of dispensing with the law.'

Om. 'a gentleman . . . concerned. He'; 'and to claim . . . turned out'; 'and others of more pliable . . . scandal'; 'and feeble.'

Om. (*at this point*) 'There was a new chief justice . . . on design to expose and betray it.'

[*f.* 145 (*b*)] *After* 'dispense with them' *add* 'And whereas an act of parliament was alleged, it was shewed [that].'

For 'it was said . . . town' *read* 'it was to be [said].'

Om. 'both constituted and.'

For 'laws, made . . . dispensed with' *read* 'all penal laws, which were the security of the people as well as the crown, [especially] the act for the test.'

For 'but to the informer . . . because his' *read* 'but one part went to the informer and another to other uses.'

Om. 'and take away property.'

Om. 'for the intention . . . law.'

For 'should be made so precarious a thing' *read* 'should be thus dissolved by a decision of the judges.'

ᵃ Cf. *Hist.* i. 646.   ᵇ *Ibid.*

---

[1] The *History* ascribes his reprieve to a stipulation made by Lord Grey.

Om. ' It was said, that, though this was now . . . mouths were now filled.'

For 'even by the strongest . . . cause of course' *read* 'arguments; nor indeed were these alleged with that force that will be perhaps made use of when these judges come to be tried for this decision; which they all (one only excepted) gave as frankly as if it had been a matter of no sort of difficulty; though the same grounds upon which this sentence was founded will bear a much more extended one, and give the king an absolute disposal of the life and properties of all his subjects [cf. *Hist.* i. 671, *supra*]. And now the books of policy writ by some of our clergy concerning the imperial crown were turned upon them.'

[*Character of the chief justice; conduct of his brother; views of the papists; the king proselytizes.*]

[a] The chief justice at this time was sir Edward Herbert [a], son to the lord keeper Herbert and [b] brother to admiral Herbert, who has shewed much greater sense both of law and religion by leaving all his employments rather than promise to give his vote in parliament for that which his brother did now destroy in a much more irregular manner. [c] Yet the chief justice is a virtuous man of an obliging temper and a true protestant; but he has very high [*f.* 146 (*a*)] principles concerning the prerogative, and is very ignorant in the law. [d] Upon the decision many papists were brought into employments [d]; yet some of them that have great estates do still avoid them, for they know that they may be brought to a severe reckoning for that in another reign. The king declared himself now highly zealous for his religion, and great pains were taken to make many converts.

[*The controversial war.*]

Cf. *Hist.* i. 673 ('And upon that there followed . . . books'), *where add* 'upon the point of controversy'; *then proceed to* p. 674, 'There were but very few proselytes . . . church of Rome'; *then revert to* p. 673, *and for* 'Many of the clergy acted . . . They examined' *read* 'Upon this the English clergy began to declare highly against the church of Rome, and both in their sermons and writings they managed'; *and for* 'The truth is' *to end of paragraph read* 'So that it was scarce possible to be so partial but that upon the reading of the books of both sides, every one must acknowledge, that, of which side soever the truth lies, yet there is a dull flatness in the one, and a life and beauty in the other, which gives a strange [strong?] prejudice for the cause that is so well defended.' *Then return to* p. 674 ('The popish priests . . . contempt'), *and for* 'made by the clergy . . . despised' *read* 'and at the advantages that all the nation observed in the books that were writ against them.'

[a] Cf. *Hist.* i. 669.   [b] *Ibid.* 671.   [c] *Ibid.* 669.   [d] *Ibid.* 672.

[*Dr. Sharp in trouble.*]

Cf. *Hist.* i. 674–5 (*to* 'for contempt ').

Before 'It was resolved' *insert* 'And because some in their sermons pressed these matters home.'

Om. 'was the rector . . . zeal. He.'

Om. 'as he believed' *and* 'touched by him . . . sermons' *and* 'not knowing . . . answer' *and* 'and, after . . . concluded.'

Om. 'as he himself assured me.'

Om. 'immediately . . . matter.'

Om. 'yet, he said, he would . . . better understood.'

For 'Sharp went to court . . . read it' *read* 'yet he did all he could do ; for he advised Sharp to give over preaching for some time, and to go to court to justify himself.'

[*f.* 146 (*b*)] *For* 'yet he was let . . . contempt' *read* 'Upon this the king, who had for a great while looked upon the bishop of London with a very ill eye, resolved to lay hold on this matter.'

[*An ecclesiastical commission set up.*]

Cf. *Hist.* i. 675 ('Jeffreys . . . first sacrifice ').

For 'to recommend himself . . . with full power' *read* 'made a proposition that recovered him his favour. He said the king, as supreme head of the church, could erect a court that might take cognizance of all ecclesiastical matters; and though the excess of the High Commission Court in king Charles the First's time had drawn a law upon them extinguishing that or any such court in all time to come (so that now the clergy were only liable to the court of the King's Bench, as all the rest of the subjects are, to be tried there according to law), yet it was resolved now to erect a new court.'

For 'without limitations . . . proceedings' *read* 'The patent that constituted them gave them a full power clogged with no limitations.'

For 'so contrary to law' *read* 'as contrary to law as it was to religion.'

Om. 'for they would trust . . . management.'

[*Conduct of Sancroft*[1]*.*]

Yet the authority of this court received a great blow in this, that [a] the archbishop of Canterbury refused to come and sit in it ; which though he did not do with that vigour that became his post in going to the court and declaring the reasons for which he could not come and[2] [*f.* 219 (*a*)] sit among them[a], yet still his refusing to act did very much derogate from the credit of this new court.

* Cf. *Hist.* i. 676.

---

[1] The alterations in the corresponding passage of the printed *History* give the first hint of the strong antipathy which Burnet, after the Revolution, conceived for Sancroft.

[2] At this point there is a lengthy

[Trial of] the bishop of London; [he] is suspended.

Cf. *Hist.* i. 676-7 *(from* 'The bishop of London was the first' *to end of paragraph).*

Om. 'was the first person that.'

For 'He was attended ... offence ; and' *read* 'was accompanied with such numbers of his clergy and other persons of quality, that it seemed rather to shew the great interest he had in the nation than to lessen him in any manner.' *(N.B. This occurs later on in the folio.)*

For 'that brutal ... natural to him' *read* 'in his abuseful way, very rudely.'

Om. 'said, here ... nothing ; so he.'

Om. 'hoping that the king ... fall, at last' *and* 'all secret methods . . . ineffectual.'

Om. 'poor spirited' *and* 'There was not so much . . . . given.'

[Character of the bishop of Durham.]

This last, though ᵃ descended from a puritan family ᵃ, and though the lord Crew, both father and son (his father and his brother), were two very worthy persons, yet he is in all respects a reproach to his birth and family ; he is a very weak man, ᵇ has no learning and less virtue, and is a fawning abject flatterer ᵇ. He was raised by the king's ¹ favour in the former reign ; but he found quickly that he was an insignificant man ; he desired me in the time of his favour to go much to the bishop of Durham to make somewhat of him. I went once or twice, but I found him so excessively weak that I told the duke that nothing could be made of him, so I gave over all further commerce with him. He waits only for a fair opportunity to declare himself a papist ; for he has no religion at all. Yet when the business of the exclusion was on foot the earl of Essex assured me that they knew if it had come near an equal division that he would have voted for it.

ᵃ Cf. *Hist.* i. 392.   ᵇ *Ibid.* 392, 676.

hiatus in Transcript A ; no. 4 (in Dr. Gifford's arrangement) ending abruptly at the middle of the sentence, half-way down f. 146 (*b*). In Transcript B, f. 218 (*b*), there is also a break at exactly the same word; but fortunately for us, there is no *lacuna* ; the narrative being continued on f. 219 (*a*) by the hand of a fresh copyist (see Introd. *supra*. We therefore give from this point forwards, till further notice, the rendering and foliation of this inferior version ; which, as the reader will notice, has required much emendation.

¹ He apparently means by the favour of the actual king (James), while Duke of York ; see below, next sentence.

The bishop of London is suspended.

Cf. *Hist.* i. 677 ('But the king . . . legality and justice of the sentence ').
For 'But the king . . . point and ' *read* 'When the king found that he was like to be baffled in the business of the bishop of London, he,' *&c.*

The princess of Orange intercedes for the bishop of London,
but without success.

[*f.*219 (*b*)] [a]While it was in dependence the princess of Orange writ earnestly to the king in his favours[a]. He had instructed her in her youth, [b]he had confirmed her and had married her[b]; the matter for which he was accused was no great crime. [c]Both the prince and princess writ to himself expressing the share they took in the trouble that was then given him. And the princess also writ to the king[c]: it was the first intercession she had ever made in a thing of this consequence, and it deserved well she should begin with it. [d]She was for some days in doubt whether she should write or not, fearing that instead of doing him service it might do him hurt; yet she ventured on it. [e]But the king was not wrought on by her intercession, unless it were to write her an answer that was very sharp on the bishop of London, and not very obliging to herself.

[*Fate of the two divines.*]

Cf. *Hist.* i. 677 (*from* 'Dr. Sharp was admitted' *to* p. 678, 'lay still on him ',
Before ' Dr. Sharp' *add* 'Some months after this.'
Om. ' dismissed with a gentle reprimand and.'
For ' only the suspension lay still . . . eighty-seven ' *read* 'and so this matter stands to this day. The bishop does no act of jurisdiction ; but really his clergy depend more on him than ever ' (*with the substance of the sentence of* p. 677, ' His clergy . . . before,' *in present tense*[1]).

[*Reflections on the king's policy.*]

It was presently given out, upon the suspension of the bishop, [that] this new court would proceed to many high things, and all the clergy feared this was to be carried much further than has been done since that time ; for there have been but two matters of any consequence before them, in both

[a] Cf. *Hist.* i. 677.   [b] *Ibid.*   [c] *Ibid.*   [d] *Ibid.* 692.   [be] *Ibid.* 677.

---

[1] For a strong letter of remonstrance against the course pursued by the bishop in petitioning, see *Life of Halifax*, i. 472-3.

which [a] they have shewed the weakness of the counsels by which they are governed. For whereas in all countries the rights of colleges are such sacred things that these are never disturbed [a] even when other things are broke in upon, and Oxford and Cambridge are two such vast bodies, in which the whole nation is so much concerned that one would have thought that these should have been the last of all to whom this new commission should have given any trouble, yet [b] they have begun just where they should have ended.

[*Nature of the attack on the universities. 1. Cambridge.*]

Cf. *Hist.* i. 697 (*from* 'The Jesuits fancied' *to* p. 699, ' greater effects ').

Before 'The Jesuits' *insert* 'Cambridge was first taken to task. It was resolved to have a college in every one of the universities ; for.'

[*f.* 220 (*a*)] *Om.* ' who were certainly too remiss.'

For ' which needed not . . . to work ' *read* ' [to do ?] which both in Oxford and Cambridge would [not ?] have raised [the king's charge ?] to above £500 a year.' (*The words in brackets are conjectural ; the passage is evidently corrupt ; and the sums given in the MS. and History do not correspond.*)

For ' or his priests . . . great bodies ' *read* ' or his inclinations carr[y] him naturally to violent counsels.'

Om. ' Which yet would have made . . . rest.'

Om. ' which might occasion . . . contention among them.'

[*f.* 220 (*b*)] *Om.* ' He was treated . . . person of that body.'

For ' either of their weakness . . . talked so much about it ' *read* ' of their weakness ; for a prince ought never to begin a hard thing unless he is either sure of the justice of it, or that he is resolved to go through with it right or wrong ; since nothing diminishes him more than the beginning such a thing and then the letting it fall. The beginning it shews his ill intentions, and the letting it fall his feebleness.'

For ' And now all people . . . taken ' *read* ' And in this I find that I took ' ; *for* ' they thought ' *read* ' I thought.'

For ' that might attend them ' *read* ' (for he himself does not see the consequences of many propositions that are made him).'

After ' by yielding to it ' *add* ' Yet I see in a great many instances that the power which his priests have over him is such that they make him venture on many things which he quits a little too poorly when he meets with a vigorous opposition.'

For ' lasted longer . . . effects ' *read* ' has made more noise.'

[*Preface to the attack on Oxford ; ecclesiastical vacancies filled.*]

[c] The bishop of Oxford and the learned bishop of Chester died both in a little time one of another, [d] as Dolben, archbishop of York, had died the year before. [e] Dolben was highly

[a] Cf. *Hist.* i. 697.　[b] *Ibid.*　[c] *Ibid.* 694.　[d] *Ibid.* 676.　[e] *Ibid.* 590.

esteemed in the north, for he performed his office very worthily[a] and he had appeared in the parliament with great vigour, so that his death was a very considerable loss to the church.   [b]Pearson, bishop of Chester, was the learnedest man of the age ; he was likewise a man of a very good life, and of a gentle, sweet temper ; but though he reasoned very well of all things in general, yet he understood not the governing part of his function ; and was so [? too] easy[b] and credulous, and too much in the power of those whom he trusted.   [c]The archbishopric of York is still vacant[c], and it is believed the revenue is sent over to cardinal Howard ; though others believe that the Jesuits have it put in their hands ; which is more credible than the other, for the king is wholly guided by their counsels in all matters that relate to religion.   [d]Cartwright was made bishop of Chester, who is a man of parts, and had [*f.* 221 (*a*)] good beginnings of learning, but he is a most illi[beral][1] person, and a brutal, ill-natured man.   He has valued himself now for many years upon his carrying the king's authority above all the restraints of law, which, according to his divinity, are only rules fo which the king submits himself as long as he thinks fit ; but the divine authority that is lodged in him is above all law, and can warrant him to break through all them when he thinks fit to exert his authority to the full[d].   This is good for the present occasion, so it is no wonder, though it recommends him now at court. He is an exact flatterer, and though it is not likely that he, being a married man, will change his religion, yet [e]he will contribute as vigorously to advance popery as if he were one of that religion.   The other vacancy in Oxford was filled by Dr. Parker, who was at first an independent ; but on the king's restoration he found his account in changing and striking up to the violentest form of the church of England.   [f]He is a

---

[a] *Hist.* i. 590.   [b] *Ibid.* 694-5.   [c] *Ibid.* 676.   [d] *Ibid.* 695.   [e] *Ibid.* 696.   [f] *Ibid.* 260.

---

[1] The reading of the MS. ('illiterate') seems incompatible with even the 'beginnings of learning' mentioned above ; and 'illiberal' in the sense of 'miserly' seems the simplest emendation.

man that has no regard either to religion or virtue, [a] but will accommodate himself to everything that may gratify either his covetousness or his ambition. He has writ many books; there is a liveliness in his style that is more entertaining than either grave or correct [a]. He has raised the king's authority in ecclesiastical matters and depressed it by turns, as he was pleased or displeased with the court; for though [b] once he carried the king's power to that height of impiety as to say in so many plain words that the form of naming the king in our prayers as under God and Christ our supreme governor in all causes was a cursed [1] and a profane expression (since he said that though the king was indeed under God, yet he was not under Christ, but above him), yet, not being preferred as he expected, he has writ many books to raise the power of the church to an independence on the civil authority. [c] His extravagant way of writing gave occasion to the wittiest books that have appeared in this age, for Mr. Marvell [2] undertook him and treated him in ridicule in the severest but pleasantest manner possible [c], and by this one character one may judge how pleasant these books were; for the last king, that was not a great reader of books, read them over and over again. [d] These twin instruments, who were picked out of the body of the English clergy to betray and destroy it [d], deserved not that a character should be given them, if it had not been that they are likely to do things that may be remembered by posterity; so that I thought it worth the while to dwell a little upon them, though I thought to have avoided it, for they are persons that have upon all occasions done me all the ill offices that were in their power. On my part, though I have no acquaintance [*f.* 221 (*b*)] with either of them, yet I look on them both as [such?] very ill men that I am perhaps so [? too] easily carried to say the worst of them that is possible [3].

[a] Cf. *Hist.* i. 696. [b] *Ibid.* [c] *Ibid.* 260. [d] *Ibid.* 696.

---

[1] The *History* reads 'crude.'
[2] In the *History* 'the liveliest,' &c.
[3] Here again the reader will notice that an insinuation against Sancroft was subsequently inserted in the narrative.

[*Attacks on Christ Church and Magdalen College.*]

Cf. *Hist.* i. 696–7 ('The deanery . . . into their lands').

Begin 'But though Parker[1] was made bishop of Oxford, yet.'

Om. 'Massey.'

For 'not long after this' *read* 'a year after this.'

For 'That is esteemed . . . wonder that' *read* 'so that being the second place of importance in the university.'

Next proceed from Hist. i. 699 ('The presidentship of Magdalen') *to* p. 701 ('And all the temporalities of the church').

After 'of Magdalen was' *insert* 'not simply at the king's gift as the deanery of Christ's Church was, but.'

Om. 'Mandamus letters . . . such a letter.'

For 'so that matter . . . settled' *read* 'for the endowment having been given by one of his predecessors, the college was tied to a great dependence upon that see.'

For 'It was said . . . pleasure' *read* 'for though the king's recommendation did not so bind them that it was a punishable thing to disobey it, yet that respect had always been paid to it, that colleges did not proceed to elections till they had so represented the matter to the court, that by the intercession of their chancellor the mandamus was withdrawn. And.'

For 'and was declining . . . country' *read* 'and this was a point too big for any man's credit; so it was resolved to carry the matter very fair.'

Om. 'both in their addresses . . . uncontrollable tyranny.'

[*f.* 222 (*a*)] *After* 'contempt of it' *insert* 'and therefore.'

For 'that the design . . . papist' *read* 'that the proceedings might have some colour as if the point that was carried on had not been so much a matter of religion as of maintaining the king's authority.'

After 'in some court of law' *read* 'For a statute passed by the commissioners was not [of] strength enough to divest a man of his freehold; and.'

Om. 'in the year 1687[2].'

For 'ill-suited to' *read* 'that shewed more the heat of an impotent passion than.'

Om. 'though with a humility . . . mollified him.'

Om. 'as sir Charles Hedges . . . matter.'

For 'acted . . . manner' *read* 'behaved himself on this occasion with that obsequious servility'; *and for* 'to the king's pleasure' *read* 'to his interest.'

For 'were all turned out' *read* 'are now all turned out.'

For 'So it was expected . . . that house' *read* [*f.* 222 (*b*)] 'So that that house will be in a very little time very probably.'

For 'The nation . . . It was thought an open' *read* 'It is said that Hough intends to plead his rights in the court[s] of justice against this.'

For 'when men' *read* 'for it can be esteemed no other in law. Upon this, and the decision that the court[s] in Westminster give in, the whole legal settlement of the church of England will depend; for if commissioners'; *and for*

---

[1] An ostensible Protestant.

[2] It took place in September, 1687; this passage therefore was written towards the close of that year.

'came' *and* 'turned' *read* 'can come' *and* 'turn'; *and after* 'freehold' *read* 'then the present constitution will subsist only upon the king's pleasure.'

After 'making' *insert* 'both in his private discourse and in his public declarations,' *and om.* 'for this struck . . . temporalities of the church.'

[*The king's advances to the dissenters.*]

But I turn next to open a new scene of politics, by which, as it has appeared on the one hand that the king has not that steady firmness to which he has pretended, so he has discovered great weakness in it. In England, as the main body of the nation was that of the church of England, so there were great numbers of dissenters that were ᵃ formed into four bodies; presbyterians, the independents, the anabaptists, and the quakers. The two former, not [maintaining?]¹ the usual distinction of different [rites?]², and their depressed estate keeping them from the dispute of the constitution of the church, upon which they had broke in the year 1645, were generally considered as one body, and made above two-thirds of the dissenters ᵃ. They were not numerous in the country or in the small towns, but their interest lay chiefly in the great towns. ᵇ The anabaptists and quakers were not very numerous, but they were more united; the former [were] men of great virtue and of a universal charity; and the latter had so many little distinctions in their whole deportment that they were everywhere known ᵇ; they lived in great simplicity and equality among themselves so, and [and so?] were all as one man. ᶜ Among them William Penn, son to the vice-admiral, had great credit. He is a man of good parts, but extremely vain; he loves mightily to hear himself talk ᶜ; he has a flourishing of learning, and with it a copious fancy; and his head is much turned to the notion of government. ᵈ He has been long and much in the king's confidence, which has brought great suspicion as if he were secretly a papist ᵈ; but I have known him long, and I think myself bound to acquit him as far as one man can judge of another. He has protested to me that the foundation of the king's kindness to

ᵃ *Hist.* i. 701, *infra.*   ᵇ *Ibid.* 702.   ᶜ *Ibid.* 693, 702.   ᵈ *Ibid.* 693-4.

¹ The MS. reads 'notwithstanding.'   ² The MS. reads 'rules.'

him was the sense that he retained [*f.* 223 (*a*)] of some
services that his father[1] did him when he went to sea in
[16]65, and from whom he learned much as to naval affairs.
Penn has been likewise a zealous promoter of liberty of
conscience, which was all that the popish party thought fit
to pretend to at first; and since he was considered as a man
that had the conduct of the whole party of the quakers, and
had likewise great credit with some of the leaders of the
other sects, the king made great use of him, and seemed to
depend much on his advice. [a] So a design was laid for inviting
all the nonconformists to join interests with the papists for
perceiving [? procuring] a general liberty to be established with
all the solemnities of a perpetual law, as the Magna Charta
had been; by which not only all penal laws in the matters
of religion should be for ever repealed, but public employments should be opened to men of all persuasions without
requiring any tests or oaths of them[a] relating to opinions
in matter of religion[2]. And this was thought so plausible
a thing at court that they did not doubt but their offer of
liberty of conscience would take the effect that they desired;
[b] though it was somewhat unnatural to the king[b], who had
made the presbyterians the chief subject of his anger and
raillery for his whole life, to turn all of a sudden and become
so very tender of them. [c] Nor was it very likely that a body
of men who had broke with the church of England for some
small approaches to popery in a few ceremonies should go
into a design that would naturally carry us to popery[c], and
they that had been always so jealous of the extent of the
prerogative must have very much changed their nature before
they could be brought to concur with the designs of the
court, which were become now very visible. Yet here was
a new game to be played. The king saw that nothing could
be done with the men of the church of England and the old

[a] *Hist.* i. 702.   [b] *Ibid.*   [c] *Ibid.*

---

[1] For Admiral Sir William Penn
see his *Memorials* by G[ranville]
P[enn].

[2] This was the scheme against
which Halifax directed his *Anatomy
of an Equivalent.*

royalists; and resolved to turn himself to gain the favour of a party that had been so long despised and ill-used by him.

[*Firmness of the nobility.*]

ᵃ All the nobility was tried if they could be engaged to change their religion ᵃ, so that popery might begin to make a better figure in the nation. ᵇ The firmness the duke of Norfolk, the earl of Shrewsbury, and the lord Lumley shewed surprised many. They had changed their religion ᵇ during the late heats that had been against popery ¹, so that it was generally believed that they would be the first that would return ; but they, on the contrary, declared that they had forsaken popery upon a full intention not to return, and that the court might endeavour to make [*f.* 223 (*b*)] them change their religion, but without effect ; and that, as they had been the last that had left it, so they would be the last that should return to it. ᶜ The earl of Mu[l]grave, that was made lord chamberlain, and was believed so compliant that, having little or no religion of his own, he might the more easily accommodate himself to the king['s], made a lively answer to the priest that [came] to instruct him. He said he had with a great deal of difficulty brought himself to believe that God had made man ; but it would be much harder to bring him to think that man was equal with God and that he made God ᶜ. The salt that was in this expression made it go far, and be in all people's mouths ; and there are times in which an apt answer has a greater effect than volumes of controversies, for every one understands and remembers it.

[*Lord Rochester is tempted; his former services in mobilizing the fleet; object of this move; our cause of quarrel against the States.*]

ᵈ But the business of the earl of Rochester made more noise ᵈ. He was become extreme insolent, and so was much hated ; yet he had established himself so well in the king's favour ᵉ by

---

ᵃ Cf. *Hist.* i. 683.   ᵇ *Ibid.* 684, 762, 763.   ᶜ *Ibid.* 683.   ᵈ *Ibid.* 684.
ᵉ *Ibid.* 684 and 685.

¹ Cf. the account of Norfolk and Shrewsbury given (with Dartmouth's note) in *Hist.* i. 762.

his borrowing £400,000 upon a [? the] credit or [? of] some branches of the revenue ^a that both he and his brother seemed to be confirmed in their employments. ^bThe use for which that money was raised was for putting the fleet in a [good ?] condition ; for both the several stores were unfurnished and the vessels themselves were in a decay ; and the king gave orders to put the whole fleet in a condition to go to sea. This made noise all Europe over, since the king was in full peace with all his neighbours, so that his preparations seemed to have some great design under them ; and the priests said everywhere, but chiefly in Rome, that the designs were against the States, and that both France and England would make war upon them all of a sudden, for it was generally [known] that the Dutch fleet was in no good condition. In this both the interest of France and that of the priests concurred ; for as they had the prospect of an advantageous war against the Dutch, so the embroiling the king with the prince of Orange was the main point that France drove at ; since that quarrel might probably have such effects that if the war proved successful, the king might have been carried to set on a new [expedient ? *or* exclusion ?[1]]^b. The pretence the king had for a war was the business of Bantam, in which there was a great deal to be said on both hands[2]. The old king of Bantam had resigned his crown to his son, who was acknowledged king by the king of England [*f.* 224 (*a*)], for he received an embassy from him. This young king happened to fall into the hands of some that were governed by the Du[tch][3] of Batavia ; so that the English began to fear that he would use them ill. Now our company had hopes of making themselves more considerable by this means, and that he would have sold Bantam or some other place to them to be fortified by them. They had also some prospect of getting into the trade of Japan by his [? this] means ; and the old king had been always so much in their interests that

---

^a Cf. *Hist.* i. 684 and 685. ^b *Ibid.* 685–6.

---

[1] Conjectural emendation of 'expedition.'
[2] There is a curious account of this affair from the Dutch standpoint quoted in Story's *Carstares*, pp. 112–3.
[3] The MS. reads 'Duke.'

they hoped to have met with the same favour from his son.
But finding that they were mistaken, and that the practices
and presents of the Dutch were like to be too hard for them,
they set on the old king to come and reassume the government, and promised to assist him effectually ; and the son
having failed in some things to [his] [1] father, this was the
more easily effected. So the old king came to Bantam, being
assisted by the English ; he drave out his son, but the Dutch
being much more powerful than the English they put the
young king again into possession, who was no sooner at
Bantam than he drove out all the English, pretending that
they had rebelled against him whom they had acknowledged
for the lawful king of that place. No doubt the Dutch set
on this, for the footing that the English had got in Bantam
had been long very uneasy to them ; so it was not doubted
but that underhand they had engaged the king of Bantam to
banish the English. Yet it went as his own act, in which
the Dutch seemed to have no other share but that they
acted as auxiliaries to the young king. And when he had
banished the English they offered them harbour, and carried
away both their effects and their persons to Batavia till
English ships came to carry them elsewhere. And they pretended to have acted in this matter as good and friendly
neighbours. So that though it was sure enough that they
had procured the banishment of the English out of Bantam,
yet they had done it in such a manner that it was hard to
make it appear, or to found a breach or a war upon it ; unless
it were resolved to follow the pattern of [16]72. But this has
drawn on a long negotiation between the companies, which
is still in dependence and is so kept up by the king that it is
plain he intends [*f.* 224 (*b*)] to make a quarrel of it as soon as
his affairs put him in a condition to begin a war. The French
were at the same time making preparation at Toulon, and it
was generally believed also [that ?] the two kings were resolved
again to fall upon the States. I do not yet certainly know

---

[1] The MS. reads 'this.'

whether the king ever intended it; it is generally believed he
did, and that he spake to some of the sea officers concerning
it, but the answer was melancholy; for Herbert and some
others told him that the seamen were generally so ill-affected
that there was no trust[ing] them in a case in which they
might believe that religion was concerned; for they who sailed
up and down the world, and so knew more of that religion
than the rest of the people of England did, had so great an
aversion to popery that there might be reason enough to fear
a revolt of the whole fleet, which is very easily done by seamen when they are unanimous. Whether this diverted the
king, or if the concurrence of other things mixed with it, I
do not know; but after a very vigorous preparation of the fleet
all was let fall of the sudden. But these discourses had a
very good effect in Holland, and made the States reflect so
seriously on the condition in which their fleet was, that [a] they
consented to the new levying of the 200th penny [a], by which
their fleet is like to be put in so good a case that they will
be no more in danger of being surprised. I made all this
digression upon the mention of the money that the earl of
Rochester borrowed [for] setting forward the king's preparations. He upon that reckoned himself very sure in the
king's favour. Yet he was soon after surprised with [b] an information that was brought him that he was to be turned out
of the treasury; upon which his enemies say that his lady
let some words fall to the queen intimating that he was tractable in matters of religion. [c] So the king spoke to him of it
and proposed it to him, the suffering himself to be instructed;
he desired a conference [c], and it was appointed that it should
be in the king's presence. [d] All conferences are thought to be
intended only to give the party to which one is resolved to
go over a greater triumph [d], as if the change had been an effect
of the victory that was gained; this was also managed with
all possible disadvantage on the side of ·our church, [since] [1]

---

[a] Cf. *Hist.* i. 692.   [b] *Ibid.* 684.   [c] *Ibid. supra.*   [d] *Ibid.* 685.

---

[1] The MS. reads 'sure.'

the king's presence was as great a restraint upon our divines, as it gave on the other hand great courage to his priests; so Rochester [*f.*225 (*a*)] was looked on as lost to us. The king did in this matter great honour to my two friends [a] Tillotson and Stillingfleet, for he excepted against them. So Rochester pitched on Jane and Patrick [a]; on the other side their [? there were] two priests, whose names I have forgot[1], to manage the debate. This dispute was not at all to the advantage of the priests, for [b] Rochester himself answered all the priests proposed, and treated them with so much neglect, that he would scarce suffer the doctors to speak; for he said he found himself strong enough against all that was offered to him, so that he needed not the assistance of the divines. [c] Rochester's enemies say that he was to be turned out whether he changed or not[c], so he chose rather to go out with [the] honour of being disgraced for his religion than to be turned out after the infamy of giving it up to preserve his white staff. [d] The king broke up the conference decently enough, but charged all parties to make no noise of what had passed in it[d]. So I do not know the particulars of it; yet the conclusion of it was, that Rochester stood firm. And a few days after, [e] the treasury was put in commission and Rochester was dismissed with a great pension[e]. The king said that he had resolved long before the conference to put the treasury in commission; so the pains that was taken to make him change, when his disgrace was resolved on before, was compared to the Italian's revenge, who having got his enemy in his power, made him first renounce God, and then murdered him, that so he might kill both soul and body. The king said he found the treasury was too great a post for one man, so he put it in commission. Others believed that this was set on by those that intended to carry the king to an exclusion. It could not be thought that Rochester could be engaged in that matter, and a

---

[a] Cf. *Hist.* i. 684.　　[b] *Ibid.* 685.　　[c] *Ibid. supra.*　　[d] *Ibid. infra.*　　[e] *Ibid.*

---

[1] Leyburn and Godden; see Routh's note (*Hist. in loco*, and *Burnet's James II in loco*).

treasurer, who pays all the pensions of the court, naturally finds out all the secrets that are in it, and therefore he could not be trusted with such a post.

[*Changes in the government of Ireland.*]

Soon after this ᵃ Clarendon was recalled out of Ireland and Tyrconnell was sent in his place. Porter was also turned out from being chancellor, and Fitton, an English papist that was not at all skilled in the law, succeeded him ᵃ, which put all the protestants in Ireland under no small apprehensions.

[*Political position of Fitz-James.*]

All the papist party begin to look on Fitz-James, that was the king's son by Mrs. Church[ill], as their chief hope[1]. The king sent him ᵇ for two campaigns into Hungary, to gain honour there. He is a soft good-natured youth, but either he or his governor took greater care of his person than of his honour; for notwithstanding all the occasions that the siege of Buda offered him of [distinguishing himself?] [*f.* 225 (*b*)], yet he appeared in none of them; nor did he so much as keep a table, but did eat always at other men's tables, though an allowance was given him by the king. Yet his governor found it more convenient for himself to put it in his own purse; and his brother is a Jesuit that is [in] the secret, so he knew that all things would be excused to one that had so sure protection. The queen declares herself wholly against Fitz-James, who is now made duke of Berwick; and that ᵇ [and ?] his own weaknesses are like to ᶜ keep him from making any great figure ᶜ.

[*The king's first marriage questioned.*]

The priests also began to call in question the validity of the king's first marriage with the duchess, but Dr. Crowder that

---

ᵃ Cf. *Hist.* i. 682.   ᵇ *Ibid.* 749.   ᶜ *Ibid.*

[1] See for this Macaulay, ed. 1858, iii. 64 (quoting Bonrepaux's despatch of July ₁₁, 1687); the *Marchmont Papers,* iii. 71–2 (letter of Jan. 1627); Story's *Life of Carstares,* p. 152, note (quoting McCormick's *Carstairs Papers,* pp. 27–8, and Fountainhall, p. 842).

married him being yet alive, Rochester got a new attestation of the marriage to be signed by him. Yet the French ambassador seemed once to fancy that he had good proof to invalidate the marriage.

[*Proposals of compromise rejected.*]

The eyes of all England were now turned towards the princess of Orange, and the popish party having broken so many of the laws and caused themselves to lie under a hard fate if a revolution should happen before they can procure some abatement of the laws, or at least an indemnity for what they have done against law, began now to try what could be done for bringing matters to some agreement; and, if some small mitigation of the rigour of the penal laws would have contented the court, many were brought to think that it might be a wise bargain to give the king somewhat in favour of his party, provided he would be contented with that; but, on the other hand, ᵃ the court resolved to have all or nothing ᵃ, and would not accept of the repeal of some of the penal laws unless all were taken away, and the tests also abolished.

[*The king and his army.*]

The king tried unsuccessfully how far he might trust his army; ᵇ he brought it together into a camp both in [16]86 and [16]87; but the aversion to popery appeared as eminently amongst them as it did amongst all other ranks of people; and though the king set up mass in it, yet so few went to it, and those who went were treated with so much scorn by the rest, that the king saw there was no trusting to them in that quarrel; for the papists that were in the army were an unequal match to the rest, and the heats concerning religion put them so near a mutiny ᵇ that it soon appeared how far they would be from assisting the king if he should go about to change the religion. All these things concurred

---

ᵃ Cf. *Hist.* i. 694, 733.   ᵇ *Ibid.* 703.

to put the king upon this new project of balancing the
[*f. 226 (a)*] church of England by setting up the dissenters
against them.

[*Penn's embassy.*]

But before this was opened ᵃ Penn was sent over to Holland
to try how the prince of Orange would resist the proposition.
So he, who is a man of many words and much vanity in his
discourse, had a long conversation with the prince ; ᵇwho
answered him very frankly that he himself was as great an
enemy to persecution upon the account of religion as any
man could possibly be, and therefore he should be very glad
to see such methods taken that none should be disturbed for
his conscience ; but at the same time he showed as great an
aversion to the admitting of papists into any share of the
government ; and all that Penn could say did not carry him
further ᵇ. This fell out soon after I was come into Holland,
and was the first piece of ᶜ confidence which the prince
honoured me with ᶜ, and ever since that time I have known
a good deal that has passed between the prince and the court
of England.

[*Burnet's own experience.*]

But this leads me back to my old [? own] story, and to give
an account of all that I had met with in ᵈ the year of ramble that
I made between my coming out of England and my coming
to settle in Holland.   ᵉ I avoided the making much acquaintance in Paris ᵉ, for the king had expressed to Mr. Barillon how
ill he took the kindness that had been shewed me by Mr. de
Schomberg and some others in France, so that I did not
think it expedient to converse with any but men of learning.
ᶠ I spent much time with my lord Montagu, and by his
means I knew many of the secrets of the court of England ᶠ,
and was confirmed in almost all things that are in the former
part of this work [1]. ᵍHe told me that during his embassy

ᵃ Cf. *Hist.* i. 693.   ᵇ *Ibid.* 693–4.   ᶜ *Ibid.* 693.   ᵈ *Ibid.* 686.   ᵉ *Ib:d.*
655.   ᶠ *Ibid.*   ᵍ *Ibid.* 391.

---

[1] It certainly does not add to the
authenticity of Burnet's information
that it should have obtained the *impri-
matur* of so accomplished a liar ; a

he could never enter into the secret of the money that the king had underhand from France, [a] for that was all managed by the duchess of Portsmouth. He often tried the king upon that head, and said that he would undertake to procure him the double of all that he had from thence. Yet the king was so ashamed 'of it that he would never own it to him ; so he believed all that was given came as a present to the duchess of Portsmouth [a].

[*Characters of Louis XIV and madame de Maintenon.*]

Both he and Mr. de Schomberg told me many things of the king of France, by which I saw how little he deserved the great character that is generally given of him ; for, as his extraordinary ignorance makes that he knows nothing but the present course of his affairs, so there is no way of dealing with him [*f.* 226 (*b*)] but by most abject flattery. Nor has he a true judgement. Schomberg told me that when he was called to speak to him of matters of war, he saw that he understood them not. The chief maxim he has is to put nothing to hazard ; he chooses always the way of corruption before gallanter methods ; and in all his undertakings he will play at small game that is sure rather than at any great project ; and yet he is so ignorant of history that he believes himself to be the greatest hero that ever was. Madame de Maintenon, that is a person of much wit and of a good proportion of beauty for her age, has risen up by many steps. First, from being a poor young gentlewoman, she got to be Scarron's wife ; who was a true Esop, and had the most wit with the worst and most misshapen body that ever met together. After his death she became so celebrated for her wit that she was made *gouvernante* to the king's daughters by madame de Montespan, and this gave her frequent opportunity of speaking with the king ; and she, who has a tone of flattery that is fine as well as bewitching, got so

[a] Cf. *Hist.* i. 392.

---

very flagrant instance of whose habitual mendacity is, in point of fact, immediately and confidently quoted by the ingenuous doctor.

much into his favours, that notwithstanding all the decay of her beauty, and of his age, she now governs him more absolutely than all his mistresses or ministers ever did. He spends many hours a day with her, and she employs all her wit in making him fancy that he is in all respects the greatest king that ever reigned. The matter is gone so far between them that it is generally believed that she not only hinders the king from marrying, but that there is a secret marriage or at least an engagement between them[1]. The king's life is writing by Mr. Racine and Mr. Despréaux (or Boileau); the [latt]er[2] has a good judgement, and the [form]er[2] a great life and diversity of thoughts; so that between them they are very likely to compose a work that will have as much beauty and force as is consistent with those schemes of flattery that must run through it. It is believed that mad. de Maintenon has her share in this work, and that she reads it to the king. It seems they design to have the king's life writ in all languages; for a creature of the archbishop's of Paris came to me and told me if I would undertake to write the king's history in English [*f.* 227 (*a*)] I might have what rewards I pleased. But I cut off the proposition very abruptly; I said the religion that I professed made that I could not employ my pen for the honour of a prince that was employing his whole force for the destruction of it.

[*Burnet becomes acquainted with Stoupe.*]

I made another acquaintance in Paris with [a] col. Stoupe[3], [b] that was once the minister of the French congregation in London, and that was much employed and trusted by Cromwell[b]; but upon the king's restoration he, refusing to receive the communion in the Walloon church, was informed

[a] Cf. *Hist.* i. 65, 660 ; ii. 692.   [b] *Ibid.* i. 65.

---

[1] The king's marriage to her is supposed to have taken place soon after the queen's death, July 30, 1683. In any case, she was almost certainly his wife by 1685.

[2] The transcriber has accidentally transposed these words in the MS.

[3] Mr. Airy's note in vol. i. pp. 115-6 of his edition gives a long list of authorities concerning this unprincipled intriguer.

against as a man dangerous to the state; so he was forced to go out of England. After some years' stay in Paris he quitted his first employment and turned a soldier, and he is now both colonel of a regiment of Switzers and ᵃa brigadier ᵃ. He is a man of pleasure and expense, and of such morals that everything goes easily down with him in which he finds his advantage. ᵇ He hath loose opinions in matters of religion, and is rather no papist than a good protestant ᵇ. He has been long in affairs, and has a searching curiosity after secrets; so ᶜ I learnt many things from him relating to Cromwell's maxims and designs ᶜ.

[*Cromwell's character and career.*]

Cromwell was a man of a str[a]ng[e]¹ composition, and there was in him as great a mixture of good and bad as perhaps ever met together in one man. He lived long a private gentleman, upon a small estate, in a high strain of strictness and piety; and was for about ten years together thought by all his neighbours the best and the wisest man that was in all that country. He had scarce any knowledge of affairs, except what related to the constitution of the English government and the temper of the nation. He had also read the Scriptures and the books of practical divinity with so much care that he was able to run out both in prayers and discourse on these heads without bounds. ᵈ He had a very hot and enthusiastical temper ᵈ, and could have prayed himself into so much warmth that he seemed to melt away in tears; and if he had found that which they of that time called an enlargement of heart, then he reckoned that God was well-pleased with him, and that he heard his prayers and would answer them; but if his spirits continued still cold and oppressed in prayer, then he reckoned that God was not pleased with him and that which he offered to him in prayer. He got into the house of commons by the credit which the opinion of his party had procured him; and being

ᵃ Cf. *Hist.* i. 65.   ᵇ *Ibid.*   ᶜ *Ibid.*   ᵈ *Ibid.* 79.

---

¹ The transcriber has written 'strong.'

Hampden's near kinsman, he was by his means made a colonel in the army that was raised against [*f.* 227 (*b*)] the king. The parliament's army went on very ill the first year; they had entertained many officers that had been in Gustavus's army, for that alone served then to raise a man; but these being accustomed to the German way of plunder, thought more of their own advantages than of the services. So after a conversation that was between Hampden and Cromwell upon the misfortunes that they had met with, and their forces not being able to stand before the king's (which seemed to flow from this, that the king had the gentry on his side who were pressed on by a principle of honour, whereas the commons that were with them had not such elevated thoughts), Cromwell set himself to model his own regiment, so that they should be all saints. He set on among them much praying and discoursing of spiritual matters, and he used to go up and down among them himself, leading them on to those exercises, with which they became so acquainted that upon all occasions his regiment distinguished itself from all the rest. This led others to follow his example, and by this means that army was wrought up to a pitch of zeal, that nothing could stand before them; and he himself quickly got up to be lieutenant-general, and upon Hampden's death he became the head of the party. [a] In the matter of the king's death he was rather pushed on by Ireton (that was his son-in-law and a severe bloody commonwealth's man) than by his own inclinations [a]; for it is said that he had once made his own bargain with the king, and was to be made earl of Essex, and to have a considerable estate given him in recompense of the service which he undertook of setting the king again upon the throne. But he durst not go on in his design when he saw that Ireton would not agree to it. Fairfax soon after that quitting his employment of general of the army, [b] Cromwell was set at the head of a great but a very factious army [b]. The disputes that he had with the Long Parliament and with the other parliaments that he called are generally known. It

[a] Cf. *Hist.* i. 46.　　[b] *Ibid.* 65.

appeared what a [stubborn?] thing the English [temper?][1] is during his government; for though he had a great and a brave army and was successful in all his foreign affairs, yet he could neither form [?force] a parliament to that point of delivering up the government to him, nor could he bring the army to concur with him in the design, though invited to it by the hopes of a share in the spoil. [a]They had filled their heads so with the notion not only of a commonwealth, but of Christ's coming to reign his reign of a thousand years[a], and was [?were] so sensible of the oaths they had made to be true to the commonwealth of England, that all he could say in those [b]long [*f.* 228 (*a*)] and dark speeches that he often made to them[b] could not work upon them. [c]The lawyers that were among them told them that they could never be secured from what they had done, nor covered from the bloodshed that was during the war, nor from the king's death, [d]nor be assured of the crown lands, and the church lands that were divided among them[d], nor the settlement of Ireland, [e]without an act of parliament passed by the king, lords, and commons[e]; and therefore it was necessary to place the shadow at least of kingship somewhere. And this was that at which Cromwell aimed; he knew well that the name of a king would in a course of some time fetch the power after it, and this would set the nation once again upon the old loyal constitution; and if that were done, there was no great reason of apprehending more danger from the old royalists, since the nobility and gentry, whose interest made them desire a kingly government to distinguish them from the commons, would be in a great measure satisfied when they saw a king and a court again, and would lose their affections to the race of the Stewarts. The fifth-monarchy men (the chief of whom were Lambert, Harrison, and Overton), that were in the best posts, stood firm to their resolutions and oaths, and entered into

[a] Cf. *Hist.* i. 67, 68.   [b] *Ibid.* 65.   [c] *Ibid.* 68.   [d] *Ibid.* 69.   [e] *Ibid.* 68.

[1] Some words have evidently been omitted by the transcriber, and are here conjecturally restored.

consultations of dismounting Cromwell ; but though he turned them out and clapt some of them in prison, the common-wealth humour was sunk too deep into the hearts of the whole army ever to endure that he, who had preached and prayed so much against tyranny, should be in a capacity of assuming that dignity [a] which he [1] had often declared to be the great obstacle to the kingdom of Christ [a]. And all the offers he made of limiting the royal power so that the king should be a duke of Venice were looked on as the acts of an ambitious usurper ; and though he did often in his family devotions, which he performed commonly himself, and in his household fasts protest to God [b] with many tears that he would choose a shepherd's staff rather than a sceptre, and that he had nothing before his eyes but the settlement of the nation [b], yet all this passed for hypocrisy.   And when he argued with any of these people to show them the necessity of having a king for settling the nation, they re[ject ?]ed [2] all that, and [c] said he was looking to the arm of flesh [c], whereas they ought to trust to the living God.   [d] Yet after all it is probable that if he had lived to another sessions of parliament he had carried his point [d] in the army as well as he had already done it in the parliament, for [e] the kingship was offered him [e], though it was carried against a vigorous [*f.* 228 (*b*)] opposition that was made to it.   [f] He hid his mind so artificially in that matter [f], that though it was so plain that he desired it, because all that were in his particular confidence set it on [3], yet [g] there fell not a word from himself intimating his inclinations [g] to accept of it ; for he always said in his canting way that he would seek the Lord, and that his mind was not yet opened to him.   [h] But that which determined him not to adventure

[a] Cf. *Hist.* i. 68.   [b] *Ibid.*   [c] *Ibid.* 69.   [d] *Ibid.* 70.   [e] *Ibid. supra.*
[f] *Ibid.*   [g] *Ibid.*   [h] *Ibid.*

---

[1] The *History* gives this to Goodwin.

[2] The MS. has 'recited.'

[3] It is curious to realize that the whole of this passage on the motives which might induce a successful soldier to assume the title of king (when offered it by Parliament) rather than any lesser title was written before the Revolution had made the question once more acute (*Hist.* i. 813, 814) ; and that the preceding clause may have been deliberately deleted, on ac-count of the curious parallel it suggests to the incidents given in *ibid.* 818, 820.

on the accepting the crown was that the morning in which
he was to give his answer to the parliament, both Fleetwood
and Desborough (the one being his son-in-law and the other
his brother-in-law) came to him, and after they had expressed
their great aversion to the design, they offered up their commissions to him; for they said they could no longer serve
him [a]. The one was lieutenant-general and the other major-
general, so this affrighted him, since [b] he saw he was like to
be deserted by those who above all others were most concerned in his exaltation [b]. While he was managing [this] [1] great
project, death surprised him and put an end to it.

[*Cromwell's foreign policy; its problem.*]

Cf. *Hist.* i. 72 (*from* 'The greatest difficulty' *to* p. 73, 'correspondence with
him ').

After ' Spain ' *add* ' for they both courted him.'

For 'The prince of Condé . . . Cardenas : he ' *read* 'and as Spain by a solemn
embassy congratulated him on his being made protector, so both the courts
allowed the same rank and precedence to his ambassadors that had ever been
given to the ambassadors of the kings of England [cf. *Hist.* i. 80]; nor would he
be contented with the honours given to commonwealths. Spain.'

For ' if he could restore . . . French ' *read* ' if he could again be master of that
key into France and of the channel.'

' Mazarin . . . character ' *is omitted, apparently by the transcriber's error.*

After ' Condé.' *add* ' that was then in the Spanish service.'

For ' he would make a descent . . . dictate ' *read only* ' to set himself at the
head of that party.'

Om. 'to talk . . . men ' *and* ' the oppressions . . . everywhere.'

For ' for Mazarin . . . particular' *read* ' and enjoyed the protection of the edicts
in so ample and undisturbed a manner that there was no reason to expect they
would interrupt their own peace, or so far trust the prince of Condé as to
declare for him.'

For ' He also ' *read* ' Stoupe added to me that Cromwell,' *&c.*

[*f.* 229 (*a*)] *After* ' on that prince ' *add* 'and [that he] was so little careful of
his secret or sure of those about him '; *and om.* 'he said upon that . . . *cardinali.*'

[*The deciding motives.*]

Cromwell saw well enough that in the balance of Europe,
France was become already too hard a match for Spain; yet
as he hoped his having once footing in Flanders would put
him in condition to turn the balance which way he pleased,
so [c] some private considerations of his own determined him to

[a] Cf. *Hist.* i. 70.   [b] *Ibid.*   [c] *Ibid.* 73.

[1] ' The' in the MS., corrected by a later hand.

side with the French; the royal family was then in France,
so if he had broken with that crown, it was in a condition
to assist the king in making a descent in England, which
would have put Cromwell's affairs in great disorder; for not
only the royalists would have gone to him, but even ᵃ many
of the commonwealth's men were so irritated against him,
seeing the steps he was making for his own advancement,
that they began generally to say that if they must return
back to a monarchy, it was better to call in the righteous heir ᵃ.
Cromwell saw this danger well, ᵇ and he knew, on the other
hand, that the Spaniards were in no condition to support the
king in so great a design. So that this particular interest of
his own was so suitable [? sensible] to him that he sacrificed the
interest of the nation to it [1]. ᶜ But while he was balancing all
those matters, Gage, a priest (that had been for many years in
the West Indies) ᶜ, being struck, as he said, with an accident by
a mouse's carrying away the sacrament, was upon that moved
to doubt of his religion; and, he having obtained leave to
come over to Spain, when he was there he goes on board
an English ship, and so came over to England. ᵈ He gave an
account to Cromwell of the feebleness of the Spaniards in
America, and showed him how easy a conquest that would be.
Cromwell saw well that if he succeeded in this he would have
such a treasure in his hands that he could carry on all his
designs without needing the assistance of a parliament ᵈ. This
would also raise his fame and recommend him extremely to
the English nation. So this determined him to join with the
French against the Spaniards, which was the greatest error
he committed in his whole conduct; for as [*f.* 229 (*b*)] ᵉ his
design of Hispaniola failed ᵉ, so the [Biscainers] [2] and the

---

ᵃ Cf. *Hist.* i. 69.   ᵇ *Ibid.* 73.   ᶜ *Ibid.* 74.   ᵈ *Ibid.*   ᵉ *Ibid.* 76.

---

[1] This passage was probably suggested, not by Stoupe's reminiscences, but by the *Character of a Trimmer*, published in 1684; see *Life of Halifax*, ii. 324.

[2] The word was omitted by the original transcriber and 'Buckaniers or Biscainers' is filled in by another hand. 'Biscainer' or 'Biscayneer' (an obsolete synonym for Basque or Biscayan) is evidently the true reading; the inhabitants of the province of Biscay being noted seamen and privateers: see Dr. Murray's *New English Dictionary.*

Ostenders [a] took so many of the merchant ships, that by this means he lost the hearts of the city of London.

[*Stoupe's anecdote concerning the Hispaniola affair.*]

Cf. *Hist.* i. 74 (*from* 'Stoupe, being on another' *to* p. 76, 'esteemed so much as he had been').

Begin 'Stoupe told me a curious thing concerning the design of Hispaniola.'

For 'in measuring distances' *read* 'which he continued to examine very exactly for some time after Stoupe was admitted.'

After 'Mexico, and' *insert* 'having a good sight.'

For 'some fancied . . . element' *read only* 'some said it was to take Cadiz; others that it was to land either at Naples or Ostia, to rob the churches of Italy.'

After 'ambassador' *add* 'Don Alonzo de Cardenas.'

For '£10,000' *read* 'ten thousand pistoles.'

For 'Stoupe owned . . . secret, and' *read only* 'but though Stoupe was not trusted with this secret, yet he was so true to Cromwell that he.'

For 'nor did he think . . . Brussells about it' *read* 'finding the offer of such a sum could draw no discovery from him.'

For 'Stoupe writ it' *to end of incident read only* 'Yet Stoupe writ it to the prince of Condé, with whom he had kept a correspondence; and when the event discovered that he had guessed right, this raised his credit so with the Spaniards that he had many good presents after that from them; and the ambassador was disgraced for not being able to penetrate into the secret.'

[*England's American policy.*]

[b] Thus it appeared that so indifferent a thing as Cromwell looking upon a map might have discovered the great secret which Cromwell kept even from the French; [c] for if he had succeeded in it, this would have put them upon new measures, since it would have raised England so high [c]. And indeed the beating of the Spaniards out of America is as [? so] easy a thing for a king of England (who has so many of [his] subjects already in the northern parts of that new-found world) that, as they will [*f*. 230 (*a*)] very willingly change their states to go into richer countries, so the feebleness of the Spaniards appears so evidently in the faint resistance that they make to the pirates called Buccaniers, that it is plain they could not stand before those armies that could be drawn out of our plantations. But this is a great thing that perhaps is reserved for a high-spirited king of England.

[a] Cf. *Hist.* i. 76.   [b] *Ibid.*   [c] *Ibid.*

[*Cromwell and the foreign protestants.*]

Cromwell made it the first article of his alliance with France that the protestants should be maintained in the full enjoyment of all their edicts, which he took care to see so well observed, that[a] they, finding the happiness of the protection that they enjoyed by his means, were very naturally caused [? carried] to speak well of him that had procured it for them. This increased very much the prejudice that our princes had to the protestant religion; for the king that now reigns told myself that he saw all the protestants of France were rebels in their hearts, and gave this their kindness to Cromwell as the chief evidence of it. Cromwell not only protected the protestants in France, but [b] he interposed so [? as] effectually for those in the valley of Piedmont. The duke of Savoy set on a violent persecution against them; and he obliged the court of France to put a stop to it[b]; and he was so lifted up with the acknowledgements that these things drew to him from beyond sea, that [c] he projected the setting [up] of a council that should watch over the interest of the protestant religion everywhere, that should be like that at Rome, *de propaganda fide.* He had marked out a fund of £200,000[1] per ann. to be disposed of by them as their service should require it. They were to have correspondents in all the places of consideration where the protestant religion was settled. Stoupe was to have been their secretary for France, Switzerland, Geneva, and those of Piedmont[2]; and Cromwell seemed to reserve the settling of it to his exaltation, for if he had been made king he resolved to have begun his government with this[c], which would have raised its credit very much both at home and abroad.

[*Stoupe's anecdote concerning Thurloe.*]

Stoupe told me another particular, that though in itself it does not deserve to be mentioned in history, yet the speculations that arise out of it make me judge it worth the setting

[a] Cf. *Hist.* i. 73.　　[b] *Ibid.* 76.　　[c] *Ibid.* 77.

[1] The *History* says £10,000.
[2] The distribution in the *History* differs.

down. ᵃ Stoupe received an advertisement from him by whose means he kept correspondence with the prince of Condé at Brussells, that an Irishman was gone over with a design to assassinate Cromwell, and that he was to lodge in King street. ᵇ Cromwell had often said that he abhorred [*f*. 230 (*b*)] assassination, and therefore, though it was in his power to destroy the king and both his brothers, yet he would never hearken to so base a proposition ; but he said withal that if any of the royal family began with him and set on men to murder him, he would then reckon himself absolved from all measures, and that he would take care to have the whole race murdered, for he would consider that step as a state of war. It was wisely done of him to declare this so publicly, for that restrained many ᵇ brutal men who otherwise might have set on a practice which cannot be enough detested, since it tends to the destruction of mankind. Yet this Irishman resolved to undertake the business, though it seems he could not keep his own secret. ᶜ Stoupe went with this notice to Cromwell, who happened then to be shut up with his council. Stoupe writ him a note that he had a matter of great consequence to communicate to him that did not admit of delays; yet Cromwell, fancying it was only a piece of news relating to the foreign protestants, sent his secretary Thurloe to see what it was. Stoupe shewed him his letter, but to his great amazement Thurloe took little notice of it, and said such a general story could lead them to no discovery ; the searching of so great a street could not be managed secretly, and if there were a guilty man in it he might make his escape, and the Protector's enemies would say that he was either haunted with needless fears and feigned plots to cover his designs. And Thurloe made so little account of this that he did not so much as speak of it to Cromwell. Stoupe was mortified to see so little notice taken of his news, and spoke of it to the earl of Leicester ᶜ, who was then of Cromwell's council and hated Thurloe. Some weeks after this, Syndercomb (for this was the Irishman's name) watched his opportunity and

ᵃ Cf. *Hist.* i. 78.   ᵇ *Ibid.* 65.   ᶜ *Ibid.* 78.

had laid it so well, that [he had very near succeeded in it; but ᵃhe being discoveredᵃ so critically ¹], Cromwell considered his preservation as a great stroke of Providence.   ᵇWhen Syndercomb was examined, it appeared he was the person concerning whom Stoupe had received the advertisement; so that Leicester said this was the same man that had been marked in Stoupe's letter. Cromwell was amazed to find that Stoupe had given him no notice of this matter; so he sent for him and began to expostulate with him upon it. But when Stoupe put him in mind of the note that he had writ him and of his sending Thurloe to him, he was yet more surprised to find that Thurloe had not said a word [*f.* 231 (*a*)] of it to himself. He sent for him in Stoupe's presence to see if he owned that which Stoupe charged him with; he confessed the matter was true, but he did not think the matter of so much consequence. Cromwell told him sternly enough that he ought to have acquainted him with itᵇ; but added that he saw that advertisements that related to his life were of no consequence. ᶜSo Stoupe came away concluding that Thurloe was ruinedᶜ, and that his credit with Cromwell would be greater than ever it was; but he found Macchiavel's reflection prove true in this case, which is, that a man must be perfectly a good man or perfectly a wicked man, and that many ill men spoil their designs because they have some reserves of goodness which restrained them from some ill actions which their other wicked actions had rendered necessary.   In this case ᵈCromwell had trusted ᵈ this great secret concerning the kingship to ᵉThurloe, so that it was not safe to disgrace him without murdering himᵉ; and therefore Cromwell, not being bad enough for that, saw that it was necessary both to forgive and to employ Thurloe.   ᶠAnd Thurloe (re-established in his favour) made it his business to lessen Stoupe so much in Cromwell's opinion, that he told me he was never used by him after that as he had been formerlyᶠ. So that Stoupe found that a discovery

ᵃ Cf. *Hist.* i. 78.   ᵇ *Ibid.*   ᶜ *Ibid.*   ᵈ *Ibid.*   ᵉ *Ibid.*   ᶠ *Ibid.*

¹ The passage in brackets (probably a marginal insertion) is erroneously placed by the transcriber *supra*, between 'Thurloe' and 'Some weeks.'

which he hoped would have raised his fortune extremely, set him so far back that he was almost forgot ever after this.

[Cromwell and the cavaliers.]

[a] Cromwell had found a way to corrupt him that had the secret of all the king's correspondency in England, who was one sir Richard Willis, that was particularly trusted by Clarendon and had the management of all the consultations that were among the royalists [a]. The corruption was somewhat extraordinary, and deserves to be mentioned. Cromwell had no mind to have any of their lives, but only to traverse all their designs, so that they should be in no condition to do him any hurt, and that they should fall in such jealousies one of another that without any violent remedies all their counsels should be defeated. [b] Willis had assurances given him that no hurt should be done to any of the party; and upon this he entered into a secret commerce with Thurloe [b]; so that the royalists found that everything that they did or said was discovered; and when they were near the executing of any project, [c] some of the chief of them were put in prison, but let out within a few days [c]. So that they suspected there were [f. 231 (b)] some imperfect discoveries made, and this kept them from suspecting Willis; for they knew that he could have made a more ample discovery. Thus Cromwell was often putting them in prison and letting them out again, which made those that did not know his secret affairs conclude that these were the effects of his fear and his hearkening after little whispers [1].

[Final reflections on Cromwell.]

Thus [? But] Cromwell saw that [d] his bearing up the honour of the nation [d] and his supporting of the protestant religion were so [e] apt to give him the hearts of the English [e],

[a] Cf. *Hist.* i. 65.   [b] *Ibid.*   [c] *Ibid.*   [d] *Ibid.* 80.   [e] *Ibid.*

---

[1] The reader will notice how greatly this anecdote is amplified in the *History,* which continues the career of Willis after Cromwell's death.

that he reckoned that if he had but life enough before him
he must at last overcome all the opposition that was made
to him ; and in this appears the greatness of the English
nation (when it is in the hands of one that can manage it
right), that though Cromwell had the whole Scottish and
Irish nation[s] and both the royalists and the commonwealth's
men against him, yet he was clearly the master of the sea.
He beat the Dutch severely ; he was the umpire of the Baltic
Sea and ᵃ the terror of all the Mediterranean ª ; he made the
two great crowns court him by turns in a most abject manner,
and had the luck to die in the midst of all his success, when
ᵇ he had brought his matters to an issue either of setting
himself on the throne or of losing all, by a general revolt ᵇ ;
so that since Caesar's days no man has appeared that had
the true genius of a wise usurper so much as he had. He
was very false, but he managed very artificially ; and in the
midst of all his exaltation, ᶜ when he was in private with
his old acquaintances he conversed with them in the old
familiarity, making them sit down and be covered by him,
reasoning with them in all the freedom of an equality ᶜ. He
had two notions that supported him against all the accusations
of conscience that returned oft upon him ; the one was ᵈ that
he that was once a child of God was always a child of God ;
so he reckoned that having been once in a state of grace, he
could not perish ᵈ ; and it appeared on many occasions, but
chiefly in his last sickness, that ᵉ no doctrine was so clear
[dear ?] to him as that of the perseverance of the saints ᵉ.
The other thing was that ᶠ he thought in extraordinary cases
men were dispensed with, even from the laws of God, which
he thought were rules only [*f.* 232 (*a*)] for ordinary cases ᶠ.
By this he excused both the putting the king to death and
the falsifying his oaths in so many instances, and gave himself
a sort of quiet ; since the necessity of affairs and the public
good required that things should be done which could not
be justified in calmer times. Thus I have given a larger

ᵃ Cf. *Hist.* i. 81–2.   ᵇ *Ibid.* 70.   ᶜ *Ibid.* 68.   ᵈ *Ibid.* 67.
ᵉ *Ibid.*   ᶠ *Ibid.* 46, 79.

character of Cromwell than I intended, but [a] having learnt
a great deal of his private concerns, not only from Stoupe but
from the earl[s] of Carlisle and Orrery [a], who were trusted
much by him, I thought this account of him might be no unpleasant entertainment to the reader.   Yet notwithstanding
all his crimes he will make such a figure in history, that (since
none that I know of have yet given a true representation
of his spirit and designs) this must needs be very acceptable
to those who desire to know the truth of history [1]

[Reflections of the count of Dohna on European revolutions.]

And upon the great figure to which he raised England
all Europe over, and the low one to which the two lawful
kings that have come since have let it sink, I will here
set down a pleasant reflection that the old count of Dohna
(whom I knew at Geneva [2]) ma[d]e [3] on the revolutions that
had fallen out in Europe in his time ; he having seen all the
states of Europe have their turns of being both very high

[a] Cf. *Hist.* i. 65.

---

[1] This long excursus on the career
of Cromwell (which was no doubt modified after the publication of Clarendon's
History in 1702) seems to have been
transferred to its present position in
the *History* by a late after-thought; see
Mr. Airy's note in his ed., vol. i. p. 3.
    [2] Evidently 'Friedrich, Reichsburg-
graf und Graf zu Dohna aus dem
Hause Schlobitten' (born 1621, died
1688), whose memoirs, in French,
have been lately published by H.
Borkowski (1898). His mother having
been a sister of Amelia de Solmes,
Princess of Orange, he was first
cousin once removed to William III ;
while his father, a Prussian nobleman,
the chamberlain and faithful follower
of the hapless Frederic of Bohemia
(being compelled, on the final ruin of
his master, to take refuge in Holland),
was eventually appointed Governor of
the Principality of Orange.   To this
charge, after a military apprenticeship
in the service of the States, Friedrich
succeeded, and retained the post from
1649 to 1662.   He was subsequently
employed in various private negotiations on behalf of his young kinsman
William ; from 1666 to 1668 he served
the state of Geneva, and from 1668 to
1673 held diplomatic posts in Switzerland.   From 1673 until his death in
1688 he lived in retirement, first at
the castle of Coppet, and during the
last few months of his life at Lutry,
near Lausanne. Bayle, who was at one
time tutor to his sons, speaks highly
of the count ; and he seems in fact to
have been a man of high character,
good abilities, agreeable manners, and
extensive cultivation. The memoirs of
his son Christophe (envoy from Brandenburg to the court of St. James,
1698–1700), which contain frequent
allusions to the father, are repeatedly
quoted by Macaulay ; and a brother of
the old count seems to have been at
one time the Swedish representative
at our court.
    [3] The MS. has 'make'; 'I have heard'
may be supplied before 'the old count.'

and very low. When he was a child Spain and the house of Austria were the terror of Europe, and since that time they had sunk extremely ; and now again the emperor, who in [16]83 was upon the point of being utterly ruined (if Vienna had been taken), is beginning to recover again. He saw France in the minority of the present king very near a precipice ; but it is now the terror of all its neighbours. He saw England laid low during the wars, and recover its lustre in Cromwell's time (which has been much eclipsed by the feebleness of the late king and the bigotry of him that now reigns) ; the crown of Sweden rise to such a degree [*f.* 232 (*b*)] that there is nothing in story like it, and maintain[1] its greatness long, and the late king overrun the two neighbouring kingdoms of Poland and Denmark ; and that crown was in the end of the last war laid so low that it was reduced to its first contemptibleness. Denmark was so near being quite conquered that every day the news of the taking of Copenhagen was expected, which was only wanting to complete the conquest ; and since that time the king of Denmark is become both hereditary and absolute. The States of Holland, after they had held the balance of Europe in their hands, were in [16]72 reduced to those extremities that it looks like a dream that they have got out of them. The Venetians were laid extreme low by the wars of Candy, and begin now to grow very formidable ; and in fine the Turk, who had given a terrible blow to the emperor twice in the distance of twenty years' time (in [16]62 and [16]83), and who this last time had brought the war to an end if the grand vizier had not strangely neglected the advantages he had of coming almost to the ports of Vienna, where they had no garrison but companies of burgesses to defend the place (for if he had come on and pressed the siege vigorously it could not have held a week, but his feebleness gave them time to have troops sent in to them, and he lingered so long that at last the king of Poland came and raised the siege), has[2] been followed ever since with

---

[1] The transcript reads 'maintained.'   [2] We delete a superfluous ' which.'

such a constant series of misfortunes, that nothing preserves the Ottoman family but the weakness of those who attack it ; for a vigorous enemy would put an end to it. He had also seen Portugal recover and be again on the point of being conquered by the Spaniards.

[*Strange story of the Portuguese court*[1].]

And this causes me to tell a curious passage relating to the revolution that happened then when the late king was engaged in prison and the present king had both the crown and the queen[2], which I had from Mr. [*f. 233 (a)*] de Schomberg. He being then general of the army and having gained so much credit by his success against the Spaniards, the queen sent her confessor to him to open her secret to him ; for she was then very ill treated by the king that was governed by the marquess of Castelmelhor, who has lived since that time in England ; and the king had really fits of

---

[1] The extraordinary story here told is also given on pp. 78-81 of the anonymous *Account of the Court of Portugal*, published in 1700 and ascribed to Dr. John Colbatch, who had been chaplain to the British factory at Lisbon, and in that capacity had corresponded with Burnet (Brit. Mus. Add. MSS. 22908, ff. 14, 25) ; but was at the period when the book appeared tutor to Burnet's son, at Trinity College, Cambridge (*ibid.* ff. 33, 43, 45, 47, and Autobiography, *infra*, f. 217). As the writer of the *Account* maintains that he is assured the substance of the anecdote ' came from the late duke of Schomberg's own mouth,' it is presumable that he derived it through Burnet, which explains its omission from the *History*.

[2] For this consult, beside the work mentioned in the preceding note, *The Portugal History*, 1677, ascribed to S[amuel?] P[epys?], and the contemporary letters of Sir Robert Southwell (published in 1740 as an appendix to [Carte's] *History of the Revolutions of Portugal*), which are curiously interesting. The facts of the case are, that Dom Alfonzo VI (brother of Catherine of Braganza, queen of Charles II of England), who was born Aug. 21, 1643, and succeeded Nov. 6, 1656, married, in Aug., 1666, Marie Françoise Elisabeth de Savoie : a few months later (Nov. 23, 1667) he was deposed ; his brother, the infante, was declared Prince Regent ; on March 24 following the queen obtained a decree of nullity of marriage from the chapter of Lisbon ; and a few days later, under a legate's dispensation previously obtained, she contracted a marriage with the Regent, which was confirmed by a papal dispensation of Dec. 10, 1668. The deposed king, who was at first confined in the Azores, died in the castle of Cintra fifteen years later, Dec. 11, 1683. The author of the *Account*, who is very severe upon the queen, regards the whole transaction and the evidence brought to invalidate the marriage as the figments of political ambition ; Southwell supposes that the original motive was political, but that the infante eventually fell in love with the queen : it is clear, however, that Alfonzo was eccentric to the verge of madness, if not beyond it.

madness, and being impotent, he was set on by his ministers
to force the queen to admit of another man, by whom she
might have children; and upon many other occasions his
madness shewed itself very evidently. Schomberg saw there
was reason enough to resolve on removing the king from the
government, and he went to the army to dispose them to
concur in the design. The queen sent one with him, by whom
he writ her a plain account of what he had done, and of the
posture in which the army was; this letter was brought her
just as she was going into her bed, so she, that lay then
alone, would not trust the letter to those who laid her to bed,
but put it under her pillow. The next morning, when she
was called on to go to mass, the king being already gone to
it, she rose in so much haste that she forgot her letters.
The king's mass was almost done before she got to chapel,
and he went from it into her apartment. She quickly called
to mind what an error she had committed and sent her confessor to her bedchamber to fetch her letters, but the king
was in it, and seemed to be in such a rage that the confessor
durst not go in, but believed he had discovered all. The
queen sent a lady of her bedchamber, who was likewise upon
the secret; but though she went in she durst not go near
the bed, for the king lay upon it. This was dreadful to the
queen, for if the king had found the letters she and all her
party must have expected to be presently discovered. So
she did not know what course to take; she could not decently
leave the mass till it was done [*f.* 233 (*b*)], and in that while
the king might even by chance find the letter though he
sought not after it. The father confessor advised her to fall
as it were into a sounding [*sic*] fit, since that was the only
pretence that could excuse her leaving the mass before it was
quite done. This was very easy for her to counterfeit, since
the concern in which she was put her very near it. So she
seemed to fall down along upon the ground, and was taken
up in haste, and carried to her bedchamber, at which the king
started up. She lay down and quickly felt for her letters and
found they were still there, by which she got out of her fit;

and as the king had not looked after them, so it was his coming into the bedchamber that kept them from being discovered, since if he had not come in, her bed had been put in order, as it used to be when she went to mass, and so the secret had been discovered. Things of this kind ought to be put in history, because they tend to make people wise and cautious.

[*The intrigue of the Spanish letter.*]

Cf. Hist. i. 302-3.

Begin 'And the offering [? affinity] of the matter makes me set down another secret of the French court which I had from Stoupe [cf. *Hist.* i. 301]. It is ordinary for all persons to tear off the outward cover of letters, and to let them fall carelessly about them,' *and then proceed from* 'Count de Guiche watched,' &c.

Om. 'by the Spanish ambassador.'

Om. 'they sent to Holland.'

For 'in such an affront . . . king' *read* 'in suffering the king to live as he did. His amours with La Vallière were mentioned ; and many sharp reflections on the king's person were mixed in the letter.'

For 'The lady suspected . . . about it' *read* 'The lady, apprehending there was an intrigue in this matter, in which she was to be the tool, carried the letter to the king.'

For 'saw he was . . . So the king' *read* 'was questioned, but shewed evidently that he had been abused in it, as well as the king was. This [*f.* 234 (*a*)] vexed the king out of measure, so he took all the methods he could think on to discover the secret of this matter ; the number of those who could write Spanish was not great ; so the marquis des Vardes (that was then a favourite) being one that could do it [cf. *Hist.* i. 302, *supra*], the king,' &c.

After 'put on him' *read* 'He was indeed upon the secret' *and revert to beginning of* p. 302 ; *and for* 'The king . . . graceful person' *read* 'For as the king had abandoned the countess of Soissons when he took to La Vallière, so she had entered into an intrigue with Des Vardes ; [and] she, being set on revenge[1], had joined with the count de Guiche, who acted likewise in complacency with the duchess of Orleans ; to whom likewise the king, in the beginning of his amour with La Vallière, who was then about her, seemed to make love ; though, as it proved afterwards, it was only a blind to hide the other ; and she took this so ill, that she likewise vowed a revenge.'

Om. 'When the treaty . . . weak a woman she was,' *and proceed from* 'The ladies now rejoiced,' *for from here to the end of the story reading only,* 'So the secret lying amongst those two ladies and their two gallants, the king could not find it out ; but the duchess of Orleans came to like Des Vardes ; and because he did not answer her invitations, but pretended a fidelity to madame de Soissons, she in revenge discovered all to the king.'

---

[1] The transcript places the 'and' after 'revenge.'

[*Burnet's travels; his reflections on the religious state of Europe.*]

I will say nothing more of the "ramble that I made over Italy ", having writ a book [1] upon it with all possible freedom and sincerity, and having since that time put several things that were too mean [2] to be owned by me in some other letters [3] concerning the present state of Italy, which I have not owned, but which I writ out of the memoirs that Mr. Sidney [4] and Dr. Hutton [5] brought me out of Italy, in which I mixed several things that I had found out myself. I shall only add one thing here, which has given me many sad thoughts. [b] I have seen now the greatest part of all the reformed churches. I saw those of France in their best state, that is when they were looking for this sad storm that has scattered them up and down the world. I came and stayed at Geneva, where the miseries of the refugees that were coming thither every day out of France and the apprehen-

---

[a] *Hist.* i. 661–2, 686.   [b] *Ibid.* 686.

---

[1] The well-known *Letters* (to Mr. Boyle), published in 1686 and frequently reprinted under the title *Travels.*

[2] We should perhaps read ' main.' It was the significance, not the insignificance of the subjects in question (Quietism, the Inquisition, and the politics of Italy), which made Burnet, whose avowed *Travels* had excited sufficient irritation at the English court (*Hist.* i. 726), afraid of handling them. Johnson gives ' important' as the final synonym of ' main '; and quotes Milton, ' so *main* to our success.'

[3] These are the anonymous ' Three Letters concerning the present state of Italy, written in the year 1687. I. Relating to the affair of Molinos and the Quietists. II. Relating to the Inquisition and the state of Religion. III. Relating to the policy and interests of some of the States of Italy. Being a supplement to Dr. Burnet's letters. Printed in the year 1688.' There are said to have been two English editions in 1688, and in the same year a translation was appended to a German version of the acknowledged letters ; while in 1689 they were republished, together with the acknowledged letters and some other short pieces, in a two-volume English publication entitled *Dr. Burnet's Tracts.* They are not however included in most editions of the acknowledged letters, though it is probable they have been generally ascribed to him. With the object no doubt of diverting suspicion, Burnet assumes in them the character of a layman, who describes Dr. Burnet's as a ' better pen ' than his own.

[4] Henry Sidney, afterwards earl of Romney, who spent the early part of James II's reign in Italy.

[5] John Hutton, a Scotch herd-boy, graduated M.D. at Padua. Chancing to be in Holland, and at hand when the Princess of Orange had a fall from her horse, he obtained the favour of William, who on coming to the crown made him his first physician. Hutton seems to have subsequently accompanied the king on his campaigns, and gave Burnet some account of William's behaviour at the Boyne (*Hist.* ii. 59-60). Anne continued him in his post, and he died in 1712 (*Dict. Nat. Biog.*).

sions in which they themselves were [of][1] falling under that
tyranny[a] should have awakened them in a signal manner.
[b] I from that went over Switzerland, which except Basel is
not [*f.* 234 (*b*)] indeed in such danger as Geneva is, yet had
still the dismal calamity of the French before their eyes, and
Basel is every day in danger of being swallowed up. After
that I saw those of Strasburg begin already to feel the storm[h]
which [is?] gathering, which will very probably break out
quickly; [c] those of the palatinate see themselves also reduced
to great dangers, and brought under a very bigoted family[c];
and from thence I am now come into [d] Holland, wh[ich][2]
having so lately come out of so great a danger of losing both
their religion and liberty, [e] so that one should have expected
to have found among them, at least at such a time (in which
the whole protestant religion run[s?] such a risk), a more
extraordinary spirit of piety and devotion. There has indeed
appeared a very high degree of charity towards the French
that have left their country[e]; and there is a great deal of
angry zeal against popery; but among those with whom
I have conversed, I must confess with great regret that
I have not found a spirit thriving that either agrees with
the name of the reformed churches or with the present
gloomy times; few are repenting of their sins and forsaking
them; even public and scandalous vices are not corrected,
and [in?] most places are not so much as covered, but are
acted with a bare face and a high hand. Few seem very
sensible of that laziness that is upon people's spirits in the
concerns of religion; few are setting themselves by a sublime
piety and a shining conversation to recover the credit and
beauty of our religion, which is so much darkened, or to
engage God to be again of our side, whom we have highly
dishonoured; and churchmen seem more generally concerned
to engage men to espouse their interests, as they are a party,

[a] Cf. *Hist.* i. 686.   [b] *Ibid.*   [c] *Ibid.*   [d] *Ibid.*   [e] *Ibid.* 687.

[1] Omitted by the transcriber; 'a' is erroneously inserted in a later hand.
[2] The transcriber wrote 'who.'

than either to reform themselves or the flocks committed to their charge. [a] Sermons are for the most part dry and dull things [a], and rather essays of wit, eloquence, and learning, than divine instructions and exhortations. They have lost both the beauty of a primitive simplicity and the overcoming force of true preaching; and though [b] matters in England have taken a different quality [b] from that in which I left them, yet I do not hear [c] that there is any great change wrought as to the religious part, or that men grow better Christians, though they are more steady [*f.* 235 (*a*)] protestants than I fancied they would have been. [d] These things affect me very sensibly, and make me often conclude that for as melancholy as the outward state of the protestant religion is at present, the inward symptoms are yet much worse [d] and more desperate; and [though?] the prospect of the exaltation of [the] prince and princess of Orange is very promising, yet the depraved state of the protestant churches, especially of the clergy, makes me fear after all that we are not yet ripe for a deliverance. [e] The Lutherans in Germany are as averse as ever to all sort of reconciliation with the Calvinists, [f] and the clergy of Holland are as rigid as they, in all their little opinions, and as apt to quarrel about them, and are now broken all into factions, [g] and upon the smallest occasions are falling into most intemperate heats [g]; and that which is yet the most astonishing part of all this sad scene, is that [h] the French, who have forsaken their country to the hazard of the severest punishments, who have abandoned their estates and left that which was dearer, their children, behind them, many of them having suffered much hardship, that these, I say, are much less affected with all this than ought to be exp[ect]ed [1]. Their ministers preach as coldly as ever, and though one is bound in charity to believe that they have made this sacrifice of all that was dear to them out of a good principle [h], yet by

[a] Cf. *Hist.* i. 687.   [b] *Ibid. infra.*   [c] *Ibid.* 688.   [d] *Ibid.* 687.   [e] *Ibid. supra.*   [f] *Ibid. infra.*   [g] *Ibid. supra.*   [h] *Ibid.*

---

[1] The transcriber has written 'expressed.'

seeing and conversing with the greatest part of them one is
not much edified, though I must add, I know many very
extraordinary persons among them, which act upon the best
motives, and are indeed great examples.   While I reflect on
all these things, I do not know what to think; how strange
a matter is it, while we are very hot in disputing about some
controverted points, we as it were all agree to neglect the
great and uncontroverted duties of true holiness and a sublime
morality; but if one wonder drives out another, I give myself
a little ease from the pain which these melancholy thoughts
raise in me by considering that it was so at all times.   In the
very days of the apostles what strange corruptions both in
doctrine and morality were breaking in upon the churches
(which appears from all the epistles, and more evidently from
those short ones that are in the beginning of the Revelations);
in all which it appears that man is (and has been at all times)
a strange, foolish, and mad creature, and that the providence
of God and the conduct of the world are the greatest of all
mysteries.

[*Burnet's reception at the Hague.*]

[a] At my [*f.* 235 (*b*)] coming to Holland I found that the
prince and princess of Orange were so favourably disposed [1]
towards me that they suffered me to speak freely to them
of our affairs [a]; so that for some [time [2]] [b] I had a free access
to them [b].   I knew what would become of this; for [c] the king
began quickly to express his displeasure [c] at the credit which
he apprehended that I might have with them; though I am
perhaps one of the clergymen in the world that am most
against all severity on the account of religion; and [d] I studied
to encourage the prince and princess in their resolutions of
consenting to liberty of conscience [d] with all possible zeal.   Yet
the king, who is vehement in everything that he once under-
takes, [e] continued by frequent repeated instances to press my

[a] *Hist.* i. 688.   [b] *Ibid.* 691.   [c] *Ibid.* 692.   [d] *Ibid.* 691.   [e] *Ibid.* 708.

---

[1] The Life, following the Autobiography, ascribes this to the influence
of Lord Halifax and Lady Russell.
[2] Inserted; qu. by the writer of f. 2?

being forbid their presence; and in both his letters which the prince[ss?][1] hath showed me, [a]and in his discourse of me, he seemed to forget his own greatness[a], and spake and writ of me in a style that had more of anger and ill-nature than of modesty in it. He gained his point, and [b]I went no more to court. [c]But, after that, the book I writ concerning Italy appeared, in which my chief design was to lay open the misery of those who lived under absolute government and a devouring superstition; there were many passages in it that offended the court highly. Next after that some papers appeared against the abolishing the test, and upon the declarations for liberty of conscience both in England and Scotland[1]. These took so much with the nation, that the king believed they crossed his designs; he suspected me to be the author, as I was indeed, though he could never find proofs of it. This sharpened a displeasure which was already quick enough; but he understanding that I was like to have one of the best matches in the Hague[c] (and a person[2] that was originally descended from a Scotch family, and that had in her all the qualities that I could have proposed to myself in a wife, besides a very fair estate), [d]he thought to have broke this by accusing me of high treason for having had a correspondence with Argyll, and for having conversed with some that were condemned of high treason. The truth was, the king writ himself to Scotland ordering his advocate to prosecute me[d]; and his advocate having no matter against me, threw together such things as he could fancy might be true. [a]I had the news of this from Scotland before the king's envoy had it[e]; and it came to me just the night before I was to be [*f.* 236 (*a*)] contracted; so Mr. Halewyn proposed an

---

[a] *Hist.* i. 726.   [b] *Ibid.* 708.   [c] *Ibid.* 726.   [d] *Ibid.*   [e] *Ibid.*

---

[1] Mr. Flexman's list, appended to *Hist.* ed. 1833, vi. 357, enumerates six such pamphlets. See also the *Collection of Eighteen Papers . . .* by Gilbert Burnet, D.D., 1689.

[2] For Mary Scott, second wife of Burnet and mother of all his surviving children, see Autobiography, *infra*, f. 210; *infra*, App. II (Meditation by Burnet on his wedding-day, May 25, 1687); *infra*, App. III.; Life of the Bishop, by her son Thomas (appended to *Hist.* ii), p. 695; art. *Dict. Nat. Biog.*

expedient, of which the prince approved, which was that the next morning I should ª petition the States of Holland to be naturalized. This was so reasonable, and seemed to be so much of a piece with my contract that was to be signed in the afternoon, that it passed without opposition ; for it was not known that there was any other design in it ; and by this means I came under the protection of the States. But I studied to soften the court, and writ several letters to the earl of Middleton in my own justification. I showed that all the matters that were laid against me were notoriously false in all the branches of it [*sic*], which appeared so plainly that the court let fall the pursuit. But because in my first letter I had writ that by my naturalization my allegiance in these provinces translated me from his majesty to the States, and because I added that if a sentence should pass against me I should be forced to justify myself and give an account of that share which I had in affairs these twenty years past, in which I might be led to mention some things that I was afraid might displease the king, upon this the court ordered a citation ª ; though it seemed strange to see the king, who had naturalized so many strangers, make a crime of my saying that I was at present become a subject to the States ; and it was also absurd to say that I threatened the king, in saying that I would be forced to write a history in my own justification. Yet this being more specious than the matter laid against me in the first citation, ᵇ the court has still kept up this against me, but has delayed proceeding to a sentence now for several months ᵇ, to see if the terror of it would bring me to make submission. And to frighten me the more, ᶜ the English envoy has talked with several of his spies of a design he had to carry me away, though the methods that he proposed were so ridiculous, and he opened it to so many persons, that all came to my knowledge ; from which I must conclude that he either spoke of it to frighten me ᶜ, or that he is one of the unfittest men in the world to manage such a design. I have taken my own way, and ᵈ have not entered

ª Cf. *Hist.* i. 726-7.   ᵇ *Ibid.* 727.   ᶜ *Ibid.*   ᵈ *Ibid.*

into any state óf treaty, though my friends in London have
writ me word that several overtures have been made to
reconcile me to the court ; but since I have not hearkened
to any of them, I hear now sentence is passed ; and whether
[*f.* 236 (*b*)] upon this any of the brutal Irish that are here
in the service will endeavour to merit at the king's hands
by destroying me [1], I do not know, nor am I much concerned[a] ;
for I am weary of life and of the world. So all my apprehensions are that they may make an attempt upon me, that
shall go only half way, and of all the things in the world
an operation of surgery is that which I apprehend the most ;
but for this and all that relates to myself, [b] I resign myself
up entirely to that providence that has hitherto watched over
me with such an indulgent care, that what my enemies have
designed against me [b], as the greatest mischief they could do
me by driving me out of England, [c] has produced the happiest
alteration [c] in the course of my life that could have befallen me,
and that which gives me the perfectest quiet and content [2].
But now I return to the secrets of public affairs.

[*The Scotch declaration of indulgence.*]

[Cf. *Hist.* i. 712 (*from* ' He sent a proclamation ' *to* p. 714, ' cold and general
words ').

For 'in February' *read* 'in the beginning of the year [16]87.'

Om. ' This was published . . . England.'

After ' The king' *insert* 'who is bound to maintain the laws.'

For ' not only . . . authority' *read only* [of] claim[ing] a power superior
to the laws.'

After ' sacred' *add* '[so] that though many princes have in effect claimed this
power, yet none that I know [*f.* 237 (*a*)] of have ever declared so much in
plain words.'

After ' rested in him ' *add* 'but as this is the only precedent that I could

[a] Cf. *Hist.* i. 727.　　　[b] *Ibid.*　　　[c] *Ibid.*

---

[1] See Luttrell, i. 433, 434, March,
1687-8 ; *Portland MSS.* (H. M. C.), iii.
405, for a report (in March, 1687-8) that
an attack had been made upon a Scotch
gentleman (identified with Sir Robert
Hamilton) who had been severely
wounded coming out of Burnet's
house ; that it was supposed the assault
had been intended for Burnet ; that the
States had offered £100 for the apprehension of the three ruffians concerned,
and that Burnet was given a guard of
soldiers. The report can hardly have
been true, or Burnet would surely
have mentioned it in his subsequent
narrative.

[2] He alludes of course to his second
marriage.

ever find of kings pretending to absolute power in any legal government (of which our court will have no reason to boast much).'

For 'The requiring' *read* 'Yet our court carried the matter much further by requiring'; *and after* 'this' *add* 'absolute power; which.'

Om. '(as indeed [that it seemed]¹ . . . jealousies).'

Om. 'to set up conventicles . . . way.'

[*f.* 237 (*b*)] *For* 'addresses' *read* 'an address.'

For 'they answered . . . words' *read only* 'they could not prevail so far with them.'

[*A parliament in Scotland.*]

Cf. *Hist.* i. 679 ('In summer . . . prevail on a majority') *and* 680–1.

For 'In summer . . . parliament had been' *read* 'There had been a trial made of a sessions of parliament in summer [16]86, to which the earl of Murray was sent down commissioner.'

Om. 'and tests . . . religion.'

After 'methods' *insert* 'both of fear and hope.'

After 'majority' *add* 'But Murray was too weak a man to manage such a matter'; *and om. entirely from* p. 679 ('But two accidents') *to* p. 680 ('who had it from the earl himself'), *and begin again at* 'When the session' (p. 680) *and go on to end of paragraph.*

Om. 'he promised.'

Om. 'and so did the bishop of Galloway.'

Om. 'were silent but'; *and after* 'laws' *add* 'but only one or two had the courage to speak for them.'

For 'meanness' *read* 'poorness,' *and for* 'of the other members' *read* 'the meanness of the commissioners for the burghs.'

After 'maintained' *for* 'yet' *read* 'It went otherwise for.'

After 'from the king' *add* 'without any reason assigned'; *and om.* 'And Paterson . . . Dunkeld.'

[*Reflections on the foregoing; state of Ireland.*]

Upon this ᵃ the nation, that was become extremely corrupt, and both ignorant and insensible as to the matters of religion, began to recover its old hatred against popery ᵃ. And though some ᵇ few ᵇ of the ruined nobility ᵇ have changed their religion ᵇ in hopes of favour from the court, yet popery is not like to make any great progression in Scotland. ᶜ It is true the episcopal clergy there is so rank, that as they are not able to [*f.* 238 (*a*)] animate the nation much ᶜ, so few of them have the zeal or the courage that is necessary for it. But, on the other hand, ᵈ the Presbyterians maintain their rooted aversion to popery to so high a degree, that the court has no great reason to depend

ᵃ *Hist.* i, 681.   ᵇ *Ibid.*   ᶜ *Ibid.*   ᵈ *Ibid.*

---

¹ The second reading is that of Routh's *Burnet's James II.*

upon them[a]; and it is not understood whether the king will go on to maintain their liberty that he has granted by his absolute power, or whether he will try another parliament. Yet Scotland is considered as an accessory to England, which will follow his [? her] fortune; [b] but Ireland is in a much more dangerous condition; for the lord deputy goes on in his brutal way[b], and now matters are there going on fast to a crisis; since the sheriffs, being generally Irish papists, have now begun in several countries to turn the English out of possession of their estates, which they hold by virtue of the act of settlement, and repossess the Irish; this is already done in a great many countries, and according to the success they find in these small attempts, they may probably go on to act more boldly. Yet the king continues to say that he will maintain the settlement of Ireland, just as he says he will maintain the church of England, at the same time that he is doing all he can to destroy it. [c] The English papists are sensible enough of Tyrconnell's brutality[c], and they thought to have got him to be recalled, and Powis was to go in his stead; of which he thought himself so sure, that he owned it to a friend of mine that he was to go thither; but this was eight months ago. Tyrconnell has, it seems, so established himself in the king's confidence that there is no appearance of a change.

[*The king and the English dissenters; characters of D'Albeville and Skelton.*]

But for the affairs of England, the king finding the church of England so firm that he had small hopes of prevailing on them, and [? he] resolved next to change his course, and to try what he could expect from the dissenters. He sent over [d] Mr. D'Albeville, or rather one Mr. White, an Irish papist, who had been for many years a spy[d] in the court of England. He began the trade in Cromwell's days, whose spy he was, as Stoupe told me; after that he was [e]employed by the Spaniards, by whose means he had obtained that empty

[a] *Hist.* i. 681.   [b] *Ibid.*   [c] *Ibid.* 682.   [d] *Ibid.* 707, 708.   [e] *Ibid.*

title of marquess [a]. He served also to the States in the same quality, but it was believed that [a]he was corrupted [*f.* 238 (*b*)] by the French [a] to give them false intelligence. [b] Mr. Skelton was envoy before [b]; and if a judgement is to be made of men by their employments through which they pass, one should conceive a very high opinion of him, for he has been now many years in foreign negotiations. He was first sent to Vienna to dispose the emperor to a peace to be made at Nimeguen ; then he was sent to reside in Hamburgh and to negotiate the affairs of the North ; after that he was brought to Holland, and he is now in Savoy, [c] and in France [c]. And yet after all this [d] he is a very weak [d] and passionate man, who neither understands the conduct of affairs, nor can govern his tongue with any sort of temper ; for as his passion carries him to fly out on all occasions, so his vanity is so little governed that [e] he discovers all sorts of secrets [e], even when he can have no other design in it but to let it appear that he knows them. [f] He had committed so many errors in Holland, and had given [f] the prince of Orange [f] such particular reasons of being displeased at him, that D'Albeville was sent in his room [f] ; who had a sort of fawning and smooth [way] with him [1], and who had made this his chief maxim, to say to every man that which he thinks will please him ; but he doth this so coarsely that he is soon discovered. He has all the boldness that he thinks necessary to get through in lying and dissembling. [g] He assured the States that the king was firmly resolved to maintain his alliance with them, and that his naval provisions had no relation to them, but were only intended to preserve the peace of Europe ; and he seemed troubled to find the States so possessed with the apprehensions of those preparations that they had already [h] ordered Mr. Dyckveldt to go over [h] and observe the king's motion. [i] This he endeavoured all he could to divert, for Dyckveldt was not yet gone. [k] It was but in

[a] Cf. *Hist.* i. 708. [b] *Ibid.* 623, 707. [c] *Ibid.* 707. [d] *Ibid.* 623. [e] *Ibid.* 624. [f] *Ibid.* 707. [g] *Ibid.* 709. [h] *Ibid.* 708. [i] *Ibid.* 709. [k] *Ibid.* 708.

---

[1] The transcript reads ' fawning and smoothing with him.'

vain, for ªthe prince had a particular design in sending him
over, which was to speak freely to the king ª, and to engage
the king to speak freely likewise[1].

[*D'Albeville's negotiation with the prince and princess;
Dyckveldt's report.*]

Cf. Hist. i. 709 (*from* 'In his secret negotiations' *to* p. 711, 'brought to
hearken to them ').

Om. ' secret'; *and after* ' assurances ' *add* ' in the king's name.'

[*f.* 239 (*a*)] *After* ' crown' *add* ' and to make it more absolute.'

For ' who had served . . . conscience' *read* ' and of whose loyalty and fidelity
he was well assured; but he added, that the king was [al]so resolved to
maintain the establishment of the church of England, and never to use any
violence in matters of conscience.'

For ' and that he spoke' *read* ' and not only spoke'; *after* ' bigot' *add* ' that
had lost his reason and'; *and for* ' whereas . . . maxims, and therefore he'
read ' but he had.'

After ' relief' *add* ' 'Tis true in this he shewed his concern for the order of
the Jesuits ; for he said P. de la Chaise,' *&c. as above.*

After ' subjects' *add* ' when he went over ; to whom he gave a good reception and to whom he spake very freely, and for the most part calmly, of all those
matters.   He was very earnest to gain the princess's consent.'

For ' At that time' *read* ' And when D'Albeville came over.'

After ' assurances ' *add* ' in his name.'

For ' But the king had reckoned . . . put off' *read* ' This was founded on the
easiness of some members who gave the king secret assurances ; but as the king
went on trying the temper of more members he found he could not come within
a great way [*f.* 239 (*b*)] of the majority of either [of the] houses, so he
dissolved the parliament.'

After ' reasonable ' *for* ' to let papists in to sit' *read* ' to [take] away the tests
by which papists might come into.'

For ' of some . . . particular' *read only* ' of the men of that religion.'

After ' jealousy ' *add* ' for the time to come.'

Om. ' it appeared . . . desired.'

For ' in so tender . . . ill from them' *read only* ' in matters of religion, so that
his throwing them off upon that account.'

For ' the king . . . improve the' *read* ' They were sorry to see the king
neglect the great'; *and for* ' might be . . . and great' *read* ' of being happy.'

Om. ' best, and now the only.'

After ' true' *add* ' they were extreme sorry to see the king involve himself in
designs in which he was like to meet with great difficulties at home, and in
which [*f.* 240 (*a*)] the[y] could not at all concur with him.'

For ' of their answers . . . D'Albeville' *read* ' of all that was said in that
matter.'

ª Cf. *Hist.* i. 708.

---

[1] The reader will observe that there
is here no mention of Dyckveldt's
errand to the opposition, mentioned in
the *History*, i. 708-9.

For 'he found . . . resolution' *read* 'he never found anything like good reasoning, but only a stiff firmness.'

After 'He said' *add* 'often.'

For 'so the king saw . . . Sunderland' *read only* 'since that might look like a reproaching of the king. Upon this Dyckveldt, that gave me an account of all that negotiation, told me that Sunderland'; *after* 'prince' *add* 'and princess'; *and after* 'concur with the king' *add* 'in the matter of the tests; that he should have the chief stroke in all affairs.'

For 'And they engaged . . . settled' *read* 'And some carried this so far as to offer that.'

[*Dyckveldt and the English opposition.*]

[a] Dyckveldt came at this time to enter into great confidences with many in England [a]; and he gave them righter impressions of the prince, [b] for many were possessed with hard thoughts of him, as though he had arbitrary notions of government [b], and these [*f. 240 (b)*] reports were studiously enforced into the minds of the country party by the papists, who seemed generally to wish for a commonwealth rather than see the prince upon the throne.

[*The Liège letter.*]

Cf. *Hist.* i. 711-2.

For 'great discovery' *read* 'pretty discovery.'

For 'by the Jesuits' *read* 'by the indiscretion of the Jesuits.'

For 'in Switzerland' *read* 'in Alsatia.'

After the second 'to kiss his hand' *read* 'which was indeed a high strain of bigotry.'

Om. 'The Jesuits at Fribourg . . . Geneva and Switzerland.'

For 'One of those . . . named the Liège letter' *read* 'Dyckveldt mentioned this letter to the king to convince him that the priests would not be contented with liberty.'

Om. 'made to make . . . odious.'

Om. 'Dyckveldt thought.'

[*Origin of the Fagel-Stewart correspondence.*]

[c] But because the court of England might have misrepresented the prince's thoughts in this matter [*f. 241 (a)*] either to other popish princes with whom he was united in the common concerns of Europe or to the English nation, the prince laid hold of an opportunity that was offered him by [d] some letters that were writ to Mr. Fagel by one Stewart, an advocate of great esteem of the Scottish nation, who had

[a] Cf. *Hist.* i. 712.　　　[b] *Ibid.* 709.　　　[c] *Ibid.* 732.　　　[d] *Ibid.* 731-2.

been engaged in Argyll's business, and was now invited out
of Holland, where he had stayed for some years, and had got
into some degrees of confidence with the pensioner[a]. The
court thought that he might be of great use to them in
disposing the presbyterians in Scotland to concur with the
king in taking off the penal laws. [b] He spake with the prince
before he left Holland, and gave him very positive assurances
of his fidelity to the common interest of religion. Yet when
he came to the court, the king possessed him with such an
opinion of his sincerity, and that he had no other design but
to establish a general liberty of conscience, that he undertook
to serve him in it both in Scotland and in the Hague.

[*Stewart's letters.*]

Cf. *Hist.* i. 731-2 (*from* 'He opened' *to* 'gained by the court').
Om. 'at another time.'
For 'Stewart after . . . But he found there, that' *read* 'but as he found no
success in his negotiation in Scotland, [where]'; *after* 'court' *add* 'so his letters
to the pensioner had no effect, which has very much displeased the court.'
For from 'The pensioner laid' *to end of paragraph read only* 'for he writ a
long and full answer to them.'

[*Fagel's letter.*]

Cf. *Hist.* i. 732 (*from* 'He began it' *to* p. 733, 'all or nothing').
[*f.* 241 (*b*)] *For* 'carried by . . . brought by him into' *read only* 'was read in.'
For 'but nothing . . . upon it' *read* 'but hitherto it has had no effect.'
For 'ordered Stewart . . . back' *read* 'said plainly to Stewart.'

[*Probable issue of the affair; position of father Petre; imprudence of D'Albeville.*]

This letter, which will be published ere long, will probably
have both a great effect on the nation and [c] all the moderate
catholics both within and without the kingdom, and by what
I have seen writ from Rome, the pope will very probably
advise the king to accept of it. But the king is now in the
hands of the Jesuits and the French ambassador[c], who has
more credit at present in our court than he had during the
last reign ; and as the king's confessor is a Jesuit, so [d] he has
taken F. Petre into his particular confidence, as he hath
been long in the secret of affairs, and is now made a privy
councillor[d]. He is a weak and [e] an ignorant man[e], but is all

---

[a] Cf. *Hist.* i. 732.   [b] *Ibid.*   [c] *Ibid.* 733.   [d] *Ibid.*   [e] *Ibid.* 672.

made up of a violent and meddling temper, which had rendered him formerly unacceptable to all the families in which he had lived. [a] He pretends now to be made arch-bishop of York and a cardinal ; but that is not like to be obtained during the present pontific[ate] [1], [*f*. 242 (*a*)] [b] for the pope is so possessed against the whole order that it will not be easy to bring him to advance any of them ; and as he has already refused to do it very flatly, though it was most earnestly desired of him by the king, so it is not like he will ever be brought to grant it. [c] But the king, though he is really governed by the Jesuits' cabal, yet would not absolutely disgust the secular priests, whose head is Leyborne, that was sent over by cardinal Howard ; so he is likewise made a privy councillor, though he has not so great a share in the counsels as the other has. This creates a faction among them which has been sometimes upon the point of breaking out very grossly ; but the king is so partial to the Jesuits that the other must be contented. D'Albeville is now coming over again, having been five months in England ; for it seems the papists have no other whom they will trust with the negotia-tion but him, which shows how low they are, and how much they want men, for he has not at all the address that is necessary for such tender matters, of which I will only set down [one ?] instance. [d] When the prince was once pressing him upon the promises that the king had made and sworn, to maintain the laws and the established religion, he, [instead of] pretending that the king still kept his word [d] by giving some ambiguous sense to his promises, [e] said roundly that upon such and such occasions, which he named, other princes [2] had forgot their promises [e]. But though in the avowing this so frankly there was much sincerity, [f] yet the prudence of a minister will appear as little in it [f] as in that which followed : [g] when the prince was arguing that the church of England being the main body of the nation the king ought to have

---

[a] Cf. *Hist.* i. 733.　　[b] *Ibid.* 704.　　[c] *Ibid.* 733.　　[d] *Ibid. infra.*
[e] *Ibid.* 734.　　[f] *Ibid.* 733.　　[g] *Ibid.* 734.

---

[1] The transcript reads 'pontificall.'　　　　[2] The *History* differs.

more regard to them, D'Albeville answered that the body
which he called the church of England would not have a being
two years to an end; which was to speak out the designs of
the court a little too plainly[a].

[*Burnet reflects: I. on these negotiations, as they affect the European
situation; II. on English affairs, and the prince's dilemma; III.
on the report that the queen is with child*[1].]

I give the account of this negotiation the more particularly,
both because I am certainly informed of it by messages which
the prince sends me, and because this is like to be the
occasion of a rupture which may have great consequences.
France apprehends the prince's being on the throne of
England above all things; so they will certainly push
[*f.* 242 (*b*)] on the king as far as is possible to embroil
matters both in England and between the king and prince;
since as this keeps the king still in a dependence on them,
so it may in the end produce somewhat in which they find
their account. On the other hand, the extremity to which
the king has driven matters will throw the nation into great
confusions, which it will be very hard to manage. For either
the nation will lose heart, and then a multitude will become
the feeblest thing in the world; or if the vigour of the
subjects is still kept up, it will be hard to govern this and
to keep it from breaking out upon great provocations, chiefly
if a force is put upon the elections of parliament men, which
strikes at all. And if there should be a comm[otion[2]], or
if the violence of the Irish should create a disorder in that
island, the prince will be reduced to great difficulties; the
ties of nature will make it hard for him to head a rising
against his father-in-law; but, on the other hand, if the king's
ill conduct throws the nation into such a violent fermentation,

[a] Cf. *Hist.* i. 734.

[1] The significance of this passage
is discussed in the *Life of Halifax*, i.
492–4. The views there defended
derive extraneous support from the
valuable authority of Herr Onno Klopp
(*Der Fall des Hauses Stuart*, vols. iii and
iv, *passim*), with whose important work
the author was unfortunately not acquainted. Klopp, iv. 497–9, shows that
the D'Estrees letters (Dalrymple, pt. i.
bk. i. App. pp. 122–30) are a forgery.

[2] The MS. reads 'a commission.'

then a rebellion that prospers will turn to a commonwealth; and if it is subdued it will put all things in the king's hands. So that the difficulties will be great on all hands; for [where] nature and honour, religion and interest, pull all different ways it will not be easy to come to a resolution. A war at home of any continuance will naturally bring over a French army, in whose hands the king will put such places as are in his power. And thus we are like to become a scene of blood and horror again; and the outrageous counsels of a few priests about the king are like to bring England again to the very brink of the precipice and very near its ruin. It is true there is a report[1], now generally believed to be true, which may change the whole scene. It is said that the queen is with child. This piece of news is so fit for their affairs at present that this tempts many to doubt of it. Yet it seems to be true; and if [it] proves in conclusion such as they desire, it will extremely feed the superstition of the party; for (besides the seasonableness of it [since][2] it comes at a juncture in which without this small hope their affairs were quite desperate [3]) ᵃ they give out that this conception was the effect of a vow ᵃ the queen [4] made ᵃ to the Virgin ᵃ. [*f.* 243 (a)] And indeed if the queen, that brought a great many children in the freshness of her youth, when she came first over, which were all so unhealthy that they died quickly, should now after so much sickness, that has brought her so very low, bear a healthy son, it would look on all hands as a very particular stroke of providence that was almost a miracle. But the history of the following years must determine this matter, which I must now leave in the uncertainty in which it is at present. But I go on to finish the present period of my history.

ᵃ Cf. *Hist.* i. 749.

---

[1] This passage, being written on or before Dec. 26, 1687 (see *infra*), seems to have been recorded before the proclamation of Dec. 23, 1687, ordering prayers for the queen's safe delivery, reached Holland. The reports had circulated as early as Nov. 14 (see *Hist. MSS. Comm. Rep.* xv. pt. 2, p. 72); and the Princess of Orange had been informed of her stepmother's expectations before Nov. 29, O. S. (Strickland, *Q. of Eng.*, ed. 1851-2, vi. 202).

[2] The transcript reads 'sure.'

[3] The transcript inserts 'and.'

[4] The *History* says, 'her mother.'

[*The English declaration of indulgence.*]

Cf. *Hist.* i. 714 (*from* 'In April' *to* 'concur with him in it ').
After 'that limited this' *read* 'for all time to come.'
Om. 'as well as to . . . church party.'
For 'yet no limitation . . . suspension' *read* 'yet this was not only pretended to be done only [*sic*] in the intervals of parliament.'
Om. 'And the promise . . . any such thing.'

[*Addresses made upon it.*]

Cf. *Hist.* i. 714-6 (*to* 'changed likewise ').
Begin 'Yet though this was a subverting the whole constitution of the English government.'
[*f.* 243 (*b*)] *After* 'dissenters' *add* 'to thank the king for the grace that was contained in it.'
Om. 'being penned . . . gained.'
For 'on the clergy . . . proceedings' *read* 'on the church of England men.'
After 'favour' *add* 'and offered up their lives and fortunes to the king.'
For 'made the cruelty . . . discourse' *read* 'broke with the church of England in a most unmerciful manner.'
For 'to show favour . . . propositions to him' *read* 'to do what he desired.'
For 'for as the persons . . . defame them' *read* 'for whatsoever some violent men might say, yet it was well known that the eminent men of the church of England had made no such advances; and this way of using them was thought an extraordinary return for their past services.'
For 'But, to carry this further . . . themselves had been lately treated' *read* 'Yet the design of this was clearly seen ; for the court thought to have engaged the church of England men and dissenters into new contentions; and they knew that they must needs gain by that. But both sides were wiser upon this occasion.'
Om. [*f.* 244 (*a*)] 'that were gained by the court.'
For 'though it was visible . . . church' *read* 'as if the chief hold by which their establishment was preserved had been that promise, and as if a general promise that was put in a declaration whose chief intent was to destroy the church of England had been so much to be magnified.'
For 'But the bishop . . . with him in it' *read* 'Yet when the bishop of Oxford sent one to the university it was rejected there with much vigour, only one person out of the whole body signing it ; and the reasons upon which they refused to do it were so strong, that these addresses were not any more encouraged by the clergy.'
For 'Some foolish men . . . peevishness' *read* 'The foolish angry men that were amongst [them [1]] were really vexed because they could not persecute their brethren any more.'
For 'But the far greater part . . . remembered this' *read* 'But the wiser and better part began now to see what advantages their animosities had given the papists ; and so they became much more moderate on those heads. If this temper continues, so that all men grow convinced that the papists have all along

---

[1] Inserted ; qu. by the writer of f. 2?

fomented our differences for their own ends, this may have a very happy effect on us in the next probable revolution [1].'

For 'Now the bedchamber . . . dissenters' *read* 'But now the tables were strangely turned at court, for the church of England men were extremely decried'; *and om.* 'and was venturing . . . account.'

After 'changed likewise' *add* 'Upon which a new set of pamphlets came out; yet all this went soon over.'

[*A progress arranged.*]

Cf. *Hist.* i. 716 ('The king seeing no hope . . . counties'); *for which read* 'But the main thing was the preparation of the nation for a new election of parliament men, and in order to the softening of men's minds, the king resolved on a progress through many of the western counties; the queen's ill health made it necessary for her to stay at The Bath.'

[*Reception of the nuncio.*]

Cf. *Hist.* i. 716-7.

[*f.* 244 (*b*)] *For* 'laws were repealed' *read* 'laws were ready to be repealed.'

For 'The duke of Somerset' *read* 'But of all the courtiers the duke of Somerset was the only person that refused to assist in the ceremony. [He].'

For 'that no person could hear it' *read* 'that I could not learn what the substance of it was.'

[*The king's progress; a supposed result of the Bath.*]

Cf. *Hist.* i. 717 (*from* 'When this was over' *to* 'her course of bathing').

For 'to all sorts of people' *read* 'unto them.'

For 'He ran out . . . conscience' *read* 'and was always magnifying the liberty that he had granted, and showed how much it was the interest of the nation.'

[*f.* 245 (*a*)] *For* 'at The Bath . . . bathing' *read* 'and it is now given out, that The Bath had so good an effect that upon their meeting she conceived.'

[*A pamphlet war [2].*]

Cf. *Hist.* i. 717 (*from* 'Many books' *to end of paragraph*).

For 'Many books were now writ for' *read* 'All [? At] this time all that intended to merit at court were writing little books to persuade people to accept of the proffer of a general'; *and omit* 'and since . . . tests gave.'

Om. 'It was never explained . . . word.'

Om. 'ever since the Oxford parliament.'

After 'upon this' *add* 'and the civilities that the king had shewed to those of the commonwealth's party'; *and om.* 'sort of.'

For 'began to talk . . . nation' *read* 'cherished the discourse, in order to the gaining of that party.'

---

[1] i.e. the political transformation which must result from the princess's eventual accession. It must be remembered, that since, even accepting the report of the queen's pregnancy as true, all depended on the sex and vitality of the expected offspring, the odds were still in favour of this contingency.

[2] See *The Anatomy of an Equivalent*, by the Marquis of Halifax.

[*Changes in the magistracy.*]

Cf. *Hist.* i. 718–9 (*to* 'reserved in the new charters').
Om. 'For great powers . . . severity and contempt.'
For 'threw off' *read* 'throws off.'
Om. 'which they did . . . upon the invitation.'
[*f.* 245 (*b*)] *For* 'dissenters' *read* 'presbyterians.'
For 'put the decision . . . exception' *read* 'took a very prudent method to make those of [the] church of England concur with him; for.'
For 'behaved himself . . . of him' *read* 'has hitherto behaved himself much more prudently than could have been expected from so weak a man.'
Place next paragraph in present tense, and for 'These regulators . . . in another' *read* 'which were at first pretended to be put in them only to make the corporation feel their dependence on the court, and not as if they had been intended to be ever made use of' (cf. p. 718).

[*Electors questioned.*]

Cf. *Hist.* i. 719 (*to end of page in present tense*).
Om. 'and freeholders.'
[*f.* 246 (*a*)] *Om.* 'They said this was . . . engagement.'
For 'This, as all . . . themselves from it: for' *read* 'So that the king finds that this new and illegal way that he has taken of asking the minds of the gentry beforehand has been so far from succeeding with them that.'

[*Reflections on the foregoing.*]

For the present state of affairs is such that [a] the king must either resolve on doing some very violent thing, either in forcing elections, or in forcing the parliament when it meets, by his soldiers [a], as Cromwell did; or if [after] all [b] the threatenings that he lets fall every day that he [is] king and must be obeyed, and that he will make those who will not consent to that feel that he is their king [b], he lets the whole matter fall and comes to treat upon the overtures which the prince has made to him, he will indeed sink much in the character of a hero, both at home and abroad; and will give credit to the insinuations of those that do not love him, [*f.* 246 (*b*)] who say that he is the severest man in the world when danger is far off, but that when it comes near him he is as much disturbed at it as other men. It is true if he lets all his attempts upon the religion and liberty of his people fall it will be a great happiness to them; for if once he lets it go he can never hope to return to it again; and, on the other hand, [c] he has run his ministers and

[a] Cf. *Hist.* i. 720.   [b] *Ibid. infra.*   [c] *Ibid. supra.*

his party into so many illegal things that they are certainly very uneasy till either he goes through stitch with his designs and subdues the nation (that so they may be safe in their crimes), or till he bring matters to an agreement (so that an act of indemnity may be passed which may secure them for the time to come[a], since the king's life and the doubtful prospect of the queen's being with child are too uncertain tenures for them to hold their safety by). But I am an historian to relate what is past, and not a prophet to look into what is to come; therefore I must here break off and stay till time opens up all that cloud that is at present over England; and having continued this history now till the end of the year [16]87, I give over writing on St. Stephen's Day, new style [Dec. 26, 1687–Jan. 5, 1688]. I have endeavoured all I could to watch over myself and not to suffer the great concerns which I have for the public or the particular injuries that are done myself to sour my temper too much; and as far as I can judge of my [heart ?], I have writ with [the] equality and sincerity of a faithful and unbiassed historian; but it must be considered that I am out of England, so that I now see things by other men's eyes[1].

[*Supplement begun in Jan.*, 168⅞; *correspondence between king and princess, &c.*]

Here I had put a stop to this work, but a transaction that fell out this year being communicated to me in the beginning of the next, seemed to me too important not to be set down, and therefore I have resolved not to delay the inserting it to the next time that I begin to write. But I do it now in the beginning of January, 1688. [*f.* 247 (*a*)][b] The king writ a letter to the princess of Orange, bearing date the fourth of November, which yet was not delivered to her before the 24th of De-

---

[a] Cf. *Hist.* i. 720.   [b] *Ibid.*

---

[1] There is no break in the transcript. The following supplement was written at intervals during the first three months of 1688; see *infra*, and also f. 254 (*b*).

cember, that Mr. D'Albeville returning from England brought it to her. ᵃ The prince was pleased to send me both the letter and the *brouillon* of the princess' answer, all writ with her own hand ᵃ. I had but time to read them twice over, yet ᵇ I have carried the most considerable points of them so well in my memory ᵇ that I am very confident I shall give a very faithful abstract of them, and that for a great part in the words of the letters themselves[1].

[*Abstract of the king's letter.*]

Cf. *Hist.* i. 720-2 (*the verbal differences are trifling, though numerous*).
[*f.* 247 (*b*)] *For* 'atheism' *read* 'schism.'

[*Reflections on the above.*]

Cf. *Hist.* i. 722 (*from* 'It was easy for me' *to* 'greater length').
[*f.* 248 (*a*)] *After* 'for I had' *add* 'upon many occasions.'

For 'was writ very decently and' *read* 'how weak soever in the reasoning part.'

[*f.* 248 (*b*)] *After* 'altered' *add* 'so that her spirits [must] have been pretty warm all the while that she writ it.'

[*Abstract of the princess Mary's answer.*]

Cf. *Hist.* i. 722-5 (*numerous trifling verbal variations*).

For 'for failing' *read* 'for forgetting the post day, and so failed[2].'

[249 (*a*)] *After* 'professed it led ill lives' *read* 'Those were indeed a scandal to it, but there were many ill men of all persuasions, though those who were called reformed ought to shew it in their lives[2].'

[*Abstract of the king's answer.*]

Cf. *Hist.* i. 725.

[*Burnet's reflections.*]

Cf. *Hist.* i. 725-6.

[*f.* 250 (*b*)] *For* 'often and it' *read* 'so oft, that he might have conned it by heart as a lesson which.'

[*f.* 251 (*a*)] *For* 'did let . . . that she' *read* 'must needs put those who

ᵃ Cf. *Hist.* i. 722.   ᵇ *Ibid.*

---

[1] French translations of these letters, with that of a second from the princess, were published in 1880, from the Bentinck archives, at pp. 4-24 of the *Lettres et Mémoires de Marie Reine d'Angleterre.* Burnet's account (which as far as concerns the princess's letter was, so he tells us in the printed *History*, subsequently revised by her) is a very fair version, especially regarding the fact that it was written from memory. The order of the arguments differs a little ; in a few cases Burnet has omitted or misconstrued a point ; and he has inadvertently admitted a reference to the story of the nun, which he had had from James himself, and to which no allusion is made in the letter.

[2] Both of these additions are found in the translation from the original.

managed the popish designs on desperate counsels, since they found by the letters that were sent on this occasion that they had to do with a princess that.'

[*D'Albeville's memorials concerning Bantam.*]

Cf. *Hist.* i. 728 (*from* ' I begin ' *to* ' matter was let fall ').

For ' I begin the year . . . Hague. He ' *read only* ' D'Albeville.'

Om. ' but nothing followed upon it.'

For ' with another . . . decently expressed ' *read* ' pretty high.'

[*f.* 251 (*b*)] *For* ' D'Albeville after this gave in ' *read* ' With this D'Albeville went away, and now he brought over.'

After ' was conceived ' *add* ' and thus the king was made appear very contemptible ; [since] after so high a threatening he came to desire a treaty.'

For ' Yet in this . . . read it ' *read only* ' But in this the king has also mistaken his measures.'

For ' When this memorial . . . let fall ' *read* ' So this business sleeps still.'

[*D'Albeville's memorials concerning Burnet.*]

Cf. *Hist.* i. 728-31 (*to* ' fright me into some mean submission ').

After ' in a memorial ' *add* ' had, before he went over.'

[*f.* 252 (*a*)] *After* ' on the king ' *add* ' but only, on my enemies.'

Om. ' and no person . . . persecute.'

After ' alive ' *add* ' But upon the first memorial I added that.'

For ' was charged with ' *read* ' have published.'

For ' two memorials ' *read* ' second memorial.'

For ' and three ' *read* ' [and] almost three.'

For ' I had lived . . . openly ' *read* ' I have lived a year [*f.* 252 (*b*)] here in the Hague in the sight of the king's envoys.'

Om. ' and ordered a memorial . . . according to them.'

After ' subjects ' *add* ' and settlement in the country.'

After ' to my charge ' *add* ' according to the grounds of their law.'

For ' an affront to him ' *read* ' a breach of the treaty.'

[*f.* 253 (*a*)] *For* ' and not according . . . lie ' *read* ' but not according to the sense which may be used in any of the king's courts of justice ; for the lawyers of one country are not bound to know the sense of those words that are in the treaties, otherwise than as common use explains them.   Therefore since.'

After ' from justice ' *add* ' the treaty must ònly [be][1] applied to such persons, and is not to be explained by a trick of the law of Scotland, in which a man that being cited does not appear is declared a fugitive and the king's rebel.'

After ' honour ' *add* ' for all this appears to be the effect of [unjust][2] and impotent passion[3].'

After ' murder me ' *add* ' I do not believe all that has been writ to me upon this head, [al]though[4] it has come from very good hands.'

Om. ' by accident ' *and* ' but not yet signed.'

After ' destroy me ' *add* ' which as he writes did so surprise him that he could scarce believe his own eyes.'

---

[1] Inserted ; qu. in hand of f. 2 ?

[2] The transcript reads ' a Jesuit.'

[3] This passage remains in the Bodleian autograph of the *History*; see Routh's *Burnet's James II*, p. 240, note.

[4] The transcript reads ' and though.'

For 'affirmed' *read* 'in his letter.'

For 'had heard . . . to convey the notice of it to me' *read only* 'told the same thing to one [1].'

After 'send the notice to me' *insert* '[an intimation was also sent me by the chancellor of England] that has made some more impressions upon me [2].'

For 'in a private way . . . his hands' *read only* 'now.'

For 'than he had done . . . send it to me, for he concluded' *read* 'since the States had given me their protection. [*f.* 253 (*b*)] The king seemed angry that he answered so, which made a friend of mine [3], to whom the chancellor told the design to have it conveyed to me, conclude.'

[*Effects upon Burnet himself.*]

[a] But I thank God this has given me no sort of disorder; it has obliged me to use a little more than ordinary caution, and that is all the effect it has had. I offer myself up to God, and am very willing to resign up my life to him [a], if he suffers me to fall into the hands of mine enemies. I have writ a paper which I have ordered to be published as my dying words [4], and have settled all things that relate to me as if I f[eare]d [5] present death; but (with all this) I must add this to the praise of true Christianity and of philosophy, that [b] I never possessed myself during my whole life in a more pleasant and clearer cheerfulness of spirit [b] than I do at present [6].

[*Publication of Fagel's letter; consequent recall of the six regiments.*]

Cf. *Hist.* i. 734-5 (*from* 'What he wrote' *to* 'persons in the States' pay').

For 'What he wrote . . . industry' *read* 'The letter that Mr. Fagel had writ lay dead as a secret for some months, but the court of England spread a report over the nation.'

Om. 'This was writ . . . Hague.'

After 'prince' *add* 'and princess'; *and for* 'gave orders' *read* 'gave secret orders.'

[a] Cf. *Hist.* i. 731.   [b] *Ibid.*

---

[1] Thus the sentence in the original does not convey the impression that Prince George sent the message; nor is this asserted in the letter (Life in *Hist.* ii. 695). As however the allusion to the letter does not occur in this sentence as eventually revised, Captain Baxter may have asserted this subsequently.

[2] The transcriber places that part of the sentence here printed in brackets between 'very good hands' *and* 'a [gentle]man of an unblemished reputation.' The present arrangement seems preferable.

[3] By these words he signifies Kirk; see *History in loco*, and cf. with *Hist.* i. 647.

[4] This paper, which is missing, is mentioned in a subsequent paper printed *infra*, as Appendix III.

[5] The transcript reads 'found.'

[6] See Macaulay, ed. 1858, ii. 505, note.

For 'saw themselves safe . . . them' *read* 'were now taken out of the hands of the court.'

For 'lay-papists seemed' *read* 'moderate papists were'; *for* 'with it' *read* 'with the proposition that was made on their behalf'; *and omit* 'though a freedom . . . appearance.'

[*f.* 254 (*a*)] *After* 'foreign ministers' *add* 'Some of the ill-natured priests took hold of this, to drive on the king to some extreme measures; but the expectation of the queen's big belly put a stop to all these; since it was said by those who offered softer counsels[1] that if the queen bore a son, the greater part of the nation would, upon that change of the prospect of succession, change their measures; and this is the chief argument now made use of, to divert all violent propositions.'

For 'and resolved . . . deep it was' *read* 'Yet one thing followed upon it, in which the king hearkened more to his passion than to his reason.'

After 'lend them to him' *add* 'which was presently done.'

Om. 'were so jealous of the king and.'

For 'the prince . . . in obtaining' *read* 'the interest that the prince had in that matter made him not without some difficulty obtain.'

Om. 'There was no distinction . . . armies: so'; *and for* 'in those' *read* 'in command among the.'

For 'England . . . among them' *read* 'though upon the breaking of that rebellion he sent them back, yet many of them were so much wrought on that factions were formed in most of the regiments between the popish and the protestant officers.'

For 'prince, who' *read* 'prince; who, as he'; *and for* 'between the king and him . . . command' *read* 'so he found the inconveniency of their being so much divided and of the many creatures that the king had among them.'

[*f.* 254 (*b*)] *For* 'The States pretended . . . part with them' *read only* 'would not part with the regiments.'

[*Situation March* 15, 1688; *Supplement concludes.*]

[a] In England the discourse of a parliament is taken up and let fall so often that it is not easy to know in what all those fluctuating counsels will end [a]. The Jesuits hope to get a cardinal's hat for F. Petre, and when that is done it is believed that he will be made [b] the chief minister. The king has refused accommodating the difference that is between the pope and the king of France, upon this reason, because the pope has refused to gratify him in that promotion; so that if the pope finds himself pressed by the king of France, then he will be forced to fly to the mediation of England, which will serve to advance F. Petre, and this will very probably precipitate our

[a] Cf. *Hist.* i. 735.   [b] *Ibid.* 735-6.

---

[1] The advice is that of Sunderland.

affairs extremely, for he is a weak but passionate and hot-headed man, who is both hardy and indiscreet and has all the ill qualities that are requisite to make him the incendiary of those kingdoms, and to drive both the king and his party to their ruin[a]. And with this I end for this time, on the 15th of March, 1688[1].

[*Burnet resumes his pen, Sept.*, 1688.]

I do again sit down to carry on this work, since the importance of [the] expedition that is now upon the point of breaking out requires it; and since I myself am to go in it, I thought it fit to carry on this history to the end of September, in which I am writing it. [*f.* 255 (*a*)] The affairs of England went on till the end of April without any considerable accident.

[*The second declaration of indulgence.*]

Cf. *Hist.* i. 736-8 (*to* 'proved in conclusion that they were').

Om. 'as if none were intended . . . ripe.'

Om. 'saw that the king . . . uneasy to them. They.'

For 'They began to apprehend' *to end of paragraph read only* 'As long as the king was entertained with hopes of carrying his point in a parliamentary way, it was not possible to push him on to extravagancies; therefore they had a mind to see the end of all those expectations, that in case they failed in them, they might take new measures.'

Om. 'And now it appeared . . . parliament[2].'

Om. 'And they were at first . . . London.'

For 'that was not strong . . . breach' *read only* 'since.'

For 'So it was proposed . . . by making' *read* 'And this made many at first [*f.* 255 (*b*)] to obey it, adding.'

Om. 'that they were bound . . . sent to them'; *and* 'and they could not see . . . not now'; *and* 'The point at present . . . expedient thing.'

Om. 'which the king . . . assume' *and* 'and the making it . . . administration.'

Om. 'and nothing they could do . . . interests' *and* 'it was therefore fit . . . enemies.'

After 'prevailed' *add* 'with the most eminent of the clergy.'

Om. 'if any considerable . . . refuse to obey.'

[*f.* 256 (*a*)] *For* 'The court depended upon this' *read* 'And it is certain that the court depended upon this and reckoned.'

After 'managed' *read* 'with so much prudence and.'

[a] Cf. *Hist.* i. 736.

---

[1] The transcript has no break; and places the full stop after 'for this time'; running '1688' on to 'I do again.'

[2] Here again, as the reader will observe, an insinuation against Sancroft was subsequently inserted.

[The bishops petition the king; their trial.]

Cf. *Hist.* i. 738-40; 40-44 (*to* 'as if it had been a victory obtained ').

For ' eighteen' *read* ' most'; *and for* ' concurred' *read* ' concurred with him.'

For ' and was a matter . . . must amount to' *read only* ' they could not concur in any act relating to that.'

For ' by his spies . . . secret and cautious ' *read only* ' with other hopes.'

Om. ' And they came . . . temper of the nation.'

Om. ' Lobb.'

[*f.* 256 (*b*)] *After* ' before the second' *add* ' and so gave but a half obedience.'

On p. 740 *omit entirely from* ' The king did what he could' *to* ' college their president' (*near end of page*), *beginning again* ' Thus the sense of the nation.'

For ' of father Petre . . . party' *read only* ' of the priests.'

Om. ' for it was then printed' *and* ' that must have been done . . . shewed it.'

[*f.* 257 (*a*)] *After* ' city' *add* ' and country.'

Om. ' and with loud shouts . . . preservation.'

For ' pretended delivery' *read only* ' delivery.'

For ' and it was given . . . vehemently' *read only* ' which was much pressed by the more moderate papists.'

Om. ' upon a *habeas corpus*.'

Om. ' St. Peter's . . . or not [1].'

Om. ' and people . . . went out.'

After ' solemn' *add* ' for there was not only an incredible crowd about Westminster Hall and on the river, but.'

For ' All the streets . . . at night' *read* ' And there appeared a most excessive joy upon their being set at liberty, and many bonefires were made upon it, both in London and all England over.'

After ' trial came' *add* ' which was the 29th of June.'

Om. ' Westminster Hall . . . affected with the matter.'

Om. ' The trial came on . . . their being the king's counsel.'

[*f.* 257 (*b*)] *Om.* ' though it did not appear . . . confession.'

Om. ' in which . . . satisfied.'

For ' that this petition was a libel, tending' *read* ' that by this petition they had questioned the king's power; [this tended].'

After ' answered' *add* ' [by] their counsel.'

After ' those matters :' *insert* ' they also shewed from the journals of parliament that.'

For ' so they thought they had a right' *read* ' and therefore, since these things were so well known to them, they had all reason.'

After ' reflect on the dispensing power' *add* ' as that which struck at the root of the whole government.'

Om. ' and the late king's . . . time.'

Om. ' that a paper . . . libel.'

After ' parliament' *insert* ' Sawyer and Finch (being the king's attorney and solicitor very lately) were now for the bishops; and Williams (that had been Speaker) was now gained to the court, who took great advantages against the

---

[1] See Routh's note, *Burnet's James II*, p. 265.

others, to let them see how their present pleadings contradicted their former actions' (cf. *Hist.* i. 742).

[*f.* 258 (*a*)] *For* 'that the witnesses . . . passage' *read* 'that Sunderland [1], being sent for as a witness against them, was not only treated with much scorn, but was believed to be in danger of his life by a tumult; but he escaped another way.'

Om. 'and that it was no libel.'

For '[chief justice] Wright [2] . . . proved' *read* 'Allibone, a professed papist, thought it was otherwise; so did the chief justice; yet in his charge to the jury he represented the matter of fact fairly, and did not think the publication was proved.'

For 'The jury . . . when they were' *read only* 'The jury being.'

For 'but it was thought . . . morning' *read* 'but [3] they resolved to continue shut up till next morning, that so they might give their verdict to the court [with more solemnity and gravity?] [4]; since that there was a danger of suffering any of their number to be practised upon if they had done it sooner; and if any juror had denied that he had agreed in the verdict, all must begin anew.'

Om. 'so long continued . . . city.'

[*Further proceedings.*]

Cf. *Hist.* i. 744 (*from* 'And so fatally' *to* p. 745, 'never sat any more').

Om. 'which they hoped . . . venture on.'

After 'order of council' *add* 'but this was likewise disobeyed.'

Om. 'were now so much animated . . . trial, that they.'

Om. 'but had always voted . . . side.'

[*f.* 258 (*b*)] *For* 'This stopped . . . stand' *read* 'This gave the king a new displeasure.'

Om. 'and they never sat any more.'

[*Burnet's reflections.*]

Thus the king has been prevailed on to put the whole kingdom in a flame, and that for a point in which (if he had been successful) he could have gained nothing by it; for the clergy obeying might have rendered themselves very odious to the nation, but would not at all have advantaged his design; whereas, on the other hand, his failing in it has both given the alarm to the whole clergy and has animated the whole nation against him beyond anything that could have been [i]ma[gin]ed [5]; nor could it have been thought that anything

---

[1] The reader will note that Sunderland's appearance at the trial is suppressed in the final version.

[2] See Routh's *Burnet's James II*, p. 268, note.

[3] The transcript here inserts a superfluous 'that.'

[4] The transcriber seems to have omitted words to this effect.

[5] The transcript has 'managed.'

was wanting to carry the discontent of the nation further; but the address of Jesuits has a depth beyond all ordinary measures [1].

[*The queen's delivery* [2].]

Cf. Hist. i. 748; 749-50; 750-2 (*to* 'base imposture now put on the nation ').

For 'I must now look back . . . afterwards' *read* 'I have already named the queen's delivery; but it is too important a piece of history to be passed over slightly; therefore since there has been no small pains taken to gather together all the circumstances of that whole matter which have been communicated to me, I will give them with [the] copiousness that such a thing, that is like to produce such consequences, deserves.'

For 'that every winter . . . having any children' *read* 'and every winter was brought so low, that all people who wished her to live (since all apprehensions of any more children by her seemed gone) were extreme [*f.* 259 (*a*)] apprehensive of her; and some thought that even the priests were weary of her, and were contriving to get rid of her; she had great and frequent loosenesses, and it is said she was extremely weakened by that [form] of women's disease called fluor albus, so that it was universally taken for granted in all lands [? on all hands] [3] that no more children were to be expected from her, or at least if they [she] [3] had any they could not be healthy, since all those she had in her youth had languished and died soon after they were born.'

Om. here from 'Her spirits were now much on the fret' *to* p. 749, 'all was forgiven him' (*for Berwick, see supra,* p. 225).

After 'bathing' *add* 'while the king went his progress.'

For 'She came to Windsor . . . October. It was said' *read* 'and [she] met the king at Windsor the sixth of October. Upon their meeting they were presently shut up for some considerable time alone, and it happening'; *and after* 'son' *om.* 'And.'

For 'A conception . . . suspicious' *read* 'The conception was attributed by naturalists to the virtue of The Bath; but by the bigots to the Virgin's intercession.'

Before 'She was not dressed' *add* 'for many months.'

For 'Prince George . . . acquiesced' *it is merely intimated that no demonstration was given, either to the princess Anne or to* 'the other protestant ladies that [were] beyond suspicion' (*for which see infra,* p. 296).

Om. from 'How [just] soever this might be' *to* p. 750, 'held on her course.'

For 'Lower, one of her physicians . . . upon them to advise it' *read only* [*f.* 259 (*b*)] 'but the king's vehemence carried the point' (*see however infra,* pp. 296-7, *for the physicians' reports*).

After 'May' *add* 'reckoning that she would be back again many days before the queen's time.'

---

[1] The allusion may be to the supposed imposture; since in the transcript there is no break between this and the following sentence.

[2] The reader will observe that such particulars as are contained in this section were all recorded previous to the sitting of the English Privy Council, before which the king produced the proofs of his son's birth.

[3] The first reading is that of the transcript; the second that of a corrector (qu. the writer of f. 2?).

After 'given' *add* 'and all possible endeavours were used.'

After 'ready' *add* 'while this was doing.'

Om. after 'Bath water' *the word* 'either,' *and after* 'agree with the princess' *om.* 'or the advisers . . . it did not'; *and for* 'and that therefore' *read* 'and so writ to court that.'

For 'to St. James's . . . good hour' *read* 'that night, it being Saturday, the ninth of June, and lie at St. James's.'

Om. 'from Whitehall' *and* 'and she always went that way'; *and for* 'by Charing Cross . . . Pall Mall' *read* 'through the streets.'

After 'to the king' *add* 'to Whitehall.'

For 'no women were' *read* 'no women were at first'; *and for* 'two dressers' *read* 'two of the queen dowager's.'

After 'Arran' *add* 'her son-in-law.'

Om. 'for it happened . . . tenth of June.'

· [*f.* 260 (*a*)] *For* 'so here was . . . filled' *read* 'so some have suspected that a child was perhaps brought in it.'

For 'with the child . . . else' *read only* 'with somewhat.'

Om. 'Chamberlain . . . could not find that any had it' (*but see infra*, p. 296).

For 'still in the dark' *read* 'with the same mysteriousness that had been observed in the whole progress of this matter.'

For 'This made all . . . nation' *read* 'so that upon the first notice that was given of this birth all people began to doubt of the truth of it and to suspect an imposture.'

Om. from 'That still increased' *to* p. 753, 'another child was found.'

[*Health of the child.*]

[a] The child was strong and vigorous, and did not look like a new-born child, as some that saw it [within][1] two days have assured me [a]. On the Tuesday it was given out that the child was dying; and often since that time it has been said by the papists all about the town [b] that he had convulsion fits and could not live [b]. It was also resolved at first to breed him up by the hand without giving him suck; but about two months after a nurse was given him, and since that time [c] he thrives very well; but there has been so great a secret made of all things that even those fits [*f.* 260 (*b*)] are looked on by some as a part of the court's device to make the child pass the better for the queen's, since he has so ill health; and it hath been observed that none of his fits came upon him when the princess was at court, whose quality was such that they could not deny her admittance; and in these fits all others are denied access [c],

[a] Cf. *Hist.* i. 753.   [b] *Ibid.*   [c] *Ibid.*

[1] A word is omitted; and a later hand supplied 'in.

so it is doubtful whether anything of all this is to be believed or not. ᵃ Thus I have related all the particulars of this matter, which came from such hands that I have good reason to believe them all true[1]; but I do not enter into the various reports which have been made ᵃ, some naming both father and mother of the child, some thinking that it was a child of the king's by one of the maids of honour, while others have said that the first child died and that a second was put in his room[2]; but I only name the reports without giving any credit to them, for when there is such an occasion given to discourse in a matter of such consequence, stories will always be made to supply all defects.

[*Reflections on the event.*]

Cf. *Hist.* i. 754 (*from* 'What truth soever' *to end of paragraph*).

After 'in some places' *add* 'but all that outward show of joy was far short of that [which] appeared a few days after upon the enlargement and acquitting of the bishops'; *and for* 'and' *read* 'yet.'

[*Reception of the news by the prince and princess* [3].]

Cf. *Hist.* i. 754.

[*f.* 261 (*a*)] *Om.* 'Upon this occasion . . . condition she was then in' (cf. *supra*, p. 195).

For 'The advertisements . . . prince upon which' *read only* 'but upon the advertisements that were afterwards conveyed to them.'

After 'rupture' *add* 'before he was ready for it.'

[*The prince designs an expedition.*]

Cf. *Hist.* i. 754–5 (*to* 'to make war on them').

For 'The prince set himself . . . fixed in his purpose' *read* 'And at this time he entereth [? entered] into this great design, which is now so near its execution.'

ᵃ Cf. *Hist.* i. 753–4.

---

[1] By this he probably indicates the reports sent by the Princess Anne to her sister, given in Dalrymple's *Memoirs*; see *Hist. in loco*.

[2] e. g. histories of Hemmings and Lady Clarendon (not given in the original memoirs, but subsequently obtained from Lloyd; see *Hist.* ii. 752–3, and Routh's note to *Burnet's James II*, p. 293).

[3] See Dr. Routh's note, *Burnet's James II*, p. 295; and Mary's own *Lettres et Mémoires*, pp. 72–6. It is absolutely certain that Mary, greatly preoccupied by a sense of the political import of the event and of the strong politico-ecclesiastical motives which might have induced the king to countenance an imposture, was completely convinced by the various suspicious circumstances attending the birth, and by the report of her sister, who was no doubt at the time a blind and passive tool of Lady Churchill's ambition, that a fraud had been practised.

For ' And if this heat . . . heart' *read* ' and that though all men had hitherto stuck together and stood firm, yet if the prince did not now show himself, the nation would lose heart ; and many of those who considered religion very little would [tr]eat[1] for themselves' (cf. *Hist.* i. 746).

For ' It was also visible . . . well affected' *read* ' It was also manifest that the king could not at all depend upon his army ; for [though] they were a company of very vicious and dissolute men, and had as it were been let loose to all sorts of disorders, and not only covered from justice [for] the crimes which they were everywhere committing, but even encouraged in them (it being hoped that as those disorders rendered them odious to the country, so they would come to hate the nation, and become the instruments of enslaving it) ; yet for all [that], they were zealous protestants, though bad Englishmen, and worse Christians' (cf. *ibid.* i. 746).

For ' The king . . . visibly' *read* ' and were much concerned at the imprisonment of the bishops, and grew so disorderly' ; *and for* ' quarters' *read* [*f.* 261 (*b*)] ' winter quarters.'

Om. ' and it was believed . . . mind.'

For ' on pretence . . . resolved' *read* ' so this obliged the king.'

For ' such offices . . . war' *read* ' other offices aboard.'

For ' upon a slight pretence' *read* ' upon the pretence of some indiscretion.'

For ' when some gained' *to end of paragraph, read only* ' and the having a quarrel with the Dutch.'

[*Motives for haste.*]

This being the state of the king's force both by sea and land, it was thought that [if] a vigorous impression could be made this year [it] would carry all before it ; but if the king had another year given him he would apply himself to model both his army and fleet, [a] and perhaps he might by some deceitful promises lay the fears of the nation asleep[a]. Therefore it seemed necessary to set about it this year. Some of the bishops also sent the prince their opinion that they thought he had a just cause of making a war on the king, in which opinion I likewise was ; for it was plain that the king was now settling about the total subversion of the government. There was a committee appointed for regulating the corporations, who were putting in and turning out every day as they found men compliant or obstinate, and who were resolved to change on till they could find such a number of men for the magistracy that would be sure to choose according to their directions.

[a] Cf. *Hist.* i. 756.

---

[1] The transcript has ' heat' corrected (qu. in the same hand as f. 2?) to 'shift.'

Many emissaries were sent over England to persuade all people of the sincerity of the king's intentions, and that it was the interest of the [*f.* 262 (*a*)] nation to comply with him in his designs for abolishing the tests and penal laws ; but these, though they were all dissenters, were men of no figure, and the little which any of them had formerly was quite lost by this employment. [a] The judges, when they went the circuits, met with eminent [ma]rks [of contempt] [1] everywhere ; and they saw that the presentments of grand juries and the verdict of other juries were no more at their disposal [a]. All things concurred to determine the prince to resolve on an expedition, in which hitherto all things have been successful. No wonder if he who believes an absolute predestination is much wrought on by them ; for though I have no belief of that, I cannot hinder my[self] [2] from being struck with the success of so many happy steps in the whole matter.

[*Death of the elector of Brandenburg; his character.*]

Cf. *Hist.* i. 746 (*from* 'He was then ill' *to* p. 748, 'recommended to them the concerns of the protestant religion ').

For 'He was then ill . . . at Cleve' *read* 'In May [3] the old elector of Brandenburg died, whom I had the honour to see for a great many days when he [was] last at Cleve.'

For 'his interest' *read* 'the sense of his judgement.'

For 'He was . . . religion' *read* 'He was a very religious man, and had a great zeal for all the concerns of the protestant religion ; which, upon the occasion of the persecution of France, he expressed with all [the] nobleness and bounty that became so great a prince' (cf. *ibid. infra*).

For 'His own life . . . blemishes' *read* 'He was a man of great personal virtues, and free of all those disorders [*f.* 262 (*b*)] that are too ordinary in princes ; and if in his youth he went into the German custom of drinking, yet the gout had obliged him to be temperate.'

For 'He tried all . . . reconciling' *read* 'He had a very ill opinion of the Lutherans as an ill-natured sort of people ; yet he was much set on reconciling the difference between the Calvinists and them ; and he disliked extremely the rigidity of the divines of Holland, and of the divines [? synod] of Dort [on the points of predestination and grace ?]; for he told me the reconciling of the two parties struck [? stuck] only at those points ; therefore.'

[a] Cf. *Hist.* i. 756.

---

[1] The transcript reads 'such eminent works everywhere.'

[2] The transcript reads ' my life.'

[3] $\frac{\text{April 30}}{\text{May 10}}$. See Routh's note from Ralph, *Hist. in loco.*

For 'He had a . . . taxes' *read only* 'He affected much greatness in his court, and it was indeed a very splendid one.'

Om. 'in all lesser . . . greater.'

For 'that the electoral . . . depend' *read only* 'never to dismember any of his dominions from his family; having observed how both the house of Saxe and palatine were sunk by those divisions.'

For 'And the elector having . . . great a prince' (*see supra*) *read only* 'for wh[ich][1] his honour was oft sacrificed; for it was believed that she received great presents from France. And to this all the ill steps that he made in his last years ought to be ascribed; yet it was no easy thing to soften him with relation to that court after they had set on the persecution.'

Om. 'and infirmities . . . gout.'

For 'had so disjointed his court' *read* 'put such a stop to the elector's good intentions.'

For 'Death . . . looked for' *read* 'He had long been gouty, and at last a dropsy came which carried him off' (cf. *Hist.* i. 747).

For 'to them' *read* 'to his son,' *and om.* 'then in such universal danger.'

[*Character of the new elector.*]

[He] upon his death began his government in such a manner as made all people consider him as one that was not like to make so great a figure in the affairs of Europe as his father. He is a prince of great piety and virtue, and free of all blemishes of all sorts[2]. [*f.* 264 (*a*)] His ministers govern him much, particularly [a] Dankleman, who is like to have the greatest share of his favour and confidence, and will probably bring all the rest into a dependence upon him. He is zealous for the common concerns of religion and the liberty of Europe, and will probably make as good a minister as can be expected in a favourite. [b] As the elector is the prince of Orange's cousin-germane [b] by his mother and is heir by provision if he has no children, so he not only [c] has a particular friendship for him [c], but he agrees with him in the same notions and designs.

[*The prince consults the new elector; conduct of the German princes.*]

Cf. *Hist.* i. 757 (*from* 'Upon the elector' *to end of paragraph*).

For 'He offered' *read* 'for in general the prince said, upon Bentinck's return, that he offered.'

[a] Cf. *Hist.* i. 748.   [b] *Ibid. supra.*   [c] *Ibid.*

---

[1] The transcript reads 'while.'

[2] Here breaks off abruptly the portion described by Dr. Gifford as No. 7, on f. 262 (*b*); for f. 263 see *supra*, p. 130. The transcript continues unbroken on f. 264 (*a*) (beginning of No. 8 in Dr. Gifford's arrangement) in a fresh hand.

For 'an army . . . all occasions' *read only* '13,000 with him, he laid down a method for procuring the same number of men from the elector and some German princes ; who were the landgrave of Hesse and the dukes of Lunen-burg-Zell, and the Wolfenbuttel.'

For the whole of the next paragraph (relating to Burnet's message to the court of Hanover) read only 'Only Hanover, though the most concerned by his near-ness to the crown of England, excused himself.'

The affairs of Cologne.

Cf. *Hist.* i. 758 *to end of* 761. (There are a number of slight variations between the accounts, principally due to corrections or amplifications of statements in-serted in the later version, but only the following need be noticed.)

For 'but while . . . management' *read* 'but while the prince was designing this.'

After 'Hildesheim' *insert* '[though] neither the revenue nor the importance of it are such as to be named with the other three.'

Om. 'much set . . . philosopher's stone.'

[*f.* 264 (*b*)] *After* 'elector died' *add* 'which fell out this year in June.'

Om. 'which the French had forced . . . bishopric.'

[*f.* 265 (*a*)] *For* 'so he was fixed to his interests' *read* 'so he could not accept of that proposition, which probably would have taken away all occasion of dispute.'

After 'this matter' *add* '(though foreign to the affairs of England) both.'

For 'and it had . . . inconsiderable beginnings' *read* 'and because.'

For 'it was necessary . . . France' *read* 'therefore it was of the greatest im-portance for the States to bestir themselves vigorously on this occasion.'

Character of admiral Herbert.

[*f.* 265 (*b*)] While those preparations were carried on [a] ad-miral Herbert came over out of England[a] ; and since he is like to bear a very considerable share in this undertaking, I shall here give [his][1] story. His father was lord keeper[2], and had followed the late king in his exile ; so he was bred in Holland. He went very young into the fleet, and has [b] served long in it with a high reputation[b] both for his valour and his conduct, and has escaped such extraordinary dangers that one would think him preserved for some great ends. Once a cannon ball passed between his legs, and another time between his thighs, but if the first did him no hurt the second was thought mortal, yet it only carried off all the flesh between his thighs, so that he escaped after a long and painful cure. [c] He had attached himself to the king when he was duke of York, so

---

[a] Cf. *Hist.* i. 762.   [b] *Ibid.* 671.   [c] *Ibid.*

---

[1] The transcript reads 'this story.'
[2] (To the exiled court) from April 6, 1653, to June, 1654.

that no man stuck more firmly to him [a] when the nation run so violently upon the exclusion ; and was much considered by the king, who made him rear admiral of England, and gave him several other good employments ; and it was chiefly upon his interest that his brother was promoted to be lord chief justice.   He was indeed ill-shaped to be a courtier, for he valued himself upon his merit and services, and so he took no great care in courting the ministers or indeed of courting the king himself; for as [b] he is naturally very haughty [b], so it was not easy for him to see others more considered than himself. But, as he stuck to the king when he thought the nation was pushing at him unjustly, so, as soon as he began to see that the king was going off from the promises that he had made, he grew sullen, and was highly offended at his brother for the judgement he gave in favour of the dispensing power ; and being a man that scorns to dissemble his thoughts, it came to the king's ears that he would not concur in the design of repealing of the test, at the time when the king was examining all the members of parliament in the beginning of [16]86 ; [c] and when the king questioned him upon it he very frankly owned to him that he could not do it [c].   The king seemed surprised, both at his answer and at the readiness of giving it ; for he neither asked him to think on it nor did he put him off with general words.   Herbert alleged among other things that [d] he could not in conscience do it ; at which the king laughed, for in the point of pleasure he has been much a libertine.   So the king told him that his course of life did not look like a man of a very strict conscience ; upon which he answered that he could charge himself with nothing but that of which many were as guilty as he was [d].   The conversation ended very sourly, and next day he was turned out of all ; upon which he withdrew with a greatness of mind that deserves so much the higher commendations, because [*f.* 266 (*a*)] it set an example to many others to stand firm.   He pressed after that [e] the clearing his accounts with the king, in all which he was used not only very hardly but very unjustly ; and when those were

[a] Cf. *Hist.* i. 671.   [b] *Ibid.* 762.   [c] *Ibid.* 671.   [d] *Ibid.*   [e] *Ibid.* 762.

ended he came out of England in the beginning of July and the prince received him very kindly. He is too much a slave to pleasure, and too barefaced in owning it.

The prince his design breaks out.

Cf. *Hist.* i. 766 (*from* ' Matters went on in Holland' *to* p. 767, ' appeared in everything').

For ' many arms' *read* ' some thousands of arms and saddles.'

After ' suspicion' *insert* ' It was indeed strange to see a secret of this nature, which must be put in several hands, notwithstanding all the precautions that could possibl[y] be used, so well kept, that, till the preparations themselves discovered a design in general, nothing was found.'

For ' D'Avaux . . . hand' *read only* ' which the king presently published.'

Om. ' shewed . . . fears ; for he.'

Om. ' He recalled . . . at all hazards.'

For ' The seamen . . . slowly' *read* ' No seamen came in, at least very few that were expert,' *and for* ' in everything' *read* ' in all his people.'

The king saw the backwardness of the army to all mixtures of Irish among them.

Cf. *Hist.* i. 767-8.

For ' A new . . . Irish one' *read* ' He met with a great mortification from the officers of the duke of Berwick's regiment ; for he intended to model his army and to bring in insensibly a number of Irish into every company ; and when that had passed, it was believed that he intended to bring French papists next. So.'

Om. ' which being already . . . everything.'

[*f.* 266 (*b*)] *After* ' council of war, where' *read* ' all that was done against them was that.'

For from ' that as no more attempts were' *to* p. 768, ' died soon after,' *read only* ' that it was believed they diverted the king from all thoughts of bringing over a French army ; for there had been a discourse, formerly, of hiring an hundred ships, which plainly imported the design of transporting an army ; but that was now let fall, since the king saw that if he went about any such thing he would be forsaken of all the English.'

The French and English ministers give in memorials at the Hague.

Cf. *Hist.* i. 768 (*from* ' D'Albeville came over' *to* p. 769, ' weaken that proof').

For ' fully persuaded that the Dutch . . . laughed at' *read* ' to England and seemed fully persuaded that the Dutch had no designs upon England. But by the advertisements that were sent by the French ambassador, the court began to apprehend somewhat ; so.'

For ' who was disowned . . . weaken that proof' *read* ' who, as it is given out, will be disgraced upon it ; though it is visible that (how foolish soever he has been in procuring orders to be sent to the French ambassador at the Hague for owning this matter), yet it is certain that the alliance is really made between the two crowns : otherwise no instances that he could have made could have engaged that court to have published it.'

[*Strange conduct of the French court.*]

Cf. *Hist.* i. 769–70 (*from* ' The conduct' *to end of paragraph*).

After ' in France' *add* ' pretending that this was necessary for encouraging the manufacture of France.'

For ' cured with French salt' *read* ' carried with French ships' (*probably a clerical error*).

[*f.* 267 (*a*)] *After* ' manufacture' *add* ' at Leyden.'

For ' great bodies . . . wars' *read* ' what by the aversion the States naturally have to all wars'; *and for* ' but the height . . . fear it' *read* ' what by the instruments that France has everywhere to have put a stop to all the prince's proceedings.'

After ' the rest' *add* ' But the prohibition of the French commodities stuck a little; [for].'

For ' This . . . amuse' *read* ' by which means neither the empire nor the States should have any reason to be afraid of the French, by reason of the cardinal's being confirmed elector.'

The king of France declares war, both to the emperor and to the pope.

Cf. *Hist.* i. 770–4 (*to* ' practicable and safe').

[*f.* 267 (*b*)] *On* p. 771, *after* ' turned into a peace,' *add* ' provided that those forts which he had built for the security of his subjects might be included in it.' (*This clause appears in Routh's Burnet's James II, in loco.*)

Om. ' I have given . . . just one or not.'

On p. 772 *om.* ' which was like to prove fatal . . . begin a war on his part.'

[*f.* 268 (*a*)] *On* p. 773 *for* ' This was the first public . . . birth' *read* ' This last was an odd step, for this was the first paper that appeared by authority in which that birth was said to be questioned.'

[*f.* 268 (*b*)] *After* ' prince Clement' *add* ' upon great occasions, especially in favour of sovereign princes.'

On p. 774, *after* ' alarm the States,' *add* ' and all the fears that some had of a catholic league being made up between France, Spain, and the house of Austria in opposition to the protestant interest were now at an end.'

[*Schomberg sent to Cleve.*]

Cf. *Hist.* i. 774.

For ' Marshal Schomberg . . . denied him' *read* ' The marshal de Schomberg had been received by the old elector of Brandenburg in a most obliging manner; he refused to turn when the persecution was begun in France; upon which.'

After ' of popery' *add* ' and so ungrateful.'

Om. ' being invited . . . Brandenburg.'

For ' By these means . . . England' *read only* ' So that the States run no danger this winter.'

Om. from ' The seas were then' *to end of paragraph.*

[*Henry*] *Sidney's character*

" A great many persons of quality had come over to him, and both in their own names and in the names of many others they had pressed him to undertake it. But he that was trusted with most of those messages [*f.* 269 (*a*)] was Henry Sidney, youngest brother to the earl of Leicester and to Algernon Sidney. He was a graceful man, and coming in very young into the court he had passed through many adventures in it [a] with all the advantages that lewd youth could desire ; [b] some of those were very public [b], but of too great consequence to be mentioned by me. He had in him all that could recommend one in a court, for [c] he had a sweetness in his temper and was the furthest from doing mischiefs to any [c], and the readiest to do good to all of any man of his age ; but he had another quality very seldom to be found in courtiers, for he was a man of great truth and candour. [d] He was sent over as envoy to Holland in [16]79, whence he entered into particular confidences with the prince, [so] that he has been ever since entirely both in his interests and in his favour ; and this being generally understood all England over, as it has exposed him to a very particular jealousy from the court, so all those who desired to signify their affection to the prince have centered on him and everything of that kind has passed through his hands [d]. He will probably be in high favour, and he has all the qualities in him that are to be wished for in a man of that post ; for he is neither imperious nor insolent, revengeful nor covetous. He has a true judgement in affairs, and all his inclinations are noble. He may be too easy to those he loves and trusts, and too much carried away from business to pleasure, but it is a great happiness when all that is to be apprehended in a man of favour is an excess of gentleness and good-nature.

[*General scheme of the expedition.*]

The design is thus laid by the prince ; [e] he has equipped out a fleet of about [51][1] sail, of which the greatest part are third

[a] Cf. *Hist.* i. 762, 763.   [b] *Ibid.* ; see also *ibid.* 227, and note.   [c] *Ibid.* 763.
[d] *Ibid.* 763-4.   [e] *Ibid.* 774.

---

[1] The transcript appears to read ' 151 ' ; probably a clerical error.

and fourth rates, which is to be commanded by Dutch officers ; only upon this occasion Herbert is to command as representing the prince's person [1]. [a] This fleet is to conduct and defend another fleet of merchant vessels that are to carry over 13,000 horse and foot [a], who are to land either in the west or north, and either all in one body, or in one great body with one or two detachments in different places, according as the last advices from England that will be given may determine the matter ; [b] with these the prince carries a provision of arms for about 20,000 men [b] that he expects may come in to him.

[*The prince's declaration.*]

Cf. *Hist.* i. 775-6 (*to* 'tenth of October').

For 'The declaration . . . too long' *read only* 'He has already prepared a declaration which was put in force by Fagel the pensioner, and was put into English by me.'   (*The abstract of the declaration is of course given in the present tense.*)

Om. 'according to the obligations . . . his own.'

[*f.* 269 (*b*)] *After* 'happiness of the nation' *add* 'he promises also the like both for Scotland aud Ireland.'

Om. from ' and he promised' *to* p. 776, ' acquiesce in its decision.'

For 'This the prince . . . October' *read* 'This he is to sign and seal the tenth of October, for it is already printed with that date to it.'

Om. remainder of paragraph.

[*Herbert puts to sea.*]

Cf. *Hist.* i. 779 (*from* 'Herbert went to sea' *to end of paragraph*).

For 'Herbert went to sea' *read* 'He has likewise instructed Herbert to go over.'

Om. 'of which . . . given.'

For ' or to engage . . . strong' *read* 'or if they cannot be prevailed on to do that, then to fall upon them; for at present there are not above eighteen ships out ; and a good blow given them [will settle ?] [2] the whole business.'

For from 'but the contrary winds' *to end of paragraph read only* 'But the wind that has been in the west above six weeks is not favourable.'

[*Burnet's concluding reflections, Oct.* 3, 1688.]

And now the whole matter will be brought to its full ripeness within a week or two ; so that one of the greatest designs that has been undertaken now for many ages is

[a] Cf. *Hist.* i. 775.   [b] *Ibid.*

---

[1] The *History* criticizes this arrangement.
[2] Blank space in transcript.

brought very near a point. [a] I intend to go along with the prince as his chaplain [a]; for as I have been made acquainted with his purpose ever since the beginning of July, so I made the offer of my poor person to go along with him [1]; [b] for having thought that it was lawful, I judged it had been a very unbecoming fear in me to have taken care of mine own person, when the prince ventured his. I have in one paper [b], which is now in the press[2], [c] writ a justification of the whole design [c]; and I have in another [3] (which I have left sealed up with my wife) set down a very particular account of all the thoughts which I have had upon this matter, and which I have ordered to be published in case I should not outlive the expedition. The design is as just as it is great, and the prince, as far as it is possible to see into a man's heart, goes into it with great and noble intentions; and he seems to be marked out by Providence for the doing of wonders; and as his first essay was the saving of this state, when it was almost quite overrun by the French, so he now seems to be led by Providence to a much nobler undertaking, in which, if God bless him with success, and if he manages the English nation as dexterously as he hath hitherto done the Dutch, he will be the arbiter of all Europe, and will very quickly bring Lewis the Great to a much humbler posture, and will acquire a much juster right to the title of Great than the other has ever yet done. But I must remember that I am a historian, not a prophet; therefore I do now interrupt the thread of this history. Whether I shall live ever to carry it on any more is only known to that God to whom I most humbly resign myself, my life, and all that is dear to me. Thus I conclude at the Hague the 3rd of October [4].

[a] Cf. *Hist.* i. 776.   [b] *Ibid. supra.*   [c] *Ibid.*

[1] In the *History* it is said the prince asked him, in the meditation (see Appendix III, *infra*) that he offered himself.

[2] The 'Enquiry'; see *infra*, Appendix I.

[3] Printed *infra*, as Appendix III, from the Morrison collection.

[4] There is no white line in the transcript.

[Burnet resumes his pen, June, 1691, and tells how] the prince
was invited to come to England,

I begin now again in June, 1691, to continue this work, and
have the account of a revolution to write that will appear to
posterity one of the most extraordinary scenes in history; and
this I am better able to give since I bore a considerable share
in it myself and was acquainted with all the [*f.* 270 (*a*)] steps of
it. I have told already many of the previous parts of it ; but
the most important of all was that of which [a] I then took care
to be ignorant, because I resolved to know as little of the
secret of the men of England who favoured our designs as was
possible; that so in case all had miscarried or that I had fallen
into the hands of our enemies, it had not been in my power,
though put to the torture, to have discovered any person[a].
Therefore I took care to know nothing of any but those who
came openly over to us and joined with us. But [b] Mr. Russell,
who managed the invitation that was sent to the prince from
England[b], has given me a particular account of it since we came
into England.

by the lord Mordaunt.

[c] The lord Mordaunt was the first man of quality that came
over to try the prince with relation to the affairs of England.
He is a man of much heat, many notions, and full of discourse ;
he is both brave and generous ; but he is not a man of solid
judgement nor of a firm virtue[c]. He has republican principles
in him to a very high degree, but all [d] his thoughts are crude
and indigested, and a little heat brings secrets easily from
him, especially to those who go into his notions and flatter
him ; for vanity is his weak side. He told the prince many
things of the affairs of England, and represented the thing [as]
so easy, that all this appeared extremely romantical to the
prince[d]. In conclusion, the prince told him that so great an
undertaking must not be set about but upon a high and just
provocation and with a strength proportioned to the resistance
that might be apprehended from so great a force and so vast
a treasure as the king then had ; and [e] he should have his eye

[a] Cf. *Hist.* i. 776.   [b] *Ibid.* 763, 766.   [c] *Ibid.* 762.   [d] *Ibid.*   [e] *Ibid.*

still upon England, and should endeavour to put the affairs in
Holland in the best posture he could to be ready when necessity should force a breach ; and said that if either the king went
about the overturning the established religion, or the wronging
the princess in her right of succession, or if he went about by
forged (or as the new word was, sham) plots to destroy his
friends, he would then see what might be possible for him to do.

The earl of Shrewsbury.

This was in the year 1686; but in summer [16]87
a man of a far different temper came over to the prince;
the earl of Shrewsbury, who, as was told formerly, had been
bred a papist, but had forsaken the church of Rome upon
a very critical and anxious inquiry into matters of controversy[a]. He certainly forsook popery with all his heart,
but it is not so easy for me to affirm that he became a hearty
protestant; I am afraid [b] he is too sceptical in matters of
religion[b]; but as to all other things he is the worthiest man
I know. [c] He has a considerable tincture of learning, a true
exactness of judgement, is a man of much honour and of great
integrity and truth, and of so sweet a temper that he charms
all that know him. He is so far from haughtiness and
impatience of spirit, which are the common frailties of young
men that are far above the common level of mankind, that
during his ministry I never heard that the indiscretion of
those who came to him, especially of importunate suitors,
drew one passionate answer from him. He has true notions
of government with generous principles, and a wit that is
as lively as it is [*f.* 270 (*b*)] soft. His gentleness and modesty
suited better with the prince's temper than Mordaunt's fire
and fierceness ; yet even with him the prince went not further
than to give general assurances.

Master Russell[1].

[d]But in May [16]88 the matter was brought nearer an issue;
for then Mr. Russell came over, that was cousin-germane to the

[a] Cf. *Hist.* i. 762.   [b] *Ibid.*   [c] *Ibid.* 762-3.   [d] *Ibid.* 763, 746.

---

[1] The reader will remark, as a sign
of the carelessness with which the
revision of Burnet was conducted,
that the printed *History* contains *two*

lord Russell; and having served long at sea, and having been
of the bedchamber to the king while he was duke of York,
had upon the lord Russell's death left the court and all his
employments.   He is a man of much honour and of very
worthy principles ; of a good temper, and very firm and
resolute; but he is both too haughty and too lazy. [a] He
pressed the prince to come to a speedy resolution ; he told him
there were a great many, both courtiers, and officers at sea and
land, that stood yet firm to the interests of their religion and
country, but he durst not answer for them that they would
stand out long ; they saw plainly the design of the court was
to model the army, that quarrels would be picked against all
that showed a firmness, and that it would be impossible to
persuade them to continue steady unless they saw a certainty
of his design to appear in the quarrel. [b] To this the prince
answered more positively than before, that he could not
meddle in [the] affairs of England unless he should be invited
to it by some of the chief men of the nation.   In this he said
he must satisfy both his conscience and his honour ; and he
protested (as he had often done) that no private ambition or
resentment of his own should ever prevail so far over him as
to make him break with so near a relation, or engage in a war
of which the consequences must be of the last importance to
the interest of Europe and of the protestant religion.   And
when Russell laid before him the danger of putting too great
numbers upon so critical a secret ; [c] he said, if the invitation
came from a considerable number of the men that might be
supposed to understand best the sense of the nation he would
be satisfied[c]. Russell spake to me of this in more general
terms.   I told him if the old elector of Brandenburg should
happen to die, I [d] believed they might depend upon the prince's
being able to come over by the end [1] of the year [d] ; but [e] if he

[a] Cf. *Hist.* i. 746.   [b] *Ibid.* 763.   [c] *Ibid.* 763, 746.   [d] *Ibid.* 746.
[e] *Ibid.*

accounts of Russell's mission (vol. i.
pp. 746 and 763), both apparently
founded on portions (sometimes identical portions) of the above original

relation.
[1] Two remarks may be made on this
passage : 1. Burnet has told us (*supra*,
p. 286) that he was inducted into the

should happen to languish long, I should scarce hope that the thing could be performed. [a]Russell upon his return communicated the matter first with Shrewsbury, Lumley, and Mr. Sidney; [b]next it was opened to Danby (and many others), who went into it heartily, and got the bishop of London to join in it.

[*Character of the earl of Nottingham*[1].]

It was by their advice communicated to Nottingham [b], who was the heir of his father's virtues and knowledge as well as of his honours. [c]He was much considered by the clergy and church of England party; his life was in all parts regular and exemplary; he is learned in the law, he has a noble way of expressing himself, but it is a little too long and too laboured[c], and not enough neglected in common discourse; he has very high notions of the prerogative and is too much soured against the Whigs; he is a very firm friend, and was the best son, and is the best brother [*f.* 271 (*a*)] I ever knew; and being free from vices and passions, and a man of great application and true judgement, was thought capable of the chief posts in the government. The king, who neither loved him nor his father, yet seemed willing to employ him; but [d]he hath kept himself at a great distance from the court all this reign[d]; yet they had [that?] regard to him and to that high reputation in which he was that [e]his name was still left among the privy councillors, though he never went to that board. He upon the first proposition that was made to him of this matter agreed to their inviting the prince; but at their next meeting he said he had considered further of it, and found his conscience so straitened that he could not go on in that affair. He confessed those with whom he had gone so far had a right to kill him

[a] Cf. *Hist.* i. 763.   [b] *Ibid.* 764.   [c] *Ibid.*   [d] *Ibid.*   [e] *Ibid.*

prince's secrets in July, while Russell's mission took place in April; 2. That in the printed *History* the assertion as to the probable date of the expedition is ascribed not to him, but to the prince.

[1] For the importance of the changes introduced into this character and that of Churchill in the printed *History* (revised when Nottingham was out of favour with the Whigs and Churchill in credit), see Von Ranke, ed. 1868, vol. vii. App. ii. pp. 186–8; and *supra*, Introduction.

according to Italian notions, but he assured them he would be no informer, and that though his principles restrained him from joining with them, yet his affections would force him to wish well to them.

[*The marquis of Halifax.*]

[a] Halifax was tried at a distance, but he did not encourage a further freedom; and upon general discourse he expressed his dislike of the design as impracticable and depending upon so many accidents that he thought it was a needless putting of all things upon so dangerous an issue.

[*The army tried; conduct of Churchill.*]

[b] Next to these the chief officers of the army were tried; Churchill, Kirk, and Trelawny went into it; and Trelawny got his brother that was bishop of Bristol to join in it. [c] Churchill did likewise undertake for prince George and the princess Anne [c]; and those officers said they durst answer for the much greatest part of the army, and promised to do their utmost endeavours to bring as many as possibly they could into it. [d] Churchill has been much censured [d]; for as he had risen in the king's service through several degrees up to be a favourite, so a kindness which had begun upon the king's commerce with his sister was now so well fixed, that [e] no man had more of personal favour and had found greater effects of it than he had. His coming into this design had the appearance of treachery and ingratitude, which has brought him under much reproach. But as he never betrayed any of the king's secrets to the prince, so he never set the king on violent measures, but on the contrary, as oft as he spake to him of his affairs (which was indeed but seldom), he gave him always moderate counsels [e]. He had kept himself wholly out of the counsels, and so set himself to manage his post in the army, [f] in which he made great advantages [f], for money had as much power over him as he had over the king. [g] His wife is about the princess and has gained such an ascendant over her [g], that

[a] Cf. *Hist.* i. 764, *supra.*   [b] *Ibid.* 764–5.   [c] *Ibid.* 766.   [d] *Ibid.* 765.   [e] *Ibid.*
[f] *Ibid. supra.*   [g] *Ibid. infra.*

there never was a more absolute favourite in a court; she is indeed become the mistress of her thoughts and affections, and does with her, both in her court and in all her affairs, what she pleases. ᵃ Churchill is a very smooth man, made for a court ᵃ, and very fit for business if his own interests prevailed not [*f.* 271 (*b*)] too much over him. ᵇ These were the persons that sent an invitation in writing ¹ to the prince by Sidney; and every one of them assured him in their letters that they writ to him what was the universal sense of all the good and wise men that they knew.

[*Tenor of the advice sent to Holland.*]

Cf. *Hist.* i. 776 (*from* 'They advised' *to* p. 777, *end of paragraph*).
Om. 'The earl of Danby . . . country.'
For 'the king . . . slowly' *read* 'that so the king might be surprised before a greater fleet could be equipped out.'

[*Herbert's criticisms.*]

Cf. *Hist.* i. 778.
Om. 'and the other seamen' *and read the whole passage in the singular.*
After 'assistance from France' *add* 'The roads were also much better up to London. It is true the passage of the Thames might have been a matter of much difficulty in a winter campaign; but if all had been carried on to the Thames the main part of the work had been done.'
For 'to have split . . . channel' *read* 'to steer that way.'

[*The prince's views as to his force.*]

Cf. *Hist.* i. 777.
For 'When these things . . . he could' *read* 'But he would.'
For 'to the king's own . . . stick to him' *read* 'to anything the king could bring against him; therefore he thought 10,000 foot and 3,000 horse and dragoons was the smallest force he could carry with him.'
Om. 'in the north'; *and for* 'to the west' *read* 'to some other place.'
Om. 'They pressed . . . carry him over with him.'
For 'in any one part . . . whole' *read* 'might turn the people to the prevailing side.'

The expedition was carried on with great secrecy.

Cf. *Hist.* i. 778 (*from* 'The prince continued' *to end of* p. 779).
For 'The prince . . . Cologne. He' *read* 'But to cover his design the better he.'

ᵃ Cf. *Hist.* i. 765, *supra.*   ᵇ *Ibid.* 776.

---

¹ This celebrated invitation, signed in cipher by Shrewsbury, Devonshire (whose name, accidentally omitted above, was subsequently inserted in the *History*), Danby, Lumley, Bishop of London, Russell, and Sidney, and first published by Dalrymple (see pp. 107-10 of Appendix to Book V in edition 1790), from the original in 'King William's chest,' is not specifically mentioned in Burnet's final version.

After 'was also ordered' *add* 'to be carried thither.'

[*f.* 272 *a*] *For* 'for so long a time' *read* 'for a winter's campaign.'

For 'The main point . . . expedition' *read* 'He also found a way to be furnished with money which was managed with great dexterity.'

For 'or at least to create a delay' *read* 'upon a point that goes always hardly in a [popular?] government.'

Om. 'But Fagel . . . prevent this.'

For 'of the neighbourhood . . . arise there' *read* '[that] the French were then possessed of the bishopric of Cologne.'

For 'their places . . . bad condition' *read* 'the fortified places on their frontiers.'

For 'in four days' *read* 'presently.'

For from 'About the end' *to* 'necessity of the undertaking' *read* 'And being now raised, the States ordered it to go to the English expedition; for the elector of Brandenburg had undertaken the war of Cologne, with the assistance of the northern princes, so that the States reckoned themselves safe on that side and diverted the money to another use. And though the government of Holland consists of many negative voices, and every one of their towns being governed by a council that consists of thirty or more persons, it could not be imagined that a body so variously composed should have so unanimously consented to an expedition in winter, that besides all other dangers had the seas and seasons to wrestle with; yet there was not in the Hague or in any of the towns of Holland one dissenting voice; nor was there any so averse to it that it was necessary to lose any time for working on them underhand; for all came in frankly and readily.'

For 'Fagel . . . concurrence in this design' *read only* 'The persecution of France had united all the protestants in Holland in this design; and the ministers were secretly directed to take all possible methods in the several towns to possess all people with a sense of the present extremity, and that now or never the protestant religion must be recovered out of the extrème danger to which it was reduced.'

For 'But I was never . . . have there' *read* 'yet they have generally great credit with their people.'

For 'Those' *read* 'Those among the Dutch.'

After 'religion, yet' *add* 'concurred heartily in this matter; they.'

For 'And the publication . . . they reckoned' *read* 'They reckoned that if England joined with France.'

For 'All the English . . . Amsterdam' *read* 'And all advices from England, as well as all the English who lived at Amsterdam.'

For 'had such positive advices . . . hand of heaven' *read* 'represented this undertaking as so sure and so easy that all went to it as the only means of their preservation.'

For 'Herbert . . . impracticable, but' (*see supra*, p. 285) *read only* 'The Dutch fleet was ordered to go to sea; but the wind stood long at north-west, and for some days there was so violent a storm, that [it].'

[*f.* 272 (*b*)] *Om.* 'and gave us . . . prospect.'

For 'Herbert . . . expected' *read* 'The fleet also was much weaker than had been promised by the admiralties, and it was generally but indifferently manned.'

Debates concerning the declaration.

Cf. *Hist.* i. 780–1.

For 'All the English ... Hague' *read* 'These were melancholy things, and this put many of the English, who were then all come to the Hague, in very ill-humour.'

Om. 'Among these ... discontent.'

For 'and on what ... bishops' *read* 'and the other violences that had been set on against the church party.'

For 'in all which' *read* 'so whatever the designs of the court might have been.'

For 'mysterious, when' *read* 'mysterious for a great while; and it was not easy to comprehend how.'

For 'the church party' *read* 'the Tory party.'

After 'by the prince' *add* 'since there was nothing in it that reflected on them.'

For 'made to secure ... religion' *read* 'and suspend [*f.* 273 (*a*)] them in all time to come, which concerned the public safety and security.'

For 'would not only carry ... army' *read* 'or on the Tory party in general, would unite the army in England.'

For 'that was to be left to the parliament' *read* 'since he was a stranger to them.'

Om. 'as they were transmitted ... going over.'

The army all shipped.

Cf. *Hist.* i. 781 (*to* 'attendance at the Hague').

For 'In the beginning of October' *read* 'The fleet, after it had been out a fortnight, was ordered in again; and about the third of October.'

After 'Texel' *add* 'which was much censured; for though the season was pretty cool, yet diseases are apt to break in upon multitudes that are aboard; for before we got to England they had been a month at sea.'

For 'Never was ... It is true some' *read* 'It appeared upon this occasion that Holland is the only country in the world in which such a design could have been executed all of the sudden; for the shipping is so vast that in three days' time they had hired almost 500 ships, and everything was so soon ready that though our impatience and the season made us complain [that] many'; *and for* 'forgot' *read* 'ill-ordered.'

For 'it seemed much more ... forgot' *read* 'the diligence of those who managed it deserves great commendation.'

For 'Van Hulst' *read* 'Mr. Harbord[1].'

Om. altogether 'I waited on the princess ... direct us.'

[*The prince takes leave.*]

Cf. *Hist.* i. 782 (*from* 'On the sixteenth of October' *to end of paragraph*).

For 'in the west' *read* 'at W. and NW., that it began to make us all melancholy.'

---

[1] Commissary-general to the force from the time of its landing to the arrival at St. James'. See *Life of* *Halifax*, i. 253 sq., 259, 272, 471 *n.*; ii. 81, 217, 225, 226.

[*f.* 273 (*b*)] *After* 'manner' *add* 'he said her deportment among them had been such, that he need not say much concerning her ; only as to one thing.'

Om. 'but a kind.'

After 'when he came' *add* 'that night.'

The fleet sailed, but beat back with little loss.

Cf. *Hist.* i. 782-3.

For 'But the next day' *read* 'But before next day at noon.'

After 'want of air' *add* 'but that was soon made up.'

For 'but was calm and silent. The States' *read* 'she showed great courage [1], and began to be much esteemed by the States, who.'

Disorders in the council in England.

Cf. *Hist.* i. 783-5.

[*f.* 274 (*a*)] *For* 'He proposed rather . . . importunities' *read* 'so he diverted that which afterwards was represented as a sign of his being in the prince's secret [2]; to this was added his great friendship with Sidney, and his constant converse with him. [Cf. *Hist.* i. 756.] [By] these things.'

For 'The fleet . . . so strong' *read* 'Dartmouth was sent to command the fleet; great diligence was used in equipping out so many ships.'

For 'the Dutch fleet' *read* 'ours'; *for* 'them' *read* 'us'; *for* 'they were' *read* 'our fleet had.'

Om. 'But, in order . . . nation.'

Om. 'They wished . . . protestant wind.'

After 'city of London' *add* 'which had an ill grace notwithstanding'; *for* 'and' *read* '[that he]'; *and om.* 'All men . . . affectation.'

Om. 'that order not being executed' *and* 'which plainly showed . . . last.'

Witnesses examined concerning the birth of the prince of Wales.

Cf. *Hist.* i. 785-6 (*to* 'who named the month of May ').

[*f.* 274 (*b*)] *For* 'The matter . . . supported' *read* 'The thing that was most in all people's mouths.'

Om. 'now in an after-game.'

After 'together, that they' *add* 'and all his people.'

[The countess of Clarendon's story; that of Windebank.]

Cf. *Hist.* i. 750.

Begin 'Upon which I think fit to set down a passage which I had from the countess of Clarendon's own mouth.'

For 'On the same day . . . admittance' *read* 'She told me that on Easter Monday she, hearing the queen was ill, came into the bedchamber, where she found the queen with very little company with her.'

---

[1] For Mary's own account of her conduct see *Lettres et Mémoires* (1880), pp. 76-92 ; Doebner's *Memoirs of Mary Queen of England* (1886), pp. 3-6.

[2] Sunderland himself, as is well known, in the vindicatory letter published (by Blencowe) in H. Sidney's *Diary* and elsewhere, made a merit of it.

After 'Undone' *add* 'and there was a great stir about her bed, she herself and all about her seeming to be in an agony.'

For 'which she believed . . . queen' *read* 'but whether it was only [linen] or anything else she could not tell.'

For 'She was upon this . . . course' *read* ' She saw she was not a welcome person there ; so she withdrew ; and that day or the next one came to her and desired her not to speak of that accident ; which went so far that the king, who was gone to Chatham to view the naval preparations, was sent for [cf. *ibid. supra*]; and [*f.* 275 (*a*)] Dr. Walgrave [then in chief charge of her] did own to Dr. Windebank [*as ibid.*]. This I had from Mr. Geddes, chancellor of the church of Salisbury, who told me he had it from Windebank's own mouth.' (*The certificate mentioned in the History was signed in* 1702 ; *see note, Hist. in loco.*)

[*Effect of this on the evidence.*]

Cf. *Hist.* i. 785 (*from* 'But if the particulars' *to* p. 786, 'nation was possessed').

For 'since . . . considered' *read* 'for upon such occasions as these modesty must be for a while laid aside.' (A trivial detail follows, quoted from the evidence of Mrs. Dawson, which proves, in Burnet's estimation, that the queen could not then have been in the condition pretended.)

Om. 'She was a bedchamber woman . . . witness.'

Om. 'So that the proof . . . question.'

Om. 'for all people concluded . . . world.'

[*Absence of the princess; various stories on this topic.*]

Cf. *Hist.* i. 786, 749, 752, 750–1, 754.

Begin (p. 786) 'It was much observed . . . could not hurt her' (*omitting last sentence of paragraph*), *and add* 'The truth was she had been strangely used in this matter, for though when she was a maid the queen had made her [satisfy herself], yet now that she was a competent judge and a witness who alone would have satisfied the whole world in the matter, she was never desired to do it.'

Then return to p. 749 ('Prince George . . . breaking with her') *and add* 'nor did it appear that any woman of rank or reputation of any of the religions had been either called on to [receive demonstrative proof, before or after].'

Then return to p. 752, *reading* 'And to end this matter altogether Chamberlain,' *&c.*

For 'wondered' *read* 'told me.'

[*f.* 275 (*b*)] *After* 'custom' *add* 'three days after.'

After 'plaisters' *add* 'for which he had a fee of 100 guineas.'

For 'He fancied . . . had it' *read* 'Upon which he, fancying that one Dr. Brady had thrust himself into this matter, went to expostulate it with him ; but he protested to him he knew nothing of it. My lady Bellasis, who was of the bedchamber, told me that for three months before the birth the ladies of the bedchamber never gave the queen her smock; but that was always so managed, that it was done before they came in the morning or after they were dismissed at night.' (Cf. *Hist.* i. 749.)

Then return and take from p. 750 ('Lower') *to* p. 751 ('to advise it') ; *after* 'told me' *adding* 'that he was present at the consultation concerning the princess's going to The Bath'; *for* 'he was against it; he' *reading* 'he and another (I think it was Radcliffe)'; *after* 'vehemence' *adding* 'not without showing anger against those who were of another mind'; *for* 'Millington, another physician' *reading* 'Sir Thomas Millington, a learned physician'; *omitting* 'from whom I had it.'

Then add 'I pass over all conjectural proofs, of which the bishop of St. Asaph has gathered a vast number [cf. *Hist.* i. 754]; because these amount to nothing unless it be to weaken a matter [1].'

Debates at Helvoetsluys [2]

Cf. *Hist.* i. 786 (*from* 'This was the state' *to* p. 787, *end of paragraph*).

For 'Here Wildman ... entertained by many' *read only* 'It was visible that many of our English heroes were upon this occasion much dejected.'

After 'fleets' *insert* 'especially when the seas are rough.'

Om. 'though both sides ... avoided.'

After 'ship them again' *add* 'it would dishearten not only the army but the States, and all their allies, to see much time lost.'

[*f.* 276 (*a*)] *Om.* 'with these things ... quieted them.'

After 'six hours together' *add* 'all the morning long.'

For 'Many that have passed for heroes, yet' *read* 'In all this time when most men.'

Om. 'it calmed a little and' *and* 'third rate.'

[*The fleet sails again; the landing;*] *remarkable providences in that voyage.*

Cf. *Hist.* i. 787–90 (*to* 'to guide thee right').

For 'on the third' *read* 'on Saturday morning.'

After 'horses' *add* 'and everything else that we needed.'

For 'at noon on the fourth' *read* 'on Sunday night.'

For 'The pilot thought he' *read* 'he thought the pilot'; *and om.* 'and believed ... orders.'

[*f.* 276 (*b*)] *Om.* 'whereas ... decided.'

---

[1] The result of the differences between the earlier version and the *History* proves (*a*) that the original story, which reached Burnet in Holland, treated the entire episode as a case of fraud; and (*b*) that after the examination before the council had disposed of this suggestion, and had proved the reality of the queen's expectations, all reports were collected and believed, which tended to show that her hopes had been prematurely blasted, and that a recourse had been then had to imposture.

[2] We must here remind the reader of a remarkable series of letters from Burnet to Admiral Herbert (mentioned in Mr. Airy's article *Dict. Nat. Biog.*) contained in Egerton MSS. (Brit. Mus.) 2621, ff. 49–83, and printed *infra*, as Appendix IV, which relate incidents from Oct. to Dec. 1688. Their genesis is described in *Hist.* i. 762: 'The managing [Herbert] was in a great measure put on me, and it was no easy thing.' The first (undated, f. 49) was written after the storm had beaten back the expedition, and contains a most amusing mixture of civilities, clerical expostulation on the recipient's vices, and the last news from England. He relates the king's interview with the bishops; changes in the command of the English fleet; the affections of the city; for German news his correspondent, like Mr. Sidney, will not care.

Om. '(upon which . . . lost).'

After 'aboard the prince' *add* 'to see for new orders.'

For 'which they found . . . season' *read* 'All the foot were landed that night.'

After 'cold night' *add* 'which might have been expected at that time'; *and after* 'much by it' *add* '[whereas] it proved to be one of the warmest nights I ever knew in that season, and was indeed like a summer's night.'

For 'shook me . . . hand' *read* 'looked very kindly to me.'

For 'The prince . . . asked them' *read* 'The prince ordered all the fishermen of the bay to be brought to him next morning, that he might know.'

For 'with as much baggage . . . Exeter' *read* 'which were above 7,000 ; for though our cavalry and dragoons were not half so many, yet the officers' horses, besides those which belonged to the train of artillery and the waggons, grew up to that number.'

After 'seaport to Exeter' *add* 'which was but [*f.* 277 (*a*)] a little way by sea.'

For 'philosophical' *read* 'too philosophical.'

After 'venti' *add* 'which at that time was Englished thus.'

Many come to him from the king's army[1].

Cf. *Hist.* i. 790 (*from* 'The prince made haste' *to* p. 792, 'great an effect').

For 'Both the clergy and magistrates . . . what they did eat we' *read only* 'The people came in to him in great numbers ; but as the magistrates of Exeter were very backward, so we.'

For 'Every day . . . Abingdon' *read* 'Every day some came [to him] from London ; the first were the lord Colchester, Mr. Edward Russell, and col. Godfrey.'

For 'The king came down . . . further' *read* 'In the meanwhile the king sent his troops westward.'

After 'dragoons' *add* 'that were sent as far as Salisbury.'

Om. 'the lord Cornbury . . . Langston.'

For 'But because . . . made' *read* 'they did not discover it to the subaltern officers, for they durst not trust them, but they still advanced as if they had been sent to view our army.'

After 'Exeter and' *add* 'as they were marching in the night.'

After 'Cornbury' *add* 'that commanded this [*f.* 277 (*b*)] body.'

For 'So they fell . . . rode back' *read* 'Many that came unto us soon after turned back then, they being in a confusion and apprehending they were falling into a trap, through the unskilfulness of their leaders.'

---

[1] These events are described in Burnet's second letter to Herbert, Eg. MSS. 2621, f. 51 (Exeter, Friday, Nov. 16, 1688). This mentions the want of transport, the Cornbury fiasco ('We had swallowed down in our hopes three of the king's best regiments,' lost by 'the confusion of the night, with Sir Fran[cis] Compton's want of head or heart, together with the vigour of some popish officers among them '), the expected defection of Kirk and the forces at Plymouth, the better temper among the clergy, and the fact that Portsmouth would have surrendered had they landed there. See also the third letter (an intervening one having been lost in the post), which describes the situation from Sherborne, Nov. 29 (Thursday). *Ibid.* f. 67.

For 'Yet, on the other hand ... flatteries' *read* 'It struck the king at first; till flatterers (who will always abound about courts that love them and that hearken to them).'

For 'The king wanted support ... Exeter' *read* 'This gave the king some quiet; but that was quickly disturbed, for.'

After 'bodies together' *add* 'in the north.'

Om. 'And the ill disposition ... depend on them.'

After 'at once' *add* 'and his health suffered so much that it was generally believed he could not hold out long. The last three days in which the prince stayed at Exeter the whole country came in [cf. *Hist.* i. 792], being the more encouraged to do it because the earl of Bath with the garrison of Plymouth had declared for him [*ibid.* 793]. And if he had not received daily assurances that the greater part of the army would have declared for him, he intended to have gone to Bristol and have secured both that town and Gloucester [*ibid. supra*]; for by that means the whole west was in his hands; and not have ventured through the great plains of Wiltshire, where the king, that was so superior to him in horse, would have had a vast advantage [*ibid.*] if he had been sure of them. But though the king sent men every hour to bring intelligence, they took his money and came with it over to the prince, but not one of them returned' (*ibid.* 791). *Then proceed,* · At Salisbury the lord Churchill,' &c. (*ibid.* 791, *infra*).

Om. 'At Axminster ... king's sons [1].'

For 'took notice ... factious' *read* 'The king was expostulating with him upon the zeal he showed for religion, which in him could be nothing but faction.'

Om. 'for he had been so ... less.'

After 'had conscience' *add* 'This of Churchill's coming over put the king in a vast disorder; and within a day after, some country people came into Salisbury and gave the alarm that the prince's army was marching with all possible haste over the plains; upon which the king went to London with all the confusion imaginable' (cf. *Hist.* i. 793).

For 'Soon after that' *read* 'Next night.'

[*f.* 278 (a)] *For* 'left him ... Sherburn' *read* 'and some others, left him.'

For 'When the news ... easily accepted [2]' *read only* 'And as soon as the princess Anne knew this she left the court and put herself into the bishop of London's hands, who carried her first to the earl of Dorset's, and from thence to the north.'

For 'not only ... but even' *read* 'by all persons, and particularly.'

After 'treating' *add* 'both him and.'

Om. 'which had a burden ... lilibulero.'

[*The prentices; the forged declaration.*]

Begin 'The prentices of London began to run together in great bodies, and fell upon all the mass-houses, and broke down everything belonging to them' (cf. *Hist.* i. 794).

Then revert to beginning of paragraph, p. 793, *and proceed from* 'A bold man' *to* 'nor whom to trust' (p. 794).

For 'A bold man ... name' *read* 'There was also a new declaration printed in the prince's name, which set London in flame.'

[1] Routh's *Burnet's James II* reads 'spurious race.'

[2] Routh's *Burnet's James II* adds 'and was by that exposed to much censure.'

Om. 'And it had as great . . . by their means.'

For 'that was in . . . channels' *read* 'that might secure the nation from them.'

Om. 'And it was never . . . thing.'

After 'consternation' *add* 'upon all things,' *and om.* 'nor whom . . . shed.'

Commissioners sent from the king to treat with the prince[1].

Cf. *Hist.* i. 794 (*from* 'The king now sent' *to* p. 795, *end of paragraph*).

For 'The king now sent . . . one opinion' *read only* 'All the protestants who were firm to him advised him.'

After 'consent to it. So' *insert* 'another meeting of the nobility was called, where the king expressed himself with much passion and confusion.'

After 'demanded' *add* 'In the meanwhile the prince advanced with his army, and every day great numbers were coming in to him ; among the rest' ; *and after* 'Clarendon' *insert* '[who].'

For 'reflected . . . condemned' *read* 'had answered the king very peevishly at the meeting of the nobility and came down full of wrath against him.'

Om. 'A day . . . answer.'

For 'The marquis of Halifax . . . both my answers' *read only* 'Halifax desired earnestly to speak with me in private ; but when I asked the prince's order, he forbid me to do it. Yet in the crowd he asked me, but so as nobody perceived it, whether we had a mind to have the king in our hands, or to let him go. I answered nothing could [*f.* 278 (*b*)] be so happy as to let him go, if he had a mind to it. Nottingham said also to me, if the prince did not take his measures right, he would find the hardest part of his work before him at London, when perhaps we might think he had all in his hands.'

Om. 'The prince ordered . . . had sent.'

Articles are proposed.

Cf. *Hist.* i. 795 (*to* 'satisfied with this answer').

For 'thirty miles' *read* 'twenty' (*see Routh's note in Burnet's James II in loco*).

Om. 'come on to London and.'

Om. last sentence of paragraph.

---

[1] This treaty is described in Burnet's fourth letter to Herbert (Eg. MSS. 2621,f. 69), a long and important missive dated Hungerford, Dec. 9, 1688. He states that Halifax and Nottingham 'seem very little fond of the employment, and say that it was put on them by their enemies' ; that the trumpeter was detained two nights while the prince consulted his followers ; that till all papists are turned out, the prince will hold on his march, for (f. 70) 'the true design of this treaty is to amuse the nation, and to stop the prince's march, in which the court will be deceived, for we will still go on. The commissioners desired to speak in private with the prince, but he declined it, for he said he was come upon the business of the nation and that he had no private concern of his own. The two first in the commission behaved themselves so, and talked so freely to myself and several others in a public room, that we saw they were condemned to act a part that was very unnatural to them.'

[*Flight of queen.*]

Cf. *Hist.* i. 795 (' But now strange counsels . . . such good terms ').

For ' But now . . . for ever' *read* ' But in the meantime things took a strange turn at London. The whole popish party saw that if a treaty was set on foot both they and their religion would be extirpated ; and the severest laws that could be contrived would be made against them ; and that many of them would be made sacrifices for what they had done.'

For 'the king's mother . . . violence' *read* '[and] the impeaching queen Mary in king Charles the First's time was not forgot; for they clearly saw that nothing could preserve the king in a parliament but the making a sacrifice both of his party and the interest of his religion.'

Om. ' The midwife . . . afterwards.'

Om. ' So she went . . . France.'

After ' disguise' *add* ' This was kept secret from all but those that were to have a share in it.'

After ' answer ' *add* ' for the lqrds, who had it on the Monday morning, sent it up by a courier ' (cf. *Hist.* i. 795, *supra*) ; *and om.* ' He ordered . . . great seal.'

The king flies away in disguise.

Cf. *Hist.* i. 796 (' And the next morning . . . scene which he then acted ').

Before ' And the next morning ' *insert* ' But these did not hinder him.'

Om. ' They passed . . . Foxhall.'

After ' France ' *add* ' And he got in it out to sea. But before he went it seems he disposed of the great seal ; for it was cast into the river above Foxhall ; and was some months after that by accident drawn to the shore by some fishermen ; but whether it was dropped there on design or lost is not yet known.'

[*f.* 279 *a*] *For* ' and of some black . . . support himself' *read* ' upon the account of the child ' *and om. following paragraph.*

But is taken and brought to Feversham.

Cf. *Hist.* i. 796 (*from* ' He was not got far' *to* p. 797, *end of paragraph*).

After ' far' *add* ' to sea'; *for* 'watching' *read* ' searching all boats '; *and for* ' came up to him' *read* 'got up to the boat in which he was.'

For ' who had ruled . . . Europe' *read* ' who had a few days before carried matters so high.'

Om. ' Here was an accident . . . active for his interests.'

Om. ' who had been a little quieted . . . prince.'

For ' where they believed . . . management ' *read* ' in a most outrageous manner.'

For ' finding . . . he was now' *read* ' whom the king had left behind.'

Om. ' he had disguised . . . But he.'

For ' and after many hours . . . died soon after' *read* ' and was at last committed to the Tower, which had been seized on by the lord Lucas without any opposition.'

The prince is invited to come to London.

Cf. *Hist.* i. 797-8 (*to* ' and ran away ').

For ' he called' *read* ' the lord mayor called.'

Om. ' They gave . . . peace.'

For 'This they all signed . . . Culpepper' *read* 'This message was sent by some of the peers, of whom the bishop of Ely was one'; *and insert from* p. 793, 'Dr. Finch . . . he needed it' (*after* 'heads of colleges' *adding* [*f.* 279 (*b*)] 'to congratulate his coming to England,' *and omitting* 'and inviting . . . thither'); *and at the end of this add* 'And Mr. Seymour having proposed an association (which contained an obligation never to separate nor depart from that undertaking till a free parliament should be called, and that they should revenge any attempt that might be made upon the person of the prince upon all the other party) that was signed by all that came in to the prince [cf. *Hist.* i. 792–3], those of Oxford were willing to enter into this bond likewise, which they afterwards signed'; *then return to* p. 798, 'The prince went.'

After 'thither' *add* 'he was willing not to make too much haste, since there was a treaty set on foot'; *for* 'of the strange catastrophe . . . till he had' *read* 'of the king's leaving Whitehall, which were brought him first by flying reports, and confirmed by.'

After 'from the king' *add* 'Upon which he told me, that though I was not much disposed to believe king Charles a prophet, yet the last time he had seen him at Windsor he had, among other expressions of his displeasure at his brother's heat, said he was confident that if he were once a king he would never be able to hold it out four years to an end' (cf. *Hist.* i. 575).

Om. 'so he sent . . . implacable enemies'; *but see supra*, ll. 9–11.

Om. 'One of the prince's officers . . . expedition.'

[*Various advices.*]

Cf. *Hist.* i. 798 (*to end of* p. 800).

For 'desertion' *read* 'withdrawal.'

After 'London' *add* 'to prevent the mischiefs that might arise from those multitudes of people that in a tumultuous way were daily committing new disorders; and, which was much more formidable, to hinder the army's disbanding itself according to the orders that the king had left for the earl of Feversham, which was like to have proved the turning loose 30,000 robbers upon the nation' (cf. *Hist.* i. 796).

Om. 'otherwise . . . killed him.'

[*f.* 280 (*a*)] *For* 'Two gentlemen . . . met upon it' *read* 'For as he came on in three days to Windsor the privy council at London, hearing that the king was at Feversham, met to consider what was fit to be done.'

After 'about him' *add* 'that night.'

For 'when the news . . . Windsor' *read* 'The prince was much troubled when he heard of the accident at Feversham, and sent Mr. Zulestein immediately with orders to set the king at liberty and to let him do what he pleased [cf. *Hist.* i. 799, *supra*]. But the privy council had prevented him, with which he was much displeased, for.'

After 'now come to him' *add* 'from London.'

Om. 'and the officious flatterers.'

After 'deserting his people' *add* '[which] was looked on as so great an advantage against him according to [*f.* 280 (*b*)] the sense of all who have writ concerning government.'

After 'secured' *add* 'or at least that he should be kept till a parliament should meet.'

For 'It was thought . . . hearken' *read* 'and of this opinion was Clarendon not without great sharpness. But since his being a prisoner in England might raise great discontents, or perhaps a violent party might in parliament move in relation to his person, to which they saw the prince would never consent, therefore they advised the prince to send him over to Breda ; where, as he could keep him more securely than he could in England, so his restraint, not being exposed to the view of the whole nation, would not raise that compassion which his being a prisoner within England must have occasioned. Few argued against this till the prince himself declared his opinion ; which was that though.'

For 'now he had him in his power' *read* 'the case was different.'

For 'nor did he know . . . called' *read* 'and if the king were made a prisoner, as that would beget a great party to him, so the disposing of his person might cause such disputes in parliament as might ruin all ; for.'

[*The mission of the three lords.*]

Cf. *Hist.* i. 801 (*to* 'a guard went with him ').

After 'drawn off' *add* 'in the night,'

Om. 'but not . . . murmuring.'

[*f.* 281 (*a*)] *After* 'asked them' *add* 'in the king's name.'

For 'escape. They' *read* 'escape ; so they.'

For 'very readily' *read* 'before morning.'

For 'having ordered . . . came about him' *read* 'with a small guard and a few servants.'

The prince comes to St. James'.

Cf. *Hist.* i. 801 (*from* 'On the same day' *to* p. 802, 'this winter ').

Om. 'And even this trifle . . . edge.'

After 'fermentation' *add* 'among some of the nobility and clergy.'

Om. 'when he was ready . . . everything.'

For 'the saying of' *read* 'that old saying made use of by.'

Om. 'disguised and designed.'

For 'the nation had never known' *read* 'The country was so little accustomed to '; *and after* 'army' *add* 'that generally they took nothing for their quarters.'

Om. 'and the freedom . . . markets '; *and after* 'maintained' *add* 'by them during this interval of government.'

After 'winter' *add* 'But upon all these accounts a discontent began to spread itself through the whole army. It was certain that if the king had stayed at Whitehall there might have been so high a fermentation upon it, that from thence disorders would have arisen which would have endangered both his life and the prince's ; and [*f.* 281 (*b*)] have exposed the city both to fire and pillage '; *and om. next two paragraphs.*

[*Consultations about a settlement*[1].]

Cf. *Hist.* i. 803 (' The first thing . . . against that proposition ').

For 'The first thing . . . settled' *read* 'And now every man was ready and forward to propose his scheme.'

---

[1] Burnet's final letter to Herbert (Eg. MSS. 2621, f. 83), dated St. James',   Christmas Day, 1688, reflects on the Feversham incident, the king's second

Om. 'which might otherwise . . . tedious.'

For 'such a step . . . to raise himself; and' *read* 'the government was first dissolved, and then deserted by king James; and therefore if the prince should now assume the kingship to himself, as it would very much disparage his honour, so.'

He [is] addressed to assume the administration, and to call a convention of estates.

(From above, to end of paragraph.)

Om. 'When these were . . . nation.'

For 'It was agreed . . . to make an' *read only* 'who did all.'

For 'though without . . . earl of Nottingham' *read only* 'Some'; *and omit* 'he' *before* 'moved.'

For 'Few were of his mind . . . nation' *read only* 'for.'

The king went to France.

Cf. *Hist.* i. 804.

For 'Many that were . . . went to him, and' *read* 'The prince wished him gone; but all his own party.'

Om. 'and to see . . . agreement.'

For 'The queen . . . ordered it to be' *read* 'But letters that he got from his queen which, with great vehemency, pressed his coming over to her, happened to be intercepted; they being writ in so imperious a strain for a point that was wished for, they were.'

For 'So he gave . . . table' *read* 'So he left behind him a paper.'

For 'And so . . . secretly' *read* 'And a vessel being provided for him he went.'

Scotland declares for the prince.

Cf. *Hist.* i. 804-5 *(to* 'copy after it in England').

For 'But before . . . governor' *read* 'The affairs of Scotland were very near in the same condition with those of England; all the forces of that kingdom had been brought into England, and so it was left in the hands of the militia, only the duke of Gordon was governor of the castle of Edinburgh.'

For 'spirit' *read* 'parts.'

---

withdrawal ('yesterday'), the discussions as to the next step (some maintain that the princess becomes queen and should issue writs for a Parliament; others advise a convention to make a settlement; 'This last is liable to this exception, that the slowness of it may expose Holland to be lost before England can be settled or ready to act'). He expresses an evidently sincere commiseration for the 'poor king's' situation, which Herbert he knows shares ('I know it was not possible for you to have acted as some others have done, but whatever one may think of that we must now shut our mouths, for there is discontent enough already, and the army seem generally out of humour and uneasy at what they have done, and you know we have not the arts of cajolery . . . it is now time for you to be for a while at rest till we make a new expedition into France, for I do verily believe the prince designs it this summer').

[*f.* 282 (*a*)] *Om.* 'particularly . . . England.'

Om. 'disguised himself and.'

For 'and put in prison' *read* 'and has continued a prisoner ever since.'

After 'popery' *add* 'and that received the news of this deliverance with joy.'

Om. 'and was printed . . . gazette.'

[*The episcopalians coalesce with Dundee, in favour of James.*]

[This] had rendered them very odious in Scotland; so they, finding that the presbyterians were like to carry all before them, resolved to make what party they could for king James and to stick to his interests. [a]There was one Graham, who had served some years in Holland, and was both a very good officer and a man of great parts. King James had given him considerable employments and made him earl of Dundee; he had taken up a violent hatred against the whole presbyterian party, and being a proud and passionate man, though in all other respects a man of virtue and probity, he had executed the law and obeyed his orders when he was quartered in the western parts of Scotland with great rigour and severity[a]. So that now both his engagements to king James, his principles, and his passions threw him into that party, [b]who received him as their head[b]; and thus the disposition of matters in Scotland looked very favourable to the prince, but very cloudy towards the episcopal interest there.

[*The meeting in London.*]

Cf. *Hist.* i. 805 ('The duke of Hamilton . . . prince's hands').

The dangerous state of Ireland.

Cf. *Hist.* i. 805-6 (*to* 'supplies should come to them from England').

Om. 'and full of . . . behind them.'

[*f.* 282 (*b*)] *For* 'Tyrconnell . . . Upon which' *read* 'After the faint resistance that the protestants made in the field to the troops that Tyrconnell sent to reduce the country.'

After 'military men' *add* 'who came over into England.'

Om. entirely from 'I will not enlarge' *to end of following paragraph.*

[*Subject continued.*]

Cf. *Hist.* i. 806 (*from* 'As for the affairs' *to* p. 809, 'and was drowned').

After 'among them' *add* 'at London.'

[a] Cf. *Hist.* i. 805.   [b] *Ibid.*

Om. ' The earl of Clarendon . . . come to a composition ¹.'

Om. ' and it was like him ².'

O.n. ' Probably . . . Tyrconnell.'

[*f.* 283 (*a*)] *Om.* ' (For sir William . . . figure).'

For ' officers' *read* ' best officers.'

For ' He had served . . . together with a' *read* ' There was a great.'

For ' Hamilton . . . of war' *read* ' He with the other Irish officers were then, in a sort, prisoners of war.'

Om. ' looking . . . terms that he could.'

After ' papist' *add* ' (Mountjoy was the protestant).'

Om. ' The earl of Tyrconnell pretended . . . all that he asked.'

For ' And he now fancied' *read* ' or was quite altered by Hamilton's going over; [Hamilton assured him] that there would be great divisions in the convention of estates, and that king James' party would be very strong in it; and therefore if he stood firm.'

[*f.* 283 (*b*)] *Om.* ' and the earl of Clarendon . . . against it.'

A convention of estates called.

Cf. *Hist.* i. 809 (' The sitting . . . formed about the town ').

Om. ' about the town.'

Some were for bringing back king James.

Cf. *Hist.* i. 809 (*from* ' The one' *to* ' their doctrine ').

Others are for naming a prince regent.

Cf. *Hist.* i. 809 (*to* p. 811, ' could be according to their own principles ').

Om. ' A third party . . . throne'; *and for* ' When the archbishop . . . benches of the temporal lords' *read* ' All the bishops, the archbishop of Canterbury ³ only excepted, went into this; for he would not appear at the convention.'

Om. ' in opposition . . . king.'

Om. ' and of men of no religion.'

[*f.* 284 (*a*)] *After* ' house of commons' *add* ' who were all those who were called the high court party.'

For ' seemed to' *read* ' did.'

But the greatest part were for declaring the throne vacant.

Cf. *Hist.* i. 811 (*from* ' The third' *to* p. 815, ' tragically represent the matter ').

[*f.* 284 (*b*)] *Om.* ' This was often renewed . . . successors.'

Om. ' Nor was . . . disowned.'

Om. ' by a gentleman . . . came by it ⁴.'

---

¹ It should perhaps be noted that a very rude note of Swift's on this omitted passage has no justification; Burnet evidently means that Temple had been long in credit with the prince.

² Some comments on this charge will be found in the *Life of Halifax*.

³ The writer will again observe that reflections on Sancroft are omitted.

⁴ Cf. *Hist.* i. 32, 33, with Dartmouth's, Cole's, and Airy's notes.

[*f.* 285 (*a*)] *For* 'the dispensing . . . continued in it' *read* '[These things] were thought a dissolution of the contract between him and his people ; which was completed by his deserting of his people; upon all which they inferred that he had abdicated the government and left the throne vacant.'

Om. 'By this proposition . . . power of a king.'

For 'And it was to be presumed . . . will' *read* 'The weakness of childhood or the disorders of lunacy might be provided for this way.'

[*f.* 285 (*b*)] *For* 'Some among . . . rest' *read* 'Two different parties appeared.'

Om. 'had his power . . . by the law, and' ; *and after* 'govern by law' *add* 'and to protect his people.'

Om. 'In extreme . . . allowed of them.'

Om. next two paragraphs.

[*Discussion as to a successor.*]

Cf. *Hist.* i. 815-6 ('It was a more important debate . . . strictly bound to it ').

For ' It was a more important debate . . . successors' *read* 'This was therefore the motion that grew most naturally to be entertained ; but in the management of this a new debate arose : Whether upon the judging or declaring king James to have abdicated they should not inquire who was the next heir, and put that person on the throne. All that were against the abdication stood upon this, that the oaths of allegiance binding the nation to the king and his heirs, then if it could be supposed that the king had absolved the nation from their tie to himself, yet they were still bound to his heirs ; and upon this ground they intended to have had the business of the prince of Wales examined ; and in this matter men were much divided.'

Om. ' it being a maxim . . . living man.'

And [*the majority*], *without examining the birth of the prince of Wales,*

Cf. *Hist.* i. 816 (*from* ' It was proposed' *to* p. 817, 'laid before me as to that matter ').

[*f.* 286 (*a*)] *For* 'And it would have gone far . . . king James' *read only* 'And it would be a great article with relation to king James; but others did not approve of this.'

For ' Upon which I was ordered . . . It is true' *read* 'There were many presumptive proofs brought, which I have in the former part of this history set down very carefully ; but.'

For ' But, when this matter . . . some observed' *read* 'It was said by the prince's friends.'

For ' so, if there' *read* 'so since there'; *and for* 'and then . . . birth' *read* ' would do as much harm on the other side.'

For ' When this debate . . . indignation' *read only* ' It took much with many that.' *This passage down to* 'enemies' *occurs on f.* 286 (*b*).

Om. ' it was also known, that . . . out.'

For 'But while these things . . . in this matter. They' *read only* ' But there were others who.'

For 'Wildman thought . . . matter' *read only* 'This was thought by some men a deep piece of policy and they valued themselves upon it. So.'

were for putting the princess in the throne.

Cf. *Hist.* i. 818 (*from* 'The next thing in' *to* p. 819, 'others for the princess ').

[*f.* 286 (*b*)] *Om.* 'and, that he might get . . . credit with the prince.'

Om. entirely from 'How far the prince' *to* p. 819, 'and died about the end of them.'

For 'The agents . . . knew nothing of it' *read* 'and here the princess of Denmark began to make some stir, that the prince might not be set before her; but she quickly desisted.'

For 'The proposition . . . sovereigns' *read* 'Others were for putting both the prince and princess in the throne.'

After 'others for the princess' *read* 'Danby, Shrewsbury, Sidney, and all the moderate church of England men were for putting both in the throne. The debate stood for several days at this.'

The prince was long silent.

Cf. *Hist.* i. 820 (*to end of first paragraph*).

[*f.* 287 (*a*)] *Om.* 'affectation and as a disguised.'

For 'he called for . . . some others' *read* 'he was prevailed on to call together five or six of those on whom he relied most.'

But at last he declared his own sense of those debates.

Cf. *Hist.* i. 820 (*from* 'He told them' *to* p. 821, 'concur in such a design ').

Om. 'he himself saw . . . accept of it.'

After 'did the princess' *add* 'nor reckon himself surer in her than he did.'

For 'in so cold . . . contrivance' *read* 'in so unconcerned and so stoical a manner, that as many of those who were there have told me, never was anything said with a more cold and indifferent air than all this was.'

For 'helped not a little to bring' *read only* 'brought.'

After 'design' *add* 'This was in great part removed by myself, who had a full occasion given me to know her mind in that matter.'

The princess's sense of putting the prince in the administration.

[a] For two years before, after my coming to Holland and that I was admitted to talk with the prince and princess of the affairs of England, [b] I had [*f.* 287 (*b*)] taken the liberty to lay before her the state of our affairs in case the succession should descend on her; that the prince would be only her husband with the title but without the power of a king, and that, as in the case of king Philip, even the title would fall with her life. This I shewed her was a very ridiculous posture for a man, and that therefore the jealousy of this had made Henry VII put his right to the crown on another foot. The princess answered me that she had never thought of that before, and so she asked what remedy there could be found

[a] Cf. *Hist.* i. 688.   [b] *Ibid.* 692.

for it ; [a] I replied that as no mortal knew that I was to speak to her on this subject, so I protested solemnly that if she did not like that which I was to lay before her no mortal should ever know it. [b] It was that she should resolve to have the crown vested in the prince during his life [b] and to reign in conjunction with her ; I told her nobody could suffer by this but she and her sister, and it was but too probable that her sister could never be concerned in it. It would put the prince in a posture becoming him ; [c] and therefore I begged she would consider well of it ; for if she once made the step to assure the prince that she would do it, she was never to think of retreating again. She immediately answered me very frankly, that she would take no time to consider of any-thing by which she might express her respect and kindness to the prince ; for she was resolved, whatsoever change might happen to her, she would be no more but his wife, and that she would do all that lay in her power to make him king for life. She allowed me to discourse the matter to the prince ; and I discoursed it afterwards to them both together, and she gave him the assurance very heartily that nothing could happen to her that should ever make her more than his wife [c]. It seemed necessary at this time to let this be known, upon which I desired by Bentinck [d] to know whether the prince would allow me to speak of it [d]. Bentinck told me that [e] the prince would not talk with me upon that subject nor give me any orders concerning it, but left me to my own thoughts [e] ; and so I presumed upon the prince's[s's ?] goodness, and told it to those who had the greatest stroke in business. And they assured me [f] it helped not a little to settle all people's minds ; and it made every one that heard of it conclude that either the princess was a wonderful good woman or a very weak one ; for they reckoned that such an indifferency for power and rule must either flow from an excess of goodness or of simplicity. At her coming to England [f] I told her that the critical state of our affairs had made me venture in publishing

[a] Cf. *Hist.* i. 692-3.   [b] *Ibid.* 692.   [c] *Ibid.* 693.   [d] *Ibid.* 821.
[e] *Ibid.*   [f] *Ibid.*

what I knew concerning her intentions[1]; ᵃand she justified me in it, and seemed not only satisfied but pleasedⁿ with the settlement that had been made. I have since my first writing of this learned a very important piece of [*f.* 288 (*a*)] the secret of this history.

[*Danby's letter to the princess.*]

Cf. *Hist.* i. 819 (*from* 'Upon this the earl of Danby' *to end of paragraph*).

After 'Danby' *add* 'was so much set on having the right of the crown vested in the princess that he'; *and after* 'over' *add* 'express.'

After 'answer to the prince' *insert* 'This on both sides is no inconsiderable part of their character.'

For 'The prince bore . . . duke' *read* 'and the prince his employing and trusting Danby after this was a very extraordinary thing likewise in him.'

[*Further debates.*]

Cf. *Hist.* i. 821 (*from* 'There were other differences' *to* p. 822, 'declared to be king and queen').

For 'But that was overruled . . . declared to be king and queen' *read only* 'But a safer way was taken, which was to declare that king James had abdicated the government, and that the throne was vacant; and upon that the prince and princess of Orange were desired to accept of it; and both houses declared them to be their king and queen. There were many conferences between the two houses, not only upon the main point of exauctorating king James, but likewise upon the words Original Contract, Abdicate and Vacant. But the commons adhered firmly to their vote, at which the lords stuck almost three weeks' (cf. *Hist.* ii. 815 *and* 821).

[*The bill of rights.*]

Cf. *Hist.* i. 822 (*from* 'But before matters' *to* p. 823, *end of paragraph*).

Om. 'Some officious . . . Magna Charta.'

For 'simply . . . taken away' *read* 'as illegal.'

Om. 'though the main clamour . . . so that.'

Om. 'upon the opposition that was made.'

After 'disputable points' *add* 'Some thought that the stating the liberties of England in the same instrument in which the crown was offered to the king and queen, looked like an imposing of conditions on them; and some that pretended [*f.* 288 (*b*)] much zeal for them pressed, even a little indecently, that it might not be done; but this was soon set aside.'

The oaths are appointed to be altered.

Cf. *Hist.* i. 823–5 (*to* 'The far greater part of the clergy').

For 'Many arguments . . . agree to the new settlement' *read only* 'Those who had opposed the settlement said.'

ⁿ Cf. Hist. ii. 821.

---

[1] For the misrepresentation subsequently placed on his incidence see Hickes, *Some discourses upon Dr.* *Burnet*, &c., p. 12. See also Doebner, *Memoirs*, p. 10.

For 'just and reasonable' *read* 'expedient.'

For 'This tenderness . . . much abused by' *read only* 'But there arose afterwards.'

Om. 'and that they might act . . . de jure.'

Om. 'The truth was . . . honour or conscience.'

For 'which by its agreement . . . among them' *read* 'which is both more subtile and more sincere.'

For 'of those . . . new government' *read* 'of the clergy who had been so entangled concerning their opinions [*f.* 289 (*a*)] concerning sovereign power, and were so engaged by having asserted them so often and so publicly [cf. *ibid.* above], that without the help of this new theory they had all gone off in a body.'

Om. 'This was chiefly managed . . . Worcester.'

After 'Heaven' *add* 'especially when it fell on the just side.'

For 'This might . . . clergy' *read* 'besides several other difficulties.'

Conclusion [1].

[a] And thus I have opened the grounds on which the several parties proceeded more fully than might have been expected from me ; [b] but, as I was in this whole matter and so spent a great part of my time during these debates in arguing with several sorts of people, so that I was well acquainted with men's schemes and reasonings, so I hope it may be both a pleasant and useful instruction to posterity to open it with all possible clearness and fulness. After many debates in both houses and many conferences between them, at last a great protestation having been made against king James' abdication, and the throne's being vacant, [c] the offer of the crown was made and accepted by the prince and princess on the 13th of February [c]. It happened to be Ash Wednesday ; so some wished it might be delayed a day, and imagined it would look inauspicious to begin a reign on a day of fasting ; others thought it had a particular decency in it, that princes immediately after they were set on the throne should come and humble themselves in dust and ashes before God ; and thought that the concurrent devotions of the nation at that time was no unbecoming circumstance for the beginning of a government.

[a] Cf. *Hist.* i. 822, 825. [b] *Ibid.* 821-2. [c] *Ibid.* 825.

---

[1] The defence of the princess's cheerfulness, subsequently inserted, was no doubt evoked by Jacobite comments on her behaviour and by distorted Whig versions of his remonstrance ; see Cunningham, i. 103.

*[Reign of William and Mary]: the king and queen
are proclaimed.*

The king and queen were immediately proclaimed in
London ; and as soon as was possible over all England with
great demonstrations of joy ; for though there was a party for
king James among the nobility and gentry and clergy, yet
the body of the nation [*f.* 289 (*b*)] had never been observed
to be so universally well satisfied with any government as
they were with this. [a] The king did not change his way in
any sort upon this new dignity ; he became only a little more
visible and accessible than he had been, but his cold silent
way was too deeply rooted in him to be changed ; he was
then in a very ill state of health ; the air and smoke of
London did not agree with him ; he had been long out
of exercise, and was fallen so very low that few believed
he should easily recover his strength again ; so he chose to
retire to Hampton Court, and there he spent the summer ;
and since he found that air agreed with him, he designed
to rebuild that old and irregular palace. [b] All this was
censured [b] as a withdrawing from business and the giving
himself up to ease and laziness. Nor did he study much to
accommodate himself to the humours of the nation.

A ministry is formed.

The ministry that he first made choice of was not of
a piece, and wrought different ways. [c] Danby was made
marquess of Carmarthen and president of the council;
Halifax was privy seal ; [d] Shrewsbury and Nottingham were
secretaries of state ; [e] Mordaunt (now made earl of Monmouth) was first commissioner of the treasury ; [f] the great
seal was put in commission, [g] and so was the admiralty ; but
though Herbert, who was made earl of Torrington, was set
at the head of it, he (who designed to be lord admiral) left his
post there [g], and Pembroke was put in it. [h] Almost all the
chief places, both in the government [i] and household, were filled

---

[a] Cf. *Hist.* ii. 2.   [b] *Ibid.* 3.   [c] *Ibid.* 4.   [d] *Ibid.* 3.   [e] *Ibid.* 4.
[f] *Ibid.* 3.   [g] *Ibid.* 5.   [h] *Ibid. supra.*   [i] *Ibid. infra.*

with Whigs[a], yet they were highly displeased that they had
not them all. [b] Godolphin was thought necessary for the
treasury, since all the rest were strangers to the revenue,
which he understood well. Yet this gave Monmouth great
offence[b]; who set himself at the head of the republican party,
and had great credit among the citizens, which he at first
employed to move them to lend the king money; but afterwards, when he saw that the king would not go into all his
notions, he hindered the advances of money so effectually
that the king turned him soon out of the treasury. [c] He was
not corrupt in disposing that vast number of places[c] which
in a great measure depended upon him, and by this he got
great reputation; but as [d] he picked out commonwealth's men
for them all[d], so in everything he grew imperious and insolent,
and neglecting his own province of the treasury, he set up
cabals everywhere in order to the breaking of the prerogative,
and the putting all Tories out of employment. [e] Halifax had
gone into the Whigs' measures during the late debates, and
had totally lost the Tories; but he found soon that the
business of the exclusion still stuck in their hearts; the
delivering up of charters and the quo warrantos were chiefly
imputed to him, and the slowness of relieving Ireland was
ascribed to him. He was observed to have great credit with
the king, but nobody thought that his mercurial wit would
suit the king's phlegm long[e]. So the Whigs were inflamed
to a mighty violence against him. [f] Carmarthen could not
bear the equality, or rather preference [*f.* 290 (*a*)], that seemed
to be given to Halifax[f]; so he meddled little and complained
of everything that was done; and by Monmouth's means,
upon whom he had great influence as was believed, [g] he raised
the storm in the house of commons against Halifax[g].
Shrewsbury was the best beloved of the whole ministry, and
deserved to be so; [h] there lay no prejudice against him but
that of his youth, which was soon overcome by his great
application and wonderful temper.

ª Cf. *Hist.* ii. 5.   ᵇ *Ibid.* 4.   ᶜ *Ibid.* 5.   ᵈ *Ibid.*   ᵉ *Ibid.* 4.
ᶠ *Ibid.*   ᵍ *Ibid.*   ʰ *Ibid.* 3.

The consequences upon Nottingham's being employed.

[a] The employing of Nottingham was very unacceptable to all that party that had shewed the greatest zeal for the king [a], and it gave a present and sensible change to the state of affairs ; for [b] the Whigs grew sullen and became jealous upon it [b], that the king would fall in with the church party and grow fond of prerogative motions. On the other hand, it had a very sensible effect on the church party ; [c] they had concluded that the opposition they had given to the king's coming to the throne, and the zeal that others had showed for it, would throw him entirely into their hands [c]; this they thought would be so managed by the commonwealth party that they, finding they had the king wholly in their power, would undermine the prerogative and rob the crown of its most important rights, and by this means they apprehended both a subversion of the church and change of government in the state ; they also knew that the commonwealth party were violent and implacable, so [d] they looked for severe revenges from them for the hardships they had suffered at their hands in king Charles' reign. This begot in them great apprehensions, and put them generally in a disposition of looking towards king James ; so Nottingham's being in the ministry was looked upon by them as no small part of their security. They knew that he would lay before the king the rights and prerogatives of the crown [d], and that he would represent to him that the church party were those he must trust, who would prove his surest and firmest friends. At the same time that Nottingham was discoursing those things to the king he took much pains, both by himself and all his friends, to persuade all the clergy and the friends of the church to take the oaths and to come into the interests of the government; and his endeavour had so good effects that I reckon I do not exceed the severe rules of history when I say that Nottingham's being in the ministry, together with the effects that it had, first preserved the church and then the crown. And

[a] Cf. *Hist.* ii. 3-4.   [b] *Ibid.* 4.   [c] *Ibid.* 3.   [d] *Ibid.*

therefore those who intended to ruin both were not without reason much troubled at his being employed ; but he went on through the rest of the parts of this settlement in pursuance to his own principles, which made him be still looked on as an enemy to the government, that opposed everything that was proposed for its defence ; and his enemies, that could not deny that he was zealous in his office for it, said that out of parliament he was for the king but in parliament he was against him.   And this made some impressions even on the king himself, who looked on him as one that was too much a bigot and too passionately wedded to a party ; this did indeed show itself upon many occasions, but all that had a good effect upon the whole; for it gained him so much credit, that it put him in a capacity afterwards to bring them almost entirely over to the king's interests.   He told the king when he entered into his service that he foresaw there were many steps yet to be made in which he [*f.* 290 (*b*)] would oppose that which would be pretended to be his service ; but he would follow his own sense of things in parliament, though he would be guided by the king's sense out of it [1].

The convention turned into a parliament.

Cf. *Hist.* ii. 5–6 (*to end of paragraph*).
For 'the Tories.   They said ' *read* 'those who thought that.'
Om. ' So it was moved . . . election.'

[*Some bishops refused the oaths.*]

Cf. *Hist.* ii. 6 (*from* 'Eight bishops' *to* p. 7, *end of paragraph*), *for which read* 'Eight bishops absented themselves, of whom two died soon after; and about twelve temporal lords and a very few of the house of commons withdrew : all the rest took the oaths.'

An act obliging all persons to take the oaths.

[a] The first thing upon this that was proposed was an act obliging all such persons to take the new oaths as had been by law obliged to take the old ones, together with penalties and incapacities upon those that took them not by a prefixed

[a] Cf. *Hist.* ii. 7.

---

[1] See Von Ranke, ed. 1868, vol. vii. App. ii. pp. 187–8.

day; and in particular such of the clergy as took them not were to be put under a suspension for the space of six months, and deprivation afterwards (if they took them not within that time). This was looked on by all the church party as a design against the church of England; for it was then given out that the greater party would refuse the oaths; and this, they hoped, would either quite break or divide the church. [a] Others of the Whig party hoped at least to bring this matter to such a composition that the church party to save this storm from themselves should have consented to have taken away the sacrament test, without which no man was capable of holding public employments. This would have let in dissenters into places of trust [a], and it was represented as a thing of such advantage to the king in the present juncture, that [b] he was advised by Mr. Hampden to recommend it from the throne to both houses, [c] which he did without communicating it to his other ministers; this was a great error, for there not being any one thing upon which the church party reckoned that their security depended more than this, they became very jealous of the king as willing to sacrifice the church to the dissenters. It was rejected by both houses with so great an inequality [c] that the king had reason to look better to the motions that came from the throne. [d] But the party, finding they had [*f.* 291 (*a*)] failed in this, set on the act about the oaths with more heat than before.

[*Debates concerning the oaths.*]

Cf. *Hist.* ii. 8 (*from* 'That which was long' *to* p. 9, 'and so it passed').

Begin 'So a great debate and many conferences followed upon it' (*vide ibid. supra*).

After 'oblige' *for* 'them' *read* 'such as gave cause of suspicion.'

After 'by it' *add* 'which was enough for the safety of the government.'

Om. 'distinctions . . . strength from them.'

Om. 'especially . . . general terms.'

Om. 'An exception . . . rejected.

Om. from 'I was the chief' *to end of paragraph.*

[a] Cf. *Hist.* ii. 8.   [b] *Ibid.* 7.   [c] *Ibid.* 8.   [d] *Ibid.*

An act for a toleration.

At the same time [a] an act passed for the toleration of all protestant dissenters [a], which gave a new disgust to all those violent churchmen [b] who retained still an implacable hatred to the nonconformists, and were longing for occasion to put the laws in execution against them. [c] Yet this act was both penned and offered first in the house of lords by Nottingham [c], who, notwithstanding his zeal for the church, had been always both for toleration and comprehension, and [d] had offered the same act to the house of commons during the debates concerning the exclusion.

[*Views of the wiser party and of the king.*]

Cf. *Hist.* ii. 12 ('But wise and good . . . statute that enacted it ').

For 'Christian religion . . . nation' *read* 'Christianity, and to the interest of the protestant religion.'

Om. 'chiefly . . . nation.'

For 'gave . . . content' *read* 'was very agreeable to the king's inclinations and interest,' *and place next sentence in present tense.*

Om. 'and he was much troubled . . . nation.'

[*f.* 291 (*b*)] *Om.* 'in many places of Germany and.'

Propositions for a comprehension.

[e] At the same time that the toleration was proposed to both houses, the bishops who resolved to adhere to king James's interest, moved before they left the house of lords that heads of a comprehension might likewise be considered [e] for taking in the presbyterians; [f] which consisted chiefly in moderating the rigour of the subscriptions, and in admitting children to be baptized without the cross, and persons to the sacrament without obliging them to kneel. [g] Those who proposed this acted very disingenuously; for not only they opposed it underhand and set on all their friends against it, but they represented such as were cordially for it as the enemies and betrayers of the church, who intended to subvert it. [h] This, which was likewise prepared and offered to the house of lords by Nottingham, [i] passed through that house,

[a] Cf. *Hist.* ii. 10.   [b] *Ibid.* 11.   [c] *Ibid.* 6.   [d] *Ibid.*   [e] *Ibid.*   [f] *Ibid.* 10-1.   [g] *Ibid.* 11.   [h] *Ibid.* 6.   [i] *Ibid.* 11.

[a] but was let lie on the table of the house of commons [a] ; and so it fell with the prorogation. [b] A party began to be formed in the house of commons that was secretly against the government ; but they pretended they were for the church of England [b] ; and they carried several smaller matters which the other party did not much oppose, on design to represent this to the king as [c] a cabal formed against him by Nottingham. That party carried an address for a convocation of the clergy; they went heavily into the toleration, and laid aside the comprehension.

[*The dissenters, and the comprehension bill.*]

Cf. *Hist.* ii. 11 ('Nor was this bill . . . fell to the ground').

Debates concerning the revenue.

Cf. *Hist.* ii. 12 (*from* 'and the necessary supplies' *to* p. 13, 'have refused it').
For 'both for the quota . . . Ireland' *read only* 'for the war.'
For 'The next care . . . shown for him. But' *read* 'But as for the main branch of the revenue that arose out of the customs, and which was usually granted to our kings for life.'
For 'Some Whigs . . . come off for them' *read only* 'The republican party.'
Om. 'or, at most . . . years.'
Om. 'and oblige . . . grant.'
Om. 'made great use . . . success. They.'

The chimney money surrendered.

The king had good reason to expect a good return from his people; for though [d] the chimney money was a part of the standing revenue and was a sure article upon which in time of war money could always be raised, for it never sunk, [e] yet he, understanding that this was a great grievance to the people of England, had promised to the people in the west as he marched through it that it should be taken away, and pursuant to that he offered to the parliament to have it taken away, which was done accordingly; but was much opposed by all that were of king James's party, who thought that both it would endear the king to [*f.* 292 (*a*)] the body of the people, and also that if king James should be restored it would lay

[a] Cf. *Hist.* ii. 11, *infra.*   [b] *Ibid.*   [c] *Ibid. infra.*   [d] *Ibid.* 13.
[e] *Ibid. supra.*

an obligation of him not to claim it ; yet it was carried and passed [a]. Now it seemed very unjust and indecent in the commons, who had received such an extraordinary favour from the king, to deny him that which had been given to all former kings; yet they were resolved not to grant it ; so it was pretended that [b] there were many anticipations and assignations upon the customs; and since the petitions of all persons concerned in those could not be considered, they granted the customs for one year to the king, as a provisional act till that whole matter should be settled ; but they intended never to carry it further than from year to year.

And an act of indemnity.

Cf. *Hist.* ii. 14 (*to* p. 15, 'merciful a prince').

For 'They could not be brought . . . set this on' *read* 'The king did likewise press for an act of indemnity for settling the minds of all that were either criminals, or that apprehended they might be made so ; and here the violent party by their fury lost the king upon another head ; or they had no mind to pass the act of indemnity.'

For 'severe revenges . . . unjust things' *read* 'to take revenge of the Tories for many things.'

Om. 'till a better . . . offer itself.'

[*The militia bill.*]

Cf. *Hist.* ii. 14 ('A bill . . . exalted his person ').

For 'both from the crown . . . house of lords' *read* 'out of the crown ; but this was so foolishly contrived that it was taken likewise out of the hands of the lords lieutenants and put in the hands of the deputy lieutenants; by this means the peers, who are generally the lords lieutenants, were concerned.'

After 'table' *add* '[and] it fell with the prorogation.'

[*The Dutch costs.*]

Cf. *Hist.* ii. 14 (*from* ' One thing the house of commons' *to end of paragraph*).

For 'One thing . . . the king; they gave' *read* 'The last act of this session was for repaying.'

For 'revolution' *read* 'for the late expedition '; *and conclude* 'and so the session ended in August.'

The state of Ireland ; [*Derry and Inniskilling*].

During this session [c] king James was got to Ireland [c]; and that whole kingdom, except the two places formerly mentioned of Londonderry and Inniskilling, submitted to him ; [d] he had raised a vastly numerous army there [d], that lived upon

[a] Cf. *Hist.* ii. 13.   [b] *Ibid.*   [c] *Ibid.*   [d] *Ibid.*

the spoil of the protestants, who were falling under an unspeakable misery. A parliament was summoned to meet at Dublin ; by it all the English of Ireland that had come over to England were attainted ; the act of settlement was reversed ; only the ancient legal settlement of the protestant religion there was not thought fit to be fallen upon at that time, though the popish clergy pressed earnestly for it. [a] Some officers [*f.* 292 (*b*)] and provisions were sent thither from France, but very little money [a] ; so that king James was put on coining brass money. [b] There were two contrary advices offered him for the reduction of Derry ; the one was to send the strength of his whole army against it and to press it so hard that, cost what lives it would, it should be carried ; the other was to block it up so that it should be starved [b], and to carry over the rest of his army into Scotland. [c] Any of these advices, if followed, might have had great effect ; but king James followed a middle advice of oppressing it slowly [c], which ruined his affairs. The king sent a relief of powder to Derry in the beginning of March ; [d] after that two regiments were sent over, but all the military men [d], considering the place and the public stores that were in it, [e] judged that it was not tenable [e], and reckoned that there were not provisions for above a week ; [f] so the military men that were in it came back with the two regiments to England [f], not doubting but those of the town would be forced very quickly to accept of such conditions as they could obtain. [g] In this they were abused by colonel Lundy the governor, who was in a secret treaty with king James, and had engaged himself to let the town fall into his hands [g] in such a way that he should not seem to have betrayed it, but should go over to England and keep himself in a condition to commit new treacheries. [h] But they, not daunted at this, resolved to stand it out to the last [h] ; and there being great store of provisions in private hands, all was brought out ; and they resolved to send once more to England, and to live and die together. [i] Those of Inniskilling entered

[a] Cf. *Hist.* ii. 17-8.   [b] *Ibid.* 18.   [c] *Ibid.* 18-9.   [d] *Ibid.* 19.   [e] *Ibid.*
[f] *Ibid.*   [g] *Ibid.*   [h] *Ibid.*   [i] *Ibid.*

into the same resolutions. A considerable force was sent against them, but through their courage and the cowardice of the Irish they held out till the end of July, [a] that Kirk being sent with a fleet and army to their relief the siege was raised and the place relieved, [b] many thousands having died of hunger [b], which grew at last to all extremities possible.   There was a minister in the place, Dr. Walker [1], who acted a very noble part in the government and defence of the town; he was but a man of ordinary parts, but they were suited to this work, for he did wonders in this siege. I will not go further in the particulars of this history which were very variously represented; those I leave to ordinary writers; my chief end of writing being very different from that of putting gazette[s] together. Those of Inniskilling had some [time?] after this, besides many small advantages, one very considerable victory over a great part of the Irish army; and about a month after that, [c] Schomberg, whom the king had made a duke, sailed over with an army of 10,000 men; [d] most of these were new levied, and both officers and men had as much of courage as they wanted in skill [d]. Ulster was quickly reduced, except the fort of Charlemont, which held out till next year.

No action, but our men suffered much.

Cf. *Hist.* ii. 20 (*from* 'He marched on to Dundalk' *to end of paragraph*).
After 'his number' *add* ' and particularly they excelled in horse.'
Om. ' much treachery . . . employed.'
Om. ' for want . . . management.'
[*f.* 293 (*a*)] *Om.* ' Such complaints . . . venture.'
After ' retreat' *add* ' and if he had succeeded, yet he could never have justified the rashness of his venturing too much.'
For ' better judges' *read* ' some military men.'
After ' quarters' *add* ' and then those who had formerly blamed his caution were forced to confess that his care in looking after his army justified all the high character that the world had of him.'

[Affairs at sea.]

Cf. *Hist.* ii. 20-1.
Om. 'Herbert . . . Ireland.'
After ' some of his ships ; and' *add* ' they went back to Brest.   Our fleet.'

[a] Cf. *Hist.* ii. 19, *supra.*   [b] *Ibid. supra.*   [c] *Ibid.* 19.   [d] *Ibid.*

[1] See Routh's note *in loco*; and Macaulay, v. 133, note.

For 'But, if we lost . . . designs' *read* 'And the fleet having been victualled at an improper season, our provisions were so soon spoiled, that more seamen died of ill food than we could have lost in a very great battle.'

The settlement of Scotland.

[a] At the opening the winter session of parliament in Scotland there was likewise some disorder in our affairs. [b] In the convention the bishops and all their party opposed all the proceedings against king James. [c] The castle of Edinburgh was in the duke of Gordon's hands, who acted but faintly, and studied rather to gain time [c] than to do much mischief. The presbyterian party struck in with zeal to make a change of government in the church, and [d] came in great numbers armed to Edinburgh, pretending it was necessary to guard the convention when the castle was in an enemy's hands [d]; they talked big and threatened high, but did no harm to any, even to those they hated most. [e] Yet Dundee and some others left the convention, pretending that they were in danger of their lives. [f] There was among [them] a great variety of opinions; some were plainly for king James, others were for following the method taken in England.

[The third party.]

Cf. *Hist.* ii. 21 (*from* 'A third party' *to* p. 22, *end of paragraph*).
[*f.* 293 (*b*)] *Om.* 'and were for maintaining ... interregnum,' *and* 'perfected or.'
Om. 'and many . . . into it.'
Om. 'since many . . . whereas.'
For from 'and quick provision' *to end of paragraph read* 'It was also visible, that since the presbyterian party was like to prevail, those in England that were for the church, and were then jealous of the interest that the dissenters had gained with the present government, would never consent to have a great many more presbyterian members sent from Scotland[1].'

[The settlement.]

Cf. *Hist.* ii. 22 (*from* 'They passed' *to* p. 23, *end of paragraph*).
For 'They passed ... tendered to them' *read* 'So at last on the 13th [2] of April, which was the day on which the king and queen were crowned at Westminster, they declared that king James had so broken all the laws of Scotland,

[a] Cf. *Hist.* ii. 25.   [b] *Ibid.* 21.   [c] *Ibid.* 22.   [d] *Ibid. supra.*   [e] *Ibid. infra.*
[f] *Ibid.* 21.

---

[1] The reason for modifying this passage in 1705 is obvious.

[2] Corrected in margin (qu. in hand of f. 2?) to '11' (the true date).

that he had thereby lost his right to the kingdom, so that the throne was vacant.'

For 'which they pretended . . . kingdom' *read* 'and another petition of grievances, which were occasioned by some oppressive laws of which they desired a redress ; among the [first[1]] of these they had put the abolishing the order of bishops.'

For 'though . . . grievance' *read* 'though the king and parliament might afterwards do in it what they pleased[2]' ; *and omit* 'whereas . . . see cause.'

Om. 'to carry . . . unreasonable soever.'

After 'settlement' *add* 'and thus they claimed many rights, and petitioned for the redress of several grievances.'

[*The new ministry.*]

In all this matter duke Hamilton showed great zeal for the king, and as [a] he was chosen the president of the convention, so [b] he carried matters in it with much dexterity and courage, so that the chief merit in procuring the settlement fell to his share ; [c] and he was immediately upon it made the king's commissioner ; the convention being turned to a parliament. [d] Sir James Montgomery had been the busiest man in managing and haranguing the members [d], and was much relied on by the presbyterian party. [e] He was a man of parts, but fierce and violent ; [f] and all the episcopal party were very apprehensive of his coming into a great post, [g] with which he flattered himself. [h] Stair was the man the king intended chiefly to trust in Scottish matters, but so many complaints were brought against him [h], particularly in the administration of justice, that it was not advisable to make him secretary.

Melville, a severe presbyterian, made secretary.

[i] So the lord Melville, who had married the duchess of Monmouth's sister [3], and that had been all along a zealous presbyterian, but was thought a cautious and moderate man, and that had been driven out of his estate, and had continued some years

[a] Cf. *Hist.* ii. 21.　　[b] *Ibid.* 23.　　[c] *Ibid.* 24.　　[d] *Ibid.* 23.　　[e] *Ibid.*
[f] *Ibid.* 24.　　[g] *Ibid.* 23.　　[h] *Ibid.* 24.　　[i] *Ibid.*

[1] The 'last' of the MS. is nonsense.
[2] These words originally, no doubt, a marginal addition) were misplaced by the transcriber (between ' order of bishops ' and ' and yet' in the MS.).
[3] Lady Katharine Lesley, cousin of the duchess.

in Holland, was made [sole (?)]¹ secretary. This has proved the worse choice of any the king has yet made; for as .he is a superstitious bigot ready to [*f.* 294 *a*] sacrifice all things to the interest of presbytery, so he is a weak, narrow-hearted ᵃ, and low-minded man, not capable of taking wise measures himself, and yet jealous of everybody else. ᵇ This choice ᵇ, and the having a sole secretary, ᶜgave a universal dista[s]te. ᵈ Montgomery was angry to find himself disappointed, and duke Hamilton was not pleased.

Great discontent given by that.

Cf. *Hist.* ii. 25 (*from* ' The parliament there was opened' *to* p. 26, *end of paragraph*).

For ' The parliament . . . resolved to ' *read* ' So a great party was formed in the parliament of Scotland that was resolved to oppose everything and.'

For ' the majority ' *read* ' the party against him.'

Om. ' that relating . . . parliament itself.'

Om. ' proper.'

After ' desire it ' *add* ' and not continue during the whole parliament.'

Om. ' just '; *and for* ' pretended ' *read* ' believed.'

After ' away ' *add* ' and all the factious party struck in with them.'

For ' both to the king . . . like to have ' *read* ' upon everything.'

Before ' dark ' *read* ' such '; *and after* ' orders ' *read* ' that he saw clearly he was resolved to expose him.'

Om. ' The revenue . . . England. But even.'

For ' though of himself . . . easily borne ' *read* ' was himself against it and complained still of defective orders.'

For from ' and I took ' *to* p. 26, ' adhered to it there,' *read only* ' and I spake to the king once or twice about it; but I found the king had no mind to talk with me on those matters, so I gave over any further meddling in them.'

For ' It was expected . . . instead of that' *read* ' But now, though the king had changed many of those who had been judges before, yet.'

After ' done ' *add* ' in the ordinary way.'

For ' those who opposed everything ' *read* ' the parliament '; *for* ' in parliament ' *read* ' by them '; *for* ' they had prepared ' *read* ' many of the members had prepared.'

After ' list' *add* ' chiefly against Stair, that was named for president.'

For ᶠ intending . . . government' *read* ' this would have been a very invidious matter, to have a whole nomination [*f.* 294 (*b*)] that was made by the king to be thus publicly canvassed and exposed. So.'

For ' nor did he himself' *read* ' and he himself, who did not '; *and for* ' chiefly . . . president. So he discontinued ' (*see supra*) *read* ' not being ill-pleased to find it so unacceptable, he obtained leave to discontinue.'

ᵃ Cf. *Hist.* ii. 24.   ᵇ *Ibid.*   ᶜ *Ibid.*   ᵈ *Ibid.* 25.

---

¹ The transcript has ' lord secretary ' (a clerical error).

A great rising there against the government [*Killiecrankie*].

[a] But while they were falling into those heats Dundee went about the highlands and got together a considerable body of men, many gentlemen of the low country running in to him ; [b] he was supplied from Ireland with powder and arms. [c] He pressed king James very earnestly to come over[c], which if he had done in time he had probably thrown us into a long and dangerous war, but the ill-conduct of the siege of Derry hindered this. [d] Mackay commanded the king's forces[d], which were then about 6,000, [e] most of them raw and new-levied men ; he made many motions from north to south, and found the heads of the clans so doubtful that the most of them promised to come to his assistance ; yet they generally went in to Dundee. At last, he pursuing him, they at last came to an engagement at Killiecrankie, a place some miles above Dunkeld[e]. Many blamed Mackay for drawing up his army as he did ; others justified him ; but success failed him, for [f] Dundee broke through his army, so that they run for it, and probably, if Dundee had outlived that day, the victory might have been far pursued ; but his side suffered more in losing him than they gained by the victory. For Mackay rallied his men quickly and made a good stand[f] ; so that after that, the highlanders, being ill-commanded, were beaten in every engagement. Thus Dundee fell with great fame, and was esteemed a second Montrose. Scotland suffered much by this summer's war ; [g] a fort was built at Inverlochy, called from the king's name Fort William, that did so cut off all communication between the northern and southern highlanders, that they were never able after this to appear in any considerable body.

[*Affairs at sea.*]

Cf. *Hist.* ii. 28.
Om. 'not setting . . . any more.'
Om. 'We seemed . . . there.'

[*Foreign affairs.*]

Cf. *Hist.* ii. 28.
Om. 'which the French . . covered.'

[a] Cf. *Hist.* ii. 26.   [b] *Ibid.* 27.   [c] *Ibid.* 26.   [d] *Ibid.* 27.   [e] *Ibid. infra.*
[f] *Ibid.*   [g] *Ibid.*

For ' Keiserwart . . . misfortunes on that side ' *read* ' The king was now acknowledged by all the courts of Europe, except the allies of France, and this was the state of affairs as to civil matters in the winter [16]89.'

The state of the clergy in England.

Cf. *Hist.* ii. 28 (' I now return . . . would be preferred ').

For ' I now return . . . recess ' *read* ' I must in the next place say somewhat of church matters.'

For ' though with many . . . conscience ' *read only* ' yet.'

For ' that were with great industry . . . church of England ' *read* ' [that] all king James' party spread over England, that the king was a presbyterian in his heart.'

[*The latitudinarians charged with Socinianism.*]

[*f.* 295 (*a*)] And because many of those were men that studied to make out all things by principles of reason, and had with great success both proved the truth of the Christian religion and the grounds of morality from rational principles, [a] it was said they denied mysteries and were Socinians ; this aspersion had been first cast on them by papists, on design to disgrace a knot of divines that had both written and acted with much strength against them ; and it was now taken up by some at Oxford. All which was managed and secretly set on by Clarendon and some of the bishops that were now falling under deprivation [a]. The promotions that were made increased those jealousies. A great many bishops happened to die in a few months ; so that [b] the king made six bishops in the space of so many months—Salisbury, Chester, Bangor, Worcester, [Chichester,] and Bristol [b].

I was made bishop of Salisbury.

To the first of these, that was the first that fell, the king thought fit to promote me ; he did it of his own motion ; for though [c] a great many of my friends, without any encouragement from me, moved him in it, he made them no manner of answer till he took occasion to speak to myself ; and he did it in a way that was much more obliging than I could have expected from him. When I waited on the queen she told me she hoped I [c] would set a pattern to others, and [d] would

[a] Cf. *Hist.* ii. 28–9.   [b] *Ibid.* 29.   [c] *Ibid.* 8.   [d] *Ibid.*

put in practice those notions with which I had taken the
liberty sometimes to entertain her [a].   She also recommended
to me the making my wife an example to other clergymen's
wives, both in the simplicity and plainness of her clothes and
in the humility of her deportment [1].   This I mention to show
what is the queen's sense of the duties of clergymen and of
the behaviour of their wives ; the vanity and pride of those
has risen to a great excess, and I have put many out of
countenance, and have freed either them of their vanity, or
at least their husbands of the expense of it, by letting this
rule that the queen gave me be known.   [b] I came into the
house of lords [2] when the matter of comprehension and
toleration was in debate [b], and I went so high in those points,
that I was sometimes upon the division of the house single
against the whole bench of bishops.   [c] But in the point of
tendering the oaths to all the clergy I did indeed oppose
that [c], upon this ground, that I thought [d] if they joined in the
public offices of the church, and performed them sometimes
themselves, this must needs bind them as firmly to the
government as any oaths whatsoever.   [e] But in the progress
of the debate I changed my mind when I understood
[*f.* 295 (*b*)] that the non-swearing bishops did not pray
for the king and queen by name, but only prayed for the
king without naming him, which was plainly the praying
for king James : and so it was generally understood.   [f] Now
it seemed contrary to the rules of government to suffer men
to minister in holy things and to be in such eminent stations
who considered themselves under another allegiance.   Upon
this I changed my mind [f].   By those things [g] I fell under great
prejudices [g] ; but that which was the greatest of all was that
[h] it was generally thought that I could have hindered the
change of the government of the church that was made in
Scotland [h], and that I went into it too easily.   The truth was,

[a] Cf. *Hist.* ii. 8.   [b] *Ibid.*   [c] *Ibid.* 9.   [d] *Ibid. supra.*   [e] *Ibid.* 9–10.
[f] *Ibid.* 9.   [g] *Ibid.* 10.   [h] *Ibid.* 26.

---

[1] See Autobiography, *infra*, f. 212.
[2] Here too a reflection upon Sancroft has been inserted in the *History*.

the king desired me to let the clergy of England understand the necessity he lay under to consent to it, [a] since the whole episcopal party, a very few only excepted, went into king James's interest: and therefore, since the presbyterians were the only party that he had there, the granting of their desires at that time were unavoidable. But he assured me he would take care to moderate the violence of presbytery, and this was likewise promised very solemnly to me by Melvillè, who I believe did intend it at first; but, he seeing that those who were engaged in a faction against him built their hopes chiefly on their interest in that party, he resolved to take the party out of their hands; and that, he knew, could not be done but by proceeding with great rigour against all the ministers of the episcopal persuasion; and in order to this he entered into a close correspondence with the earl of Crawford, whom he got to be made president of the parliament. And, it being universally understood that he had Melville's secret, he came to bear great sway, though he is a very weak and passionate man in his temper, and is become furious by his principles; [b] so he upon every address turned out ministers and encouraged the rabble to fall on such as gave no occasion of complaint against them.

[Crawford's conduct; effect in England.]

Cf. *Hist.* ii. 29 (*from* 'the convention, when they passed' *to* p. 30, 'episcopal persuasion').

For 'the next Sunday' *read* 'the very next day (for they voted it on a Saturday).'

Om. 'for the most part . . . read.'

After 'queen' *add* 'by name.'

For 'much eagerness . . . afterwards. And upon' *read* 'so much eagerness and rudeness that all the violent men of the party brought in complaints to the council of their ministers, for not reading it [*f.* 296 (*a*)] on the day appointed, [or] for.'

After 'government' *add* 'and all those were so well received that upon the slightest proofs.'

[Burnet blamed for this.]

And because I had to a great many of the clergy [c] excused what the king had done in Scotland from the necessity of his

[a] Cf. *Hist.* ii. 29.   [b] *Ibid.* 30.   [c] *Ibid.*

affairs, and had assured them that the king would moderate the fury of presbytery, this gave very bad impressions of me [a] to the whole body of the clergy; and the sense of this, together with the principles which I had been so long forming of the function of a bishop, made me [b] lay down a scheme to myself [b] which I write here as that which shall be a witness against me if ever I depart from it.

[*Burnet draws up a scheme of his duties* [1].]

[c] I reckoned that the beginning of all the reformations was to be laid down in the education of those who were to serve in the church; and therefore I resolved to choose ten students of divinity, to whom I would give 30 lib. a year apiece, and whom I would train up at hard study, and in a course of as much devotion as they could be brought to, with whom I would discourse an hour a day of matters of learning and piety, and particularly of such things as related to the pastoral care; that so I might have a sufficient number of persons ready to be put in such cures as fell to my disposing [c]; and this I have hitherto kept to, and have seen the good effects of it [2]. [d] I resolved in the next place to go round my diocese once every year (in a private visitation) in eleven different places, where I should order the clergy of that division to meet me. I intended to preach and confirm, and after that to hold conferences with them concerning some points of divinity, that so I might grow acquainted with my clergy and with the state of my diocese, and that I might have frequent opportunities to set the clergy to their studies and to the discharge of their pastoral care. I judged that nothing would be a likelier means to raise the spirit of religion (that was generally sunk and dead) than the calling on persons to be confirmed, not in their childhood upon their

[a] Cf. *Hist.* ii. 30. [b] Cf. Life (appended to *Hist.* ii), p. 706.
[c] *Ibid.* 708–9. [d] *Ibid.* 706.

---

[1] This should be compared, not only with the Life, but with the Autobiography (*infra*), ff. 211–5 (which, based on the above, forms the foundation of the Life); with App. V, *infra*; and with the *Pastoral Care.*
[2] But see Autobiography, *infra*, f. 213; Life (in *Hist.* ii.), p. 709.

having the church catechism by rote, but when they were come to the years of discretion; that so by an act and sponsion of their own they might engage themselves to Christianity [a]. I thought this would likewise give the clergy an opportunity of going from house to house about their parishes and of inquiring into their deportment, and so entering upon such methods of treating with them as they should find to be most effectual. [*f.* 296 (*b*)] This I have observed on my part; but it is not easy to bring the clergy to desire to take pains among their people, nor are the people very willing to submit to it, so this goes on but slowly. [b] I resolved likewise to preach constantly every Lord's day, not only at the place of my residence, but in as many churches as lay within such a distance that I could decently go to them and return on a Sunday [b]. And because my diocese consisted of two counties, Wiltshire and Berkshire, I resolved to divide the year between them. The former is much the bigger county, and is my seat, so I intended to be eight months of the year at Salisbury and four at Windsor; and by this means I have already preached in above fifty churches of my diocese, and confirmed at them all. [c] I resolved to ordain no persons without knowing them well, and examining them strictly myself, and after I was satisfied by examining them in private, I resolved to do it with the concurrence of as great a number of the clergy as I could gather about me, without whose approbation and consent I resolved never to ordain any [c]. And this I have hitherto observed; but I find that the strictness of my examinations frightens the clergy, so that few come to me. These were the rules that I set to myself at first, and in which I do hitherto continue. [d] I thank God I have not met with much scandal among my clergy, but many of them are too ignorant; they seem to have no great sense of devotion, and none at all of the pastoral care, but imagine they acquit themselves well when they perform the public functions [d]. Covetousness, aspiring to preferments, and a restless seeking after great livings, which

[a] Cf. Life in *Hist.* ii. 706.   [b] *Ibid.* 707.   [c] *Ibid.* 707-8.   [d] Cf. *Hist.* ii. 640-1.

they desire to hold one upon another, has often made my
life a burden to me among them ; ᵃ and the foul suspicion
of simony in the disposal of most benefices (which by
a carnal and secular word are called livings) is a dreadful
thing ᵃ.

Great abuses of the church courts.

But the worst part of all is the horrid abuse of the bishops'
courts, which ought to be the means of reclaiming sinners, at
least of making them ashamed of their sins ; but they are the
most corrupt courts of the nation, ᵇ in which they think of
nothing but of squeezing and oppressing people by all the
dilatory and fraudulent ways that are possible ; and I do
not see how it is possible to reform them ᵇ, for they seem to
subsist upon nothing but disorder ; and whether in this age
we shall be able to find out an effectual remedy to those or
not, is that which I do much doubt.

A comprehension of dissenters endeavoured.

The first business that we had with the clergy related to
the heads of ᶜ a comprehension of the presbyterians ; it had
been set forth in the petition which the bishops had given to
king James ᶜ, that they were ready to come to a temper in
those matters in convocation and parliament ; and all
messages that come over from them to us in the Hague
carried many positive assurances that almost all people were
come off from their stiffness in those matters and were
ashamed of [it], so that we had assured all the Dutch
ministers that [*f.* 297 (*a*)] we should take care of their
brethren the presbyterians ; for none of them (in some conferences that I had with them) desired that we would change
any of the foundations of our church, only they wished that
in indifferent matters some regard might be had to the
scruples of men of tender consciences. ᵈ By many advices
from England the prince was also moved to send to the chief
of the presbyterians advising them not to comply with the
offers that king James was a-making them, but to join with

ᵃ Cf. *Hist.* ii. 645-6.   ᵇ Life in *Hist.* ii. 707.   ᶜ *Hist.* ii. 30.   ᵈ *Ibid.* i. 708 ; ii. 30.

the church of England for the supporting the interest of the protestant religion ; upon which he assured them that in due time regard should be had to them.   Upon all those reasons it was that [a] the prince had promised in his declaration that he would endeavour all that in him lay to procure an union between those of the church of England and all protestant dissenters [a].   Therefore it was resolved to lay that matter before a convocation.

[*The preliminary conference.*]

Cf. *Hist.* ii. 30 (*from* ' but it seemed necessary ' *to* p. 33, *end of paragraph*).

For ' but it seemed necessary . . . So ' *read only* ' But to prepare it to them a committee was named.'

On p. 31, *for* ' a number of ' *read* ' a commission of the most eminent.'

After ' several weeks ' *add* ' and digested an entire correction of everything that seemed liable to any just objection in the whole common prayer-book. [Cf. *ibid. infra.*] All that lies together in Dr. Tenison's hands[1], and I make no doubt but it will be preserved till a fit opportunity comes for making use of it. The whole was very carefully weighed, as became scholars and divines.'

For ' they ' (*bis*) *read* ' we ' ; *for* ' them ' *read* ' us.'

For ' matters . . . objection ' *read* ' everything was inquired into very critically, for.'

Om. ' as well as very learned.'

Om. ' who showed herself . . . children.'

Before ' It was not offered ' *add* ' For instance.'

For ' that so we might draw over . . . gaining of them ' *read* [*f.* 297 (*b*)] ' and therefore the present occasion was not to be neglected.'

[2] [*f.* 47 (*a*)] *After* ' on both sides ' *add* ' Clarendon and others of.'

Om. ' and presbytery . . . set up.'

For ' while it went off . . . concessions ' *read* ' by the corrections that were made.'

After ' universities ' *add* ' particularly Oxford.'

For ' severe reflections . . . shelter themselves ' *read* ' and the king's interest came to suffer considerably by it.'

[a] Cf. *Hist.* i. 776 ; ii. 30.

----

[1] In Birch's valuable account of this preliminary conference, *Life of Tillotson,*&c., 1753, pp. 166-83, mention is made of the scrupulous reticence observed by Tenison with regard to these papers, of which he had the custody (p. 176). They were published in a Parliamentary Blue Book in 1854.

[2] At the words ' could not appoint a [select] number ' (which occur on p. 32, vol. ii. of the published *History*) Transcript A becomes again available ; since here begins (at Harl. MSS. 6584, f. 47) No. 2 in Dr. Gifford's arrangement, and the narrative is continued in duplicate.   We shall however only give the foliation of the earlier and better version.   Folios 47 *et sqq.* are lettered in the transcriber's hand *a et sqq.* successively.   Folio 46 and the upper part of f. 47 contain some notes of the discrepancies between this portion and the printed *History*, in the hand of Dr. Gifford.

For 'a thing not known . . . times ; so ' *read* 'and they were so much heated by those instruments who hoped to have weakened (if not pulled down) the government by their means.'

[*A convocation met*] *and the matter was let fall.*

Cf. *Hist.* ii. 33–4 (*to* ' more hurt than good ').

Before ' message ' *insert* ' kind and gracious.'

Om. ' But the lower house . . . message ; and.'

For 'their owning some . . . not agree to it ' *read* 'an expression favourable to those churches that had not bishops ; and though the avoiding to name the protestant religion seemed to be a very invidious thing at that time, yet they refused to do it rather than give the least advantage to any healing propositions.'

Om. ' and they had not their metropolitan with them.'

For 'to set things forward ' *read* 'to govern the lower.'

For ' and thus . . . to no purpose ' *read* 'which was done, and they have never met since.'

After ' entirely forgot' *add* 'The clergy, on the other hand, said (to justify themselves) that it was very visible from all the proceedings in Scotland that the king was no friend to the church, and that therefore it was necessary for them to stand their ground, and to stick firm to one another. By this means the high church party became very jealous of the court.'

For ' in this matter' *read* 'in the miscarriage of the convocation and of the design of comprehension.'

Om. ' Jacobite.'

A session of parliament.

Cf. *Hist.* ii. 34 (*to* ' could be grounded ').

[*f.* 47 (*b*)] *For* 'In winter . . . ill-humour' *read only* 'which was the parliament.'

Om. 'The ill-conduct . . . made on him.'

After ' Bolton' *add* ' and the other Whig lords.'

After ' reign ' *add* ' (the lord Russell's, Col. Sidney['s], and others).'

After ' charters' *add* ' It appeared visibly that all this was levelled at Halifax.'

[*Halifax retires; the king annoyed with the Whigs.*]

So nothing came of it, only Halifax saw such a tide raised against him in both houses, that [a] he thought fit soon after to quit his place and withdraw from business ; and ever since he has seemed to lean to king James' party ; he has always favoured them, and he is finding fault with everything the government does [a] ; so that he is thought a Jacobite. Yet I believe his commerce that way goes no further than that he is laying in for a pardon, and perhaps for favour if a revolution should happen, for he is neither a firm nor a stout man. [b] Yet the party that was thus pursuing their old resentments with so much violence [b] when the necessity of affairs

[a] Cf. *Hist.* ii. 34.   [b] *Ibid.*

called all that wished well to the government to a more entire union in their councils, ᵃ lost much in the king's good opinion ᵃ. But as the house of commons is the chief scene, so the proceedings there did quite alienate the king from them.

[*The king demands the revenue.*]

Cf. *Hist.* ii. 34 (' He expressed . . . unless that was done ').

For ' without that ' *read* ' without the power and the necessary means to support it.'

For ' And he spoke of this . . . vehemence ' *read* ' And he seemed so much set on this.'

For ' an empty name ' *read* ' the government.'

Om. ' he said once . . . without power.'

Jealousies of the king.

ᵇ But a jealousy was raised as if he would grow very arbitrary if the revenue were once settled ; some began to give out that he was hearkening after prerogative notions, and that if he were settled on the throne he would strain for as high a stretch of his authority ᵇ as any that had gone before him had done ; and both he himself and Bentinck, whom he had made earl of Portland, spake to a great many upon this subject in a style of such earnestness and positiveness that all this tended to increase the jealousy. ᶜ Those of the Whigs who had lived long at Amsterdam ᶜ and had been there possessed with the jealousies of that city ᵈ told about all the little stories they had heard of the king's sullenness and arbitrariness.

[*Intrigues between St. Germain and the Scots malcontents.*]

Cf. *Hist.* ii. 35 (*from* ' the Scotch, who were now come up,' *to end of paragraph*).

For ' the Scotch . . . apprehensions ' *read* ' but that which made the greatest impression came from the Scots.'

Om. ' so he was oft admitted . . . good spy.'

After ' agents ' *add* ' he was [*f.* 48 (*a*)] a papist.'

For ' the best spy the court had ' *read only* ' a good spy.'

For ' When he had gained . . . Portland ' *read only* ' When he [had] told as much truth as served to give him credit, he began to tell stories for raising.'

For ' so by other hands it was ' *read* ' he by Payne's means got it to be.'

For ' that the court . . . them and ' *read only* ' that Portland.'

ᵃ Cf. *Hist.* ii. 34.   ᵇ *Ibid.* 35.   ᶜ *Ibid.*   ᵈ *Ibid.*

Many turn about to king James.

Cf. *Hist.* ii. 35 (*from* 'Sir James Montgomery' *to* p. 37, *end of paragraph*).

For 'Sir James Montgomery . . . management' *read* 'When sir James Montgomery with the other lords of his party came up to justify themselves they found the king was so possessed against them that they by Simpson's means.'

For 'princes in exile . . . power' *read only* 'so this being easily granted them.'

After 'close treaty' *add* ' with Payne.'

Om. 'because, by duke Schomberg's . . . cut off.'

For ' and on both sides . . . secure them ' *read* ' who saw themselves marked out for destruction by the violence of presbytery ; and so they pretended that self-preservation forced them to join with any party that might secure them. At first they seemed to design nothing by their uniting together, but the joining interests in parliament to oppose Melville ; and this was all that the leading men set out to those of their party; but king James was at the bottom of it all ' (cf. *ibid. infra*).

For 'against Montgomery' *read* 'against them, particularly sir James Montgomery.'

Om. 'who did not know . . . lord Stair ' (*but see supra*).

Om. ' particularly . . . Bolton.'

For 'this wrought . . . trust him' *read* 'who seemed marked out to be the next person to be fallen upon after they had got rid of Halifax. Many of the Whigs went much further and entered into treaty with king James.'

For ' and who endeavoured to prevent it ' *read* ' for he did not think it safe to go further with me.'

After 'faintly' *add* ' I let the first proposition he made of this pass as a ramble of discourse, upon which I made no reflection ; but the second conversation upon that subject gave me greater cause to apprehend that he was engaged in the thing.'

For 'matters were trusted to' *read* ' He trusted [*f.* 48 (*b*)] himself in it to.'

For 'and Ferguson . . . they were given' *read* 'and [Monmouth] undertook to engage a great part of the citizens into it.'

For 'weary' *read* ' so weary '; *for* ' and saw his error . . . as he had done ' *read* ' that he might be well trusted on that head.'

For 'This corrupted party . . . that the restoring him' *read* 'and in a word the restoring him was represented as that which.'

For 'that the matter . . . convinced of it' *read* 'that this was more than an idle way of talking, set forth to frighten the court.'

A conspiracy discovered.

[a] But at last a brother of one of the chief plotters [a], whose name for certain reasons I do not think fit to write down [1], [b] sent me some letters by a disguised name : he asked a pardon for himself, and such of his friends as he should afterwards

[a] Cf. *Hist.* ii. 37.   [b] *Ibid.*

---

[1] Montgomery's brother ; see *Hist. in loco.*

name; not to be made evidence; and never to be named in the whole matter; and he undertook to discover the whole negotiation, the articles agreed to, the methods that were concerted; and added that an invitation was subscribed by the whole cabal to king James to come over[a]; and he charged me, if discoveries were expected from him, to speak of the matter to no person but the king only. When I showed his letters to the king, I saw he was not surprised at it, but was well prepared to believe all except that of subscribing a paper. [b] He did not think that probable[b]; but [c] he gave me leave to promise everything that had been asked, only he stuck at the indefinite demand of his friends' pardon. He would make no such general promise; but even in that the discoverer might trust his inclinations[c], which were not cruel, as all the world saw. [d] So upon those assurances he came to me and told me many particulars[d] which I do not yet think fit to mention; [e] he was in hope of putting me on a way of finding out the original paper signed by them all; and after a few days he came and told me that one Williamson was gone down that day to Dover on his way to France with all the papers; he told me where he was to lie. So I acquainted Shrewsbury with this, and he took care to send one down in such haste that he found Williamson abed next morning; there were other suspicions against him, for he had procured a pass for Flanders, but was treating with some to carry him to France. All his clothes and his portmantle were strictly visited, but nothing was found. This did so vex the discoverer, who reckoned that upon that he would be ill looked at[e], that he never came near me more, and he is now at St. Germain. The truth was the papers were signed and given to Williamson; king James' party pressed that they might be signed; for some supplies from France and the French fleet's coming into our seas were necessary for the design; those of St. Germain thought it necessary for giving them credit in the court of France to be able to show the subscriptions of many who [were] formerly thought enemies,

[a] Cf. *Hist.* ii. 37.   [b] *Ibid.*   [c] *Ibid. supra.*   [d] *Ibid.*   [e] *Ibid.*

to persuade that court that the nations were coming about
to them. But unknown to my discoverer, ª Simpson, who
resolved to go over with Williamson, told him that he knew
Kent well, and so would go down in byways to Dover
whereas the other, trusting to his pass, was to go down in the
stage-coach ; therefore he thought it was safer to trust the
papers to him. To [*f.* 49 (*a*)] this Williamson consented
so Simpson had them ; and according to appointment he
came to Dover, when Williamson was in arrest, and upon
that he got out of the way, and so carried the letters safe to
St. Germain ; upon which money was sent over, together
with the promise of a larger supply ; ᵇ but all this was afterwards discovered ᵇ. The only thing that the plotters could do
in winter was to alienate those with whom they had credit
all that was possible from the king, and to create ᶜ jealousies
in the city ᶜ, especially in the rich citizens who made the
advances of money. ᵈ The house of commons granted the
supplies that were demanded for the reduction of Ireland
and for the fleet, and continued the gift of the revenue for
another year ᵈ ; and this was all that could be obtained from
them.

A bill concerning corporations.

Cf. *Hist.* ii. 38-9 (*to* ' little doubt was made of the passing of the act ').

For ' The Tories . . . a bill, by which ' *read only* ' At the same time they
carried a bill by which they thought to have established their party and.'

For ' mayors and recorders . . . London ' *read only* ' who had been concerned
by voting to, or procuring, the [late ¹] surrenders of charters.'

Om. ' for six years.'

Om. ' for they saw . . . kingdom.'

After ' severity ' *add* ' it was pretended in most corporations it would not be
possible to find a sufficient number to serve, if all should be incapacitated that
had acted in that matter.'

For ' And now . . . king ' *read* ' So now both parties looked on this as a crisis
The Tories looked upon themselves as ruined if the bill should pass.'

After ' bill passed ' *add* ' in the house of lords, where it was like to meet
with great difficulty.'

Om. ' And the Tories . . . dissolved.'

ª Cf. *Hist.* ii. 38.   ᵇ *Ibid. supra.*   ᶜ *Ibid. infra.*   ᵈ *Ibid.*

---

¹ Transcript A reads, erroneously, ' later.'

For 'The bill . . . surrendered' *read* 'For upon the first points (whether corporations could be surrendered up or not) there was a great opposition made.'

After 'Holt' *add* 'that was chief justice.'

For 'in which the abbeys . . . regular times' *read* 'in which the surrenders of abbeys had been so much supported, that upon that all other ecclesiastical corporations were also surrendered ; for there were no other precedents brought but of those.'

For 'for the bill' *read* 'in favour of the surrender.'

For 'after which . . . act' *read* 'yet it was visible that the weight of the house of commons would have carried the matter at last.'

The king was in great straits.

[a] But now the king was much pressed by Nottingham and all the Tory party to dissolve the parliament, and call a new one. It was said that the corporations who saw themselves struck at by the change which this act would have made would not choose any of those violent men whose heat was like to set all on fire ; the breaking upon this point, as it would make the new elections sure to the church party in many places, so it would oblige them to the king, since he preserved them from the fury of this bill[a]. This state of affairs looked very melancholy. The king saw the Whigs would not trust him nor indeed support him, but in a dependence upon their passions and humours ; on the other hand he thought he could not trust the Tories, they seemed all linked to king James' interests and to be jealous of him.

[He resolves for Holland.]

Cf. *Hist.* ii. 39-40 (*to* 'to put an end to the war in Ireland ').

For 'He was once . . . resolution' *read* 'He for some days took [*f.* 49 (*b*)] up a resolution that had been fatal if he had followed it.'

Om. 'he thought . . . the Whigs.'

For 'the Tories . . . confide in her' *read* 'the church party would trust the queen.'

For 'So he called . . . few more' *read* 'He went so far in this that he called some of those he trusted most about him.'

For 'a convoy' *read* 'three or four good ships.'

For 'since . . . brought him' *read* 'This was a great surprise to them all.'

For 'to lay aside . . . necessity' *read* 'not to think more of it, since it would certainly ruin all the affairs of Europe.'

For 'among them . . . resolution' *read* 'on all hands upon this occasion, but

[a] Cf. *Hist.* ii. 39.

it ended well; for the king was prevailed on to lay aside all those thoughts, and to go on with the resolution he had taken.'

Om. ' this was told me . . . so nearly.'

He designed to go in person to Ireland.

^aBut when this came to be known a great many of both sides were resolving to oppose it^a; the Jacobites could not be supposed to be much concerned for his person, so their secret reason was believed to be that ^bthey were afraid he should have too good success there^b, and bring that war too soon to an end. ^cThe rest were really concerned for his person^c, since they reckoned that all their safety depended upon it. ^dBut upon the first motions that were made in both houses (for by consent it was proposed in both on the same day) the king, seeing that it would certainly have ended in an address to him against it, came next day and prorogued the parliament. There was not money enough given for the whole campaign^d, so it was necessary to have another session before the king should go; or dissolve the parliament and call a new one. The king by this time saw that the leading men of the Whig party were not only resolved not to give him the revenue, but that they were beginning to treat with king James, and were generally standing off from advancing money upon the credit of the money bills; and therefore he thought the safest course was to trust the promises that the Tories were making him and to try a new parliament. ^eSo the parliament was dissolved and a new one was called^e.

New parliament called.

Cf. *Hist.* ii. 40 (*from* 'There was a great struggle' *to* p. 41, 'how to manage matters for him').

For ' One thing . . . Tories had made' *read* ' Among other things that they had proposed to the king, to give their party a confidence in him, one.'

For ' given . . . excluded' *read* ' put the military power of London into the hands of the Whigs.'

For ' which was such a mortification . . . commission ' *read* ' so a change was desired to such a degree, that the Tories should be the stronger.'

For ' the bishop' *read* ' but he, who is apt to do things without advice.'

Om. ' who had been engaged . . . reign.'

^a Cf. *Hist.* ii. 40.   ^b *Ibid.*   ^c *Ibid.*   ^d *Ibid.*   ^e *Ibid.*

For 'to examine the list . . . approved of it' *read* 'to examine and settle that matter, and they agreed to the list. They seemed to blame the bishop of London for taking so little care in the preparing of it; but they thought since such persons [*f*. 50 (*a*)] were once named it would be an affront that would be resented by the whole party if their names should be struck out[1].'

For 'a set of officers . . . king James' *read* 'those very men who had been the wickedest instruments in the end of king Charles, and the beginning of king James' reign.'

For 'This matter . . . government' *read only* 'Here Shrewsbury began first to show his discontent; for all this matter was managed by Carmarthen and Nottingham.'

For 'The elections . . . declared' *read* 'When the list of elections of parliament appeared, all that loved the government were under great apprehensions; for it was generally believed that the far greater part of them were in their hearts.'

Om. 'The king made a change . . . money bills.'

[*The 'recognizing' bill.*]

Cf. *Hist.* ii. 41 (*from* 'The first great debate' *to* p. 42, 'it passed in two days in that house').

For 'The first part passed . . . warm debate' *read only* 'This held long in the house of lords.'

After 'declaratory way' *add* '[for if so] the strength of the crown was broke.'

Om. 'and brought . . . . question.'

For 'times : but . . . juncture' *read* 'times, [so] the want of the writs could not be supposed to carry in it a nullity in such a juncture.'

For 'when all' *read* 'It was called in an interregnum, in the best method that could then be thought of; all.'

Om. 'both' *and* 'and people.'

For 'a long debate' *read* 'a fourth night's debate.'

Om. 'declaring and' (*see Speaker Onslow's note, Hist. in loco*).

For 'many lords . . . at court' *read only* 'a great part of the house of lords not only opposed it, but protested against it.' (*This appears earlier in the passage.*)

Om. 'It was expected . . . act. But'; *and for* 'in that house' *read* 'in the house of commons.'

For from 'without any debate or opposition' *to end of paragraph, read only* 'but the party that prevailed in it was willing to give the king this early assurance of their fidelity to him; and the leaders of the Tory party drew in their followers (before they were aware of it) to consent to it'; *and om. next paragraph.*

The revenue granted for a term of years.

Cf. *Hist.* 42-3 (*from* 'The house of commons' *to end of paragraph*).

For 'The house of commons' *read* 'They also.'

After 'frequent parliaments' *add* 'and they thought that such a precedent

---

[1] In the *History* this passage is shortened to such an extent as to become meaningless.

might be begun with greater advantages [*f.* 50 (*b*)] in the present reign than in any other.'

For 'and if he ' *read* ' and since this was thought a greater security than any bills for triennial parliaments, if he, that was our deliverer.'

For ' which probably . . . done ' *read* 'nor could the revenue have been granted for life.'

Om. 'which they thought . . . running into a great arrear.'

After ' king's absence ' *add* ' at any time.'

For ' to take no notice . . . nor of those who ' *read* ' to be so unconcerned that she never asked after the bill, and took no notice of any person's behaviour whether they.'

Place ' to the great grief of the Whigs' *after* ' lieutenancy of London,' *and proceed* : ' who were now in so high a ferment that they hindered all their party in London from advancing more money ; nor did the other party lend so liberally as had been promised ; so that between the two, the government for some time was at a stand.'

Debates for abjuring king James.

Cf. *Hist.* ii. 43-5 (*to* ' affront of its being rejected ').

For ' But the greatest debate . . . session ' *read* 'And then came on in both houses a great debate.'

After ' Whigs ' *add* ' and some votes were passed for it.'

For ' with a great copiousness . . . arguing ' *read only* ' with all their strength.'

For ' and that all . . . settlement' *read* ' and therefore they would not consent to any new imposition.'

[*f.* 51 (*a*)] *For* 'The Whigs pressed the king' *read* 'But in private the Whigs pressed the king vehemently.'

For ' At the same time . . . bestowed on it, or not' *read* ' On the other hand, it was laid before the king that this could not be easily carried ; much time would be lost in the debates, and much heat would be raised by them ; for a great number of men can hang long upon a debate.'

After ' service' *add* ' so that it would rend both the parliament and the nation.'

After ' carried ' *add* ' (of which great doubt was made).'

Om. ' who might otherwise . . . neutrals.'

For ' intimation ' *read* ' indirect message.'

For ' and go to other matters . . . Tories' *read* ' which was a wise and good resolution, though I myself was at that time of another mind. And this, though it enraged the Whigs, who hoped now to have all the places of trust or profit, and by consequence the government again into their hands, yet generally it had a good effect ; it gained the Tories more entirely to the king.'

For ' it had indeed . . . people' *read* ' It gave indeed great hopes to the French, and was given out there as a certain sign that the parliament was for king James.'

After ' rejected' *add* ' so it animated them extremely.'

Shrewsbury withdrew from business.

Cf. *Hist.* ii. 45 (' The earl of Shrewsbury was at the head . . . could not be prevailed on ').

Om. ' or success.'

For ' such things as should have . . . too much ' *read* ' those things that should have broken him quite with the king.'

After ' word of it ' *add* ' as soon as might be.'

Om. ' who thought him before . . . how firm he was.'

After ' ever ' *add* ' it would make them conclude that the king was so entirely gone in to the Tories, that for that reason he had withdrawn himself from the public counsels.'

After ' purpose ' *add* ' for he was fixed in his resolution, though [*f.* 51 (*b*)].'

For ' though he should not act . . . prevailed on ' *read* ' to which once he seemed to have consented; yet the night before the king went he sent them to him by Russell. Thus by a very unreasonable peevishness, the best minister that I know about the king left his service in so disobliging a manner that I am afraid the king will not easily forget it.'

[*The second abjuration bill; end of session.*]

Cf. *Hist.* ii. 45 (*from* ' The debate for the abjuration lasted ' *to* p. 46, ' generally Whigs ').

For ' The debate . . . king James ' *read* ' But to return to the public; after the business of the abjuration was laid aside by the commons, the lords took up a debate very like it, for such an engagement as should bind all that were in public trust to be faithful to the government in opposition to king James. This was long and warmly debated. Halifax began upon this occasion to discover himself, for he has ever since appeared to be in king James' interests ; though I believe he will put nothing to hazard for them.'

For ' The Tories offered ' *read* ' The party that opposed all these motions offered.'

For ' with severe penalties . . . refuse it ' *read* ' and offered to put this to all persons whatsoever [1].'

After ' lost the next ' *add* ' so that it was impossible to make any progress in it.'

[*Jacobite intrigues; Fuller.*]

[a] Many little discoveries were now made of the correspondences and motions of the Jacobites [a], for so king James's party came to be named. A little boy [2] that had been a page and had turned papist went over to St. Germain, and offered himself with so much spirit to manage for them that he was trusted; he brought over with him one Crone, an Irishman, with many letters. It was pity that so much life as he had

[a]   Cf. *s.* i. 46.

---

[1] There is an obvious hiatus in the transcript at this passage, clearly due to the accidental identification of two successive ' whatsoevers ' in the

original MS.

[2] Fuller. See Macaulay, ed. 1858, 221–4, 233–5 ; *Life of Halifax,* ii. 147–8.

was so ill-turned.   He discovered Crone and all that negotiation.   Crone was condemned, but has since saved himself by
ⁿa discovery ; it was chiefly about providing money and arms,
and the putting the party in a readiness to appear upon
a call.

The queen in the administration.

Cf. *Hist.* ii. 48 (*from* 'the queen was now' *to* p. 49, 'happy under her').
After 'administration' *add* 'by the king's going for Ireland, in which she was
so exact to the law, that she would not enter upon it till she heard that he was
upon the sea.'

[*f.* 52 (*a*)] *Before* 'all this was nothing to the public' *insert* 'nor was she ever
uneasy or displeased with any that brought new objects in her way ;'
Om. from 'The king named' *to end of paragraph.*

[The king's sense of affairs.]

Cf. *Hist.* ii. 46 (*from* 'the day before' *to* 'all that he had said').

The king's tenderness of king James.

Cf. *Hist.* ii. 47 (*first paragraph*).
For 'having learned . . . made to the king' *read* 'for one had sent by me
a proposition to him, which seemed fair.'
For '(for he was well known to him)' *read* '(for he had served at sea and was
known to him).'
For 'as the king should desire . . . ashore' *read* 'for he would not engage in
it unless he were assured that he were not to be made a prisoner.   When
I carried this to the king,' *&c.*
For 'king James would certainly' *read* 'if king James should.'
After 'the king had made' *insert* 'me.'

The king goes for Ireland.

Cf. *Hist.* ii. 47–8 (*to* 'things went far otherwise').
Before 'Charlemont' *insert* 'save that' ; *and om.* 'which was . . . hands.'
[*f.* 52 (*b*)] *For* 'they flattered . . . false hopes' *read* 'as he loves to be flattered
with false news, so he was filled with them [*sic*] upon this occasion and
[believed].'
After 'days come, before' *add* 'by a prisoner that was taken.'
After 'immediately' *add* 'drew back his army [and].'
After 'French foot' *add* 'that Lauzun had brought over.'
For 'country on to Dublin' *read* 'plain country to Dublin.'
For 'the strengthening . . . body of foot' *read* 'the marching away towards
the Shannon ; the strengthening their garrisons; and keeping only a flying
camp together.'
After 'king's transports.   This' *add* 'was a great design and.'

ⁿ Cf. *Hist.* ii. 46.

The state of affairs at sea; [and on land].

Cf. *Hist.* ii. 49–50 ('an unhappy compliment ... and then a rising ground').

For 'and it was joined ... chief command, was' *read* 'And Herbert, whom the king had made earl of Torrington, was ordered to go about with the rest of our fleet to join both the squadron at Plymouth and that which Shovel was to bring him out of the Irish seas. He [was].'

For 'our main fleet lay long' *read* 'he was forced to lie some days.'

[*f.* 53 (*a*)] *For* 'so they ... Channel' *read* 'Upon this advice from England their fleet (consisting of eighty capital ships) was ordered to sail into the Channel, which they did on the twenty-second of June.'

For 'near the Isle' *read* 'at the bight of the Isle.'

For 'surprised' *read* 'both surprised and destroyed.'

For 'and abandoned Dublin' *read* 'they would be forced to abandon Dublin and.'

Om. 'it would also ... England.'

For 'for his crown' *read* 'for it; for he said he forgave the prince of Oranje all he had done against him, since he was now come to give him battle.'

Om. 'of the struggle and even.'

For 'rose ... tide' *read* 'swelled twice a day with the tide.'

The king was wounded with a cannon-ball.

Cf. *Hist.* ii. 50 (*from* 'On the last of June' *to* p. 51, 'military men').

For 'a great body' *read* 'his body'; *for* 'in the face of the enemy' *read only* 'in another place'; *om.* 'a little below him.'

The battle of the Boyne.

Cf. *Hist.* ii. 51 (*from* 'It was a complete victory' *to* p. 52, 'did also capitulate').

[*f.* 53 (*b*)] *Before* 'threw down' *insert* 'very soon.'

For 'The army of the Irish ... king thought' *read* 'Besides, it was generally believed that, considering the cowardice of the Irish.'

For 'a party' *read* 'twenty or thirty.'

Om. 'for most ... cut off,' *and* 'like another Epaminondas.'

For 'a very indecent' *read* 'a great.'

Om. 'This was not ... fled.'

For 'he rode ... parts of his life' *read* 'and left Dublin early next morning, and rid with all the haste that was possible to Duncannon, which was about seventy Irish miles from Dublin; he had been so provident that he had sent sir Patrick Trant thither to have a ship ready for him, and all the way as he rid he was taking care to have bridges cut, and was in so much dread that when he came to Duncannon, though the fort was of a considerable strength, yet he would not trust himself to it, but lay aboard. Thus did his courage sink with his affairs to so great a degree that those who believed he was brave before concluded that there was now some extraordinary guilt upon him which has brought him under so much fear.'

For 'their officers' *read* 'their general officers.'

For 'and king James's officers ... revenges after it' *read* 'The Irish marched in their flight through Dublin in so much haste, and with so much disorder, that whereas it was much feared that if they had been beat they would have taken their revenges upon that town, and have plundered and burnt it, they were now so far from that, that they made all the haste possible to be gone.'

For ' declared for the king' *read* ' declared presently for the king, who sent immediately some troops thither to secure that city.'

A battle in Flanders [Fleurus] and at sea [Beachy Head].

Cf. *Hist.* ii. 52 (*from* ' But to balance' *to* p. 53, ' pursuing his victory').

[*f.* 54 (*a*)] *Om.* ' did at the first charge.'

For ' yet the stand . . . they able' *read* ' yet their loss was believed greater ; they were certainly so much weakened that they were not able.'

For ' This was the battle . . . consequence of it ' *read* ' This weakening of their army.'

For ' On the day . . . Boyne' *read* ' For about a week after that, on the last of June.'

After ' at sea' *add* ' Our fleet got under sail upon the news of the arrival of the French fleet.'

After ' at Plymouth ' *add* ' and that which was commanded by Shovel.'

For ' what was fittest to be done' *read* ' whether our fleet [without them] should be ordered to make towards the French and to engage them or not.'

After ' his coming in' *add* ' for some time.'

For ' some began to call' *read* ' Now his enemies began to spread about stories that brought.'

For ' they thought . . . mischievous to us' *read* ' It was looked on as extremely unbecoming for us to bring in our fleet upon the French coming into our seas, and to leave them masters of our coast and trade. For all our fleets of merchantmen (reckoning that the two royal fleets would be at that time waiting upon one another) were then coming home, and would be by this means exposed to the enemy. It would have raised the credit of the arms of France, and sunk ours, if we should have fled from them.'

For ' that it was reasonable . . . admiral' *read* ' that we might well fight them ; and in this they were seconded by some on whom the administration relied much, who writ from the fleet that though the enemy exceeded them in number, yet they took ours to be the stronger fleet. It is true in the council of war the much greater number were of Torrington's opinion. But in conclusion he had orders.'

For ' to a council of war' *read* ' to him. So on the 30th of June.'

For ' both the Dutch . . . general opinion' *read* ' The Dutch, as they had suffered much, so they complained that they had been abandoned by Torrington ; those of the blue squadron complained as much ; and all (except his friends) who were in that action do still say.'

[*f.* 54 (*b*)] *For* ' many of our ships ' *read* ' our fleet quite.'
After ' his victory' *add* ' So.'

[The French masters of the sea.]

Cf. *Hist.* ii. 53 (*from* ' Our fleet came in ' *to* p. 55, ' French should prevail ').

After ' refitting it' *add* ' and great care was had of the sick and wounded of the Dutch.'

For 'seven thousand' *read* 'a thousand[1].'

After 'raised' *insert* 'and continued out a month.'

For 'in this melancholy . . . expected' *read* 'The Scotch plot, as shall be afterwards told, was both discovered and broke ; and now it appeared that neither the taxes nor the ill success could alienate the nation from the government, for though it was now harvest-time, yet the militias continued together with great cheerfulness, and showed a great zeal for the service.'

Om. 'kept out of the way'; *and after* 'rabble' *add* 'again.'

After 'coast' *add* 'and then returned again to ours.'

After 'confederate armies' *om.* 'when . . . direction.'

For 'The French . . . understood afterwards, that' *read* 'During the fitting out of our fleet, the French rid triumphing in our seas, but did us no harm. All the while.'

For 'excused' *read* 'were glad to excuse.'

For 'weakened' *read* 'much weakened ; they had many sick men aboard.'

[*The queen's behaviour upon this occasion.*]

Cf. *Hist.* ii. 55 (*from* 'In all this time' *to middle of following paragraph*, 'required his presence here ').

[*f.* 55 (*a*)] *Om.* 'for I . . . Windsor.'

Om. 'she apprehended . . . danger.'

Om. 'For she told me . . . king was in Ireland.'

For 'and acquainted her' *read* 'he gave it her with the letters.'

After 'presence here' *add* 'more than Ireland could then do.'

[*Affairs abroad.*]

Cf. *Hist.* ii. 64–5 (*from* 'As for affairs' *to* 'carrying on the war ').

For 'As for affairs . . . alliance' *read* 'At this time the allies gained upon the duke of Savoy to enter into a confederacy.'

Om. 'with the emperor.'

For 'ripe for it. They demanded' *read* 'ready for it, by demanding'; *and after* 'in their hands' *add* 'during the war.'

Om. 'This was . . . vassal prince.'

Om. 'when their affairs require it' *and* 'who had promised him nothing.'

After 'prey to the French' *add* 'The war upon the Upper Rhine, where the elector of Bavaria commanded, produced no actions, but many marches backwards and forwards ; and.'

Om. 'yet he . . . on the war.'

The affairs of Scotland.

Cf. *Hist.* ii. 61 (*from* 'From the affairs of Ireland' *to* p. 62, 'his instructions ').

Om. 'From the affairs . . . what passed.'

For 'by a Dutch officer . . . forces in Scotland' *read only* 'by sir Thomas Livingstone.'

[*f.* 55 (*b*)] *For* 'Lord Melville . . . post himself' *read* 'Melville was sent down

---

[1] ' 7000 sais [*sic*] the printed edition ' (note by Dr. Gifford). See also f. 2 (in Appendix VII, *infra*).

with powers to be high commissioner for the parliament, but he stayed there some weeks before he made use of them.'

For 'assured the king' *read* 'had told the king before he had went down.'

After 'carry anything' *add* 'So the matter was secretly managed.'

For 'would not consent' *read* 'stuck a little.'

For from 'yet he found' *to end of paragraph read* 'And for those he was forced to send one over to Ireland ; and it is generally said that though he ventured to give up those, yet he had no instructions for it. But the king is so secret in those matters that it is not possible to find them out ; only it is visible that he is not pleased with Melville's behaviour in parliament.'

[*A parliament thère.*]

Cf. *Hist.* ii. 62 ('The Jacobites ... second message').

For 'for many ... swear to him' *read* 'on design that thereby they might have the greater number there, and be able to break that which they sware to maintain.'

For 'by Paterson ... archbishops' *read* 'even [by] one of the bishops that was in that party.'

Om. 'for he thought ... parliament.'

After 'prerogative' *add* 'even in the point of the dispensing power.'

[*A plot discovered.*]

Cf. *Hist.* ii. 62-3 (*to* 'ruined his fortune,' *near end of paragraph*).

Om. all allusions to Argyll.

Om. 'pretending, as they said afterwards, that.'

After 'pressed the king' *add* 'since all was broken.'

After 'upon a full discovery' *add* 'This he refused to do.'

For 'discovered all ... Scotch' *read only* 'made discoveries.'

After 'against others' *add* 'This was granted him, so he told all he knew.'

Before 'treated' *insert* 'immediately.'

[*f.* 56 (*a*)] *Om.* 'He continued ... life.'

[*Results of the plot.*]

Cf. *Hist.* ii. 63 (*from* 'The lord Melville had now' *to* p. 64, *end of paragraph*).

For 'by which ... condemnation of it' *read only* 'was the settling of presbytery.'

For 'But it was not so easy ... ; if' *read* 'But this could not be safely done, if.'

For 'the pattern ... 1638' *read* 'any of the former patterns ; for then.'

Before 'episcopal' *read* 'for the greater part.'

For 'and all those who ... presbyterian way' *read* 'who had taken presbyterian ordination of late.'

For 'this was like ... the old men' *read* 'by an error that may prove fatal to the whole party ; [because] many of the old men.'

For 'so these broke out ... defame them' *read* 'they began to raise accusations against the episcopal clergy ; some were grounded only upon their being of that persuasion, others were charged with scandalous disorders ; but in many places these were not pretended to be proved, but were only made use of to defame those whom they intended to deprive.'

The progress of the war in Ireland.

Cf. *Hist.* ii. 55 (*from* 'for it was hoped the reduction of Ireland' *to* p. 57, 'decently towards him').

For 'for' *read* 'But while affairs went thus in all other places.'

[*f.* 56 (*b*)] *For* 'By these he understood ... and ended it thus' *read* 'By these it appeared that they looked upon their business as desperate before the battle. Tyrconnell's last letter to queen Mary that had not been sent ended thus.'

Om. 'the king went to Ireland' *and* 'an Irishman ... languages well'; *and for* 'was to be' *read* 'had been sent'; *and after* 'murder the king' *add* 'which seemed to be much confirmed by this letter.'

Om. 'sir Robert Southwell ... retaliating in that way.'

For 'The escape ... at the battle of the Boyne' *read* 'But as God preserved the king from the many dangers through which he passed at the last battle [when]'; *and after* 'friends' *add* 'so God has likewise preserved him hitherto from all secret practices.'

For 'the king was pressed ... apprehend' *read* 'The king's chief care was now to secure a station for his transport ships; for as he found by the letters that had fallen into his hands that the French intended to send over some frigates and fireships to burn them, so their advantage at sea made the execution of this easy to them; and therefore, finding Dublin was no safe station for them, and that Waterford was the nearest place where they could lie securely, instead of pursuing the Irish during their first consternation to Athlone or Limerick, to which their main body had retired, he sent only a detachment to Athlone, and he marched himself towards Waterford; both the town, and Duncannon fort, which commanded the port, capitulated; so that now his transport fleet was safe; though indeed it was not in so much danger as was believed.'

[*f.* 57 (*a*)] *For* 'He fell under' *read* 'And ever since that time he has been under.'

[The situation in Ireland.]

Douglas, who led the detachment to Athlone, said he could do nothing for want of great cannon; though others thought he had no mind to make too quick an end of the war. [a] The king sent his army forward [a] to Golding bridge near Cashill; [b] and he himself came back to Dublin in order to his return to England, to which he had been pressed [b] by many letters from England. This had a very ill effect on his affairs; for the Irish (who are apt to believe all the lies that their priests set on among them) were persuaded that he was forced to go to England to defend it against the French, and that he would be obliged to carry over his army very soon thither; therefore they were made believe that if they could but stand

[a] Cf. *Hist.* ii. 57.   [b] *Ibid.*

out a little while, the island would be soon their own again. By these means they were wrought on to make a stand. [a]But when the king came to Dublin he found letters of another strain from England; the fitting out of the fleet went on apace; the militias were all up, and expressed much zeal for the government; the most dangerous men were secured; and there was now no reason to apprehend a descent from the French. So the king went back to his army, and moved towards Limerick.

Limerick besieged.

Cf. *Hist.* ii. 57 (*from* 'Upon this, Lauzun' *to* p. 59, *end of first paragraph*).

For 'It was hoped' *read* 'There was good reason to hope[1].'

For 'he had left' *read* 'he [had been] obliged to leave.'

Om. 'best.'

After 'and scarce' *insert* 'possible to work in [or].'

After 'some great guns' *add* 'which were brought very near him.'

For 'who despised . . . distance that they' *read only* 'who thinking themselves secure'; *and for* 'and went to bed' *read* 'all night, and kept very little order.'

For 'Sarsfield . . . in time' *read only* 'The king had a timous advertisement that Sarsfield with a body of horse had passed the Shannon.'

[*f.* 57 (*b*)] *For* 'the convoy . . . morning but they' *read* 'the ammunition; for he believed the design must be upon that; yet (by whose fault I do not know, for when I asked the king about it he did not answer) the orders which he gave in the morning were not executed till it were midnight. Lanier commanded it; he marched slow and.'

Om. 'the general observation . . . side) was, that'; *for* 'they had' *read* 'he had'; *for* 'themselves' *read* 'himself'; *for* 'their master' *read* 'his master'; *and after* 'conclusion of it' *read* 'so he came back without doing anything.'

After 'channel. Yet' *insert* 'as soon as the cannon came up.'

After 'retired' *add* 'by which the garrison took heart.'

For 'the king saw that . . . he must leave' *read* 'and if another body had come the king had been forced to have left.'

For 'and it was thought . . . too much' *read* 'and had exposed his person so often that it appeared upon many new occasions that the providence of God was as watchful over his person as he seemed careless in exposing it.'

The siege raised.

Cf. *Hist.* ii. 59 (*from* 'The king lay' *to end of third clause*, 'disorder the retreat'); *for which read* 'Upon all this the king saw the necessity of raising the siege, after three weeks lost before it. They within were very happy in their own thoughts that they had scaped so great a danger; and, content with

[a] Cf. *Hist.* ii. 57.

---

[1] Dr. Gifford notes this difference.

that, they did not think fit to venture out and disturb the king as he marched off. He presently ordered the army to go into quarters; only some bodies were drawn near Cork.'

[*Marlborough's campaign.*]

Cf. *Hist.* ii. 60 (*from* 'While he lay' *to* p. 61, *end of first paragraph*).

For 'While he . . . proposed that' *read* 'For Marlborough had offered an advice, that when our fleet should be ready to go out (upon which we had reason to believe that the French would go in).'

Om. 'and with the assistance . . . should try.'

For 'and ordered . . . with them' *read only* 'and gave orders for it.'

Om. (*at this point*) 'And so he broke . . . London.'

Before 'person' *add* 'only'; *and for* 'the greatest' *read* 'any.' (*This occurs on f.* 58 (*a*).)

Om. 'in a season so far advanced.'

For 'The Irish . . . divert it' *read only* 'But during the siege, the Irish, in order to the diverting the forces.'

[*f.* 58 (*a*)] *Om.* 'which cut off . . . Ireland.'

For 'without staying . . . orders' *read* 'with the first wind.'

After 'submitted to the king' *add* 'and lived in his quarters.'

For 'had a sad time' *read* 'were like to have a terrible winter of it'; *for* 'almost quite destroyed in many places' *read* 'so destroyed that a famine was generally apprehended for the next year.'

[*The king's return.*]

The king came over to England within a few days after the siege was raised; and though [a] the last action of Limerick as coming latest had very much damped the joy of the former successes [a], yet he was everywhere received with great expressions of joy in the countries through which he passed from [b] the place where he landed, which was near Bristol, till he came to London [b]; his behaviour in small as well as in greater matters had begotten in all that were about him a vast esteem of him.

The equality of the king's temper.

Cf. *Hist.* ii. 59 (*from* 'Dr. Hutton' *to* p. 60, 'in restraining or concealing them').

After 'near him' *add* 'in all the dangers through which he passed.'

For 'joy' *read* 'any indecent joy'; *and om.* 'only . . . cheerful.'

After 'compliments, as' *add* 'upon much less occasions.'

For 'As soon . . . physician, he ordered' *read* 'In the midst of all that were [*sic*] then said to him, he did not forget to order his physician.'

[*f.* 58 (*b*)] *After* 'Limerick' *add* 'he took notice of his behaviour in every little thing after that.'

[a] Cf. *Hist.* ii. 59.　　　　[b] *Ibid.* 60.

[The king's arrangements.]

Cf. *Hist.* ii. 65 (*from* 'The king, at his first' *to end of paragraph*).
For 'at his first coming . . . campaign that he' *read only* 'had once.'
Om. 'about the beginning of October.'

Great supplies granted by the parliament.

Cf. *Hist.* ii. 65 (*from* 'Both houses' *to end of paragraph*).
After 'inconsiderable ; and' *read* 'they set about the ways of raising it ; and after a variety of propositions which were long canvassed.'
Om. 'though these proved . . . defective.'

[Various complaints.]

Cf. *Hist.* ii. 65 (*from* 'Some indeed' *to* p. 66, *end of paragraph*).
For 'but the ministry . . . should name' *read* 'that had been given since the beginning of this reign ; but this lasted not long ; for the privy councillors that were in the house consented that an act should be prepared empowering so many members of that house.'
Om. 'with all particulars . . . scandalous reports.'
For 'When this bill . . . of their own house' *read* 'This was like to have been stopped in the house of lords ; for there it was thought that the dignity of that house required.'
For 'this was done by ballot' *read* 'And this was carried ; to which probably the commons would not have consented. The peers were to be named by billet.'
For 'firmness' *read* 'obstinacy.'
For 'as it was sent up' *read* 'without that addition ; which gave great content to the commons.'
After 'against them. But' *insert* 'though upon another occasion it is not to be doubted but the house of commons will be careful to maintain the habeas corpus bill yet.'
After 'house of commons' *insert* 'though they would not justify illegal imprisonments, yet.'
Om. 'and yet maintained . . . act' *and* 'contrary to that act.'

[Anecdote concerning the habeas corpus act.]

[*f.* 59 (*a*)] And since I am now upon this point (which is the chief fence of the liberty of England), I will tell [a] a very odd account of the way in which the act for the *habeas corpus* was carried [a]. It was vehemently pressed by the country party, but as vehemently opposed by the court, as that which would be a great diminution of the prerogative ; so the much greater part of the house of lords opposed it. When it came to the final vote the house divided upon it, and there being

[a] Cf. *Hist.* i. 485.

always two named to be the tellers of the house, one of either side,[a] the lords Norris (now earl of Abingdon) and Grey were the men. Grey[a] believing that his side, which was for the bill, had lost it, leaped from twenty-four to thirty-five, and so [b]told ten wrong[1]; which the other not perceiving, the report was made for the bill; so by this artifice, though it was indeed cast out by the lords, it was passed[b], and the royal assent was given to it in the year 1679[2].

[*Irish debates.*]

Cf. *Hist.* ii. 66 (*from* 'Great complaints' *to* p. 67, 'state of his affairs should require').

Before 'Great complaints' *insert* 'But to return to the house of commons.'

Before 'there was a great arrear' *insert* 'When the king left Ireland'; *and after* 'due to them' *add* 'no pay had been sent to them all the while he was there.'

After 'lords justices' *add* 'who were the lord Sidney, sir Charles Porter (who was made chancellor of the kingdom again), and one Coningsby, the choice of whom was much censured, for he was a vicious man[3] and his parts were very indifferent.'

For 'and punished accordingly' *read* 'and a legal government. But, on the other hand.'

After 'oppressed it' *add* 'in a very intolerable manner.'

For 'of a very gallant . . . Wirtemberg' *read* 'a German, the duke of Wirtemberg[4].'

For 'so the country . . . forces' *read* 'so this did not give a full remedy to that great grievance; yet the house of commons did not think fit to take up this matter.'

After 'in the rebellion of Ireland' *add* 'since the beginning of the present reign.'

Om. 'to grant away . . . served in the war, and.'

For 'petitions were offered' *read* 'difficulties arose.'

Om. 'imitating . . . against in Ireland.'

For 'and the matter . . . commons' *read* 'This was near the end of the session; so the whole matter was let fall on [*f.* 59 (*b*)] a message sent by the king to the commons.'

For 'assure them . . . officers' *read* 'to secure them from the fears that were suggested, that those estates would be divided among favourites, courtiers, and officers.'

[a] Cf. *Hist.* i. 485.   [b] *Ibid.*

---

[1] The printed *History* makes the fraud of Lord Grey less deliberate.

[2] His friends asserted that the royal assent was obtained by the exertions of the Viscount (afterwards Marquis of) Halifax (Grey's *Debates*, vol. viii, Debate of Nov. 22, 1680).

[3] See Macaulay, ed. 1858, vi. 72, 375; Dalrymple, *Memoirs*, ed. 1790, vol. iii. part iii. book i. p. 29.

[4] Burnet's own correction for 'a gallant pr[ince] of Wirtemberg.' The *History* reads 'a gallant prince, one of the dukes of Wirtemberg.'

[The earl of Torrington is tried.]

Cf. *Hist.* ii. 67-8 (*to end of paragraph*).

After 'vest in the commissioners' *add* 'The privileges of peers are things of which the house is so tender, that these debates took up much time ; but.'

For 'who intended . . . matters' *read* 'who seemed, or at least pretended, to be highly irritated against Torrington.'

For 'which did . . . rupture' *read* 'which might have broke the session.'

For 'the king was apprehensive' *read* 'the government was [apprehensive]' ; *and for* 'though he' *read* 'though the king.'

For 'so that' *read* 'This was so highly resented by the Dutch, that.'

After 'repent of it' *add* 'He is now given up to luxury and is wallowing in it.'

[Designs against the marquis of Carmarthen.]

Cf. *Hist.* i. 68 (*from* 'Another debate' *to* 'universal hatred').

For 'so they did not come home to the present case' *read* 'so that these made indeed against this.'

After 'act of parliament' *add* 'So this was let fall.'

For 'to have the greatest credit' *read* 'the only man in credit.'

For 'hatred' *read* 'envy and hatred.'

[The king's tactics regarding him.]

And though the king brought over the lord Sidney from Ireland and made him secretary of state, and made the lord Godolphin first commissioner of the treasury without communicating the matter to him (these two being [*f.* 60 (*a*)] likewise known to be his enemies), yet this did not lay the jealousy that was taken up of his great interest at court.

[The design fails.]

Cf. *Hist.* i. 68 (*from* 'In a house of commons every motion' *to* p. 69, *end of paragraph*).

Om. 'envy him ; others.'

Om. 'The thing was . . . king and his affairs.'

For 'at this time' *read* 'a few days before the session was ended.'

For 'so that put an end . . . present' *read* '[so] it was not thought decent to attack a man who was serving the government so faithfully ; so he was not named.'

A new plot discovered and the lord Preston taken.

Cf. *Hist.* ii. 69 (*from* 'The session of parliament' *to* p. 70, 'some in Ashton's hand').

For 'so they got . . . negotiation' *read* 'It was thought a matter of such consequence, that Preston undertook to go over and persuade[1] king James to hearken to it.'

---

[1] The transcript says 'persuaded.'

Om. 'no time . . . James; but.'

Om. 'if he surprised . . . news of it.'

For 'more easy' *read* 'as easy'; *for* 'more sudden' *read* 'as quick.'

Before 'quaker' *om.* 'famous'; *and after it add* 'it is not yet known how many more were concerned in it.'

For 'they would' *read* 'he would'; *for* 'with that' *read* '[with] his principles, that tied him to her service'; *and for* 'their' *read* 'his.'

For 'a vessel' *read* 'a small vessel.'

Om. 'which was only . . . France.'

For 'a young man' *read* 'a young sea-officer.'

For 'the hold . . . hid' *read* 'a hole that was made to hide them.'

For 'behind him . . . signet' *read* 'and seals [1] (among which one was king James' signet) in the hole behind him.'

For 'them' *read* 'the papers'; *and for* 'from him' *read* 'out of his armpit; and both Preston and he used all possible endeavours to persuade him to let them be thrown in the sea ; but.'

Before 'Lord Preston's mind' *add* 'From the beginning.'

And [two are] condemned.

[*f.* 60 (*b*)] At their trial they were fully and fairly heard, but [a] made a poor defence [a]. It was said that the papers were found in Ashton's hands; upon which Preston pretended that he was not concerned in them ; but it was proved he treated with the officer to throw them in the river. Some [b] pretended that a part of the evidence being a similitude of hands, the same practice that had been condemned in Sidney's trial was now followed ; but this was only a circumstance in the proof; for the treason was the carrying over such advice and papers to the king's enemies which, whether they had writ them or not, made them still guilty [b]; so though this was an aggravation of the matter, yet the weight of evidence did not turn upon it, but upon things that were fully proved.

Cf. *Hist.* ii. 70.

[Ashton suffers.]

But Preston discovered all.

[c] Preston had no mind to confess all, and yet he was resolved not to die [c]. He made half-confessions, which he enlarged twice or thrice, after he had with imprecations protested that

[a] Cf. *Hist.* ii. 70.   [b] *Ibid.*   [c] *Ibid.* 70.

---

[1] See Routh's note (from Ralph), *History, in lco.*

he knew no more. In conclusion, the government was so far satisfied of his having told all he knew that he had both his pardon and liberty; but this whole matter is yet a secret, so I can say nothing of it till it comes to be more public. Preston's behaviour brought him under a great deal of contempt from all hands; for he was above two months in a great distraction of mind. [a] Sometimes, when he was heated with the importunities of his friends who were all of that party, and his spirits were exalted with wine, he resolved to die heroically; but when that heat went off and he saw death before him his heart failed him [a]; for without doubt a man in those circumstances ought either to resolve to die and to enter into no treaty for life, or he ought at first frankly to tell all he knows.

[*General reflections; treatment of those implicated.*]

Cf. *Hist.* ii. 71 (*from* 'The scheme he carried over' *to end of following paragraph*).

After 'secret' *insert* 'of his confession [1].'

Om. 'would proceed . . . against him, but.'

Before 'The king had suffered' *read* 'This discovery gave the king a very just ground for filling the sees of the deprived bishops.' (Cf. *Hist.* ii. 71, *infra.*)

For 'they all the while . . . palaces' *read* 'to see if any of them would change their mind; there was still a body of men in the nation and in the parliament that had a tenderness for them.'

Om. entirely 'I had, by . . . he withdrew.'

For 'The discovery . . . sees' *read* 'So the king did want so fair an opportunity as this gave him to fill their sees.'

The king went to meet some princes at the Hague.

Cf. *Hist.* ii. 71-2 (*to end of paragraph*).

For 'he ran . . . hazard' *read* 'he met with a new instance of that careful providence that has been observed still to watch over him.'

[*f.* 61 (*a*)] *For* 'some of his lords' *read* 'five or six of his court.'

For 'And, when' *read* 'He said upon that occasion a word which deserves to be put in history as well as Caesar's; for when.'

For 'He soon settled . . . year' *read* 'At the Hague he quickly brought the councils of state [counsels of the States?] to the point he aimed at; nor were there any disputes among them this year, as there had been the former year. Before that was over.'

[a] Cf. *Hist.* ii. 71.

---

[1] This confession has not been recovered. Some details are given by Dalrymple, part ii. book vi. Appendix, p. 185.

For 'that his affairs ... promising face' *read* 'that the state of his affairs is now as promising as it seemed then ruinous.'

For 'that they did not trust ... came back' *read* 'that they resolved not to communicate them to their own ministers, till the time of execution should make that necessary ; I am sure the king kept the secret as to his part exactly ; for Nottingham, upon his return, told me that he knew nothing of it. All our court was much taken with the duke of Bavaria, in whose air and whole deportment they said there was somewhat that was great and heroical ; so that the best judges of men who saw him, believed that if the crown of Spain should devolve on him he might put new life in that great but paralytic body [1].'

Om. 'they lived ... that' ; *and for* 'upon ... interviews' *read* 'at a meeting of so many princes.'

The election of a new pope.

Cf. *Hist.* 72-3.

For 'the formulary ... 1682' *read only* 'those articles (which all the clergy of France were required to sign).'

Om. 'This he did ... feared them.'

For 'who had' *read* 'who has.'

After 'Spaniards' *add* 'in the conclave.'

For 'assumed' *read* 'has assumed' ; *for* 'seemed' *read* 'seems' ; *for* 'for he did not seek ... raise his family' *read* 'He seems not to be concerned in his family, so probably he will stand firmly upon pope Innocent's pretensions.'

Om. 'of which the king ... notice of that.'

Mons is taken.

Cf. *Hist.* ii. 73.

[*f.* 61 (*b*)] *For* 'To return ... besieged' *read only* 'While the princes were with the king at the Hague the French besieged Mons.'

Om. 'broke up the congress and' ; *and for* 'very soon' *read* 'in a very few days.'

After 'battle' *for* 'But' *read* 'The siege was carried on very slowly ; but the secret of this afterwards appeared ; for.'

For 'Upon that ... the king' *read* 'And upon the French going into quarters for some weeks, the king put likewise his army into quarters and.'

For 'a few' *read* 'three.'

[Preparations for the next campaign.]

Cf. *Hist.* ii. 73 ('He gave all necessary' *to end of paragraph*).

After 'chief command' *add* 'He had made duke Schomberg's eldest son duke of Leinster, and he left him to command in England [2].'

For 'which was soon ready ... time' *read* 'which was the strongest, the best, and soonest equipped that had ever been known ; and he was joined with a squadron of very good ships that was sent over from the States.'

---

[1] See Macaulay, ed. 1858, vi. 276, note.

[2] A pencil note in the MS. (qu. by Gifford?) draws attention to this insertion.

A stop is put to the violence of presbytery in Scotland.

Cf. *Hist.* ii. 74 (*to end of first paragraph*).

Before ' lords' *add* ' Jacobite' ; *and for* ' who had been concerned . . . came up and' *read* ' that came up the former winter, had.'

For ' to ruin' *read* ' to the revenges of their enemies.'

Om. ' who stood . . . parties.'

For ' and they undertook . . . serve him' *read* ' and the whole episcopal party (if they might be sure of the king's protection) would not only acknowledge his authority, but serve him with much more zeal than could be expected from the other party.'

For ' episcopal ministers . . . to serve' *read* ' the episcopal party might be protected.'

Om. ' without . . . opinion.'

[*The changes made in Scotland.*]

[a] All this did agree so well with the king's temper and sense of things that he very easily hearkened to it[a]; but Melville being so entirely wedded to the presbyterian party, it was necessary to employ another instrument for managing it. So [b] Dalrymple, that was son to Stairs the president, now made a viscount, was made conjunct secretary[b]; and he, with several others of the nobility, were employed to bring men's minds of all hands to a greater temper in those matters. [c] The presbyterians had held a general assembly in winter, in which they did very much expose themselves by the weakness and peevishness of their conduct; so little learning or prudence, such poor preaching and wretched haranguing as was among them, their partialities to one another and their violence against all that differed from them, and the gross injustice of their proceedings did so sink their reputation, that [d] all that had been done against presbytery in a course of [*f.* 62 (*a*)] many years had not so [e] effectually weaned the nation from the fondness it had to their government[e] as their own heat and folly had now done. But though the king is resolved to stop the fury of their proceedings, yet he finds it no easy thing to do it; there is a present cessation of violence, but that is all; and I will now leave that scene till the next time I sit down to prosecute this work.

[a] Cf. *Hist.* ii. 74.   [b] *Ibid. infra.*   [c] *Ibid.* 75.   [d] *Ibid.*   [e] *Ibid.*

The sees of the deprived bishops are filled.

Cf. *Hist.* ii. 75 (*from* 'The next thing', *to* p. 76, 'violence and severities on those heads ').

For 'The next thing the king did' *read* 'But the chief thing that the king did during his short stay in England.'

Om. 'He judged right, that.'

For 'a high party . . . hated him' *read only* 'the high church party.'

For 'Dr. Tillotson' *read* 'He pitched on Tillotson, who was then dean of St. Paul's and clerk of the closet; who.'

Om. 'both' *and* 'and queen'; *and for* 'They had both . . . pressed him' *read* 'The king had declared his intentions to him above a year before this.'

Om. 'and slander.'

Om. 'that the Jacobites . . . people with'; *for* 'whom they called' *read* 'that was looked on by his party [as]'; *and for* 'began . . . compassion' *read* 'and that would have the compassions for the unfortunate.'

For 'He had large' *read* 'But he [had] large.'

After 'superstition' *add* '[and] heat.'

For 'a good correspondence' *read* 'great friendship.'

After 'heads' *add* 'which drew the hatred of all our violent men upon him.'

[*Same subject continued.*]

And this they laboured to lay very heavy upon him; but [though] he had still gone on in his way without taking much pains to gain them, yet he had never done anything that was provoking to them as I had done. [a] Among other prejudices against him one was that he and I had been observed to live for many years in close and strict friendship. He laid all this before the king [a]; he acknowledged that the leaving the quiet station in which he then was gave him many uneasy thoughts, but as for that which concerned himself he went soon over it, and laid himself at the king's feet; but he continued long after that [b] to represent to him how much he thought it against the king's service to promote him [b]; and laid this matter so often and so fully before the king, that though it was not strong enough to divert him from his intentions (since [c] it increased his esteem of him [c]), yet it served to gain a delay. A full year was now granted, and all people were of opinion that [d] the bishop of Ely's letters gave the king so fair an occasion of doing it at this time that it was by no means to be let go. So the king named him; and the

[a] Cf. *Hist.* ii. 76.   [b] *Ibid.*   [c] *Ibid.*   [d] *Ibid.*

archbishop of York dying soon after, Sharp (now dean of Canterbury) was promoted to that see; so that these two sees were in a month's time filled with two of [a] the greatest prelates, [b] the [*f.* 62 (*b*)] best preachers [b], and the wisest and worthiest men [1] that perhaps ever sat in them. [c] Patrick was translated from Chichester to Ely, Grove was made bishop of Chichester, Cumberland was made bishop of Peterborough, More bishop of Norwich, Fowler bishop of Gloucester [c], and Kidder bishop of Bath and Wells. That see had been first offered to Beveridge, who is a man of great learning, a very practical preacher, and a devout man, but in the monastic way, too superstitious and singular. He accepted of it; but he leaned much to the other side; and when he understood that Ken, who held that see, was resolved to continue in possession, he afterwards refused it; he is a very weak man and very rough, but honest and sincere [2]. Stillingfleet had been made the year before bishop of Worcester; and [d] Hough, that was president of Magdalen, was made bishop of Oxford [d]. Ironside, that had been vice-chancellor of the university of Oxford [3], had been made bishop of Bristol; Chester and Bangor had fallen vacant the first year of the reign, and Stratford [4] and Humphreys [5] had been promoted to those sees. [e] Thus in two years' time the king has made fifteen bishops [e], and excepting what is to be said as to myself, [f] it is visible that they are the worthiest and learnedest men, the best preachers, and the men of the gentlest and prudentest tempers that could be found [f]. And it could not be otherwise, for both the king and queen showed that they would have the best and fittest men sought out

[a] Cf. *Hist.* ii. 76.   [b] *Ibid.*   [c] *Ibid.*   [d] *Ibid.*   [e] *Ibid.*   [f] *Ibid.*

[1] Political motives subsequently lessened Burnet's esteem for Sharp; see Autobiography (1710), f. 214; the printed *History* also modifies the eulogy in this place.

[2] For the importance of Beveridge's refusal (the omission of which from the pages of the printed *History* draws forth a comment from Dr. Routh *in loco*) see Lathbury's *Nonjurors*, pp. 87-91.

[3] See Birch's *Tillotson*, 1753, p. 214.

[4] Bishop of Chester, Sept. 15, 1689–1707. There is a eulogistic notice of him in the *Dict. Nat. Biog.*, by Rev. F. Sanders.

[5] Bishop of Bangor, 1689-1701; of Hereford, 1701-12. Mr. Thompson Cooper in *Dict. Nat. Biog.* describes him as a good Celtic scholar.

for the service of the church; they declared they would discourage all ambition and aspiring among the clergy, and would have the worthiest [a] men searched for and brought out of their retirements to be raised to the most eminent posts in the church, and that all men that pressed their own advancement should be kept back [a] for that very reason. It was also observed that most of these were men not past fifty, whereas generally men had not been promoted formerly till their strength and parts began to sink with age, which made them incapable of doing those services to the church that might have been expected from men whose parts were more lively and whose strength was more entire. [b] There was also great care had in filling the livings and dignities which the persons now promoted had formerly held; and generally the choice fell upon eminent preachers and moderate men; so that in this whole matter the king discovered both his own temper and the measures that he intended to take in the government of the church [b]; for he had made now so many good and moderate bishops that he had rendered it unpracticable to think of violent and high counsels for want of proper instruments.

The king went to command the army in Flanders.

Cf. *Hist.* ii. 76–7 (*to* ' between the Sambre and the Maese ').

For ' had yet learned to be ' *read only* ' could be.'

For ' came up to ' *read* ' marched in all haste to have surprised.'

After ' Waldeck ' *add* ' abandoned Halle and.'

[*f.* 63 (*a*)] *For* 'kept' *read* ' have kept '; *for* 'all the . . . campaign ' *read* 'ever since'; *for* 'made' *read* 'has made'; *and for* 'yet he could not do it' *read* ' yet hitherto he has not been able to do it.'

For 'Signal preservations . . . guarding him' *read* 'Two particulars which the last post brought show how much both he and his army are still under the same watchful providence that has hitherto appeared in so many signal instances.'

After ' under a tree' *add* 'looking upon the enemy.'

Om. ' drawn up . . . effects.'

After 'providence' *read* '[rather] than only among singular and great blessings.'

For 'The two armies . . . followed' *read* 'The two armies are now between the Sambre and the Meuse; and there I leave them for this time'; *and om. at this place remainder of paragraph.*

[a] Cf. *Hist.* ii. 76.　　　[b] *Ibid.*

[Affairs at sea.]

^a At sea matters go much as they do at land ^a. The French had some capital ships, with great stores at Dunkirk, which cannot be brought out but at spring-tides and must come out empty for want of water ; they receiving their loading in the road. So a ^b squadron of our ships have blocked it up. The rest of our fleet is seeking the French, but have not been able in two months' time to come up to them ; for they go off still in the night, and it seems are resolved to avoid an engagement ^b, which, though it cannot be so easily done in narrow seas, yet in the ocean it is not practicable to force a fleet to come to a battle that has orders to decline it. ^c The Smyrna fleet, both Dutch and English, which was then coming home and was valued at near four millions sterling, gave much disquiet to the trading part of the nation ; for though they had a strong convoy, yet the French fleet had stood out to the sea to intercept them ; but they had orders to make to Kinsale, which they did, and so got safe into port ^c. Thus our fleet has hitherto secured our quiet at home, ^d and has covered our merchantmen ^d ; but whether it is to meet with the French before the end of the campaign is that which cannot be now determined.

The success in Ireland.

Cf. *Hist.* ii. 78 (*to end of* p. 79).

After ' in France ' *add* ' being esteemed a good officer.'

[*f.* 63 (*b*)] *For* ' Parties were sent out ' *read* ' Ginkell was ordering some motions of his troops.'

Om. ' by Mackay.'

Om. ' taken the most . . . he had.'

For ' very favourable . . . advantages, they ' *read* ' very unfavourable to our men ; but they broke through everything till they came at the Irish, who.'

For ' and every' *read* ' and that happened upon this occasion which is not ordinary, that [every].'

For ' so that now . . . the river' *read* ' and he is now marching to Limerick ; a squadron of our ships is also gone to Shannon, to press it on that side.'

After ' lords justices' *add* ' after the business of Athlone.'

[Reflections on the situation.]

[This] they have since that time enlarged ten days further, for the sake of Limerick ; but it does not yet appear that they

^a Cf. *Hist.* ii. 78.   ^b *Ibid.*   ^c *Ibid.*   ^d *Ibid.*

intend to accept of it. A little time must tell how that matter (which concludes the war of Ireland) will end. The king has ordered those large offers to be made both out of his [*f. 64 (a)*] natural inclinations to mercy and [a] that he may be able to make use of some part of that army elsewhere[a]; for ships are now preparing to transport seven or eight thousand of them. But all this I must now leave to time, as also the prospect of the other parts of the confederacy. Spain seems to be in some disposition to awaken itself out of the lethargy in which it has slept so long. There is a fair prospect of a peace with the Ottoman court ; for the war in Hungary has been now so unsuccessful to the Turks (in a course of eight campaigns) that they have lost, not only Hungary itself, but several of the adjacent provinces. The Vizier Bassa has received the king's ambassador (who is gone to offer his mediation[1] for a peace) not only with all the public honours that were due to him, but with all the most particular demonstrations of a willingness to put an end to that war, and a project of peace is concerted between the emperor, the crown of Poland, and the republic of Venice ; upon which if a peace is obtained, the face of affairs in these parts will receive great alterations by it. Matters have gone of late very ill for the French in Piedmont ; they had in the end of the former campaign taken Susa, which opened a passage to their troops, and in the beginning of this they took Nizza, the only strong place which that prince had upon the Mediterranean sea ; and several lesser places were taken. At last they besieged Coni, a small place from which little was expected ; but they defended themselves so well, and held out so long, that, after the French had lost 4,000 men before it, upon [learning[2]] that Prince Eugene was coming with a body of horse to raise the siege, they prevented him ; and went off with so much precipitation that they left their sick men, their provisions, and some of their cannon, behind them. They lie now upon a defensive ;

[a] Cf. *Hist.* ii. 81.

---

[1] See note to *Hist.* ii. 83, inserted by Routh from Ralph.

[2] The transcript erroneously reads ' leaving.'

but it is probable the duke of Savoy will quickly change the scene, and fall upon them; for he had now an army of 16,000 Germans come up to him, a great part of which is upon the king's pay; and the duke of Bavaria will be soon with them. This I must leave likewise to time, as also the fate of the army on the Rhine (commanded by the duke of Saxe) that passed the Rhine, being led with conduct and courage. The French army, commanded by marshal de Lorge, marched off as they advanced; but now they have passed the Rhine, and have obliged the Germans to go after them, for the covering their own country. There is now a third party forming in Germany by the practices of the French who declare for a peace; the chief of these are the king of Sweden [and?] the duke of Hanover; and they hope to draw both the king of Denmark and the bishop of Munster into their interests; and if this campaign end unfortunately for the French, probably they will interpose in the consultations next winter to procure a favourable peace to them. The two northern crowns have complained much of the interruption of their trade with France (for there was a secret treaty between England and Holland to hinder all trade with France); upon this they have complained much, and threatened high; but there is a project now on foot to regulate the number of the ships that shall be allowed to trade, which will accommodate that matter if French money does not overbalance their counsels. The French ministry is now almost wholly changed. Mr. de Seignelay, that was the minister for the marine, died some months ago; and about a month ago Mr. de Louvois died suddenly; upon this the king has brought in the dauphin to the cabinet council; he has also put Mr. de Pomponne and the duke of Beauvilliers into the ministry; if this new set of men do [*f.* 64 (*b*)] as well as the old, then the world will believe that it has been the king's own genius that has hitherto supported an[d] animated his affairs; and if the counsels grow hereafter feebler and less successful, then the glory to which the success of that king's affairs has hitherto raised him will receive a great diminution.

With this I give over writing for this time on the 13th of August, 169[1][1].

[*Burnet resumes his pen, September* 1, 1693.]

I began again to continue this work on the first of September, 1693; so that I have now the transactions of two years before me.

Limerick is taken, and Ireland wholly reduced.

Cf. *Hist.* ii. 80-1 (*from* 'Ginkell pursued' *to* 'our civil war came to a final end ').

For 'Ginkell ... open' *read* 'The siege of Limerick went on but slowly for some weeks; the town was bombarded; but it being so large, and the Irish and the French accustomed to hardships, the beating down the houses had no great effect; and they being besieged only on the side of Munster, Connaught was still open to them, so that.'

For 'When the men-of-war ... Ginkell' *read* 'but Ginkell having ordered the men-of-war and the other ships to come near the place, he.'

For 'The earl of Tyrconnell ... inevitable' *read* 'For Tyrconnell, when he had carried the point in the court of France, that no soldiers, but only officers, should be sent over to them (in which the great difficulties that the French began to feel in making their levies made it easy for him to succeed), thought that he had it now in his power to treat with the king; and did not doubt but the Irish would be easily engaged, when they saw their ruin unavoidable, to accept of a treaty and good terms; for he had resolved to preserve himself.'

For 'his words ... for' *read* 'as men's last words have commonly more weight after they are dead.'

For 'They wanted ... Limerick' *read* 'We hoped that their provisions would have failed them; but they had great stores for many weeks.'

For 'To hinder that ... Yet the French' *read* 'but a squadron of the English ships, that was sent after the French, secured that fear; since it was visible that they.'

[*f.* 65 (*a*)] *For* 'three years' *read* 'two years'; *then insert* 'all provisions were to be carried a great way'; *and before* 'When they came' *insert* 'So.'

Om. from 'which was set on' *to* 'Limerick treated.'

The errors of the French in the war.

In the progress of this the French had committed several great errors. They did not enough consider into what distraction that put all our affairs, and so did not support it as they ought to have done; but their main error was that they did not consider the importance of Cork and Kinsale. For

---

[1] The transcript has '1690'; an obvious clerical error.

these deserved to be fortified to the utmost degree possible : since they were ports of that security, and so well situated, that it had been easy to have fortified them to such a degree that the taking of them must have cost England many campaigns.   Nor were these places that only concerned Ireland ; but looking over into England must have put the whole west of England into a constant terror and many alarms ; and such a part of the French fleet might have been laid in those parts that the whole trade of England would have been ruined by it.   This was such an omission (in a matter that was both so obvious and so practicable) that I have taken some pains to inquire into it.   All the account that I could ever get of it is this.   [a] There was a great emulation in the French ministry ; Louvois, that had the concerns of the war in his hands, was certainly the most esteemed by the French king ; but Mr. Seignelay had more personal favour ; he was more united to madame de Maintenon [a], and his own wife was believed to have a great share in the king's heart, so Louvois was jealous of such things as raised his credit.   [b] Now the war in Ireland (being chiefly to be managed by the marine forces) fell to Seignelay's province ; this, as it led king James to make more court to him, so it engaged Louvois to obstruct it all he could [b].   And this probably diverted him from forming any great project in the progress of that war ; and therefore they went no further than to entertain the propositions that the Irish made them, which went only to the fortifying Limerick ; though that place had no relation to England, and was too high in the river to be relieved by sea.   Now it was in the king's hands.

[*The articles of Limerick.*]

Cf. *Hist.* ii. 81 (*from* 'The articles of capitulation' *to* p. 82, 'of the general officers ').

Om. ' and some doubts . . . Irish.'

For ' So earnestly . . . done them' *read* ' to the great grief of the English in Ireland, who were too much exasperated with the wrongs that had been done them by the Irish, to be easily satisfied with the good conditions that were now given them ; but wise men saw what a happiness it was to have matters

[a] Cf. *Hist.* ii. 17.   [b] *Ibid.*

quieted at home, and to be able to send all our strength abroad against the common enemy; no part of these dominions being any longer the seat of the war; and though some violent men.'

[*f.* 65 (*b*)] *For from* 'noble rewards' *to end of paragraph read* 'and had other rewards, though far below his merits; which some [affect]ed[1] to lessen by ascribing the chief share of those great actions to the subaltern officers; for now a national jealousy began to arise between the English and the Dutch, which has already produced very ill effects and may in time produce worse.'

Affairs at sea.

Cf. *Hist.* ii. 78 (*from* ' The season went over' *to* ' maintained ').

For ' The season . . . action' *read* 'At sea nothing considerable was done: the French declined an engagement; and our fleet was not able to force them to it'; *and for* ' at the end of it' *read only* ' also.'

For ' among the flag officers' *read* ' against the flag officers.'

Om. 'by this great equipment.'

In Flanders.

Cf. *Hist.* ii. 77 (*from* ' When the time came' *to* p. 78, *end of paragraph*).

Before ' When the time' *insert* ' The campaign in Flanders was spent in the motions of both armies.'

After ' marched off, and' *add* ' as was generally reckoned they.'

For 'Auverquerque . . . service' *read* ' The honour of this action was due chiefly to Mr. Auverquerque.'

And Hungary.

Cf. *Hist.* ii. 82 (*from* ' The emperor's affairs in Hungary' *to* p. 83, 'those he esteemed heretics ').

For ' The emperor's . . . fatal to him' *read* ' At this time the emperor's army, commanded by prince Lewis of Baden, advanced near Belgrade; the grand vizier (as was found afterwards, having designed nothing by the good reception he gave our ambassador, but to make the imperialists more secure by the shows of peace) came up to them.'

For 'so he attacked . . . fury that' *read* 'so after a short resistance'; *place last sentence of paragraph in present tense; and for* 'of those . . . about him' *read* ' of the French in that court of Vienna, engaging him to continue that war.'

Before ' The news' *insert* ' It has also been said that'; *and after* ' Ireland' *add* ' (coming at this time to that court).'

Om. ' with the rest . . . allies.'

For ' it was said . . . heretics' *read* ' it is said, that he is not ill-pleased to see the weight of the war against France lie on those whom he accounts heretics '; *omit remainder of paragraph.*

[*Affairs of Germany.*]

Cf. *Hist.* ii. 83 (*from* ' Germany was now' *to* p. 84, ' must be first had ').

For ' the third party . . . war' *read* ' The f[resh][2] party that the French were forming.'

---

[1] The transcript reads ' ascribed.'   [2] The transcript reads ' first.'

[*f.* 66 (*a*)] *Om.* 'that so . . . engaged with them.'

Om. 'whom the French . . . peace.'

For 'who had been long . . . court' *read* 'came now over entirely into the confederacy '

For ' in which . . . to it' *read only* 'This was easily consented to by the court of Vienna.'

For 'and they moved' *read* 'and sometimes the archbishop of Salzbourg was spoke of; but the court of Vienna designed.'

For 'The French . . . first had' *read* 'and though upon that the French endeavoured to have formed a new party that should not acknowledge him, yet all that fell to the ground; which was managed by the new elector with great skill and much vigour, he being without doubt the ablest prince now in Germany.'

Affairs in Savoy.

Cf. *Hist.* ii. 84.

For ' Montmelian . . . Caraffa' *read* ' so that the campaign [indeed?] ended with the taking of Carmagnola, but Montmelian was lost, which was of much greater consequence; and was abandoned by Caraffa's counsels upon this account, as was suggested.'

Om. ' He was recalled . . . room.'

The elector of Bavaria comes into Flanders.

Cf. *Hist.* ii. 84-5.

[*f.* 66 (*b*)] *For* ' seemed . . . signalizing ' *read* ' he found had all the ambition of a gallant young prince to signalize.'

For ' he could support' *read* ' he would not be a charge to the country, but would support.'

For ' in the right. . . succession ' *read* ' (that king having no children, nor being like to live long).'

After ' proposal ' *add* ' and so did the duke of Bavaria.'

For 'but the court of Vienna ' *read* ' so the king was upon sending an embassy thither to propose it, when the court of Vienna.'

After ' provinces ' *add* ' and was certainly the best expedient possible for the preserving them.'

A session of parliament; [jealousies concerning the king].

Cf. *Hist.* ii. 85 (' This was the general state . . . as if they had been denied it ').

After ' affairs ' *add* ' in winter 1691.'

For 'and then it appeared . . . infuse into all people, that ' *read* 'who began to be possessed with two notions; the one was, that, since the war of Ireland was now ended.'

After ' troops ' *add* ' [in] Flanders.'

After ' at sea' *add* 'This was so suitable to the genius of the nation that.'

For from 'But it was not easy' *to end of paragraph read* ' So though it seemed at first view very strange that the king should propose the keeping up the same land army after the reduction of Ireland with a very small diminution, yet the thing was made so plain, that, after a little struggle, they all went into it.'

For 'Another prejudice . . . effects' *read* 'But the other was not so easily overcome.'

Om. 'to trust . . . with him.'

After 'pains' *add* 'to constrain his humour.'

For 'he was shut . . . long' *read* 'he spent most part of his time in his closet and was almost inaccessible.'

For 'as much as' *read* 'more than.'

[*Additional reasons; Marlborough and the malcontents.*]

The frankness with which the two last kings had lived among them was remembered ; and this sudden and extreme difference was very sensible and distasteful. Of all those that were displeased at this Marlborough was he that spake loudest ; [a] he had pretended to great rewards ; upon his service [a] at Cork and Kinsale he hoped to have had an increase of title, and to be made master of the ordnance. But finding this was denied him, and that he had not so absolute a disposal of all employments in the English army as he expected, he set himself to decry the king's conduct and to lessen him in all his discourses, and [b] to possess all the English with an aversion to the Dutch, who, as he pretended, had a much larger share of the king's favour and confidence than they had. This was a point in which the English, who are too apt to despise all other nations [b] [*f.* 67 (*a*)] and to overvalue themselves, [c] were easily enough influenced, so it grew to be the universal subject of discourse [c], and was the constant entertainment at Marlborough's, where there was a constant rendezvous of the English officers. The only thing that made that this did not spread so universally over England was that the Dutch were under so good a discipline and [d] behaved themselves so regularly in their quarters and paid so punctually, whereas the English were very rude and exacting, and especially the bodies that were all this winter coming over from Ireland, who had been so long in an enemy's country that they could not be soon brought into order [d] ; which made the people everywhere

[a] Cf. *Hist.* ii. 85.　　[b] *Ibid.*　　[c] *Ibid.*　　[d] *Ibid.* 85–6.

[1] wish that as long as we had a standing army it might consist chiefly of the Dutch [1]; and this indeed increased the hatred that our soldiers bore the Dutch, since their deportment was made a subject of reproach to them. [a] All these things concurred to make matters go slowly in the house of commons [a].

[*The king charged with despotic leanings; political bribery; the judges' salaries.*]

Cf. *Hist.* ii. 86 (*from* 'The king was also believed' *to* p. 87, 'affairs would permit').

For 'The king was also believed to be' *read* 'But that which was yet more uneasy was that it came to be understood that the king was.'

After 'persons that were' *add* 'in all other respects.'

After 'highest' *add* 'had been in the interest of the former courts, and.'

For 'as the Whigs said' *read* 'as was believed'; *for* 'such jealousies' *read* 'such apprehensions of a commonwealth as made him grow jealous'; *for* 'some . . . enemies' *read* 'those who at best were but cold friends if not secret enemies. And all these things came to have the more credit because it was observed that'; *and for* 'was believed . . . practised' *read* 'was again begun.'

After 'Seymour, who had' *read* 'of all others.'

For 'yet though . . . contrived' *read* 'These things begun all to work in this session, but they did not so plainly show themselves as afterwards ; so that the business of the parliament went on smoothly.'

For 'Among the bills . . . one' *read* 'And all bills were passed except one, that.'

After 'king's pleasure' *read* 'so it was thought but half work to secure to them their continuance in their places, unless they were also made sure of their salaries ; since this did otherwise bind an employment on them, without the profits of it.'

Om. 'by some of the judges themselves'; *and for* 'that it was not fit they should' *read* 'that by this act the judges would.'

For 'A parliament . . . to annul' *read* 'This was likewise laid to Nottingham's charge, who was now again for another year sole secretary; the lord Sidney being sent lord lieutenant into Ireland, where he was to prepare matters for a parliament, that should repeal.'

[*f.* 67 (*b*)] *For* 'and as the state . . . permit' *read* 'and as the present occasions required.'

Affairs in Scotland; [character of secretary Johnstone [2]*].*

[b] The affairs of Scotland were also put in another method ; Tweeddale was made chancellor [b], and Tarbot and Linlithgow

[a] Cf. *Hist.* ii. 86.   [b] *Ibid.* 87.

---

[1] This passage is among the 'suppressed' passages of the *Hist.*, vol. ii, which will be published for the first time in the edition now in progress.
[2] For these incidents see Appendix VI, *infra.*

with Breadálbane [a] were brought into the ministry; and Melville being made privy seal, the king brought over Mr. Johnstone, that had been envoy at the court of Brandenburg, and made him secretary of state for that kingdom [a]. I may perhaps be partial to him, because he is not only my cousin-germane but has been bred and formed by me. He has a very good understanding, and a great dexterity in managing business, and is a man of an entire virtue; and though the engagements of his family has obliged him to espouse the presbyterian interests (it being also the king's pleasure that he should enter into the confidence of that party), yet he has none of their narrow notions, but is rather too loose as to the doctrinal part of religion, though that is much balanced (at least covered) by the strictness of his life. In Scotland things were like to fall into great disorders; the king had hoped to have brought the episcopal party to his service by [b] putting some of the leaders into the chief posts; but as by doing this he disgusted the presbyterians, so it quickly appeared those men came only into employments on design to betray him and to deliver up the kingdom to king James [b]; and it appeared to be an extraordinary piece of confidence to take men out of a plot to betray the government and put them in the chief places of trust. This heightened the reports, that began generally to be believed, that such men as seemed resolved to advance the prerogative would be always trusted beyond all others. [c] And indeed they were so barefaced in avowing their designs for king James, that the trusting them did very much lessen the reputation of the government [c]. The presbyterians had by their foolish heats and obstinate stiffness [d] very much offended the king. A general assembly was held [d], to which the earl of Lothian was sent down commissioner.

[His instructions; course of the assembly.]

Cf. *Hist.* ii. 87 (*from* 'And therefore he recommended' *to* p. 88, *end of paragraph*).

For 'and therefore . . . winter' *read* 'The main instruction he had was to bring the assembly.'

[a] Cf. *Hist.* ii. 87.   [b] *Ibia.*   [c] *Ibid.*   [d] *Ibid.*

For 'were stiff' *read* 'are stiff'; *and om.* 'they were jealous of the king.'
Om. 'and would abate ... government.'

[*f.* 68 (*a*)] *After* 'themselves' *add* 'to August [16]93.'

For 'in which he was so far . . . from him' *read* 'into which he went very easily; and, as they gained their end, in making him lose the affections of those who had hitherto adhered most firmly to him, so the king's taking in a set of men into [*sic*] his affairs, who, to the observation of that whole kingdom, were designing to betray him, did very much sink his credit with that nation.'

A massacre committed in the Highlands [1].

ᵃ At this time there was a very horrid murder committed in that kingdom ᵃ, which has been so often objected to this government that I cannot pass it over; though it is so black that it is with some pain that I find myself obliged to leave such a blemish upon the present administration. ᵇ Breadalbane had been negotiating with the Highlanders to bring them into the present government ᵇ; but in this he played double; for he proposed it to the king as a great service in which he would bestir himself, and for which he promised himself great rewards; ᶜ he did at the same time propose it to the Jacobites as a service to that interest ᶜ; for he said the Highlanders would be still firm to them; that if they did not now submit they would be overrun, ᵈ and therefore he proposed this only as a means to preserve them to a better opportunity ᵈ. But in managing this, he had framed such a scheme of the Highlands as ᵉ did not satisfy some of the leaders of the clans; particularly one tribe of the Macdonalds that lived in Glencoe, and who had indeed been guilty of many black murders ᵉ. They refused long to accept of ᶠ the indemnity, the offer of which was to end with the year 1691 ᶠ.

[*Glencoe comes in; preparations for the massacre.*]

Cf. *Hist.* ii. 88 (*from* 'All were so terrified' *to* p. 89, 'who knew the country well').

For 'All were . . . them to him' *read* 'Yet, on the last of December, the head of that tribe came [in], and offered to take the oaths, by which he was [to be] comprehended within the indemnity. But he came to a military man, who, not being empowered to tender him the oaths, addressed him to a proper magistrate.'

ᵃ Cf. *Hist.* ii. 88. ᵇ *Ibid.* ᶜ *Ibid.* ᵈ *Ibid.* ᵉ *Ibid.* ᶠ *Ibid.*

---

[1] Macaulay made use of this account; see *Hist.* ed. 1858, vol. vi. pp. 207, 211.

Om. 'and the person . . . past.'

Om. 'came to court . . . design; and'; *and after* 'revenge and' *add* 'as it is surmised intending to.'

For 'he proposed . . . Glencoe' *read* 'represented to the Master of Stair the necessity of making examples.'

Om. 'be shut . . . indemnity and.'

Om. 'in order . . . the rest.'

For 'The king signed . . . about it' *read* 'All this went easily from the king '; *and place from* 'for he was' *to* 'precipitately' *in present tense.*

[*Responsibility for them.*]

[*f.* 68 (*b*)] This shows that Breadalbane was in the secret of that matter. In every letter of the secretary's he gives ᵃ strict orders that no prisoners should be taken ᵃ; he also encouraged Livingstone to go about it carefully, with great assurances of his friendship and kindness when it should be done; and knowing that Livingstone was faithful to the king, ᵇ he expressed in his letters a great zeal for the king's service, as if his designs in this were only to destroy those that were still in rebellion ᵇ and who were expecting assistance from France.

[*The massacre takes place.*]

Cf. *Hist.* ii. 90 (*from* 'In February' *to* 'and escaping ').

[*Callousness of Stair; outcry; investigation.*]

And when this massacre began to raise that outcry which so barbarous a thing had justly occasioned, the secretary writ down (to quiet the persons that were concerned in it) that they had obeyed orders and so had no reason to be concerned at the clamour which was raised; and for his part he was only sorry the execution had not been fuller, for some had escaped. ᶜ This matter was presently published both in France and England; and did cast such a reproach on a government that in all other instances has been very gentle ᶜ, that the king, being still ignorant of the truth of the matter, ᵈ gave an instruction ᵈ by Mr. Johnstone ᵉ to examine the whole secrets [1] of that affair ᵉ; which was done this summer;

ᵃ Cf. *Hist.* ii. 89.   ᵇ *Ibid.* 90.   ᶜ *Ibid.*   ᵈ *Ibid.*   ᵉ *Ibid.*

---

[1] See Appendix VI, *infra.*

ᵃ and then all these letters and orders were showed ᵃ of which the officers concerned have given him copies to lay before the king, which will be showed him when he returns from the campaign. ᵇ This did wonderfully inflame that nation, and put the Highlanders in the best disposition that the Jacobites could have wished for to have revolted again as soon as a fit opportunity should have presented itself ᵇ.

Marlborough is disgraced.

ᶜ About the end of the session of parliament in England the king called for Marlborough's commissions and dismissed him out of his service ᶜ; the king said to myself upon it that he had very good reason to believe that he had made his peace with king James and was engaged in a correspondence with France [1]; it is certain he was doing all he could to set on a faction in the army and nation ᵈ against the Dutch and to lessen the king ᵈ; [and that he] as well as ᵉ his wife, who was so absolute a favourite with the princess ᵉ that she seemed [2] to be the mistress of her whole heart and thoughts, ᵉ were alienating her both from the king and queen ᵉ.

[*f.* 69 (*a*)] The queen had taken all possible methods to gain her sister, and had left no mean unessayed, except the purchasing her favourite, which she thought below her to do; but, that being the strongest passion in the princess's breast, all other ways proved ineffectual, ᶠ so a visible coolness grew between the sisters ᶠ. Many rude things were daily said at that court, and they studied to render themselves very popular, though with very ill success; for the queen grew to be so universally beloved that nothing could stand against her in the affections of the nation.

ᵍ Upon Marlborough's disgrace his wife was ordered to leave

ᵃ Cf. *Hist.* ii. 90.   ᵇ *Ibid.*   ᶜ *Ibid.*   ᵈ *Ibid.*   ᵉ *Ibid.* 91.   ᶠ *Ibid.*
ᵍ *Ibid.*

---

[1] On this see Dartmouth's note to *Hist.* ii. 487; and Macaulay, ed. 1858, vol. ii. pp. 171–2, 176. The corresponding 'suppressed passage' of the *History*, not yet printed, is very curious; and gives an account midway between that of the original Memoirs and the final version.

[2] See Von Ranke, ed. 1868, vol. vii. Appendix ii. p. 187.

the court; this the princess resented so highly that she left the court likewise; for she said she would not have her servants taken from her. All persons that had credit with her tried what could be done to make her submit to the queen, but to no purpose [a]; she has since that time lived in a private house, and [b] the distance between the sisters is now risen so high [b], that the visiting the princess is looked on as a neglect of the queen's displeasure; so that she is now as much alone as can be imagined. [c] The enemies of the government began to make a great court to her [c], but they fell off from her soon; and she fell under so great a neglect, that, if she did not please herself in an inflexible stiffness of humour, it would be very uneasy to her.

[*Russell and the fleet.*]

Before the king went beyond sea [d] the command of the fleet was lodged with Russell [d], but he fell under a great peevishness of spirit; [e] he owned a high friendship for Marlborough after his disgrace, and expostulated upon it with the king in a strain that was not acceptable, for he pressed somewhat rudely to know what secret information there was against him [e]: he had this to say that seemed to justify it, for [f] he had carried the messages between the king and him before the king came into England, and so had formed the confidence between them. Russell was also in very ill terms with Nottingham; and he seemed to be in so ill an humour, in all respects [f], that nothing but the confidence in his fidelity made it reasonable to trust the fleet to his conduct. I had more than ordinary occasion to know this; for [g] I was desired by some of his family to try if I could soften his temper, but without success [g].

England was to have been invaded.

Cf. *Hist.* ii. 92 (*from* 'The king went over' *to* p. 93, *end of paragraph*).
For 'to prepare . . . but we had' *read* 'and he had given orders to make a show of a descent designed against France, which he intimated in his speech to the parliament; but it was visible we had.'

[a] Cf. *Hist.* ii. 91.   [b] *Ibid.*   [c] *Ibid.*   [d] *Ibid.* 92.   [e] *Ibid.*   [f] *Ibid.*   [g] *Ibid.*

For 'king James was preparing for' *read* 'they had contrived, and were very near the executing.'

Om. 'the end of.'

[*f.* 69 (*b*)] *After* 'Luxembourg' *add* 'no doubt by the king's direction.'

After 'intelligence' *add* 'It is certain there is not care enough nor expense enough laid out in this ; and that appeared very signally upon this occasion ; for.'

Om. 'a Scotchman.'

For 'but the heavens . . . such a storm' *read* 'but that which totally broke their design was that for a month together the weather was so rude, and so full in the north, making indeed a perpetual storm.'

After 'there, that' *insert* 'as it stopped them from coming further, so.'

A great victory at sea [off La Hogue].

Cf. *Hist.* ii. 93 (*from* 'On the 19th' *to* p. 95, 'securing the trade').

Om. 'Rooke . . . fault[1].'

Om. 'our men said that.'

For 'but Russell . . . French did' *read* 'which was their ruin ; for those who stood by the sea westward got off. If Russell had lain at anchor that night, as the French did, he had been upon them next morning ; but he.'

For 'A great part . . . pursue them' *read only* 'He sent Ashby to pursue those that went into the Race of Alderney.'

After 'St. Malo's' *add* 'to the river [*f.* 70 (*a*)] Dinant.'

For 'and the other ships' *read* 'and many of the capital ships.'

After 'La Hogue' *add* 'so that if Ashby had been as successful as they were, here had been an end of the French power at sea.'

For 'that if this success . . . that' *read* 'that if, while the consternation that the French were under continued, Russell had followed either to St. Malo's or to Brest.'

For 'But Russell' *read* 'But whether he thought he had done enough by so signal a victory or whether he' ; *and for* 'which he thought . . . upon that' *read* 'or whether the imprisonment of Marlborough, with several other suspected persons, added to his ill-humour, certain it is that.'

For 'the rest' *read* 'the greater part.'

Om. 'a great part . . . was spent.'

For 'came . . . late' *read* 'was proposed.'

For 'about seven thousand . . . St. Malo's, but' *read* 'fourteen thousand was all the strength that England or Ireland could spare, but not above half of these was got ready. If those had been shipped in the first heat, somewhat might have been done ; but as the best part of the summer was over before they could be all shipped, so when they were sent out (on design to try a descent on St. Malo's).'

Om. 'They complained . . . whole fleet.'

For 'two years before' *read* 'when Torrington commanded.'

Om. 'nor seamen.'

---

[1] Burnet no doubt conceived a subsequent prejudice against Rooke, who was in opinion a Tory. See *Hist.* ii. 388–91, and notes; also *Biog. Brit.*, 2nd ed. iii. 35. In the 'suppressed passage' of the *History* which represents the sentence given above the censure is intensified.

A design to assassinate the king discovered.

Cf. *Hist.* ii. 95–6 (*to end of paragraph*).

For 'the design . . . was laid' *read* 'the first design was.'

Om. 'in his ordinary . . . slowly and.'

Om. 'The king of France . . . equal to the post. He,' *for which read only* Barbesieux, that succeeded his father in his employment.'

Om. 'as one . . . French service' *and* 'practices and.'

[*f.* 70 (*b*)] *For* 'both king James . . . Grandval said' *read* 'The blackest part of this was that king James and his queen were.'

For 'one Parker . . . designs' *read only* 'Parker.'

Om. 'for some years'; *and for* 'but being . . . left Paris' *read only* '(was upon the persecution put up [? shut up] and kept a prisoner in the Bastille till April, 1692) writ me a long account of [how].'

Om. 'not knowing . . . court.'

Om. 'This Morel . . . safe to me' (*see supra, line* 13).

Before 'The king gave orders' *insert* 'In Grandval's trial.'

For 'had drawn' *read* 'had been given to draw'; *and for* 'nor was . . . pleased himself' *read* 'or to make him name persons; [and] it is very visible from what is printed that in the interrogatories there was not care enough to circumstantiate the particulars that he told, so minutely as was necessary.'

After 'represented' *insert* 'king James and.'

Namur taken.

Cf. *Hist.* ii. 96 (*to* p. 97, 'waiting on one another').

For 'But though this miscarried, the French' *read* 'But if the French miscarried in this, as well as they were beat at sea (so that the main parts of their design for this year had failed), yet they.'

After 'some days' *add* 'this was a fatal stop.'

For 'his measures' *read* 'the spirit of his army.'

After 'great army' *add* 'And it very much sunk the elevation that the victory at sea had begot in the English.'

For 'The king's conduct . . . it was said, he' *read only* 'It was generally thought that the king.'

For 'this action' *read* 'that' (? the performance); *and after* 'defensive and' *insert* 'for many weeks.'

The battle of Steinkirk.

Cf. *Hist.* ii. 97–8 (*to end of paragraph*).

[*f.* 71 (*a*)] *For* 'At Steinkirk' *read* 'At last.'

For 'a brave attempt' *read* 'very successful.'

For 'and the men . . . done' *read* 'and so much time ought not to have been lost; for all men believed that if it had been better maintained.'

After 'Solms' *add* 'that was the general of the infantry.'

For 'here Mackay . . . principles that he' *read* 'One Mackay in particular ought not to be forgot by me, not so much because he was a Scotchman, as because he was the most conscientious man that I ever knew in an army [cf. *Hist.* ii. 27]; he was in all respects a man of strict morals and.'

For 'The king often observed' *read only* 'it was observed.'

After 'courage. He' *add* 'was lieutenant-general of the foot and'; *and after* 'quality' *add* 'in which young Rouvigny (now made viscount of Galway) told me he was singular.'

For 'that came from England' *read* 'that had been prepared for the descent.'

For 'The command . . . given to' *read* 'But the king put the government of those parts into the hands of.'

For 'who said' *read* 'to see.'

For 'the reputation . . . sunk' *read* 'we suffered much in point of reputation.'

Affairs upon the Rhine.

Cf. *Hist.* ii. 98-9.

[*f.* 71 (*b*)] *For* 'was gained' *read* 'was, as it is given out, gained'; *and after* 'design' *add* 'it was certainly broken.'

Place from 'upon this occasion' *to end of sentence in present tense.*

For 'upon which . . . passed' *read* 'So the rest of the summer was spent in complaints.'

For 'but they were not . . . and' *read* 'they did nothing considerable; they could not so much as cover their own country; for.'

For 'totally' *read* 'surprised and entirely.'

In Hungary.

Cf. *Hist.* ii. 99 (*to* p. 100, 'So the war was still carried on there').

For 'But, though . . . Hungary' *read only* 'There was no considerable action in Hungary.'

For 'lay . . . defensive' *read* 'pretended only to lie on the defensive and to preserve what they had; Waradin was lost before the campaign was opened.'

For 'by the Dutch ambassador' *read* 'by the unskilfulness of the Dutch ambassador.'

After 'Podolia' *add* 'with the castles on the Borysthenes; together.'

For 'Achaia and Livadia' *read* 'Livadia, Achaia, and Thebes.'

For 'the ministers' *read* 'the corrupt ministers.'

After 'another project' *add* 'to which the king had brought the court of Vienna.'

For 'the Ottoman court . . . refused it' *read* 'it had given much trouble to the Ottoman court.'

Om. 'how ignorant . . . court.'

For 'so the war . . . there' *read* 'so that [*f.* 72 (*a*)] the war was like to go [on] there till some great misfortunes should make them listen to the mediation from England.'

[*Trumball's reports and advice.*]

[a] At this time sir William Trumball was come over, [b] who had been ambassador from king James in Constantinople. He was a man of great capacity as well as learning, and had been envoy in France during the persecution [b] and the

[a] Cf. *Hist.* ii. 100.   [b] *Ibid.* i. 769.

scattering the protestants there, for whom he had expressed such tenderness, and to whom [a]he had given so much protection[a], that though the court of England had a due esteem for him, yet they found he was not fit for that post; [b]so he was sent to Constantinople [b] a little before the last revolution in England. [c]The French ambassador came to him and congratulated upon the league[c] both offensive and defensive [d]that was concluded between their masters, and showed him Croissy's letter to him in which it was[d]. This gave Trumball very melancholy thoughts ([e]for he told me this passage himself), and I set it down here as a convincing proof of that matter[e], though both kings have since that time denied there was any such alliance; and it is a point still insisted on here, by the Jacobites, that the nation was cheated into a revolt from king James by the false suggestions of that alliance upon the revolution. Trumball was much pressed to act still as ambassador from England in king James's name, by which our trade must have been ruined; but he refused to act in opposition to the interest of his country and to the present establishment; yet he, who went so far that he might be at a great distance from the storm that he saw ready to break into his country, desired to be recalled. [f]The chief advice that he offered upon his coming over to force the Turks into a reasonable peace was that we should send a powerful fleet into the Mediterranean and destroy the French trade there[f]; this he said would effectuate a mediation more than all our embassies could do; for as long as the French were the masters in the Mediterranean, the Turks considered them chiefly; and as soon as ever we were the strongest there [g]we might then be able either to turn that court, or to form seditions by stopping their trade, and to set Constantinople itself in a flame[g] as oft as we pleased. But this advice has not been yet followed.

[a] Cf. *Hist.* i. 769.　　[b] *Ibid.*　　[c] *Ibid.*　　[d] *Ibid.*　　[e] *Ibid.*
[f] *Ibid.* ii. 100.　　[g] *Ibid.*

And [affairs] in Piedmont.

Cf. *Hist.* ii. 100.

For 'and the French . . . defensive : so' *read* 'and after some motions and amusements.'

For ' with an army ; and ' *read* ' with so considerable a force that.'

After ' betrayed in it ' *add* ' for instead of marching forward (which he might have done which way he pleased upon the first consternation).'

For '[that] there was either a great feebleness or ' *read* 'that either he had not strength enough in his own genius to conduct his affairs, or that [there] was.'

For ' that and . . . provinces into ' *read* ' that province [into], and the prejudice that it received by it.'

[*f.* 72 (*b*)] *From* ' but a ferment' *to end of sentence is in present tense ; for* 'Many months . . . danger ' *read* ' and though the Jesuits' powder has stopped these, yet they have returned so oft that his health was long very broken and uncertain.'

After ' there ' *add* ' likewise.'

For ' and no vintage . . . northern parts ' *read* ' almost no vintage at all.'

[*An earthquake ; a general corruption of manners.*]

Cf. *Hist.* ii. 101–2 (*to end of paragraph*).

After ' Jamaica ' *add* ' with about 2,000 people.'

From ' We were indeed brought ' *to end of sentence is in present tense.*

From ' Yet the reformation ' *to end of paragraph is in present tense ; om.* which some zealous . . . promote,' *and* 'in some places . . . censured ' ; *and after* ' all sorts ' *for* ' of people ' *read* [*f.* 73 (*a*)] ' and parties.'

[*Reflections on the above.*]

It is not safe to argue from our notions to what may be expected from the providence of God, which is an unsearchable abyss ; yet I am often forced to think, that unless God is making use of England to carry on some other great design which he is to bring about, we must be cast into some dismal calamities, which as a furnace may purify us and melt us down ; yet God's ways are past finding out ; they are not as our ways ; because his thoughts are not as our thoughts. But I leave this sad scene and go on [1].

A session of parliament.

Cf. *Hist.* ii. 102 (*to* p. 106, ' trusted by the other,' *at the end of a paragraph*).

For ' The session . . . disadvantages ' *read* ' The parliament met in winter [16]92 ; the first debates were in the house of lords.'

---

[1] A similar passage is among the yet unpublished ' suppressions ' of the second folio volume.

For 'put in the Tower . . . bail, so' *read* 'kept in prison a great part of the summer, and were still under bail when the house met; so great complaints were made of this.'

After 'suspected' *add* 'though contrary to law.'

For 'There was' *read* 'There were some rogues in the gaol that had forged a writing like.' (Cf. *Hist.* ii. 102, *supra.*)

For 'ordered' *read* 'had given orders for.'

For 'passed some votes' *read* 'upon these debates, went high in'; *and om.* 'for detaining some in prison.'

For 'They thought' *read* 'which judged better that.'

For 'was more set on it . . . formerly' *read* 'seemed very much set upon it; yet in both houses it was opposed by the greater part of the ministry.'

[*f.* 73 (*b*)] *After* 'great, that it' *insert* 'was visible it would not pass; so [it].'

For 'The king . . . into the hands of' *read* 'Yet the king, it seems, was not of their minds; for after the thing was kept long in suspense, the king dismissed Russell from the command of the fleet, and put it in commission to.'

For 'the two first . . . it was said he' *read* 'the first of these had not so fair a character as the last had; he was believed to lean much to king James; and Delaval was thought a weak man, who would be much influenced by him; so that it was said Shovel'; *and om.* 'and that . . . anything.'

After 'possessed with it' *add* 'but he took no notice of all this.'

Om. 'both king . . . judgement'; *and for* 'with a . . . smallest matters' *read* 'and [he] went higher than ever against all that were called Whigs.'

For from 'The bills for the supply' *to end of paragraph read* 'In the house of commons the bills of supply went on very cheerfully, so that they gave near five millions towards the charge of the next year's war. But during this session a very ill-humour began to show itself in both houses; the party of Whig and Tory was higher than ever, and showed itself almost in every question.'

For 'The ill-humour . . . made to' *read* 'In the house of lords a party was formed that opposed.'

For 'the king from the Dutch' *read* 'the English from the Dutch. The king had in his speech desired the advice of his parliament; so.'

After 'Steinkirk' *add* '[which] was laid on the count de Solms.'

For 'by a secret management' *read* 'according to what was usual to them.'

For 'and they drew . . . persecuted' *read only* 'and Shrewsbury.'

For 'These lords . . . jealous of the ministry' *read* 'And as all that favoured king James went always with them, so many of the Whigs that were discontented because they had not got what they pretended to.'

After 'money-bills' *add* 'but that they must either be passed or thrown out by them as they were sent up.'

After 'drawn up' *insert* 'they saw plainly afterwards that'; *and after* 'bill' *add* 'upon that account.'

[*f.* 74 (*a*)] *Om.* 'which was . . . pageant.'

For 'that had never . . . civil wars' *read only* 'when they were upon the heads of advices to be offered to the king.'

For 'and they would . . . fall' *read only* 'it was opposed with much zeal.'

For 'in either house of parliament' *read* 'in the house of commons, where the scene of business lay.'

Om. 'The truth was . . . places and pensions.'

For 'When this bill . . . difficulty' *read* 'This was set on by a few in the house of commons, and was opposed by none at all.'

For 'had not strength . . . parties' *read only* 'had not credit enough to stop it.'

After 'establish' *add* 'for ever.'

The triennial bill.

Cf. *Hist.* ii. 106-7 (*to* ' refused to pass it ').

After 'was offered' *add* 'by Shrewsbury.'

For 'within a limited time' *read* 'by or before the first of January next.'

Om. 'in king Edward . . . these acts.'

For 'as a grievance . . . three years' *read* 'till king Charles the First's time.'

After 'insupportable grievance' *insert* 'But.'

Om. 'and were to be made . . . tyranny.'

[*f.* 74 (*b*)] *For* 'so well . . . only of themselves' *read only* 'well, and not to cover themselves from just debts by privilege if they were to continue but for three years.'

Om. 'All that was objected . . . come round.'

For 'yet it was said . . . continue longer. So' *read* 'yet the main design of the act being the dissolution of the present parliament.'

For 'and fixed' *read* 'only they prolonged'; *and omit* 'so that . . . themselves.'

For 'for some time' *read* 'till the end of the session.'

. *from* 'so the session ended' *to end of paragraph.*

A change in the ministry.

[a] Some alterations that were made did in a great measure quiet the murmuring that was like to have risen upon the denial of the bill. [b] Upon the king's coming to the crown all people desired to see the chancery in commission; they fancied it was too great a trust for one man; so it was put in three persons. [c] But as this bred great delays, so the charge of the court was much increased [c] when three sets of servants were to be gratified. [d] Many of their decrees were also much complained of, and were every day reversed [d] by the lords; whereas when one man bore the judgements of the court, he was more circumspect. And the greatest business of all was that, whereas a chancellor is to bear a great part of the load of the government (especially in all related to law and justice), the commissioners, being equal in power, considered themselves only as so many judges in chancery;

[a] Cf. *Hist.* ii. 107.　　[b] *Ibid.* 3.　　[c] *Ibid.* 107.　　[d] *Ibid.*

and never thought on the general concerns of the justice and
policy of the nation. So this whole matter becoming on so
many accounts a common grievance, ªthe king made sir John
Somers, that was his attorney-general, lord keeper. He was
a man that had all the learning necessary to his profession
and a great deal more in other professions. He had great
capacities for business and eminent virtues; he was modest
and gentle to a high degree, so that he had all the patience
and softness which that post required. He had always
stuck to ª the interests of the country, so that ª one side ª
confided entirely in him, and his justice and probity made
him to be not unacceptable to the other party. ᵇ Sir John
Trenchard was also made secretary of state. ᶜ He had been
much concerned in the business of the exclusion, and had
afterwards ᵈ gone into the duke of Monmouth's concerns ᵈ,
but had come in very early to the king, and was made
chief justice of Chester; he was much considered in the
house of commons, and was a dexterous man in business; ᵉ he
was very calm and sedate, and was much more moderate
than could have been expected from a leading man in a party.
The trusting of these men gave a great content to the whole
party. ᶠ There was indeed nothing in the administration
of the present government that pleased the nation so well
as the justice of the bench; [*f. 75 (a)*] for the judges were
generally men of integrity and virtue and competently learned
in their professions ᶠ; so the nominating of the judges depending so much upon the lord keeper, all people reckoned
they should see a succession of able and just judges.

[*Preparations for a descent in France.*]

Cf. *Hist.* ii. 110 (*from* 'But now I go' *to* 'whole nation ').
After 'So' *add* 'immediately.'
For 'this was very acceptable . . . any effect' *read* 'This did so please the
English, that all the anger for not granting the triennial bill did immediately
vanish; and with this the king went beyond sea.'

ª Cf. *Hist.* ii. 107–8.   ᵇ *Ibid.* 108.   ᶜ *Ibid.* i. 548.   ᵈ *Ibid.* ii. 108.
ᵉ *Ibid.*   ᶠ *Ibid.* 5.

[Affairs on the Rhine.]

Cf. *Hist.* ii. 110 (*from* 'The French had attempted' *to* 'the like success').

For 'and by it Franconia . . . Rhine' *read* 'but they had taken no care of the Rhine.'

After 'the like success' *add* 'but count Horn yielded Furnes and Dixmuyden more easily to them' (see *supra*, p. 377, *Hist.* ii. 98).

Affairs in Flanders.

Cf. *Hist.* ii. 110 (*from* 'The campaign' *to end of page*).

For 'In the meanwhile . . . with the States' *read* 'and if Liège had been taken, it was given out that Maestricht would have been besieged next, to have struck the more terror into the Dutch ; whom the French were trying by all possible practices to draw into a separated peace ; and who had reason given them to be jealous of England, by the humour that had lately appeared in both houses against them.'

Intrigues of Halewyn [the younger].

There was also a secret negotiation set on by the burgo-master of Dort, brother to that Halewyn whom I have formerly mentioned [1]. It was believed that he had hoped to have succeeded Fagel (he being then the pensioner of Dort), and that he was in an ill-humour ever after that disappointment. He went secretly into Switzerland and treated with Amelot the French ambassador for bringing about a peace. Amelot promised him that one should be sent to him from France to concert a project and the methods of composing it ; who came soon after, but [brought] no project. So this matter was in its first fermentation, when it was discovered ; Halewyn and Roberti (the Frenchman) confessed the whole matter without torture. Halewyn was condemned to a perpetual imprisonment, and Roberti was to remain prisoner during the war, and after that to be banished the States' dominions. The elder Halewyn was suspected to be in the matter, and was long under arrest ; but no proofs appearing against him he was set at liberty, but put out of all his employments ; for the suspicion lies still very heavy [*f.* 75 (*b*)] upon him since it was known that he had his brother very much under his management.

---

[1] See pp. 179, 198, 200, 251-2, *supra*.

[Affairs in Flanders resumed.]

Cf. *Hist.* ii. (*from beginning of* p. 111 *to end of paragraph*).

And [affairs] on the Rhine.

Cf. *Hist.* ii. 111 (*from* 'The dauphin' *to* 'all this campaign ').
Om. 'the town . . . resistance.'

For from 'The French were not able' *to end of sentence read* 'That town was sacked, and from thence de Lorge was moving towards Frankfort ; but he was obliged to retire, and so they joined ; and in a little time the dauphin came up to them.'

For 'but no action . . . campaign' *read* 'but that is all that this campaign has hitherto produced upon the Rhine.'

In Spain.

Cf. *Hist.* ii. 111 (*from* 'The French had better' *to end of paragraph*).
Om. 'and less opposition.'

After 'Rosas' *add* '(which commands a bay ; but I do not know whether it is a good station for ships or not).'

And Piedmont.

Cf. *Hist.* ii. 111 (*from* 'Affairs in Piedmont' *to* 'the siege of Pignerol ').
For 'they expected' *read* 'it seems they expected.'
After 'And then' *add* 'in the beginning of August.'

For 'and he was master . . . siege of Pignerol' *read* 'so now he is master of it ; but it is uncertain whether he will abandon it, or whether he intends to besiege Pignerol itself or not.'

The battle of Landen.

Cf. *Hist.* ii. 112[1] (*to* p. 113, 'the battalions he had sent to Liège ').
For 'lay long' *read* 'lay for many weeks.'

[*f.* 76 (*a*)] *For* 'and his conduct . . . enemy's' *read* 'which lay just behind him.'

For 'with the loss . . . officers' *read only* 'with a vast loss.'

For 'in a place . . . gave way' *read only* 'some bodies both of German and Spanish horse giving way.'

For 'and so the French . . . cannon : but the king' *read* 'In conclusion, when he saw the French could not be beaten out, he retired, leaving most part of his cannon behind him ; and so.'

After 'out of reach' *add* 'and the other parts of his army which came off in different bodies, came all together, and joined him in a few days.'

For 'that it was thought . . . Boyne' *read only* 'that [they] have very much increased his reputation.'

For 'hours' *read* 'days.'

For 'with a vastly . . . officers' *read* 'in officers and soldiers.'

---

[1] The commencement of p. 112 is not indicated in the edition of 1833.

For 'The king's behaviour . . . side' *read* 'The king has never, upon any occasion, signalized himself more eminently than upon this; so that his enemies, as well as his own army, acknowledge that both the supporting the action so long, and the prudent retreat when it was necessary, were wholly due to him.'

Om. (*here*) *from* 'and some other bodies' *to end of paragraph.*

[*Position of affairs; remarks on Waldeck's death.*]

And the French have not undertaken anything since that time; and in this state both armies lie when I am now writing: they are moving from one camp to another, watching one another's motions. This campaign has proved the more honourable to the king because he alone has conducted it; for prince Waldeck, who had first formed him to war and [a] had a great genius though with a very bad fortune in military matters, [b] had died the former winter [b]. He was the only man with whom it was observed that the king advised[1]; and so, upon his death, many dreaded that the king's way of resolving with himself, without talking [*f.* 76 (*b*)] with any of his general officers, might have proved as fatal as it was distasteful to his officers, especially the English; who could not bear the contempt (as they fancied it to be) of never being let into any of the counsels, though they were raised to great posts in the army.

Affairs at sea.

Cf. *Hist.* ii. 114–6 (*to* 'trading part of the nation').

For 'two great ports' *read* 'two ports where their great ships lay'; *and for* 'fleet together' *read* 'great ships from Toulo[n]'; *and after* 'again' *add* 'every year.'

For 'was watching this carefully' *read* 'were known to have an eye on this in winter.'

For 'a spy . . . certain persons' *read* 'one being.'

For 'that kingdom' *read* 'this kingdom' (*probably a clerical error*).

Om. 'new excuses . . . made; for.'

For 'a new delay . . . staying' *read* 'but he was still delayed.'

For 'Yet these . . . design' *read* 'Yet it was still believed that they were to come about. In conclusion.'

Om. 'from England . . . designs.'

[a] Cf. *Hist.* i. 328.   [b] *Ibid.* ii. 150.

---

[1] For the relations between the two consult D. P. L. Müller's *Wilhelm III von Oranien und Georg Friedrich von Waldeck*, Haag, 1873.

For 'But at the secretary's . . . fleet, but' *read* 'And to complete our misfortunes, we did for some weeks after this know so little of the French motions, that we believed them to be still in Brest; and'; *and after* 'believed' *insert* 'So that.'

Om. 'when they thought . . . danger.'

[*f.* 77 (*a*)] *For* 'but from the Toulon . . . information' *read* 'but from D'Estrees' fleet. And his scouts, that were out, discovering a great many ships, and taking a fire-ship, the captain told them such a plausible story of fifteen ships of war that lay there, to go and join D'Estrees, that notwithstanding the improbability of it (for he told them that three French admirals were there), yet it was too easily believed; and though Rooke was for standing out in the sea, yet the merchants pressed that they might hold on their voyage. The Dutch and most of the captains were of the same mind.'

For 'some got to Gibraltar' *read* 'some few, but of great value, got to Gibraltar.'

After 'sail away' *add* 'for water.'

For 'first to . . . England' *read* 'to Kinsale with many of the merchants.'

After 'practicable' *insert* 'So after they had stayed for some time there.'

Om. 'and in some other places.'

For 'the trading part of the nation' *read* 'the whole nation.'

[*Suspicions of the ministry; Rochester; his attitude towards the new bishops; their conduct.*]

Cf. *Hist.* ii. 116 (*from* 'The appearances' *to* p. 118, 'very uneasy in his great post').

For 'rose high . . . office' *read only* 'went much higher.'

Om. 'It was said, that'; *and for* 'many particulars . . . acted like enemies' *read* '[These] were such amazing things, that I never knew men's minds more possessed with the belief of the king and the nation's being betrayed, than at that time. This made people lay not only all these [but many other?] particulars together; [which] (with the putting many men in subaltern employments through the [*f.* 77 (*b*)] whole kingdom, who discover so violent a hatred to the government, and talk and act as if they were open enemies) are like to raise much heat in the approaching sessions.'

From 'Our want of intelligence' *to end of paragraph is in present tense; for* 'a good share' *read* 'the heaviest part'; *for* 'the Whigs' *read* 'all that are called Whigs'; *for* 'for being naturally . . . company' *read* 'for, as he allows himself great liberties in drinking, so.'

After 'queen herself' (*omitting entirely* 'I was in some sort . . . would have pursued') *proceed from* 'He talked' *to* 'methods they were taking' *in present tense; for* 'which he had so much promoted in' *reading only* 'of' *and omitting conclusion of paragraph.*

For 'The king had left . . . church' *read* 'The matters of the church are now almost'; *and after* 'hands' *add* 'for the king has turned them over to her.'

From 'so he devolved' *to end of passage* ('great post') *is in present tense; after* 'prudence' *add* 'and so due a weighing of men's merits, that this gives indeed great hopes'; *for* 'for a party was formed . . . who set themselves' *read* 'for the clergy seemed to have combined'; *after* 'promoting them' *add* 'with a strictness that we never saw before'; *om.* 'if it was not . . . way'; *for* 'He did not enter . . . all they could' *read* 'His not entering into an union with the ministry, but living in a great freedom and equality with them, makes that they seem all to dislike him'; *and for* 'He grew . . . post' *read* '[so] that if he could decently do it, he would much more cheerfully retire from that post, than he came into it.'

[*Burnet's own experience.*]

[a] I have also received my share of mortifications[a]; I continue still (I thank God) as I began; going every year round the greatest part of my diocese, preaching constantly, and wasting my wife's estate besides the spending my whole income; yet I find the high [b] sort of churchmen cannot be gained; till the toleration is broke and a persecution of dissenters is set on foot, they will still conclude that the church of England is persecuted or at best neglected: and they cannot with any patience bear a man that has declared himself so openly against those things[b] as I have done; and yet by the pains I take [c] to gain upon that party[c] I have [d] fallen under the displeasure of the other party; [e] so hard a thing it is in such divided times to resolve to be of no parties; for a man of that temper is protected by none, and pushed at by a great many[e]. For, in the last sessions of [*f.* 78 (*a*)] parliament, some began to find fault with a notion by which some divines had urged obedience to the present government; that here was a conquest over king James, and that conquests in a just war gave a good title. This some had carried so far as to say, in all wars (just or unjust) conquests were to be considered as God's transferring the dominion from the conquered to the conqueror; yet all these writers had taken care to distinguish between a conquest of the nation and a conquest of king James; the latter being only that which was pretended. That, as they said, gave the king all king James's rights. This doctrine was condemned by a vote of both houses, and a book that had set it forth with great modesty and judgement[1] was in a heat condemned to be

[a] Cf. *Hist.* ii. 118.   [b] *Ibid. supra.*   [c] *Ibid.*   [d] *Ibid.*   [e] *Ibid. infra.*

[1] *King William and Queen Mary Conquerors*, the anonymous tract attributed to Charles Blount, of which Macaulay gives so spirited an account (*Hist.* ed. 1858, vol. vi. pp. 367–9).

burnt; and because, in a treatise that I had writ immediately after I was a bishop to persuade my clergy to take the oaths [1], I had only mentioned this as a received opinion among lawyers and put it in among other topics, but had put the strength of all upon the lawfulness and justice of the present establishment, they fell upon that little book and ordered it likewise to be burnt. So it looked somewhat extraordinary that I, who perhaps was the greatest assertor of public liberty, from my first setting out [2], of any writer in the age, should be so severely treated as an enemy to it. But the truth was the Tories never liked me, and the Whigs hated me because I went not into their notions and passions; but even this and worse things that may happen to me shall not, I hope, be able to make me depart from moderate principles and the just asserting the liberty of mankind [3]. I now leave all that remains of our affairs to the approaching sessions which I see ᵃcoming on with great apprehensions of the ill effects that are like to rise, partly from the king's humour, partly from the ill-conduct of our affairs, and from the bad disposition of our minds ᵃ.

[*The affairs of Ireland.*]

Cf. *Hist.* ii. 118 (*to* p. 119, *ending with* 'Christian princes' *at conclusion of next paragraph*).

After 'the lord lieutenant was' *insert* 'so little fitted to struggle with peevishness, and so.'

For 'and were much sharpened against them' *read* 'and took all possible advantages to fall on them.'

For 'The protecting . . . necessary' *read* 'Those who protected the Irish said they did it for the good of the nation.'

After 'ill administration' *insert* 'in almost all parts of the government.'

After 'stores' *add* 'and of other oppressions, in all which it was thought that Sidney was too remiss and too gentle to those that were complained of.'

For 'in England, which drew' *read* 'here also in both houses; but at that

ᵃ Cf. *Hist.* ii. 118.

---

[1] 'A pastoral letter writ by . . . Gilbert, Lord Bishop of Sarum, to the clergy of his diocese, concerning the oaths of allegiance to K[ing] William and Q[ueen] Mary . . . 1689.'

[2] Burnet's memory seems to have failed him at this point; see *supra*, pp. 32-9; and *infra*, Appendix I.

[3] This passage ('it looked somewhat extraordinary . . . mankind') is quoted by Macaulay (*Hist.* ed. 1858, vi. 372 note) in his account of this affair (*ibid.* 369-72). He comments on the expressive reticence of the published *History*.

time the session was near an end; so all they did was that the matters were laid before the king in.'

[*f.* 78 (*b*)] *For* 'lord Capel . . . Essex' *read* 'sir Henry Capel, lately made a lord'; *for* 'sir Cyril . . . Duncombe' *read* ' Mr. Duncombe that had been envoy in Sweden, and sir Cyril Wyche, who had been secretary to several lords lieutenants; they are all men of virtue and probity, and of good capacity for affairs.'

After 'disorders' *add* 'and immoralities'; *after* 'poverty' *add* ' or other miseries'; *and after* 'expected' *add* 'They were rather worse than ever.'

After 'vacant see' *add* 'The queen was then in the administration.'

After 'understood' *add* 'by many hands.'

After 'fit to promote him' *add* 'Some attempts were made to purge him, but the bad character could not be so easily taken off.'

[*The William and Mary college.*]

[a]"Another piece of the queen's piety was finished this year[a], which probably may have great and good effects. [b]There came over a minister from Virginia[b], who was a man of another stamp than commonly go to plantations; since, to our reproach, it must be owned, that for [the] most part very undeserving men and such as can find no sort of employment in England go over; and the bishops of London[1] have never yet thought fit to take care of those colonies. Mr. Blair had gone over in king James's time and became quickly the most acceptable man that had been in Virginia for a great while. He observed that the want of schools and a college there was a vast prejudice to all their youth. [c]He thought those born there had from the climate all the advantages of genius[c], while they lay under the greatest disadvantages by an ill education. He also thought that [d]a good foundation in Virginia might be of great use to all the other plantations. [e]So after he had engaged the planters to a very liberal subscription, he came over with a project of a public school and college, which might be endued out of some branches of the king's revenue there that went all into private hands, and had never been accounted for; [f]yet those who were concerned in the plantations having made

[a] Cf. *Hist.* ii. 119.   [b] *Ibid.*   [c] *Ibid.* 120.   [d] *Ibid.*   [e] *Ibid.* 119–20.
[f] *Ibid.* 120.

[1] Titular diocesans of the plantations at the period in question.

advantage of those matters, here was great opposition to be
looked [for] [a]. The archbishop of Canterbury did highly
approve of this motion; and laid it before the queen, [b] who
liked it so well [b] that she gave orders to have it particularly
examined; and informed herself so exactly of the whole
matter that she was able to argue with such as did oppose it;
[*f.* 79 (*a*)] who though that they clogged it with all possible
delays, yet were not able to hinder it. [c] The queen saw such
a probability in it of having a very good effect on the
morals and religion of those colonies, and perhaps of preparing men to propagate the gospel among the natives, that
she resolved to set it on; and she very easily persuaded the
king upon his coming over to be of her mind. So the patent
founding a college, together with a good revenue for its endowment of £600 a year; was passed [c]; and the good man who
projected it is now gone over to see it put in execution.

[*Virtues of the queen; Burnet's reflections on the same.*]

Cf. *Hist.* ii. 133 (*from* 'The queen continued' *to* p. 134, 'I had large opportunities to observe ').

For ' The queen continued to set' *read* ' Thus the queen was not satisfied with
setting '; *and after* ' parts of it ' *add* ' but.'

Om. 'both to read and.'

From ' but she freed' *to end of passage is in present tense.*

After ' promise she made' *add* ' and so careful to remember well the promises
she makes.'

After ' opportunities to observe ' *proceed as follows :*

As I am sensible that I perhaps return too oft to this, so
I acknowledge it is so [d] pleasant to myself, that as it is almost
the only thing that supports my thoughts against the melancholy prospect which all other views of our affairs gives [d], so,
since I intend this work not only as a bare recital of history,
but as a means of conveying the best instructions that I can
to posterity, I think the setting out this pattern in the best
and fullest lights the most useful part of my whole work.
And as I thank God that I do still feel the sense of the
Christian religion and of the reformation of it from popery to
be that which lies nearer my heart than all the things of this

[a] Cf. *Hist.* ii. 120.   [b] *Ibid.*   [c] *Ibid.*   [d] *Ibid.* 134.

world put together; so [a] I cannot without a very particular joy see that person whose present circumstances mark her out to be both the defender and perfecter of that blessed work to be such, in all the parts both of her private deportment and the public administration of the government, that she seems to be in all points fitted for that work for which she seems to have been born [a].

[*And the affairs of Scotland* [1].]

But now I leave this subject to give an account of [b] a very disorderly scene [b] with which I will end my writing for this time, and that is of Scotland. The king had ordered Johnstone to go down to Scotland in summer 1692, [*f.*79 (*b*)] and to bring him up a particular account of the state of that kingdom. He found the whole nation so full of [c] distrust of the men that had been newly put in the government [c] that they thought the king had abandoned Scotland. [d] When the invasion was looked for, they had taken so little care to conceal their inclinations [d], that those who were true to the king intended if any such thing had happened to have begun with them, and seized on them. And [e] it looked to be unaccountable to take men out of a plot, a part of which was to persuade many to take the oaths to the present government with design to betray it, and yet to trust the kingdom to them, for they were now the masters of the counsels. [f] Hamilton was discontented and came no more to town [f]; and many others absented themselves, so that a very small force sent from France would have mastered that kingdom. [g] The presbyterians saw they had lost the king and began to be sensible of their folly, and were willing to carry themselves more gently for the future [g]. Johnstone gave them all possible assurances that upon their submission and moderation they might regain the king's confidence; he also engaged [h] Hamilton to return to the council [h], and got some men whom the presbyterians trusted to be put in employments. He laid

[a] Cf. *Hist.* ii. 134.   [b] *Ibid.* 120.   [c] *Ibid.*   [d] *Ibid.*   [e] *Ibid.*   [f] *Ibid. infra.*   [g] *Ibid. supra.*   [h] *Ibid. infra.*

[1] See for all this Appendix VI, *infra*.

before the king [a] the correspondence between France and Scotland ; in all which the easiness of the undertaking was often insisted on if no time were lost [a]. And indeed the generality of the gentry and nobility became so open in declaring for king James, that [b] it was necessary to put some stop to it [b]. More forces seemed necessary, and some parts of the revenue were near falling off ; which were granted for years. So [c] a session of parliament [c] was proposed ; this was much opposed by the other party, who knew they could not be the masters there : yet the state of affairs made the king resolve on it. [d] Hamilton was commissioner [d], and Johnstone went down, who principally managed the sessions, and acquired by it a very high reputation ; for he showed great abilities in all debates, with great dexterity in the conduct of business, and carried everything as the king had desired ; he laid before the parliament all the letters that had been intercepted. Most of them were writ by Neville Payne, from which a design of bringing in a foreign force plain appeared. He made this out by so many circumstances that the parliament was convinced of it, and upon that [e] voted supplies [e] for maintaining 6,000 men for eighteen months. [f] All went visibly by the strength of the presbyterian interest [f] ; yet, according to the king's desire, Johnstone kept them from making a representation against the ministry, which they had a great mind to have done.

[*Ecclesiastical affairs in Scotland.*]

Cf. *Hist.* ii. 121 (*from* ' The matters of the church ' *to* p. 122, *end of paragraph*).

For ' than was expected ' *read* ' beyond what could have been expected from presbyterians.'

After ' scandal ' *add* ' in their life or doctrine.'

[*f.* 80 (*a*)] *After* ' assurance ' *add* ' by a day prefixed ' ; *and om.* ' owning . . . adherents.'

For ' when the session was near an end ' *read* ' The parliament also addressed to the king to call a general assembly ; and thus all things went very smoothly ; only [when] the time limited to their sitting was near expired '; *and om.* ' upon the many letters . . . intercepted.'

For ' in many of his own letters . . . reconciling one ' *read* ' ready to be offered ; but both the commissioner and the chancellor had reason to apprehend that their sons were in the plot, and Payne said, as long as his life was his own he would say nothing ; but if it were once the king's, he would save it by telling

[a] Cf. *Hist.* ii. 120.   [b] *Ibid.*   [c] *Ibid.* 121.   [d] *Ibid.*   [e] *Ibid.*   [f] *Ibid.*

all he knew. This terrified many who were concerned; his pretences for a delay were easily admitted; and his trial put off. So the session was ended, which was the smoothest and the kindest the king had held in any of his dominions. But upon the conclusion of that meeting, when it was expected that the king should have given orders for the levies, and for the other parts of the administration, he has not yet thought fit these three months to take any notice of their affairs or to give any orders about them.'

Place from ' so they could claim ' *to end of paragraph in present tense; and for* ' so they could claim . . . benefices' *read only* ' so that they are now out of their churches by law.'

Om. ' so they were easily . . . whispers.'

[*General view of the situation; with which Burnet concludes for the time, Sept.* 9, 1693.]

[Mean]while he seems averse to those whose interests are twisted with his, and grows jealous of them. This becomes now the subject of all people's observations and censure; and seems to be the greatest of all those dangers that hang over his government. This winter is like to prove critical; the Whigs are studying to inflame all people against the ministry; and as that is a thing in which the house of commons is always very easily engaged, so the misfortunes of this summer gave a handle to all attempts against them; and the Jacobites will go into anything that may embroil us, hoping that the king's stiffness on the one hand and the eagerness of the commons on the other may throw us into distrusts and confusions. [a] Middleton has been sent over to king James by the party, [b] who found great fault with a declaration that he had prepared for the invasion of the last year in which he promised nothing and pardoned nobody. It was indeed calculated to so high a note that it is plain from it that his council then thought that the design was so well laid that it could not miscarry; so that he talked in the strain of a conqueror that had all things in his power. But this year he has sent over one, [c] that as far as words can go, give[s] a full security, for he pardons all persons, and promises everything. [*f.* 80 (*b*)] And this the party think they have in their hands, to offer to the nation [c], if they can but once throw us into convulsions. Arise then, O God, and

[a] Cf. *Hist.* ii. 122.   [b] *Ibid. infra.*   [c] *Ibid.* 123.

perfect thou that which concerns us : and do thou prosper and establish the work of thy hands among us. So I give over on the ninth of September, 1693.

[*Burnet resumes his pen in April,* 1695.]

I do begin again in April, 1695, to prosecute this history. There was a new misfortune that concluded the campaign of 1693 ; ᵃ Charleroi was besieged ᵃ in September.

Charleroi taken.

Cf. *Hist.* ii. 113 (*from* ' the country' *to* ' at last ').

[*Situation in France.*]

Cf. *Hist.* ii. 113 (*from* ' Thus the French' *to* p. 114, *end of paragraph*).

For ' but their successes . . . balanced by' *read* ' but at home '; *and om.* ' that.'

For ' strict' *read* ' very good.'

For ' steps' *read* ' faint steps.'

After ' posture' *add* ' The allies entered into a new concert for the year [16]94, and there was little to be feared, either in Holland or Germany.'

[*Overtures to Spain.*]

Cf. *Hist.* ii. 123 (*from* ' We were also' *to end of paragraph*).

For ' We were also . . . Madrid' *read* ' In Spain their affairs were so low that they were in a great disposition to hearken to a proposition made them by the French, which seemed much to their advantage.'

For ' the grandees of Spain' *read* ' the greatest part there.'

After ' allies' *add* ' at least for once [1].'

For ' watching their conduct' *read* ' the mending of matters.'

Om. ' The Spaniards . . . Madrid.'

A session of parliament [*expected* ; *a change in the ministry*].

Cf. *Hist.* ii. 123 (*from* ' The king came over' *to* ' satisfaction of the Whigs,').

Before ' The king' *insert* ' When '; *and before* ' saw' *insert* ' quickly.'

[*f.* 81 (*a*)] *For* ' so that went off' *read* ' so that matter lay in suspense for some months.'

For ' yet the king . . . assurances that' *read* ' but in conclusion '; *and for* ' of the Whigs' *read* ' of the nation.'

Sunderland in credit.

Cf. *Hist.* ii. 123 (' But the person . . . could and would support him ').

For the initial ' But' *read* ' Yet, after all' (i. e. all his former conduct?).

ᵃ Cf. *Hist.* ii. 113.

---

[1] The use of ' once' (i. e. ' one time' or ' a time') as a synonym for ' some time,' though not recognized by Johnson, is still common in Somersetshire.

Om. 'who, by his long . . . ever had'; *before* 'he had brought' '*insert* 'It was thought'; *and for* 'both trust and satisfy' *read* 'comply with.'

[*Comments made.*]

His behaviour in former reigns made people conclude that he could not be firm himself to principles of public liberty ; and therefore, though they were glad that, at any rate, the king was brought about, yet a deep jealousy still remained of the king's own inclinations.

[*The Whigs in power ; a session.*]

Cf. *Hist.* ii. 124 (*from* 'so the Whigs' *to* p. 125, 'end of April ').
Om. 'perhaps.'
For from 'so that the king' *to end of paragraph read* 'so they grew to be very hearty for the king when they saw he intended to put himself into their hands ; they resolved to use him well ; for men grow to be either patriots or courtiers as they happen to be well or ill used by the government. All the money that was necessary for the war was granted by this session of parliament ; and.'
Om. 'at least in bank-notes.'
For from 'It was visible' *to end of paragraph, read* 'This matter was so strongly argued on both sides, that, I confess, I understand it not enough to form a sure judgement upon it ; I do rather think the bank will be an advantage to the nation, as it is certainly a great one to the king, since they furnish him with money on much easier terms than it was formerly borrowed on.'
For 'took up . . . long' *read* '[was] the most troublesome business of this session.'
For 'it seemed . . . get out' *read* 'it was said that it was not sent out.'
For 'for it was now the . . . favour' *read* 'for it was become the business of a party ; [so] the examination held long in both houses ; in conclusion they were acquitted.'

[*Visit of the prince of Baden.*]

[*f.* 81 (*b*)] [a] The prince of Baden came into England this winter ; he stayed above two months [a], much longer than he had intended ; [b] he was treated by the king in an extraordinary manner and at a vast expense [b] ; he seemed to be much pleased with it, and he was the most universally esteemed stranger that I have ever known come into England.

[*The Tories attack the judges ; eulogy of Somers.*]

[c] The Tories began now to grow very backward in the king's business.   Rochester and Nottingham obstructed it [c] as much

[a] Cf. *Hist.* ii. 125.   [b] *Ibid.*   [c] *Ibid.*

as any, though more covertly at first, but afterwards they laid aside the mask and opposed everything openly. ᵃ The judges gave great credit to the government by their fair and impartial administration of justice ; and no man had ever kept the seal ¹ with a higher reputation than Somers ᵃ. He showed great justice and temper, discretion and good judgement, in everything that came before him ; and was in all respects the man whom I have ever known in a high post with the least censure or reproach cast on him. He is really as much and as universally esteemed as he deserves to be ; and though the enemies of the government see what strength and lustre he gives to it, and so hate him in proportion to that, yet they have not hitherto found matter for slander to work upon ² ; but the other ᵇ judges have been often and unmercifully but most undeservedly fallen upon by the enemies of the government ᵇ ; but there was so little grounds for all their complaints that were made that they suffered little by them in the esteem of the nation.

[*The bishops censured ;*] *debates concerning divorce.*

Cf. *Hist.* ii. 126 (*from* ' The bishops' *to* p. 127, *end of paragraph*).

Om. entirely ' it was visible . . . despised and ' ; *and for* ' who designed . . . betray it' *read only* ' not true to the interest of the church of England.'

After ' parliament' *insert* ' in order to the opening of which I must take a large compass ' ; *and om.* ' it related . . . him to marry again ' (*see infra*).

For ' the party that was injured ' *read* ' either party.'

For ' At that time . . . marriage only as ' *read* ' Upon that occasion many profane people began to question the whole doctrine of marriage ; they said it was.'

For ' the consequence . . . have ' *read* ' that' (i. e. the king's divorce) ; *and for* ' many ' *read* ' some.'

After ' allowed ' *add* ' This being premised, I come now to the present time. The duke of Norfolk had married the earl of Peterborough's daughter, and being very ill satisfied with her conduct had parted with her and moved,' *&c., as in Hist.* ii. 126, *supra* ; *then return to* p. 127, ' a great party ' ; *omitting* ' In the duke . . . Jacobite ; so.'

[*f.* 82 (*a*)] *For* ' who were thought engaged in lewd practices ' *read* ' who had been in secret engagements with her, or that were in the like with other women.'

After ' in the bill ' *insert* ' ; every step that the bill made was disputed with much heat.'

ᵃ Cf. *Hist.* ii. 125–6.   ᵇ *Ibid.* 126.

---

¹ The transcript erroneously reads ' the seals.'

² The attacks on Somers date of course from 1699.

After 'too plain' *add* '; though a great deal was brought to lessen the credit of the witnesses.'

After 'reasons' *add* 'and it happening that.'

Om. 'and that the contrary . . . dark ages'; *and* 'though some . . . were so.'

For 'Here was . . . inferred' *read* 'Here was a plausible colour for saying.'

After 'Rochester' *add* 'and some others.'

For 'The bill . . . time' *read* 'The bill could not go on in the session of [16]92 ; and it being again taken up in that of [16]9[3] ¹ it so plainly appeared that it could not be carried through, that it was let fall'; *and for* 'of either side' *read* '[by] the divines of that party.'

The campaign, 1694.

Cf. *Hist.* ii. 127 (*from* 'The king went' *to end of* p. 128, 'everywhere').

For 'The king . . . May' *read* 'The sessions being ended, the king went beyond sea.'

After 'they lay' *insert* 'for a great while'; *and after* 'that they intended' *insert* 'after the country was eat up.'

For 'in the ordinary . . . one another' *read* 'in marches and countermarches.'

For 'This design . . . Huy, who' *read* 'The king followed his detachment, but finding the design lost he sent another, commanded by the duke of Holstein Ploen (whom he had brought to command the Dutch forces in the room of prince Waldeck). He was ordered to attack Huy; which he did so successfully that [he].'

After 'bishop' *insert* 'who had stuck firm to the alliance.'

For 'but that for . . . favour' *read* 'The cardinal of Bouillon had tried what interest he could make, but with no success. The dispute was soon over; it was judged at Rome, after some delays, in favour of the elector of Cologne; for though.'

Om. 'upon the submission . . . 1682.'

For 'The confederates . . . but lay' *read* 'And with this the campaign in Flanders ended; great armies laying'; *before* 'advantageously' *insert* [*f.* 82 (*b*)] 'so'; *and for* 'without any action' *read* 'that it was not possible to engage in any action.'

For 'in the usual manner' *read* 'at the same rate.'

Om. 'which the French . . . battle.'

Om. 'only there appeared . . . Savoy.'

For 'were beat . . . posts' *read* 'lost a small battle.'

For 'The court of Madrid' *read* 'There was an inconceivable terror at the court of Madrid; they.'

Om. 'All this was intended . . . make them.'

Our fleet in the Mediterranean.

Cf. *Hist.* ii. 129 (*from* 'but to prevent' *to end of paragraph*).

For 'a great fleet . . . home' (*last sentence of passage*) *read* 'and the whole measures, that France was in, are disconcerted by this means. And, while I am writing this, the news is come, that the great convoy which carried

---

¹ The transcript erroneously repeats '[16]92.'

to them stores and bomb vessels, together with all necessaries till September, is happily arrived ; so that we are now in expectation of somewhat considerable, besides the preserving of Spain.'

Attempt on Camaret.

Cf. *Hist.* ii. 129 (*from* ' But while' *to end of* p. 130).

For ' Camaret . . . Brest' *read* ' a neck of land in Camaret Bay which might have been easily kept.'

[*f.* 83 (*a*)] *After* ' Russell' *add* ' in the house of lords.'

After ' 600 men' *add* ' but a wrong time of the tide was taken, and their orders were changed just as they were going to land' ; *and for* ' and ' *read* ' He.'

For ' it was needlessly . . . undertaking' *read* ' that nothing could be done.'

Om. ' very fit . . . soldiers.'

For ' so that . . . good service' *read* ' That, joined with his other qualities, made him appear so dangerous a man, that some thought his loss might be more easily borne with.'

For ' must . . . effects' *read* ' might have made an end of the war.'

The French coast bombarded.

Cf. *Hist.* ii. 131 (*to* ' sunk our enemies ').

For ' did great execution' *read* ' set them on fire. The loss they made was considerable ; but the terror that this gave them put them into greater distractions.'

After ' had first begun' *add* ' This destruction was the more considerable because it was the first essay we had made in that way, [*f.* 83 (*b*)] and that success in it would probably encourage us to go on in another season, and to become more expert in the conduct and management of such designs for the future.'

For ' The campaign . . . arms' *read* ' Thus this campaign ended the most to our advantage of any we had during the war.'

The affairs of Turkey.

Cf. *Hist.* ii. 131 (*from* ' The war in Turkey' *to* p. 132, *end of paragraph*).

For ' The war in Turkey . . . made themselves masters of' *read* ' The only confederate the French had was also very unfortunate at the end of the campaign. The Venetians did not only take Ciclut[1] in Dalmatia, but.'

For ' that wanted people. The Turks' *read* ' which it was believed they intended to do. But some months after, the Turks.'

For ' but their abandoning . . . balance' *read* ' but this has come to us only through their hands while I am now writing this, so it is not authentical ; it may be perhaps given out to cover their abandoning of Scio, which they did in a very few days after the second engagement.'

Om. ' as they did every year.'

After ' provisions ; ' *for* but' *read* ' so it was thought that Caminieck would quickly fall. But a few months after.'

---

[1] A frontier fort ; the Turks strained every nerve to take it. See Daru, *Histoire de . . . Venise,* v. 119.

Om. 'their queen's ... jealousy'; *and after* 'business' *add* '[So] the Tartarians made great excursions, and much waste, and got safe home again.'

After 'Temeswaer' *add* 'It is true all Germany was put in a mighty terror, [for].'

For 'the grand signior ... present' *read* 'Whether the grand signior's death will change their counsels, and if the present successor will carry on the war more successfully, or take more pains to compass a peace, must be left to time to determine it.'

[*French attempts to procure peace.*]

Cf. *Hist.* ii. 132 (*from* 'At the end' *to end of paragraph*).

[*f.* 84 (*a*)] *For* 'the States sent ... errand ; and' *read* '[so] that this attempt had not success enough to make it certain whether it was made or not ; some affirming that men of note came as far as Maestricht desiring passports to come further, and that the States sent some to meet with them secretly, but that upon seeing their powers and instructions passports were denied them ; while the whole matter has been disowned and denied by the French emissaries among us ; they.'

A session of parliament.

[a] The king came over in the beginning of November, and the parliament was opened with a calmer face than had ever yet appeared in any session. The supplies which were demanded amounted very near to five millions, and were agreed to without any opposition [a]; but the party that was against the court put their strength to [b] the opposing of good and easy *fonds* for the money; everything that looked like an excise was desired [? decried] [b]; and though some steps were made in some of those propositions, yet they were all laid aside ; but in conclusion, after a long and tedious session, the *fonds* were all found and clauses were put in the act, of a public faith, for making them good according to the estimates that were set upon them.

An act for triennial parliaments.

In this parliament a bill passed which by all the present views we have of things will be a great happiness and security to England. There were no limits yet set to the continuance of a parliament, so that our princes, finding one to their mind, might continue it, and practise so [on ?] the members of it as long as they pleased ; and since this had been the method in

---

[a] Cf. *Hist.* ii. 132–3.   [b] *Ibid.* 133.

king Charles the Second's time, and was generally believed to
be the practice of the present reign, it was thought reasonable
to put an effectual stop to all such methods for the future.   So
ᵃ a bill was brought in for frequent parliaments ᵃ, for yearly
sessions, and a new parliament every third year ; but many
thought there might be as much danger from too many as
from too few sessions of parliament.   This had been in debate
two former sessions, but the court had stopped it ; now the
act was prepared only ᵇ with a relation to a new parliament
every third year ᵇ without any clause for an annual session,
ᶜ and the present parliament was to be dissolved at the furthest
in the beginning of the year 1696 [1] ; to this the royal assent
was given.   It was very acceptable to the nation ᶜ to come
to a new election of their representatives every third year ; it
would oblige the members to have more regard to their own
credit in common matters of justice, as well as to their voting
in the house, when, at the end of three years, they were to be
all canvassed over again in their countries.   It was also hoped
that when it was evident that parliaments could not be of
a long continuance ᵈ men would not be at such an excessive
charge in procuring themselves to be chosen.   This had very
much corrupted the whole nation ; and it seemed reasonable
to believe that those who bought the votes of others intended
to sell their own when they should come to be chosen ; so it
was hoped that when men came to be chosen without expense
the character they were in and the reputation which they had
would come again to be prevailing considerations in elections ;
and this is all that can be wished for, in order to the recover-
ing the credit and integrity of a house of commons which was
now so much lost, that it was generally believed that corruption
prevailed to such a [*f.* 84 (*b*)] degree that even in the com-
monest matters money carried everything ᵈ.

ᵃ Cf. *Hist.* ii. 133.   ᵇ *Ibid.*   ᶜ *Ibid.*   ᵈ *Ibid.*

---

[1] Some such ambiguous term (which might indicate either Jan. 1 or March 25 of the year 1696, N. S.) no doubt accounts for Burnet's discrepant statements as to the determining date (cf. *Hist.* ii. 133 and *ibid.* 160). Both dates are really wrong ; the statute as eventually passed points to November, 1696.

[*The treason bill.*]

^a A bill for regulating trials of treason was much pressed in this session ^a upon this particular occasion.

Trials in Lancashire examined.

Cf. *Hist.* ii. 141 (*from* 'Lunt, an Irishman' *to end of* p. 143).

Begin 'There had been a discovery of treason in the former summer by an Irishman Lunt,' &*c.*, &*c.* ; *om.* 'of a mean understanding [1]'; *and for* 'letters and messages' *read* 'instructions and commissions.'

For 'so he' *read* 'so there was reason to believe that he.'

After 'present government' *add* 'with much officious zeal.'

Om. 'the imposture . . . in discovering.'

After 'houses for arms' *add* 'some few were found.'

After 'depositions' *add* 'which the ministry had kept very secret and.'

[*f.* 85 (*a*)] *Om.* 'very idly'; *and for* 'to make a fortune . . . among many till' *read* 'to be another Oates, and to spread his discoveries far till.'

For 'this was sworn . . . given to him' *read* 'Now though he denied this, yet two witnesses affirmed it against him.'

After 'Chester' *add* 'together with some of the king's learned counsel.'

For 'of late' *read* 'in all my time, at least.'

After 'found to be' *add* 'in a great measure.'

For 'after them' *read* 'after the first day.'

For 'examined into by' *read* 'brought under a long examination in.'

After 'proceedings' *add* 'with the concurrence only of two others, who did them but little honour.'

[*Complaints of the bank.*]

Cf. *Hist.* ii. 144 (*to* 'shaken in another').

For 'When this design . . . set up' *read* 'Great noise was also made'; *and for* 'which began . . . credit' *read* 'which had been settled in the former sessions.'

The bad state of the coin.

We had fallen under another real and great mischief; there had been for six years together ^b such a general clipping of money that it was fallen above a third part below its just value; ^c and it was not possible to give an effectual remedy to this, but by a recoining the whole money of England and the having no money to pass but what was milled. This required a great *fonds*, and that could not be come at in the end of a session;

---

^a Cf. *Hist.* ii. 141.   ^b *Ibid.* 140.   ^c *Ibid. infra.*

---

[1] The corresponding 'suppressed passage' of the *History* (preserved in the Bodleian autograph) is very curious.

D d

so Rochester, who together with Nottingham [a]led everything which might obstruct business, [b]made a loud complaint of this; yet all that it produced was only an act with stricter clauses and penalties against clippers; [*f.* 85 (*b*)] it did very much alarm people, and sunk the value of our money at a time when it could not be effectually cured. [c]A great point was [thus] carried by those who were now engaged in an opposition to the government[c]; and it appeared very evidently that those who had pretended to a zeal in general for the prerogative could act against it with as much heat as any others had ever done when they themselves had not the management of it.

Discoveries of corruption.

Cf. *Hist.* ii. 144 (*from* 'Towards the end of the session' *to* 'expelled the house ').

Begin 'But to conclude all that relates to this session of parliament, towards,' *&c.*

For 'Upon this' *read* 'This coming with a general complaint of corruption everywhere.'

For 'the secretary to the treasury' *read* 'Mr. Guy, who had been secretary to the treasury both in king Charles' and king James' time, and had also got in again in this reign' (cf. *Hist.* ii. 144, *infra*).

For 'turned out of his place' *read* 'another got his place, though it is generally believed he has it only in trust for him.'

Om. 'many were the more . . . because'; *and* 'he had held . . . methods' (*see supra*).

For 'But the house . . . further' *read* 'So from a very casual discovery the house resolved to enquire into corruption.'

For 'so that full . . . appeared' *read* 'but besides this, a great deal had been given secretly both by the chamber and by the orphans; of which no discovery has been yet made.'

[Foley becomes Speaker; his character.]

[d]And Mr. P[aul] Foley was chosen Speaker[d]: though the court named Littleton. [e]Foley is a man of integrity[e] and of particular notions, to which he is much addicted. He is zealous for the present government, but [f]much dissatisfied with the administration. [g]He had set up for a patriot[g]; he opposed most things; and he had been every year one of the commissioners for the public accounts.

[a] Cf. *Hist.* ii. 140, *supra*.　　[b] *Ibid. infra.*　　[c] *Ibid.* 141.　　[d] *Ibid.* 144.
[e] *Ibid.*　　[f] *Ibid.*　　[g] *Ibid.* 109.

[*The East India company scandals.*]

Cf. *Hist.* ii. 145–6 (*to* ' desired a present trial ').

For ' the greatest part . . . among ' *read* ' that this had been between the court and.'

For ' for the two preceding . . . stifle this enquiry; but' *read only* ' so they resolved to enquire into that matter '; *and for* ' curiosity . . . enquiries' *read only* ' The curiosity of an enquiry will always prevail.'

For ' and was like . . . came in, and' *read only* ' he '; *and after* ' matter' *add* [*f.* 86 (*a*)] ' This act passed and the day came.'

Om. ' that should disgrace . . . favourites.'

For ' There were indeed presumptions' *read* ' Only it appeared by other examinations '; *and for* ' £5,000 ' *read* ' 8,000 guineas.'

For ' felt that he was' *read* ' is.'

For ' while the act . . . house of lords ' *read* ' in opposing the act.'

For ' but now all had broke out . . . Bates swore, that he' *read* ' and now both Bates (who had managed the matter between him and Firebrace, a man employed by the company) and he himself told a very incredible story; that Bates.'

After ' keep it to himself' *insert* ' but that Bates desired he would order one of his servants to receive the money, which had been done ; the money being kept by the servant till it was restored.'

For ' it did also appear . . . come at' *read* ' yet that servant, in whose breast the whole matter lay, and who, it seems, had not so tractable a conscience as others had who were examined in this matter, was of the sudden conveyed out of the way'[1] (cf. *Hist.* ii. 146, *infra*).

For ' he, to prevent . . . justification ' *read* ' he had the tacit permission of the lords to go and speak to them; which he did.'

After ' the nation' *add* ' and this government'; *and for* ' in terms . . . to himself' *read* ' in terms that seemed to assume too much to himself.'

Om. ' from which . . . in the end.'

[*Conclusion of the matter; the session ends.*]

[a] The articles were brought to the lords ; all was denied by the duke of Leeds[a]; but it was too late in the session. So [b] the matter was hung up till another session[b]; and it came to be generally believed that the chief design of this enquiry was to blast him. [c] An act of grace came in the end of all[c]; and thus the session of parliament was concluded. There was nothing of importance either in Scotland or Ireland within this period that deserves to be [*f.* 86 (*b*)] mentioned;

[a] Cf. *Hist.* ii. 146.   [b] *Ibid.* 147.   [c] *Ibid.*

---

[1] A ' suppressed passage ' of the *History*, still legible in the autograph and transcript, resembles this.

so I come to end this part of my relation with a very melancholy scene. I have kept it last that I may conclude with it, and enlarge upon it without interrupting the thread of the history.

Tillotson's death.

Cf. *Hist.* ii. 134-5 (*to* 'shortened his days').

For 'It was preceded . . . November' *read* 'About the middle of November Tillotson, archbishop of Canterbury, was taken with a fit of a dead palsy.'

For 'but not thinking . . . too long' *read only* 'but neglected it for many hours.'

After 'will of Heaven' *add* 'thus he died.'

For 'it was more decent . . . safe' *read* 'it became me.'

Om. 'affectation.'

For 'sublime' *read* 'true'; *and om.* 'his thread . . . solid'; *for* 'it was thought' *read* 'I believe.'

[Sancroft's death.]

Cf. *Hist.* ii. 135.

Om. 'and despicable.'

For 'that some . . . raise' *read* 'which the Jacobites had set on foot.'

Om. 'a parliamentary . . . and therefore.'

For 'and all that joined . . . tacit yielding to it' *read only* 'And now, by Tillotson's death, the colour of a separation was taken away'; *for* 'to embroil church and state' *read* 'to separate'; *and om.* 'and no arguments . . . from it.'

[Tenison succeeds.]

Cf. *Hist.* ii. 136 (*from* 'Both king' *to* 'desire Tenison').

For 'so generous . . . good works' *read only* 'He was eminently generous and charitable[1].'

Om. 'she spoke . . . earnestly for him.'

For 'and all concurred . . . no enemies' *read* 'so they [i. e. the Whigs?] all concurred [*f.* 87 (*a*)] to desire Tenison, who I hope will prove very worthy of it.'

[Small-pox in London.]

Cf. *Hist.* ii. 136 ('The small-pox . . . never had them').

The queen's sickness and death.

Cf. *Hist.* ii. 136-8 (*to* 'but that which I knew to be strictly true').

Om. 'but the next day . . . off.'

After 'following' *add* 'which was the 20th of December'; *and om.* 'her illness . . . on her that.'

For 'imputed . . . Radcliffe' *read* 'generally imputed to the unskilfulness and wilfulness of Radcliffe, an impious and vicious man, who hated the queen much, but virtue and religion more. He was a professed Jacobite; and was by many

---

[1] The baselessness of the insinuation against Sancroft, here inserted in the *History*, is well shown by D'Oyley, *Life of Sancroft*, ii. 89-92.

thought a very bad physician; but others cried him up to the highest degree imaginable[1].'

After ' too late ' *add* ' All symptoms were bad; only the queen still felt herself well[2].'

Om. ' he came, on . . . passed it.'

For ' The day after ' *read* ' The second day of her illness '; *and for* ' a most tender passion ' *read* ' the tenderest passion I had ever seen in man '; *and for* ' he burst . . . hope of the queen ' *read* ' he cried out very violently ; he told me he had no hope.'

For ' could scarce refrain from ' *read* ' bursting out into '; *and for* ' This hope ' *read* ' [so] there was an inconceivable joy spread everywhere.   It.'

Om. ' whatever effect it might have.'

Om. ' it went . . . for.'

[*f.* 87 (*b*)] *For* ' composed . . . die ' *read* ' gave herself wholly to prayer '; *for* ' but said ' *read* ' but wished she might not ; she '; *and om. here* ' and said often . . . prayer.'

For ' such passages ' *read* ' such prayers [and] such passages.'

After ' ineffectual ' *add* ' she said all the while, she found nothing did her good but prayer ; in that and nothing else she found a sensible [effect or recruit[3]] that refreshed even her body.'

For ' and some words . . . break ' *read* ' some broken words of delirium came sometimes from her.'

Om. ' I will add . . . character ' *and* ' without . . . rhetoric.'

[*Burnet's own grief for her loss.*]

I never admired any person so entirely as I did her.   In the course of above eight years' very particular knowledge of her, I never saw any one thing that I could have wished to be otherwise than it was in her.   The more I knew her, I still saw the more reason to admire both her understanding, her piety, and her virtue, without discovering the least defect or fault in her.   The purity and the sublimity of her mind was the perfectest thing I ever saw ; I never felt myself sink so much under anything that had happened to me as by her death ; it is a daily load upon my thoughts, and gives me great apprehensions of very heavy judgements hanging over us, for I am afraid that in losing her we have lost both our strength and our glory[4].

[1] This passage has been quoted by Miss Strickland ; and a similar, though even stronger character is among the still ' suppressed ' passages of the *History*, second volume.

[2] The queen's freedom from suffering is mentioned more than once in Burnet's *Essay* on her memory.

[3] The words in brackets were inserted by Burnet, in emendation of the transcriber's ' reflect.'   A similar passage occurs in the *Essay on . . . the late Queen.*

[4] Two passages, containing similar

[*The king's grief.*]

Cf. *Hist.* ii. 138 (*from* 'The king's affliction' *to* 'long with him').

[*His good resolutions.*]

He began then the custom which he has observed ever since very exactly, of going to prayers twice a day; [a] he entered upon very solemn and serious resolutions of becoming in all things an exact Christian [a], and of breaking off all bad practices whatsoever[1]. He expressed a particular regard to all the queen's inclinations [and?] intentions; he resolved to keep up her family, and to carry on her charities; and that he might pursue that design (which of all others was the deepest in her) of encouraging a pious and a laborious clergy, and might [*f.* 88 (*a*)] also deliver himself from importunities which he was not at all times able to resist, [b] he granted a commission[2] to the two archbishops, the bishop[s] of Lichfield, Worcester, Ely, and myself, to recommend fit persons to all ecclesiastical preferments [b]; and did charge us to seek out the best and worthiest men we could find, that such and only such might be promoted. This has a very good appearance, and if it is continued by the king, and is well managed by us, it may have happy effects; though I confess my hopes are so sunk with the queen's death that I do not flatter myself with further expectations. If things can be kept in tolerable order, so that we have peace and quiet in our days, I dare

[a] Cf. *Hist.* ii. 138.   [b] Cf. *Life* appended to *Hist.* ii. 715-6.

---

fears, are deleted, both in the Bodleian autograph and the Bodleian transcript of the *History*, and very similar apprehensions conclude the *Essay on . . . the late Queen.*

[1] There can be little doubt that this expression refers to the intrigue with Elizabeth Villiers. It is surmised that the 'scrutoir' brought by Tenison to the king contained the 'letter of strong but decent admonition' seen by Lord Hardwicke (see note to *Hist.* ii. 138), and that this was a remonstrance (reserved till no personal animus could be suspected) against the relation in

question. Certain it is that p. 23 of Tenison's very significant sermon 'On Holy Resolutions,' preached before the king two days after his wife's death, and published by special royal command, contains a marked allusion to the perils of illicit ties; and that William within the year gave an almost ostentatious countenance to the marriage of Elizabeth Villiers (see Mr. Seccombe in *Dict. Nat. Biog.* lviii. 326).

[2] Incidental allusions to this will be found in *Hist.* ii. 285, 317, and Luttrell, iii. 466. It was signed in April, 1695.

look for no more ; so black a scene of providence as is now upon us gives me "many dismal apprehensions ᵃ. But I must now turn from this gloomy prospect¹.

[*Deaths of the dukes of Hamilton and Queensberry.*]

Cf. *Hist*. ii. 149.

For ' the former winter' *read* ' within some months of one another.'

After 'enemies' *add* 'They were both proud and imperious, much set on raising their families, and very prosperous in it.'

After 'genius' *add* 'and better notions ; but the other understood our law better.'

Lord Halifax died; [*Burnet lays down his pen for the time, May 2, 1695*].

In England ᵇ the marquis of Halifax died in April, 1695. He had gone into the interests of the Jacobites after he was put out of employments, and though he took care to preserve himself from dangerous or criminal engagements, yet it very visibly appeared that he studied to embroil matters all he could ᵇ, and to shelter that party upon all occasions. ᶜ His spirit was restless ᶜ, and in spite of all his pretences to philosophy ᶜ he could not bear to be out of business ᶜ. He struck up, as all discontented men do, to be a patriot, but he discovered too manifestly what lay at bottom ; ᵈ his vivacity and judgement did seem to sink very much ᵈ; but while he studied to support all with wit and mirth, without considering what became his age and post, he lost a great deal of that esteem which he had formerly both as to his parts and his integrity. ᵉ He died of a gangrene occasioned by a long neglected rupture². When he was warned that his condition

---

ᵃ Cf. *Hist*. ii. 138.   ᵇ *Ibid*. 149.   ᶜ *Ibid*.   ᵈ *Ibid*.   ᵉ *Ibid*. 149–150.

¹ See p. 405, note 4. Burnet's lugubrious prophecies became, as time went on, a fertile source of amusement to his more malicious contemporaries ; see *More News from Salisbury*, 1714.

² A most amusing story concerning the unwillingness of Halifax to accept the death-bed ministrations of Burnet, ' lest,' as he himself said, ' he should triumph over him after his death,' i. e. claim for himself the credit of any penitence the marquis might express, is related by Cunningham (*Hist*. i. 146) ; whose rooted antipathy to Burnet compels us, however, to receive the anecdote with some ' grains of salt.' An allusion to the dying declarations of Halifax can be almost certainly traced in a very excellent letter from Burnet to Dr. Colbatch, written about eighteen months later (Brit. Mus. Add. MSS. 22908, ff. 14, 25).

was hopeless he showed a great firmness of mind, and composed himself to die with a calm that had much of a true philosopher in it. He professed himself to be a sincere Christian, and expressed great resentment of many former parts of his life, with settled resolutions of becoming quite another man, if God should have raised him up[a]. With this I end writing on the 2nd of May, 1695.

[Burnet resumes his pen.]

I begin writing again in February, [16]96[1].

Lords justices [appointed] in king's absence.

Cf. *Hist.* ii. 150 (*from* 'The seven lords justices were' *to end of paragraph*).

At the beginning insert 'As soon as the business of the parliament was over, the king settled the government during his absence in seven persons, who, according to the states [? style] of Ireland, were called lords justices' (cf. *Hist.* ii. 149).

Om. 'and they avoided . . . necessary' (*see infra*).

[*f.* 88 (*b*)] *After* 'preference' *add* 'They assumed no sort of state, and went nowhere in ceremony; so that except at the council board, where it was unavoidable, they had no sort of distinction upon them [*see supra*]. This made that.'

After 'trusted with them' *add* 'The king was naturally so jealous that as they had observed in the queen's administration a great tenderness in doing nothing but upon express directions and orders, so.'

After 'bounds' *insert* 'and to be very slow and cautious.'

Om. 'till they had . . . exactly' *and* 'because . . . orders.'

For 'for though . . . disorder, when' *read* 'for we being absolute masters at sea everywhere, the Jacobites were quiet, seeing that.'

The campaign in Flanders.

Cf. *Hist.* ii. 150.

Om. 'Luxembourg . . . winter, so.'

For 'An attempt was made on . . . lines' *read* 'It seemed of importance to take . . . lines; so an attempt was made upon it.'

Om. 'who was . . . before this' (*vide supra*, p. 385).

Namur is besieged.

Cf. *Hist.* ii. 150–2 (*to* 'came and joined the king's army').

For 'his [Vaudemont's] army' *read* 'his little army.'

[a] Cf. *Hist.* ii. 150.

---

[1] i.e. February, 1696, N.S.; as Johnstone was dismissed (see *infra*, p. 415) in January, 1696, N.S.; and the bill mentioned *infra*, p. 414, note 1, passed the Commons, February 23, 1696, N.S.

For 'but without cause . . . lost' *read* 'he laid the blame on the duke of Maine, the French king's beloved son.'

For 'the garrisons' *read* 'two advanced garrisons that.'

[*f.* 89 (*a*)] *Om.* 'without either colour or shame.'

For 'and sold . . . disgrace' *read only* 'but the contrary appeared afterwards' (cf. *infra*).

After 'Villeroy' *add* 'finding he could attempt nothing else.'

For 'the assistance . . . of them' *read* 'some small assistance.'

After 'time to retire;' *for* 'but' *read* 'it was pretended that this was a necessary reprisal upon our bombarding their sea-towns, and [he].'

Om. 'and troops . . . garrisons.'

After 'credit' *add* 'he could do nothing.'

After 'Villeroy;' *for* 'and' *read* 'The prince of Baden at the same time sent'; *and for* 'came and joined' *read* 'which came in time to join.'

Namur taken.

Cf. *Hist.* ii. 152–3 (*to* 'according to promise').

For 'with an army of' *read* 'his army was [*f.* 89 (*b*)] not much above.'

For 'the French gave it out' *read* 'and the French sent many surgeons to lie in the neighbourhood of their army, giving it out.'

After 'during the siege; and' *add* 'all the military men do affirm that.'

Om. 'Cohorn . . . perfection during this siege.'

For 'Boufflers was first' *read* 'so after he had been kept a few days he was.'

Great disorders in the army.

Cf. *Hist.* ii. 153 (*from* 'The officers were tried' *to* p. 154, *end of paragraph*).

For 'The officers . . . they were raised' *read* 'The officers were tried by a council of war; Ellenberg, who commanded in Dixmuyden, was beheaded; and O'Farrell, who commanded in Deinse, was broke with infamy [cf. *Hist.* ii. 152]. Many of the other officers were also broke. Men rise' (*putting remainder of sentence in present tense*).

For 'corruption . . . army' *read* 'employments are generally sold.'

For 'the king did not approve . . . severity' *read* 'it has been oft laid before the king, but he is little touched with it, and does not seem to apprehend the consequences that it may have'; *for* 'subalterns' *read* [*f.* 90 (*a*)] 'subaltern officers and their soldiers.'

Casale is surrendered.

Cf. *Hist.* ii. 154 (*from* 'In Italy' *to end of paragraph*).

Om. 'and in conclusion, that duke himself.'

After 'in Europe.' *add* 'More did not happen in Piedmont.'

We are everywhere masters at sea.

Cf. *Hist.* ii. 154 (*from* 'Our fleet was' *to* p. 155, 'squadron became useless').

For 'the French . . . than once;' *read* 'We designed to destroy Marseilles and Toulon if it was but possible; but the French had been at an incredible charge to defend them; and, besides that, we had no calm nor favourable weather. Our fleet came no sooner before them than'; *for* 'him' *read* 'them'; *and for* 'he himself' *read* 'Russell.'

For ' to our affairs' *read* 'to all the affairs of the allies.'

After ' no progress' *add* ' and could not maintain what they had formerly got ; so '; *and after* ' abandoned ' *add* ' both Hostalrick and.'

Om. ' for he had regiments . . . board.'

Om. 'of themselves . . . place ; for'; *for* 'in Catalonia' *read* 'in a hot and deserted country'; *and after* ' Barcelona ' *add* ' which was the only undertaking that could answer the charge and fatigue they were at.'

After ' own channel' *add* ' commanded by the lord Berkeley.'

[*f.* 90 (*b*)] *After* ' Grandville' *add* 'a big town.'

Om. ' (whose father . . . title)' *and* ' to secure . . . merchants.'

For ' he was . . . man ' *read* ' but he is a man, though of great courage yet very extravagant.'

For ' of merchant ships ' *read* ' of our merchantmen.'

The losses of our merchants.

Cf. *Hist.* ii. 155-6.

After ' also taken' *add* ' by Nesmond.'

After ' ocean' *add* ' and few ships are taken in so open a sea.'

For ' at a million ' *read* ' much above a million.'

For ' our factory' *read* ' the factory that the African company had '; *and om.* ' he took . . . had there.'

The war of Hungary.

Cf. *Hist.* ii. 156.

[*f.* 91 (*a*)] *For* 'some slight engagements' *read* 'two actions that followed one another.'

For 'in which' *read* ' the first ended almost equally ; in the second.'

For 'but nothing followed upon them' *read* ' But next to the Spaniards they are the least to be believed, in the news that is publicly given out by them, of any in Europe ; and, in that, follow the maxims of all commonwealths, magnifying their advantages, and concealing their losses.'

Affairs in Scotland.

Cf. *Hist.* ii. 156–7 (*to* ' a new pardon to be passed for him ').

For ' the marquis of Tweeddale' *read* 'Tweeddale, now created a marquis.'

After ' commissioner' *add* ' and Johnstone went thither by the king's direction.'

For 'supply' *read* 'levies.'

For ' in enquiring into it' *read* ' in ordering a further enquiry to be made into it.'

For ' without . . . matter' *read* ' but that some motions would be made to enquire into it.'

For ' This was looked on as ' *read* ' This looked ill, and seemed.'

For ' yet when it was complained of. . . examining into it' *read* 'but high motions were made about it in parliament, all which were quieted [when].'

For ' a new practice' *read* 'a treasonable practice.'

After ' castle of Edinburgh' *add* ' and he was ordered to be proceeded against for high treason '; *and om.* ' to say anything . . . credit with them.'

[*State of parties in Scotland*[1].]

[a] But now a great party was formed in the parliament of a very odd mixture; the high presbyterians and the Jacobites joining together to oppose everything [a]; and this was managed by those who knew the secret of Portland's intentions, which made some conclude that he had a particular reason to hinder the enquiry into the Glencoe business; and has brought a great load of censure and reproach, not only on himself, but on the king. [b] The opposition that was made was not strong enough to carry the vote; but great heats arose [b] upon it, and the managers of it were much encouraged by Portland's emissaries. In conclusion [c] the report of the whole enquiry was made in parliament [c], after it had been delayed long enough for the king to have countermanded it if he had thought fit so to do; but the court would not venture upon that.

[*The Glencoe report; the episcopal clergy.*]

Cf. *Hist.* ii. 157 (*from* 'by that it appeared' *to* p. 158, 'promised them by the act').

After 'was laid' *add* 'by the Master of Stair[2].'

[*f.* 91 (*b*)] *After* 'secretary of state's' *add* 'private.'

After 'law : this' *insert* 'was much opposed; but it.'

For 'with some address' *read* 'by Johnstone with great address.'

For 'and by a very zealous . . . were brought' *read* 'but this would have had little effect if Johnstone had not gone to several of the northern counties, where the episcopal clergy were both the most numerous and the most esteemed; he engaged above seventy of them.'

A Scottish East India company.

- Cf. *Hist.* ii. 158 (*from* 'Another act' *to* p. 159, *end of paragraph*).

For 'that has already . . . worse after it' *read* 'that is like to have some consequences; and therefore I have reserved it to the last place.'

For 'and with all . . . projects' *read* 'with the highest privileges possible.'

Om. 'at court.'

For 'There was one Paterson . . . East India trade might be set up; so' *read* 'And one Paterson, a Scotchman of mean extraction and no education, but very good sense, with great notions of trade, and a compass of project (for he projected the Bank of England), had been long in the West Indies; and had a secret that he valued very much; it is thought to be a rich mine somewhere

[a] Cf. *Hist.* ii. 157.   [b] *Ibid.*   [c] *Ibid.*

---

[1] See *infra*, Appendix VI.   [2] 'Suppressed' in *Hist* vol. ii.

in America. So he got the West Indies to be put in the draught of the act, as well as others took care of the East Indies. Johnstone heard there was a design projecting among the merchants, of which nothing was communicated to him[1]; but he (apprehending that this might disorder the king's affairs in England) acquainted him with it; and whereas, by all former instructions, full power had been given by our kings to their commissioners to pass such bills of trade as should be offered to them[2].'

Parliament in Ireland.

Cf. *Hist.* ii. 159 (*from* 'In Ireland' *to* p. 160, 'entirely on himself').

[*f.* 349 (*a*)] *For* 'he was too easily . . . end in it' *read* 'and, as he was naturally a vain, as well as a weak man, some who hoped to govern him, and Ireland by his means, set him on[3].'

For 'of severe . . . administration' *read* 'of severer tempers; they favoured the English, but would not opp[ress][4] the Irish; and took little pains to court the *mobile.*'

For 'all the English in Ireland' *read* 'all that came from Ireland.'

Om. in loco 'was made lord deputy and'; *and for* 'this was agreed to' *read* 'and he was so much supported by the Whig party at court, that the other two were recalled, and he was made lord deputy.'

After 'removes' *add* 'among the judges and in some other employments.'

For 'who had' *read* 'who were believed to have.'

For 'who was beginning . . . house of commons' *read only* 'it was moved.'

For 'by a majority of two to one' *read* 'by a great majority; above 140 were for him, and about 70 only were against him; so that matter fell.'

For from 'at so great a distance' *to end of next paragraph read* 'at a great distance from one another; and in that broken state does Ireland lie at present; two factions are formed in it, which seem to be the following a maxim that the king had set to himself, in all his affairs, as if *Divide et impera* were a sure method to keep all in a balance and in a dependence on himself. But the state of his affairs is such, that he is much liker to lose all than to gain any by this means.'

New parliament in England.

Cf. *Hist.* ii. 160 (*from* 'As soon' *to* 'high favour he was in').

For 'intended' *read* 'left the army, designing'; *and for* 'long' *read* 'many weeks.'

For 'till Lady Day' *read* 'yet one winter more[5].'

[*f.* 349 (*b*)] *For* 'all men except the merchants' *read* 'the nation.'

For 'Thus' *read* 'As soon as the king came over, [by] a proclamation.'

---

[1] This contradicts Dalrymple, *Memoirs*, ed. 1790, vol. iii. part iii. book vi. p. 129.

[2] After the words 'trade of England' (see *Hist.* ii, end of p. 158 and beginning of p. 159) f. 91 (*b*) of Harl. MSS. 6584, and, with it, no. 2 in Dr. Gifford's arrangement, come to an abrupt end; nor is anything further of Transcript A forthcoming. The narrative is however continued for a few pages by Transcript B; f. 349 (*a*) of which begins at the same point.

[3] A 'suppressed passage' of the second volume.

[4] The transcript has 'oppose.'

[5] See *supra*, p. 400, note.

[*The king's behaviour; elections; the session begins.*]

The country came in very thick to see the king; for the taking of Namur had raised his character very much; but though " he forced himself to a little more civility than was natural to him, yet his cold and disobliging way had too deep a root in him not to return too oft and too deep upon him ". The elections went generally for men that loved the present constitution. In many places, those who pretended to be chosen put themselves and their competitors likewise to a great charge; and everywhere there was more spent than could have been expected in elections to a parliament that could not sit above three years. ᵇ The Jacobites were so generally decried that very few of them were chosen; but many others were chosen, who ᵇ though they were resolved to preserve the constitution against France and king James, yet some from their inclinations to republican principles, others from dislike of the king's methods, ᶜ were in no good temper with relation to the administration of affairs. Generally they were men of estates, and many of them were young men ᶜ. At their first opening, the court, seeing a great disposition in many to continue Mr. Foley, would not raise a heat by opposing him, that so [? so that] he ᵈ was chosen Speaker. The demands of the court were very great ᵈ; five millions were asked to carry on the war, and ᵉ all was granted and lodged on good *fonds* ᵉ in as calm a manner as could have been expected. ᶠ The state of the coin was also considered; the difficulty of the remedy occasioned great and long debating upon this; many were for raising the value of the money ᶠ, and this seemed to be so specious that it is scarce to be imagined how many were inclined to follow it; for certainly both our exchange with all other nations must rise, as well as the price of all things whatsoever, as much as money is raised above its just value; so that it might well be the interest of tenants to have the money raised; yet it was unaccountable how a parliament that consists all of men of estates could give any favour or even a patient hearing to

ᵃ Cf. *Hist.* ii. 160.　　ᵇ *Ibid.*　　ᶜ *Ibid.*　　ᵈ *Ibid.* 161.　　ᵉ *Ibid.*　　ᶠ *Ibid.*

such a motion; yet this stuck long and went [*f.* 350 *(a)*] on slowly, though the ᵃ nation was everywhere so much alarmed with the apprehensions of the calling in of the clipped and bad money, that few would take money in any payment; the markets were not supplied and all things at a stand, that if there had been ill-humour then stirring in the nation, many disorders might have been justly looked for in the different parts of the kingdom; but none happened, to the great disappointment of the Jacobites, who were full of hopes upon this occasion ᵃ

[*System of recoinage adopted.*]

Cf. *Hist.* ii. 161 (*from* 'All came in the end' *to end of paragraph*).
Om. 'wise and happy.'
Om. 'thought' *and* 'that it.'
For 'happily settled . . . apprehended from it' *read* 'despatched in the parliament; but many are still full of fears, lest there may come some new disorders in the execution of it, and that the new money will not be ready in time.'

[*The treasons bill.*]

Cf. *Hist.* ii. 161 (*from* 'The bill of trials' *to* 'the royal assent').
Om. 'as no doubt it was' *and* 'were so desirous . . . down to them, they.'

[*Election bills.*]

Cf. *Hist.* ii. 161–2 (*to end of paragraph*).
Om. 'and the house judged the matter.'
Om. 'it had been happy . . . last was'; *and after* 'future parliaments' *add* 'Another bill was brought in regulating elections, of which I shall say nothing in this place, because though the commons have done with it the lords have not yet agreed to it ¹.'

[*Complaints of the East India act.*]

Cf. *Hist.* ii. 162 (*from* 'Great complaints' *to* 'in England,' *end of first clause*).

[*The king's response; changes in Scotland ².*]

The king made an answer that did very much disoblige all his ministers in Scotland; ᵇ he said he had been ill-served in Scotland, but he hoped remedies should be found [*f.* 350 *(b)*] to the inconveniences of that act. And a few days after that he turned out both the secretaries ᵇ, and it is to be believed

---

ᵃ Cf. *Hist.* ii. 161.   ᵇ *Ibid.* 162.

¹ This Act was no doubt that exacting a qualification in real property from all candidates. William refused the royal assent, April 10, 1696 (see *supra*, p. 408, note; Macaulay, vii. 319–22, 404–6; *Hist.* ii. 181).
² See Appendix VI, *infra*.

that [a] Tweeddale [a] is also to be [b] turned out [b]; and some others were also turned out of the treasury. So this opportunity was taken to make [c] a great change of the ministry of Scotland [c], and a new set of men are put in who will generally depend on Portland ; for as he had that nation once wholly in his hands, so he seemed uneasy that he had let it go out of his dependence. The enquiry into the Glencoe business gave great offence, and as [d] motions concerning that matter had been ill entertained [d], so it was visible that Johnstone had lost his favour for his zeal in that matter ; [e] which made it be concluded that it was some way favoured either by the king [e] or Portland ; and thus, though the enquiry that had been made into it by the parliament had cleared the king of it, and left the load wholly on Stair and some subaltern officers, yet this method of proceeding did fetch it back on the court again. The king called his new set of ministers together, and charged them to avoid heats and divisions, and to go on vigorously in his service. [f] But when it was known in Scotland that the king had disowned the act from which the nation expected so much wealth to flow into it, a very high fermentation arose upon it [f]. The turning Johnstone out in so rough a manner was a little irregular ; for as he had as great a share in managing the revolution as any person whatsoever ([g] having been upon the secret of Sidney's whole negotiation [g]), so he had served the king ever since with so particular a zeal as well as fidelity, and with equal success ; not any one thing failing that had been ever committed to him. He had also broke the whole practice of corruption and bribery during the time of his ministry ; and with relation to the East India act his caution had been great and meritorious ; but he had trusted to his integrity and services, and had not been so obsequious and dependent as the court expected ; and his principles with relation to public liberty had been well known, having been ever avowed by him. So though he preserved his reputation, he lost his employment.

---

[a] Cf. *Hist.* ii. 162.   [b] *Ibid.*   [c] *Ibid.*   [d] *Ibid.*   [e] *Ibid.*   [f] *Ibid.*
[g] *Ibid.* i. 764.

[CONNECTING NOTE.

Here, abruptly, about two-thirds down f. 350 (*b*), with a transverse stroke of the pen, ends the Harl. MSS. 6584. It is probable (as we have argued in the Preface) that the narrative was soon continued from Feb., 1696, to the Peace of Ryswick ; and that it had reached that stage, when the MS. of the original Memoirs (or *Secret History*) was entrusted to Lord W[illiam] P[aulet]. The date and length of the various subsequent instalments by which the narrative was carried up to the period of the battle of Oudenarde cannot even be conjectured ; since the original draught of Burnet's *History*, so far as it relates to the events of the interval between Jan., 1696, and Aug., 1708, and answers to *Hist.* ii. 162–505, is missing. We therefore proceed direct to the hitherto unnoticed fragment of the original draught, preserved in the Bodleian Library (Add. MSS. D. 21, rectos of ff. 1–63, versos of ff. 63–21), which retails the events included between the battle of Oudenarde (June 30, 1708) and the Peace of Utrecht ; with which event, like the printed *History*, the original narrative concludes. It therefore answers to pp. 505–632 of the *History*, second volume. The substantial variations are of far inferior extent and importance to those which occur in the earlier portions of the Memoirs ; since (in the very short period which intervened between composition and revision) the standpoint and method of the writer had undergone comparatively little transformation. Such really significant alterations as occur, usually relate to the conduct of the duke of Marlborough, the behaviour of the Whigs, and the necessity for a prolongation of the war after the French proposals of 1709 ; with regard to none of which topics does Burnet display quite so much complacency as is evinced in the revised version. Both the fragment of the original Memoirs, and the rough draught of the 'Conclusion,' by which it is followed (and which, except in the instances quoted *infra*, differs very little indeed from the printed version), are in the autograph of Burnet. The historical fragment opens abruptly ; in the middle of a sentence which describes the conclusion of the battle of Oudenarde.]

[Conclusion of the battle of Oudenarde; and events of the campaign, up to the investment of Ghent.]

Cf. *Hist.* ii. 505 (*from* '[the French] posted themselves on the great canal' *to* p. 511, 'from Lisle, the army marched to invest Ghent.'

[*f.* 1 (*a*)] *Om.* 'of about 30,000 men' ; *and from* p. 505, 'but he himself,' *to* p. 506, 'fit to attack them.'

Om. 'with a very strong . . . dominions' ; *and* 'of the best.'

For from p. 506, 'but when he saw,' *to* p. 507, 'made in that,' *read* ' But when he saw he continued looking on without coming to an engagement, he drew a line before his army. This obliged him to call away so many men from the siege that it went on slowly for some weeks.'

[*f.* 2 (*a*)] *Om.* 'but as their behaviour was not a little censured, so.'

Om. 'had sent some ammunition . . . enterprise depended ; he.'

On p. 508, *after* ' number,' *add* ' otherwise the loss in the pursuit might have been greater.'

For 'saw of what importance . . . attacked that' *read only* 'attacked Leffingen.'

[*f.* 3 (*a*)] *Om.* 'the place was weak . . . resistance.'

For 'insomuch . . . Vendôme' *read* 'they'; *and for* 'his hands' *read* 'their hands.'

Om. 'but that could not last long.'

On p. 509, *after* 'the latter' *add* 'had full powers from Versailles and'; *om.* 'of his neglecting them . . . Vendôme'; *from* 'He kept close' *to* 'Versailles' *is deleted; and for* 'where the accounts . . . uneasy to him' *read* 'The former was often disgusted.'

Om. 'but by the accounts we had from France.'

After 'upper Rhine' *insert* 'on pretence that it was proper for him to act there'; *and reverse the order of the two following clauses.*

Before 'army of 14,000 men' *insert* 'small.'

Om. 'but to deceive . . . carried to the enemy; for.'

Om. 'he advanced . . . artillery.'

On p. 510, *om.* 'some of the general . . . 10,000 men'; *and for* 'their great' *read* 'his great.'

[*f.* 4 (*a*)] *Om.* 'Whether the notice . . . the world'; *for* 'their' *read* '[The French].'

Om. 'Those who thought of presages . . . happy one.'

On p. 511, *om.* 'but that in which . . . till it was taken' (*for which see infra,* p. 418).

[*The campaign elsewhere.*]

Cf. *Hist.* ii. 512 (*from* 'The campaign in Spain' *to* p. 515, *end of first paragraph*).

On p. 512, *for* 'Tortosa' *read* 'Lerida.'

[*f.* 5 (*a*)] *After* 'all was carried' *add* 'by a very small force.'

Between 'for this service' *and* 'Many were afraid' *insert* 'and there was everywhere such a motion of troops that.'

On p. 513, *after* 'took them both' *add* 'after some weeks in the siege.'

For 'he was also master of the valley of Pragelas' *read* 'without apprehending anything behind him, while he should advance.'

Om. 'and at the apprehensions . . . German army.'

For 'to see if matters . . . demands' *read* 'with offers of an [*f.* 6 (*a*)] accommodation, or rather an entire submission.'

On p. 514, *for from* 'In conclusion' *to end of paragraph read only* 'A little time will show how this matter will come to a conclusion.'

After 'through the Ukraine' *add* 'to the Borysthenes [1].'

For 'only a part' *read* 'a great part.'

For from 'After that, we were' *to end of paragraph read only* 'We have no certain news from thence now for six months. I must leave him far engaged in a very wild country; so that he must either go through with his design, and succeed, or perish in it.'

For 'formerly' *read* 'some years past.'

After 'losses' *add* 'We missed some great prizes.'

[*Prince George's death and character.*]

Cf. *Hist.* ii. 515–6.

After 'in this respect' *add* 'as in many others.'

---

[1] i. e. the Dnieper; see *supra,* p. 377.

[*f.* 7 (*a*)] *After* 'all vice' *add* 'and had no spite nor revenges in his temper.'

For 'by those who had credit with him, who had not all of them' *read* 'by a brother of the duke of Marlborough, who had not one of' (*N.B. It is thus possible to take* 'his being bred . . . matters' *as referring to Churchill*); *and for* 'his favourite's' *read* 'Mr. Churchill's.'

[*A new ministry; parliament meets; Scotch business.*]

Cf. *Hist.* ii. 516 (*from* 'The earl of Pembroke' *to* p. 517, 'to have been returned ').

After 'Europe depended' *insert* 'and which was to be the fruit of this long and expensive war'; *and om.* 'neither ill practices nor' *and* 'though their jealousies . . . removed.'

For 'to come to Parliament . . . managed' *read only* 'to come and open the parliament; so it was done.'

Om. 'he was a worthy . . . to the Whigs, and'; *and* (*at this place*) *from* ' In the house of commons' *to end of paragraph.*

[*f.* 8 (*a*)] *For from* 'the duke of Queensberry' *onward read* (*at this place*) *only* 'and the proceedings in that matter were not ended before February.'

[*Ghent and Bruges retaken; a very hard winter.*]

Cf. *Hist.* ii. 511-2 (*from* 'From Lisle' *to end of next paragraph*); *and* p. 511 ('but that in which . . . taken'); *for* 'From Lisle . . . December' *reading* 'The duke of Marlborough marched with his whole army to Ghent about the end of December,' *omitting* 'This coming on . . . campaign,' *and for* 'many of the chief . . . least' *reading only* 'the most irreligious persons of the army'; *after which return to* p. 511, *from* 'but that in which the observers' *to end of paragraph.*

[*Complaints concerning this campaign.*]

Severe observers found matter for censure, even in this campaign; our not following the French after the battle of Oudenarde (when they were [in] a great consternation, so that probably their whole army might have been destroyed) was much complained of; instead of that, parties were sent to raise contributions, which was thought the common practice of generals who love to enrich themselves by war, and not to put an end to it. If Lisle had been invested as soon as the resolution was taken to besiege it, so great a garrison had not got into it; and the sending so small a force with Webbe (where the [*f.* 9 (*a*)] enemy was so very powerful that they might have been overpowered by a vastly superior strength), and the not sending a second great body to support them in that case, was thought the putting the success of the whole campaign upon too doubtful an issue. But though the great successes of this year silenced all complaints at this time, yet unkind observers laid them up in their minds to make use of them when they found a proper time for it.

[*Parliamentary proceedings.*]

Cf. *Hist.* ii. 516 (*from* 'In the house of commons' *to* p. 525, 'that which was called high church') [1].

On p. 516, *om.* 'as the surest way . . . speedy peace.'

For 'The French . . . gave out' *read* 'We know little yet of the counsels of France; they continue to talk very confidently'; *and finish sentence in present tense.*

For 'by the Jacobites' *read* '[by] some'; *and on* p. 517 *after* 'Ireland' *add* 'so it is to be hoped an equal care is taken to prevent their designs.'

For 'things went on' *read* 'things go on.'

For 'were not so much as out of countenance . . . friends' *read* 'are now guilty of the same excesses, for which they made complaints formerly. Some few men of great integrity, who cannot allow themselves in a matter of justice (such as an election is) to give their vote implicitly because their party would have it so, are reproached for their integrity in that matter. Everything is carried as the court would have it.'

For 'A petition . . . returned' (*see supra, f.* 8 (*a*)) *read* 'In the elections of the Scotch peers great exception was taken to the duke of Queensberry's voting among the lords of Scotland.'

[*f.* 10 (*a*)] *On* p. 518, *for* 'As to the duke . . . it was said, that' *read* 'The first point was of the greatest consequence; for.'

Om. 'a peer of England . . . seals; but'; *and.after* 'in that of Great Britain' *add* 'as a lower rank in peerage sinks into a higher when advanced by the crown. On the other hand, it was urged that the clause for electing was general for all the peers of Scotland; so here was a right that still remained not cut off'; *and om.* 'besides, that.'

After 'against the duke of Queensberry' *add* 'and the proxy he had.'

For 'some had signed these' *read* 'some proxies were signed'; *and after* 'subscribing witnesses' *add* 'which was prescribed by the act of the union; so these were set aside.'

[*f.* 11 (*a*)] *On* p. 519, *after* 'carried many elections against him' *add* 'and joined entirely with the Whigs of England.'

After 'a breach' *add* 'yet they bore what they saw could not be helped'; *and for* 'continued still to be' *read* 'grew to be' (*instead of* 'were,' *which is deleted*).

For from p. 519, 'Another act,' *to* p. 520, 'was from a trial,' *read only* 'And to end all that related to Scotland at once, there had been a trial ordered.'

Om. 'he did not upon that move . . . trial went on and.'

Om. 'they complained . . . fixed or certain.'

Om. 'by the Scotch members'; *and after* 'by the lords' *add* 'and occasioned long and warm debates there.'

[*f.* 12 (*a*)] *Om.* 'might' *before* 'put such'; *and before* 'court' *for* 'a bad' *read only* 'the.'

On p. 521, *after* 'proved immediately' *add* 'the court being the judges.'

---

[1] p. 525 is not indicated in the 1833 edition of the *History.*

Om. 'who were to be twelve ... verdict.'

After 'signed by the witnesses' *add* 'and the pleadings in point of law were given in writing.'

For 'whereas ... Reformation' *read only* 'which gave great light to one who was to write history.'

[*f.* 14 (*a*)] *On* p. 523, *after* 'pretender : it was said' *add* 'with great force.'

Om. 'it was considered ... formal laws.'

On p. 524, *after* 'set on foot' *add* 'so that many might be brought into danger by it.'

[*f.* 15 (*a*)] *For* 'gold in their mines' *read* 'gold dust in their rivers.'

On p. 525, *for* 'which was called high church ... opposition' *read only* 'the high church.'

[*The state of France.*]

There was a great dearth (next to a famine) in many parts of Europe; [*f.* 16 (*a*)] but it rose to such [a] a degree of misery in France [a] that many died in the extremities of cold and hunger; and there were great disorders in many parts of that oppressed kingdom. The people broke into the towns, robbed the markets and the king's magazines; so that a general desolation threatened that whole kingdom; and some undertakers who had, by great premiums and a high interest, got great sums into their hands (by which the king's affairs had been hitherto supported) could maintain their credit no longer; so they broke with a debt of many millions (some called them forty and some fifty millions). This made such a general breaking among all those who had trusted them, that it was scarce[1] possible for the ministers to carry on the war any longer. The ill state of the affairs of that kingdom was kept from the king as long as was possible by those who considered his health and quiet more than the interests of his people, and, indeed, more than his own true interests; but this could be no longer concealed. They were now run aground; so the ministry possessed both madame de Maintenon and the duke of Burgundy with the absolute [b] necessity of procuring a peace[b], since it seemed not possible to carry on the war; but the king could not be easily brought to resolve on submitting to the terms that he had reason to expect the allies would insist on.

[a] Cf. *Hist.* ii. 525.   [b] *Ibid.*

---

[1] Substituted by Burnet for his original 'not.'

[*The Halifax address.*]

Cf. *Hist.* ii. 525 (*from* 'this gave occasion' *to end of paragraph*).

For 'this gave occasion . . . lord Halifax' *read* 'while we had this prospect of an approaching peace, the lord Halifax moved the house of lords.'

For 'None durst . . . oppose this' *read* 'This was opposed by none.'

For 'so both . . . allies' *read* 'which was entertained by all, both within and without doors, with an universal approbation and joy.'

[*Overtures of the French.*]

In the meanwhile [a] the French court begun to make steps towards a peace[a], but in so ungracious a manner that [b] they designed to try if the Dutch could be brought into a separate treaty. So one Rouillé[b], a president of the court of parliament, came to Antwerp, and sent to the States for a passport. They sent two deputies to hear what his propositions were, but they were so short of what they knew the allies would insist on, that he sent back his secretary for fuller powers ; and upon his return he was suffered to come nearer; but still all that was offered came so far short of what would satisfy, that he sent his secretary three or four times to Versailles. And now, as I am writing this, it seems a negotiation is like to be opened ; for [c] Mon. Torcy (secretary of state for foreign affairs)[c], with some other ministers, is [d] come to the Hague, and give (*sic*) great hope of a speedy peace[d]. [*f.* 17 (*a*)] Upon prince Eugene's return from Vienna [e] the duke of Marlborough came over to England[e], but did not stay above three weeks ; for [f] Rouillé had begun his negotiation in his absence[f] ; and it was much feared that the States might go in too hastily to the overtures made by the French for a peace. So he (to put a stop to any such resolution) went soon back, and he found [g] the Dutch in a very good disposition to adhere to their allies, and to enter upon no negotiation but in concurrence with them[g], and after a fortnight's stay there, [h] he came back again[h], which has made all people conclude that the offers are such that a treaty will be opened, and that he came over [i] to procure full instructions[i] and powers. [k] He went back in

---

[a] Cf. *Hist.* ii. 526. [b] *Ibid.* 527. [c] *Ibid. infra.* [d] *Ibid.* 528. [e] *Ibid.* 527. [f] *Ibid.* [g] *Ibid.* [h] *Ibid. infra.* [i] *Ibid.* [k] *Ibid.* 528.

the beginning of May, with the lord Townsend joined in commission with him; who is the most shining person of all our young noblemen ª, being both learned and virtuous, of a clear understanding and a fine expression. He has for several years appeared with great advantage in the house .of lords, and is very much considered in Norfolk, which is his country. ᵇ He is free from all vice ᵇ, and seems to have a true sense of religion, ᶜ with very good principles ᶜ. I do not yet mention what offers the French are making for a peace. It is yet a secret, and is variously reported; so I reserve the particulars till I am more certainly informed about them; and it will be more proper to mention them when they are either entertained or rejected.

[*Convocation meets; Burnet concludes for the time, May 8, 1709.*]

Cf. *Hist.* ii. 525-6 (*to* 'and under very bad influences').

Om. 'though not with such a majority.'

For 'to recommend . . . church' *read only* 'to embroil us.'

For 'and so catching . . . clergy of Ireland' *read* 'and they had set the same spirit aworking in Ireland.'

Om. 'as they had no . . . convocations.'

For 'the succeeding governors' *read* 'the duke of Ormond.'

Om. 'This was received . . . triumph' *and* 'but though . . . another.'

For 'and that though the war . . . these hopes; but' *read only* 'though the state of her affairs obliged her to act otherwise. It is not certain that this is not so; for though I believe they have no hopes given them by her, yet' (*and continue in present tense*).

For 'enemies . . . dissenters' *read* 'But here I stop, the 8th of May, 1709.'

[*Burnet resumes his pen; the preliminaries of peace are settled.*]

Cf. *Hist.* ii. 528 (*from* 'The foundation' *to* p. 530, 'was dismissed').

[*f.* 18 (*a*)] *Before* 'The foundation' *insert* 'The preliminaries in order to a treaty were agreed on at the Hague.'

Om. 'within two months' *and* 'the time was too short, and that perhaps.'

For 'It was, upon this, insisted on . . . bringing it about' *read* 'To this it was answered, that he must first withdraw all his force from him, and must not only suffer the allies to march through France for the reduction of Spain, but likewise assist in it with a force of his own, and give some places as a security for observing this; for it was remembered how in the peace of the Pyrenees he had sworn not to assist the Portuguese; yet he had no regard to that, but sent Schomberg with an army to Portugal' (cf. *Hist.* ii. 529).

ª Cf. *Hist.* ii. 528.   ᵇ *Ibid.*   ᶜ *Ibid.*

After 'the other preliminaries' *add* 'were easily yielded ; [they].'

For 'As all the great interests . . . entirely restored' *read only* 'and no material thing was omitted; lesser pretensions were reserved to a treaty.'

After 'excepted' *add* 'only.'

For from 'but in conclusion' (*end of* p. 528) *to* p. 530, 'the supporting of the king of Spain : it was said,' *read only* 'But the allies were firm ; so all being settled, those who had treated about this were by a day prefixed to procure the ratification of these preliminaries from their masters. Ratifications came from the allies; but the court of France refused to ratify them, insisting on the article with relation to the Spanish monarchy, in which the dauphin expressed great heat ; so it was resolved to carry on the war. There was a fermentation in the court at Versailles, of which I know not yet the particulars; only it is said.'

For 'appeared' *read* 'appears'; *and for* 'Chamillard . . . dismissed' *read only* 'Chamillard quitted all his employments.'

Om. entirely from 'but it is not certain what influence' *to* p. 531, 'on that occasion'; *and* (*at this place*) *from* 'The miseries of France' *to* 'miseries of his people.'

[*The war is resumed; campaign in Portugal and Spain.*]

Cf. *Hist.* ii. 531 (*from* 'Villars was sent' *to end of paragraph*).

Om. (*at this place*) 'of whom . . . never beaten.'

For 'upon some part of their southern coast' *read* 'on Cadiz or some part of Andalusia.'

[*f.* 19 (*a*)] *For* 'though we gave them no disturbance on that side' *read* 'Baker was kept so long by westerly winds (and so long at Cork to take in some more bodies from Ireland), that he could not sail towards Spain before the beginning of September ; so the issue of this design cannot yet be known.'

[*Campaign in Dauphiné and in Germany.*]

Cf. *Hist.* ii. 531 (*from* 'Nothing of any importance' *to end of paragraph, omitting only the final sentence*).

[*Misery of France.*]

Cf. *Hist.* ii. 531 (*from* 'The miseries of France' *to* 'miseries of his people').

For 'that they saw no hope nor relief' *read* 'that they saw their miseries were like to last another year.'

After 'men of war' *add* 'in many places the people eat grass with their cattle.'

[*The campaign in Flanders, including the battle of Malplaquet; Mons is invested.*]

Cf. *Hist.* ii. 532 (*from* 'The chief scene' *to* p. 533, 'the outworks were carried with little resistance ').

For 'The chief scene . . . shows of peace' *read* 'The duke of Marlborough trusted so little to the steps they seemed to be making towards a peace, that he.'

For 'The army . . . Lisle' *read* 'Mar[shal] Villars was sent to command the French army ; he had been hitherto successful, for the French king said of him he was never yet beaten [cf. *Hist.* ii. 531], so he was thought the fittest for this command; the elector of Bavaria had no command this year, but stayed at Mons. The duke of Marlborough and prince Eugene drew their army together near Lisle.'

For ' near Douay' *read* ' between La Bassée and Douay.'

For ' which was counted . . . all the ground' *read* ' which [*f.* 20 (*a*)] was not only fortified with the utmost exactness, but (it standing on an eminence) all the ground about [it].'

After ' cease till then' *add* ' only a body of the troops was still to lie before the place, and were to have one of the gates put into their hands.'

After ' lost in it' *add* ' by the springing of mines.'

For ' saw plainly . . . dislodge them' *read* ' ordered the troops employed in the siege of Tournay to join them, and resolved to attack the French camp.'

Om. ' and cost them many men.'

For ' have always talked of this as the sharpest' *read* ' reckoned this the greatest'; *om.* ' not without reflecting . . . attack.'

For ' without giving them . . . Brussels' *read* ' they offered no disturbance to the train of artillery that was brought from Brussels. As soon as it arrived.'

Om. (*at this place*) ' and Mons capitulated . . . quarters.'

[*Affairs in Spain.*]

Cf. *Hist.* ii. 533-4.

[*f.* 21 (*a*)] *For* ' In Catalonia' *read* ' While this went on, we understood from Catalonia that'; *om.* ' after he received . . . Italy,' *and* ' with which he . . . mortified,' *and* ' and with that . . . end.'

[*Fortunes and character of the king of Sweden.*]

Cf. *Hist.* ii. 534-6.

Om. ' resolved . . . Muscovy, and.'

Om. ' who were easily . . . czar.'

For ' and settled . . . Moldavia' *read* ' who [*sic*] have him now in their hands; a little time will let us see how they will use him.'

Om. ' and that it was not . . . consent.'

For ' and Stanislaus . . . fortune' *read* ' Stanislaus was soon forsaken by his own party; what figure he will hereafter make must be left to time.'

For ' that the extravagant . . . Germany' *read* ' that the Swedes are like to suffer severely for the extravagant humours of their king; but since England and the States were the *guarants* of the peace made in 1701, and since their interests will lead them to maintain the balance in those seas, this may perhaps involve us in a new war by the time that we get out of our present war.'

For ' Dantzic was at this time' *read* ' Dantzic has been of late'; *om.* ' though few . . . infection'; *for* ' put' *read* ' puts'; *om.* ' but it pleased . . . no further.'

[*f.* 22 (*a*)] *For* ' many years' *read* ' seven years.'

For ' Dr. Robinson . . . Bristol' *read* ' the present dean of Windsor, Dr. Robinson, who has been long the minister of this crown in those parts [1].'

---

[1] Dr. Robinson's letter, undated, is among the miscellaneous Burnet papers in the Bodleian (Add. MSS. D. 23, f. 67); and concludes with the request that it may be regarded as strictly confidential.

[*Mons falls.*]

Cf. *Hist.* ii. 533 (*from* '[the French] left our army' *to* 'winter quarters') (*see supra*, p. 424).

[*f.* 23 (*a*)] *For* 'left our army . . . little resistance' *read* 'The siege of Mons was carried on in form without any disturbance from the French army. They were employed in making lines of an unusual strength, and they lay close within them.'

[*Affairs in Italy; with which Burnet concludes for the time.*]

Cf. *Hist.* ii. 533 (*from* 'the pope delayed' *to* 'acknowledged him' *only*). *For* 'by several . . . campaign' *read only* 'as long as he could.'

[*Burnet resumes his pen, May* 30, 1710; *the pope sends an embassy.*]

Cf. *Hist.* ii. 533 (*from* 'He sent also' *to* 'nepotism').

Before 'He sent also' *insert* 'I begin now, on May 30, 1710, to prosecute this work; the period that I had prefixed to myself is now out; but since the war does still go on I intend to continue writing till I can end it with the relation of the conclusion of the war and of a general peace' (cf. *Hist.* ii. 548); *and for* 'He sent also' *read* 'The pope sent.'

After 'Vienna' *insert* 'from thence to Saxony.'

[*Affairs in the north.*]

Cf. *Hist.* ii. 536 (*from* 'The king of Denmark' *to* 'the peace of the northern parts of the empire was secured').

For 'it was believed . . . Rome' *read* 'was diverted from going to Rome.'

After 'home' *add* 'calling in at several courts there' (*sic*).

Before 'king Augustus' *insert* 'the czar and'; *and after* 'Augustus' *add* 'There was a small Swedish army still in Poland, and it was thought that it would not be easy for it to penetrate into Pomerania; but Cressaw, who commanded it, marched thither, and king Stanislaus with him, and then it was pretended that king Augustus' resignation was null and void, since the diet of Poland had not accepted of it, nor renounced their right to him, so he was recalled and held a diet,' &*c.* (*Cf. with all this Hist.* ii. 536 *infra*, 534.)

For 'upon his return home' *read* 'in the beginning of winter.'

[*Affairs of Charles XII; and of the Hungarians.*]

[*f.* 24 (*a*)] [a] A peace was made up between the czar and the Turk [a], and it was thought that the keeping the king of Sweden still a prisoner was a secret article in that agreement; for [b] he continues still at Bender [b], under the show of liberty; but since his affairs require his hasting home, and since he does not stir from Bender, it is concluded he

[a] Cf. *Hist.* ii. 536.   [b] *Ibid.*

is a prisoner there. [a] The war in Hungary went on still, and though the court of Vienna published great successes that their arms had there [a], yet there was reason to suspect the relations they give out, [b] for one sent from Hungary [b] by prince Rafalsi [1] to beg the protection and mediation of our court [c] assured me that their pretended victories were either nothing at all, or they were real losses and defeats [c]; but perhaps he might exceed as much in lessening as they do in raising their successes too much. He told me they asked nothing but the performing those capitulations to which both this emperor and his father had agreed; but added that the court of Vienna laid aside all those agreements at pleasure, and that they could not trust them any more; so unless they had a distinct prince in Transylvania, and the queen and States guaranty, they could not think themselves safe in any promises that might be made them. He concluded they were Christians, and so they begun with Christians, and begged their protection; and if this could not be obtained they must cast themselves on the Turk, who they knew would take them into his protection, upon their delivering up those places of which they were possessed. This was the last remedy; but rather than perish they were resolved to cast themselves upon it. The queen and the States are sending to the emperor, to offer their mediation [2]: time must shew if it will be accepted, and what effects it will have.

[*Our fleet well conducted.*]

Cf. *Hist.* ii. 537 (*from* 'Nothing of importance' *to end of paragraph*).

For 'so he desired . . . down' *read* 'so he withdrew from it, and had a good pension assigned him.'

For 'at the head of' *read* 'in'; *and after* 'a commission' *read* 'with such as he should think proper for it.'

[*The session; and Sacheverell's business.*]

Cf. *Hist.* ii. (*from* p. 537 *to* p. 546, *end of first paragraph*).

[*f.* 25 (*a*)] *On* p. 538, *om.* 'pretending it was.'

[a] Cf. *Hist.* ii. 536.　　[b] *Ibid.*　　[c] *Ibid.* 536–7.

[1] *Sic* MS.; probably an error for Ragotski.
[2] Are these the 'secret negotiations' to which vague reference is made in *Hist.* ii. 537?

For 'The queen seemed ... despised' *read only* 'The queen and the ministry were highly offended at it.'

Om. 'Eyre, then solicitor-general, and.'

Before 'chosen' *om.* 'unhappily'; *and after* 'chosen' *add* 'I was then in my diocese, so I had no share in the deliberation. The reason that made the solemn way be resolved on was this.'

[*f.* 26 (*a*)] *Om.* 'dignities ... hold it.'

For 'under his own hand' *read* 'corrected by Lesley's own hand.'

After 'judicious' *add* 'and learned'; *and after* 'divine' *add* 'who had writ with great temper and moderation, as well as with great force, against the separation from the church.'

On p. 539, *for* 'with a visible superiority of argument to them all, and' *read* 'and (the *Rehearsal* continuing to attack him).'

For 'When it was moved' *read* 'In the beginning of the session of parliament the sermon was complained of; and it was moved.'

[*f.* 27 (*a*)] *Om.* 'and the tools ... not then known.'

On p. 540, *for* 'with unthinking people' *read* 'with all the young unthinking members'; *om.* 'though the effects ... foreseen'; *and after* 'some weeks' *add* 'and the emissaries set out by the Jacobites were everywhere at work to give strange apprehensions of ill designs.'

[*f.* 29 (*a*)] *On* p. 542, *for* 'before my own door ... they did' *read* 'one was killed before my door; his skull was cleft with a spade.'

After 'public peace' *insert* 'In some places resistance was made and prisoners were taken; but in most places.'

[*f.* 30 (*a*)] *On* p. 543, *om. at end of paragraph* 'and would take the first occasion to shew it.'

[*f.* 31 (*a*)] *On* p. 544, *om.* 'and though he submitted ... passed upon him.'

On p. 545, *for* 'to others it was said' *read* 'to some it was secretly said.'

[*f.* 32 (*a*)] *For* 'not only in London' *read* 'nor did this madness only shew itself in London.'

For 'greater effects' *read* 'worse effects.'

[*The queen's speech; changes in the ministry.*]

Cf. *Hist.* ii. 546–7.

The queen's speech has the epithet 'very good.'

Om. 'as he gave out.'

[*f.* 33 (*a*)] *For* 'the change of principles that he had discovered in the trial was imputed' *read* 'and that he was to be the chief minister. It was said that the view of this had made him vote as he did in the trial; and all was imputed'; *om.* 'him and'; *for* 'with' *read* 'and.'

For 'upon that ... no more at it' *read* 'upon which she has retired from the court for some months.'

For 'but there was now too much ground given for suspicion' *read* 'nothing has yet followed upon this step; so those who judge the most favourably of it think it is done on design to have a protection to the new favourite.'

[*Burnet remonstrates with the queen.*]

Cf. *Hist.* ii. 547–8.

Om. 'who was in great esteem among them'; *and for* 'some' *read* 'two.'

Burnet's Original Memoirs [1710

[*f.* 34 (*a*)] *On* p. 548, *after* 'before the queen' *add* 'all this winter'; *om.* 'but I found . . . effect upon her; yet'; *and after* 'I had to her' *add* 'Things are yet in the dark; the design of that party is to have a new ministry and a new parliament; but how far they are like to succeed must be left to time.

[*Marlborough goes abroad; negotiations at Gertruydenberg.*]

[a] The duke of Marlborough went beyond sea in February to prepare for an early campaign [a]; great care was taken to have such magazines laid in, [b] that our army might be brought together in April [b]. The disorders into which the party broke out in England gave great joy to the courts of St. Germain and Versailles, and though the miseries of France were so great that it seemed necessary for them to put an end to the war, [c] yet the hopes they had from the ill-temper that showed itself among us made them slower in their advances to a peace. [d] There were messages all this winter going between Paris and the Hague; [e] the French pressed the States to open a negotiation of peace, and to admit of plenipotentiaries from France; [f] but the States came to vigorous resolutions to admit of no treaty till the preliminaries concerted the former year should be first agreed to. [g] The French said they had an equivalent to offer with relation to that concerning the Spanish monarchy; but the States would not hearken any further to this than to suffer the French to send plenipotentiaries [h] to Gertruydenberg, to make those propositions to such deputies as they should send to them [h]; and upon their [*f.* 35 (*a*)] report they would examine the propositions before they would open a treaty. They have been now above two months at Gertruydenberg, and have often sent for a conference with the deputies of the States, but all the propositions they have hitherto made have not given any satisfaction to the States.

[*Operations in Flanders; siege of Douay.*]

Cf. *Hist.* ii. 548 (*from* 'in April [the campaign was opened]' *to* 'he drew off'). *For* 'though they had' *read* 'everywhere else; so they by draining their garrisons and drawing their troops from all other places.' *For* 'they lay before' *read* 'they were brought to Bouchain, from thence to.'

[a] Cf. *Hist.* ii. 548.   [b] *Ibid.*   [c] *Ibid.* 552.   [d] *Ibid.* 549.   [e] *Ibid.* 550. [f] *Ibid. infra.*   [g] *Ibid. infra.*   [h] *Ibid.* 551.

After 'he drew off' *add* 'towards Arras; and in that state they were the 9th of June, N. S., when the last letters came from thence.'

Om. (*at this place*) 'so the siege . . . 14th of June.'

[*Disgrace of Medina Celi; conduct of king Charles; Burnet concludes for the time, June 8, 1710, but adds a postscript.*]

In Spain (as king Philip was going to set out to open the campaign) [a]a discovery was made of some conspiracy of the duke of Medina Celi's, then the chief minister[a]; the thing is yet secret; [b]he was sent a prisoner to Segovia, where he is kept very strictly, none being admitted to speak to him, but no examination is yet made[b] into the discoveries pretended to be made; this retarded the king's journey to Arragon till the middle of May. It is given out that he intends to besiege Balaguer. King Charles his army is drawing together, and recruits are brought over from Italy to him. His counsels are very weak; he is much in the power of his Germans, and seems to hate the Spanish nation, and cannot yet be prevailed on to offer an indemnity to king Philip's party; who, on the other hand, renders himself very popular in Spain. This is the present state of affairs, 8 June, 1710. I only add to this that [c]Douay with the Fort Escarp both capitulated on the 14th of June[c]; and though [d]king Philip went to his army on the Segre to fight king Charles (who likewise came to his army), yet after a short cannonading of his camp, in which he lost some hundreds, he[1] went back[2].

[*Battle of Almanara.*]

Cf. *Hist.* ii. 555 (*from* 'Before the end of July' *to end of page*).

[*f.* 36 (*a*)] *Om.* 'he drew his whole body together.'

After '20th of August' *add* ' N. S.'

For '10,000 men' *read* '9,000 men, [who joined him at] Tudela.'

After 'face of an army' *add* 'and advanced to the Tago.'

[*King Charles at Madrid.*]

Cf. *Hist.* ii. 556 (*to* 'supply or support him' *only*).

After 'hazards' *add* 'From Madrid he went to Toledo, which he is fortifying ;

[a] Cf. *Hist.* ii. 557.   [b] *Ibid.*   [c] *Ibid.* 548.   [d] *Ibid.* 555.

[1] 'broke off the campaign and' is deleted.
[2] 'So I end(?) 1 July (?)' is deleted.

but whether he can maintain the ground he has gained seems uncertain. The allies have not yet sent him any reinforcements, though it is now above three months since the battle of Saragossa.

For 'The king of France . . . supply or support him' *read* 'The king of France seems resolved to support king Philip; he sent the duke of Vendôme to command his army; and now that the campaign is everywhere at an end he will probably[1] order troops to march into Spain.'

[*Bethune, Aire, and St. Venant taken.*]

Cf. *Hist.* ii. 557.
After 'of the Lys' *add* 'and all the places on that river.'
Om. 'though not of such lustre . . . fought, yet[2].'
Om. 'Nothing considerable . . . both sides.'

[*The Gertruydenberg conferences.*]

[*f.* 37 (*a*)] [a] Their plenipotentiaries stayed some weeks at Gertruydenberg, and treated upon an equivalent for that preliminary that related to the delivering up of Spain, and the obliging king Philip to withdraw from it; but their negotiation was so apparently frau[du]lent that [b] in conclusion all treaty with them was given up, and the States published a full deduction of the steps they made; by which it appeared there was no sincere intentions in the French court to evacuate Spain. The court of France published nothing on their part; for they would not openly own that they had entered on any treaty to abandon Spain [b], lest that should have provoked the Spaniards to abandon king Philip.

[*State of Europe.*]

There was a great change at Constantinople; a new grand vizier seemed resolved to break with the czar, and to set the king of Sweden upon him with a great force; but he was soon removed; so that design vanished, and the king of Sweden continued still at Bender. [c] The czar has reduced all Livonia; he took both Riga and Revel; and now there is a great plague in Sweden which sweeps away many of their people. [d] There is a guarantee settled between the emperor,

---

[a] Cf. *Hist.* ii. 551.   [b] *Ibid.* 552.   [c] *Ibid.* 557.   [d] *Ibid.* 534, 536, 557.

---

[1] Burnet's own correction of his earlier 'without doubt.'
[2] The remainder of the sentence is an afterthought, inserted at the bottom of f. 35 (*b*).

the queen, the States, and the princes of the north of Germany for securing the peace of the empire; so though Sweden is left exposed, their dominions in Germany will be by this means preserved, yet it is not without difficulty that the king of Sweden is brought to give way [1] to this [a]. The war in Hungary has gone on slowly this year; the court of Vienna publishes their successes; but there has been no deciding action in those parts. And now having taken a general view of the state of Europe, I return back to England.

[*Change of ministry.*]

Cf. *Hist.* ii. 552-3 (*from* 'In June [the queen] dismissed' *to end of paragraph*).

Om. 'without pretending any malversation in him' *and* 'in particular . . . bank of England'; *for* 'and said this herself . . . in such cases' *read only* 'but'; *and om.* 'lord Poulett . . . form, but.'

For 'and it was visible . . . minister; and' *read* 'This raised the alarm again, and carried the jealousy much further; for.'

[*Sacheverell's progress; fresh ministerial changes.*]

Cf. *Hist.* ii. 553 (*to beginning of* p. 554, 'distaste to the old ones').

[*f.* 38 (*a*)] *After* 'champion of the church' *add* 'and was the idol of a mad party.'

For 'they were rather favoured . . . than checked' *read* 'and those who were condemned for the riots in London were, after some reprieves, at last pardoned, and set at liberty.'

Om. 'which Harcourt . . . had prepared.'

For 'the queen did not look . . . readily; and' *read* 'which [was] for some time lodged with four judges; but.'

Om. 'with some of the commissioners of the admiralty'; *and for* 'in whose room others were put' *read* 'but there is none yet put in his place.'

For from 'All this rose' *to* 'distaste to the old one' *read* 'Mr. Harley and Mrs. Masham are looked on as the persons whose credit with the queen is now so entire, that all these changes are ascribed wholly to them.'

[*The elections; the lieutenancy of London.*]

Cf. *Hist.* ii. 554 (*from* 'The next' *to* 'Whigs were left out').

[*General political situation; sinking of credit; Burnet concludes for the time, Nov. 16, 1710.*]

[*f.* 39 (*a*)] [b] These practices had never been known in England before; and by these means three parts in four of the elections [b] went for Tories; so we are now in a gaze

[a] Cf. *Hist.* ii. 557.   [b] *Ibid.* 554.

---

[1] Burnet had originally written 'consent.'

to see how they will proceed when the parliament is opened.
ᵃ The queen is at present much pleased with the changes she
has made ᵃ, and with the prospect she has of the approaching
parliament. ᵇ The new scene of the ministers talk as if they
intended to act very moderately at home, and very steadily
with relation to the war and to the alliances abroad ᵇ; but
they are under great difficulties for money.   ᶜ The bank (that
used to furnish the government) is no more in condition to do
it ᶜ, for a jealousy of the present ministry is so spread (not
only through the nation but over all Europe), that many
concerned in the bank are calling out their money and selling
actions; which has made ᵈ such a fall of actions that what
sold some months ago at 130 has fallen to 95; that is now
raised a little to 102 ᵈ, while I am ending to write at this time,
on the 16th of November, 1710.

[*Opening of parliament.*]

Cf. *Hist.* ii. 557–8 (*to* 'Christmas ').
Om. 'which shewed . . . former addresses' *and* 'as if they had apprehended
. . . asked of them.'
[*f.* 40 (*a*)] *After* 'Christmas' *add* 'but all this while the credit did not rise.'

[*Affairs in Spain; French account of the battle of Villa Viciosa.*]

At Christmas we had news of a great change of affairs in
Spain.   ᵉ King Charles continued till the beginning of
December in the neighbourhood of Madrid ᵉ and Toledo.
Then he thought fit to retire to Barcelona, and got safe
thither.   ᶠ The army (after a show of fortifying Toledo and
giving out that they would take their winter quarters in
Castile) found such difficulties in subsisting there, and had
such apprehensions of the French coming to the Ebro and
cutting them off from Catalonia, that they resolved to march
back ᶠ. We have yet no account from them, but the French
news is that king Philip (finding they were marching back
to Catalonia) ᵍ pursued them close in great marches; and
overtook the rear, commanded by Stanhope, in an unfortified

ᵃ Cf. *Hist.* ii. 554, *supra*.   ᵇ *Ibid.* 555.   ᶜ *Ibid. supra.*   ᵈ *Ibid.*
ᵉ *Ibid.* 556.   ᶠ *Ibid. infra.*   ᵍ *Ibid.*

town ; ª where by casting up entrenchments they defended
themselves as long as they could, but were made prisoners
of war. Staremberg, who was advanced before them, came
upon that back ª to their relief, and drew up in order to fight
king Philip's army. It is acknowledged the action was sharp,
with advantage to Staremberg on one wing, but they give
out that he was routed and lost both his cannon and baggage.
This is so differently related that, till we have the account
given by both sides, we must suspend our belief. These
actions happened on the 9th and 20th December, N. S. ᵇ Soon
after the French had filled all places with an account of their
success in Spain, we had a truer account of it ᵇ.

[*Second version of the battle of Villa Viciosa.*]

Cf. *Hist.* ii. 556 (*from* '[Stanhope] finding king Philip' *to* p. 557, *end of
paragraph*).

After 'to desire his assistance' *Burnet originally wrote* 'who fatally missed
his way a whole day'; *which he has deleted.*

For 'Staremberg might . . . that it was conjectured' *read* 'Staremberg, when
he understood the danger Stanhope was in, he drew his forces together, though
but slowly ; for.'

For 'Stanhope and his men . . . Staremberg came up' *read* 'So though he
marched back he came some hours too late for that.'

For 'but Staremberg . . . nor could he' *read* '[Staremberg was not] able to.'

Om. 'the enemy . . . disturbance.'

[*Debate in parliament concerning the war in Spain; abuses censured; supply.*]

Cf. *Hist.* ii. 558 (*from* 'During that time' *to* p. 563, 'prospect of a peace ').

[*f.* 41 (*a*)] *For* 'During that time . . . so' *read* 'The queen, upon the first news
from France'; *and om.* 'as the public . . . particulars.'

Om. 'ordered some regiments . . . Spain, and.'

On p. 559 *om.* 'and that little regard . . . opposition.'

Om. 'for he told them . . . agreed to there.'

[*f.* 42 (*a*)] *On* p. 560, *after* 'it was carried' *insert* 'by a majority of twenty-one.'

[*f.* 43 (*a*)] *On* p. 561, *after* 'in the January' *insert* '; the act passed in February,
and the money was to be raised the 25th of March.'

After 'for that service' *add* 'both in the year 1706 and in the year 1707.'

[*f.* 44 (*a*)] *After* 'examination had been made' *add* 'in the committee.'

On p. 562, *for* 'some, who voted . . . ashamed of it ; they said' *read* 'all that
I heard was said in secret to excuse it, was that.'

For 'and had made a good retreat . . . diligence' *read only* 'on that unhappy
occasion.'

ª Cf. *Hist.* ii. 556 *infra.*   ᵇ *Ibid.* 558.

[*f.* 45 (*a*)] *For from* 'We had likewise,' *to end of paragraph read* 'but it was resolved to lay much load on him, so they put a censure upon this. How much further they may carry their enquiries a little time must show.'

For 'Harley . . . enquire' *read* 'There was an enquiry made in the house of commons.'

Om. 'the abuse . . . some have said that.'

On p. 563, *for from* 'but the abuse' *to end of paragraph read* 'If this is carried through all who practise it, it will save much money to the public; and oblige those who serve at sea to much frugality.'

Before 'The money did not' *insert* 'All this while credit did not rise; the actions of the bank did not rise above 103.'

Om. 'neither' *and* 'nor on the duty laid on malt' (*for which see infra*); *for from* 'so to raise' *to end of paragraph read* 'several duties (as upon hops, coals, and candles) are voted for 32 years, for a *fonds* to a new lottery; but men's minds are possessed with such jealousies of the new ministry, that it is apprehended money will not be brought in, but upon great and exorbitant premiums, so that a black cloud seems to hang over all our affairs' [*see also infra*, p. 435].

[*The duke of Marlborough still commanded our armies; Burnet concludes for the time, Feb.* 16, 17$\frac{10}{11}$]

Cf. *Hist.* ii. 563-4.

Om. 'For this the duke . . . ministry.'

For 'for all the ill usage . . . carrying on the war' *read only* 'but was willing to continue in the command of the army, to which he was much pressed by the States and our other allies'; *and om.* 'and finding . . . overcome.'

Om. 'in all which . . . dealt with the crown.'

After 'the last' *add* 'Thus affairs stand the 16th February, 17$\frac{10}{11}$.'

[*Complaints concerning the Palatines.*]

Cf. *Hist.* ii. 564-5.

[*f.* 46 (*a*)] *For* 'The house of commons found . . . story was, that' *read* 'The next thing the house of commons took under their consideration was the encouragement that had been given to about 10,000 poor Palatines, who being reduced to extreme poverty (what by the miseries of war, what by the severities of the government) came over to England in summer 1709' (*then proceed as in Hist. from* 'In the year 1708').

After 'recommended' *add* '[by] the Lutheran ministers.'

After 'that the queen' *add* 'upon his application.'

After 'of that country to' *add* 'leave their poor ruined habitations and.'

Om. 'the time of our fleet's . . . distance.'

[*f.* 47 (*a*)] *For* 'in the queen's name' *read* 'by order of the cabinet council.'

[*A bill to repeal the general naturalization; and the place bill.*]

Cf. *Hist.* ii. 565.

For 'for disabling . . . places' *read* 'disabling persons in any employments (excepting only such a number as was allowed) to sit in the house of commons.'

[*A bill qualifying members to be chosen passed.*]

Cf. *Hist.* ii. 565.

After 'Another bill' *add* 'to the same intent.'

For '£600' *read* '£500.'

Om. 'it being pretended, that.'

For from 'This was thought' *to end of paragraph read only* 'When this was brought up to the lords it appeared that the ministry (who usually opposed such acts) did all favour it; so that the attempt to extend the qualifications to Scotland was not entertained ; so the bill passed.'

[*An act for French wines; character of the extreme Tories; Guiscard's attempt.*]

Cf. *Hist.* ii. 565–7 (*to* 'stopped by the bark ').

For 'delicate' *read* 'vitiated.'

[*f.* 48 (*a*)] *After* 'but his own :' *add* 'for he will have us trade with him.'

Om. 'that had been almost . . . happy to him ; it.'

After 'of a design' *add* 'as if.'

After 'insurrection' *add* 'of the papists.'

For 'with those' *read* 'with the Huguenots.'

After 'in favour of the Huguenots' *add* 'to draw them back again into France.'

For 'and he seemed . . . liberty' *read* 'He talked of public liberty with the zeal of a Roman, and.'

For 'he seemed forward . . . put on' *read* 'he seemed a desperate man and ready to venture on any design for invading France '; *and for* 'for some years ' *read* 'for four or five years '; *and after* 'increased' *add* 'and that he was deep in debt.'

[*f.* 49 (*a*)] *On* p. 567, *for* ' some imputed this to' *read* 'he being in.'

For 'others thought it was an artifice' *read* 'which his enemies said was one of his artifices.'

For 'It was not known . . . confessed' *read* 'It is yet a secret whether he confessed anything or not; it is certain he seemed not disposed to tell all he knew.'

For 'her health . . . shaken' *read* 'The queen's health was at this time in some disorder, which was probably heightened by this accident.'

[*The lottery bills.*]

Cf. *Hist.* ii. 563 (*from* 'The duty laid on malt' *to end of paragraph*) ; *but read instead* 'In the meanwhile the subsidy bills went on ; the duty on malt was continued, and two lotteries were raised successively, one after another, the first of £1,500,000 and the second for about £2,000,000, and the hope of benefit tickets wrought so on the nation that the first was over-subscribed by a fifth part, which was ordered to be returned back ; and the second is secretly subscribed, though the bill is not yet passed' (*see also supra*, p. 434).

[*King William's grants.*]

Cf. *Hist.* ii. 567.

For 'and against those who had served him best' *read* 'few appeared for it.'

[Inquiries into the accounts.]

Cf. *Hist.* ii. 567-8.

For ' Their malice . . . counsel on every article ' *read only* ' When this failed, then they fell to examine the returns that had been made into the exchequer of the supplies given by parliament' (*and see infra*, pp. 437-8).

[*f.* 50 (*a*)] *For* ' diligence ' *read* ' skill.'

Om. ' or on any of the Whigs.'

[Deaths of the dauphin and the emperor [1].]

Cf. *Hist.* ii. 568.

Om. ' and the emperor both ' ; *after* ' died ' *insert* ' suddenly ' ; *and after* ' small-pox ' *add* ' a defluxion falling down and suffocating him ; and three days after that, the emperor likewise died of the small-pox ; thus the two most eminent princes of Europe died of the same disease ' ; *and after* ' of the month' *add* ' The duke of Burgundy is now dauphin.'

For ' the one or the other will have . . . affairs ' *read* ' this will have on the counsels of France.'

For ' The electors were all resolved to ' *read* ' Upon the notice given of the emperor's death, all the electors have already given assurances that they will.'

For ' A little before . . . kept up from them ' *read* ' And the council at Vienna has so dexterously managed matters in Hungary, that they have prevailed on the malcontents to receive the offers made by them of a general amnesty ; they kept up the news of the emperor's death.'

[War imminent between the Turk and the czar; affairs in Spain and the Netherlands.]

Cf. *Hist.* ii. 509.

Om. ' the Crim Tartar.'

After ' new war ' *insert* ' till he had filled his treasury and.'

For ' It did not yet appear . . . nor was it yet known ' *read* ' The differences between the courts of Vienna and Turin are now fully settled ; so probably the war will be carried on more vigorously on that side ; and king Charles has [*f.* 51 (*a*)] such reinforcements already sent him (and more from Italy are believed now to have joined him), that, as king Philip has not attempted anything, so it is believed this time king Charles has the superior force and will be in a condition to attack him ; but it is not yet known,' *&c.* (*to end of paragraph*).

Put next paragraph in present tense ; and for from ' nothing was yet attempted ' *to* ' From our temporal concerns ' *read* ' It is very probable that (the weather being now so happily changed) somewhat will be soon attempted ; and this is the present situation of our affairs with relation to our temporal concerns.'

[A convocation; Burnet lays down his pen for the time, May 14, 1711.]

Cf. *from Hist.* ii. p. 569 *to end of* p. 572 *only.*

[*f.* 52 (*a*)] *On* p. 570, *for from* ' and because the other bishops had maintained' *to end of paragraph read* ' it seemed strange to put such a mark of contempt on so many bishops ; but it was understood that they had been better pleased with

---

[1] The intervening paragraph of *History* (on building churches) does not appear.

the former than with the present ministry; so it was thought fit to let them see who were the conductors of the queen's favour and confidence.'.

On p. 571, *om.* 'into this he brought . . . agreed to his draught; but.'

For 'it was not settled' *read* 'It is not yet settled'; *and om.* 'for it was known . . . former reign.'

For 'but none of these . . . houses' *read* 'but they are not agreed to; so I say nothing in this place concerning them.'

Om. 'the professor . . . exemplary life, but.'

For 'nous' *read* 'logos.'

After 'body' *add* 'but thought that [?the logos] was a creature.'

[*f.* 53 (*a*)] *Om.* 'a reference . . . at a stand.'

On p. 572, *for* 'what should be judged heresy' *read* 'that nothing should be esteemed heresy but what was plainly contrary to the scriptures, or the first four general councils' (cf. *end of page in History*).

Om. 'to be laid before the two houses of convocation.'

At the end of p. 572 *add* 'Here I left it, May 14, 1711.'

[*Burnet, in Jan.* 1711–2, *continues his account of convocation.*]

Cf. *Hist.* ii. 573 (*to* 'came to an end').

[*f.* 54 (*a*)] *Begin* 'I begin now in January, 1711, by our style, to continue this work'; *and for rest of paragraph read* 'The upper house of convocation drew some propositions out of Mr. Whiston's book on which they passed a censure; to which the lower house did not entirely agree; but the prorogation of parliament put a stop to the progress of this matter for that time.'

For 'but both . . . to an end' *read* 'the prorogation put an end to the session; and, soon after, the representation penned by Atterbury was printed, and that gave occasion to the printing that agreed to by the bishops; both were censured as men stood affected.'

[*Act for the South Sea trade.*]

Cf. *Hist.* ii. 573.

For 'aboard; where . . . by credit' *read* 'abroad; where we could not carry on the war' ('aboard,' *though in ed.* 1833, *seems to be a printer's error; see Hist. ed.* 1823 *in loco*).

For 'high' *read* 'so high that there was great loss made by it.'

[*Reflections on the old ministry fully cleared.*]

Cf. *Hist.* ii. 573–4.

For 'so to keep up a clamour . . . power of conviction' *read* 'They found that many accounts were not regularly passed in the exchequer; though the money collected was all brought in and well managed, yet the accounts being so vast, with the vouchers, were not regularly passed. [*f.* 55 (*a*)] The methods of passing accounts are very sure but very slow, calculated to such a small revenue as our princes had anciently; but the supplies being now so great, it was not possible to pass them in haste, when they had so much business on their hands. They knew that in the gross they were right; and thus the accounts of about thirty millions lay before them, which being to go through, so many clerks could not be all examined; so here a clamour was raised that five and thirty millions of the public money were not accounted for, and this was so artificially spread through the nation, that the unthinking multitudes were made believe that the nation was cheated of all that vast sum, and so the nation was confirmed in their aversion to the late administration' (cf. *with all this Hist.* ii. 567–8).

[*Affairs in Spain.*]

Cf. *Hist.* ii. 574–5.

For 'The business . . . hopes failed' *read only* 'Nothing was done in Spain, either on the side of Portugal, or of Catalonia.'

After 'had been supported' *add* 'as he expected.'

Om. 'for the parliament . . . examination'; *and (at this place)* 'the duke of Argyll . . . forces; and.'

After 'two small places' *we find deleted* 'and took them after some time'; *from* 'That of Cardona' *to* 'baggage' *is inserted on f.* 54 (*b*), *with the addition* 'In the relation we have of this action no mention is made of any of the queen's troops.'

For 'and the duke of Vendôme's army . . . on that side' *read* 'The duke of Argyll was sent to command there; he did nothing, but wrote over heavy complaints that he was not supplied as he expected [cf. *Hist.* ii. 574]; and he fell into a quarrelling humour with Staremberg.'

[*The election of king Charles to be emperor.*]

Cf. *Hist.* ii. 575–6.

Om. 'We hoped . . . common cause'; *and (at this place)* 'And Mr. St. John . . . nothing.'

For 'was not then known' *read* 'is not yet known.'

[*f.* 56 (*a*)] *Om.* 'being now safe . . . previous to an election; and'; *and after* 'solemnity' *add* 'in the end of December.'

[*The duke of Marlborough passed the French lines; siege of Bouchain.*]

Cf. *Hist.* ii. 576–7.

For 'and it was said, that Villars . . . to the duke of Marlborough' *read* 'and after some weeks spent in small motions, it was generally thought nothing was to be done there; which seemed to be designed by our ministry and was spoke aloud in the house of commons in a rash sally of Mr. St. John's, in which he told them nothing was to be expected in Flanders' (cf. *Hist.* ii. 575).

From 'the army was much fatigued' *to* 'allowed for refreshment' *is added on f.* 56 (*b*).

[*f.* 57 (*a*)] *After* 'venture on it; the French' *insert* 'brought their army within a mile of the place and.'

From 'was more fatigued' *to* 'the whole war. He' *is added on f.* 56 (*b*).

Om. 'seemed to be very busy . . . purpose; yet.'

After 'reckoned' *insert* 'by all military men'; *and for* 'in the whole . . . war' *read* 'they had ever known in war.'

For 'in those parts' *read* 'gloriously.'

[*An expedition by sea to Canada.*]

Cf. *Hist.* ii. 577–8.

For 'No action . . . command' *read* 'I shall next give an account of the use

that was made of the 5,000 men that were drawn out of his army. An expedition was designed by general Hill (brother to the favourite) ; [he] had the command.'
[*f.* 58 (*a*) *For* 'They sailed . . . to stay' *read* 'and [need] not have lost so.'
Om. 'it was the more . . . the end of the session'; *and* 'the merchants . . . cruisers.'

[*Affairs in Turkey.*]

Cf. Hist. ii. 578–9.
Om. 'not without suspicion . . . money to it.'
For from 'being highly' *to end of paragraph, read only* 'pretends the grand vizier had the czar and his whole army at mercy ; and he studies to infuse this into the grand signior; the reports are various, as is natural in things at such a distance from us.'

[*And in Pomerania.*]

Cf. Hist. ii. 579.
For 'They sat down . . . which rendered' *read* 'They are now before Wismar, trying if they can succeed better there ; if that attempt fails likewise' ; *and after* 'Denmark' *add* 'will become.'

[*Harley's promotion.*]

Cf. Hist. ii. 579 (*to* 'must bring upon him ').
[*f.* 59 (*a*)] *Om.* 'and important' ; *and after* 'at home' *add* 'that will probably bring me to a speedy conclusion of this work.'
Om. 'and, by consequence . . . war.'
For 'flatterers' *read* 'some aspiring scholars[1]'; *and om.* 'and being pre-pared . . . direction.'
Transpose 'He saw the load . . . bring upon him' *and* 'It soon appeared . . . in the favourite'; *for* 'rewards' *read* 'fair appearances'; *and for* 'foreign affairs' *read* 'affairs, now that he was at the head of them.'

[*Negotiations.*]

Cf. Hist. ii. 579 (*from* 'so he resolved' *to* p. 582, *end of second paragraph*).
For 'The earl of Jersey . . . expect a peace' *read* 'And in order to that, in September he sent over one Prior to the court of France, who had been once a boy in a tavern, into which the earl of Dorset happening to come, he saw him reading Horace; so he, who was a very generous [man], took him away from that mean estate, and bred him up in literature ; his genius lay particularly to poetry, and some of his composures were much esteemed. He was earl Jersey's secretary when he was ambassador in France, and it was believed that he (as well as the lord Jersey) continued in a close correspondence both with that court and with the court at St. Germain.'
After 'at Dover' *add* 'because he had not a pass' ; *and for* 'to set him free' *read* 'for his coming up.'
After 'Mesnager' *add* 'now made the count of St. John.'
[*f.* 60 (*a*)] *Om.* 'The court . . . Windsor'; *after* 'copy of them was' *add* 'some days afterwards'; *and om.* 'and printed . . . newspapers'; *adding after* 'out of England' *these words,* 'The grounds of such a severity are not yet

---

[1] Probably a hit at Swift, by whom the patent was drawn.

certainly known, therefore I write of them in these general terms' (*omitting the following paragraph entirely*).

For 'so well . . . their ends' *read* 'would not be a complying tool to ill designs.'

After 'to Holland' *add* '; who had nothing in him to qualify him for that post, but a ready obedience with a bold insolence in his conduct[1].'

For 'It was not then known' *read* 'It is not yet certain.'

For 'to justify . . . work' *read* 'on design to show the impossibility of conquering Spain, or driving the French to better terms' (*omitting thus all reference to Swift's tract*).

After 'hereditary dominions' *add* 'Many reproaches were thrown on the late ministry for the conduct of the war and the alliances'; *om.* 'zealously, though most falsely'; *and after* 'and failed us' *add* 'in not furnishing their quotas.'

[*f.* 61 (*a*)] *For* 'which made them conclude . . . pretender's affairs' *read* 'which seemed to confirm the reports we had from Paris by many hands that it was given out that by a secret article the pretender was to be declared heir of the crown after the queen.'

Om. 'and by the wealth . . . all about them.'

For 'but the memorial was' *read* 'but his ministers took care to have the memorial; and.'

After 'proposed' *add* 'It was well drawn, full and clear; and showed a great dislike of the designs of our court, but in terms full of respect to the queen.'

Om. '(seeing . . . steps)'; *and place* 'the session . . . granted them' *after* 'queen's determination.'

Om. 'this was offered . . . court to' *and* 'they'; *and for* 'then' *read* 'would have.'

[*Preparations for the session; its history.*]

Cf. *Hist.* ii. 582 (*from* 'Before the opening' *to* p. 589, 'proxies were called for'; *and from* p. 590, 'When the fourteenth,' *to* p. 599, 'in thirty-two years').

[*f.* 62 (*a*)] *On* p. 583, *after* 'carrying on the war' *add* 'with vigour.'

[*f.* 63 (*a*)] *For* 'for her speech' *read* 'for the gracious assurances in her speech.'

Om. 'officious courtiers.'

On p. 584, *for* 'three voices' *read* 'five voices.'

[*f.* 63 (*b*)] *On* p. 585, *for* 'the high men in the house of commons' *read* 'the body of the house of commons that went by the name of the October club.'

[*f.* 62 (*b*)] *After* 'part of England' *add* 'these two last clauses were in favour of the dissenters.'

For 'and the court had agents' *read* 'and it was said that the lord treasurer [had] agents.'

On p. 586, *om.* 'and thereby . . . before them.'

For 'a duke in England' *read* 'duke of Brandon.'

Om. 'the queen might give . . . pleased.'

On p. 587, *after* 'constant dependence' *insert* 'at so low a rate'; *and at end of paragraph after* 'might be' *add* [*f.* 61 (*b*)] 'The servile union observed to be among them in voting in every question as the court was inclined had very much prejudiced indifferent men against them.'

---

[1] A suppressed passage of the second volume.

[*f.* 60 (*b*)] *Before* ' On the twenty-second of December ' *read* ' The bill for four shillings in the pound went through the house of commons so quick that.'

For ' this was granted ' *read* ' to this the court agreed.'

On p. 588, *for* ' to proceed at their next meeting' *read* ' to make great noise.'

Om. ' and who had appeared . . . ministry.'

For ' a matter ' *read* ' a man.'

After ' army in Flanders ' *for* ' made ' *read* ' made before with the States, was to give.'

For ' He heard his enemies . . beyond sea : so he wrote to them ' *read* ' Upon which, when he heard his enemies were taking advantages to his prejudice, he wrote to the commissioners of accounts.'

[*f.* 59 (*b*)] *For* ' which they chiefly aimed at ' *read* ' as if he had enriched himself by starving the army.'

For ' But they ' *read* ' But the lord treasurer.'

On p. 589, *for* ' sir Miles Wharton ' *read* ' one '; *and for* ' and that, whereas . . . done by him ' *read* ' as if his vote was to be depended on.'

Om. ' And whereas formerly Jeffreys . . . advanced to be a peer.'

For ' nor was it possible . . . ancient peers, a sense ' *read* ' and a great number of the ancient peers were so entirely brought, or as some said, *bought* over to the court, that it was not possible to raise in them a just sense.'

[*f.* 58 (*b*)] *On* pp. 589-90, *om. paragraph about prince Eugene.*

After ' fourteenth of January came ' *insert* ' the queen was indisposed and.'

After ' they were made ' *insert* ' [and] referring the treaty to her majesty's wisdom.'

For ' assured them ' *read* ' assured us ' (*which shows Burnet was present*).

[*f.* 57 (*b*)] *On* p. 591, *for* ' There were two . . . by the one ' *read* ' [By] a second article in the queen's message '; *and omit* ' by the other . . . put upon it.'

For ' whom they resolved . . . stood thus ' *read* ' a gentleman of Norfolk, who had distinguished himself eminently for many years in the house of commons and had gone through great posts ; he had been secretary of war and treasurer of the navy.'

After ' friend of his own ' *add* ' one Mann.'

On p. 592, *for* ' the person concerned ' *read* ' Mann.'

[*f.* 55 (*b*)[1]] *For* ' insisted . . . the bill ' *read* ' being weary of the opposition that he gave them, and to put him out of the way, that he might not oppose them [cf. *Hist.* ii. 591] in that which was to come next before them.'

Om. ' it was often . . . much more.'

For ' so that it appeared . . . denied ' *read* ' yet they would not let that be put to the vote, that the paying this to the general had been customary.'

Om. ' and paid so well for it '; *and for* ' by a great majority ' *read* ' by a majority of above a hundred.'

[*f.* 53 (*b*)[2]] *On* p. 593, *om.* ' but what this will end in . . . time.'

After ' ordnance in his room ' *add* ' but he found that whereas the old establishment settled £10 a day on that office when the master of it travelled, duke Marlborough had reduced it to four.'

---

[1] f. 56 (*b*), we remember, contains only some additions to f. 57 (*a*).

[2] f. 54 (*b*) has likewise only the addition to f. 55 (*a*).

For 'in the late king's time' *read* 'long before he had the command.'

For 'for it was . . . producing nothing' *read* 'even those who favoured him thought somewhat of this sort might have been discovered that way. He appearing so clear in the only thing of which he was suspected, his enemies.'

After 'administration' *read* 'by finding nothing when they searched so narrowly for it.'

For 'could have expected' *read* 'could have done.'

Om. 'happy does . . . whole transaction.'

'Impudent' *is correct.*

[*f.* 52 (*b*)] *On* p. 594, *om.* 'though it exceeded . . . very far.'

For 'Those who . . . designs' *read* 'Those who managed Scottish affairs.'

Om. 'this seemed so reasonable that.'

Om. 'which in most places . . . church power'; *and substitute* 'yet it passed with this extent.'

Om. 'it was well known . . . cover them from it'; *and for* 'since it seemed . . . It was well understood' *read* 'because it was known.'

[*f.* 51 (*b*)] *On* p. 595, *for* 'but those who intended to excuse . . . up from the commons' *read* 'but those who intended to irritate them carried it against this; so the act passed ; what effect it will have must appear when the day limited for taking the abjuration comes.'

After 'irritate them' *add* 'so no opposition was made to this.'

For 'by an act of' *read* 'in the second year of.'

For 'of a more public nature' *read* '[which] gave a more general alarm.'

Om. 'but had been taken . . . agreements with us' *and* 'these were chiefly . . . by them.'

On p. 596, *om.* 'from the time . . . Pyrenees.'

[*f.* 50 (*b*)] *Om.* 'during this war.'

For 'for the maintaining this' *read* 'for communication with them and for defending those places.'

For 'they also asked' *read* 'they only asked [further].'

Before 'the trade' *add* 'insensibly.'

After 'was made' *read* '[anno] 1609.'

On p. 597, *for* 'The mercenary writers . . . to defend' *read* 'The writers that favoured.'

[*f.* 49 (*b*)] *For* 'whereas . . . counsels' *read* 'This pointed plainly to the pretender.'

Om. 'and might erect . . . capable of them'; *and for* 'but it was answered that' *read* 'though.'

For 'But reason . . . taken so' *read* 'But on those occasions men love not to speak plain ; yet.'

On p. 598, *for* 'strange preludes . . . peace' *read* 'a prelude to a bad peace.'

[*f.* 48 (*b*)] *Om.* 'but no notice . . . drew it.'

For 'This was a confutation . . . made, yet' *read* 'Yet this did them little service.'

For 'in which . . . no opposition' *read* 'with success ; for the Whigs, seeing the earl of Nottingham and his friends set on carrying it, made no opposition to it.'

Om. 'as was ordinary.'

After 'easily there' *add* 'for it was reckoned that it would be rejected by the lords ; but.'

On p. 599, *after* ' so many there, that' *add* 'as the Whigs who had formerly opposed the bill now promoted it, so.'

[*Affairs abroad.*]

Cf. *Hist.* ii. 599 (*from* 'I look next' *to* p. 602, 'conversed with her').

[*f.* 47 (*b*)] *Om.* 'and unwillingly'; *and after* 'preliminaries' *add* '[by] our court'; *and after* 'named' *add* '[by them].'

Om. 'but they waited . . . allies.'

For 'in a very high strain' *read* 'in so high a strain that, by it, they seemed to be well assured of our court's standing by them.'

Before 'These demands' *read* 'All people were amazed.'

On p. 600, *after* 'dying condition' *add* 'though he is not yet dead.'

Om. 'as is usual . . . occasions.'

Om. 'was believed . . . chemistry, and' *before* 'ambitious' *insert* 'wicked and'; *and after* 'prince' *insert* [*f.* 46 (*b*)] 'abandoned to the most execrable vices, and capable of the worst projects ; for.'

Om. 'and to marry . . . dowager.'

From 'King Philip' *to* 'the original letter' *is written on the margin.*

On p. 601, *for* 'These deaths . . . portend that' *read* 'All observers of Providence did consider these deaths in so critical a time as very amazing things by which.'

For 'But I will go . . . prospect' *read* 'But I restrain myself from looking too far into what is before me.'

For 'the lord treasurer' *read* 'the court' ; *and for* 'he saw' *read* 'there was.'

Om. 'yet the doing . . . act.'

After 'in that treaty' *add* 'who owned him king.'

[*f.* 45 (*b*)] *after* 'specific answers in writing' *add* 'Whether this was refused by the French on design, from the beginning of the treaty, on purpose to gain time and to create jealousies among the allies ; or if it arose out of the many unlooked-for deaths by which king Philip was now so near the succession to the crown of France, so that they knew not how to frame a direct answer, is not yet known ; but they have now, to the beginning of May, N.S., drawn out the matter in many fruitless meetings,' &c., *as in Hist.*

For 'the negotiation there was' *read* 'matters there are.'

On p. 602, *before* 'The preparations' *add* 'In the meanwhile.'

[*f.* 44 (*b*)] *For* 'At this time . . . with her' *read* 'The court of St. Germain was struck with great apprehension upon the pretender's having the small-pox ; but he recovered of them, and at the same time his sister died of them. She was by all that saw her admired as a most extraordinary person in all respects, so the nation here was filled with very extraordinary characters of her ; and now while I am writing we have a report very current that the pretender himself is dead. If it proves true, these deaths, as well as those of the house of Bourbon, must be looked on as very extraordinary indications of a watchful Providence, that happily interposes to save us when we had great reason to look on our affairs as almost desperate.'

[*Convocation meets.*]

Cf. *from Hist.* ii. 602 *to* p. 605, *end of first paragraph.*

For 'I turn next . . . convocation' *read* 'The convocation did little this winter.'

Om. 'in pursuance . . . amongst them.'

For 'a very defective abstract of it' *read* 'some of the weakest of our arguments.'

[*f.* 43 (*b*)] *On* p. 603, *after* 'and probably this' *read* 'will be settled during the session; which.'

For 'that he came not among us' *read* 'that he did not stir from Lambeth.'

For 'but none . . . session' *read* 'but now in the end of May we have yet received no answer'; *and end paragraph in present tense; omitting* 'I was gone . . . passed.'

After 'openly' *add* 'and severely.'

On p. 604, *om.* 'nor was the dispute . . . congregations.'

[*f.* 42 (*b*)] *For* 'among us; and the necessity' *read* '[among us,] as to the necessity.'

For 'were entertained' *read* 'and was entertained'; *and for* 'by many' *read* 'by our high clergy'; *and for* 'far out of view' *read* 'so far out of view, that this late and wild system came to work mightily on them.'

For 'but few' *read* 'and some.'

[*Supply in parliament; and events to June* 2 (1712), *when Burnet concludes for the time.*]

Cf. *Hist.* ii. 605-7 (*to* 'words he had used').

[*f.* 41 (*b*)] *On* p. 605, *for* 'demanded were given' *read* 'went on very largely.'

After 'the malt bill' *add* '[which] passed easily.'

After 'indignity on his grants:' *add* 'others in friendship to the persons concerned in those grants opposed the bill: yet'; *and after* 'two' *add* 'or at most three.'

On p. 606, *after* 'last reading of the bill' *read* 'in a very full house'; *and om.* 'so for that . . . lost.'

[*f.* 40 (*b*)] *For* 'expectation' *read* 'daily expectation.'

For 'That prince Eugene' *read* '[It] was.'

Om. 'which were not produced . . . bare reports.'

On p. 607, *for* 'and all were in great . . . produce' *read* 'and we are now all in expectation to see what a few days will bring forth.'

[*f.* 39 (*b*)] *For* 'but nothing followed . . . quick one after another' *read* 'But the day after this debate in both houses we were surprised with a relation of what passed.'

After 'he had used' *add* 'Here I stop, the 2nd of June'; *and om. rest of paragraph.*

[*Burnet resumes his pen and describes remainder of session.*]

Cf. *Hist.* ii. 608 (*from* 'On the fifth of June' *to* p. 609, 'either of their addresses').

[*f.* 38 (*b*)] *On* p. 608 *the stipulation about the succession in England is added on the margin.*

For 'for communicating' *read* 'for her condescension in communicating.'

Om. 'who had all along protested . . . taken.'

[*f.* 37 (*b*)] *On* p. 609, *for* 'the queen in her speech' *read* 'the period of the queen's speech that related to the plan of the peace was the subject of some reflections; for in it she.'

After 'either of their addresses' *add* 'but the nation was so weary of taxes that they were resolved to accept of any peace whatsoever.'

[*Events to the end of the year* 1712.]

Cf. *Hist.* ii. 609 (*from* ' The earl of Strafford ' *to* p. 614, *end of first paragraph*).

On p. 609, *after* ' in order to a general peace ' *insert* ' but when the auxiliary troops refused to conform themselves to the duke of Ormond's orders, there was for some days a stop in the offer of delivering up Dunkirk ; but ' ; *and after* ' place ' *insert* ' and then.'

[*f.* 36 (*b*)] On p. 610, *for* ' as treacherous . . . degree. The ' *read* ' with the further aggravation that the.'

Om. ' and if the auxiliary . . . prevented.'

For ' by a general voice ' *read* ' by addresses.'

From ' that lay on both sides ' *to* ' his whole army ' *is inserted on the margin.*

[*f.* 35 (*b*)] On p. 611, *for* ' would not . . . loss ' *read* ' would not consent to anything decisive ' (*the whole clause is a subsequent insertion of the bishop's*).

Om. ' with secret instructions ' ; *after* ' fully concluded ' *add* ' and is said to be since ratified on both sides ' ; *and for* ' all that was published . . . return, was ' *read* ' hitherto nothing is published but.'

After ' lord Lexington to Spain ' *add* ' and thus a most glorious war is brought to a most inglorious end. I still carry on my narrative, till a peace is publicly owned [1].'

For ' which, it was said . . . imperiousness ' *read* ' with a great indecency both of language and behaviour ' ; *om.* ' to have Valenciennes demolished ' ; *and after* ' for trade ' *add* ' between France and them.'

On p. 612, *for* ' The lord Lexington . . . and Strafford ' *read* ' With this the earl of Strafford returned ; and soon after there was a promotion [*f.* 34 (*b*)] of six knights of the garter ; for there were then nine vacant stalls ; so that the order was scarce able to furnish out a decent chapter. One of these was duke Hamilton.'

For ' high provocation ' *read* ' small provocation ' ; *and om.* ' but both . . . honour.'

On p. 613, *for* ' who was a good-natured . . . foreign affairs ' *read* ' Thus I have laid this all together, though it happened after other transactions which I am next to relate.'

Om. ' one or other of.'

For ' At the same time . . . give him ' *read* ' A little time will show how far the Swedes are in condition to pursue [*f.* 33 (*b*)] their victory, while at the same time reports from Constantinople seem to threaten a new war from thence to the czar, which the king of Sweden is still pressing, assisted by the practices of the French at the Porte.

For ' This gave ' *read* ' This must give ' ; *and for* ' that disorders . . . he had taken to ' *read* ' who is studying ' ; *for* ' that kingdom ' *read* ' Hungary ' ; *and after* ' continue the war ' *add* ' who have been for some months under great distractions with relation to that matter.'

For ' but to draw . . . the more ' *read* ' but before the negotiation for a general peace was to be entered on.'

On p. 614, *for* ' as also for obtaining . . . intercession ' *read* ' and that the emperor may be also brought into the peace. In a few days we will see what our court says in answer to this ; and in this state do our affairs now stand, in

---

[1] The second sentence probably represents a fresh start, as the ink is less faded.

the beginning of the year, a few days before the session of parliament is to be opened.'

[*Postscript: death of Godolphin; events to signing of new barrier treaty.*]

Cf. *Hist.* ii. 614-6.

Begin ' I will to this only add somewhat relating to the duke of Marlborough ; his great friend the earl of Godolphin died,' *&c., as in Hist.*

[*f.* 32 (*b*)] *Om.* ' affection and.'

For ' artful favourite ' *read only* ' waiting-woman ' ; *and for* ' of a great genius ' *read* ' of any one good quality.'

For ' some pretended ' *read* ' some thought ' ; *and for* ' of fear . . . himself ' *read* ' of a mean fear.'

For ' he would be at liberty ' *read* ' he is at liberty ' ; *and for* ' might ' *read* ' may.'

On p. 615, *for from* ' Upon his going ' *to end of paragraph read* ' How far either of these two suits will be carried on or in what they will end [*f.* 31 (*b*)] a little time will show.'

Om. ' And during that time . . . died.'

For ' to come into ' *read* ' to come in, (as the word was) into.'

After ' apprehensions of a war ' *add* ' between the Turk and the czar.'

For ' come down . . . Strasbourg ' *read* ' try if he could bring the queen to obtain better terms for him ; the States also continued to press the restoring of Strasbourg ; but that ' ; *and for* ' nor did it . . . project ' *read* ' At last the States were brought to accept of the terms that we imposed on them ; in which though they pressed much to have Condé demolished, yet the French refusing it, we did not urge it.'

After ' forced to yield ' *add* ' to us ' ; *and for* ' into some confidence with them ' *read* ' more entirely into their dependence.'

On p. 616, *for from* ' we were not able ' *to end of paragraph read* ' they seem, by their behaviour, to design another campaign ; but that will now appear very soon.'

[*Prorogations of parliament ; events up to March* 24, 171⅔ ; *when Burnet concludes for the time.*]

Cf. *Hist.* ii. 616-7 (*to* ' a house near Adrianople ').

Begin ' In the meanwhile our parliament stands prorogued now for the third time ; though a proclamation was [*f.* 30 (*b*)] set out,' *&c., as in Hist.* ; *and for* ' but though ' *read* ' and [though] ' ; *and om.* ' yet we were . . . three weeks.'

For from ' Many expresses ' *to* ' a new scene ' *read* ' The nation is full of rumours that occasion great jealousies and fears ; but till it appears what ground there is for them, I shall say no more concerning them.'

From ' The Swedes ' *to end of paragraph is in present tense ; and for* ' that their retreat . . . Baltic sea ' *read* ' that it is apprehended their retreat by land is cut off.'

Om. ' he raised . . . . dominions ' ; *and for* ' but was so apt . . . whispers, that ' *read* ' as long as they maintained their credit with him ; but.'

On p. 617, *after* ' inclination ' *read* ' and to be very firm to the alliance against

France'; *and after* 'time' *add* 'He has hitherto made the king of Sweden his pattern; it will soon appear what ply he will take in the affairs of Europe.'

For 'varied so often ... end' *read* 'do not increase, though'; *and for* 'but he threw himself ... opposed the war' *read* 'but if the general peace of Europe (which we are told is almost quite concluded) does take effect, it is not probable that the Turks will suffer themselves to be drawn into a new war. [*f.* 29 (*b*)] But as I am writing, we have an account of the king of Sweden's misfortunes. The grand signior was diverted from the war with the czar, and.'

Om. 'much superior to his'; *and for* 'a house near Adrianople' *read* '[as was at first given out] to Thessalonica[1].'

For from 'but not suffered' *to end of paragraph read* 'Whether this will prove the final catastrophe of this unquiet prince, as most people think it will, must be left to time. We are now in the sixth prorogation, and a seventh is generally expected within two days [cf. *Hist.* ii. 616], for I end 24 March, 171⅔.'

[*The signature of peace; and the debates upon treaty of commerce.*]

Cf. *Hist.* ii. 617-23 (*to* 'prayer of their address').

For '13th of March' *read* 'March 31'; *and after* 'upon this' *read* 'after a seventh prorogation' (*see Hist.* ii. 616).

On p. 618 *om.* '(which of course ... queen)'; *after* 'out of France into' *insert* 'Lorraine; but even there he was in'; *and after* 'crown of France' *add* 'but compliments are easily carried.'

[*f.* 28 (*b*)] *For* 'was not yet finished' *read* 'is not yet finished.'

For from 'the emperor' *to* p. 619 'his losses; the States' *read* 'but the empire and the emperor would not accept the terms offered them; which were, the restoring the electors of Bavaria and Cologne, with a high demand for their losses, and the mesne profits; in lieu of which the emperor was to deliver Sardinia to the elector of Bavaria. So upon the matter the empire had nothing, the emperor had only the duchy of Milan, the kingdom of Naples, and the property of the Netherlands, the States being to keep the fortified places; they.'

For 'the emperor ... accepting of it' *read* 'Reflections were soon made on the articles of peace and commerce.'

For 'no mention ... treaty' *read* 'so this was thought a delusory article, that amounted to nothing.'

Om. (*at this place*) 'at last ... made of it' (*for which see infra*, p. 448).

Om. 'The English have always ... foreigners.'

For 'these were the reflections on the treaty of peace; but' *read* 'But as these exceptions were very visible and of great importance.'

[*f.* 27 (*b*)] *For* 'but the court at that time ... still on' *read only* 'yet the trade with France being favoured by the court, trade went still on, though at a great loss'; *and om.* 'and to the end ... no more parliaments.'

On p. 620 *some provisions concerning a treaty of commerce are repeated from* p. 618; *and before* 'It was said that' *is inserted* 'Great exceptions were taken to all this.'

---

[1] The words in brackets are a subsequent insertion of Burnet's.

Om. 'which is more than double . . . Portugal' *and* 'besides a great vent of our manufactures.'

The figure is 300,000.

[*f.* 26 (*b*)] *Om.* 'since the cheapness . . . markets.'

Om. 'they called it faction.'

On p. 621, *om.* 'it was carried in the affirmative . . . could bear.'

Om. 'though it was as good . . . interpreted.'

[*f.* 25 (*b*)] *On* p. 622, *for* 'and the commissioners for trade and plantations . . . there it was settled' *read only* 'and the last project was settled without so much as consulting with the commission for trade and plantations.'

On p. 623, *for* 'it was not then' *read* '[it] is not yet.'

For 'It was brought . . . step' *read* 'The bill was reported by the committee'; *and for* 'those who' *read* 'those called Tories who'; *and after* 'division' *read* 'of a full house (near 400)'; *and after* 'importance lost' *add* 'on the 18 June. What may be further done on this head must be left to time; for I am writing this on the 23 June'; *and then add passage concerning Dunkirk address from* p. 619 ('It did not appear . . . explanation being made of it'); *for* 'Some weeks' *reading* '[They] began to think no answer was to be made; [for] a fortnight'; *and for* 'but we were still . . . made of it' *reading* [*f.* 24 (*b*)] 'This answer amazed them; it is not yet explained; so the event must declare it'; *and then return to* p. 623, *from* 'But the house of commons, to soften.'

Om. from 'It was once apprehended' *to end of paragraph, and the whole of the speech,* pp. 623–7.

[*Demands on behalf of the civil list; address for the pretender's removal; Burnet concludes for the time, July* 4, 1713.]

Cf. *Hist.* ii. 628 (*from* 'I now go on' *to* p. 629, 'with her desire on that occasion').

For 'I now go . . . session' *read* 'This [i. e. *the peculiarity of the queen's answer to the address of the house of commons*] was observed by some; but.'

For 'a large overplus' *read* '£600,000.'

Om. 'upon a new account . . . £800,000 less; and.'

After 'due to the civil list' *add* 'and the customs assigned by the civil list did increase considerably in times of peace (*see Hist.* ii. 628, *infra*); so that considering what was due to the civil list, and what was owing from it, the debt was really but about £300,000' (*this seems to represent* 'these two sums . . . £240,000,' *which does not appear*).

For 'in the end of the session . . . left' *read* 'when not above a third part of the house was in town, the greater part being gone home to look after their elections.'

For 'This was thought . . . argument' *read only* 'Some opposition was made to this' (*and* cf. *supra*).

[*f.* 23 (*b*)] *For* 'the ministers' *read* 'the house of commons.'

On p. 629, *for* 'And the weight . . . agitation' *read only* 'But when the session was near an end.'

After 'nemine contradicente' *read* 'with an offer to assist and support the queen in making those instances effectual.'

For 'all the answer . . . informed of that' *read* 'This I write on the 4th of July.'

[*Deaths of Sprat and Compton, and events to close of Burnet's historical Narrative.*]

Cf. *Hist.* ii. 629-32.

After 'died' *add* 'suddenly'; *and om.* 'to which his temper . . . profession'; *and for* 'a great' *read* 'the greatest.'

On p. 630, *after* 'power of others' *add* 'and was neither learned, lively, nor judicious[1]'; *and om.* 'he was succeeded . . . Bristol.'

[*f.* 22 (*b*)] *On* p. 631, *after* 'addresses of both houses' *add* 'To endanger advantages was an odd expression[2].'

[*f.* 21 (*b*)] *For* 'it was fit . . . close this work' *read only* 'and so have ended my design in composing this work for the use and benefit of posterity.'

For 'of above three and fifty years. I' *read only* 'which I'; *and om.* 'it.'

On p. 632, *after the last word add* 'And then I shall have attained my chief end in writing.'

The Conclusion[3].

Cf. *Hist.* ii. 633-69.

[*f.* 84 (*b*)] *On* p. 641, *for* 'and so severe . . . dissenters' *read* 'and in a disposition to severity ; that shows itself in too visible an aversion to the dissenters, and an uneasiness under the toleration.'

[*f.* 80 (*b*)] *On* p. 648, *after* 'better in their labours' *add* 'for I have much experience of this, that when I have prayed with more than ordinary earnestness for a blessing on my preaching, I have often seen signal effects of it.'

[*f.* 79 (*b*)] *On* p. 649, *for* 'the course of his reign' *read* 'his flagitious reign.'

[*f.* 73 (*b*)] *On* p. 657, 'this is not true of' *is substituted for* 'these dare not own this to' *deleted.*

After 'and destroy religion' *we find deleted* 'and by false stories and subtle methods they heighten a jealousy of them.'

After 'it is visible' *we find deleted* 'to all the world'; *and after* 'acquiesce' *we find deleted.* 'and are only on the defensive, studying to preserve it.'

[*f.* 72 (*b*)] 'when that is ended it may probably' *is substituted for* 'and that there is a foreign management in the case. Then it will' *deleted.*

On p. 658, *om.* 'perhaps' *before* 'some of their leaders.'

After 'much the greater part' (*end of a paragraph*) *add* 'This appears evidently in all the controverted elections in the house of commons, and begins to show itself too visibly in the judicature of the house of lords ; and I must say, in my observation, that the Tories are much more grossly and indecently partial, than ever I saw the Whigs.'

On p. 659, *after* 'an entire system of our laws' *add* 'There is one man yet

---

[1] A suppressed passage of the second volume.

[2] See preceding note. This passage, and the passage in the *History* from 'It was also observed' to 'protestant succession,' are added on the margin of f. 22 (*b*).

[3] Written on the versos of ff. 91-64, the book being reversed. Its date is June, 1708 ; see *supra*, p. xv. The printed version has a few grammatical corrections ; but excepting these, and the instances quoted above, the MS. and published *History* are practically identical, in wording as in substance. The deletions on ff. 73 (*b*), 72 (*b*), and 68 (*b*) resemble in form those of the autograph of the *History*, first volume.

alive, who I hope has yet many years before him, who is the fittest person of this or the former age [for this task].   [*f.* 71 (*b*)] If this is not done by the lord Somers, I know not the man that can do it[1].'

After 'for a bishop' *add* 'who has not passed for a narrow-handed man.'

[*f.* 68 (*b*)] *On* p. 664, *after* 'which render those who' *we find deleted* 'like the present king of France[2].'

_____

[1] Lord Somers survived Burnet little more than a year, dying April 26, 1716, nearly eight years before the appearance of the *History*.

[2] Louis XIV died Sept. 1, 1715, a few months after Burnet's death.

PART II

(BURNET'S AUTOBIOGRAPHY[1])

(Bodl. Add. MSS. D. 24, ff. 195–218).

[a] ROUGH DRAUGHT OF MY OWN LIFE [a].

The Introduction.

I DO not write my own life out of vanity to give my selfe
a fame and a name to posterity; but because I know I can
mix in the account I am to give of it some usefull instructions to those who may read it, and [b] since I have been so
long on the stage, and have acted in so manny different
stations and have had so large a share of favour and approbation from some, and of censure and obloquy from others [b], I
have reason to think that after my death some will write concerning me ; some in kindnes and some out of hatred, or
some only to publish a book that may have sale, therefore I
who am best acquainted with my own concerns and may be
supposed best able to judge what may be fit to be remembred
and what not, have resolved to give such an account of my
selfe, as I hope may be of some use to the world. [c] I am the
more encouraged in this because I find *Thuanus*[2] did it. I
have made him my pattern in writing [c], and as I read most of
him manny years ago, and formed my designe in writting
from that great Originall ; so after I had ended my History,

[a] Cf. Life in *Hist.* ii. 671.   [b] *Ibid.*   [c] *Ibid.*

---

[1] There is no need of any introductory note, as the circumstances
connected with the composition of
the Autobiography and its suppression
are discussed at length in the Introduction, *supra.* The MS. (Bodl. Add.
MSS. D. 24, ff. 195–218) is throughout
in the handwriting of Dr. Burnet ;
and some of the folios are misplaced.
The headings appear in the margin of
the MS.

[2] With whose standpoint (no less
than his method) our author has
something in common.

I read him all over again, to see how farre I had risen up in my imitation of him, and was not a litle pleased to find that if I did not flatter my selfe too much, I had in some degree answered my designe in resembling him. It is tru I have avoided a particular recitall of warlike actions both in battles or sieges[1], and I have not endeavoured to be so copious as he is in the relation of forreigne affairs[2] or in the lives and writtings of learned men. I have not had the opportunities that his station gave him of being informed of these things ; and have wrote on designe to be a[s] short as possible, and to point chiefly at the good and bad of what I have known, for the instruction of others. As I have followed that great man in the main of my work, so I will adde such a relation of my own particular circumstances, as I hope may serve to carry on my designe in endeavouring to make the next generation better and wiser by what I have observed and by what has occured to me.

My birth and my Parents.

[a] I was born at Edinburgh on the 18[t] of September 1643. My Father[3] was a younger son of a family of considerable antiquity and interest in Aberdeenshire. He was bred to the law and studied seven years in France. He was learned in his profession, but did not rise up to the first form in practise. His judgment was good[a], but he had not a lively imagination, nor a ready expression, and [b] his abilities were depressed by his excessive modesty. [c] He was eminent for integrity and probity[c] and spoke his thoughts freely on the tenderest subjects. When he found a cause morally injust he would not plead in it, but pressed his client to consider his conscience more then his interest, in which he often succeeded, for he spoke with great authority on those occasions : [d] he was allwaies ready to

---

[a] Cf. Life in *Hist.* ii. 672.   [b] *Ibid.*   [c] *Ibid.*, and *Hist.* i. 2.   [d] Life in *Hist.* ii. 672.

---

[1] For his reason see *supra*, p. 165.
[2] See Von Ranke, ed. 1868, vol. vii. App. ii. p. 155.
[3] For whom consult *Hist.* i. 2, 79–80 ; and Cockburn's *Specimen*, Remark, ii. pp. 25-6, with the paper mentioned *supra*, p. 12, note (to be printed by the Scottish History Society).

plead the causes of the poor, and instead of taking fees from them, he supplied such as he saw were injustly oppressed very liberally. He never took any fee from a Clergyman who sued for the rights of his Church, and he was so friendly and generous in his practise, that he told me the full halfe of his practise went for charity or for friendship [a]. He grew to be disgusted of his profession. He studied Divinity for some years and intended to change his gown, but [b] he was dissatisfied with the conduct of the Bishops. He was in high esteem for the exemplary strictnes of his life [b] and was much considered by them but [c] he was displeased with most of them and delivered him selfe so plainly that [c] he lost the favour of the governing Bishops: [d] and at the breaking out of the troubles in the year 1637 he was looked on as a Puritan.

But when he saw that instead of reforming abuses, the Order it selfe was struck at, he did adhere to it with great zeal, [e] and in the warrs that followed he stuck to the rights of the Crown without once complying in any respect with the party that then prevailed. [f] He never took the Covenant [1] and left his profession and was forced three severall times to leave the Kingdome, staying at one time five years out of it. [g] Not that he thought that it was not lawfull to rise in armes when the King broke the lawes, for he allwaies espoused Barclay and Grotius' notions in that matter, but he thought that was not the case [g] but that the King's authority was invaded against law, so he relinquished his profession for above twenty years and lived privatly up on his estate but was a preacher of righteousnes for he catechised not only his [*f.* 196] servants but his tennants frequently, at least every Lord's day of which he was a very strict observer, and indeed to all that came to him he recommended the practise of religion and vertue with great earnestnes and often with many tears. He treated those who differed from him in opinion with great gentlenes.

[a] Cf. Life in *Hist.* ii. 672.   [b] *Ibid.*, and *Hist.* i. 2.   [c] *Ibid.*   [d] *Ibid.*
[e] *Ibid.*   [f] Life in *Hist.* ii. 673.   [g] *Ibid.* 672.

---

[1] See *supra*, p. 12 and note.

My Education;

[a] I had the chieffe advantage of his retirement for he made the teaching me a great part of his care [b] I was sent to no school but was taught Latine by him with such successe that before I was ten year old I was master of that tongue and of the Classick Authors. I was five years at the Colledge of New Aberdeen and went thro the common methods of the Aristotelian Philosophy with no small applause, and passed Master of Arts some moneths before I was fourteen [b]; but all that while my Father was my chieff tutor, for he made me rise constantly about four. He perhaps loaded me with too much knowledge, for I was excessively vain of it. It is true he humbled me with much severe correction, in which how much soever I might deserve it by manny wild frolicks yet I think he carried that too farre, for the fear of that brought me under too great an uneasynes and sometimes even to a hatred of my Father. The sense of this may have perhaps carried me in the education of my children to the other extream of too much indulgence. But when I remember how near I was often to the taking desperate methods this has given me a biasse the other way.

and first studies.

When my Father desired me to choose which way I would direct my studies I saw the advantages of the profession of the law and was so sensible of the assistance my Father could give me in it, that [c] I choose that to my Father's great regret, who had allwaies designed me to be a Clergyman [c]. I had an elder brother who was a Lawier[1], and as the eldest was a Phisitian[2], so we being three my Father wished we might be all of different professions, but he would use no authority in that matter and left me to my free choice. [d] For a year together I studied the Civill and Feudall law with that advan-

---

[a] Cf. Life in *Hist.* ii. 673, and *Hist.* i. 1–2.   [b] Life in *Hist.* ii. 673.   [c] *Ibid.*
[d] *Ibid.*

---

[1] See *supra*, p. 4.
[2] Thomas Burnet, afterwards knight-

ed; see *Hist.* i. 541 ; art. on him, *Dict. Nat. Biog.* ; Cockburn, *Specimen*, p. 27.

tage that I find the good effects of it to this day, for without it I should not have had just notions of humane society and of government, and I impute the wrong notions that manny Divines have of government to their being unacquainted with the principles of law [1]. After I had for a year run thro these studies I told my Father I intended to change my designe and to apply my selfe to Divinity [a]. He was overjoied at this and ran out with manny tears into a heavenly discourse of the noblenes of a function that was dedicated to God and to the saving of souls, and charged me to study not out of vanity or ambition but to understand the Scriptures well and to have a tru sense of divine matters in my own mind. He continued to the end of his daies repeating manny good instructions to me, he told me that he had seen much ambition, great covetousnes and violent animosities among our Bishops which had ruined the Church. He charged me to treat all who differed from me with gentlenes and moderation and to apply my selfe chiefly to prayer, the reading the Scriptures, and to the practicall part. [b] I followed for some years a hard course of study, I went thro the Bible with severall Comentaries on all the parts of it. I did also study controversy and read Bellarmine and Chamier [2] in opposition to one another quite thro [b]. I fell violently into another study which had almost undone me, [c] I went thro severall bodies of School Divinity [c], and read above twenty volumes in folio of these writters and grew fond of them. This heightned my vanity and brought me into a false way of reasoning and everlasting wrangling which made me despise and triumph over all who had not suffered themselves to be entangled with that cobweb stuffe. [d] I read also manny volumes of History of all sorts [d] so that I furnished my selfe with much matter of discourse and laid it all out upon all occasions [3]. [*f.* 195 (*b*)] [e] I had a very happy constitution capable of much labour and hard study [e] and I

---

[a] Cf. Life in *Hist.* ii. 673. [b] *Ibid.* [c] *Ibid.* [d] *Ibid.* [e] *Ibid.* 676.

---

[1] See *supra*, p. 102.
[2] *D. Chamieri Panstratiae Catholicae.*
[3] The next few sentences are an addition made on the verso of preceding page.

was never the worse but the better for labour and study,
[a] I have enjoied to this day a perfect health [a], excepting only
two or three feavers which I believe fortified my constitution
so that I have often reckoned that I had a more than ordinary
account to be given of my time, since I have lived free
of all lingring indispositions and of all pains, some very
gentle fitts of the gout excepted.   This I owe to the good
constitution and regularity of my parents and to the sobriety
in which I have allwaies lived.   [b] I had with this good state
of health an extraordinary happiness of memory that took
things soon and kept them long and a quicknes of imagination,
so that my ideas very ever ready [*sic, qu.* were ever very
ready] and in order, and I had a great copiousnes of expression [b], so happily did God and his Providence furnish me [1]
to do him great service if I had made good use of them
[*f.* 196].

The trialls of Preachers in Scotland.

[c] I was desired to enter upon preaching according to the
method of Scotland as Probationer, or as they call it an
Expectant preacher, who after a course of trialls that last
about 3 moneths are allowed to preach where they are desired, and here I will give an account of these.   First they
preach only practically on a text given them, then they preach
critically on a harder text, then they are tried on a mixture
of both waies in one, then they have some head in Divinity
given them for a Latin explanation of it, upon which they give
out Theses and defend them [c], they have also some period

---

[a] Cf. Life in *Hist.* ii. 721.   [b] *Ibid.* 676.   [c] *Ibid.* 674.

---

[1] Cockburn also dilates on Burnet's early proficiency and precocious ability: 'He had good natural parts, a quick apprehension, and a prodigious memory; but too volatile for exercising a judgement and penetrating into the depth of things. He stayed no longer upon a science than after he had got some view of it, and so much as could enable him to hold some discourse upon it; and affected the appearance of knowing many things, rather than any one thing perfectly.   It was his misfortune that his father died so early, for he would have been a great curb to his youthful levities and extravagancies; but that restraint being taken off, he gave all liberty to his curious, heedless, and precipitant genius.' *Specimen*, pp. 27-8.

of the Scripture History given them to explain and clear the difficulties in it, [a] after that an Hebrew Psalm is given them to expound, and they are examined upon the Greek Testament and at last comes the questionary triall, every Clergyman of the precinct [*sic*] putting such questions out of the Scripture or the body of Divinity as he [*f.* 197] thinks fit to try the knowledge of the person. None is admitted to these trialls but upon the testimony of the Minister wher he lives of his good life and good temper, and if in the course of them any scandall breaks out upon him a stop is presently put to them. After Episcopacy was set up [a], all the alteration that the Bishops made in this was that when the Clergy did approve any person who passed thro these trialls they certified it to the Bishop and he either put him to some new triall for his own satisfaction, or he gave him a licence to preach upon the Testimoniall of the Clergy. When any person was presented to a Benefice he was to go over all these trialls again, and being approved by the Clergy they certified that to the Bishop, who upon that proceeded to Ordination. This being so much a better method than any we have [b] I set it down the more particularly [b] in case we are at any time so happy or so wise as to consider how things among us may be brought to a better state, here a sketch is given of a method for examining persons before they are ordained Deacons or Priests.   [c] I past thro these trialls some moneths before I was eighteen.

My Father was made Judge.

[d] Soon after that my Father was made a Judge [d]. When he took his place on the Bench he made a speech or rather sermon to his brethren, and opened the characters given of Judges, 18 Exod. 21, 22 v., and 2 Chron. 19, 6-7 v., in so plain and convincing a manner that some of the Bench have told me they never were so much moved with any discourse they had ever heard, and they hoped the impression that it made on them should never wear out of their minds. The greatest defect I had ever observed in my good Father was

[a] Cf. Life in *Hist.* ii. 674.   [b] *Ibid. supra.*   [c] *Ibid. bis.*   [d] *Ibid.*

his earnestnes to see me settled.   ᵃ I was presented by his
nephew Sir Alexander Burnet to a Benefice where his family
resided and in the center of all our kinred.   My Father left it
to me to consider whether I would accept of it or not ᵃ, but
plainly intimated his wishes that I would.   ᵇ There is no law
in Scotland that limits the age of a Clergy man, but by the
happy Providence of God I refused it.   I thought one that
was not yet 18 ought not to undertake a cure of souls ᵇ, persons of that age are so apt to have a good opinion of themselves and to desire a setlement, especially considering my
Father's infirmities and the value of the Benefice that I wonder
how I came to be so wise and so good as to refuse it.   But I
have often blessed God for it since, and have observed what
a happines it was not to be engaged in such a station before
I was better prepared for it.   My Father was much troubled
to see so much vice break out at the time of the Restoration,
and that men's resentments were so high for what was past.
He saw the designe laid to set up Episcopacy again in Scotland but from the channel in which things did then run he
did very much apprehend that great disorders would follow
upon it.   Tho he preferred Episcopacy to all other forms of
government and thought it was begun in the Apostles' times,
yet he did not think it so necessary but that he could live
under another form, for indeed his principle with relation to
Church Government was Erastian.   ᶜ He knew Grotius well
beyond sea ᶜ, and went in to all his notions upon those
matters.

His Death.

He did not enjoy his new dignity long, for ᵈ he died on the
24 August 1661 ᵈ.   His sicknes lasted a week in which time he
expressed great resignation to the will of God, he seemed to
rejoice that his dissolution was so near and with wonderfull
zeal recomended to us all the fear of God and the practise of
a religious and vertuous life.   I am sensible that it may be
thought I have said too much of him, but I hope the Reader

ᵃ Cf. Life in *Hist.* ii. 674.   ᵇ *Ibid.*   ᶜ *Ibid.* 672.   ᵈ *Ibid.* 674.

will allow this return of piety to one of the best Fathers that ever man was blessed with.

My mother's family.

I must next say a little of [a] my Mother[1]. She was a good religious woman but most violently engaged in the Presbiterian way[a]. Her family[2] was for above 50 years the most eminent of any in Edinburgh that way. [b] Her brother[3] Sir Archibald Johnstone known by the title of the Lord Warriston was esteemed the head of the party. [c] He commonly praied 5 or 6 hours a day[c], he had almost the whole Scripture by heart, [d] he had a heated imagination and could not sleep above 3 hours in the 24. He was eager in everything, and was a rank enthusiast [d]. He had the temper of an Inquisitor in him[4] and spared no body, for tho my Father had bred him and in his youth had managed all his affairs, [e] he thought it a crime to shew any other favour to him when he would not take their Covenant but to suffer him to go and live beyond sea[e]. He did overdrive [*f.* 198] all their councells and was the chieffe instrument of the ruine of the party by the fury and cruelty of their proceedings in which he was allwaies the principall leader. But after all that appeared in his publike actings, [f] he was a sincere and selfe denied Enthusiast, and tho he had 12 (?)[5] children he never considered his family but was generous and charitable[f].

My knowledge of the Presbyterians.

By my Mother's numerous kinred and by the great esteem they were in with the Ministers of that way I came to be well

---

[a] Cf. Life in *Hist.* ii. 672.   [b] *Ibid.* 672–3.   [c] *Hist.* i. 28.   [d] *Ibid.*
[e] Life in *Hist.* ii. 673.   [f] *Ibid.*, and *Hist.* i. 28.

---

[1] For Burnet's mother see *supra*, pp. 3, 30, 41, 86 ; *Hist.* i. 237 ; Cockburn, *Specimen*, pp. 26–7 ; Elliot, *Specimen*, p. 62 ; and the story quoted by William Morison in his *Johnston of Warriston*, p. 16, from Hailes, *Memorials*, ii. 75. The two later anecdotes suggest that the lady had a somewhat shrewish tongue.
[2] See Morison's *Johnston of Warriston*, 14–7.
[3] Mr. Airy's statement, note 2 on p. 43, vol. i. of the *Hist.* in his edition, seems to be a slip of the pen.
[4] See *Hist.*, Airy's ed. i. 43, note i.
[5] The *Hist.* says 13.

acquainted with the chieffe men of that persuasion. I could never esteem them much I thought all was low and saw litle of the sublime either of piety, vertue, or learning among them, yet I must say on the other hand I saw so much sincere zeal, such a sobriety and purety of deportment, such an application to praier, to reading the Scriptures and a tru tho' over scrupulous observance of the Lord's day, that this has for ever secured me from uncharitable thoughts of them, or severe proceedings against them. I never read their practicall Divinity books, nor their volumes of sermons, for looking sometimes accidentally into some of them I could not value them nor indeed could I ever read the sermons of the Episcopall Divines, especially the then admired Bishop Andrews. I began my study with relation to our home matters with [a] Hooker's Ecclesiasticall Policy [*sic*], which did so fixe me that I never departed from the principles laid down by him [a], nor was I a litle delighted with the modesty and charity that I observed in him which edified me as much as his book instructed me. [b] Soon after my Father's death my Brother Robert died ; he was rising up to be very eminent in the law, upon that my Mother's kinred pressed me much to return to the study of the law, but I told them I had put my hand to the plough, and so I could not look back [b].

My acquaintance with Mr. Nairn[1].

At this time I grew into an acquaintance and afterwards into a great friendship with [c] Mr. Nairn, then Minister of the Abbey Church at Edinburgh. His preaching charmed me, ther was a beauty of expression, a trueth of reasoning and a noblenes of thought in it beyond any thing I had formerly heard, so I resolved to make him my pattern [c]. He was a man of a warm but sweet temper, free and communicative and decently cheerful. [d] He opened a new scene to me and put books of another sort in my hand than those I had

---

[a] Cf. Life in *Hist.* ii. 675.   [b] *Ibid.* 674–5 ; *supra*, p. 4.   [c] Life in *Hist.* ii. 675.   [d] *Ibid.*

[1] See *supra*, p. 4.

formerly dealt in. Smith's Select Discourses and Dr. H. More's works were the first. He recomended also the reading of Plato and the Platonists [a] and here I found a noble entertainment. I observed he preached upon litle study tho by hearing him I thought every word was chosen with a particular care, upon that [b] I asked him how he could perform as he did upon so litle study. He upon that told me that he spent much time every day in meditating and accustomed him selfe to speak out his thoughts and to form them into proper expressions upon all occasions[b], he had made him selfe master of the Scriptures, and of the body of Divinity, so that he was well furnished with good materialls, he had a great purity of expression, [c] he was a man of a hevenly temper and just principles. He was more moderate in the Presbiterian way than any I had yet known among them [c]. He submitted to Episcopacy, but [d] would never be a Bishop himselfe, tho he was often pressed to it [d]. He read the epistles and letters of great men and had a great collection of them, he said in these he saw their thoughts in an originall simplicity and freedome ; with him I spent many hours. [1] At this time I applied my selfe to Philosophy and Mathematicks, and run thro Des Cartes and Gassendi and George Keith, afterwards a famous Quaker [2] and in conclusion as famous an enemy to them, led me thro all the Elementary parts but not into Algebra or the Conick Sections. [e] In the year 1662 the Bishops who had been consecrated at Westminster came down and made a pompous entry into Edinburgh. I saw it and could not help thinking that appearance of pride was no good beginning.

My happines in knowing Bishop Leighton,

[f] I soon after made my selfe acquainted with Bishop Leightoune in whom I saw a sublimity that amased me.

[a] Cf. Life in *Hist.* ii. 675.   [b] *Ibid. supra.*   [c] Cf. *Hist.* i. 215.   [d] *Ibid. supra.*
[e] Cf. Life in *Hist.* ii. 675 ; *Hist.* i. 142-3 ; *supra*, p. 17.   [f] Cf. *Hist.* i. 134-9 ;
Life in *Hist.* ii. 675 ; *supra*, pp. 9-15, 30.

[1] Here begins the portion of the Autobiography which runs parallel with the first extant fragment of the original Memoirs. See *supra*, pp. 4 seq.

[2] See *supra*, p. 30, and note 2.

I will repeat nothing concerning him that I have put in my History, he grew very soon to so particular a liking to me that it was the matter of universall observation and this continued without the least cloud or interruption for 22 years to his death. He raised in me a just sense of the great end of religion as a divine life in the soul that carried a man farre above forms or opinions [a]. I found all his words to me were as Solomon saies of the words of the wise as nailes and goads fastned in a sure place, for I never left him without carrying with me a warm sense [*f.* 199] of those divine things with which he had entertained me. [b] He advised me to read all the Apologies and the short Treatises of the Fathers of the first 3 centuries, which I did very carefully. I read also all Binius' Collection of the Councells in a series with his notes down to the 2d Councel of Nice.

And Mr. Charteris.

[c] I grew also well acquainted with Mr. Charteris, in whom I saw a grave and solemne simplicity joined with great prudence. [d] He seemed dead to the world [d], had no mixture of vanity or selfe conceit. He despised the greatest part of that the world called learning; he hated controversies and disputes as dry and lifelesse things. [e] He loved the Misticall Divines [e] and thought he found in them a better savour of divine matters than in most other writters. [f] There was no affectation in him [f], his sermons were plain and easy; litle different from common discourse, insisting chiefly on our being resigned in all things to the will of God and our loving and obeying him, and our living in the daily expectation of death and judgment. [g] He had read all the Histories Ancient and Modern that came in his way, [h] with all books of travells [i] and the lives of great men [i]; he said these books gave him an amusement without passion and a pleasant usefull entertainment.

[a] Cf. *Hist.* i. 134-9 ; Life in *Hist.* ii. 675 ; *supra*, pp. 9-15, 30.   [b] Life in *Hist.* ii. 675.   [c] *Ibid.* 675-6.   [d] Cf. *Hist.* i. 215.   [e] *Ibid.* 216.   [f] *Ibid.* 215, and Life in *Hist.* ii. 675.   [g] Cf. Life in *Hist.* ii. 676, and *Hist.* i. 216.   [h] Cf. Life in *Hist.* ii. 676.   [i] Cf. *Hist.* i. 216.

I went into England.

Thus I was prepared to go abroad into the world and I resolved to see a litle of it. [a] I came to London [a] in the year 1662 [1] and studied to know as many eminent men in it as I possibly could. [b] Thurscrosse was a devout but simple man, Thorndike was dry and sullen. [c] I grew well acquainted with Tillotson and Stillingfleet, who were then the most eminent of the young Clergy, Whitscot and Wilkins [c] were very free with me, and I easily went into the notions of the Latitudinarians. Outram [2] and [d] Patrick [d] were then very much and justly esteemed and were very moderate. I was also particularly recomended to [e] Mr. Baxter [e] having read manny of his books and having received great benefit by them, and I was often with him. He seemed very serious in the great matters of religion and very moderate in the points of conformity but I perceived he was credulous and easily heated by those who came about him. I knew also [f] Dr. Manton [f], but he seemed to be too full of intrigues and was a more artificiall man.

And saw both Universities.

[g] I staied some time at Cambridge and was much delighted with Dr. More's conversation [g]. There was a sweet simplicity in his whole manner that charmed me. [h] I shall never forget one saying of his with relation to the disputes then on foot concerning Church government and ritualls, he said none of these things were so good as to make men good, nor so bad as to make men bad, but might be either good or bad according to the hands in which they fell. [i] Guning appeared so trifling a man to me that I was amased to see him so much considered, a vein of sophistry run thro all his discourses. [k] Pearson was a man of another sort, judicious, grave and moderate. Burnet [k] who wrote the Theory of the earth [3] was the most considerable

[a] Cf. Life in *Hist.* ii. 676 ; *supra*, pp. 41, 43-7.   [b] Cf. *supra*, p. 45.   [c] *Supra*, pp. 45-6, and Life in *Hist.* ii. 676.   [d] Life in *Hist.* ii. 676.   [e] *Supra*, p. 46. [f] *Supra*, p. 46.   [g] *Supra*, p. 46, and Life in *Hist.* ii. 676.   [h] Life in *Hist.* ii. 676.   [i] *Supra*, p. 46.   [k] Life in *Hist.* ii. 676.

[1] The Memoirs and Life say 1663.   Master of the Charterhouse did not
[2] Author of *De Sacrificiis*.   appear till 1681.
[3] The *Telluris Theoria Sacra* of the

among those of the younger sort, Cudworth was in all respects a great man [a], but was then in a cloud as favouring the Nonconformists. [b] After I had staied some time at Cambridge I went to Oxford. I was particularly recomended to Dr. Wallis and was so kyndly used by him that it gave some jealousy of me to others, [c] yet my having read the Fathers and Councells so much reconciled even the highest of them to me. [d] I was much delighted with Dr. Pocock's company who was learned [d], humble [1] and moderate. [e] Dr. Fell used me very kindly, he was learned, pious and very zealous, but set too great a value on litle things. [f] There was something nobly sweet and great in Dr. Allestry [f]. Bernard had such beginnings that I thought he would have proved a greater man [2] than he afterwards appeared to be. [g] After some weeks stay at the two Universities I returned to London [g] fully undeceived of the high opinion I had formerly of them, when I came into England I thought to have made a longer stay in one or other of them, Cambridge answered my expectation more, but Guning, Sparrow and Beaumon[t] carried things so high that I saw latitude and moderation were odious to the greater part even there.

I was known to Mr. Boyle.

[h] At my return to London I was by Dr. Wallis recomended to Mr. Boyle [h] with whom I lived ever after that to his dying day, in a close and entire friendship, [i] he had the purity of an angell in him, he was modest and humble rather to a fault. He despised all earthly things [i], he was perhaps too eager in the pursute of knowledge, but his aim in it all was to raise in him a higher sense of the wisdome and glory of the Creator and to do good to mankind, he studied the Scripture with

[a] Life in *Hist*. ii. 676.   [b] *Ibid*., and *supra*, p. 47.   [c] Life in *Hist*. ii. 676.
[d] *Ibid*.   [e] *Ibid*., and *supra*, p. 47.   [f] *Supra*, p. 47.   [g] *Supra*, p. 47, and
Life in *Hist*. ii. 676.   [h] Life as above.   [i] *Hist*. i. 193.

---

[1] The modesty of the famous orient-alist seems to have been proverbial.
[2] It is not quite easy to explain the implied disparagement of this famous scholar.

great application and [a] practised universall love and goodnes
in the greatest extent possible [a], and was a great promoter of
love and charity among men and a declared ennemy to all
bitternes and most particularly to all [*f.* 200] persecution on
the account of religion.

And to S[ir] R. Murray.

[b] My chieffe acquaintance at London that proved of the
greatest use and advantage to me was with S[ir] Robert
Murray who indeed treated me as a father. I was with him
every day and was directed by him in all things, and which
was the most important as well as the most necessary thing
I was admonished and chid by him for every thing that he
knew or saw amisse in me. I was very forward and was too
apt to shew how much I knew of every thing so he gave me
great lessons of humility and modesty. He recommended
Epictetus much to me for he had poised his own mind with
his maxims so equally that he did not seem moved with any
thing that could happen to him. I never could observe the
least change of countenance or behaviour in him by any thing
that befell him, tho I know on manny occasions accidents
happened to him that would have shaken even a firm mind but
they did not so much as move him [b]. He set me a noble
scheme of life both with relation to my studies and to the
function to which he knew I intended to dedicate my selfe.

And Mr. Drummond.

[c] There was another Gentleman who seemed then dying of
a consumption but lived ten year longer, Mr. Drummond who
had lived 12 year in London [c] and was in great esteem with
all who knew him. I was particularly recommended to him
and found him in all things as a brother. He told me how
to make way to all the persons to whom he addressed me
he cautioned me as to every one of them, to engage them
upon the subjects that would be most pleasant to them, and
most usefull to my selfe, and he made strict enquiries into my

[a] *Hist.* i. 193.   [b] Life in *Hist.* ii. 676; *Hist.* i. 59–60 ; *supra*, pp. 43-6.
[c] *Supra*, pp. 44-5.

behaviour and ªused all the plaines of a kind and even of a severe monitor with me. ᵇ By these means my journey into England, tho but of six moneths continuance, was of great use to me ᵇ and though I had designed a further journey, yet I thought it best to come back to Scotland and to reflect on all that I had seen and known ; and then by the next season to travell farther. ᶜ I was much pressed to enter into Orders and to accept of a Benefice. I was invited to go into the Westerne parts with the offer of one of the best Churches in the countrey : but I was happily diverted from it ᶜ for if I had gone thither probably I might have been engaged unto the passions and interests of a party by the provocations that might have been given me by the perverse people in those parts. ᵈ Sir Robert Fletcher a Gentleman of great vertue and very learned in the Mathematicks, had while he travelled and was at Paris, been used by my Father who was then there, with such particular care and kyndnes that he owned to manny that he owed more to my Father than ever he did to man next his own Father ; so he hearing a favorable character of me desired to be acquainted with me ᵉ and invited me to his house at Saltoun.

I was offered Salton a Benefice in Scotland.

His Minister Mr. Scowgall was named to be Bishop of Aberdeen, so as soon as Sir Robert heard me preach he made the offer of that Church to me. I had indeed projected that Mr. Nairn should come into that Church and I was resolved to accept a smaller one in that neighbourhood, so I told Sir Robert I could not entertain his offer but desired him to pitch on Mr. Nairn ; I added I intended to travell for some moneths. This did not move him for he had setled his thoughts on me, and he said he would keep the place vacant till I returned, for the Bishop was not Consecrated till some moneths after that. I upon that consented to accept of it and I quickly set out to travell again.

ª *Supra*, p. 45.   ᵇ Life in *Hist.* ii. 676.   ᶜ Cf. *ibid.*; *Hist.* i. 155; *supra*, p. 28.   ᵈ Cf. Life in *Hist.* ii. 676; *supra*, pp. 85-6.   ᵉ Life in *Hist.* ii. 676-7 ; *supra*, pp. 88-9.

I went beyond sea.

[a] I went by London to Holland and after a ramble of some weeks, I setled at Amsterdam, to the wonder of all who went to Holland for their studies.   I had another designe I had a learned Jew to perfect me in the Hebrew, but my chieffe designe was to know the best men of the severall forms of religion there, to establish me in the principles of universal charity and of thinking well of those who differed from me.   I knew the Arminians, the Lutherans, the Anababtists, the Brownists, the Papists and the Unitarians ; and I must say that I saw among them all some who were so very good that I was by this not a litle confirmed in my resolutions never to go in to severe methods on the account of religion [a].   The most eminent men in Leyden were [b] Golius [b] and Heydanus [1].   Cocceius [2] was beginning to vent his singularities upon the Prophets but was then very litle considered.   [c] I saw old Voetius, who was a sour rigid man.   [d] From runing round these Provinces I went thro the Spanish Netherlands to Paris.   At Paris I made a large acquaintance I did admire Daillé's learning and Morus's eloquence Charenton was then much divided by a quarrell between those two great [*f.* 202] men. Morus's way of preaching was much admired: he had an inimitable fire with a great variety of thoughts that lay out of the common road, that both surprised and pleased the audience, his manner was lively and looked like one inspired, but he had too much of the stage in his way ; and those flights that passed well in a pathetick discourse could not bear a strict examination.   I was much improved in my scheme of preaching by what I saw in him, and found a great deal both to imitate and to correct.   [e] I could not bear the false eloquence and the forced gestures of the Monks ; I heard one Secular

---

[a] Life in *Hist.* ii. 677; *Hist.* i. 207; *supra*, pp. 90–4.   [b] *Supra*, p. 94.   [c] *Supra*, p. 91.   [d] Life in *Hist.* ii. 677 ; *Hist.* i. 207 ; *supra*, pp. 95-6.   [e] *Supra*, pp. 96-7.

[1] Abraham Heydanus (1597–1678), head of the 'Hoogeschool' at Leyden from 1648 to 1676, a moderate man, and a disciple of Descartes (Van der Aa, viii. 395–8).

[2] Johannes Cocceius (1603–69) was head of the 'Hoogeschool' at Leyden from 1650 to his death. This 'immortal writer' (*vide* Van der Aa, iii. 518-20), whose piety was as remarkable as his intellectual independence, headed the opposition to Voetius.

Priest that pleased me much. I went to manny of the Religious houses but saw nothing that pleased me among them.
·I met with none of the Mysticks: and the Jansenists were
then so much depressed that they kept them selves in great
retirement, and so I could not find a way to be admitted to
see any of them. ⁴ The Lord Hollis then Ambassadour at the
Court of France used me with great freedome and kindnes.
ᵇ After some weeks stay at Paris I returned back to England,
ᶜ I was then¹ recomended by Sir Robert Murray to be a
Fellow of the Royall Society ᶜ and after a course of these
small travells² for seven moneths I came home to Scotland in
the end of the year 1664. ᵈ A few daies after Sir Robert
Fletcher came and carried me with him to Salton.

I prepared my selfe for holy Orders.

When I was presented to that Church I choose to continue
among them 4 moneths preaching constantly before I took
Orders: I resolved to know all the parish and to be known of
them, before I would engage my selfe to them³. They all
came without any one exception to me and desired me to
come and labour among them ᵈ. So I resolved to prepare my
selfe for that the best I could. I knew I had a great deal to
answer for to God and the Church: ᵉ I had a perfeit health
capable of labour and study, I had a good memory and an
imagination that was but too lively. I had a copious fluency
of expression ᵉ, all these nature or rather the author of nature
had furnished me with. I had the greatest advantages in the
progresse of my life from my first beginings under my Father,
to that day, of any man that I knew. ᶠ Three of the greatest

ᵃ Cf. Life in *Hist.* ii. 677 ; *Hist.* i. 207 ; *supra*, p. 95.   ᵇ Cf. Life in *Hist.* ii.
677 ; *supra*, p. 98.   ᶜ Cf. Life in *Hist.* ii. 677 ; *supra*, p. 89.   ᵈ Cf. Life in
Hist. ii. 677.   ᵉ *Ibid.* 676.   ᶠ *Ibid. supra.*

---

¹ See *supra*, p. 89, note 3.
² Here concludes the portion which
runs parallel with the first Harleian
fragment.
³ The 'Extracts from the . . . proceedings of the Presbytery of Had-
dington,' printed in the *Bannatyne*

Miscellany, iii. 393–5, show that the
Bishop of Edinburgh's letter in his
favour was received Nov. 10, 1664 ;
that his 'trials' were completed by
Dec. 15, 1664 ; and that he was in-
stituted by Laurence Charteris after
June 15, 1665.

Clergymen [a] and two of the best Laymen of the age who were all eminent in different waies [b] had concurred to finish an education that was well began [b], so I had much to answer for and tho I laboured under a load of selfe conceit and vanity, and was excessivly forward in discourse, yet I thank God I had gone long under tru and deep impressions of religion, but I had not kept them up allwaies in one state I had been often under great dissipation I now entred upon a more serious view of my selfe, and of the function to which I was to be dedicated. I resolved to give my selfe wholly to it, and to direct all my studies that way. A melancholy accident happned that took out of my way the greatest diversion that seemed to lie before me. Fletcher delighted in the Mathematicks, but could not break in upon Algebra, so I had a Master at London that carried me thro Oughtred [1], and to Sir Robert's great joy I taught him that. That winter a great comet appeared and we observed it manny nights: this had so ill an effect on him that it brought a feaver on him of which he died [2], so here a full stop was put to my Mathematicall studies which was a great happines to me for I was much taken with them and I had such a memory that I could carry on a progresse of equations long without pen ink or paper, so that I was pursued with them day and night. This change put me in a better disposition to follow the duties of my function. [c] I was ordained a Priest in February 1665 [c], and I set about the care of my parish in so particular a manner and with such successe that I will set down the method I held in for the 5 years that I continued there.

.   *My labours in my parish.*

I first consider[ed] how to preach to the edification of the people who were of a low form two considerable families only

[a] Cf. Life in *Hist.* ii. 676.   [b] *Ibid.*   [c] *Ibid.* 678.

[1] The *Clavis Mathematica* of William Oughtred was the textbook of the day on Algebra and Arithmetic.
[2] See his funeral sermon (printed anonymously), Burnet's first published work; and the comments of Cockburn, *Specimen*, pp. 30-2. He says Sir Robert's family were greatly displeased with it.

excepted. [a] I saw what a labour preaching was to manny who wrote their sermons and then got them by heart, for none do read in Scotland, so I resolved to follow a freer and easier way the hints of which I had from Mr. Nairn [a]. I read the Scripture with great application and got a great deal of it by heart and accustomed my selfe as I was riding or walking to repeat parcells of it. I went thro the Bible to consider all the texts proper to be preached on and studied to understand the literall meaning of the words and the right way of expounding and applying them. [b] I accustomed my selfe on all occasions to form my meditations into discourse and spoke aloud what occurred to my thoughts [b], I went over the body of Divinity frequently, both the speculative and the practical, [*f.* 203] chiefly the last, and formed a way of explaining every part of it in the easiest and clearest way I could, and [c] I spent a great part of every day in talking over to my selfe my thoughts of those matters [c], but that which helped me most was that I studied to live in frequent recollection observing my selfe and the chain of thoughts that followed all good or bad inclinations, and thus by a course of meditation and praier I arrived at a great readines in preaching that has continued with me ever from that time. To give me more life in all this I pursued a method of praier in such a compasse that I had all my sins and infirmities all my duties and obligations daily in my view, going thro a full survey of every thing relating to my selfe and to all others in whom I was concerned with particular meditations and praiers upon them all, and this I could enlarge to manny hours or shorten so as to bring it within one hour every day.

Next to my private thoughts I resolved to make the care of my parish a constant labour to me [d] I preached twice every Lord's day and once in the week I catechised all my parish 4 times a year [d]. We catechised in Scotland all old and young, masters of families and servants, and indeed all except those whose education set them above the suspition of ignorance. [e] This I did 3 times a week [e], except in the seasons

[a] Cf. Life in *Hist.* ii. 675.   [b] *Ibid.*   [c] *Ibid.*   [d] *Ibid.* 678.   [e] *Ibid.*

of hard labour. I quickly brought all my parish to such a degree of knowledge that they answered me to the sense of the questions I asked without sticking to the words of any catechisme, and in doing this I explained things copiously to them and turned to the Scriptures proper to the severall subjects which was so well received by them that great numbers came to be catechised, and one family coming after another I have been kept often three hours in a catecheticall exercise. [a] I went round my parish at least twice a year and visited every house and spoke with every person as there was occasion for it, reproving, exhorting, or comforting them. I visited every person that was sick every day[a], for the Church and my house stood almost in the center of the parish, the remotest house not being above a mile's distance from it. [b] I gave the Sacrament 4 times a year and spoke to every individuall person that desired to receive it[b]: thus I gave my selfe up wholly to the pastorall care. [c] I knew every person in my parish and all their concerns: [d] and living frugally I gave all that was over and above my necessary subsistence in charity among them. [e] I had all their hearts to a very great degree[1], even the Presbiterians among them loved me beyond expression, tho I was the only man that I heard of in Scotland that used the forms of the Common praier[e], not reading but repeating them.

My private studies were the reading the New Testament in Greek over and over again without any Comentary to determine me, but only with dictionaries and concordances that I might by my own industry comprehend the designe of those writings. [f] I also read all the books I could find to help me to see what the Primitive Constitution of the Church was, and

---

[a] Life in *Hist.* ii. 678.   [b] *Ibid.*   [c] *Ibid. infra.*   [d] *Ibid. supra.*
[e] *Ibid. infra.*   [f] *Ibid.*

[1] Alexander Cunningham, whose writings betray a personal animus against Burnet, and who speaks of his labours in his first parish with vindictive and irrelevant disparagement, maintains that he was very unpopular (*Hist.* i. 30). Cockburn, on the other hand, fully confirms Burnet's own account of his labours, his austerities, and his self-conceit (*Specimen*, pp. 32-3). See also *Bannatyne Miscellany*, iii. 395, for the approbation expressed by Burnet's elders at the visitation of July, 1666.

what were the rules by which the Bishops and Priests of those times governed themselves. S. Cyprian was my chieffe author but I carried my search into other writters as far as I could.

I was much offended with the methode the Bishops took.

By this I saw that our Bishops observed none of the Primitive rules, while yet they fetched the chiefe arguments for their Order from those times. [a] They neglected their Dioceses [a], scarce ever preached, [b] they were raising their own families, and above all were persecuting those who would not submit to them [b]. Of the particulars relating to this I say no more in this place because they will be found in my History. [c] This heated me to a great degree so I drew up a long and warm Memoriall[1] of all their abuses and sent copies of that to all the Bishops of my acquaintance. They treated me very severly on that occasion and threatned me with high censures, but the thing had got abroad and was so well liked that they thought fit to dismisse me with a reprimend for my presumption. Upon this I resolved to let the world see that I had done nothing on designe to make my selfe popular. I retired from company, I staied constantly at home, [d] I entered into an ascetick course of life for two years till the whole masse of my blood was corrupted by my ill diet, so that two great feavers in two subsequent years convinced me that I ought not to continue longer in that course of ill food [d]. The last feaver was of 30 daies continuance and for some hours [e] I seemed to be in the last agony [e], and for some minutes lay as dead. Upon my recovery I returned to more compliance with my body. But one happy thought gave a great change to the course of my studies. I had till then pursued them in a great compasse and had the vanity to designe to be an eminent and distin-

[a] Cf. *Hist.* i. 217.   [b] *Ibid.*   [c] Cf. Life in *Hist.* ii. 678-9 ; *Hist.* i. 217.
[d] Cf. Life in *Hist.* ii. 678-9.   [e] *Ibid.*

---

[1] See Cockburn, pp. 33-43 (quoted by Mr. Airy, note, *Hist. in loco*) ; and *supra*, p. 40, note 1. There seems to be a reference to Scougall's conduct in the Preface to the *Life of Bedel.*

guished scholar. I had not the humility to repent of this
and to abhorre it and so I resolved for the [*f.* 201] remaining
part of my life no more to pursue the vanity or curiosity
of being thought a learned man, and only to read books
as an entertainment when no better thing was to be done
and to this resolution I have adhered from that time to this
day, so that any measure of knowledge I have arrived at since
that time has come on me as my station or other circumstances engaged me in my hours of leisure to study.

I studied Misticall Divinity.

With my ascetick course of life I joined the reading all
the Misticall Authors I could find ; in particular all Teresa's
works. They are all brought into a sisteme by Baker in his
Sancta Sophia[1]. I read also volumes of the Lives of the
Saints of the Church of Rome, but these are of such a
fabulous and ridiculous contexture, that it was no small
exercise to my patience to bear with them. The Misticks
are writters of a better strain: but being writ by recluse,
melancholy people they are full of rank Enthusiasme, and
if in the Church of Rome they had not set up the principle
of submitting to the Church and of being resigned to the
conduct of a confessor as the superiour principle to which all
are to subject themselves, their Misticall Divinity must have
led them to all the extravagancies of Enthusiasme. I have
often wondred to find that my course of life and of study
both concurring that way, I was never in danger of being
misled. But as I had nothing of the spleen or melancholy
in my naturall constitution, so my Philosophicall studies had
taught me to distinguish between the effect of a heat in the

---

[1] He alludes to the *Sancta Sophia, or
Directions for the Prayer of Contempla-
tion,* drawn up by Father Serenus
Cressy from the writings of Father
Baker (a convert to Roman Catholi-
cism), published at Douay in 1657.
The suppression of Burnet's mystical
leanings in his son's account is no
doubt deliberate. They had given
scandal in his own day, both to a rigid
orthodoxy and to men of the world ;
see Hickes, *Some discourses,* pp. 23–5,
Leslie's *Character of an Enthusiast,*
and the ludicrous exaggerations of
Cunningham, *Hist.* i. 124, 211 ; and
they would have been yet more offensive to eighteenth-century rationalism;
see *Portland MSS.* (H. M. C.) vii.
367–8.

animal spirits, which was mechanicall and that which lay in the superiour powers of the soul.

An extraordinary effect of histericall fitts.

A happy accident at that time let me see that seeming raptures might flow from naturall causes. The Countesse of Belcarras with whom I had lived in great friendship for manny years sent for me to come to her in all hast: when I came she told me her daughter[1] had fitts of a strange nature, in which she lay waking, but knew no body: she spoke all the while like one in heaven as if she had been conversing with God and the holy Angells. She spoke without interruption as long as the fitt lasted, and said she had a vision of the number of hours in which that converse with God was to last, and when the hour she had named came, she fell into a short slumber and wakened clear in her head, but knew nothing that she had been doing or saying; her spirits were sunk, for her fits lasted manny hours, the last was about 10 hours long. She was then about 18 and was an extraordinary person in all respects. I apprehended there was something belonging to her sexe in the case, so I advised her Mother to send for a phisitian. He set nature right and she had no more fitts. I had heard of other instances of this sort, but never knew any besides this: in it I saw how Nuns by their state of life might be subject to such fits, so stories of that sort among them are not all to be rejected as fictions, nor to be entertained as things supernaturall.

Upon the whole matter I will deliver my sense of my course of life and studies very freely. I learned indeed to neglect my body and to live upon litle. I grew to dispise the world, and had so litle need of wealth that I contemned it. I loved solitude and silence and so I avoided manny

---

[1] This must have been Lady Henrietta Lindsay, her youngest daughter, whose religious zeal and supposed prophetic visions are noted in Lord Crawford's *Memoir of Lady Anna Mackenzie*, pp. 111-38 passim. She married in 1678 Sir Duncan Campbell of Auchinbreck.

tentations, but I was out of measure conceited of my selfe, vain and desirous of fame beyond expression. I grew into a superstitious overvaluing of the severities I underwent, and became very scrupulous in all the circumstances relating to them: the worst of all was I undervalued those who did not practise the same things. I never felt any internall apprehension of extraordinary impulses, tho I cannot deny but I desired mightely to feel them, if such things were to be felt, and I was sometimes very near a resolution of abandoning the world and of going into some remote places in a disguised habit where none knew me that so I might instruct poor people as being one of themselves, and a very small impulse would have carried me to this, for my imagination was much heated with it. Thus I have given a very plain and tru account of my life and labours at Salton. At the end of my stay there [a] the scene of our Ministry was much changed, for there was a great mildnes in the administration and most of those [*f.* 204] who were then put in the Ministry were my particular friends, so I was often called for and advised with by them. Moderation was then the word as much as the execution of the lawes was formerly driven on.

Great Moderation in the administration.

[b] I had been long acquainted with Lady Margaret Kennedy, a daughter of the Earle of Cassilis; [c] she was a very extraordinary woman and a most zealous Presbyterian, and in great credit and esteem with them. [d] There was some kinred between us [d], but my moderation was the chieffe thing that recommended me to her. [e] She lived in a most particular friendship with the Dutchesse of Hamilton, [f] who is[1] a woman of a great understanding, eminently devout and charitable and indeed a pattern of vertue. She would never medle to

---

[a] Cf. Life in *Hist.* ii. 679.   [b] *Supra*, pp. 84-5.   [c] *Supra*, pp. 84-5 ; Life in *Hist.* ii. 681.   [d] *Supra*, p. 84.   [e] Life in *Hist.* ii. 681.   [f] *Hist.* i. 276.

---

[1] Anne, Duchess of Hamilton in her own right (married April 29, 1656, to William Douglas, Earl of Selkirk, created Duke of Hamilton), survived Burnet, dying in 1716 at the age of 80.

dispute in matters of speculation, but went on this ground that the Presbiterians were better men, better preachers and more successefull in their labours than the Episcopall Clergy[a]. Sir Robert Murray had given her such a character of me that she being at Edinburgh [b] desired my acquaintance and after some conversation with her she desired me to come on a visit to Hamilton. [c] I staied there for some daies and I had a very particular information of the state of the Countrey brought me by manny hands of different sorts; [d] things there were in a very lamentable condition, the Clergy were a sad pack of people and were so much hated that upon the slackning the rigorous execution of the lawes they were universally deserted by their people. Scandalous reports passed upon most of them and they were generally believed, the people were running either into grosse ignorance or into wild fanaticisme, some of the most extravagant of their teachers drew multitudes after them and filled their heads with manny strange conceits, while the more sober of that persuasion were cautious and looked on without interposing; [e] so it was proposed that these who were the more moderate of the Presbiterians might be put into some of the vacant Churches to keep the people in some order, [f] and I was so farre convinced of this that I made the motion in a letter that I wrote to the court.

[g] This came afterwards to be known and drew the hatred of the Episcopall party on me to such a degree that I could never overcome it. [h] While I was at Hamilton I became acquainted with him that was Rector of the University of Glasgow. He was so well pleased with me that he proposed to that body to choose me to be Divinity Professor there, in this he prevailed so that they sent him to me with a Decree choosing me to fill that chair. All my friends[1] advised me

---

[a] Cf. *Hist.* i. 276. [b] Life in *Hist.* ii. 679. [c] Cf. *Hist.* i. 280.
[d] *Ibid.* 247, 273, 276-7. [e] *Ibid.* 276-7. [f] *Ibid.* 280. [g] *Ibid.* 281.
[h] Life in *Hist.* ii. 679; *Hist.* i. 287.

---

[1] Cockburn maintains that Leighton on this occasion urged Burnet to refrain from politics (*Specimen*, pp. 45-6).

to accept of it[a]. They thought me capable of filling the post and of doing the Church great service in it. [b] I confesse the lamentations of the good people of Salton made my parting with them very hard to me[b]. It is not easy for me to expresse the violence of the passion they expressed nor the manny tears that they shed on that occasion.

I was made Divinity Professor at Glasgow.

But at last I left them tho not without great uneasines, and [c] in November, 1669, I removed to Glasgow. I continued 4 year and a halfe there in no small exercise of my patience. The Presbiterians hated me because they thought I was taking methods to establish Episcopacy among them, the Episcopall party did not love moderation nor the slackning the execution of the lawes[c], so between them I had few friends and manny enemies. The violent prejudices they took up against Bishop Leightoun with whom I lived in an entire confidence encreased their ill opinion of me. I preached constantly in the town and in the places about it, and went oft to Hamilton but I could never overcome the prejudices of the Presbiterians. [d] My chieffe busines was to form the students of Divinity right, and I laid down a plann for it[d] which made all my friends uneasy because they thought it was not possible for me to hold out long in it, yet [e] I let no part of it fall all the while I staied there. I will set it all down, because every one approved of the scheme, only they thought it ought to be the work of two or three men and that it was too much for one.

My performances there.

On Moonday I made all the students in course explain a part of the body of Divinity in Latine with a Thesis and answer all the arguments that the rest could make against it, and I concluded it with a determination of my own in Latine. On Tuesday I had a Prelection in Latine in which I designed

---

[a] Cf. Life in *Hist.* ii. 679 ; *Hist.* i. 287.   [b] Life, as above.   [c] *Ibid.*, and *Hist.* i. 287-8.   [d] Life in *Hist.* ii. 679.   [e] *Ibid.* 679-80.

to go thro a body of Divinity in about 10 or 12 years time, so that I was not gone halfe way when I left the place, On Wednesday I went thro a Criticall Commentary on St. Mathews Gospell for a whole hour which I delivered in English and went quite thro that Gospell. On Thursday I expounded a Psalm in Hebrew, comparing it with the 70, the vulgar and our version and explained the meaning of it, and by turns on the next Thursday I explain[ed] the constitution and the rituall [*f.* 206] of the Primitive Church and made the Aposticall Canons my text bringing every particular that I opened to them to one of these Canons. On Fryday I made the students in course preach a short sermon upon a text that I gave them; and when that was ended I shewed them what was defective or amisse in the sermon and how the text ought to have been opened and applied. Besides all this I called them all together in the evening every day to praiers, and after praiers I read a parcell of Scripture to them, and after I had explained it I made a short sermon for a quarter an hour [*sic*] upon it. I then asked them what difficulties they met with in their studies, and answered such questions as they put to me. Thus I applied my selfe for 8 moneths in a year to answer the ends of a professor with the diligence of a schoolmaster[1]. This obliged me to much hard study. I rose early and studied close from 4 to 10 for six hours, but was forced to throw up the rest of the day, partly for the use of students and partly for hearing the complaints of the Clergy and for receiving the applications made to me, for it was understood that I had some credit with those who governed, so this drew much trouble upon me.

---

[1] Burnet, like Arnold, was clearly in his element as a pedagogue. Cunningham, as usual, makes Burnet's conduct at this time the text for ill-natured gibes; says he preached a compound of Arminianism and Calvinism 'to the no small admiration of the vulgar'; and that his praises of virginity and the state of widowhood (after the manner of St. Jerome) rendered his subsequent marriages very ridiculous (*Hist.* i. 30).

I wrote the memoirs of the dukes of Hamilton.

I made manny visits to Hamilton [a] which lay within 8 mile of Glasgow, and [b] growing into a high measure of favour with the Duke and Dutchesse [b], and having a just esteem of them I took pleasure to be for some daies there wher I was very easy and free. [c] I offered my service to the Dutchesse to examine the papers she had with relation to her Father and her Uncle's ministry. She had kept them carefully but had not till then found a person that she thought fit to trust them to. She had such an entire confidence in me that she put them all in my hands [c], and I read them with great care. I saw by all the common books that her Father had been hated by both parties, so this inclined me to think he was the moderate man who has comonly that fate. This gave me first the curiosity to examine into all his actions. I say no more here of that work having said so much of it in my other works. Besides all that was fit to be published, I saw manny other particulars that gave me a clear view into those times and to the chieffe actors in them. [d] This brought the character of King Charles the first very low with me [d], but the Earl of Clarendon's History [1] sunk it quite. [e] As soon as the L[ord] Lawderdale knew that I had entred on this work, he desired me to come up to London and to lay it before him for he was sure he could give it a finishing.

Upon that I went to Court.

Upon that I went to Court where I was treated by him with so particular a confidence that if I had pleased and would have followed the methods of a Court, I could easily have made a great fortune under him. All the addition he gave to my work was with relation to those passages in which he had a share. I took them all readily from him, but could not bring my selfe to comply with his brutall imperious humours. One

---

[a] Cf. Life in *Hist.* ii. 679–80.   [b] *Ibid.*, and *Hist.* i. 298.   [c] *Ibid.*
[d] Cf. *Hist.* i. 298.   [e] *Ibid.* 298-9, and Life in *Hist.* ii. 680–1.

---

[1] See *supra*, p. 53, note 3.

thing I did effectually. D[uke] Hamilton and he had been at a great distance so I had powers to reconcile them entirely. D[uke] Hamilton got assignations to satisfy his pretensions on the Crown, of which I had found authentick vouchers among the papers trusted to me. He on the other hand promised to concurre in Parliament with the D[uke] of Lawderdail[a]. The King took particular notice of me[1] and gave me great assurances of favour and preferment. But I thank God these things made no impression on me. [b] I liked Court favour only because it put me in a capacity of serving other people and a great deal of that passed thro my hands. [c] I was offered a Bishoprick but refused it[c]. So farre I have given the fair side of my selfe, but now I will open another scene not very bright.

My first marriage.

[d] I lived manny years in great freindship with L[ady] Margaret Kennedy. I had a high esteem of her understanding and a much greater one of her generosity, vertue and piety[d], and had in great measure brought her off from the rigidity of the Presbiterian way so that our friendship was observed to be very extraordinary. From a high esteem it grew into an affection so that I courted her. She was much concerned at that for as she had no mind to lose my company she had as little mind to marry me. She was 18 year elder then I and having lived till then in a high reputation she saw a marriage on such an inequality would much lessen her, nor did she think it decent in me it would have a face of ambition and covetousness; and of all this I was so convinced that I resolved often to break it off, but my affection was so strong that it returned upon me allwaies and at last after two years sute [e] we were [2] married[e]

---

[a] Cf. *Hist.* i. 298-9, and Life in *Hist.* ii. 680-1. [b] Cf. *Hist.* i. 298. [c] Life in *Hist.* ii. 681; *Hist.* i. 298, 300. [d] *Supra*, pp. 84-5. [e] Life in *Hist.* ii. 681.

---

[1] See Mr. Airy's note, *Hist.* i. 533 in his edition.

[2] It is difficult to fix the exact date of this marriage. Mr. Airy we find, in different articles, assigns it to the years 1672 and 1670-1 respectively (*Dict. Nat. Biog.* vii. 397, 407). Burnet himself states (*a*) that he was married thirteen years—which, as his wife died in May, 1685, would place the marriage in 1672; and (*b*) that the marriage remained a secret two years—which,

but so privatly that none but the Bishop of [*f.* 208]
Ed[inbu]r[gh] who wrot the license and Mr. Charteris who
married us and two other witnesses knew any thing of it, and
it continued a secret for two year. This was an inexcusable
piece of folly in me for which when it broke out we were both
severly censured. She lived with me 13 years but fell under
such a decay of memory and understanding that for some
years she knew nothing and no body. [a] In this I had a large
occasion for patience and for a tender return of care [a] to one
that had laid so great an obligation on me, and I thank God
I went thro that in a very singular manner. [b] When I first
married her she had no thought of securing her fortune to her
selfe so that it would have all fallen into my hands, but I prepared a deed which I delivered to her before our marriage
by which I renounced all pretensions to it [b]. This in great
measure softned her friends when our marriage came to be
known. But I must now open another scene of my life.

My medling in busines much censured.

[c] When I was in London in the year 1671 reading my History to the L[ord] Lauderdale I saw then that there was a
secret negotiation between our Court and the Court of France,
this broke out terribly in the year 1672, [d] and then the Duke
of Lauderdale came down to Scotland in a vast magnificence
with his new lady, I was looked on by all as a favourite and
continued to do all poor sutors good offices, [e] but I saw such

[a] Life in *Hist.* ii. 722.   [b] *Ibid.* 681.   [c] Cf. *Hist.* i. 300–1, 303–10.
[d] *Ibid.* 338–9, and Life in *Hist.* ii. 681.   [e] *Hist.* i. 339.

as it became public during the same
week as his appointment to the Rolls
Chapel in the Long Vacation, 1675,
would place the ceremony in 1673 or
at least in 167⅔. The skill with which
Mr. Thomas Burnet has glided over
the less agreeable features of this
alliance, and has altogether suppressed
its clandestine character, gives us a
high opinion of his qualifications as
an advocate. For the adverse comments on the match to which Dr. Burnet refers see Swift, *Works*, ed. 1824,
xii. 188; Cunningham, i. 30; and Cockburn, pp. 46–7 (whose information, derived in part from Mr. Charteris, is
extraordinarily correct). Cockburn
mentions that the Hamiltons had calculated upon their wealthy kinswoman portioning some of their children; which suggests an additional
motive for Burnet's renunciation of
her fortune. The final illness of
Lady Margaret (for which see *supra*,
p. 151, *infra*, p. 490) is mentioned in
one of Dr. Leighton's letters (described
supra, p. 9, note 1) with characteristic
comments.

a spirit of violence and injustice and such a ravenous sale of all things among them that I came to abhorre their methods. [a] I did what I could to keep him and D[uke] Hamilton in a good understanding during that Session of Parliament. This was imputed to the offices done by me for they were often upon the point of breaking out and I was thought the instrument of setting them right, for which I was bitterly censured by those who intended to have made a rupture between them, for nothing could have been then done in opposition to D[uke] Lauderdale unlesse D[uke] Hamilton would have headed the party against him [a]. I was blamed as an aspiring man. [b] I was again offered a Bishoprick and promised the first Archbishoprick that should fall, and their particular confidence. I thank God I refused it. I saw I could not hold long with them [b] nor could I go in to the measures taken by the other Bishops who for the greater part were set in violent methods.

[c] In the year 1673 I went up again to print the Memoirs of the Dukes of Hamilton [d] and to break off from the Court and all further medling with matters of state. [e] I saw Popery was at Court the prevailing interest, the failing in the designe of destroying Holland the former year had indeed put them to a stand and forced a Session of Parliament in which the Sacramentall Test was set up chiefly to turn out the D[uke] of York and the Lord Clifford with the other Papists who had got into imployments, the price of obtaining this was 1200000 lib. which helped the King to go thro that Summer with the warre [e] and to get a peace with the States in the following winter. [f] When I was at London I used all proper freedome with the Duke of Lauderdale and his Dutchesse, but all was in vain he was so drunk with his prosperity that he despised every thing that was said to him. [g] All his enemies at Court who knew my freedome with him and the union I was in

[a] *Hist.* i. 338-9, and Life in *Hist.* ii. 681.   [b] *Ibid.* 682 ; *Hist.* i. 339.
[c] Life in *Hist.* ii. 682 ; *Hist.* i. 354.   [d] Life in *Hist.* ii. 682 ; *Hist.* i. 355.
[e] Life in *Hist.* ii. 682.   [f] *Hist.* i. 355-6 ; Life in *Hist.* ii. 682.   [g] *Ibid.* ;
Hist. i. 359-60.

to the family of Hamilton used me in an extraordinary manner, they magnified the credit I had in Scotland so to the King and the Duke that I found my selfe engaged deeper in the Court then ever.   ·

I was known to the King and to his Brother.

The King talked often to me but the Duke much oftener and that with a very extraordinary opennes and freedome [a], but I will say no more of this having said enough of it in my History.   [b] I saw a visible alteration in the behaviour of the D[uke] and D[utche]sse of Lauderdale towards me, [c] they thought I was sent up to manage intrigues at Court [c] and they began to talk of me as a proud and medling man, and as they were allwaies in extreams with all people I grew to be as much hated and mistrusted as ever I had been confided in by them.   [d] I followed them to Scotland and seeing the breach between D[uke] Hamilton and them was so laid that it could not be prevented I resolved to retire to my busnes at Glasgow and past the winter there.   [e] They now railed at me as one that had been undermining them both at Court and in Scotland, [f] and at their return to London they infused it into the King that I had been the chieffe author of all the opposition that had been made to them in Scotland, and the King having known the active and turbulent spirit of my Uncle Warriston he assured him I was a man of the same capacity and temper.   This went easily with the King who never troubled himselfe to examine any thing that his Ministers suggested to him as long [*f.* 205] as they maintained their credit with him [f], so I was under a long disgrace with him.   [g] The Duke of York stuck firmer to me [h] and gave me very extraordinary demonstrations of it.   The most important was he told me if I returned to Scotland I would be put in prison and he could not think but I would lie long in it [h].

[a] Life in *Hist.* ii. 682 ; *Hist.* i. 359-60.   [b] *Ibid.* i. 362.   [c] *Ibid.* 363.
[d] Life in *Hist.* ii. 683 ; *Hist.* i. 362-3.   [e] Life in *Hist.* ii. 683 ; *Hist.* i. 363, ·
in'ra.   [f] Cf. *Hist.* i. 363.   [g] Life in *Hist.* ii. 683 ; *Hist.* i. 363.
[h] Life in *Hist.* ii. 683 ; *Hist.* i. 372.

I fell in Disgrace at Court.

The trueth was the D[uke] of Lauderdale had put himselfe so much in my power by speaking so freely to me that I had reason to believe he would shut me up and keep me close, [a] so upon that I resigned my Professorship [a] and resolved to cast my selfe on the Providence of God.

[*f.* 204 (*b*)] [b] At this time the open breach between the Duke of Lauderdale and me exposed me to an examination before the House of Commons concerning him [b]. I say no more of that in this place having said so much of it in my History that I have nothing to adde here concerning it. It was a great errour in me to appear in that matter and seemed to be a great misfortune, but it has proved since a very great blessing to me, it raised such a spirit in the Court against me that it obliged me to so much diligence and to such caution that in the series of my life I thank God [c] it has proved a happy deliverance from Courts and intrigues in which I was at that time so farre engaged that it was not easy by any other way to free me from them [c]. This delivered me from them all. [*f.* 205 *resumed.*]

I preached long at the Rolls.

[d] Not long after that the L[ord] Holles sent for me and directed me to go to S[i]r Harbottle Grimston M[aste]r of the Rolls and he presently entertained [me] to be Preacher at the Rolls. The Court thought me a man of that consequence that they sent first a Bishop and then a Secretary of State to prevail with him to dismisse me, but he was not to be moved in the matter. By this means I had a settlement in London in which I continued ten year all to one Term [*sic*] [d]. That which made this look to me like somewhat of a very particular Providence was, that as it came to me without any thought or procurement of my own, so it happned at the very time I think in the very week that my marriage came to be

---

[a] Life in *Hist.* ii. 683 ; *Hist.* i. 372.   [b] Cf. *Hist.* i. 373, 379-80.   [c] Life in *Hist.* ii. 684 ;*Hist.* i. 380.   [d] *Ibid.*, and Life in *Hist.* ii. 684.

known in Scotland, so it looked as if God was watching over me for good since I had the face of a small subsistance to bring my wife to. Here I applied my selfe to preach with great care, it was only in Term time that I was obliged to preach but I was imploid in one place or another in the vacation time. I hope I did some good there as appeared not only by the croud at the Chappell of the Rolls but by manny who seemed to have arrived at a better sense of things and a change of life by my ministry there. [a] I happned also in looking for a house to fall accidentally on the next house[1] to S[i]r Tho. Litleton [a] knowing nothing concerning him. But I soon found that he was one of the considerablest men in the Nation. He was at the head of the opposition that was made to the Court[2] and [b] living constantly in Town he was exactly informed of every thing that past [b]. He came to have an entire confidence in me so that for six year together [c] we were seldome two daies without spending some hours together. I was by his means let in to all their secrets [c], and indeed without the assistance I had from him I could never have seen so clearly into affairs as I did. [d] We argued all the matters that he perceived were to be moved in the House of Commons [d] till he thought he was a master of all that could be said on the subject, and [e] it was observed of him that in all debates in the House of Commons he reserved himselfe to the conclusion and what he spoke commonly determined the matter [e]. But tho my spirits were much dissipated upon my coming to England for a year or two, yet I thank God I recovered my selfe and returned to my profession and the exercises and studies belonging to it.

[f] The apprehensions of Popery obliged us to study these controversies with application, [g] and the conference in which

---

[a] Cf. *Hist.* i. 389.   [b] *Ibid.*   [c] *Ibid.*   [d] *Ibid.*   [e] *Ibid. supra.*
[f] Life in *Hist.* ii. 685.   [g] *Ibid.*, and *Hist.* i. 395.

---

[1] It was in Lincoln's Inn Fields, 'near the Plow Inn' (see the *Criminal Letters* against Dr. Burnet). He remained there from 1674 or 1675 till the winter of 1681-2, when he removed to Brook Buildings (see his Answer to the *Criminal Letters*).
[2] For Littleton see *Hist.*, Mr. Airy's ed., i. 414 (and notes a and 2), 415 (and notes a and 1); Dalrymple, ed. 1790, vol. i. Review, chap. iv. App. p. 381.

Dr. Stillingfleet and my selfe were engaged with Mr. Coleman and others as it made for some time great noise so it set me as in the front of those who opposed Popery.

I wrote severall books.

[a] The publishing the Memoires of the Dukes of Hamilton made some think me capable of writting History, and that set my friends on engaging me to write [b] the History of our Reformation in which I took so particular a method and succeeded so well in it, that it gave me a very generall reputation. [c] I was called on to assist manny who lay a dying particularly one with whom Wilmot E[arl] of Rochester had an ill concern. He heard that in a long attendance on her I treated her neither with a slack indulgence nor an affrighting severity, upon that he sent for me and in manny discourses with him I saw into the depths of Satan, and by a winter's conversation generally once a week I went thro much ground with him, and as he owned to me I subdued his understanding [c] but the touching his heart was that which God reserved to himselfe and which followed some time after that [1]. He had been a malicious observer of the applications the Clergy made at Court for preferment, and fortified himselfe and others with prejudices against religion by the observations he made on their behaviour, and this made him so partiall [*f.* 207] to me because he observed nothing of aspiring to preferment in me. He told me he said to King Charles after the 1st Volume of my History of the Reformation came out, he wondered why he would use a writer of History ill, for such people can revenge themselves, the King answered I durst say nothing while he was alive when he was dead he should not be the worse for what I said. He gave me very strange impressions of that King and indeed of the

[a] Cf. *Hist.* i. 395-6.   [b] *Ibid.*, and Life in *Hist.* ii. 685.   [c] Cf. Life in *Hist.* ii. 685.

---

[1] Burnet frequently alludes to this subject in his contemporary letters to the Marquis of Halifax (then reputed an atheist), which are to be published by the Historical Society. For unfavourable comments on the affair, see Cunningham, i. 50.

whole Court. [a] After his death I was advised to write a book, what I published concerning him [a], I wrote it with the utmost sincerity and trueth. I began now to have some fame by writing, and I will give an account of the rules I governed myselfe by in writting.

My rules as to the writing of Books.

[b] The Bishop of Worcester Dr. Lloyd had studied the nature of language in generall and of ours in particular very exactly when he drew the Tables for Wilkins' Philosophicall language and Reall Character and had the truest notions of a correct stile of any man I ever saw. He opened all these to me [b] which helped me to see manny errours that had run thro all my former writtings. [c] I kept close to his rules and so came to have the reputation of a correct writter as to stile [c]. I used likewise another method. I never published any book without shewing it to severall persons before it went to the presse, and I was very implicite in submitting to their censure in every thing. Tillotson and Lloyd were the persons I generally made use of this way. I also shewed what I wrot to some persons of a lesse knowing but judicious sort with this intention that if they found any thing too dark or too short I might consider how to correct that. I considered that if I wrote any thing that my friends did not approve of, certainly my Enemies or envious Criticks would be severe on me for it. This in a great measure saved me from reflections on the things that I wrote. I wrote manny litle books which were all so well received that they sold well and helped to support me, so that tho I had no great plenty about me yet I was in no want of anything. I had great presents often offered to me but refused them all except those which were made to help me to bear the charge I was put to while I was preparing materialls for the History of the Reformation [1]. Upon all other occasions I excused my selfe in particular to the sick

---

[a] Cf. Life in *Hist.* ii. 685 ; *Hist.* i. 265.   [b] *Ibid.* 191.   [c] *Ibid.*

[1] Robert Boyle contributed towards his expenses in that matter.

ª who sent much for me ª. I got thro all these years in a very easy manner.

I sought for no preferment.

I never sued for preferment and was so tru to my principles that ᵇ when the E[arl] of Essex offered me the best Benefice in his gift worth about 300 lib a year, but upon this condition that I would not live upon it, but stay still in town where he said they could not bear my absence, I plainly refused it. ᶜ K[ing] Charles¹ sent me the offer of the Bishoprick of Chichester if I would come intirely into his interests. I said I understood not the importance of those words, I knew what the Oaths were which I was to take, these I should observe faithfully but for other promises I would make none. ᵈ He took great pains on me to give me good impressions of him ᵈ, but I knew him too well to let good words overcome me. This made him wish to have me in his power, he said once to D[uke] Hamilton then E[arl] of Aran after the L[ord] Russell's death, he beleeved I would be content to be hanged to have the pleasure to make a speech on the scaffold, but he would order drums so that I should not be heard. I answered when it came to that I should put my speech in such hands that the world should see it if they could not hear it. ᵉ When that unhappy matter of the E[arl] of Essex and the L[ord] Russell broke out, those who knew in what friendship I had lived with them did all expect to see me clapt up.

I was strict to my principles of Loyalty.

ᶠ But I had plainly told them my opinion was that remote fears and bad practises, tho the tendency of them was ever so evident, were not a just cause of resistance when the root of our Constitution was struck at, then and not till then it seemed to me lawfull to enter upon such consultations ᵍ and till that

---

ª Life in *Hist.* ii. 685.   ᵇ *Ibid.* 691.   ᶜ *Ibid.* 685-6 ; *Hist.* i. 434.
ᵈ *Ibid.* 508.   ᵉ Life in *Hist.* ii. 691.   ᶠ *Ibid.* ; *Hist.* i. 540.   ᵍ Life in
Hist. ii. 691 ; *Hist.* i. 585 ; *supra*, p. 130.

---

¹ Mr. Airy's note, *Hist. in loco*, seems written under a misapprehension. The 'He' of the paragraph is clearly the king, to whom the last clause of the preceding paragraph refers.

was lawfull I did not think it lawfull to conceal any thing that might be told me of such councils. This did effectually secure me from having any thing of that sort comunicated to me, so that I was never charged with any thing, ᵃexcept my accession to the making the L[ord] Russell's speech ᵃ of which I have given a full account in my History. One particular I will adde because the conjuncture of Providence seemed to be [*f.* 209] particular. I had bound my selfe in 150 lib. for a kinsman of mine who was setting up in a way of trade, he broke and I was called on to pay the money which at any other time would have been uneasy to me, but upon L[ord] Russell's death his Lady made me a present by his order of 100 guineas and his Father gave me 50 guineas so I was delivered out of that difficulty, but it taught me a piece of wisedome, never to be bound again for any person whatsoever. ᵇ I grew to be much visited and to defend my selfe against the obligation of returning visits, I built a Laboratory ¹ and for above a year I run thro some courses of Chimistry which helped me in my Philosophicall notions, was a pleasant amusement to me and furnished me with a good excuse for staying much at home. ᶜ Manny from the Court came oft to see me and they all studied to possesse me with the apprehensions of the severities that were designed against me. I made one answer to all, that I never troubled my selfe with the fear of what false witnesses might swear against me for that was without all bounds, and I was very sure no body could with trueth lay any thing to my charge ᶜ, so I continued not only in quiet but with that naturall cheerfullnes that arose from a good constitution and a clear conscience. I writ then a large book concerning the trueth of religion and the authority of the books of the Scripture ², with all the freedome of one that was

ᵃ *Hist.* i. 562; Life in *Hist.* ii. 691.   ᵇ *Hist.* i. 499-500; Life in *Hist.* ii. 690.   ᶜ *Ibid.* 692.

¹ Thomas Burnet places this before the Rye House Plot; following on this point the order of the *History*.

² It is possible that this work may be the MS. for the publication of which Burnet, both on the eve of the Revolution (see *infra*, App. III) and in his last will (see Introduction, *supra*), left strict directions, but which seems to have been suppressed by the family, as it has entirely disappeared.

disengaged from parties and interest which I have lately read over and am of the same opinion I was then as to the main of it. In some particulars I have seen further than I did then.

My sense of King Charles's death.

[a] I continued at the Rolls till December 1684 the[n] I was by a speciall order from the Court forbid to preach more there[a]. When K[ing] Charles lay a dying I saw manny under a great terrour about it. I heartily pitied him for the state his soul was in but with relation to the publike I could not but think it was a deliverance, his smooth and cautious way might have undermined us I knew what he was at bottom but he would never have put things to hasard wheras I knew his Brother's hot and eager temper would soon open the eyes of the Nation. [b] I saw it was convenient for me to go abroad for some time, [c] but Lady Margaret tho then brought very low was yet alive [c], she knew me not for above a year before so I was not able to minister any comfort to her, but [d] I got her friends' consent to trust her to the care of some in whom they had great confidence, so I left England in May but before I got to Paris she died.

I went beyond Sea.

[e] At Paris I lived by my selfe retired from company being jealous indeed of all our countreymen. [f] When the journey into Italy was proposed to me all my friends at Paris had great apprehensions of danger in it none encouraged me to it but the L[ord] Mountague. [g] I have said so much of that journey in my letters that I will repeat nothing here. [h] At Geneva I was much grieved to see them insist so much upon their consent of doctrine so that some were forced to leave their countrey while others perhaps subscribed it with equivocations. I spoke much to all who came to me of the folly and wickednes of those impositions. I had then such credit

---

[a] Life in *Hist.* ii. 692; *Hist.* i. 596-7.   [b] Life in *Hist.* ii. 692; *Hist.* i. 597. [c] *Supra*, p. 151.   [d] *Ibid.*   [e] Life in *Hist.* ii. 692; *Hist.* i. 628, 655; *supra*, p. 157.   [f] Cf. *Hist.* i. 661; Life in *Hist.* ii. 692; *supra*, p. 205.   [g] Life as above.   [h] Life in *Hist.* ii. 692-3; and see *Hist.* i. 687.

among them that I have understood since that what I spoke
upon that subject was not without effect for they are now
released from those fetters, they are obliged to no subscriptions
but are only liable to censure if they write or preach against
the established doctrine. ᵃ The multitude and length of their
sermons disgusted me muchᵃ, I thought fewer and shorter
sermons would do much better and that instead of a sermon
on one verse an explanation of a whole chapter would be
more usefull both to the preacher and the people and would
make them understand and love the Scripture the better. At
Bern they were dissolved into luxury and were very haughty
except those who had learned more civility in the French
service but if they were more civill they were likewise more
corrupt then the rest, the Divines seemed dry and conceited
Zurich and Basil had men of another temper among them.

And came and settled in Holland.

ᵇ I came thro Germany to Holland designing upon my
coming thither an absolute retreat, but the Lady Russell and
the Lord Halifax (Saville) had got such a character of me to
be infused into the Prince and the Princesse of Orange that
I found upon my first admittance to them so full a freedome
and so entire a confidence that I saw pains had been taken to
prepare them to receive me well.   I was soon taken into all
their councells.   ᶜ The first thing that I proposed to the Prince
was to put the Fleet of Holland in a good case for that would
give England good hopes that they were preparing for a
rupture.   I prevailed with the Princesse to write to the King
in favour of the B[isho]p of London.   She ventured on it not
without a great fear of offending the King and he answered
her sharply.   He began to look on me as that which he called
an ill Instrument and he wrote her some very severe letters
against meᶜ which she shewed me and was pleased to ask me
how to [*f.* 210] answer them.   An accident happned to me
at this time which gave a great turn to the rest of my life.

ᵃ *Hist.* i. 687; *supra*, p. 249.   ᵇ Life in *Hist.* ii. 693; *Hist.* i. 688 ; *supra*,
p. 250.   ᶜ Life in *Hist.* ii. 693 ; *Hist.* i. 692.

My second marriage.

Hitherto I had lived without children and by consequence without any great concern with relation to other persons except it was for a few friends whom I esteemed and loved very tenderly, but now a new scene was opened to me. ᵃ There was a gentlewoman at the Hague originally of Scotch extraction but of a family long setled in Holland ᵃ. She was an only child and was bred at a great expence as ᵇ one of the best fortunes at the Hague, she was very perfect in Musick of all sorts, she both drew and painted to great perfection. She spoke French, Dutch, and English equally well, she had a very good understanding and a very sweet temper, and was well instructed in religion rather like one that had studied Divinity than barely to be a good Christian ᵇ. She had continued unmaried till she was 27 year old resolving not to marry till she saw a person that she could like. If she was not a perfect beauty ᶜ she was very agreable and was well shaped ᶜ. I was desired to visit her but declined it for I had no thoughts of marriage but was then looking for a dismall overturning of religion and liberty, yet seeing her accidentally I liked her conversation so well that [1] I went to visit her and continued to see her often. I came to like her so well and was so acceptable to her that we were married in May 1687 [2].

I must here set down somewhat that I hope will not be unaccep[tab]le to the Reader. I was farre from the beliefe of Absolute Predestination but the beleife of it brought me both my wives. L[ady] Margaret being young and in a frolick of a divination by letters G B came up to her as the letters of her husband's name. She knew none so named but S[i]r Gideon Barly who had married her near kinswoman, he was dead long before she knew me but she could not put out of her mind the letters of my name ̄and that made her think I was appointed to be her husband which as she told me after

---

ᵃ Life in *Hist.* ii. 695.   ᵇ *Ibid.*   ᶜ *Ibid.*

---

[1] ' Upon her invitation ' is here deleted.   [2] See *infra*, App. II.

our marriag[e] had gone a great way to determine her to it. My 2d wife had manny sutors but could not bring her mind to consent to any of them. In that time which was manny years before I knew her one of whom she had a greate opinion told her she would be married to a Clergy man of another Countrey, so upon seeing me and receiving my addresse she came to think I was that person and that I was appointed to be her husband. [a] As soon as King James heard of my intentions to marry he fancied as that would fixe me at the Hague, so the threatning to proceed criminally against me would terrify her and break that designe [a]. I was so happy in her temper that she was not frighted, on the contrary that brought our marriage on the sooner. [b] I found in her a religious, discreet and good tempered friend[1] who was a prudent manager of my affairs and a very good mistris of a family [b], and she had a very particular art of making her selfe acceptable to all people. She bore me seven children 5 boies and two daughters that were born twins, two of the boies died the rest are still alive she gave them all suck her selfe as long as her health did allow of it [c] and was a tender mother [c] to them all. She lived with me eleven year and then after the peace she went over to Holland to setle matters relating to her estate, but being in a house at Rotterdam where the small pox was, [d] she was taken with the infection and died [d] on the 4th or 5th day [e] in the year 1698 [2].

I was then named by the King to be Tutor or Preceptor to the D[uke] of Glocester [e]. I had some intimations that I was not acceptable to the Princesse and tho she by my L[ord] Godolphin [f] sent me assurances to the contrary [f], yet [g] I had reason to beleive there was some ground for it, so [h] I laid hold on this domestick affliction to desire to be excused from

---

[a] Life in *Hist.* ii. 694 ; *Hist.* i. 726 ; *supra*, p. 251.   [b] Life in *Hist.* ii. 695.
[c] *Ibid.*   [d] *Ibid.* 716.   [e] *Ibid.*, and *Hist.* ii. 210.   [f] Life as above.
[g] *Hist.* ii. 210.   [h] Life in *Hist.* ii. 716-17.

---

[1] See *infra*, App. II and III.
[2] She died June 18, 1698, N. S. (Bodl. Add. MSS. D. 23, ff. 77-8). Her fortune, which seems to have amounted to £30,000 (Luttrell, vi. 177), forms the subject of much business correspondence among the Burnet family papers in the British Museum.

it, and I wrote earnestly to that effect to my best friends but all that was imputed to melancholy so I submitted to the King's pleasure[a]. I saw all that Court except L[or]d Marlborogh and his Lady were against me, I lived very well with them and I thought that was enough[1]. But I do now return to affairs as they stood at the time of my marriage.

The steps made to the Revolution.

[b] The E[arl] of Danby the Marquis of Halifax and the B[isho]p of London were the persons that corresponded with the Pr[ince] of Orange, [c] Mr. Sidney was the man most trusted[c] and Mon Benthink afterwards Earle of Portland answered their letters, [d] the E[arl] of Shrewsbury and the E[arl] of Devonshire came also into the correspondence, [e] they represented on the one hand the desperate designs of the Court and on the other hand the firmnes of the Nation. But [the] danger lay in the Army which tho it stood firm yet military men have seldome such a principle of regeneration that they can be much depended on, and if they begun once to break there was r[eason][2] [*f.* 211] to apprehend that manny might be prevailed on to follow. [f] Among other things to persuade the Prince they wrote to him that all the anger that the Church party bore to the Dissenters was now much allaied so that he would find the reconciling them a very easy matter. Upon this he was desired to use the best means he could to keep them from going in to the measures of the Court by assuring them of the good disposition the Clergy were then in to an union with them [g] and the Pensionary Fagell on whom the Preachers in Holland depended entirely when he directed them to visit all their people and to possesse them with the

[a] Life in *Hist.* ii. 716-17.   [b] *Hist.* i. 712; *supra*, pp. 290-1.   [c] *Hist.* i. 756; *supra*, p. 284.   [d] *Hist.* i. 712; *supra*, p. 288.   [e] Cf. *Hist.* i. 746; *supra*, p. 289.   [f] Cf. *Hist.* ii. 30; *supra*, pp. 331-2.   [g] *Hist.* i. 778-9; *supra*, p. 293.

[1] This circumstance, together with the charm of Marlborough's manner and the energy shown by him in defence of Burnet, when attacked by the House of Commons in 1700 (Macaulay, viii. 249-51), no doubt concurred with political sympathies to modify the unfavourable and more correct estimate which Burnet had at first formed of the famous soldier.

[2] There is a tear here in the MS.

necessity of a rupture with England, [a]among other things said one effect of it would be the freeing their brethren the Presbiterians of England from any farther vexation and persecution[a]. I confesse I did not easily beleeve this, I knew the virulence of some men's tempers and the narrownes of their thoughts in those matters too well easily to believe any thing could so entirely change them, yet upon those assurances often repeated from manny different hands [b]the Prince in his Declaration promised to endeavour a reconciliation of all Protestants[b].

The different views of some who joined in it.

I saw even in Holland those who met and joined with Wildman were utterly against this, [c]they desired only a tolleration but seemed to apprehend the Church would be too secure and grow too strong if united, and they seemed to make it a Maxisme to keep the Church as much divided as could be and by that means to hold it in a dependance, and to keep up a party in opposition to the Church[c]. I suspected manny of these were in their hearts enemies to the Christian religion so their views might be the enervating Christianity by keeping up of parties among us. I say no more of the Prince's Declaration nor of our expedition to England in this place having said all I can say of these matters in my History. [d]We soon found a coldnes in manny of the Clergy which gave us the just apprehensions of what quickly followed, [e]tho the Heads of the University of Oxford declared zealously for the Prince[e]. It was much censured that all the way as we came to London the Prince had on Sundaies sermons and praiers in the Dutch way by a French minister, but he was then acting as Statholder of the States so he continued in their way till he came to Windsor after that he was constant at Church. [1]If K[ing] James had to any tollerable degree kept up his spirits the work would have

[a] *Supra*, p. 331.   [b] *Hist.* i. 776; *supra*, p. 332.   [c] *Hist.* ii. 11 ; *supra*, p. 318.   [d] Cf. *Hist.* i. 790.   [e] *Ibid.* 793; *supra*, p. 302.

[1] From here to the word 'roughness' is one of the two quotations from the Autobiography made in Routh's *Burnet's James II* (p. 412, note).

been difficult if not doubtfull for [a] we saw how variable multitudes are by the joy that was in London upon the King's return from Feversham, [b] and the message sent by the Prince to the King at midnight to withdraw from Whithall, [c] struck a generall damp upon manny not only in London but over the whole Nation, the compassion turned then to his side [c] and if he had staied at Rochester the difficulty in the Convention would have become insuperable.   This gave the Earles of Clarendon and Nottingham the handle to make great opposition in the House of Lords, the Pr[ince] of Orange's cold riserved way disobliged all that came near him while his favourite Benthing provoked them beyond expression by his roughnes.   I say no more of the debates in the Convention having given those so fully in my History that I can adde nothing here.

The King's cold way a prejudice to his affairs.

[d] The trueth was the King for now the Prince was by Declaration of Parliament put in the Throne, was under such an ill state of health that tho it was necessary to conceal it he was sinking under a cold and ill habit of body occasioned by a stay of 10 weeks at S. James, the air of Hampton Court relieved and restored him [d].   I was set on by manny to speak to him to change his cold way, but he cut me off when I entred upon a freedome with him, so that I could not go thro with it.   I wrote him a very plain letter to let him see the turn the Nation was making from him, this offended him so that for some moneths after I was not admitted to speak to him [1].   All our friends had designed that I should be made B[isho]p of Durham, [e] Crew having rendred himselfe

[a] Cf. *Hist.* ii. 799 ; *supra*, p. 302.   [b] Cf. *Hist.* ii. 801 ; *supra*, p. 303.
[c] *Hist.* i. 802.   [d] *Hist.* ii. 2 ; *supra*, p. 312.   [e] Life in *Hist.* ii. 696.

---

[1] This incident, together with Burnet's advocacy of the princess's right (*Hist.* i. 818) and his garrulity, account for the strong dislike which William III, immediately after the Revolution, expressed for Burnet (*Life of Halifax*, ii. 216, 222, 229, 232).   Later on, William probably appreciated Burnet's fidelity and his devotion to the queen (*Hist.* ii. 137), though he still resented his intrusiveness.   See Routh's and Dartmouth's notes to *Hist.* ii. 211 ; Life in *Hist.* ii. 699 ; Cunningham, i. 103, 130.

so obnoxious that he seemed unpardonable, the L[ord]
Mountague brought a message from him both to the Prince
and to my selfe that he would resigne in my favour, trusting
to my generosity of allowing him a thousand pound a year[a].
But[1] the Bishop of London who had then great merit had
asked that Bishoprick of the Prince a few daies after he came
to S. James's and he could not well deny him any thing.
Upon this the B[isho]p of Durham refused to retire and so
that matter fell, and [b]soon after the Prince was put in the
Throne, I was made Bishop of Salisbury[b].

I was named to be Bishop of Salisbury.

[*f.* 212] When I saw that was resolved on [c]I set my selfe
seriously to form a method how I would behave my selfe in
that station[c]. I spent a whole week in retirement and sat up
the whole night before I was Consecrated. I set my selfe
to examine all the sins of my former life and to renew my
mournings for them I run over all the thoughts I had at any
time entertained of the duty of Bishops and made solemne
vows to God to put them in practise[2]. I resolved never to
indulge losenes or luxury nor to raise fortunes to my children
out of the revenues of the Church. I resolved to abstract my
selfe from Courts and secular affairs as much as was possible,
and never to engage in the persecuting of any of what side
soever on the account of differences of religion, and to
dedicate my selfe to the functions belonging to the Order,
preaching, catechising, confirming, and ordaining and governing the Clergy in the best manner I could. Thus I studied
to prepare my selfe for taking that character upon me.
[d]I told all this to the Queen who was much pleased with
it, [e]and added only her desire that my wife should wear plain

---

[a] Cf. Life in *Hist.* ii. 696. [b] *Ibid.*; *Hist.* ii. 8; *supra*, p. 326.
[c] *Supra*, p. 329. [d] *Supra*, pp. 326-7; *Hist.* ii. 8. [e] Cf. *supra*, p. 327.

---

[1] Dr. Routh's second and last allusion
to the Autobiography (*Burnet's James
II*, p. 457, note) refers to this passage;
but he fails to notice that the accounts
in the Autobiography and Life do not
quite tally.
[2] His meditation on this occasion will
be found *infra* as App. V.

clothes[a] suteable rather to what became a Bishop's wife, than to her education, in which she found a very ready and entire compliance with so reasonable a command.

Debates in the House of Lords concerning Comprehension.

[b] I was brought in to the House of Lords at the time that the debates both about Comprehension and Tolleration and about obliging all persons to take the Oaths to the Government were on foot. I was according to my fixed principle much for gentlenes in this last particular but my zeal for the other two took off the merit of this so entirely, that I was scarce thanked for it. [c] In another particular I judged wrong, I thought we might have gained the majority of the Clergy in Convocation to have consented to some moderate things, that we were preparing to lay before them, so when it was moved in the H[ouse] of Lords to appoint in imitation of what had been done in K[ing] Henry the 8 and Edward the 6th's time a select number of both Houses of Parliament, with a select number of both Houses of Convocation to setle a body of Ecclesiasticall lawes, I opposed this with such zeal that I very much lost the good opinion of the Whigs by it. I am now convinced that if ever our Church is to be set right, it must be by some such method, and not by a majority in Convocation[c], for litle good is to be expected from the Sinodicall meetings of the Clergy ; there is so much ambition, presumption and envy among them, that they may do much mischieffe, but there is no probability of their being either inclined to do much good, or of their being able to execute it.

I went to my Diocesse to do my duty there.

[d] But now I was to go into my Diocesse, and for that end I formed my designe thus ; [e] I resolvd to preach constantly every Lord's day [f] and also to preach the weekly lecture at Salisbury. [g] I resolved to go round my Diocesse about three weeks or a moneth once a year, preaching and confirming every day from Church to Church. I resolved thus once

[a] Cf. *supra*, p. 327.   [b] *Hist.* ii. 8-11 ; *supra*, p. 327.   [c] Cf. *Hist.* ii. 10.
[d] Life in *Hist.* ii. 706 ; *supra*, p. 329.   [e] Life in *Hist.* ii. 707 ; *supra*, p. 330.
[f] Life as above.   [g] Life in *Hist.* ii. 706 ; *supra*, p. 329.

in three years besides the formality of the Trienniall Visitation to go round to all the chieffe parts of my Diocesse and to hold conferences with my Clergy upon the chieffe heads of Divinity, [a] in which in a discourse of about two hours length I opened all that related to the head proposed, and encouraged them to object or propose questions relating to the subject. In this I continued till I published my Explanation of the Articles, and then I did not think it necessary to continue those conferences any longer[a]. I found the Clergy were not much the better for them, and false stories were made and believed of what I delivered in those conferences[1]; and tho [b] as I went round I kept an open table to all the Clergy[b], yet nothing could mollify their aversion to a man that was for tolleration and for treating the Dissenters with gentlenes. [c] I continued still to go about preaching and confirming[c], so that I have confirmed and preached in 275 Churches of my Diocesse, and 10 or 12 times in all the market touns and considerable places.   [d] I look upon confirmation if rightly managed as the most effectuall mean possible for reviving Christianity[d], but I could never prevail with the greater part of my Clergy to think of any other way of preparing their youth to it but to hear them repeat their catechism, they did not study to make them consider it as the becoming a Christian by an act of their own.   [e] I have now setled upon a method in which I intend to continue as long as God continues my strength to execute it. I stay a week in a place where every morning I go and [*f.* 213] preach and confirm in some Church within 6 or 7 mile of the place, and then at 5 a clock after evening praier I catechise some children and explain the whole Catechisme to them, so that I go thro it all

---

[a] Life in *Hist.* ii. 706.   [b] Cf. Life as above.   [c] *Ibid.*   [d] *Ibid.*, and *supra*, pp. 329-30.   [e] Life in *Hist.* ii. 706-7.

---

[1] He obviously alludes to Leslie's 'Tempora Mutantur or the great change from 73 to 93. In the travels of a Professor of Theology at Glasgow from the Primitive and Episcopal Loyalty, through Italy, Geneva, &c., to the deposing doctrines under Papistico-Phanatico-Prelatio Colours at Salisbury ; together with his great improvement during his short stay at Cracovia. [Dedicated] to the Clergy of the Diocese of Sarum' [1694]; see *infra*, p. 506 and note.

in six daies and confirm there next Lord's day, and make
presents to the value of about a crown a child to all whom
I catechised, and I have them all to dine with me on the
Lord's day. This seems to be the most profitable method
I can devise both for instructing as well as provoking the
Clergy to catechise much, and for setting a good emulation
among the younger sort to be well instructed. [a] I have likewise set up a school for 50 poor children at Salisbury who
are taught and clothed at my charge[a], and to whom I go
once a moneth and hear 10 of them repeat such Psalms and
parts of the New Testament as I prescribe, and give them
18 pence a piece for a reward, this is a mean to keep them in
good order. I set my selfe to encourage my Clergy not only
by my going often about among them [b] and by assisting them
kyndly in all their concerns, but by a large share of my
income with which I have relieved their necessities[b]. I never
renewed a lease but [c] I gave a considerable share of the fine
either to the Minister of the Parish [c], or if he was well provided to some neighbooring charity, so that I can reckon
3000 lib. given by me in larger sums among them besides
smaller ones that occurre daily.

That on which my heart was most set was that which
raised such hatred against me especially at Oxford, and
answered my expectation so litle that after I had kept it
up 5 year at the rate of 300 lib. a year I saw it was expedient
to let it fall. [d] I thought the greatest prejudice the Church
was under was from the ill education of the Clergy[d].   In the
Universities they for most part lost the learning they brought
with them from schools, and learned so very litle in them that
too commonly they came from them lesse knowing than
when they went to them, especially the servitors, who if they
had not a very good capacity and were very well disposed
of themselves were generally neglected by their Tutors.
They likewise learned the airs of vanity and insolence at
the Universities so that [e] I resolved to have a nursery at

[a] Cf. Life in *Hist.* ii. 723.   [b] *Ibid.*   [c] *Ibid.* 724.   [d] *Ibid.* 708 ; *supra*, p. 329.
[e] Life in *Hist.* ii. 709 ; *supra*, p. 329.

Salisbury of students in Divinity who should follow their studies and devotions till I could provide them. I allowed them 30 lib. a piece, and during my stay at Salisbury I ordered them to come to me once a day and then I answered such difficulties as occurred to them in their studies and entertained them with some discourses either on the Speculative or Practicall part of Divinity or some branch of the Pastorall care. This lasted an hour, and thus I hoped to have formed some to have served to good purpose in the Church ; some of these have answered my expectation to the full and continue still labouring in the Gospell. [a] But they were not all equally well chosen; this was considered as a present setlement that drew a better one after it, so I was prevailed on by importu[n]ity to receive some who did not answer expectation. Those at Oxford looked on this as a publike affront to them and to their way of education [a], so that they railed at me not only in secret but in their Acts [1] unmercifully for it.

Another thing encreased their prejudices against me, [b] I never refused to consent to a plurality where the Churches lay near one another and where the endowment was small, but promoted these all I could ; but for the heaping up of benefice upon benefice that were well endowed, I not only would consent to none of these but opposed them and I openly declared against such as I found possessed of them as robbers of the Church [b], and as living in a spirituall poligamy. This irritated not only all those who were concerned but all who aspired to the like accumulation of benefices so I was considered by them as a common ennemy and they set themselves in a violent opposition to me. [c] I was very gentle to the Dissenters and received them kyndly when they came to see me, but I took much pains to convince them of the sin and the bad consequences of separation and I brought manny off from that way [c]. The Dissenters all

---

[a] Cf. Life in *Hist.* ii. 709.   [b] *Ibid.* ; *Hist.* ii. 646.   [c] Life in *Hist.* ii. 711.

[1] The general allusion is to the ' Terrae filius ' ; see Wordsworth, *Social Life at the English Universities,* p. 26 and index. (*Note kindly contributed by Mr. Doble.*)

over my Diocesse treated me with great respect, they thought it due to me in gratitude because I used them well ; they were also well pleased to see a Bishop set himselfe as they thought I did to advance religion. Upon this a jealousy was taken up of me as being secretly in an understanding with them which the malice of some carried so farre as to give it out that I was in a secret designe to betray the Church to them, [*f.* 214] and this got such credit that above halfe my Clergy acted in such an opposition to me as if they had believed it, but I resolved patiently to bear with what I could not correct. All this gained yet more credit with them by ᵃthe opposition I gave to the Bill against Occasionall Conformity, ᵇ on which they had set their hearts as a breach begun upon the Tolleration and as a mean to manage Elections of Parliament. ᶜ I shewed all possible moderation to a Jacobite meeting that was opened at Salisbury and obtained a secret consent from the King and Queen to connive at it, yet this did no way soften themᶜ. They thought this was only a justice due to them, ᵈwheras it was a betraying the Church to be gentle to Dissenters.

ᵉ I looked on Ordinations as the most important part of a Bishop's care and that on which the law had laid no restraints, for it was absolutely in the Bishop's power to ordain or not as he judged a person qualified for it, and so I resolved to take that matter to heart. I never turned over the examining those who came to me for orders to a Chaplain or an Archdeacon, ᶠ I examined them very carefully my selfe. ᵍ I began allwaies to examine them concerning the proof of the Christian religion and the authority of the Scriptures and the nature of the Gospell Covenant in Christ ; if they understood not these aright I dismissed them, but upon a competent understanding of these I went thro the other parts of Divinity and soon saw into the measure of their knowledgeᵍ. One defect run through them all, even those who could not be called ignorant, they read the Scriptures so litle that they scarce knew the most common things

ᵃ *Hist.* ii. 364.   ᵇ *Ibid.* 337.   ᶜ Life in *Hist.* ii. 710.   ᵈ *Ibid.* 711.   ᵉ *Ibid.* 707 ;
Hist. ii. 638, 643.   ᶠ Life in *Hist.* ii. 707 ; *supra*, p. 330.   ᵍ Life in *Hist.* ii. 707-8.

in them, but ^a when I was satisfied that they had a competent
measure of knowledge, I directed the rest of my discourse
to their consciences and went thro all the parts of the Pastorall
Care to give them good directions and to awaken in them
a right sense of things ^a. I pressed them to imploy their time
in praier, fasting and meditation and in reading carefully the
Epistles to Timothy and Titus. I spoke copiously to them
every day for four daies together upon these subjects, sometimes to them alltogether and some times singly. ^b I referred
the examining them in Greek and Latin to the Archdeacon
and brought them to a publike examination in the Chapter-
house before the Dean and Prebendaries ^b. As for their
moralls we were forced to take that implicitly from the Testi-
monialls signed by the Clergy in whose neighbourhood they
had lived, in which I have found such an easines of signing
these, that unlesse I knew the men I grew to regard them
very little. This was the best method that in the present
state of our affairs I could take, yet I found it so defective
and so farre short of a due exactnes that I must confesse
the Ordination weeks were much dreaded by me and were
the most afflicting part of the whole year and of the whole
Episcopall duty. ^c I tried next how to regulate my Consis-
toriall Court and for some years I went constantly to it but
I found that which is crooked cannot be made straight, all
our proceedings are so dilatory and engage men into such
an expence that I did not wonder to hear them so much
cried out on as they were, they are a great Grievance both
to the Clergy and Laity so I gave over all hope of doing any
good in them and gave over going more to them ^c. Thus
I laid my plan and have now followed it executing it almost
22 years, but I must say doing litle good with all this agitation
I have put my selfe in, yet since this is the best thing I can
do I am resolved to continue thus doing till I can see any
thing that is better.

^d When a Convocation was opened in the year 1689 we

^a Life in *Hist.* ii. 707-8.   ^b *Ibid.* 708 ; *supra*, p. 330.   ^c Life in *Hist.* ii.
707 ; *Hist.* ii. 634 ; *supra*, p. 331.   ^d *Hist.* ii. 33 ; *supra*, pp. 331-3.

saw the old ill humour of the Clergy shew it selfe. All the good temper they were in and the promises they had made in K. James's time were now forgot, they would not so much as enter on the considerations of any alterations but resolved to adhere firmly to the establishment made by the Act of Uniformity, so all the hopes of a union or coalition vanished[a]. The Queen hoped to have overcome the peevishnes of the leaders of the party by preferring them but nothing could soften them after they saw Tillotson promoted to be Archbishop of Canterbury, Sharp by a great errour of Tillotson's was made Archbishop of York. He has proved an ill instrument and has set himselfe at the head of the party but has suffered much by it in the opinion of manny who looked on him before as a man of integrity and simplicity, but few do now retain that opinion as with regret I confesse I do not I have observed too much art and [1   ] [*f.* 215] and designe in him to be able to think of him as I wish I could do[2]. I saw no good could be done in that present conjuncture for the healing of our breaches, this made me apply my selfe more diligently to do all the good I could in my own Diocesse. [b] I observed that the strength of the Dissenters was in the market touns where the Ministers provision was so small that according to the common observation a poor living had as poor a Clark. I resolved to remedy this all I could, and there being manny Prebends in the Church of Salisbury all in the Bishop's gift, I resolved to give these to the Ministers of the market touns, but thought it reasonable to demand a bond of them that in case they should leave the market town they would resigne the Preband, that so the Prebend might be as it were annexed to the Church in the market town. This was done by the advice of manny eminent Bishops and others who highly applauded my designe, but when some[b] virulent Clergy men began to

[a] *Hist.* ii. 33; *supra*, pp. 331-3.　　[b] Life in *Hist.* ii.712.

[1] A word torn off.
[2] Sharp had voted against Fenwick's attainder; and after the accession of Anne, over whom he possessed much influence, was regarded as a Tory. He died in 1714.

open against me they finding no other matter to fixe their censures on, [a]declaimed against this[a] and in severall prints charged it with simony. Upon which [b]to withdraw all occasion from their malice I gave up all the bonds I had taken[b], and finding some whom I had provided with the best things in my gift, had withdrawn from the poor provisions in touns to better livings, I upon that let my designe fall[1].

I know I have said that which may seem too much of my labours in my Diocesse, if it were not to lay open the injustice and malice of those angry men who studied to represent me as a favourer of Dissenters, who was betraying the Church into their hands. I had indeed considered much thro the whole course of my life and studies what a Bishop ought to be, and how he ought to labour so that it would have been most inexcusable in me to have gone in the beaten road and have followed common methods. I thought my selfe under an indispensabl[e] obligation of applying my selfe by the best waies I could think on to build up and heal the breaches of this Church. So that what sins soever I have to humble me before God I do not know any I am guilty of with relation to the Church, unless it be sins of omission for I might still have done more in every particular than I have done. But this comfort I have, that I have studied to put in practise the best things done by any of our Bishops since the Reformation, and have not spared my person nor my purse[2], but have laid them out very liberally at all times. Thus I have lived and laboured manny years and have not abated in any one particular of my first designes, but have rather increased in them all, for at this age both memory and strength of body are still entire, [*f.* 214 (*b*)] and I have been so [c]farre from encreasing my estate[c] that I have not saved all the produce of my temporall estate. [*f.* 215] [d]The attendance on Parliaments is a great distraction and put us to a great

---

[a] Life in *Hist.* ii. 712.   [b] *Ibid.*   [c] *Ibid.* 723-4.   [d] *Hist.* ii. 660.

---

[1] See *Hist.* ed. 1833, vi. 367, and the catalogue of the University Library, Cambridge, ed. 1856, &c., iv. 437.

[2] See Bodl. MSS. Rawl. D. 1172, ff. 2-3.

charge, besides the calling us off the halfe of the year from doing our duty. [a] I do indeed continue my practise of preaching constantly while I am at London [a].

I wrote concerning the Pastorall care

I set my selfe soon after I was Consecrated to write of [b] the Pastorall care, and that is the book that of all my other writtings pleases myselfe best[1]. I wrote it under deep and serious impressions of the duties incumbent on Pastors, and I thank God it has had a very good effect on manny persons, but it helped not a litle to heighten the indignation of bad Clergymen against me, they lookt on it as writ on designe to expose them to the nation, for reformation and moderation are the two things that bad Clergymen hate the most of all things. A man that will magnify the authority of the Clergy and assert all the rights of the Church how much soever he may extend them, and that declaims bitterly against Dissenters how weakly soever he argues, and how falsely soever he charges them, will passe for a tru Churchman and a champion among corrupt Clergy men. It is tru that they will not attack a man who writes for Reformation tho they will hate him, for they know that the world will be against them in that. They will wait for some doctrinall point that they may more safely charge him with Heresy. At this time they raised a clamour against Socinianisme which was levelled chiefly at Tillotson, and after him at my selfe, for no tru reason but it was a word of an ill sound and so they made noise with it, and [c] I publishing 4 discourses that I had made to my Clergy, one against Infidelity, another against Socinianisme a 3d against Popery and a 4th against Dissenters [c] to give my Clergy some instructions, for I saw much ignorance among them, they found a rude pretender to learning who fell on me in a very petulant stile[2] but so poorly in point

[a] Cf. Life in *Hist.* ii. 721.   [b] *Hist.* ii. 637.   [c] Life in *Hist.* ii. 707.

---

[1] Burnet's judgement may be here applauded.

[2] See *supra*, p. 499, note. For Burnet's special grudge against Leslie consult the Introduction.

of argument that he seemed [*f.* 216] to have no other designe in writing but to rail at me, I would not answer him, two others did very fully.

and an exposition of the 39 *Articles.*

[a] These short treatises moved both the Queen and Tillotson to set me on a greater work to write on the 39 Articles. [b] I set about it and by the helps my former writtings and my papers gave me I finished it within a year after I undertook it. Tillotson read it all over and corrected it in manny places and approved of it all, only he thought I put a force upon the condemnatory versicles in Athanasius' Creed which the words could not bear ; he thought that Creed, especially those damning propositions in it was a heavy load on our Church [b]. He confessed since we retained it the best sense possible ought to be put on every part of it. [c] I kept that work seven year by me before I put it in the presse, [d] manny Bishops read it Tennison, Sharp, Stillingfleet, Patrick, Hall, and Williams. It lay some considerable time in both Universities and was read by manny, all approving of it and des[i]ring me to print it. Williams only pressed me much to consider these as Articles of peace and not as Articles of doctrine. The meaning of which was that they were Articles which all men were bound to acquiesse in and not to contradict, but were not bound to believe them. I considered this as carefully as I could, but tho I wish they had been so setled, I could not think according to our Law and Constitution that they could be so understood. At last I published that work, for a while all were silent about it. They who on other accounts set themselves against me when they saw it generally well received were for a while at a stand, [e] but when they were suffered to meet in Convocation they resolved to vent their ill humours upon me [e]. They thought it a presumption for any single person to expound the doctrine of

[a] Cf. Life in *Hist.* ii. 719 ; *Hist.* ii. 228.   [b] Life in *Hist.* ii. 719.   [c] *Ibid.* 719-20 ; *Hist.* ii. 227.   [d] Life in *Hist.* ii. 720.   [e] *Ibid.* ; *Hist.* ii. 284.

the Church. ª They did not like a latitude of sense in which
I had expounded the Articles ª chiefly those that related to
Predestination to shew that men of both sides might with
a good conscience signe them. This had been more excus-
able [if] it had come from Calvinists, for the words of the
Articles do plainly favour most of their tenets, but it was
very strange when it came from Arminians and shewed they
would even wound themselves to thrust at me. That which
was most at heart with them was that I had not carried
Church power higher, that I had owned the forreigne Churches
to be tru Churches, and that I had so flatly condemned the
reall presence in the Sacrament. These were tender points
with them, but they resolved to raise a clamour and ᵇ they
brought up a generall charge against that book to the Upper
House, but when they were pressed to assigne speciall matter
they let it all fall. ᶜ Severall books were writ against it[1],
and it was reflected on in manny sermons but tho answers
were writ to these I despised them all, for indeed tho I had
read them carefully yet I did not find reason from any thing
that any of them wrot to alter so much as one period or
to change one word in my whole work ᶜ. The matter has
been let sleep now these ten years, but whither they will
revive it or not I cannot tell. My being set about the D[uke]
of Glocester increased their indignation, they thought I would
infuse ill principles in him, so ᵈ an attempt that they set on
in the H[ouse] of Commons [2] against me failing ᵈ they continued very ineasy, ᵉ but that Prince's death put an end to
that service.

My third marriage.

ᶠ At that time I saw it was convenient for me to marry
again. I had 5 children; the eldest was but 10 years old
when his mother died, and being now to live in a Court and
in a constant attendance it seemed necessary to provide a

ª Life in *Hist.* ii. 720 ; *Hist.* ii. 284-5.   ᵇ *Ibid.*   ᶜ *Hist.* ii. 228.
ᵈ *Ibid.* 237.   ᵉ *Ibid.* 245-6.   ᶠ Life in *Hist.* ii. 718-9.

[1] The British Museum *Catalogue* specifies three such, dated 1702 or 1703.
[2] See Luttrell, iv. 592-3.

Mistris to my family and a mother to my children ª. But whither these reasons would have determined me or not I cannot tell, if I had not known ᵇ one of the most extraordinary persons that has lived in this age both for great knowledge and descretion, a sublime piety, a sweet temper and one whose deportment shined in a most exemplary manner ᵇ in all the places wher she had lived. She had been particularly known to my former wife, who used allwaies to say she was a woman fitted to be my wife, and when she went to Holland she said if she never came back she wished me to get her to be her children's mother. I had known her manny years, so after she had been seven year a widdow, and I two year a widdower we were married, and both I and my children were happy in her beyond expression, for she was one of the strictest Christians and one of the most heavenly minded persons I have ever known. ᶜ Her Method of Devotion gives her tru character ᶜ, she practised it all as well as she wrot it. I know some think I assisted her in it, but they are mistaken, I did indeed read it over and advised her to leave out and shorten some things, and in some few places and but in few I corrected the grammar of her stile, but I gave her no other assistance in it. All [*f.* 217] came from her own heart, her head and her hand. ᵈ Before the 2d edition of that book there is an account given of her ᵈ which I dictated for the greatest part, ᵉ Dr. Godwyn whose name is to it ᵉ only writing so much of it as to give him a right to set his name to it at my desire. She lived with me 8 years and 8 monethes, and bore me two daughters, both which died soon after they were born [1].

ª Cf. Life in *Hist.* ii. 718-9.   ᵇ *Ibid.* 719.   ᶜ *Ibid.*   ᵈ *Ibid.*   ᵉ *Ibid.*

---

[1] She was Elizabeth, daughter of Richard Blake, Knt., goddaughter of Bishop Fell, and widow of Robert Berkeley of Spetchley. The account by 'T. Goodwyn, archdeacon of Oxford' (afterwards Archbishop of Cashel), prefixed to the second edition published in 1709. and summarized in the article devoted to her life by the *Dictionary of National Biography* (vii. 393-4), gives a pleasing picture of a devout, amiable, and very beneficent woman, but hints a perhaps excessive political zeal (in the Whig interest), which might also be suspected from *Jerviswood Correspondence*, pp. 169, 175. She remarried with Dr. Burnet in 1700, and from thenceforth with her husband's consent devoted four-fifths of an income estimated at £800 a year (Lut-

The education of my children.

The next part of my life relates to my children, of whom I have taken a more then ordinary care, and have, I thank God for it, been hitherto very successfull in it. I will therefore set down the methods I have followed which I hope may give some instruction to those who read this. [a] At seven year old I entered them into Latine. I had a distinct Tutor to every one to whom as I gave 30 lib. a year, so when I saw they deserved a Prebend in my Church I did not lessen their allowance [a], for I thought it simony to make them serve me in educating my children upon my giving them Church preferment. I choose my sons' Tutors with great care, and they answered my expectation. [b] I took the instructing all my children in the principles of religion into my own hands, and spent every morning about halfe a hour in that work. I went thro the whole O[ld] Testament once, and the New Testament thrice with them, giving a perpetuall Commentary [b] to make them understand and delight in those sacred writtings, and this I continue to do to this day. I watched over their moralls with all possible care. I thought the pains my Father had taken upon me laid a more then ordinary obligation on me to look carefully to my children; only remembring the ill effect his severity had on me, my biasse lay the other way to [c] a remisse gentlenes [c] of which I thank God I have not yet seen any ill effects. I determined to keep them with me at home. I know emulation and example with lively company awakens young

---

[a] Cf. Life in *Hist.* ii. 722.   [b] *Ibid.* 721.   [c] *Ibid.* 722.

---

trell, iv. 649) to good works. The *Colbatch Correspondence* (Brit. Mus. Add. MSS. 22908, f. 45) bears touching testimony to her solicitude for her step-children. She predeceased her husband, Jan. 27, 1708-9, 'very much lamented for her charity and piety' (Luttrell, vi. 403), and was buried near her first husband; in accordance with a promise, and not (as her will testifies) 'out of any want of respect or kindness to my present husband, who has by his great kindness and confidence deserved from me all the gratitude and acknowledgments of Love and Respect I can testify.' Her devotional *Method*, though distinguished, as her biographer in the *Dictionary* remarks, by the inordinate length of its devotions, is no less remarkable for a simple and elevated fervour and a refreshing common sense. Her diary when abroad in 1707, and some religious papers, are in Bodl. MSS. Rawl. D. 1902.

spirits and a Bishop's table accustomed young persons to
a great variety and to much liberty. But my sons were
lively enough and learned as quick as I desired. They in
halfe the time that they must have staied at a school learned
at least 4 times as much as they would have done at one,
and yet they were not kept so long at their books as they
must have stayd at a school, for I held them to a rule of
being kept 3 hours before dinner and two hours after dinner
to their books, so both they had a full time allowed for their
childish diversions and their tutors had time for their private
studies, but they sate by them all the while they were at
their books observing them and answering th[e] questions
they put them. In lesse then 4 years time they went thro
both Latine and Greek beside the Accidence and Grammar
much shortned they went thro Corderius, most of Erasmus's
Colloquies, Justin, Phedrus, Corn. Nepos, Terence, Cesar,
Salustius and a great part of Livy, all Virgill's Eneids, with
many of his Ecclogues, Ovid's Epistles and a great part
of his Metamorphosis, many of Horace's Odes and Satires,
some of Juvenall's Satires and manny of Buchanan's Psalmes,
and to form them to a good stile of Latin as they read Cesar
twice over so they translated some parts of him into English,
and about a week after they turned it back into Latine,
and then compared their performance with Cesar. In Greek
besides the Grammar they went thro the Gospells and Acts,
some parts of Isocrates and some of Lucian's Dialogues, and
then Homer's Iliad twice over. [a] Thus they went thro the
learning of the Languages[1] with great exactness. [b] I sent
my eldest son [2] to Trinity Colledge in Cambridge[b], and gave
him a very good Schollar for his servant and 40 lib. to his

[a] Cf. Life in *Hist.* ii. 722.   [b] *Ibid.*

---

[1] This passage relating to his sons'
education should be compared with
the *Thoughts on Education* published
in 1761 from a MS. in the possession
of Sir Alexander Dick of Prestonfield,
Bart., who had found it among the
papers of Sir John Cunninghame of
Caprington, Bart. The MS., which was
anonymous, but was believed to be in
Burnet's handwriting, must have been
written while he was minister of
Saltoun, and is addressed to a 'lord'
whose name does not transpire.

[2] For William Burnet, see Hutchinson,
History of Massachusetts Bay, ii. 336-64;
Biog. Brit. 2nd ed. vol. iii. pp. 38-9;

Tutor Dr. Colbatch [1], but after two years stay there I brought
him from thence and put him for a whole year under Mr. Craig,
who carried him a great way into Mathematicks and Philosophy. [a] My two younger sons [2] I sent to Merton Colledge at
Oxford, but kept a private Tutor with them besides a Tutor
in the Colledge [a], where they staied 3 year and I thank God
they came back to me from those places without any of those
taints that are too commonly given in them. [b] After that
I sent them beyond sea [3], where they staied a year at Leyden,
two of them were 8 moneths at Geneva, 4 moneths at Rome,
the rest was a ramble thro Italy and Germany [b]. They were
in all three years beyond sea kept by me at a great charge
that so they might go into the best companies and learn all
that was to be learned abroad. They are now come home
I thank God yet pure and free from all ill impressions, and
they have made such a progresse in knowledge that all
I shall say for them is that I do not find the labour and
expence I have been at upon them is losst. [*f.* 218] They
must say the rest for themselves in due time, and with that
I end this article.

I had kept my selfe in an abstraction from medling in the
Elections of Parliament all King William's time, but upon

[a] Cf. in *Hist.* ii. 722. [b] *Ibid.*

Dict. Nat. Biog. vii. 404 ; Brit. Mus.
Add.MSS. 22908, ff 33, 43, 45, 47 ; *Hist.
MSS. Com. Rep.* V. 215-6 ; XI. App.
iv, pp. 46, 273, 274, 296 ; XV. App. vi,
p. 61 ; Bodl. Add. MSS. D. 23, ff. 133ᵉ,
138. His will is in Somerset House,
Auber 183, dated Dec. 6, 1727.

[1] See *supra*, p. 244, note 1.

[2] (a) Gilbert Burnet, born at Salisbury,
Nov. 15, 1690 ; matr. Nov. 6, 1703 ;
B.A. 1706 ; M.A. (Cambridge) 1713 ;
became Canon of Salisbury in 1715 ;
Chaplain to the king, 1718 ; Rector of
East Barnet, 1719 (*Alum. Oxon.* i. 215);
engaged in literary pursuits (*Dict. Nat.
Biog.* vii. 404), edited the first volume
of the *History* (see *supra*, Introduction),
and died unmarried in 1726 (Brit. Mus.
Add MSS. 11404, f. 104, 113). The
will of his brother William refers to his

generosity in assisting to pay the said
brother's debts. (b) Thomas Burnet,
born Feb. 19, 1694, matr. Nov. 12, 1705,
for whom see *Alum Oxon.* i. 215 ; *Biog.
Brit.* 2nd ed. vol. iii. p. 40 ; *Dict. Nat.
Biog.* vii. 410-1 ; *Hist. MSS. Com. Rep.*
XV. App. vii, p. 212 ; Nichols, *Literary
Anecdotes,* i. 71, iii. 353 ; *True Account
of the Life and Writings of Thomas
Burnet, Esq.,* 1715 ; *Notes and Memoran-
dums of the Six Days,* 1715 ; Brit. Mus.
Add. MSS. 11569-70 ; Eg. MSS. 921,
f 87 ; Add. MSS. 27784, f. 35 ; Add.
MSS. 11394, ff. 59-61 ; Bodl. Add. MSS.
D. 23, ff. 142-5, 148, 151-6, 194-5.
His will, dated July 14, 1747, proved
Feb. 3, 1753, is in Somerset House.
See also the Introduction, *supra.*

[3] In May 1707 (Bod. MSS. Rawl. D.
1092, ff. 115-7, 125, 134).

the Queen's displeasure at the attempt to tack the Bill
against Occasionall Conformity, when that Parliament came
to its conclusion, she her selfe spoke to me with relations
to the elections. She said we saw she trusted to us, and in
particular she spoke severely of Mr. Fox [1] the Citisen for
Salisbury. This made me set my whole strength to keep
him out, for I being Lord of the whole town and having laid
manny obligations on the body in the generall, and on
most of the Electors, I thought I might for once recommend
one to them. I failed in my attempt, and it raised a most
violent storm against me from the Tories, who by manny
very bad practises are now a majority in the Corporation.
I am sensible it was an errour in me occasioned by my too
forward zeal to serve and please the Queen. Things of
that sort draw very bad consequences after them. This has
raised an anger against me which will follow me as long as
I live here. I have now gone thro the most materiall passages
of my life to this day which is the 30th of November in
the year 1710, when I am entred in the 68 year of my age,
if things hereafter shall occurre worth transmitting to posterity
I will adde them as I shall see cause. I will only now give
a Catalogue of all the Books I have written—

A Dialogue between a Conformist and Nonconformist
1669.

A Vindication of the Lawes and Constitution of Scotland
1673.

The Mystery of Iniquity Unvailed 1673.

An account given by T. K. believed to be Ken a Jesuite
of the trueth of Religion examined 1674.

The Memoirs of the Duke of Hamilton 1676 folio.

An Account of a Conference with Coleman 1676.

A Collection of Sermons and Pamphlets from the year
1678 to the year 1706 in 3 vols 4to.

---

[1] Bishop Burnet's unfriendly relations
with his Dean, Dr. Younger (*Hist.
MSS. Com. Rep.* X. App. iv. p. 341 ;
Bodl. Add. MSS. D. 23, ff. 30, 32),
seem to have originated with the
Bishop's objection to Younger's appoint-
ment, because he had been tutor to Fox
(Bodl. Add. MSS. D. 23, f. 9).

The History of the Reformation 2 vols. folio 1679, 1681.

The History abridged 1682.

An account of the Earl of Rochester 1681.

The Life of Sir Mathew Hale 1682.

The Methods of Conversion by the Clergy of France examined 1682.

The History of the Regale 1682.

The Translation of More's Utopia 1683.

The Life of Bishop Bedell 1685.

The Translation of Lactantius de mortibus Persecutorum 1687.

Letters concerning my Travells, 1687 Reflections on Varillas 2 vols 12mo 1687.

The Pastorall Care 1692.

Four Discourses to my Clergy 1693.

Essay on Q. Mary's Character 1695.

My Vindication of Archbishop Tillotson 1696.

Explanation of the 39 Articles folio 1700.

The Church Catechisme explained 1710.

Severall Sermons on particular occasions.

APPENDIX

I

ADDITIONAL NOTE ON BURNET'S CHANGE OF VIEW WITH REGARD TO PASSIVE OBEDIENCE

(See *supra*, p. 32, note 2.)

THE remarkable passage which will be found on pp. 32–9, *supra*[1], constitutes one of the most curious episodes in Burnet's original Memoirs; it is not surprising that it should have been so ruthlessly recast after the Revolution; and it appears somewhat strange that it should not have been expunged from the original Memoirs when Burnet, on the eve of the Revolution, made conditional arrangements for their posthumous publication. It is of course no news to students of Burnet that the historian (presumably about a month before the pages in question were written) had co-operated with Dr. Tillotson in an attempt to obtain from Lord Russell, while in the condemned cell, a recantation of the doctrine which admits of ultimate resistance to oppression; but the circumstances of the moment, and the somewhat disingenuous modifications introduced by Burnet into the final version of those events[2], have tended to obscure the very radical nature of the change in his views, and the very late period in life at which it occurred[3]. Macaulay (who may have read the long excursus on which we comment, though, if so, he clearly regarded it as contemporary with the events of 1661, to which it relates) confines Burnet's belief in the doctrine of passive obedience to the days of his 'early youth[4]'; and Von Ranke, who had certainly never seen either this passage or the early version of the Russell affair, regards the rendering of the latter event given in the *History* as representing

---

[1] Which offers a striking contrast to the serene impartiality with which Burnet's master, Archbishop Leighton, handles the respective obligations of rulers and people ; see *Works*, ed. 1830, i. 289, 295, 314–5; ii. 66 ; iii. 205–12.

[2] Cf. *supra*, p. 130, with *Hist.* i. 540, 557; and cf. also *supra*, p. 11,

ll. 8–9 from bottom, with *Hist.* i. 135; and *supra*, p. 24, l. 4 from bottom, with *Hist.* i. 146.

[3] As late as 1686, in an unsigned and undated letter to Dr. Fall, of great interest (Bodl. Add. MSS. D. 23, f. 1), Burnet expressed the strongest adhesion to the doctrine of non-resistance.

[4] *Hist.* ed. 1858, ii. 435.

Burnet's original view[1]. To Burnet's contemporaries, however, his change of standpoint was fully apparent; and the principal Jacobite and Tory writers of the post-Revolution period—Leslie in the *Tempora Mutantur* of 1694, Hickes in *Some discourses upon Dr. Burnet and Dr. Tillotson* (1695), the pseudonymous 'Miso-Dolos' of *The Good old Cause, or, Lying in Truth* (attributed to Leslie), and Swift in his caustic censures on the published *History* (*Works*, 1824, xii. 188)—have commented severely on a tergiversation to which their inveterate hostility was partly due. They were enabled to fortify their case by copious and compromising citations from his earlier works, many of which have long since fallen into obscurity. *The Modest and Free Conference* of 1669; a sermon on the anniversary of King Charles's Martyrdom, 1672; the *Vindication of the Church and State of Scotland*, 1673; the *Life of Bedel*, 1685[2]; various treatises and sermons, notably three discourses on Judg. xix. 30, Rom. xiii. 5, 2 Sam. i. 12, afforded peculiar opportunities for sarcasm. Burnet, on the other hand, in the curious meditation which we print *infra* as Appendix III, pathetically asserts the continuity of his own political opinions; and argues that the loophole he had always left—a very small one, as readers of the passage we are considering will be disposed to consider it—for the exercise of a right of political self-preservation *in extremis*, precludes the charge of inconsistency. Whatever view we may take of this argument, which Burnet had urged before his own contemporaries in his self-vindicatory answer to Hickes, it must at least be admitted that Burnet always repudiated the theories we associate with the name of Filmer. Like Grotius, he founds the principle of passive obedience not on an hereditary right divine, but upon motives of religious quietism and political expedience; motives to which the memories of the Civil Wars, in Scotland more especially, lent impressive force. Nor can it escape remark, that even in his unregenerate days, there is betrayed a natural bias in favour of more energetic principles (*supra*, p. 35, ll. 26–31); with a strong sense of the appalling practical arguments which must occasionally confront the extreme advocates of non-resistance (*ibid.* ll. 10–3). Burnet's own formal renunciation

---

[1] *Eng. Gesch.*, &c., ed. 1868, vol. vii. App. ii. p. 166.

[2] With regard to this work, Burnet, in his *Reflexions* in answer to Hickes (1696, pp. 69–72), successfully defends himself. In the copies possessed by the British Museum and London Libraries the most incriminating leaf (pp. 445–6) has been removed.

of the doctrines which inculcate an unconditional obedience will be found in the tract entitled 'An Enquiry into the measures of submission to the supreme authority; and of the grounds upon which it may be lawful or necessary for subjects to defend their religion, lives, and liberties,' which he published anonymously on the eve of the prince's expedition; and to which the *Meditation* already mentioned specifically refers us. This pamphlet, of which the language is in parts curiously reminiscent of the earlier, and very different, passage to which our previous observations have applied, commences (to quote its own words) with 'a true and full view of the nature of Civil Society, and more particularly of the nature of supreme power, whether it is lodged in one or more persons?'

Section I explains that the law of nature acknowledges no difference or subordination among mankind, except in respect to the relations of parent and child[1], husband and wife; all men being born free, though they may contract themselves into servitude. The Second and Third Sections state that self-preservation (whether involving the resistance of violent aggression, or the exacting of reparation for the same) is a duty imposed by the law of nature; and that government originates in a compromise, by which the second of these rights is surrendered to a national trustee. So far, Burnet is practically recapitulating the argument of his Memoirs[2]; but in the *Enquiry* we find three suggestive additions to these presuppositions, viz. (1) That the right of exacting reparation includes the right to put such unjust persons as commit unwarranted aggressions 'out of a capacity of doing the like injuries any more, either to ourselves, or to any others'; (2) That the central power may be entrusted either to 'a single person' or to 'a body of men'; (3) *That the supreme power is vested in the Legislature*; of which the *executive* (in all cases where these powers are separated) is merely the *delegate*. Section IV maintains that, on the principles of natural religion, God has vouchsafed no specific authorization to any one form of government[3]; but that national constitutions, whatever their nature, cannot be subverted without sin; since power, like property[4], is confirmed to its actual possessors by the sanctions of natural religion. The Fifth Section asserts that the authority of rulers, as of

---

[1] Cf. *supra*, p. 36, ll. 18-22.   [3] Cf. *supra*, p. 35, ll. 31-3.
[2] Cf. *supra*, from p. 36, l. 28, to   [4] Cf. *supra*, p. 38, ll. 16-22, 34-7.
p. 37, l. 12.

masters, varies in specific instances, according to the terms of the
agreement on which it is founded; there being masters of servants
and apprentices, as well as of slaves [1].   Section VI affirms that
a divine right to the supreme power could only be claimed by men
miraculously chosen; and that the divine choice is not arguable
even from possession, which may be merely due to successful
usurpation.   In Section VII we learn that the measures of obedience are laws, oaths, prescription; but with this reservation, that
'power must always be proved, but liberty proves itself; the one
being founded only upon a positive law, and the other upon the law
of nature.'   In the Eighth Section we are reminded that Old Testament instances (as depending on miraculous warrant) cannot be cited
in this connexion [2].   The Ninth Section maintains that in the New
Testament no regulations with regard to *forms* of government
can be traced; but that since by its precepts a final seal is set
upon the general rules of 'justice, order and peace [3] . . . we are most
strictly bound by it, to observe the constitution in which we are.'
The propagation of Christianity by force, the forcible resistance of
persecution, are specifically forbidden [4]; *but this last only applies to
cases where persecution is authorized by the laws of the land; for
if our religion is established by law, its undisturbed exercise becomes
a branch of our property.*   The Tenth Section urges that the submission preached by Christ to the Jews is defined by the fact that
the Jews, having appealed for the protection of Rome, had forfeited
all subsequent right to resent her domination.   Augustus himself
certainly claimed no divine right; usurpation, sanctioned by the
subsequent acts of senate and people, constituted his only title [5].
Passing thence to the English constitution, Burnet argues (Sections
XI and XII) that, since our kings admittedly possess but a *share* of
the legislative function, though the *whole* of the executive power, their
prerogative is necessarily limited, especially as regards taxation; and
that the unlawful demands of their agents (where the issue is plain
and weighty) may be lawfully resisted.   But here lies the crux (as
is acknowledged in Section XIII); the Militia Act (to one clause of
which all holding office are bound by oath) vests the right of using

---

[1] The last only are mentioned *supra*,
p. 34, ll. 9-15.
[2] Cf. *supra*, from p. 35, l. 5 from
bottom, to p. 36, l. 4.

[3] Cf. *supra*, p. 36, ll. 4-6.
[4] Cf. *supra*, p. 33, ll. 31-6.
[5] Cf. *supra*, p. 36, ll. 6-9.

force solely in the king, and explicitly condemns all resistance to his warrant[1]; 'and since this has been the constant doctrine of the Church of England, it will be a very heavy imputation on us, if it appears, that though we [have] held those opinions as long as the Court and the Crown have favoured us, yet as soon as the Court turns against us, we change our principles.' In Section XIV Burnet meets the difficulty, first, by insisting that in all obligation there is an implicit reserve. The obedience even of children and wives is not unlimited; the marriage tie is held binding till death, yet few deny that adultery dissolves the bond. Where two fundamental principles collide, we must decide which is the more important, and accommodate the lesser to the greater. In the controversy between *public liberty* and the formal *renunciation* of the right to resist (made in the official declaration above mentioned), *liberty* is no doubt the superior principle, to which, if any liberty is to be retained, the *renunciation* must be accommodated. 'Since it is by a law that resistance is condemned, we ought to understand it in such a sense, as that it does not destroy all other laws.' Thus the renunciation can only apply to cases where the executive acts within the intention of the legislature, and cannot extend to instances in which the executive usurps upon the function of the legislature. Ill administration, consequently, cannot justify resistance[2]; which is only authorized by an invasion upon legislative powers or by a 'total subversion of the government.' In these cases the agents of the invading authority may be resisted; since a king who subverts that to which he owes his own power 'ceases to be king.' In the Fifteenth Section Burnet proceeds to argue, that the greatest assertors of monarchical power necessarily admit certain cases in which a sovereign may 'fall from his power[3],' or at least from the exercise of it. Desertion of his people, an attempt to enslave, sell, or destroy his kingdom, infancy, or phrensy[4] (and in the last case he quotes the then recent instance of Portugal) are recognized as valid causes; and an attempt to subvert the foundations of the government must surely, by parity of reason, entail at least a regency under the aegis of the next heir. In the Sixteenth Section Burnet elaborately maintains that James II had actually attempted a total subversion of the constitution.

_____

[1] Cf. *supra*, p. 35, ll. 3-10. [3] *Supra*, p. 35, ll. 10-3.
[2] Cf. *supra*, p. 33, ll. 7-12. [4] *Supra*, p. 35, ll. 13-22.

II

[BURNET'S MEDITATION ON HIS SECOND MARRIAGE [1]]

*At the Hague in Holland
the 25 May, 1687.*

Vpon my second marriage into which I am now entring.

O MY God the God of my life thou hast watcht over me for good
during the whole course of my pilgrimage to this day and tho' I am
lesse then the least of all thy mercies yet thou waits to be gracious
to me. Thou hast in a cours of so many years covered me from the
rage of my enemies so that tho' their power and their malice against
me were almost equally great yet thou who stopt the mouths of lions
has so overruled all the rages of their anger that their threatnings
has only served to discover their injustice and thy goodness to me.
Thou provided plentifully for me in the midst of all their fury so
that I have lived now for many years in a decent plenty farre from
the sense or the apprehensions of the smallest uneasiness. Thou
preserved me from those engagements in England which might have
exposed me more certainly to the storm, but at last all ties that held
me there having fallen off thou led me out of England by an Indulgent
Providence that drew me out of those difficulties into which I would
have fallen quickly thou led me thro' the severall parts of Europe
with an Indulgent tenderness that I can never enough adore. Thou
preserved me from those snares that I might have justly apprehended
in France and Italy and at last brought me safe into these parts
and I was no sooner here then I found a chain of Providences
leading me thro' many steps into this which is now near its accom-
plishment. All the concurrence of circumstances that seemed to
favour it lookt like an intimation of thy holy will and thou that
knowest all things knowest that neither the follies nor heats of nature
nor the levities of a wandring fancy nor the regard to the wealth
and abundance that accompanies the person determined me to it.
It was somewhat of thy Image that I discerned in the person herselfe
and the Characters of thy Providence that were so apparently
obvious in the progresse of it that led me into it.

---

[1] Holograph, 2 pp. 4to, Morrison MSS. See *supra*, pp. 251, 492.

Thou O God sees into the secrets of all my hidden thoughts tho[u] knowest that I neither designe to live in vanity nor luxury nor do I aspire to wealth and honour, and that even the outward decencies which I am in some sort forced to are uneasy to me. My true design is to be building up my selfe with her who is now to be my other selfe in our most holy faith and to be growing up in thy love my designe is to live wholly to thee and to the advancement of thy glory and the edification of the Church which is thy body and thou my blessed Redeemer. It is to these ends that I consecrate my time and all my faculties and those few abilities that thou hast given me and if thou blessest me with abundance all that is beyond that which is in some manner needfull for my own family shall goe towards the releeving thy poor members. Thy past mercies thy conduct of this matter and that temper in which I find my thoughts makes me hope that all this matter comes from thee, so that I most humbly prostrate my selfe before thee the fountain of all blessings doe thou O God of love so knit our hearts to thee and to one another in thee that our whole life may be a continued course of advancing our selves in that blessed way that must make vs not only happy here but happy for ever hereafter. Bless vs with that calm of mind, that union of thoughts and that tender concern in one another and chiefly in one another's soul, that our chieffe study may be that neither of us sin against thee preserve us so long together till our work is done here on earth and in all the other things that relate to a married state doe to us and with us O God what seems good in thine eyes and let thy will be alwaies preferred by us to our own. If thou O God wilt hear and answer this my humble praier in which I am now pouring out my heart to thee, then doe I most solemnly vow to thee that I will be wholly thine that I will live only to Thee and if thou honourest me so farre as to call me to it, I will with joy offer up my life for thy name's sake for thou art my God and my all thro' Jesus Christ my blessed saviour and Redeemer. Amen[1].

---

[1] Endorsed (in another handwriting and erased): 'Mr. Burnet's prayer upon his marriage before he went along with the king to make his progress in England and settle the nation.'

III

[BURNET'S MEDITATION ON THE IMPENDING EXPEDITION OF 1688 [1]]

A Meditation on my voyage for England which I have writ intend-ing it for my last words in case this expedition should prove either unsuccessfull in generall or fatall to myself in my own particular.

I WILL not say anything in this paper in justification of the designe having done that so copiously in another Paper which is to be printed with this Title *An Enquiry into the measures of Submission*, that nothing is left for me to adde in this.   I have also so fully and heartily approved of the Prince's Declaration which was put in English by me, that it is to these Papers that I referré those who may desire to know the grounds upon which I have engaged in an Vndertaking of this nature.   From those and some other Papers, especially one that I seal up with this [2], which I writ when I was under some apprehensions of being killed or carried away by some emissaries of the Court of England the world will see what are the reasons that have prevailed upon me to join in this matter so fully that I can say no more of this subject.   But this I will adde, and for this I appeal to thee, O God the searcher of hearts, that no consideration either of resentment for Injuries done me, or ambition have so much as moved me in this matter.   I have so watched over my own heart, to observe if the Injustice and Violence with which the Court of England had first ordered me to be judged in Scotland, and then to be murdered in Holland, had sharpned or embittered my spirit : but I thank God that I have had no motions of either anger or resentment, And that I have considered the state of England Scotland and Ireland with the same Impartiallity and the same cold blood that I should have had if I myselfe had not at all been concerned in my own particular : Nor was I at all

---

[1] Holograph, 4 pp. folio, Morrison MSS.   See *supra*, p. 286.
[2] It is unfortunately missing.

wrought on by any ambitious or covetous prospect of raising my own fortunes, by contributing to procure a Revolution in England. It never yet appeared in [*illegible*] when I was much younger and so was pushed on with a greater heat of blood, and was pressed with a greater straitnes of fortune, that I aspired either to riches or dignity; so that being now in a plenty of fortune, and having a wife in whom I have all the satisfaction which a married state can possibly give me, and who deserves from me all the returns of kyndnes that I can ever make her, having also a young child that promises all that can be expected in his age, and seeing the probability of another that is coming, I am not so litle flesh and blood as not to feel, what it is to leave these endearments, which possesse me heare [? my heart] so much, that no earthly consideration relating to my selfe could ever make me throw my selfe thus on Providence, if a much more powerful did not determine me. Nor am I set on by any sour or ill-governed zeal against Popery. I have indeed appeared much in opposition to that Religion [*words illegible*] of heart knows that I am farre from being heated, much lesse led by any violent and ill-tempered zeal in those points. I am none of those who would aggravate matters, or that let my selfe be governed by the spirit of a party. I love all men that love God, and that live well, and can make great allowances for errours and mistakes even of the highest order; for in that I have very large notions of the goodnes of that God of love whose mercies I could never limit to any one form or party of Religion, and so I am none of those that damne all Papists: for I have known many good and religious men among them. Therefore the aversion that I bear to Popery flows not so much from their errours, tho' I think their Church is full both of great and very pernicious ones, and that both in their doctrine and worship, but above all in the casuisticall Divinity and in the conduct of souls in the manner of their confessions and absolutions. But the chieffe ground of my abhorrence of that Church, is that carnall designing Ambitious, Crafty, Perfidious, and above all that Cruell Spirit that reigns among them, chiefly among the Religious Orders, and most eminently among the Jesuites, who are the Pests of humane society, and the reproach of the Christian Religion, so that I confesse I should not dread the progresse of Mahomitanism, or the returne of Paganisme, soe much as I doe the authority which that society begins to have in all the Popish Courts of Europe. and this is the true reason of all that warmth that I have expressed against that Religion; which does not at all lessen either that moderation which I have ever professed with relation to speculative points of Controversy, nor the esteem which I bear to the good things and the good men which are still in that communion, notwithstanding all their errours and corruptions.   The only motive therefore that has caried me into this matter, was that it appeared to me very visibly by the many plain Indications that the King has given, and the many broad steps that he has made, that he designs to overturn both the Religion and the Government of those kingdomes, and that he intends to set up Popery and Tyranny, if this appeared only in a few Instances that might be the effects of Inadvertances or passions, and if the steps that are made were in matters justly doubtfull, I should still have thought that, according to our Constitution, wee had been bound to submit and suffer : but the designe being a totall subversion, the case is plainly different.   Nor have I in this departed from my former principles, for I am still as much as ever, fixed in that persuasion, that the Christian Religion gives us no warrant to defend it by armes, but on the contrary forbids all resistance but still it is to be understood that if this Religion has lawes on its side, in a legall Government, where the King's Prerogative is shut up within such limits, then as the right of professing that Religion, comes to be one of the civil liberties, so the King by breaking thro' all the limitts of Law, assumes an authority which he has not, and by consequence he may be withstood.   And all that I ever writ or preached on the subject, of non-resistance agrees exactly with this : for I ever founded obedience and submission on the Lawes and severall Constitutions of Nations and I only went on the generall Topick, that the Christian Religion gives no authority to maintain it by Armes: yet after all, tho' this both is and ever was my Principle, I have gone no further but to give my opinion both to the Prince of Orange, and some other private persons, that I looked on the thing as very Lawfull, and as aggreeing both with the Christian Religion and the Constitution of the English Government.   But I never set my selfe to advise or presse it : for I ever said to all those with whom I spoke in that matter, that I thought it neither aggreed with my character[1], nor with the Circumstances in which

---

[1] i. e. his clerical function.

I am, to advise or persuade any such thing : so I carried the matter
no further then to assert in generall the lawfullness of the undertaking. It is true having asserted that, I thought it became me to
offer to wait on the Prince of Orange and to follow him as his
Domestick Chaplain, since he had intimated to me some moneths
agoe that he Intended to have me about his person in that Capacity :
and as for the danger I run in case I fall in the hands of my
Enemies from whom I expect all sort of ill usage, and an Igno-
minious death in Conclusion, I resigne my selfe up as to that, and
to the good and holy will of the only wise God, being cheerfully
resolved to glorify him in what manner so ever he will call me to
doe it whether in life or death : I leave all the quiet and satisfaction
I enjoy at home and goe whither he in his Providence leads me.
I cast not only my selfe but that which is yet dearer to me, my
dear Wife and my son upon the mercies of that God, to whom I
have consecrated my life and all that is dear to me; and I am
confident that he will doe that which is the best for him and me.
He that knowes all things knows the sincerity of my heart, that
I have made it the busines of my whole life, tho' in the midst of
many and great Imperfections to walk before him exercising my selfe
ever in this to have in all things a good conscience both towards God
and towards man.   And as I am perfectly assured both of the truth
of the Christian Religion and of the Protestant Religion, so those
matters are so dear to me that if I had a thousand lives I would
venture them all with joy in this cause.   I say no more concerning
any of those matters which are set forth by me in the Paper that
I writ in July 1687 for my sense of all these being at present the
same with that which I writ then I avoid repeating any part of it,
only I can never enough recommend the serious practise of true
Piety and of secret Praier : and I must sincerely Protest to the
world, that all the true joies that I have ever known have flowed
from this, as all the sorrows of my life, have flowed from my strayings
out of that way, that leads to life and blessednes.   I have ever hated
and despised superstition of all sorts ; and have found a great deale
of it even among those that pretend to be the furthest from it : nor
could I ever consider Religion under any other notion, but as it
furnished me with true and solide Principles, for the Reforming my
heart, and for governing my whole life, in a course of an Exact and
sublime vertue, deadening me to the world and [*a line and a half*

illegible] and raising me to a constant love to God, and my Neighbour: and a continuall desire of doing all the Good that was possible for me to doe. I have writt the beginning of a work, which [if?] I live I intend to finish of *Essaies concerning Morality and Religion*, in which I have delivered my sense of all the things that I treat of, with the same simplicity[1] in which I think of them, without saying any thing more or lesse, upon any other Consideration, but that of Truth. I order that to be printed after my Death. I order likewise all those short Essaies of Sermons, which are near two hundred, to be also [print]ed; and I doe likewise order my secret *History* to be Print[ed], and this is all of my writting that I allow to be made Publi[ck] as for all other Papers of mine I order them to be kept for my [son's] use; but never to see the light. I recommend most earnestly to him the study of Divinity and the work of the [*words illegible*]-lest of all Imployments: and that which when rightly followed makes a man but a little lower than the Angells: but if undertaken upon Carnall Motives and secular designes, it is that which brings more Guilt on the man, and more scandall on Religion, then any other course of life whatsoever. Happy are they that love God and that pursue the gaining of souls to him, with a labour of love: how much trouble soever they may meet with in this world, Great is their reward in Heaven. I continue to the last to love all my friends, of whom I have a great many, and that with all the tendernes and concern that is possible: for as I have lived a life of friendships, so I find the endearments of those bonds will stick to me to the last moment of my life: and as no man ever had greater reasons to love a wife most tenderly then my selfe she having in all respects deserved all the acknowledgments and kyndnes possible from me so I will carry with me to the last moment of my life, all the intirest affections for her of which my heart is capable: and I doe most humbly commend her, and my son, and what she goes with, to the blessings of the God of my life; who I trust will take her and them under his most Immediat Protection: and I doe most earnestly recommend both her and them to the care and kyndnes of all my friends, not doubting but that they will continue the true friendship, which I am confident some of them bear me to them.

---

[1] That very simplicity probably accounts for the fact that the work was suppressed by Burnet's family, despite the explicit direction for its publication, reiterated in his last Will and Testament.

And now O my God I turn my thoughts wholly from the world and all worldly objects to look up to thee, and to follow thee whither soever thou leads me. Thou has dealt hitherto with me so preciously that I cannot mistrust thy Providence but cast my selfe wholly upon it: and as I dare appeal to thee of the sincerity of my heart, and of my Intentions in this matter, so I look up to thee for a blessing upon it. I dedicate my selfe to thee, and make this vow to thee that if thou blesses us with successe in this matter, and brings me safely thro' it, then I will consecrate my selfe and the rest of my life more entirely to thy service; and will study all that is possible for me to shine as a Pattern of true Religion and of Exemplary Vertue: and if thou raises me to any Eminent Post in thy Church, I will study to be an example of Humility meakness gentlenes to all men and of Contempt of all worldly Greatnes and wealth, and that I will withdraw as much as may be, from all Courts and secular affairs, and will consecrate my selfe to the work of the Gospell, to the healing of our breaches to the care of souls and to the raising of a spirit of true Holiness and piety both among clergy and laity [*words illegible*] the advantages that thou gives me for the advancing of thy Glory and the doing good to mankind all I can. But O my God I throw myselfe in the dust before thee as one that is unworthy of the meanest office in thy House: therefore let thy name be glorified and let this great Vndertaking succeed and for me let me be covered with all that shame and confusion of face which belongs to me. Let not O God my sins or the sins of any of those who goe into it provoke thee to blast it look not O God at our sins, but consider thy Truth, the Glory of thy name, the Kingdome of thy Dear son and the happines of thy poor servants, that lie in the dust before thee, and that wait for thy salvation. Arise O God and Deliver the poor and needy, that call on thee: and let not the Cruell and bloodthirsty men prevail. Let the time appointed to favour and deliver thy sion come: O God, for our eyes are towards thee. Blesse [*words illegible*] I trust thou hast made strong for thy selfe. Preserve his Person, direct his Councells, and blesse his Armes: Give him Victory in the day of battell, and set him and the Princesse in thy good time, on the Throne, make them to rule in thy fear, and make them the Deliverers and Defenders of Thy Church that their names may be blessed in the present and following Generations. But O God if our sins are such, that thou wilt not deliver thy people by our means, or if the sins of England are such that they must be severely punished, then in every thing that thou does I will submit and adore thy Providence and acquiesce in thy Wisdome and offer my selfe up to thee to be disposed of as seems good in thine eyes; and to glorify thee whether in death or in life. if thou calls me to suffer, support and lead me thro' whatsoever thou suffers my Enemies to doe to me. Give me the joies of thy salvation. Let me find in the whole course of whatsoever Trialls thou putts me to that thou art with me! Lead me if thou wilt, thro' the Valley of the Shaddow of Death: for thou art with me I fear nothing that Devills can contrive or that men can exercise against me. Bring me at l[ast] where thou art O my God and my all: for thither am I continually aspiring, and am longing daily to see and enjoy thee eternally. I am thine O my God doe with me what seems good in thine eyes my God and my Portio[n for ev]er.

Amen Amen.

IV

LETTERS FROM DR. BURNET TO ADMIRAL HERBERT, 1688 [1]

I.

[*f.* 49] 'NOBLE SIR,

'As bad a man as you are a man cannot hold being extreamely concerned for you which has been so sensible to some that even the Great and generall concern for the whole busines has not been able to swallow it up. You have put us out of a great pain for after the apprehensions into which these storms had put us the good newes of your being all safe and well is to us that which a Victory had been if you had had a happier season. I hope by this time you have got to be clean and sweet, and that if my Cosen Johnstoune has not had his share in the storm yet he will come in time to be a witnes to the Glory that I hope staies for you and after all I hope you feel sometimes somewhat within telling you that perhaps your own leud life has contributed more to stop your voyage than either Albeville's masses or his prayers. And if you would but grow a litle better if

---

[1] Eg. MSS. 2621 ; see *Hist.* i. 762, and *supra,* pp. 297–8, 300, 303.

you are not passt that you might hope that all things would go better with you. No doubt you have the last newes from England of the Kings sending for the Bishops (the Archbp. was sick and London in the Country) he confessed passt errours to them and desired their advices how to set[t]le the nation and that they would now show their loyalty. Their answer was Generall and cold only Bath and Wells told him that their were 5 things the nation could not bear 1 the putting Papists in Imployments 2 the dispensing power 3 the Ecclesiasticall Commission 4 the turning out of the Magdalen Colledge men and 5 the regulating the Corporations. The King seemed to yield up all to them except the dispensing power which he said he would reserve to a Parliament to Judge of. He sent them to the Archbishop but they did not come back that night and this was on Fryday. This must compleat his ruine and show the meannes of his soul your Noble Combattant [1] is to come and command the Fleet and if S. R. Haddock will goe Strickland as is thought will be recalled and S. J. Berry will be Rear Admirall but it is positively writ that seven ships is all that the Court can pretend to be able to set out but it is believed that they cannot go so far and that four will be all that they can go to. The affections of the city appear every day plainer and plainer and yet the King thinks fit to look on so this must needs sinck his own party extreamly and I cannot think that his softnes which comes so late can have any other effect but to make him cheaper. I will not write you a word of the newes of Germany for perhaps you are as Mr. Sidney is out of patience when you see one look after any other news but those of England the winds and the fleet. I have tried but without success again and again to find out Sr Rowland Guinne when I can find him I shall see what can be done with him. This is all that I can say at present but that in spite of all your leudness I cannot hinder myself from being with all my heart and with all possible esteem

'Right Honorable

'Your most humble most faithfull and most obedient servant

'G. BURNET.

'Tuesday Morning'

Endd. ['1688, D. Burnet to Adm^{ll} Herbert just after the Storme.']

---

[1] Lord Dartmouth; see *Hist.* i. 762.

2.

[*f.* 51] 'Noble Sir

'You are a strange bad man and nothing can mend you neither storms nor our happy passage can Reform you but yet after all one cannot hold having a most particular high value for you, though you have some reason to accuse me for not writting but the first two daies one had so much to doe that to say trueth I never minded it and then I understood that you had orders to sail: so I hope you will excuse my omission. Our numbers grow upon us every day. the Gentry of the Countrey were a little backward at first but now they come in apace and if the newes that wee have of the Intentions of the Army did not make Levies here lesse necessary it were easy to raise a great body of foot but this Countrey wants horse extreamly and wee stick here for want of carriages for tho wee are much called to come nearer the King's forces yet I doe not see how soon wee can march, but it will be I hope by the midle of the next week at furthest. Wee had swallowed doune in our hopes three of the King's best Regiments which were very near us but the Confusion of the night with Sr Fran Compton's want of head or heart together with the vigour of some Popish Officers among them put all in so much disorder that the greater part after they had marched above 60 miles to come and join us wheeled about yet Lanstoun brought of[f] the D St Albans Regiment entire 50 horse of Compton's and above an 100 of Cornbury's dragoons came in likewise and yesterday wee heard that Capt. Kirk was marching with an 100 horse Cherry [1] is just now gone to Plimouth upon an advice that wee had yesterday that it will be delivered to us and that the E[arl] of Huntingtoune cannot be suffered to come within the fort but is forced to lie in the Toune wee begin to work a litle on the Clergy for they are now promoting a Petition for a Free Parliament wch is understood by all to be a Declaring for us. In short everything goes as well as our hearts can wish I am called on to make an end so that I can adde no more but that in spite of your ill Qualities the few good ones that you have determine me to be for ever   'Sir

'Your most humble and most obedient servant

'G. BURNET.

'Fryday the 16th Nov^r

---

[1] Query, a nickname for Captain George Churchill? Cf. Darlymple, *Memoirs*, ed. 1790, vol. ii. pt. ii. bk. vi. App. p. 251, and *Dartmouth MSS.* (H.M.C.) 210. (*Note contributed by Mr. Doble.*)

' wee now know that if wee had landed at Portsmouth it had been certainly delivered to us.'

Add. ' For the Honorable Admirall Herbert.'

Endd. ' Novemb^r 16: 1688 Dr Gilbert Burnett about Publick matters of that tyme.'

3.

[*f.* 67] ' Sir

' I write you a second Letter before I left Exeter which I gave to one that called himselfe your servant but he brought it back to me to Crookhorn and said that you were under sail before he could find you, so all the last newes from Exeter were losst. Mr Seimour Sr Wm Portman and all the chiefe men of the Countrey came in and were all extream hearty. there wee begun to signe the Association of which I send you a Copy. wee left the greatest part of our Cannon and heavy baggage at Exeter where Mr Seimour staies as Governour for the civill part and Gibson for the Military. The E. of Bath has at last declared with the whole garrison at Plymouth where the E. of Huntington is prisoner who in great wrath threatens the E. of Bath that he will bring his Habeas Corpus against him. the Earle of Shrewsbury is gone with a Regiment of horse another of foot and Dragoons to possesse Bristoll and Glocester where there are none but Militias and from both the Prince has such messages that I believe wee shall have them very cheap and perhaps the D. of Beaufort into the bargain and E. Shrewsbury hopes to come and join the Prince at Oxford for wee must take that road both because the Salisbury road is quite wasted by the King's army marching backward and forward in it and likewise to join a great body of horse that comes from the North commanded by the E. of Devonshire, the E. of Danby and the L. Delamere who were when wee heard last from them by an Expresse above 2000 strong but are now as wee hear 6000 strong. The King was mightily struck when he found that the D. of Grafton and the L. Churchill had left him and next day Prince George and the D. of Ormond also left him and after wee were in great pain having no newes of him for four daies wee had the wellcome account last night of his being got to Shaftsbury. So he dines to-day with the Prince at the Earle of Bristolls where wee have been these two daies the L. Bristoll having met us as wee came into the County with a body of all the Eminent men

in it Coll Strangewaies S. Jo. Morton and 20 more, who are sitting
for raising both a force and a present in money to the Prince Coll
Trelawney L Coll Churchill and almost all their officers are [?] come
in and a great many both of Trelawneys Regiment and Kirks but
unhappily poor Kirk himselfe was taken but it was only on suspicion
for as yet they have no proof against him if the King had not taken
the allarme of Churchill's going away so hot that he presently sent
for all the forces that lay at Warminster under Kirk's command wee
had got all that body of 6 or 7 Bataillons but tho as soon as
L Churchill sent us word Mr Bentinck marched all night with 400
horse and 800 dragoons to assist our friends in case of any resistance,
yet they had marched away long before and the King went up to
London in all the Confusion that was possible. He is very ill in his
health and bleeds upon every occasion at the nose and much puru-
lent matter comes out so that it is generally thought his person is in
as ill a state as his affaires are he made a Speech to the D. of
Grafton's Regiment when he set E. Litchfield at their head that he
would defend the Prot. Religion to the last drop of his blood wee
have every day many straglers dropping in to us. This is all I can
now tell you, only Frank Russell and Mr. Jepson that found me
writing to you give you their most humble service. wee remember
you very often but no man with a more particular esteem than

'Sir
'Your most humble and most obedient servant
'G. BURNET.

'Sherborn Thursday the 29th [?] November.

Add. As the last.

Endd. 'Sherborne Novr 29: 1688 D^r. Burnett That forses came
over to ye Prince Dayly.'

4.

[*f.* 69] 'Sir

'I doe not know whether this shall have better luck then my
two last had which were both brought back to me and so were
destroied by me for it was said that you were under sail so that no
Letters could come to you. This I only say to you to excuse your
not hearing from me for tho upon all other occasions the miscarriage
of a letter from me could not deserve an Apology yet at this time

since perhaps what I write might have given you some aggreable entertainment I would have you beleeve that it was not my fault but my misfortune that denied me the pleasure of serving you which bad as you are, I cannot deny to be very great. Wee have had hitherto as prosperous a march as wee could have wished for. not one ill-accident has befallen us. the Gentry of all the Counties through which wee have marched have come in almost all of them and both in Dorsetshire and Wiltshire they have undertaken both to levy some Regiments and to raise money. The coming of the D. of Grafton and the L. Churchill did so disorder the King that he presently retired back from Salisbury in a great consternation the Pr. of Denmark and the D. of Ormonds leaving him at Andover was a new mortification and they were 4 daies gone before wee had any newes of them which troubled us not a little but they went up the London road and so fetched a great compasse and at last they joined at the Earle of Bristolls at Sherborn the Princesse of Denmark left the Cockpit the same night that the Pr. left the King and she walked afoot in slippers to the Bp of London's house who conveyed [?] her first to Copthall and then to the North where she is at present but wee are put in hope that the force which received her is moving towards us and that she may join us in three or four daies. all this you may perhaps have heard already in the Publike newes and therefore I only name it, as I will doe Glocesters declaring for us and their taking L. Lovelace out of prison and making him their Governour, and the E. of Shrewsbury's being sent to Bristoll with some troops and his being received there with all possible joy. No doubt you have heard of L. Delameir's rising in the north who with a Regiment of 400 horse after a march of about 200 mile came hither two daies agoe and joined the Prince. The D. of Beaufort has abandoned the post he had given him to keep so all these counties have declared for the Prince. The King upon all this called a Councill of all the Peers about Toune and told them that since he found that a Parliament was the generall desire of all his people he was resolved to call one but he desired their opinion of the way to make it effectuall so they advised a treaty with the Prince upon which M. Hallifax E. Nottinghame and L. Godolphin were named the two first seem very litle fond of the Employment and say that it was put on them by their Enemies. A trumpeter was sent to the Prince demanding passeports for them who was kept two nights before he had his dispatch for the Prince sent for the Nobility and communicated the matter to them before he granted it. But tho the Commissioners came to Andover while he was at Salisbury yet he sent them to a place within 3 miles of this and so he gave them audience yesterday in the presence of several of the Nobility. they brought him a letter from the King containing some kind expressions such as that as he was the King's Son in Law so he was considered by them as a Son. Their Instructions were generall that since the Prince referred all in his Declaration to a free Parliament the King was resolved to grant one but desired that all Armies might be kept at such a distance that a Parliament might be chosen and sit in free-dome. The Prince desired them to put this in writting which they did and this night an answer is to be sent them in writting to this purpose that in order to the holding a free Parliament it is necessary that all Papists be first turned out of all Imployments both in England and Ireland and both out of the Army and the Court and so till that is done the Prince will hold on his march for [*f.* 70] the true designe of this treaty is to amuse the Nation and to stop the Princes march in which the Court will be deceived for wee will still goe on. The Commissioners desired to speak in private with the Prince but he declined it for he said he was come upon the busines of the Nation and that he had no private concern of his own. The two first in the Commission behaved themselves so and talked so freely to myselfe and severall others in a publike room that wee saw they were condemned to act a part that was verry unnaturall to them. In short the King dares not trust his army nor come to meet us and yet he must either doe that very suddenly or he must leave London for wee will be very near it in 8 or 10 daies. I write this at night and was not at Court since morning which is almost two mile from home, so I cannot tell you whether wee goe to London by Newbury Reading and Maidenhead which is our nearest way or if wee crosse the Thames at Wallingford bridge and so fall in to the Oxford Road for that was then under consultation and not then resolved on. Wee heard that the King upon our advancing hither had called back 2000 of his rear that lay at Reading which made us incline to that road but an advice came this morning that 500 horse and Dragoons of the King's were come back to Reading which put them upon new Councills. And by all that wee hear the Kings Army is so litle affectionate to him that it is scarce possible to fancy that he will venture with them and yet it is hard to know what else is left him. Thus I have given you a long account of our affairs which I hope will not be unacceptable to you and tho perhaps you may have the same things much better from other hands yet at least this will let you [see?] how desirous I am to doe everything that I can Imagine will be pleasing to you. You have a more Melancholy post then wee have but with lesse fatigue for the pleasure of seeing our matter goe on so well the new faces that wee see every day of which the E. of Oxford was one of the latest and the most wellcome and the shifting of the scene makes the trouble go Insensibly tho wee have had both bad way and ill weather except these last 3 or 4 daies that I fancy the dull quiet in which you live is much more uneasy to you then all this march would have been. I hope you will still be so just as to esteem me one of your faithfullest and most humble servants.

'Hungerford the 9th of December.

'G. BURNET.'

Endd. 'Hungerford Dec: 9th 1688 Dr Gilbt Burnet to Admll Herbert.'

5.

[*f.* 83] 'Noble Sir,

'I hope you have not such hard thoughts of me as to Imagine that I doe not write but letter for letter but if I had not thought that you might have been gone I had writ to you a great many daies agoe. Wee have now turn upon luck the foolish men of Feversham by stopping the King at first have thrown us into an uneasy after-game. Compassion has begun to work especially since the Prince sent him word to leave Whithall: and now as to the settling of the Government there are two different Opinions for a third which was for treating with the king has fallen by his second withdrawing yesterday of which I say litle because you will have it all in the common newes. Some are for calling together with the Peers all such as have been Parliament men that so they may goe to declare that the King having left his people and withdrawn the pretended Prince the Princesse is Queen and so proceed to call a legall Parliament by writts in her name others think that a Parliament or rather a Convention is to be summoned which will be the true representative of the kingdome and that tho they have no legall writts yet they being returned upon a free choice this will be upon the matter a free Parliament and that this Assembly is to Judge both the King's falling from the Crown and the birth of the Pretended Prince and that then a Parliament may be legally held after they have declared in whom the right of the Crown lies. this last is liable to this exception that the slownes of it may expose Holland to be losst before England can be setled or ready to act. I have not time by reason of many Impertinent people that presse in upon me to give you a fuller detail of our affairs your Reflections on the poor King's misfortunes are worthy of you I could hardly have thought that anything relating to him could have given me so much compassion as I find his condition has done I know it was not possible for you to have acted as some others have done but whatever one may think of that wee must now shut our mouths for there is discontent enough already and the Army seem generally out of humour and uneasy at what they have done and you know wee have not the arts of cajolery.

'You will no doubt see the Resolutions of the Peers yesterday so I will say nothing of it only it was so unanimous no shew of opposition being made to it that I believe now the greatest part of our difficulty is over. I am extream glad that you put me in hope of seeing you shortly here for it is now time for you to be for a while at rest till wee make a new expedition into France for I doe verily believe the Prince designs it this summer and it is but just that after you have passt thro so much hardship you should begin to receive those returns and acknowledgements that are worthy of you. I am much more then I dare venture to tell you unless you become a better man

'Sir

'Your most humble and most obedient servant

'G. BURNET.

'St. James's
    Christmasse day

'I wish you with all my heart a merry Christmasse and a good new year.'

Endd. 'St. James : xt masse Day 1688. Dr. Burnet wth opinions of people after ye Kings w[i]th drawing.'

V

BURNET'S REFLECTIONS ON HIS ELEVATION TO THE EPISCOPATE [1]

A Meditation on my Consecration the night before being Easter Eve, March 30, 1689.

I AM now coming to thee again O my God, to be once more dedicated to thee, and to rise up to the highest station in thy house. But how does this strike me, when I that am not worthy to remain in the lowest order but deserve to be cast out, as salt that has lost its savour, am now to be exalted instead of being debased. Oh but the Judgments of men are slight and deceitfull things. I passe for somewhat in the world. But before thee to whom the secrets of my whole life are known, I am nothing and lesse then nothing. I know the corruptions of my own heart and the errours of my life, which ought rather to drive me to a wildernes to spend the rest of my life in mourning for what is past then to enter upon an Imployment that is but a little lower then that of Angells. I have had addresse enough to cover my faults, and favourable circumstances have concurred to hide them from the world : But they are all known to thee, and therefore I stand trembling in thy presence divided in my thoughts, thy Providence seems to call me out to this station and my guilt pulls me back. I know my own unworthiness, how then dare I goe on : ought not I rather to fall downe before the Bishops, as an humble penitent to subject my selfe to the utmost severities of Censure rather then suffer them to lay hands on so great a sinner. Here I fall downe before thee O God to be guided by thee, for after all how guilty soever I may be I still retain my integrity and doe offer my selfe up to thee, all that determines me now is that thy Providence wh^ch calls me to this station is publike and visible and my sins which pull me back are secret and therefore it seems to be thy will that one should be followed rather then the other. But as I came loaded with much sin before thee so thou who knows my sins knowest likewise how bitterly I have mourned for them, how heavy they lie on me and how seriously

* Holograph, Morrison MSS; see *supra*, pp. 329, 497.

I am resolved to change the whole course of my life, even to the smallest particulars. I am indeed resolved to avoid all singularities and affectations, but as I will keep sin and all objects that may lead to it at the greatest distance so I will enter on a stricter course of daily devotion and of seeking thee by secret praier of spending daies in fasting and wrestling with thee as I was wont to doe many years agoe. I will cutt off all I can the levities of vain discourse and Indecent mirth. I will avoid every thing that looks like pride and the setting a value on my selfe, or the undervaluing of others. I will study to be an example first in my family to my wife and to such children as thou shalt think fit to give me, and then to my servants whom I will take care to Instruct in thy fear. I will also study to shine before my clergy and to be an example to them of humility meeknes and charity of contempt of the world, and a neglect of my person and of all the softening as well as the defiling pleasures of life. I will visit the sick, relieve the poor, comfort the prisoners, and will Imploy the revenue that belongs to the Church, as a Trust which I am to administer and for which I know I must answer to thee, whose right it is. I will place my friendships and favours as near as I can discern, on those that fear and love thee : they shall be all my delight and I will study in all things to walk before thee and be perfect : these are my resolutions which I offer up to thee as holy vowes, doe thou O God accept of them and enable me by thy grace to pay them to thee for after all without thee I can doe nothing. And as for this Holy Function into which I enter as thou hast given me high and sublime notions concerning it, so I will by thy Grace put all these in practise I will preach in season, both in publike and from house to house : I will not spare my selfe much lesse will I lose that time which now in a more particular manner [is] thine, in following a Court or any other Impertinent cares, for I will give my [selfe?] wholly to this great work : I will go round and be frequent in inspecting my clergy and will apply reproofs and censures as well as encouragments without passion or partiality. I will be carefull not to lay hands suddenly on any, nor become partakers of other mens sins, for thou knowest that I have but too many of my own to answer for. I will harden my selfe to all entreaties and recommendations in the conferring either of Orders or of Benefices, and I will study to form as many as I can to a high sense of the care of souls and employ such in thy vineyard

I will lay aside the prejudices of a party and as I will not rule over any by force or cruelty so I will shew all kyndnes not only to such as may differ from me but even to gainsaiers: for I will love all men: I will live with my Brethren of the Clergy in all brotherly love and true humility. I will not act by my own single advice but by the concurrence of the best of my Clergy, and will doe what in me lies to carry on the Reformation of this Church to a full perfection, by cutting off the Corruptions that doe still remain among us, and by adding such things as are wanting: nor will I ever suffer my selfe to be biassed by the base considerations of Interest, and I will set my selfe to doe the work of a Bishop in my Diocesse, without ever designing to remove [or?] to aspire higher: for I hope to fall here unlesse thou for the exercise of my faith and patience calls me to suffer for thy name these are my desires and these are the vowes which I now offer up to thee in the sincerity of my heart.

All these are indeed my sincere resolutions yet I know they will be as nothing if thou doest not concurre and favour me with a most speciall measure of thy grace. O how often have I begun well but alas the end was afflicting. All my hope is now placed in this that I know I begin at thee my God and put my trust wholly in thee O let my [me?] feel this day some of the motions of that wind that blows whensoever thou pleases make me find both in my receiving this divine benediction and in being admitted to the misteries of thy sons death such a measure of thy grace that I may feel that I have a new principle within me a seed of God by which I may grow up to thee. Doe thou breath on me O thou saviour of the world and make thy spirit come and dwell in me for all my hope is in thee. Doe thou but enable me to perform my duty and then dispose of me in all other things as seems good in thine eyes for I come not to ask great things of thee for my selfe it is neither riches nor honour, ease, nor length of daies. How much a nobler portion were it if thou wouldst honour me so farre to go and carry thy crosse and to preach thy Gospell as a true follower of Christ bearing his reproach and to seal that blessed Gospell which he confirmed with his blood by my own. But thou O God knows best what I am able to do and to suffer therefore I cast my selfe on thee and dare ask thee nothing but must only say thy will be done on me and in me. I am nothing and deserve nothing but shame and wrath, but be thou my God and my all support me by thy Grace and guide me by thy Councell I come unto thee and cast my selfe downe before thee and make an entire surrender of my life time and of all those talents with which thou has blesst me to thee I will Employ them all in thy service and dwell in thy house for ever and will be for ever aspiring to that blessed hope and glorious recompense which thou the Shepherd and Bishop of souls has promised to all that wait for thee. Come Lord Jesus even so come quickly.

VI

ADDITIONAL NOTE ON BURNET'S ORIGINAL ACCOUNT OF SCOTCH AFFAIRS AFTER THE REVOLUTION; INCLUDING THE MASSACRE OF GLENCOE

THE large amount of matter, relative to affairs in Scotland after the Revolution, which Burnet appears to have suppressed when revising his original Memoirs, attracts attention, and seems to require explanation. The statements now revealed bear chiefly upon two persons: Mr. 'Secretary' Johnstone, and Lord Portland. The almost entire elimination of the former personality from the pages of the final version may be probably ascribed to a desire of averting the charge of literary nepotism[1]; since, despite a suggestive note of Lord Dartmouth's[2] and the equally suggestive character inserted by Burnet (presumably during the revision of 1704–5) into *Hist.* i. 764, there seems no reason to suppose that Burnet disapproved the subsequent career of his kinsman, whether as a member of Tweed-dale's ministry, or as a leader of the 'Squadrone' (1704–5). The exact value of the new information must be gauged by those more intimately acquainted than is the present writer with the course of Scotch intrigue during the period in question; but the following points seem clear.

1. Burnet throws into relief a fact upon which historians[3] are

[1] See Introduction, p. xviii.
[2] See *Hist.* i. 4.
[3] Dalrymple, *Memoirs*, ed. 1790,

vol. iii. pt. iii. book x. p. 237, note; Macaulay, ed. 1858, viii. 80.

content to touch—the preponderating influence over Scotch affairs
exercised, during the reign of William III, in the name, at least, of
Lord Portland. That William, who himself regarded Scotch business
with a mixture of indifference and distaste, should have welcomed
the opportunity of employing his confidential favourite in a sphere
where his Presbyterianism was rather a qualification than the reverse,
and where his foreign birth, as rendering him superior to purely
English prejudice, might be considered, even by Scotchmen themselves, as an advantage, can excite no surprise; that he affected to
do so is certain[1]. But it is a moot question how far Lord Portland
was really influential, and to what extent he was the stalking-horse of
more powerful intellects. The close alliance which existed between
Portland, Carstares[2], and Sir James and Sir John Dalrymple—the
three former of whom had been intimate during the exile of the
second and third mentioned—is undoubted; nor is it any less
clear that after the Revolution William's Scotch policy was in fact
directed by this Scoto-Dutch group, of which the ascendency excited
from the first considerable heartburnings among the magnates of
Scotland. Its members were in fact united no less by personal
devotion to William than by political aims. All were statesmen first,
and moderate Presbyterians in the second place only; and their
policy may be summed up as contemplating, (*a*) the continued
ascendency of William; (*b*) the pacification of Scotland, in so far
as this should prove compatible with the wider issues of European
politics; (*c*) the establishment of a moderate Presbyterianism, as
combined with a general toleration. It is impossible to apportion an
exact responsibility among the several members of this political
fraternity. Lord Stair, his son, and Carstares (the studied reticence
of the last notwithstanding) have riveted the attention of posterity.
Portland, on the other hand, bulked larger in the eyes of contemporaries; and in Burnet's original narrative entirely eclipses Burnet's
own co-chaplain Carstares, of whose influence he was naturally
jealous, but who, by a refinement of ill-humour, is barely mentioned[3].

   2. The fluctuations in the fortunes and policy of the brotherhood

---

[1] Balcarres, *Memoirs*, pp. 42–3; *Leven and Melville Papers*, *passim*; McCormick, *Carstairs Papers*, pp. 64, 98; Macky, *Secret Memoirs*, pp. 61–2, 209–11; *Marchmont Papers*, iii. 139, 401–7; Dalrymple, ed. 1790, vol. iii. pt. iii.

book x. p. 237, note; Story's *Carstares*, pp. 182, 205–7.

[2] Dalrymple, *Memoirs*, part i. book i. p. 39, note, describes Carstares as Portland's secretary (no reference given).

[3] See *Hist.* i. 340.

must now be traced. Its first trend was in the purely Presbyterian direction; and Melville, another member of the Scoto-Dutch alliance, between whom and Burnet there existed a mutual dislike[1], was certainly its nominee[2]. At a very early date after the new settlement the disastrous result of the Montgomery intrigue[3] clearly affected Portland's position[4]; and seems during the year 1690 to have occasioned his temporary retirement from the management of Scotch affairs[5]. Meanwhile the rather intemperate zeal of Melville for the Presbyterian economy, and his injudicious alliance with Crawford, had completely alienated the episcopal interest and rendered a ministerial reorganization necessary. The appointment of the younger Dalrymple as conjunct Secretary in the end of 1690[6] introduced a moderating influence, and was but the prelude to the entire shelving of Melville, which took place towards the close of the year 1691[7]. At the same time as this latter event two steps were taken, which proved in the end incompatible. Breadalbane and several other of the malcontent grandees—episcopal in their sympathies, and in some cases strongly suspected of Jacobite leanings—were conciliated by admission to office; and James Johnstone found himself appointed Dalrymple's co-secretary. But Johnstone (a son of Lord Warriston), who had himself ranked among the exiled Scotch of Holland and whose services to the cause of the Prince had been considerable, proved no submissive instrument; his talents, temper, and principles alike unfitting him for a purely subordinate part. A man of independent convictions, and, though at one with the moderate Presbyterianism of the governing group, in principle a strong Whig; firmly attached indeed to the Revolution settlement, but bound to the King by no ties of individual devotion, his personal relations with the junto at Whitehall and with the new Ministry in Scotland could not fail to become rapidly strained. A tragedy precipitated the breach. Within a month or two of Johnstone's appointment occurred the massacre of Glencoe, in which Secretary Dalrymple was the overt principal and Breadalbane (one of the chief among the newly 'rallied' grandees) an inciting accessory. Rumours on the subject were certainly current in London

---

[1] *Leven and Melville Papers*, Introduction, pp. xxviii–ix; Dalrymple, ed. 1790, vol. ii pt. ii. book vi. App. p. 199; Macaulay, ed. 1858, vi. 193.
[2] McCormick, p. 95; Macky, p. 203.

[3] *Hist.* ii. 35; *supra*, p. 334.
[4] *Supra*, p. 335.
[5] *Leven and Melville Papers*, p. 533.
[6] *Hist.* ii. 74; *supra*, p. 357.
[7] *Supra*, p. 370.

within the month[1]; and when some months later, on the eve of the campaign, these rumours became importunate, Johnstone, who was sent down to Scotland as representative of the junto, seems to have received from the king instructions, presumably secret, to investigate the affair[2]. The inquiry appears to have been conducted with discretion. The extremely quiet and satisfactory course of the next year's session, on which Macaulay comments[3], is ascribed by Burnet to the dexterity with which Johnstone, by whom it had been proposed, soothed the irritated susceptibilities of the Presbyterians: he adds[4] that Johnstone's influence averted an attack on the ministry, i. e. the junto[5]. The fact probably is that the public inquiry into the Glencoe affair, on the absence of which Macaulay lays stress[6], was staved off by hints of an investigation in progress. The results of the session however clearly included a dislocation of interests as between Johnstone and the junto. The energy with which Johnstone had pursued the Glencoe investigation—an energy which, though no doubt perfectly sincere, may have been spurred by personal motives—must have certainly exasperated Breadalbane and the Master of Stair; Johnstone no doubt resented, both on private and political grounds, the cold and scanty recognition accorded to the conduct of the session[7]; Carstares may have naturally disliked the self-reliant temper and independent language[8] of his supposed henchman; for even King William, though no stickler for form, was displeased by his uncourtly bearing[9]. The junto, in fact, found its power in part undermined[10], and the channel of influence usually available in the person of the second Secretary no longer open. The progress of the Glencoe affair aggravated the split. The private report for which Burnet, in

---

[1] Macaulay, vi. 220; McCormick, p. 253. Macaulay's remarks, vii. 199-200, as to the date when the outcry became urgent, are quite incompatible with Burnet's remarks, *supra*, pp. 372-3; which Macaulay must have overlooked.

[2] *Supra*, pp. 372-3, 391. Macaulay's view (vii. 200), based on the preamble to the Commission of 1695, seems misleading.

[3] *Hist.* ed. 1858, vi. 388-92. Johnstone's account of the session, in his letters to Portland and Carstares (*State Papers*, 153-84, April 18-May 27, 1693), which should be read, corroborates Burnet.

[4] *Supra*, pp. 391-2.

[5] In fact he seems to have obtained from the Parliament an address requesting the king to confer a Scotch peerage on Portland (Macaulay, vi. 390); an honour which Portland appears to have desired (McCormick, p. 155).

[6] *Hist.* ed. 1858, pp. 390-2. The observations on p. 391 and note I think quite incorrect. Cf. Johnstone to Carstares, McCormick, p. 153, last line, p. 154, first line, with Burnet's account.

[7] See *supra*, p. 393.

[8] See Johnstone's letters in McCormick.

[9] McCormick, p. 93; *supra*, p. 415.

[10] *Supra*, pp. 372-3, 415.

his original Memoirs, makes Johnstone responsible was burked; but when in the summer of 1695 the Scotch Parliament, after two years' recess, met once more, the outcry became menacing; and the Court was compelled to grant a Parliamentary investigation. The animus displayed in the prosecution of the affair was largely ascribed to Johnstone [1]; and it is not surprising, though it is regrettable, that Portland [2] and Carstares [3] should have been impelled to the discreditable policy of shielding the guilty. The fall of Stair therefore, though a censure mild indeed for the occasion, became for Johnstone [4] a triumph, for his colleagues a serious rebuff; Portland indeed in the irritation of the moment renounced all further concern with the affairs of Scotland [5]. But his retirement, if real, was at any rate temporary; for when, six months later, the Darien crisis became acute, he doubtless combined with Carstares (who disclaimed any vindictive feeling in the matter [6]) in urging that the Secretary should be 'thrown to the lions [7].' If Burnet's version of events should be even approximately correct, Johnstone's action in the Darien affair was very ill requited; and the historian's observations, *supra*, p. 415, no doubt represent the not unnatural bitterness of the discarded Secretary. After his fall, the influence of the two friends, of whom Ogilvy became the instrument, remained supreme, and was only terminated in Portland's case by his voluntary withdrawal from public life [8]; in that of Carstares by the death of William III. That Carstares, after his retirement, retained feelings of dislike to Johnstone is clear from the language used by his correspondents [9]; while Johnstone is said in his later years to have made certain insinuations adverse to Portland's fair fame [10]. These may possibly have referred to the massacre of Glencoe, though other interpretations were hazarded; but it is more probable that he merely touched upon a supposed complicity in the arts of Parliamentary corruption, as practised in Scotland.

---

[1] Cunningham, *Hist.* i. 151-2 (see also pp. 365, 412-5); Macaulay, vii. 201.

[2] *Supra*, pp. 411, 415.

[3] McCormick, pp. 236, 257.

[4] McCormick, p. 99; Burton, *Hist. Scotland*, i. 172; *Caveat against the Whigs*, pt. 3, p. 74.

[5] See McCormick, p. 263. The suggestion may have been faint. It seems to have been made to Ogilvy, Stair's successor, who, though introduced into business by Johnstone, was the creature of Portland and Carstares (McCormick, p. 94; *ibid.* pp. 269-527, *passim*; Lockhart of Carnwarth's *Memoirs*, ed. 1817, i. 72; Macky, pp. 181-2).

[6] Story, pp. 254-5.

[7] Macky, *Secret Memoirs*, p. 210 (Macky was the spy who warned Johnstone previously to La Hogue); Lord Minto's introduction to the *Jerviswood Correspondence*, second page.

[8] See *Hist.* ii. 235.

[9] McCormick, pp. 729, 736, 745.

[10] Lockhart of Carnwarth, i. 367-8.

VII

THE SHEET OF NOTES PREFIXED TO HARL. MSS.
6584; BELIEVED TO BE IN THE HAND OF ROBERT
HARLEY (see Introduction, pp. vi, ix, x).

f. 2 (a).   *Materials.*

July 17, 1699.

S^r W^r Y^e rem: away

Mr. Hampden's usage (the word abdicate was Hasty)

Whigs tho they had many places had not al, therefore
displeased [ᵃ].

A council for protecting the Prot[estant] Religion to be
established with 200000^{ll} a year &c [ᵇ].

When ministers make their masters believe, that
al they reckon to be their enemys are also the
kings, the common practice cried out ag^t in ye last
reigns [ᶜ].

That men go away w[i]th vast grants the Pillage
of ye country the reward of long service to be
swallowed in a moment.

They had ruin'd y^t by their Heats about the
Corporation Bill & self seeking &c. when ye 2^d Parl[iament]
was chosen [ᵈ]

Lieutenancy of London changed (a meer trifle)
first whigs put in, then chang[e]d for ye torys &c.
upon ye new Parliam[en]t: 1690 [ᵉ]

They outraged y^t Parlia[men]t as Jacobites, yet [? y^t]
did more for ye governm[en]t than others

How did the whiggs oppose one anothers Elections &c.

Green & Somers

The wh[igs] desire power and use it ye worst in ye world

They set on another [act?] of abjuration in order to
get al ye offices of profit in y^r hands & al power [ᶠ]

ᵃ Cf. Harl. MSS. 6584, f. 289 (*b*) (*supra,* p. 313).   ᵇ *Ibid.* f. 230 (*a*) (*supra,*
p. 237).   ᶜ *Ibid.* f. 48 (*a*) (*supra,* p. 335).   ᵈ *Ibid.* f. 49 (*b*) (*supra,* pp. 337–8).
ᵉ *Ibid.*   ᶠ *Ibid.* f. 51 (*b*) (*supra,* p. 342).

f. 2 (*b*).

July 21, 1699.

The P:[rince of] O:[range's] declaration was ag^st^ surrender of Charters and directing writts to illegal officers to choose Parlia[ment] [ᵃ] and now have not these broken through al those things treated [? cyted] on in ye declaration & ye late king

Charters
{
Bewdly
Malmesbury
Plimouth
Dunwich
Hertford
Orford
}

Instead of non obstantes did not they set up the
Royal oke lottery contrary to law
did not Judges go circuits to elude
the Law, to shew how near they
could go & not sin ; this ought
to be animadverted on.   Howe they could
dare to set such an example
Sheriffs pricked for example Carbery to serve
England & Wales.
Marshal Law exercised when no Law for it
justified by Sr R. R. & Sr S. S. [? G.]
and so their fetters struck of[f].
This faction have tryed to do what neither
they nor anything else can
bring about, to discredit ye Govern[men]t
for ye Beachy fight 1690 we had not
2000 men in England¹ & yet our beaten
fleet defended us, [ᵇ] tho[ugh after ?]² pressed for
20000 here.

ᵃ Cf. Harl. MSS. 6584, f. 269 (*supra*, p. 285).   ᵇ *Ibid*. ff. 53–4 (*supra*, pp. 344–5) ; 63 (*a*) (*supra*, p. 361) ; 70 (*a*) (*supra*, p. 375).

---

¹ From the fact that the Harleian transcripts make mention of 1000 only, Mrs. Lomas argues that Harley had access to a different copy.   This seems overstrained; 1000 *is* 'not 2000'; and the second and larger numeral may have been employed by Harley merely in antithesis to ' 20,000.'

² Letters very illegible.

INDEX

A.

[1] Where they are called ' the violent party.'
[2] *bis*; once they are called ' the party.'

THE END.

OXFORD
PRINTED AT THE CLARENDON PRESS
BY HORACE HART, M.A.
PRINTER TO THE UNIVERSITY

Recently Published, in Two vols., Demy 8vo, cloth, price 25s.

BURNET'S
HISTORY OF MY OWN TIME

A NEW EDITION BASED ON THAT OF
M. J. ROUTH, D.D.

PART I.

THE REIGN OF CHARLES THE SECOND

EDITED, WITH INDEX, ETC., BY
OSMUND AIRY, M.A., LL.D.

OXFORD
AT THE CLARENDON PRESS
LONDON, EDINBURGH, AND NEW YORK
HENRY FROWDE

15/10/02

CLARENDON PRESS, OXFORD.

SELECT LIST OF STANDARD WORKS.

1. DICTIONARIES.

A NEW ENGLISH DICTIONARY
ON HISTORICAL PRINCIPLES,

Founded mainly on the materials collected by the Philological Society.
Imperial 4to.

EDITED BY DR. MURRAY.

PRESENT STATE OF THE WORK.   £ s. d.

					£	s.	d.
Vol. I.	A, B	By Dr. Murray	Half-morocco		2	12	6
Vol. II.	C	By Dr. Murray	Half-morocco		2	12	6
Vol. III.	D, E	By Dr. Murray and Mr. Bradley	Half-morocco		2	12	6
Vol. IV.	F, G	By Mr. Bradley	Half-morocco		2	12	6
Vol. V.	H—K	By Dr. Murray	Half-morocco		2	12	6
Vol. VI.	L—N	By Mr. Bradley . .	L–Lap		0	2	6
			Lap–Leisurely . . .		0	5	0
			Leisureness–Lief .		0	2	6
Vol. VII.	O, P	By Dr. Murray . .	O–Onomastic . . .		0	5	0
Vol. VIII.	Q—S	By Mr. Craigie . . .	Q		0	2	6

The remainder of the work is in active preparation; the distribution of the letters into the volumes will be approximately as follows:

     Vol.   VIII   Q–S   By Mr. Craigie.
     Vols. IX, X   S–Z

Orders can be given through any bookseller for the delivery of the remainder of the work either in complete VOLUMES or in *Sections* or in *Parts*.

HALF-VOLUMES. The price of half-volumes, bound, with straight-grained persian leather back, cloth sides, gilt top, is £1 7s. 6d. each, or £13 15s. for the ten now ready, namely, A, B, C–Comm., Comm.–Czech, D, E, F, G, H, I–K.

SECTIONS. A single Section of 64 pages at 2s. 6d. or a double Section of 128 pages at 5s. is issued quarterly.

PARTS. A Part (which is generally the equivalent of five single Sections and is priced at 12s. 6d.) is issued whenever ready.

Nearly all the Parts and Sections in which Volumes I–V were first issued are still obtainable in the original covers.

FORTHCOMING ISSUE, JANUARY 1, 1903. Lief–Lock. By Mr. Bradley.

Oxford: Clarendon Press. London: HENRY FROWDE, Amen Corner, E.C.

A Hebrew and English Lexicon of the Old Testament, with an Appendix containing the Biblical Aramaic, based on the Thesaurus and Lexicon of Gesenius, by Francis Brown, D.D., S. R. Driver, D.D., and C. A. Briggs, D.D. Parts I-X. Small 4to, 2s. 6d. each.

Thesaurus Syriacus : collegerunt Quatremère, Bernstein, Lorsbach, Arnoldi, Agrell, Field, Roediger: edidit R. Payne Smith, S.T.P.

Vol. I, containing Fasciculi I-V, sm. fol., 5l. 5s.

Vol. II, completing the work, containing Fasciculi VI-X, 8l. 8s.

A Compendious Syriac Dictionary, founded upon the above. Edited by Mrs. Margoliouth. Parts I-III. Small 4to, 8s. 6d. net each.

The Work will be completed in Four Parts.

A Dictionary of the Dialects of Vernacular Syriac as spoken by the Eastern Syrians of Kurdistan, North-West Persia, and the Plain of Moṣul. By A. J. Maclean, M.A., F.R.G.S. Small 4to, 15s.

An English-Swahili Dictionary. By A. C. MADAN, M.A. *Second Edition, Revised.* Extra fcap. 8vo, 7s. 6d. net.

A Sanskrit-English Dictionary. Etymologically and Philologically arranged, with special reference to cognate Indo-European Languages. By Sir M. Monier-Williams, M.A., K.C.I.E.; with the collaboration of Prof. E. Leumann, Ph.D.; Prof. C. Cappeller, Ph.D.; and other scholars. *New Edition, greatly Enlarged and Improved.* Cloth, bevelled edges, 3l. 13s. 6d.; half-morocco, 4l. 4s.

A Greek-English Lexicon. By H. G. Liddell, D.D., and Robert Scott, D.D. *Eighth Edition, Revised.* 4to. 1l. 16s.

An Etymological Dictionary of the English Language, arranged on an Historical Basis. By W. W. Skeat, Litt.D. *Third Edition.* 4to. 2l. 4s.

A Middle-English Dictionary. By F. H. Stratmann. A new edition, by H. Bradley, M.A. 4to, half-morocco. 1l. 11s. 6d.

The Student's Dictionary of Anglo-Saxon. By H. Sweet, M.A., Ph.D., LL.D. Small 4to. 8s. 6d. net.

An Anglo-Saxon Dictionary, based on the MS. collections of the late Joseph Bosworth, D.D. Edited and enlarged by Prof. T. N. Toller, M.A. Parts I-III. A-SÁR. 4to, stiff covers, 15s. each. Part IV, § 1, SÁR-SWÍÐRIAN. Stiff covers, 8s. 6d. Part IV, § 2, SWÍÞ-SNEL-ÝTMEST, 18s. 6d.

An Icelandic-English Dictionary, based on the MS. collections of the late Richard Cleasby. Enlarged and completed by G. Vigfússon, M.A. 4to. 3l. 7s.

2. LAW.

Anson. *Principles of the English Law of Contract, and of Agency in its Relation to Contract.* By Sir W. R. Anson, D.C.L. *Ninth Edition.* 8vo. 10s. 6d.

Anson. *Law and Custom of the Constitution.* 2 vols. 8vo. Part I. Parliament. *Third Edition.* 12s. 6d. Part II. The Crown. *Second Ed.* 14s.

Bryce. *Studies in History and Jurisprudence.* 2 Vols. 8vo. By the Right Hon. J. Bryce, M.P. 25s. net.

Digby. *An Introduction to the History of the Law of Real Property.* By Sir Kenelm E. Digby, M.A. *Fifth Edition.* 8vo. 12s. 6d.

Grueber. *Lex Aquilia.* By Erwin Grueber, Dr. Jur., M.A. 8vo. 10s. 6d.

Hall. *International Law.* By W. E. Hall, M.A. *Fourth Edition.* 8vo. 22s. 6d.

—— *A Treatise on the Foreign Powers and Jurisdiction of the British Crown.* By W. E. Hall, M.A. 8vo. 10s. 6d.

Holland. *Elements of Jurisprudence.* By T. E. Holland, D.C.L. *Ninth Edition.* 8vo. 10s. 6d.

—— *Studies in International Law.* By T. E. Holland, D.C.L. 8vo. 10s. 6d.

—— *Gentilis, Alberici, De Iure Belli Libri Tres.* Edidit T. E. Holland, I.C.D. Small 4to, half-morocco. 21s.

—— *The Institutes of Justinian,* edited as a recension of the Institutes of Gaius, by T. E. Holland, D.C.L. *Second Edition.* Extra fcap. 8vo. 5s.

Holland and Shadwell. *Select Titles from the Digest of Justinian.* By T. E. Holland, D.C.L., and C. L. Shadwell, D.C.L. 8vo. 14s.

Also sold in Parts, in paper covers—
Part I. Introductory Titles. 2s. 6d.
Part II. Family Law. 1s.
Part III. Property Law. 2s. 6d.
Part IV. Law of Obligations (No. 1), 3s. 6d. (No. 2), 4s. 6d.

Ilbert. *The Government of India.* Being a Digest of the Statute Law relating thereto. With Historical Introduction and Illustrative Documents. By Sir Courtenay Ilbert, K.C.S.I. 8vo, half-roan. 21s.

—— *Legislative Forms and Methods.* 8vo, half-roan. 16s.

Jenks. *Modern Land Law.* By Edward Jenks, M.A. 8vo. 15s.

Jenkyns. *British Rule and Jurisdiction beyond the Seas.* By the late Sir Henry Jenkyns, K.C.B. With a Preface by Sir Courtenay Ilbert, K.C.S.I. 8vo, half-roan. 16s. net.

Markby. *Elements of Law considered with reference to Principles of General Jurisprudence.* By Sir William Markby, D.C.L. *Fifth Edition.* 8vo. 12s. 6d.

Moyle. *Imperatoris Iustiniani Institutionum Libri Quattuor,* with Introductions, Commentary, Excursus and Translation. By J. B. Moyle, D.C.L. *Third Edition.* 2 vols. 8vo. Vol. I. 16s. Vol. II. 6s.

—— *Contract of Sale in the Civil Law.* 8vo. 10s. 6d.

Pollock and Wright. *An Essay on Possession in the Common Law.* By Sir F. Pollock, Bart., M.A., and Sir R. S. Wright, B.C.L. 8vo. 8s. 6d.

Poste. *Gaii Institutionum Juris Civilis Commentarii Quattuor;* or, Elements of Roman Law by Gaius. With a Translation and Commentary by Edward Poste, M.A. *Third Edition.* 8vo. 18s.

Sohm. *The Institutes.* A Text-book of the History and System of Roman Private Law. By Rudolph Sohm. Translated by J. C. Ledlie, B.C.L. With an Introduction by Erwin Grueber, Dr. Jur., M.A. *Second Edition, revised and enlarged.* 8vo. 18s.

Stokes. *The Anglo-Indian Codes.* By Whitley Stokes, LL.D.
Vol. I. Substantive Law. 8vo. 30s.
Vol. II. Adjective Law. 8vo. 35s.
First and Second Supplements to the above, 1887-1891. 8vo. 6s. 6d.
Separately, No. 1, 2s. 6d.; No. 2, 4s. 6d.

3. HISTORY, BIOGRAPHY, ETC.

Adamnani *Vita S. Columbae.*
Ed. J. T. Fowler, D.C.L. Crown
8vo, half-bound, 8s. 6d. net (with
translation, 9s. 6d. net).

Aubrey. *'Brief Lives,' chiefly*
of Contemporaries, set down by John
Aubrey, between the Years 1669 *and*
1696. Edited from the Author's
MSS., by Andrew Clark, M.A., LL.D.
With Facsimiles. 2 vols. 8vo. 25s.

Baedae *Historia Ecclesiastica,*
etc. Edited by C. Plummer, M.A.
2 vols. Crown 8vo. 21s. net.

Barnard. *Companion to Eng-*
lish History (*Middle Ages*). With 97
Illustrations. By F. P. Barnard,
M.A. Crown 8vo. 8s. 6d. net.

Boswell's *Life of Samuel*
Johnson, LL.D. Edited by G. Birkbeck Hill, D.C.L. In six volumes,
medium 8vo. With Portraits and
Facsimiles. Half-bound. 3l. 3s.

Bright. *Chapters of Early*
English Church History. By W.
Bright, D.D. *Third Edition. Revised*
and Enlarged. With a Map. 8vo. 12s.

Bryce. *Studies in History*
and Jurisprudence. By the Right
Hon. J. Bryce, M.P. 2 Vols. 8vo.
25s. net.

Casaubon (Isaac), 1559–1614.
By Mark Pattison. 8vo. 16s.

Clarendon's *History of the*
Rebellion and Civil Wars in England.
Re-edited from a fresh collation of
the original MS. in the Bodleian
Library, with marginal dates and oc-
casional notes, by W. Dunn Macray,
M.A., F.S.A. 6 vols. Crown 8vo. 2l. 5s.

Earle. *Handbook to the Land-*
Charters, and other Saxonic Documents.
By John Earle, M.A. Crown 8vo. 16s.

—— *The Alfred Jewel:* An
Historical Essay. With Illustrations and Map. Small 4to, buck-
ram. 12s. 6d. net.

Earle and **Plummer.** *Two of*
the Saxon Chronicles, Parallel, with

Supplementary Extracts from the others.
A Revised Text, edited, with Intro-
duction, Notes, Appendices, and
Glossary, by Charles Plummer,
M.A., on the basis of an edition by
John Earle, M.A. 2 vols. Crown
8vo, half-roan.
Vol. I. Text, Appendices, and
Glossary. 10s. 6d.
Vol. II. Introduction, Notes, and
Index. 12s. 6d.

Freeman. *The History of*
Sicily from the Earliest Times.
Vols. I and II. 8vo, cloth. 2l. 2s.
Vol. III. The Athenian and
Carthaginian Invasions. 24s.
Vol. IV. From the Tyranny of
Dionysios to the Death of
Agathoklês. Edited by Arthur
J. Evans, M.A. 21s.

Freeman. *The Reign of*
William Rufus and the Accession of
Henry the First. By E. A. Freeman,
D.C.L. 2 vols. 8vo. 1l. 16s.

Gardiner. *The Constitutional*
Documents of the Puritan Revolution,
1628–1660. Selected and Edited
by Samuel Rawson Gardiner, D.C.L.
Second Edition. Crown 8vo. 10s. 6d.

Gross. *The Gild Merchant;*
a Contribution to British Municipal
History. By Charles Gross, Ph.D.
2 vols. 8vo. 24s.

Hastings. *Hastings and the*
Rohilla War. By Sir John Strachey,
G.C.S.I. 8vo, cloth. 10s. 6d.

Hill. *Sources for Greek*
History between the Persian and Pelopon-
nesian Wars. Collected and arranged
by G. F. Hill, M.A. 8vo. 10s. 6d.

Hodgkin. *Italy and her In-*
vaders. With Plates & Maps. 8 vols.
8vo. By T. Hodgkin, D.C.L.
Vols. I–II. *Second Edition.* 42s.
Vols. III–IV. *Second Edition.* 36s.
Vols. V–VI. 36s.
Vol. VII–VIII (*completing the*
work). 24s.

Johnson. *Letters of Samuel Johnson, LL.D.* Collected and Edited by G. Birkbeck Hill, D.C.L. 2 vols. half-roan. 28s.

——*Johnsonian Miscellanies.* 2 vols. Medium 8vo, half-roan. 28s.

Kitchin. *A History of France.* With Numerous Maps, Plans, and Tables. By G. W. Kitchin, D.D. In three Volumes. *New Edition.* Crown 8vo, each 10s. 6d.

> Vol. I. to 1453. Vol. II. 1453–1624. Vol. III. 1624–1793.

Kyd. *The Works of Thomas Kyd.* Edited from the original Texts, with Introduction, Notes, and Facsimiles. By F. S. Boas, M.A. 8vo. 15s. net.

Le Strange. *Baghdad during the Abbasid Caliphate.* By G. Le Strange. 8vo. 16s. net.

Lewis (*Sir G. Cornewall*). *An Essay on the Government of Dependencies.* Edited by C. P. Lucas, B.A. 8vo, half-roan. 14s.

Lucas. *Historical Geography of the British Colonies.* By C. P. Lucas, B.A. With Maps. Cr. 8vo.

> Introduction. 4s. 6d.
>
> Vol. I. The Mediterranean and Eastern Colonies (exclusive of India). 5s.
>
> Vol. II. The West Indian Colonies. 7s. 6d.
>
> Vol. III. West Africa. *Second Edition, revised to the end of* 1899, *by H. E. Egerton.* 7s. 6d.
>
> Vol. IV. South and East Africa. Historical and Geographical. 9s. 6d.
>
> Also Vol. IV in two Parts—
> Part I. Historical, 6s. 6d.
> Part II. Geographical, 3s. 6d.
>
> Vol. V. The History of Canada (Part I, New France). 6s.

Ludlow. *The Memoirs of Edmund Ludlow, Lieutenant-General of the Horse in the Army of the Commonwealth of England,* 1625–1672. Edited by C. H. Firth, M.A. 2 vols. 36s.

Machiavelli. *Il Principe.* Edited by L. Arthur Burd, M.A. With an Introduction by Lord Acton. 8vo. 14s.

Merriman. *Life and Letters of Thomas Cromwell.* With a Portrait and Facsimile. By R. B. Merriman, B.Litt. 2 vols. 8vo. 18s. net.

Morris. *The Welsh Wars of Edward I.* With a Map and Pedigrees. By J. E. Morris, M.A. 8vo. 9s. 6d. net.

Oman. *A History of the Peninsular War.* 6 vols. 8vo. With Maps, Plans, and Portraits. By C. Oman, M.A. *Just Published.* Vol. I (1807-1809. From the Treaty of Fontainebleau to the Battle of Corunna). 14s. net.

Payne. *History of the New World called America.* By E. J. Payne, M.A. 8vo.

> Vol. I, containing *The Discovery* and *Aboriginal America,* 18s.
>
> Vol. II, *Aboriginal America* (concluded), 14s.

Plummer. *The Life and Times of Alfred the Great.* With an Appendix and Map. By Charles Plummer, M.A. Crown 8vo. 5s. net.

Poole. *Historical Atlas of Modern Europe from the decline of the Roman Empire,* comprising also Maps of parts of Asia, Africa, and the New World, connected with European History. Edited by R. L. Poole, M.A. 5l. 15s. 6d. net.

Prothero. *Select Statutes and other Constitutional Documents, illustrative of the Reigns of Elizabeth and James I.* Edited by G. W. Prothero, M.A. Cr. 8vo. *Edition 2.* 10s. 6d.

Ramsay (Sir J. H.). *Lancaster and York.* (A.D. 1399–1485). 2 vols. 8vo. With Index. 37s. 6d.

Ramsay (W. M.). *The Cities and Bishoprics of Phrygia.*

> Vol. I. Part I. The Lycos Valley and South-Western Phrygia. Royal 8vo. 18s. net.
>
> Vol. I. Part II. West and West-Central Phrygia. 21s. net.

London: Henry Frowde, Amen Corner, E.C.

Ranke. *A History of Eng-land, principally in the Seventeenth Century.* By L. von Ranke. Trans-lated under the superintendence of G. W. Kitchin, D.D., and C. W. Boase, M.A. 6 vols. 8vo. 63*s.* Revised Index, separately, 1*s.*

Rashdall. *The Universities of Europe in the Middle Ages.* By Hast-ings Rashdall, M.A. 2 vols. (in 3 Parts) 8vo. With Maps. 2*l.* 5*s. net.*

Rhŷs. *Studies in the Arthur-ian Legend.* By John Rhŷs, M.A. 8vo. 12*s.* 6*d.*

——*Celtic Folklore:* Welsh and Manx. By the same. 2 vols. 8vo. 21*s.*

Scaccario. *De Necessariis Observantiis Scaccarii Dialogus.* Com-monly called Dialogus de Scaccario. By Richard, Son of Nigel, Treasurer of England and Bishop of London. Edited by Arthur Hughes, C. G. Crump, and C. Johnson. 8vo, 12*s.* 6*d. net.*

Smith's *Lectures on Justice, Police, Revenue and Arms.* Edited, with Introduction and Notes, by Edwin Cannan. 8vo. 10*s.* 6*d. net.*

—— *Wealth of Nations.* With Notes, by J. E. Thorold Rogers, M.A. 2 vols. 8vo. 21*s.*

Stephens. *The Principal Speeches of the Statesmen and Orators of the French Revolution,* 1789-1795. By H. Morse Stephens. 2 vols. Crown 8vo. 21*s.*

Stubbs. *Select Charters and other Illustrations of English Constitu-tional History, from the Earliest Times to the Reign of Edward I.* Arranged and edited by W. Stubbs, D.D., late Bishop of Oxford. *Eighth Edition.* Crown 8vo. 8*s.* 6*d.*

—— *The Constitutional His-tory of England, in its Origin and Development. Library Edition.* 3 vols. Demy 8vo. 2*l.* 8*s.*
Also in 3 vols. crown 8vo. 12*s.* each.

—— *Seventeen Lectures on the Study of Mediaeval and Modern History and kindred subjects.* Crown 8vo. *Third Edition, revised and en-larged.* 8*s.* 6*d.*

—— *Registrum Sacrum Anglicanum.* Small 4to. *Second Edition.* 10*s.* 6*d.*

Swift (F. D.). *The Life and Times of James the First of Aragon.* By F. D. Swift, B.A. 8vo. 12*s.* 6*d.*

Vinogradoff. *Villainage in England.* Essays in English Medi-aeval History. By Paul Vinogradoff. 8vo, half-bound. 16*s.*

4. PHILOSOPHY, LOGIC, ETC.

Bacon. *Novum Organum.* Edited, with Introduction, Notes, &c., by T. Fowler, D.D. *Second Edition.* 8vo. 15*s.*

Berkeley. *The Works of George Berkeley, D.D., formerly Bishop of Cloyne; including many of his writ-ings hitherto unpublished.* With Pre-faces, Annotations, Appendices, and an Account of his Life, by A. Campbell Fraser, Hon. D.C.L., LL. D. New Edition in 4 vols., crown 8vo. 24*s.*

—— *The Life and Letters, with an account of his Philosophy.* By A. Campbell Fraser. 8vo. 16*s.*

Bosanquet. *Logic; or, the Morphology of Knowledge.* By B. Bosanquet, M.A. 8vo. 21*s.*

Butler. *The Works of Joseph Butler, D.C.L.,* sometime Lord Bishop of Durham. Edited by the Right Hon. W. E. Gladstone. 2 vols. Medium 8vo. 14*s.* each.

Campagnac. *The Cambridge Platonists:* being Selections from the writings of Benjamin Whichcote, John Smith, and Nathanael Culver-wel, with Introduction by E. T. Campagnac, M.A. Crown 8vo. 6*s.* 6*d. net.*

Fowler. *Logic;* Deductive and Inductive, combined in a single volume. Extra fcap. 8vo. 7s. 6d.

Fowler and **Wilson.** *The Principles of Morals.* By T. Fowler, D.D., and J. M. Wilson, B.D. 8vo, cloth. 14s.

Green. *Prolegomena to Ethics.* By T. H. Green, M.A. Edited by A. C. Bradley, M.A. *Fourth Edition.* Crown 8vo. 7s. 6d.

Hegel. *The Logic of Hegel.* Translated from the Encyclopaedia of the Philosophical Sciences. With Prolegomena to the Study of Hegel's Logic and Philosophy. By W. Wallace, M.A. *Second Edition, Revised and Augmented.* 2 vols. Crown 8vo. 10s. 6d. each.

Hegel's *Philosophy of Mind.* Translated from the Encyclopaedia of the Philosophical Sciences. With Five Introductory Essays. By William Wallace, M.A., LL.D. Crown 8vo. 10s. 6d.

Hume's *Treatise of Human Nature.* Edited, with Analytical Index, by L. A. Selby-Bigge, M.A. *Second Edition.* Crown 8vo. 8s.

—— *Enquiry concerning the Human Understanding, and an Enquiry concerning the Principles of Morals.* Edited by L. A. Selby-Bigge, M.A. Crown 8vo. 7s. 6d.

Leibniz. *The Monadology and other Philosophical Writings.* Translated, with Introduction and Notes, by Robert Latta, M.A., D.Phil. Crown 8vo. 8s. 6d.

Locke. *An Essay Concerning Human Understanding.* By John Locke. Collated and Annotated, with Prolegomena, Biographical, Critical, and Historic, by A. Campbell Fraser, Hon. D.C.L., LL.D. 2 vols. 8vo. 1l. 12s.

Lotze's *Logic,* in Three Books —of Thought, of Investigation, and of Knowledge. English Translation; edited by B. Bosanquet. M.A. *Second Edition.* 2 vols. Cr. 8vo. 12s.

—— *Metaphysic,* in Three Books—Ontology, Cosmology, and Psychology. English Translation; edited by B. Bosanquet, M.A. *Second Edition.* 2 vols. Cr. 8vo. 12s.

Martineau. *Types of Ethical Theory.* By James Martineau, D.D. *Third Edition.* 2 vols. Cr. 8vo. 15s.

—— *A Study of Religion:* its Sources and Contents. *Second Edition.* 2 vols. Cr. 8vo. 15s.

Selby-Bigge. *British Moralists.* Selections from Writers principally of the Eighteenth Century. Edited by L. A. Selby-Bigge, M.A. 2 vols. Crown 8vo. 18s.

Spinoza. *A Study in the Ethics of Spinoza.* By Harold H. Joachim. 8vo. 10s. 6d. net.

Wallace. *Lectures and Essays on Natural Theology and Ethics.* By William Wallace, M.A., LL.D. Edited, with a Biographical Introduction, by Edward Caird, M.A., Hon. D.C.L. 8vo, with a Portrait. 12s. 6d.

5. PHYSICAL SCIENCE, ETC.

Balfour. *The Natural History* of the Musical Bow. A Chapter in the Developmental History of Stringed Instruments of Music. Part I, Primitive Types. By Henry Balfour, M.A. Royal 8vo, paper covers. 4s. 6d.

Chambers. *A Handbook of Descriptive and Practical Astronomy.* By G. F. Chambers, F.R.A.S. *Fourth Edition,* in 3 vols. Demy 8vo.
Vol. I. The Sun, Planets, and Comets. 21s.
Vol. II. Instruments and Practical Astronomy. 21s.
Vol. III. The Starry Heavens. 14s.

De Bary. *Comparative Anatomy of the Vegetative Organs of the Phanerogams and Ferns.* By Dr. A. de Bary. Translated by F. O. Bower, M.A., and D. H. Scott, M.A. Royal 8vo. 22s. 6d.

—— *Comparative Morphology and Biology of Fungi, Mycetozoa and Bacteria.* By Dr. A. de Bary. Translated by H. E. F. Garnsey, M.A. Revised by Isaac Bayley Balfour, M.A., M.D., F.R.S. Royal 8vo, half-morocco. 22s. 6d.

—— *Lectures on Bacteria.* By Dr. A. de Bary. *Second Improved Edition.* Translated and revised by the same. Crown 8vo. 6s.

Fischer. *The Structure and Functions of Bacteria.* By Alfred Fischer. Translated into English by A. Coppen Jones. Royal 8vo, with Twenty-nine Woodcuts. 8s. 6d.

Goebel. *Outlines of Classification and Special Morphology of Plants.* By Dr. K. Goebel. Translated by H. E. F. Garnsey, M.A. Revised by Isaac Bayley Balfour, M.A., M.D., F.R.S. Royal 8vo, half-morocco. 21s.

—— *Organography of Plants,* especially of the Archegoniatae and Spermaphyta. By Dr. K. Goebel. Authorized English Edition, by Isaac Bayley Balfour, M.A., M.D., F.R.S. Part I, General Organography. Royal 8vo, half-morocco. 12s. 6d.

Miall and **Hammond.** *The Structure and Life-History of the Harlequin Fly (Chironomus).* By L. C. Miall, F.R.S., and A. R. Hammond, F.L.S. 8vo. With 130 Illustrations. 7s. 6d.

Pfeffer. *The Physiology of Plants.* A Treatise upon the Metabolism and Sources of Energy in Plants. By Prof. Dr. W. Pfeffer. Second fully Revised Edition, translated and edited by Alfred J. Ewart, D.Sc., Ph.D., F.L.S. Part I. Royal 8vo, half-morocco. 28s.

Prestwich. *Geology—Chemical, Physical, and Stratigraphical.* By Sir Joseph Prestwich, M.A., F.R.S. In two Volumes. Royal 8vo. 61s.

Sachs. *A History of Botany.* Translated by H. E. F. Garnsey, M.A. Revised by I. Bayley Balfour, M.A., M.D., F.R.S. Crown 8vo. 10s.

Solms-Laubach. *Fossil Botany.* Being an Introduction to Palaeophytology from the Standpoint of the Botanist. By H. Graf zu Solms-Laubach. Translated and revised by the same. Royal 8vo, half-morocco, 18s.

OXFORD HISTORY OF MUSIC.

Edited by W. H. HADOW, M.A.

The Polyphonic Period. Part I (Method of Musical Art, 330–1330). By H. E. Wooldridge, M.A. 8vo. 15s. net.

The Seventeenth Century. By Sir C. Hubert H. Parry, M.A., D.Mus. 15s. net. (*Just Published.*)

The Age of Bach and Handel. By J. A. Fuller-Maitland, M.A. 15s. net. (*Nearly ready.*)

IN PREPARATION.

The Polyphonic Period. Part II. By H. E. Wooldridge, M.A.

The Viennese School. By W. H. Hadow, M.A.

The Romantic Period. By E. Dannreuther, M.A.

OXFORD

AT THE CLARENDON PRESS

LONDON, EDINBURGH, AND NEW YORK

HENRY FROWDE

Printed in Great Britain
by Amazon

40251047R00371